In the Beginning Was the Word

In the Beginning
Was the Word

The Bible in American Public Life,
1492–1783

MARK A. NOLL

OXFORD
UNIVERSITY PRESS

OXFORD
UNIVERSITY PRESS

Oxford University Press is a department of the
University of Oxford. It furthers the University's objective
of excellence in research, scholarship, and education
by publishing worldwide.

Oxford   New York

Auckland   Cape Town   Dar es Salaam   Hong Kong   Karachi
Kuala Lumpur   Madrid   Melbourne   Mexico City   Nairobi
New Delhi   Shanghai   Taipei   Toronto

With offices in

Argentina   Austria   Brazil   Chile   Czech Republic   France   Greece
Guatemala   Hungary   Italy   Japan   Poland   Portugal   Singapore
South Korea   Switzerland   Thailand   Turkey   Ukraine   Vietnam

Oxford is a registered trade mark of Oxford University Press
in the UK and certain other countries.

Published in the United States of America by
Oxford University Press
198 Madison Avenue, New York, NY 10016

© Oxford University Press 2016

Library of Congress Cataloging-in-Publication Data
Noll, Mark A., 1946–
In the beginning was the word : the Bible in American public life,
1492–1783 / Mark A. Noll.
pages   cm
Includes bibliographical references and index.
ISBN 978-0-19-026398-0 (cloth : alk. paper)
1. Bible. English—History.   2. Bible—Influence.   3. Bible and politics—
United States—History.   4. United States—Church history.   I. Title.
BS455.N65   2015
220.0973—dc23   2015009982

To Maggie

Contents

Acknowledgments

IN READING ABOUT, researching, and pondering issues concerning the Bible in American history for more than forty years, I have received critical assistance from a not-quite-numberless host. Here I am grateful to acknowledge much appreciated recent help from the National Endowment for the Humanities, the Notre Dame Institute for Advanced Study, and Notre Dame's College of Arts and Letters. Institutional support of a different but no less valuable kind has come from regular participants in Notre Dame's CORAH, Colloquium on Religion and History. For a book that depends entirely on works from earlier centuries, I owe an unusually significant debt to two Indianapolis publishers (Bobbs-Merrill for the American Heritage Series, and the Liberty Fund for its many editions of writings from the colonial period.) My debt is even greater to three searchable digitized resources that have made this a longer but also, hopefully, a better book: Early English Books Online (EEBO), Eighteenth-Century Collections Online (ECCO), and especially Early American Imprints.

At Notre Dame, it has been a great privilege to work with a corps of dedicated administrators who succeed at upholding the university's desire to provide a superb undergraduate education, promote specialized research at the highest level, and sustain Notre Dame's Catholic mission. Prominent in that corps for me have been John McGreevy, Patrick Griffin, Tom Noble, Ted Beatty, Dan Graff, and Father Robert Sullivan. Colleagues in the history department who offered especially welcome advice on aspects of this project include Brad Gregory, Patrick Griffin, Jim Turner, and Ben Wetzel. From doctoral students Heath Carter, Raully Donahue, Josh Kercsmar, and Laura Porter I learned much about disciplined research and effective prose. Billy Smith, with a forthcoming dissertation on Benjamin Colman, has underscored the crucial importance of New England's connections to the Old World. Peter Choi's splendid dissertation on the imperial George Whitefield provided key insights for chapters 6 and 7. From Nicholas

Miller, a lawyer whom I attempted to instruct in the ways of historians, I received the unexpected reward of finding out how much a lawyer could teach a historian; chapter 5 is particularly indebted to what that teaching meant.

My personal watchmen on the walls of Zion are historian-colleagues and friends who have provided many kinds of support for many efforts in many venues over many years. It has been an inestimable privilege to receive steady encouragement, and only an occasional question about how the Bible book is coming along, from (and at the risk of omitting someone unintentionally) Randy Balmer, Dan Bays, David Bebbington, Edith Blumhofer, Jim Bratt, Catherine Brekus, Joel Carpenter, Larry Eskridge, Darryl Hart, Nathan Hatch, David Hempton, Bruce Hindmarsh, Mark Hutchinson, David Livingstone, Kathryn Long, Roger Lundin, George Marsden, Ken Minkema, the late George Rawlyk, John Stackhouse, Harry Stout, Mark Valeri, Marguerite VanDie, Grant Wacker, and John Wilson. I am also grateful to Dr. Liana Lupas for special assistance from the collections of the American Bible Society and to my brother Craig Noll for his expertise in Greek and much else.

For this particular effort I received the best possible criticism on the whole manuscript from Mark Valeri, Grant Wacker, and Oxford's anonymous readers. At the press, I have benefited greatly from the expert assistance of Marcela Maxfield, Theo Calderara, Mary Sutherland, Joellyn Ausanka, and especially Cynthia Read. On this occasion I am also delighted to rise up and call blessed Mary, Dean, Anne, Lydia, and Irene Venables; David, Bethany, Nathaniel, and Juliana Davis Noll; and Robert and Kate Lee Noll.

In the Beginning Was the Word is dedicated to my wife, Maggie, who assisted in its production with a range of expert librarian's skills that some of us know we need but cannot master ourselves. Even more sustaining has been her own faithful engagement with Scripture and her selfless support of my writing life. Little did I realize in June 1970, when the Reverend Bob Atwell gave us a copy of *Strong's Exhaustive Concordance of the Bible*, that this seemingly eccentric gift would accompany us throughout our days, eventually play a significant part in preparing this book, and speak enduringly of the values I share most deeply with Maggie. Her price is far above rubies.

Abbreviations

ANB	American National Biography
BCP	Book of Common Prayer
KJV	King James Version (1611)
LW	Luther's Works (American Edition)
SPCK	Society for the Promotion of Christian Knowledge
SPG	Society for the Propagation of the Gospel in Foreign Parts

Gen	Genesis
Ex	Exodus
Lev	Leviticus
Num	Numbers
Deut	Deuteronomy
Judg	Judges
1&2 Sam	1&2 Samuel
1&2 Kings	1&2 Kings
Ps/Pss	Psalms
Prov	Proverbs
Isa	Isaiah
Hab	Habakkuk

Mt	Matthew
Mk	Mark
Lk	Luke
Jn	John
Acts	Acts
Rom	Romans
1&2 Cor	1&2 Corinthians

Gal	Galatians
Eph	Ephesians
Phil	Philippians
Col	Colossians
1&2 Thess	1&2 Thessalonians
1&2 Tim	1&2 Timothy
Tit	Titus
Philem	Philemon
Jas	James
Heb	Hebrews
1&2&3 Jn	1&2&3 John
Jude	Judge
Rev	Revelation

In the Beginning Was the Word

Introduction

THE BIBLE IN American history defines a subject of extraordinary depth and vast complexity. For countless Americans—of high estate and low, slave and free, male and female, red and yellow, black and white—Scripture has opened a doorway to the personal experience of God. To varying degrees for those ones and many others, the Bible has also functioned as a guide to life, sometimes with liberating or comic effects and sometimes with oppressive or tragic results. Scripture has obviously played a dominant role in the organized religious activities of all Christian and Jewish traditions, as well as with variations among Muslims and believers in other sacred texts. As a tangible object, it has been a ubiquitous physical presence—sanctifying all manner of homes, but also focusing rituals, stimulating commerce, distinguishing ethnic communities, naming the landscape, and memorializing stages on life's way. It has made an incalculably large contribution to the construction of culture—in vernacular and elite speech, in political persuasion, in iconic and literary representation, in scholarship, in legal reasoning, and in entertainment. It is no exaggeration to claim that the Bible has been—and by far—the single most widely read text, distributed object, and referenced book in all of American history.

This book about *the Book* examines the public history of America's most comprehensively present "thing" from first European contact through the American War of Independence. It goes almost without saying that a *public* history like this is possible only because of the immense significance of Scripture for *personal* histories. The Bible's message—its dynamic accounts of divine creation, divine judgment, divine mercy, and divine guidance—has been appropriated with many differences in countless variations. Yet because of the power of that message, as both actively embraced and formally recognized, Scripture has featured in public life wherever it has been heard, read, marked, learned, and inwardly digested.

To illustrate, Martin Luther early in the sixteenth century expounded the fifth chapter of the Epistle to the Galatians, with its stirring words about standing "fast in the liberty wherewith Christ hath made us free," as a thrilling description of personal redemption. Because personal appropriations of this text continued to resonate so powerfully through the generations, it stood ready in the eighteenth century for the Americans who evoked it to condemn plans for an Anglican bishop in the colonies, to attack the institution of slavery, and to promote armed rebellion against king and Parliament.[1] In other words, without ongoing personal engagement, no compelling reason would exist to attempt a public history.

For this particular attempt, three densely connected realities propel the narrative. First, if Roman Catholics introduced the Christian Scriptures to the Americas, including areas now in the United States, Protestants, professing to follow the Bible above all other authorities, dominated this early history and dominated it overwhelmingly. Although the history of Scripture in the United States even after 1776 rested on that strongly Protestant legacy, Catholics, Jews, and adherents of other holy books eventually contributed significantly to what became an ecumenically Christian and then an actively interfaith story. But the colonial history of Scripture unfolded, with very few exceptions, as a Protestant history where Protestants perceived those with other convictions about the Bible or with loyalty to other sacred texts as enemies. A primary goal of this study is to show what it meant—positively, negatively, ironically, often inadvertently—for Protestants to claim that they followed the Scripture above all other human authorities.

The second and third matters give this history its plot, as well as its contemporary relevance. The Bible occupied a central place in Protestantism because it served so well to attack the devastating errors Protestants perceived in Roman Catholicism and also because it could guide their own efforts to live as Christian believers. But—the second reality—Protestants always differed considerably among themselves concerning *how* Scripture served as a guide. Was it the primary guide? The one essential guide? The crucial guide? Or the only guide? Protestants in colonial America held all of these positions, and more. Yet attempts to live by "the Bible alone" (as the only guide) enjoyed greater currency in the colonies than in any part of Europe. This attempt—which I define as "biblicism" later in this introduction—keyed especially significant developments in American life, from the seventeenth-century Puritans who established Holy Commonwealths in New England through the eighteenth-century revivalists who proclaimed scriptural truths as bringing personal redemption to disputants in the Revolutionary era who argued about the legitimacy of slavery. Although far from the only approach to Scripture, trust in "the Bible alone" emerged by the end of the eighteenth century as one of the most important colonial legacies to the new nation. As this book's underlying second theme, I try to explain why that particular view became more powerful in the colonies than in Britain, how it related to other stances on Scripture, and what legacy these colonial developments bequeathed to the later history of the United States.

The third reality was the assumption of Christendom (also defined later) that settlers brought to the New World. Apart from a few radicals in Europe, almost all Protestants from their origin in the early sixteenth century took for granted that societies existed as organic unities. In this belief they stood with their Roman Catholic contemporaries. Since a Supreme Deity actually existed and had communicated his will by revelation to humankind, all human life should be organized in response to that revelation. To some degree before the Reformation and much more intensely after it began, Europeans differed on *how* God revealed his will and over *what* that will entailed. But the assumption of a unified social-political-cultural whole prevailed so widely that those who questioned it looked more like seditious maniacs than principled dissenters.

Christendom, too, came with European settlers to the New World. Yet because of the diversity of colonial settlements as well as the space that America opened for innovation, assumptions about Christendom eventually changed and, in some cases, drastically so. Because the Bible had always functioned as a crucial factor in those assumptions, the new-world history of Scripture and the new-world history of Christendom moved in lockstep together. The most complicated aspect of this colonial history is the way that trust in the Bible could both strengthen and weaken the Christendom heritage. Over the course of the eighteenth century, recourse to Scripture fueled rejection of church-state establishments, the most important institutional structure of Christendom. At the same time, deepened attachment to Scripture heightened the feeling that all of life required divine direction from the Bible, which allowed for what might be called "informal Christendom" to continue even when Americans rejected church-state establishments. Europeans have never fathomed this distinction between institutional and informal Christendom. But that distinction, with Scripture as key for its emergence, became a central feature of late-colonial life and exerted a tremendous influence on later American history.[2]

With this book on Protestant trust in the Bible, particular attitudes toward scriptural authority, and the new-world history of Christendom, I hope to explore questions especially relevant for those who, as the Scriptures might say, have eyes to see. For Roman Catholic and Eastern Orthodox Christians, as well as Jews and others who believe that a deity or deities actually communicate with human beings, this book can provide an instructive tale. Their religions have a place for Scripture, but not exclusively central in Protestant fashion. Colonial Protestants, with their particularly strong reliance on Scripture, did many things that strengthened their own faith and made them a blessing to society at large. Just as certainly they did other things that harmed themselves and created havoc for all. Attending to the whys and wherefores of what went right and what went wrong in Protestant attachment to Scripture should provide other kinds of believers with examples of what they might imitate and what they should at all costs avoid in living by their own understanding of divine revelation.

For Protestants in the contemporary United States who (like myself) continue to regard the Bible as definitive divine revelation, I hope the book can serve as a cautionary tale. Its narrative treats both the positive life-transforming power of Scripture along with a host of destructive or delusionary results manifest among those who believed in that power. Active trust in "the Bible alone," or in Scripture more generally, guaranteed social influence; it did not guarantee positive benefits for that influence in society.

For those with no interest or belief in divine revelation, I hope the book can illuminate aspects of the American past that for good and ill continue to bear on the present. Standards of secular morality differ as much as standards based on divine revelation, but those standards will be applied with more knowledge, insight, and perhaps empathy if they are informed by fuller historical understanding.

Public Life

The pages that follow concentrate on the Bible in *politics* and the Bible for *empire* or *nation*—that is, Scripture in the sphere of coercive power defined, defended, or contested—as well as for the processes by which political units create or articulate their own identities. *In the Beginning Was the Word* does draw freely on an inexhaustible record documenting how the Bible has been appropriated by individuals, put to use by religious institutions, found expression in other social institutions, and contributed to the meanings that make up culture. But the purpose throughout is to show how such influences shaped the history of Scripture for political, imperial, and national purposes.

As should be obvious already, the chapters in this book are pointing toward a consideration of the Bible's public history in the later United States. My hope is soon to publish an account that traces the rise and gradual decline of a "Bible civilization" in the United States' long nineteenth century. Yet that later history rests so firmly on what went before that it cannot be properly understood without reasonably full attention to developments in Europe and America before the United States came into existence.

The later history from the American Revolution through the First World War involved the continuing effort by sectarian evangelical Protestants to reestablish an "informal Christendom" even after they had helped dismantle church-state established religion. By the 1830s this informal Christendom had come to exert great influence on the nation as a whole, but then it wavered when confronted with the crises that led to the Civil War; thereafter it declined further by fits and starts through the fifty years leading up to World War I. Over the same years, the biblicist approach first came close to dominating Protestant circles, but then it too wavered. Irreconcilable quarrels among Protestants, especially over what Scripture taught concerning slavery, sped its decline, but so also did success by Catholics, Jews, and some with no interest in religion who contested the dominance of Protestant mores.

This later United States history—with the Bible as a forceful but constantly contested influence—did not emerge ex nihilo. It unfolded, instead, as the latest stage in a rich history with origins deep in the ancient Mediterranean world, redirected during the first Protestant centuries, and strongly influenced by crises in British history under the Tudors, Stuarts, and Hanoverians that provided the default cultural patterns for the American colonies. In this much longer history, the embeddedness of Scripture within Christendom was absolutely central.

Christendom, Protestantism, and the Bible

Christendom represented an ideal of civilization marked by the thorough intermingling of religion with everything else. As defined succinctly by the historian Hugh McLeod, it meant "a society where there are close ties between leaders of the church and secular elites; where the laws purport

to be based on Christian principles; where, apart from certain clearly defined outsider communities, everyone is assumed to be Christian; and
where Christianity provides a common language, shared alike by the de-
vout and the religiously lukewarm."[3]

A plethora of signal moments defined the possible variations of secular
and religious authority within Christendom: from the Emperor Constantine
in the early fourth century beginning to support the Christian churches or
Charlemagne on Christmas Day in the year 800 reluctantly accepting the
crown of the Holy Roman Empire from Pope Leo III; through Martin
Luther protected by his prince, Frederick of Saxony, after his published
opinions discredited him with pope and emperor, and John Calvin advis-
ing the Geneva city councils on the mode of execution for Michael Servetus
(sentenced to death for his religious opinions); to the sponsorship of over-
seas Christian missions by first Catholic powers (Portugal, Spain, France)
and then by Protestants (Denmark, the Netherlands, Britain, Germany)—
to the blunt prescription attributed to Denis Diderot sometime late in the
ancien regime of France that "men will never be free until the last king is
strangled with the entrails of the last priest." However much the balance
of power shifted back and forth between what we today call "church" and
"state," behind the variable disposition of those realms lay a nearly universal conviction: existence, under God, must be visibly unified, whatever the
exact configuration of that unity.

Integral to Christendom was, naturally, Christianity, and integral to
Christianity was the Bible. From the emergence of Christendom in the late-
Roman and early medieval eras, implicit, foundational trust in Scripture
remained a constant. In the late fourth century, a noted Roman rhetori-
cian and recent Christian convert penned a testimony to Scripture that
became as influential as it was typical. The following passage from *The
Confessions* of St. Augustine deserves extensive quotation since it reflects
something of the exalted regard for the Bible that informed much of
Western history:

> So, since we were too weak to discover truth by pure reason
> and therefore needed the authority of Holy Writ, I now began to
> believe that you could not possibly have given such supreme author-
> ity to these Scriptures all over the world, unless it had been your
> wish that by means of them men should both believe in you and
> seek after you.... In fact, the authority of Scripture seemed to me
> the more venerable and the more worthy of religious faith because,

while it was easy to read for everybody, it also preserved in the more profound sense of its meaning the majesty of something secret; it offers itself to all in plain words and a very simple style of speech, yet serious thinkers have to give it their closest attention. Thus its arms are wide open to receive everyone.[4]

Yet if Christendom was unimaginable without the powerful presence of Scripture, so also did Christendom shape the imagination of those who heard the Bible and acted upon its precepts. The well-established practices of Western Christian society cut the channels in which biblical usage flowed. So deep did those channels become that the Bible's central place in the terrain of Christendom could usually be taken simply for granted. Indeed, through most of the centuries from ca. 350 to ca. 1520, while the Bible remained an essential foundation, it was a foundation obscured by the public edifices built upon it. Some of those edifices were physical, like churches constructed by princes and municipalities where entire communities joined to worship God. Other edifices were conceptual, like the interpretive conventions taught in churches, monasteries, and eventually universities that governed how believers looked to the Scriptures for moral, social, and theological direction.

The taken-for-granted status of Scripture as indispensable deep structure for Christendom explains much about the very earliest career of the Bible in America. As sketched in the Prelude, that history was well underway before the rise of Protestantism complicated the story. For American history, "in the beginning" the Word was in Spanish, Latin, and native languages like Nahuatal—and no one paid much attention to the Bible as a principle in its own right. Yet for Catholic figures like Christopher Columbus or Bartholomé de las Casas, the Bible figured as centrally as for almost any later Protestant, only not as a contested object.

With the rise of Protestantism, Scripture emerged from the shadows. When Protestants attempted to rebuild the superstructures of Christendom, biblical foundations were exposed for contentious scrutiny. The controversies of the sixteenth century are the subject of chapter 1; their bequest shaped the story narrated in the rest of this book and the second volume to come on the United States' nineteenth century. After the Reformation, the long history of Protestant-Catholic strife would be defined by two first-order questions: How could humans be reconciled to God? How could we know?

The most important early leaders of the Protestant Reformation challenged neither Christendom nor Christianity's traditional deference to Scripture. They did challenge what they took to be the corrupt, enervating, hypocritical, distorted, simoniacal, neglectful, and completely indefensible abuse of Scripture in the Roman Catholic Church. That challenge concentrated on what in their eyes had become the inadequate honoring, teaching, preaching, application, and simple understanding of the Bible. In carrying out this challenge, they raised into self-consciousness what had been mostly conventional opinion about the centrality of Scripture for personal Christian existence and corporate Christian civilization.

Significantly for what came later in America, Protestant efforts to recover Scripture's true meaning and, thereby, restore Christianity to Christendom spun off two radical notions that later made a real difference. One of these notions raised the banner of biblicism. The other proclaimed the hitherto unimaginable possibility that the Bible might oppose Christendom.

Biblicism and the Protestant Trust in Scripture

As used in this book, "biblicism" means an effort to follow "the Bible alone"—absent or strongly subordinating other authorities—as the path of life with and for God. The word seems to have been used first by John Sterling, a Scottish friend of Thomas Carlyle, who applied it to the English Puritans of the seventeenth century. In 1843, Sterling made a chronological observation to Carlyle about the latter's plan to write a book on Oliver Cromwell. Sterling wrote that by the seventeenth century, the Royalists who supported King Charles I had already degenerated into a complacent "Squirism"—by contrast to the energy and dedication of the Puritans. In framing this comparison he coined the word: "One must go back to the Middle Ages to see Squirism as rampant and vivacious as Biblicism was in the Seventeenth Century."[5] He was referring to the Puritans' ardent profession to follow only the Scriptures as they pushed for further reforms of the English state-church establishment.[6]

I am using "biblicism" in this sense, but with more emphasis on the word's critical function than implied by Sterling. In his history of American fundamentalism, George Marsden emphasized that function, while specifying an important American chronology: "This Biblicism, strong among the Puritans, gained new significance in the early nineteenth century.... The true church should set aside all intervening tradition, and return to the purity of New Testament practice. The Bible alone should be one's guide."[7]

Historians have rightly linked biblicism with another abstract noun—primitivism, or the desire to shrug off the accumulated detritus of the centuries in order to recover pure Christianity as experienced by the very first believers.[8] Protestants in general rehabilitated the reputation of medieval reformers who had complained about the Catholic Church's drift away from earlier and purer Christian standards. Among English Protestants a particularly strong primitivist critique carried over from attacks on Rome to prescriptions aimed at reforming English church life. That strand, in turn, contributed much to American settlements in New England and has ever since been periodically revived by American critics disgusted by official corruption and visionaries longing for the New Jerusalem.

In the Beginning Was the Word concentrates on what it meant for biblicism to arise as a powerful force in England during the second half of the sixteenth century, to flourish there into the middle of the next century, only then to recede—though for different reasons and with quite different effects in the mother country and the colonies. The heart of the book features developments during the mid- to late-eighteenth century that led to a resurgence of this approach in the colonies. Those developments included a powerful appeal to the Bible by revivalists as well as a shift in political ideology that led colonists to view hereditary or aristocratic authority as purest evil. Only the Bible—and often in the form of "the Bible alone"—survived the Revolution's assault on old-world traditions.[9]

From the late 1510s, almost all Protestants sounded like biblicists when they addressed corruptions they perceived in the Catholic church. As with so much else, Martin Luther created the mold when at the very inception of the Reformation he took his stand against pope and emperor—against, that is, the weight of European Christendom—on the Bible alone (chapter 1). That note then reappeared consistently in Protestant history, perhaps most memorably in a famous sentence from a polemical tract published in 1638: "The BIBLE, I say, THE BIBLE only is the Religion of Protestants!"[10] (The ironical context of that statement is explored in chap. 3).

Yet for Luther, as also for most Protestants in the sixteenth century and since, biblicism served a polemical purpose more than it functioned as a practical guide. Reliance on *sola scriptura*, or "the Bible alone," worked well as a weapon of criticism wielded to draw Christendom back to Christ.

For church reform, social renewal, or the practices of piety, however, things became more complicated. From the beginning, recourse to Scripture operated on a spectrum where Protestants accepted different complements from outside the text itself. On the biblicist end of the spectrum stood those who in principle questioned any authority except the Bible, or that the Bible directly sanctioned. On the other end stood those who viewed the Bible's supreme authority as perfectly compatible with other authorities that did not contradict Scripture. "Directly sanction" as opposed to "not contradict" sounds like a small difference, but that distinction has produced a great array of intra-Protestant disputation.

As we observe in chapters 2 and 3, the main English Protestant confessions of the sixteenth and seventeenth centuries both articulated principles of supreme biblical authority and specified several appropriate secondary authorities. The Protestants who promoted these confessions were, thus, trying to be biblical, but they were not biblicists as I am defining that word.

Efforts to secure the Bible as an ultimate standard were also complicated because of implicit authorities that functioned alongside those that Europeans explicitly acknowledged. Authorities beneath the level of consciousness have played a role in all religious movements—indeed, in all human contexts. Among Protestants bent on following Scripture wherever it led, those implicit extratextual influences could be personal—for example, deference to a charismatic leader like Martin Luther or John Calvin, whose teaching became the sole possible interpretation of Scripture for those who trusted the leader's guidance. More commonly, implicit authority came from mental habits absorbed unselfconsciously. What the surrounding culture took for granted about accepted ideals of organization, conventions of interpretation (i.e., hermeneutical assumptions), and commonplace attitudes toward self or the ideal life influenced Protestant appropriation of Scripture—as similar habits have informed all humans in all settings, including the efforts of historians. The presence of implicit authorities complicates the history of the Bible among Protestants because such authorities exerted their influence at every point on the spectrum—from those who claimed to follow the Bible *only* to those who willingly accepted secondary authorities, and with many variations in between.

Examples abound. Biblicists and other Protestants often came to treat the King James Version of the Scriptures as simply "the Bible" with entire confidence that this particular translation represented the plenitude of biblical revelation. Some nonbiblicists took for granted that the conclusions of a Protestant standard like the Westminster Confession (1646) could interpret Scripture with absolute finality—despite what the Confession explicitly stated about the unique status of the sacred text. Even more widespread became the assumption that the application of a "proof text" could secure unambiguous divine sanction for a particular point of dogma or a particular action in church or society—with no apparent awareness that when Bible users cited chapter and verse by number (e.g., Gn 3:15; Mt 28:16; Rom 3:23), they employed a culturally particular way of dividing up the flow of biblical narratives that came not from the original texts but from much later editorial work. The verse divisions of sacred Scripture, and hence much use of Scripture so divided, in reality reflected human actions with no claim to inspiration by the Holy Spirit (chap. 2).

In the pages that follow I try to sort out the interplay of authorities in several intersecting planes—appeals to the Bible versus other authorities, claims and counterclaims evoking Scripture with equal fervor, controversy usually stimulated by biblicists over which secondary authorities should be allowed to stand alongside Scripture, and even deeper controversy occasioned by the operation of presupposed authorities.

Heartfelt debates over the interpretation of Scripture did not begin in the sixteenth century. Yet the rise of Protestantism manifestly expanded the scope and deepened the intensity of those debates. The precipitating spark for that expansion and intensification was everywhere the Protestant drive to purify the corruptions of Catholicism by appeal to Holy Scripture. To repeat, all Protestants sounded like biblicists when they focused on Catholic errors. Yet the Protestants who maintained biblicist principles when they turned to the restoration (or the abolition) of Christendom made the strongest appeals with the most far-reaching effects. A main purpose of this book is to show why those appeals became stronger in the colonies than in Britain, especially in the decades after 1740 that would shape cultural instincts for the new nation.

The Bible and Christendom: Protestant Variations

From within Protestantism came a second radical idea that had been all but unthinkable for at least a millennium before 1520. It was the conviction that faithfulness to Scripture demanded *opposition* to Christendom. This revolutionary idea arose when radicals transformed the biblicism with which other Protestants attacked Rome into a principle of their own for guiding Christian life. They asked, as a first instance: Where in Scripture could a specific warrant be found for the time-honored practice of baptizing infants? Once that question emerged, others followed almost immediately: Biblical warrant for paying taxes leveled by the state to support the church? Biblical warrant for going to war at the command of government? Biblical warrant for coercive discipline of citizens thought to have violated church teachings? The Anabaptists aggressively troubled Europe with such persistent questions. For their pains, the governments of Western Christendom, Catholic and Protestant alike, subjected them to imprisonment, exile, and execution. If Anabaptists were condemned as heretics for their beliefs, the more serious crime was their seditious folly of rejecting Christendom.

Protestantism began with a strong point of agreement: recovering the true message of Scripture was the essential first task for repairing the great damage done to Christianity by the Catholic church. Yet from early in the Reformation, three Protestant stances existed with respect to the Bible and Christendom. The first and most common appeared among those who believed that a clarified understanding of Scripture would restore the spiritual integrity and public virtue of Christendom. Early Protestant leaders have been called "magisterial reformers" (from "magister," or teacher) because they sought to bring Christendom back to its godly purposes through the restoration of proper biblical teaching. Their efforts contributed to the creation of "confessional states" that, along with contemporary Catholic counterparts, divided Europe into locally specific mini-Christendoms.[11] While the magisterial Protestants might have spoken like biblicists in attacking Rome, they did not carry out their work of restitution on the basis of the Bible alone. In America, the colonies with the strongest Anglican presence, especially Virginia, exemplified this stance. Their white citizens would long view the Bible as belonging to Christendom, and Christendom as the only proper frame for the Bible.

A second and opposing variation came from the Anabaptists, as well as other radicals who thought that the recovery of biblical Christianity demanded the abandonment of Christendom. When the leaders of Protestant confessional states censured their proposals for reform, these upstarts responded with words their Protestant opponents had thrown at Catholics about the need to follow only God's written word. To be sure, not all radicals were biblicists, for some believed they could receive divine revelation directly from the Holy Spirit without the mediation of a sacred book.[12] Nonetheless, the driving force behind radical Protestant attacks against organized Christendom came from the appeal to Scripture as a unique *and comprehensive* authority.

In a political Europe that was soon divided into competing confessional states, the radicals enjoyed scant opportunity to show what a post-Christendom society might look like. Instead, Bible-based protests against Christendom sustained a precarious existence on the European margins. They were also marginal in seventeenth-century colonial America. Biblicist principles did inspire the maverick Roger Williams when he protested against the Puritan Christendom of New England (chap. 5). Williams hoped his new colony, Rhode Island, would allow other biblicists to join him in displaying a better way, but most observers in Britain and America, when they noticed Rhode Island at all, considered it a byword for moral and social chaos.

Somewhat later, William Penn relied on a moderate biblicism to create a colony that moved beyond Christendom less aggressively than did Rhode Island (also chap. 5). Penn's experiment became more significant than Williams's, especially when it proved attractive to his fellow Quakers, who tried to make the colony into a "peaceable kingdom," and also to European sectarians whom authorities had hounded for not conforming to Christendom rules. Yet well into the eighteenth century, the most typical Christian movements transplanted to North America rejected the way Scripture was used in Rhode Island and Pennsylvania as whimsical, dangerous, or berserk.

Representatives of another Protestant variation tried for a third way that is now harder to grasp. They continued to take Christendom for granted even as they proposed to reform it by using Scripture in biblicist or nearly biblicist fashion. Protestants of this sort stood with the magisterial reformers in seeking a Christian commonwealth, but with the Anabaptists in using biblical authority as a principle of criticism against other Protestants. During the reign of Queen Elizabeth, 1558–1603, Protestants who believed that England remained mired in an incomplete reform, continued to push for change dictated by their strict adherence to Scripture. To advance these efforts at purifying church and nation, they returned repeatedly to the Bible as the first principle. Scripture alone—the biblicist formula—was their battle cry. From the 1570s on, the desire to burn away dross intensified in direct proportion to resistance from the regime. Elizabeth—then King James I (1603–25) and his son Charles I (1625–42/49)—maintained a moderately Protestant path, but one guided at every step by imperatives of state craft and dynastic security. From reformers came a predictable response: ever more strident appeals to the Bible alone.

As tensions continued to build under Elizabeth, James, and Charles, a few reformers gave up on nationwide reform and, functionally if not always explicitly, gave up also on Christendom; they took the pilgrim path from England to the Netherlands, back to England, and then on to the Plymouth Colony in America. A larger number of reformers continued to uphold an ideal of Christendom reformed by the Word of God but gave up on England; they set out to the New World in order to establish what they could not accomplish in the Old. These Puritans founded the colonies of Massachusetts, Connecticut, and New Haven.

In England, even more reformers held out, giving up neither on the mother country nor on Christendom. They eventually joined the Parliamentary forces offended by the actions of Charles I. After the warfare that broke out in 1640 led to the victory of Parliamentary-Puritan forces, many of these English reformers tried to refashion the church and nation on biblicist or near-biblicist terms. As a consequence with great significance for the future, they failed in that attempt. Disagreements within the Puritan-Parliamentary coalition over what the Bible required posed a first irremediable dilemma, and then in 1660 an exhausted nation welcomed back the monarchy along with its Anglican establishment. Thereafter the Bible still remained very much alive in England. Yet as an important difference with the colonies, the biblicist approach to communitywide reform did not. After the English Glorious Revolution of 1689, Parliament under the monarchs William and Mary legislated a measure of toleration for Bible believers who denounced Christendom and for biblicists disillusioned by the Anglican establishment. But the influence—especially the political influence—of the small minorities holding these two radical positions remained severely limited.

The Bible in the Colonies

In the colonies it was a different story. For New England, biblicist efforts to establish a thoroughly reformed Commonwealth seemed to succeed for thirty years or more. But from about 1660, while never dramatically quashed as in England, the biblicism of the Bible Commonwealths did begin to fade. Eventually, for reasons spelled out in chapters 6, 9, 10, and 11, colonists mostly came to use the Bible in pubic life as regulated by what could be called (after the union with Scotland in 1707) British imperial Christendom.

In the century between 1660 and 1760, Scripture remained a pervasive presence in the colonies, even as biblicist rhetoric gradually faded. New England's biblicist Christendom, Pennsylvania's post-Christendom Christianity, and the South's Anglican Christendom carried on, but all were increasingly drawn into the mother country's web of commerce, imperial struggle, political intrigue, and literary fashion. As explained in chapter 9, when considering most questions about economic life, racial hierarchy, and political principles, the Bible operated in the background as a support, rather than in the foreground as an explicit authority. Colonists also felt the effect of tectonic intellectual movements, designated by historians as the Enlightenment, that began to disaggregate religion from other spheres of life.

Yet historical development was never uncomplicated. As an important difference from Britain, the move in the colonies away from biblicism remained evolutionary, nonviolent, and did not involve a cataclysmic crisis like civil war and a monarchical Restoration. As a result, biblicism was never as thoroughly discredited in the colonies as was the case in England after 1660.

The colonies also experienced countervailing currents. Even as absorption into imperial consciousness weakened appeals to follow "the Bible alone" (for economic, political and some social purposes), Scripture appropriated very much as "the Bible alone" received a substantial boost during the 1730s and 1740s. As explained in chapters 7 and 8, evangelical revivals quickened many individuals spiritually by bringing selected scriptural themes passionately to life; it led also to self-selected communities in which heeding the particulars of Scripture as a guide for personal religious life became an urgent priority. Without questioning allegiance to the Protestant British empire, those riding the crest of evangelical renewal moved back toward biblicist norms, at least for personal and communal purposes. Much the same also characterized those in Britain affected by evangelical revival, only in a context where the biblicist option for society had been eliminated.

As a consequence, by the mid-eighteenth century, the place of Scripture in the American colonies was both narrowing and intensifying. Along with increased ardor for the Bible wherever the religion of evangelical revival took hold—often in expressly biblicist terms—came also a shrinking of the spheres to which even the most active Protestants applied the Scriptures.

The interplay of Bible and empire produced unexpected results. During the middle decades of the eighteenth century, colonial leaders deployed a full range of biblical texts to strengthen loyalty to Britain, always depicted as Protestant and freedom-loving in opposition to papal and tyrannical France. Yet in the same years—and for the first time—African Americans in substantial numbers responded positively to the Christian message (chap. 8). For this largely un-free population the biblicist or near-biblicist style of the revivalists made many more converts than had responded to earlier efforts at Christianizing the colonies' enslaved black population. Crucially, those early efforts had all presented Christianity to blacks as the religion of Christendom. With only a few exceptions, the colonial representatives of Christendom also assumed the moral legality of black chattel slavery. Revival religion did not usually call slavery into question; yet it did proclaim a biblicist form of faith with scant attention to the inherited structures of British tradition. The complex story of the colonies at mid-century must, therefore, account for the Bible both expanding its influence with a marginal people whom Christendom enslaved and intensifying its support for the British Protestant Christendom responsible for slavery.

Chapters 10 and 11 show how warfare between France and Britain, conflict between Parliament and the colonies, and then the American War of Independence moved the colonists to reject the institutionalized Christendom of the British empire. In a rapid transformation, the mother country's church-state came to be perceived as a deadly example of the malignant power that had brought the colonies to the very brink of enslavement. Given the historical centrality of Scripture in British culture, it was no surprise that American patriots found much support for their convictions in the Bible—as did the smaller number of colonists who remained loyal to the mother country.

As a rhetorical presence, the Bible became even more ubiquitous in Revolutionary America—providing texts for a great array of patriotic (and a few Loyalist) sermons, enlivening the published pamphlets that everywhere proliferated, and seasoning the formal pronouncements of the rebels' governing assemblies. Yet once past well-worn phrases and a mind-set steeped in the moral universe sustained by Bible-reading, it is much harder to discern either patriots or Loyalists seeking direct guidance from the precepts of Scripture. Where earlier in New England and the middle colonies, leaders had self-consciously tried to shape politics and social life with explicit biblical precepts, now political convictions more obviously provided the substance of arguments, though still regularly sanctioned by biblical references and allusions

It is important to remember that throughout the tumultuous changes of the period considered in this book, one Protestant feature remained rock solid. Firm anti-Catholic convictions always reinforced movement from a general trust in Scripture toward more specific trust in "the Bible alone." For most Protestants during most of the three centuries from the Diet of Worms (1521) to the final defeat of Napoleon (1815), "Antichrist," as ably summarized by historian Michael Winship "was a satanic spirit of hatred against all of God's laws, driven by an insatiable lust for power.... The culmination of this rise of the spirit of Antichrist was the Catholic church."[13] As the narrative to follow makes clear, that sentiment remained just as firm for Christendom Protestants as for those who hoped the Bible could bring institutional Christendom to an end.

But What Is *the Bible?*

Although books should be clear about what they are about, that standard poses difficulties for a history of the Bible. The Canadian literary critic Northrop Frye once described the contents of Scripture as "a mosaic." But then he went on to detail the complexity of that mosaic: "a pattern of commandments, aphorisms, epigrams, proverbs, parables, riddles, pericopes, parallel couplets, formulaic phrases, folktales, oracles, epiphanies, *Gattungen*, *Logia*, bits of occasional verse, marginal glosses, legends, snippets from historical documents, laws, letters, sermons, hymns, ecstatic visions, rituals, fables, genealogical lists, and so on almost indefinitely."[14] Notwithstanding Scripture's great internal diversity, it remains justifiable for a historical account to speak more generally of "the Bible." Generations of Americans have in fact consistently used that undifferentiated term as they referred to an abstract ideal, a weapon in disputes, a source of inspiration or guidance, an object of study or meditation, and in many other ways—even when in practice they have been referring to or thinking about only limited portions of the sacred book.[15]

For all but a scholarly few, the Bible has not been the texts that first appeared in the ancient Mediterranean world but were translations that others have made of these ancient writings. Bible translations, unlike the original, appear invariably in only one language. From the early sixteenth century, hundreds of translations have rendered all or portions of Scripture into English. Yet one of the strongest justification for a history of the Bible in America is the fact that the Authorized or King James Version (KJV) of 1611 achieved an overwhelmingly dominant position for almost all public purposes from early in the colonial period until deep into the twentieth century. Because this one version remained so prominent for so long, histories of alternative translations that sought a place alongside, or aspired to serve as a replacement, reveal much about general attitudes toward Scripture.[16]

Speaking casually of "the Bible" also obscures the fact that translated (as well as original-language) Bibles have appeared in a huge variety of physical sizes and shapes.[17] They have been cheap and expensive; bound in all manner of covers and formats; immense and microscopic and all sizes in between; fancy, ornamental, and deliberately reverent as well as plain, unadorned, and intentionally down-home. Each form of published or translated Bible carries a distinct social, economic, educational, gendered, and cultural—as well as religious—connotation.

Yet especially in a more secular age, it is important to remember the primacy of those religious meanings. Bruce Metzger, a veteran New testament scholar at Princeton Theological Seminary, long served as the chairman of the translation committee of the New Revised Standard Version (NRSV), a revision of a revision of the King James Bible. When the NRSV first appeared in the late 1980s, Metzger's introduction explained at length the complex history (linguistic, organizational, academic) that lay behind its publication. Yet he closed his introduction with a reminder pertinent for all who want to chart the course of Scripture in history: "In traditional Judaism and Christianity, the Bible has been more than a historical document to be preserved or a classic of literature to be cherished and admired; it is recognized as the unique record of God's dealing with people over the ages....The Bible carries its full message, not to those who regard it simply as a noble literary heritage of the past or who wish to use it to enhance political purposes and advance otherwise desirable goals, but to all persons and communities who read it so that they may discern and understand what God is saying to them."[18] This book mostly sidesteps the main reason why the Bible has been important in American history, which is the claim of its adherents that it tells the truth. However that claim is regarded, it remains beyond question that Scripture has occupied an important place in public life and so deserves to be examined historically, with this-worldly concerns, as I have tried to do.

Protocols and Perspectives

Scholarly and popular writings on the Bible in American history could fill a good-sized library. But even the great quantity of such works comes nowhere near the stupendous array of scriptural references, quotations, citations, allusions, evocations, disputes, and more found in the primary sources left by all sorts of Americans in all past eras and from all levels of society. In the pages that follow, almost every document, sermon, tract, statement, or treatise that I treat in some detail could be multiplied countless times over. In addition, although the notes (in abbreviated form) document where I have received special insight for particular issues, full documentation for every general or historical assertion would have resulted in an apparatus that swallowed up the narrative. In partial compensation, I have added a bibliography that provides complete bibliographical information for the book's primary sources as well as many of the works that oriented me to a subject that sprawls without limit in almost every direction.

I am fully conscious that this book overflows with quotations of scriptural passages and with much reference to specific biblical texts. What might seem like overexuberant quotation to the point of tedium is deliberate. The citations and quotations reflect a self-conscious strategy that responds to an observation from Perry Miller, one of the great American historians from the first half of the twentieth century. He once wrote that "The Old Testament is truly so omnipresent in the American culture of 1800 or 1820 that historians have as much difficulty taking cognizance of it as of the air people breathed."[19] This very difficulty in focusing on the atmospheric ubiquity of Scripture makes it all the more important to attempt its history. With a changed metaphor, historians have long recognized that ubiquity but have treated it as wallpaper, simply a backdrop for more important objects of attention. This book suggests, by contrast, that Scripture should be viewed as a sturdy piece of furniture smack in the middle of the room. If I as an author, or readers in their perusal, weary of so much quotation, we reflect a basic unwillingness to confront American history as it actually unfolded.

Where authors did not specify the source of their biblical quotations, I have tried to supply those references in brackets. For reasons that will become obvious, all biblical quotations are from the King James Version, except where specified.[20] The book also pauses at several points to explain the importance of the verse divisions of Scriptures; that formatting device factors as a neglected but unusually important aspect of the Bible's history as a public document.

Implicit as well as explicit moral judgments are inevitable in any work on a subject like the Bible. Nonetheless, since this book has been written first for historical illumination, I hope it can be understood as trying above

all to provide a responsible reading of its sources. One of the most important distinctions that struck me from those sources was the difference between turning to the Bible as a source of didactic instruction versus using
the Bible as a treasury of evocative examples. It is the difference between
basing an analysis of current events on one phrase taken from a single biblical narrative and grounding it in detailed exposition of an extended passage of scriptural instruction. From that admittedly loose distinction, the
pages that follow sometimes move to a historical judgment—that the
Protestant claim to be guided by Scripture was most convincing when Bible-
users reasoned step-by-step from scriptural texts to this-worldly applications. By contrast, when such applications rested on rhetorical, figurative, or
allegorical uses of Scripture, it is easier to conclude that something other
than biblical authority—from political, class, economic, racial, gender, or
other sources—was shaping the application of Scripture. All such historical conclusions and historical judgments are of course fallible, which is
why full documentation has been provided so that others may check, and
perhaps correct, my account of what the historical figures wrote or said.

It is also obvious that historical judgments bleed easily into moral
judgments. Probably as a result of my own convictions about the Bible, I
have been more likely to view allegorical, exemplary, or merely rhetorical
usage as somehow less authentically scriptural than usage based on didactic reasoning. For example, the fiery Boston minister Jonathan Mayhew
sometimes snatched a phrase from the Psalms on which to base entire
sermons aiming at celebrating a political event, reinforcing a political
opinion, or stirring up his hearers to political action. On another occasion,
he preached a lengthy expository sermon to argue that the thirteenth
chapter of the Epistle to the Romans did not require colonists to passively
obey the dictates of Parliament.[21] Although such distinctions can never be
entirely clear-cut, these two ways of deploying Scripture did represent em-
pirically distinguishable approaches, which in turn requires a historical
judgment about how those examples conformed to—or trivialized—the
Protestant profession to follow Scripture. If, however, I go on to imply that
Mayhew's exposition of Romans 13 deserves more serious consideration
as a possible rendering of what God through the Scriptures actually
intended, that judgment verges from the historical to the moral. Although
I have tried to differentiate such evaluations from each other, readers are
forewarned about slippage between the two.

Finally, *In the Beginning was the Word* does not affirm "American exceptionalism," except in a limited historical, as opposed to moral, sense.

Historically evaluated, certain features of American experience deserve to be considered distinctive in world history; one of the most distinctive has been the central place of Scripture in American life. From that judgment, however, I do not conclude that those distinctives have given the United States a unique claim to moral, political, or religious superiority. While I hope that those who want to make judgments about the character of American moral, political, and religious life might benefit from this book, those judgments are not my primary concern. Instead, the chief goal is an explanatory narrative about changes over time for the place of Scripture, together with an assessment of the relative influence that Scripture has exerted at different times in relation to other cultural authorities and social forces. In my view, some of this colonial American engagement with Scripture made the nation that came later a better place and left a positive influence in the world; some made it a worse place and helped unleash malevolent forces in world history.

Prelude

CATHOLIC BIBLES IN THE NEW WORLD

IN LATE 1501 and early 1502, Martin Luther was studying at the University
of Erfurt, where he had recently matriculated as a student; it would be another two or three years before he first read through the Bible in the Latin
Vulgate copy held in the university library. In England, Arthur Tudor, the
Prince of Wales and heir apparent to the English throne, had only recently
married Catherine of Aragon, daughter of Isabella and Ferdinand of Spain.
Arthur's father, King Henry VII, who hoped this marriage would cement
an Anglo-Spanish alliance to check the expansive designs of France, gave
his younger son, Henry, Duke of York, a prominent role in the wedding.
Otherwise, since this younger son was not the heir, he attracted only minimal public attention. In France, Desiderius Erasmus had recently returned
from a lengthy visit to England where he had made the acquaintance of
Thomas More and John Colet. The latter had left a particularly deep impression by a style of preaching that turned aside from scholastic authorities to speak directly from the New Testament. Inspired by Colet's example,
Erasmus dedicated himself to learning Greek and began to collect older
Greek and Latin manuscripts of the New Testament.[1] The founding events
that occasioned the rise of Protestantism with its dedication to Holy
Scripture lay still in the future.

Over that same winter and early spring, Christopher Columbus, undertook a whirlwind of activities in Spain. Despite poor health, he was
preparing for a fourth voyage to the New World, contesting judicial charges
brought against him by a rival, compiling a *Book of Privileges* to secure
grants and titles he considered his due—and revising a large manuscript
that became known as the *Libro de las profecías*.[2] The last, a motley ag-
gregation of texts, included many quotations from church fathers like
St. Augustine and Thomas Aquinas, but it mostly contained biblical passages that Columbus felt predicted either his own special role in exploring

the oceans or his contribution to the Christian recapture of Jerusalem. For this effort, Columbus drew from forty-three different books of the Bible (thirty-two Old Testament, eleven New), including selections from over half the Psalms.[3]

After dedicating the manuscript to Ferdinand and Isabella, he cited several authorities on what he explained as the standard exposition of Scripture by "four methods" (history, allegory, moral teaching, "heavenly glory"). He then began by quoting from John chapter 15: "All things, whatsoever I have heard of my Father, I have made known to you." A comment from Augustine on how Scripture sometimes used the past tense to predict "future things" supplied Columbus with his warrant for the biblical interpretations he assembled in the *Libro*: they would speak of events taking place in his lifetime or soon to unfold. The lengthy dedication to the Spanish monarchs that introduced the compilation thanked Ferdinand and Isabella for sponsoring his labors and then explained the motivation that had driven him through three voyages of discovery and now prepared him for a fourth: "Who can doubt that this fire was not merely mine, but also of the Holy Spirit who encouraged me with a radiance of marvelous illumination from his sacred Holy Scriptures, by a most clear and powerful testimony from the forty-four books of the Old Testament, from the four Gospels, from the twenty-three Epistles of the blessed Apostles— urging me to press forward? Continually, without a moment's hesitation, the Scriptures urge me to press forward with great haste."[4] As experts on the life of Columbus have shown clearly, the fixation on mystical and prophetical meanings of Scripture seen in this manuscript from 1502 represented only the last stage in a long history of intense religious experience. Often Columbus interpreted that experience with a direct application of biblical texts, or even more often by inserting himself into the scriptural record, as he did at critical moments during his first voyage in September 1492 when he likened himself to Noah and Moses.[5]

Parallels to what appeared later in American history with ardent British Protestants are unmistakable. Columbus exhibited the same mastery of content from the entire Scriptures, the same deep confidence in the Bible as divine revelation, and the same willingness to read his own experience into the scriptural story. If his hermeneutic came from the Middle Ages instead of the sixteenth century's New Learning and if his theological guides were Catholic instead of Protestant, he nonetheless embraced the Bible with what might be styled Puritan ardor. Although this book as a history of "the Bible in America" will record a mostly Protestant story, it is important to recognize who came first.

Intense Catholic engagement with Scripture marked a great deal of the initial European exploration and conquest of the New World. A notable publishing first in 1516 testified to the depth of that engagement. In that year Erasmus also published his landmark *Novum instrumentum omne* in Basel, a bilingual edition of the New Testament, featuring a Greek text that Erasmus had collated from several extant manuscripts, alongside the text of the Vulgate—and which, as the pages to come reveal, inspired many early Protestant leaders. It was two years after a team in Spain guided by Cardinal Francisco Ximénez de Cisneros completed and printed their more extensively researched Complutensian Polyglot, with an even more reliable Greek text, but four years before that Polyglot was released to the public. In 1516 Martin Luther was lecturing to students at the University of Wittenberg on the Psalms. In England, the nation had recently celebrated the birth of a royal princess, Mary, born to Henry VIII and his wife, Catherine of Aragon, whom he had married after his brother Arthur's death—and a young Master of Arts, William Tyndale, was preparing to carry on further language and biblical studies at Cambridge.

Alongside Erasmus's *Novum instrumentum*, the publishing event of 1516 was the *Polyglot Psalter* produced by a learned Genoese, Agostino Giustiniani. His beautiful volume represented probably the first printed polyglot book as well as the first printed Arabic translation of the Scriptures. The Polyglot's eight columns offered the Psalms in the Latin Vulgate, two other Latin translations by Giustiniani, Hebrew, Greek, Aramaic, and Arabic, with the eighth for the editor's wide-ranging commentaries (*scholia*). Psalm 18:5 in the Vulgate (19:4 in later Protestant Bibles) reads *in universam terram exivit sonus eorum et in finibus orbis verba eorum* ("Their sound hath gone forth into all the earth; and their words unto the ends of the world," Douay-Rheims-Challoner). It was adjacent to this sentence that Giustiniani inserted a publishing first: the substantial biography of his fellow Genoese, the Admiral of the Ocean Sea. This account, of approximately 1,600 words in English translation, lauded Columbus for his discoveries, though it did not hesitate to criticize Spanish depredations on natives ("Spain sent her poison to an innocent world"). It also spelled out clearly the connection between this comment on the Psalm and the sailor's own convictions: "Since Columbus often declared that God had chosen him to fulfill this prophecy ['to the ends of the world'] through him, I have not considered it inappropriate to insert here his biography."[6] In years to come, many other Christian inhabitants of North America would read the fate of their own communities into the Scriptures, but few by integrating modern history and ancient Scripture so thoroughly as in Giustiani's Polyglot.

The devotion to Scripture witnessed in Columbus's life continued to mark a significant minority of other Spanish settlers in the New World. Conspicuous in that number was Bartolomé de las Casas whose life shines as a rare humanitarian beacon against the darkness of Europe's cataclysmic

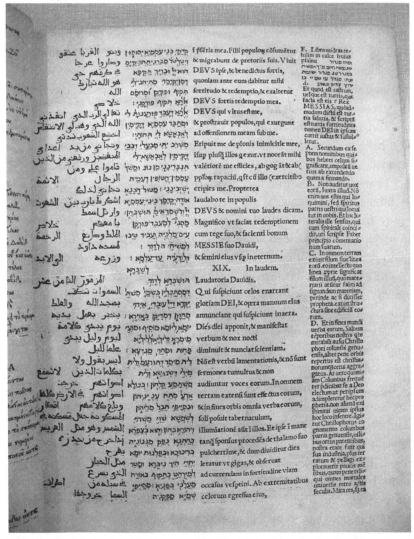

This page with Psalm 18 in Agostino Giustiniani's Polyglot Psalter of 1516 includes the first published biography of Christopher Columbus as an extensive side note. (Courtesy of the American Bible Society Library)

assault on North American native peoples. As a boy in Seville, Las Casas had witnessed the return of Columbus from his first voyage in 1493; he would later preserve for posterity primary sources documenting the admiral's voyages in his *History of the Indies*. In contrast to Columbus, however, Las Casas's application of Scripture to the New World featured direct ethical teaching rather than speculative prophetic interpretation. After traveling to Hispaniola with his merchant father and working there for a short period, Las Casas came back to Spain where he was ordained a deacon and then, in 1507, a priest. Upon his return to the Indies, especially after joining the Dominicans in 1522, he campaigned relentlessly for humane treatment of the Indians. Through a number of important publications and impassioned personal appeals to Spanish officials, in the New World as well as at the Spanish court, Las Casas became his era's most conspicuous advocate for native rights and dignity.

Guidance from the Scriptures infused all of Las Casas's activities and publications. Nowhere was that guidance more prominent than in the manuscript *De Unico Vocationis Modo* ("The Only Way to Draw All People to a Living Faith") that he first composed in 1534 and thereafter used as an intellectual warehouse supplying arguments, citations, references, and resources for later publications, letters, and public appeals.[7] In 1537 he prepared an expanded version for presentation to King Charles I of Spain (whom we will meet later as the Holy Roman Emperor Charles V).

The manuscript's two main sections explained "True Evangelization" and "False Evangelization." The first drew on patristic and medieval church authorities, but even more heavily on Scripture, to explain how the Christian gospel should be promoted; the second, with much detail specifying Spanish atrocities in the New World, he again supported from church authorities and with selective quoting from the Bible.

Early in the first part Las Casas established the Christian church's mandate for evangelism by noting "the universal command as it is stated in Matthew 28:19–20: 'Go teach all nations, baptizing them in the name of the Father, and of the son, and of the Holy Spirit, teaching them to obey all that I have commanded you.' And Paul to the Romans (10:17): 'Faith comes from hearing, hearing from the word of Christ.'" His next sentence summarized the argument of the entire work: "Therefore the way of teaching people has to be a gentle, coaxing, gracious way."[8] Within only the next few paragraphs, Las Casas cited or quoted from Matthew 10, Luke 9, Acts 13, again Matthew 10, Luke 10, again Mathew 10, and Matthew 11.

He intended the catena of quotations to explain what "It all means: learn from me [Christ] that you also may be meek and humble of heart."[9]

Las Casas of course wrote as an individual of his own times, with assumptions about power, prerogatives, people, and progress commonplace for his particular setting. Yet his reliance on traditional church teaching, including an extensive deployment of Scripture, also equipped him to stand against powerful conventions of his age and to advocate for the Indians as few other Europeans did. Whether that ability came from a quirk of personality or from the Christian sources he channeled for his advocacy cannot be determined by ordinary historical reasoning. It nonetheless remains striking that for a Continental history where Protestants long monopolized claims about allegiance to Scripture, a Catholic appearing on the scene before Protestants arrived showed clearly what that allegiance could mean as a force resisting, as well as expressing, Christendom.

Las Casas, however, was far from typical. The Franciscans, Dominicans, and eventually Jesuits who accompanied the Spanish, Portuguese, and then French to the Americas did their best to transform colonial outposts into sites of Christian civilization.[10] Yet their own weaknesses, alongside the colonizers' lust for dominion, compromised almost all of these efforts.

For a history of the Bible, the kind of easy familiarity and ready use seen in Columbus and Las Casas—and also promoted by the Bible-centered reforms of the Ximénez circle in Spain—carried on in the New World through the first half of the sixteenth century.[11] In 1548 a printed collection of sermons, *Doctrina Christiana en lengua española y Mexicana*, included the Lord's Prayer from Matthew chapter 6 as well as other brief passages in Spanish and Nahuatl.[12] Earlier, the first archbishop of Mexico, Juan de Zumárraga, encouraged the translation of selections from the New Testament gospels and epistles into Nahuatl for use in catechetical instruction. His promotion of such work paralleled his opposition to notions spread by other Spanish settlers that the Indians lacked the intelligence to understand the written Scriptures. Zumárraga's reply was unequivocal: "I do not approve the view of those who say that the simple-minded should not read the sacred text in the language that the common people use, because Jesus Christ desires that its secrets be spread abroad widely."[13]

Given these sentiments, it is not surprising that Zumárraga joined Las Casas in petitioning the Vatican to protect the Indians against imperial assaults. Their efforts prompted the landmark bull promulgated by Pope Paul III in 1537, *Sublimus Dei*, which appealed to "the testimony of the sacred scriptures" to repudiate what the pope called a satanic lie, "that the Indians of the West and South...should be treated as dumb brutes created for our [the Europeans'] service." Instead, "the Indians are truly men," they are fully capable of receiving the Catholic faith, they deserve ordinary rights to their property, "nor should they be in any way enslaved."[14] Advocacy for the Indians spilled over naturally into a desire that they hear and read church teaching, including the Scriptures, in their own languages. To that end, several other Franciscans joined Bishop Zumárraga in translating portions of the Bible, extending even to parts of the Old Testament like the Book of Proverbs.[15]

The Catholic reforms of the mid-sixteenth century redirected new-world engagement with Scripture. By tightening church organization, regularizing doctrine, and reacting to the spread of Protestantism, the church considerably restricted access to the Scriptures by the laity. Steps undertaken for European purposes soon affected the New World as well. The incorporation of natives into the universal church became focused more on proper administration of the sacraments and less on possession of biblical knowledge.[16]

The manifest Protestant enthusiasm for Bible translation into vulgar languages meant that when Casiodoro de Reina's 1569 Spanish translation appeared in Basel as a Protestant project, it immediately went on the Index of Prohibited Books that had condemned such publications for Catholics since 1559—and so was also banned in New Spain and the Indies.[17] The reassertion of bishops' control over priests and priests' control over the laity dampened impulses that had worked to put Scripture into the hands of the people at large. Tighter cooperation between church officials and Catholic regimes, often implemented by the Inquisition, also restricted the circulation of Scripture. In 1572 the Inquisition Council in New Spain prohibited the importation of vernacular Bibles. A generation later, between 1600 and 1604, the Dominican bishop of Santo Domingo, Agustín Dávila Padilla, supervised the public burning of three hundred such Bibles confiscated when merchants tried to smuggle them into Hispaniola.[18]

In the early seventeenth century when French exploration and settlement began in what is now Canada, standard Catholic practice included the reading of Scripture within religious communities. In a letter from 1639, a Jesuit reported back to superiors in France on the ordinary structure of a day: "then follows dinner, during which is read some chapters from the Bible; and at supper Father du Barry's *Philologie of Jesus* is read; the benedicte and grace is said in Huron, on account of the savages who are present."[19] As suggested by this letter, early Jesuit teaching for Indians included some biblical bits translated into native languages, but only in the church formulas prepared for the natives. For the most part, however, Scripture remained securely tethered to prescribed readings prepared for closely regulated church use. In the early 1630s the elderly Samuel Champlain, as an example, assembled and read a great deal of Christian literature in Quebec. But the biblical content of such reading lay embedded within texts that had received the imprimatur, like *Fleurs des sainctz*, *Pratique de la perfection chrestienne*, or the *Chroniques et instruction du père Sainct-François*.[20] Among native converts, relics from the early Jesuit martyrs and then a focus on their martyrologies occupied the central place roughly analogous to the place of Scripture among Protestants.[21]

For Catholics the Bible remained essential, but distinctly as the church's book. By the early seventeenth century, when the first permanent Protestant settlements were only just taking root, the earlier Bible-and-church consciousness of the Las Casas era had moved a considerable distance toward a church-as-sole-authority practice. The first Protestants in the generation of Luther, Tyndale, and Henry VIII—all of them indebted to Erasmus's biblical scholarship—were watching. As they proposed reforms based on fresh reading of Scripture, they too wanted to keep scriptural authority and church authority in balance. But once having unleashed the Scriptures, it would not be easy.

I

Protestant Beginnings

ROMAN CATHOLICS FIRST brought the Bible to the Western Hemisphere. But even as Columbus, Las Casas, and Zumáragga pioneered reading of Scripture in or about the New World, events unfolded in Europe that would one day lead to an American Bible civilization resting on strongly Protestant foundations. That story began with Martin Luther since Luther's appeal to Scripture as a corrective for church error and a sure guide for authentic Christian life became definitive for the entire history of Protestantism. A brief account short-circuits many important questions, but it can at minimum show how the reformer's early career paved the way for later American developments, while also indicating the considerable distance that divided the earliest Protestants from their later American descendents.

Martin Luther and the Dawn of the Reformation

The furor over Martin Luther's *Ninety-Five Theses* of 1517 is widely—and correctly—viewed as the flash point that instigated the Protestant Reformation.[1] That document, which pushed out from obscurity a thirty-three year-old Augustinian monk, bent the direction of European history. In light of later Protestant insistence on Scripture as the defining norm for doctrine and life, however, the compact list of arguments he proposed for debate in those *Theses* contained very little direct appeal to the Bible. Luther's title spoke plainly to what he considered the main issue at stake: "Disputation on the Power and Efficacy of Indulgences."[2] Contentions over a church practice and the theology supporting that practice, not in the first instance questions about religious authority, sparked the uproar.

The *Theses* themselves objected to practices authorized by the church to relax penalties associated with penance, the sacrament of the forgiveness of sins. In previous centuries, procedures for granting indulgences had grown increasingly formal, fiscal, and dependent on the pope. In the thirteenth century they became connected to the doctrine of merit, specifically the belief that Christ and the saints had accumulated a meritorious treasure that the papacy could tap to mitigate the satisfaction owed by repentant sinners for the remission of their sins. By Luther's day, popular beliefs held, with at least some official approval, that the time departed Christians suffered in purgatory could be reduced if a living person secured an indulgence for the sufferer. Also by Luther's day, indulgences were being sold by special preachers who secured their franchises from church officials eager to share in the profits. The trade provided spectacular returns for the sellers as well as the officials, including the pope, who oversaw the system as a whole. Luther had come to the conclusion not only that the practice had gotten out of hand but also that the theology undergirding it meant spiritual destruction.

The key thesis for his exercise in pastoral theology was number 62: "The true treasure of the church is the most holy gospel of the glory and grace of God." In Luther's judgment, the indulgence trade obscured this "glory and grace," especially when the pope silenced "the preaching of the Word of God" (no. 53) by licensing indulgence sellers to hawk their suspect wares. Luther did begin in Thesis 1 with a reference to Scripture, quoting from Matthew 4, where Jesus "begins to preach... Repentance"; in Thesis 2 he contended that "this word" was not relevant to "the sacrament of penance." In addition, Luther also appealed in another thesis (no. 18) to "reason or Scripture" in order to defend what he wanted to say about purgatory.[3] But his impassioned plea for debate remained focused on the properly Christian understanding of repentance, grace, forgiveness, and the cross of Christ that Luther felt the indulgence traffic flat out contradicted. In the *Theses* as a whole, "word" or "word of God" (*verbum dei*) could refer to the Bible, but even more particularly to broader meanings taken from the Gospel of John where the *logos* (or word) referred as much to Christ as to the written Scriptures.

Shortly before proposing the *Ninety-Five Theses*, Luther had been explaining to students at the University of Wittenberg why he considered it so vital to align proper understanding of the written Word with life-giving devotion to Christ as the living Word. In lectures on the Apostle Paul's Epistle to the Galatians, delivered from October 1516 through March 1517, Luther painstakingly described what he held the Bible taught about well-grounded faith in Christ—as when he expounded the first sentence of the fifth chapter: "For freedom Christ has set us free; stand fast, therefore, and do not submit again to a yoke of slavery."[4] To Luther, this text could only mean that "In this freedom...we must stand strongly and steadfastly, because Christ, who fulfills the Law and overcomes sin for us, sends the spirit of love into the hearts of those who believe in Him." As the vitally important consequence, "This makes them [believers] righteous and lovers of the Law, not because of their own works but freely because it is freely bestowed by Christ."[5] Patient instruction like this, however, went barely noticed amid the uproar caused by the *Ninety-Five Theses*.

When enterprising printers translated Luther's academic document from Latin into German and then marketed it aggressively as an exposé, an eager population responded with enthusiasm even as the pope responded with outrage. Two developments became immediately crucial for European religious life and would strongly influence later American history as well. First was an explosion of print. Led by Luther himself, whom controversy transformed into a literary volcano, presses in German-speaking lands and well beyond stoked intense public interest with unprecedented publishing output. Some of this publication appeared in Latin and so remained restricted to learned elites; more came in German and other vernacular languages and so reached a much wider population. What the Gutenberg Revolution meant for Western society now came into focus. Protestantism and the vigorous deployment of the press marched together in closest lockstep. The democratization of the public sphere that would later characterize American culture had launched.

The second consequence, when Luther's local protest became an international cause célèbre, was an almost inevitable shift in the controversy's center of gravity. Issues of Christian doctrine certainly remained important, but questions about how to define doctrine quickly joined and then often superseded doctrinal questions as such. The *Ninety-Five Theses* were posted on 31 October 1517; in early October of the next year Luther traveled from his home town of Wittenberg to the imperial city of Augsburg in order to confer with a representative of the pope, Cardinal Thomas Cajetan. Luther agreed to this meeting because his prince, Frederick of Saxony, an Elector of the Holy Roman Empire, had the clout to secure a safe-conduct from Emperor Maximilian for his suddenly famous theologian. At Augsburg the controversy over indulgences almost immediately expanded into a controversy over Scripture.

Near the beginning of the conference, Luther defended himself before the cardinal by asserting "that I am not conscious of having said anything contrary to Holy Scripture, the church fathers, or papal decretals."[6] As soon as the inevitable question of the pope's authority came up, Luther quoted passages from Galatians 2 and Acts 15—which speak of the Apostle Paul reproving the Apostle Peter—to prove that the popes as successors of Peter needed correction like every other Christian.[7] Then when he responded to Cajetan's objection to Luther's assertion that "no one can be justified except by faith," Luther quoted nine separate scriptural passages and added statements by Saint Augustine and Bernard of Clairvaux on two more passages to defend his understanding of the disputed points.[8] To Luther it was reprehensible that Cajetan "never produced a syllable from the Holy Scripture" to defend the practice of indulgences. Luther, naturally, did not think any such syllables could be found since "there is universal agreement that nothing is mentioned in Holy Scriptures about indulgences."[9] Luther's struggle to stop the indulgence traffic and over- throw the underlying theology of penance had turned into a controversy over religious authority.

Luther's mode of quoting the Scriptures went completely unremarked at the time, but would later bear on American history. When he cited Scripture to contend with Cajetan, he did so with general references to what was "stated in Rom. 1" or found "in the words of Christ" or based on what "Christ says in Mark."[10] Modern editors fill in the verse references that Luther himself never specified for the simple reason that versified Bibles were not printed until after Luther's death. When that significant advance in the physical layout of printed Bibles did take place, it opened up intellectual possibilities for a democratic appeal to Scripture that Protestants of all kinds eagerly exploited, and none more eagerly than in America.

Why the Bible?

Theological controversy made the Bible a highly visible property in the early sixteenth century. Catholic authorities, after initially fumbling in the face of Luther's rapid-fire enlistment of biblical texts to advance his polem- ical assaults, soon recruited their own champions to fight back. While the church's order of battle did not rely single-handedly on biblical armament, it soon marshaled what the Vatican headquarters defined as a proper de- ployment of sacred Scripture to reinforce a traditional understanding of church authority. Yet even if the pastoral concerns that had provoked Luther to pen the *Ninety-Five Theses* soon gave way to wide-ranging battles over church discipline and authority, those pastoral concerns did not dis- appear. From the very first days of the Reformation—indeed, throughout the entire history of Christianity—the public history of Scripture depended on a much less visible private history. The political, cultural, linguistic, and social influence of the Bible has always rested on such religious foundations. In the relation between the personal and the public, Luther again set the pace.

Late in his life, when he wrote a preface to an edition of his many publications in Latin, Luther offered a biographical vignette on the circumstances that led him to propose the *Ninety-Five Theses*. Historians have disputed the accuracy of Luther's memory as well as the exact sequence of events he narrated, but there can be no doubt about the importance of his reminiscences for larger purposes. He wrote in 1545 that as public controversy began, he was lecturing to students at Wittenberg's university on the Psalms. These lectures followed hard on the heels of earlier attention he had devoted to the New Testament books, including Galatians. Now late in life he reported that he had been "captivated with an extraordinary ardor for understanding Paul in the Epistle to the Romans."[11] One phrase from the epistle's first chapter, later to be identified as verse 17, transfixed the scholar-monk: "In it the righteousness of God is revealed." Later scholars have again debated whether Luther correctly understood Romans 1:17, or the Old Testament passage it references from Habakkuk 2:4. For a history of the Bible, however, it is more important that Luther read "righteousness" in this passage as the divine standard revealing to sinful humans how far short they fell of God's perfect holiness. Hence, Luther's anguished statement that "I hated that word 'righteousness of God,'" which he took to mean a condemnation for his vigorous efforts as a monk to live as a child of God. For this professor of theology, the upshot was anguished but active despair: "Thus I raged with a fierce and troubled conscience. Nevertheless, I beat importunately upon Paul at that place, most ardently desiring to know what St. Paul wanted."

Then, Luther reported, he experienced "the mercy of God," which had the immediate effect of overturning his previous understanding of the passage. That mercy enabled him to see that God's righteousness came to needy sinners as a gift—that it was "the passive righteousness with which merciful God justifies us by faith." With this fresh interpretive insight, Luther experienced the liberation he had lectured about in Galatians. He wrote in 1545 that faith in Christ, "a gift of God"—and not his own labor or mental state—enabled him to rejoice in the righteousness of God. And so he could declare exuberantly: "Here I felt that I was altogether born again and had entered paradise itself through open gates."

Then came sentences that made Luther's experience paradigmatic for Protestant history: "There a totally other face of the entire Scripture showed itself to me. Thereupon I ran through the Scriptures from memory. I also found in other terms an analogy, as, the work of God, that is, what God does in us, the power of God, with which he makes us strong, the wisdom of God, with which he makes us wise, the strength of God, the salvation of God, the glory of God." The sacred book, which had been a puzzle, an obsession, an academic challenge, and a distress, now became the book of life.

Over the centuries that followed, to be a Protestant meant to experience that same gift of life from the same source. Or at least to talk about it often. Or keep it in focus as the justification for contesting the perceived errors of Rome or fellow Protestants. The tight link that Protestants perceive between Scripture and salvation explains the great energy they have poured into studying, distributing, and translating the Scriptures, as well as producing the never-ending deluge of printed material explaining, mediating, parsing, debating, exploring, and riffing on the Bible.

The Scriptures have certainly played a huge role also among Jews, Roman Catholics, the Orthodox, and adherents of the many non-Western manifestations of Christian faith. Although a polemical climate long obscured the fact, it is also true that apprehensions of Scripture in these other traditions have also resulted in experiences of God similar to what Protestants have experienced. Nevertheless, the Bible has enjoyed a particularly momentous public history in Protestant regions of the world because of how important have been the multiplied private experiences that resemble, though with great variety, what Martin Luther discovered when he "ran through the Scriptures from memory."

Christendom

Since the spheres of religion and society intersected so intimately in early modern Europe, Luther's challenge to religious authority came quickly to be understood as a challenge to authority in general. That broader challenge emerged with sharp clarity when Luther, once again under a safe conduct secured by the Elector Frederick, traveled to an imperial Diet at Worms in April 1521. It was the first such gathering of Electors convened by Charles V, the young Habsburg king of Spain who two years before had been elected to succeed his deceased grandfather, Maximilian, as Germany's Holy Roman Emperor.

If Charles lacked experience as emperor and if everything spoken in German had to be translated for him into Latin, he nonetheless represented at Worms the personal embodiment of Christendom. Charles was not only the Holy Roman Emperor and monarch of Spain, Hungary, Austria, Burgundy, and more; he was also the inheritor of Charlemagne's grand vision for a Christianized Europe. The ideal, built up over the previous seven centuries, harmonized the interests of church and state, religion and society. Before such an august personage representing such a well-established ideal, Martin Luther appeared as a solitary monk who in his private spiritual journey had become convinced that Scripture taught much that the pope, the emperor, and all Christendom had tragically misconstrued.

When Luther on the seventeenth of April came before the imperial court, the emperor's spokesman demanded that he recant the many errors found in his writings, which lay spread out in great quantity on a table before the Diet. The pile of those writings, all published in the previous four years, rose so high that when Charles and his aides first stepped into the chamber, they scoffed at the notion that any single person could have written so much.[12]

After being allowed to retire and come back the next day, Luther told the court that he had written three kinds of books. Some were works of simple piety, some attacked abuses that all condemned, while some he conceded did perhaps contain overly aggressive material. Then Luther offered a quintessentially Protestant challenge. He would consider recantation but only under one condition: "Therefore, I ask by the mercy of God, may your most serene majesty, most illustrious lordships, or anyone at all who is able, either high or low, bear witness, expose my errors, overthrowing them by the writings of the prophets and the evangelists. Once I have been taught I shall be quite ready to renounce every error, and I shall be the first to cast my books into the fire."[13]

But Luther had not yet expressed himself clearly enough. The emperor's spokesman pressed him again to respond without ambiguity. Luther replied with these memorable words: "Since then your serene majesty and your lordships seek a simple answer, I will give it...: Unless I am convinced by the testimony of the Scriptures or by clear reason (for I do not trust either in the pope or in councils alone, since it is well known that they have often erred and contradicted themselves), I am bound by the Scriptures I have quoted and my conscience is captive to the Word of God. I cannot and I will not retract anything, since it is neither safe nor right to go against conscience."[14]

This dramatic statement in this most auspicious setting established the Protestant base line: Protestants would follow the Bible before all other authorities—even when, as many of them later concluded, the Bible taught truths about "the glory and grace of God" much different from what Luther found in Scripture. A second landmark has exerted almost as much influence: "my conscience," or the individual Bible-reader aware of standing *coram deo* (directly in the face of God, as Luther often said), would be the final guide for interpreting the supremely authoritative Scripture.

Luther and most of the leading reformers of his generation came to have second thoughts about how much scope the individual conscience should be given to interpret Scripture. Yet the principle once stated remained alive and eventually came to fullest expression in North America, a part of the world about which European Christians in the age of Luther knew very little.

Immediately after Luther had finished speaking on 18 April the emperor's spokesman called him to account for setting himself up as superior to the historical councils of the Catholic church that had already ruled on many of the issues he was addressing. "In this," the imperial secretary told Luther, "you are completely mad. For what purpose does it serve to raise a new dispute about matters condemned through so many centuries by church and council? Unless perhaps a reason must be given to just anyone about anything whatsoever." The secretary went on to what he obviously considered an absurd conclusion: "if it were granted that whoever contradicts the councils and the common understanding of the church must be overcome by Scripture passages, we will have nothing in Christianity that is certain or decided."[15]

Further comment on Luther's profession to follow the Bible above all other authorities came the next day from the emperor himself. In words written out with his own hand, Charles V reminded his German nobles about the inheritance of Christendom: he was descended from the "most Christian" monarchs of Germany, Spain, Austria, and Burgundy who, "to the honor of God, the strengthening of the faith, and the salvation of souls," had each "remained up to death faithful sons of the church." Charles, to say the least, was not impressed with what he had heard the day before. "It is certain," he concluded, "that a single friar errs in his opinion which is against all of Christendom and according to which all of Christianity will be and will always have been in error both in the past thousand years and even more in the present." Because Charles had been called as emperor to defend the true faith, he felt it would be "a great shame" to himself and all the nobles of Germany if, during their age, "not only heresy but suspicion of heresy or decrease of the Christian religion should through our negligence dwell after us in the heart of men and our successors to our perpetual dishonor."[16]

The emperor could not have been less impressed with what Luther had said. For him, Scripture was of course an indispensable resource, but a resource interpreted by the church, guided by the emperor, and remaining securely a possession of all Christendom. Despite Charles's sharp retort, he and the pope's representatives dawdled after Luther's dramatic appearance in order to determine a course of action. By the time they figured out what they wanted to do with him, Luther had long since left Worms. His prince, the Elector Frederick, was torn between a desire to protect the theologian who brought such renown to Saxony and the need to show proper deference to the emperor whom his vote had helped place on the throne. Frederick's creative response was to maintain a public position of noncommittal impartiality while arranging, under strict secrecy, for Luther to be "kidnapped" and spirited away to a secret retreat, the Castle Wartburg near Eisenach.

A Protestant Bible

As soon as Luther was settled in the Wartburg, he immediately turned his great energy to translating the New Testament into German. Several printed versions in German had already appeared, but because Luther exploited the dialect of the Saxon chancery with consummate skill, his New Testament of 1522—with its later editions and the eventual addition of the Old Testament—immediately became the standard Scripture for German-speaking Protestants, which it remains with modifications to this day. The popularity of the *Luther Bibel*, in turn, became even more important for shaping the modern High German language than the King James Version has been for the course of modern English.

Luther's 1522 New Testament stood at the head of a long line of memorable vernacular translations produced under Protestant sponsorship. Hard on its heels came within a decade translations into Danish, Dutch, English, French, Swiss-German, and Swedish. Then before the halfway mark of the century, further translations into Finnish, Flemish, Hungarian, Icelandic, and Spanish.[17] And so on in a circle that has gone on widening to the present day.

Supremely for such a translation at such a moment, much hung in the balance when Luther published his 1522 New Testament. Everyone who read it realized that Luther was taking the opportunity to accentuate the themes of Scripture that most directly fueled his reforming fire. A much-noticed instance was his translation of a key passage about faith and justification toward the end of the third chapter of Paul's Epistle to the Romans (v. 28, though none of the translations that Luther prepared would be broken into verses). Only three years later William Tyndale translated the passage into English as, "We suppose therefore that a man is iustified by fayth without the dedes of the lawe."[18] Tyndale, like Luther, was much indebted to the Latin Vulgate that had been the standard biblical text in the West for centuries; it read, "arbitramur enim iustificari hominem per fidem sine operibus legis."[19]

But both Tyndale and Luther, in their desire to recover the purity of the written word of God, owed an even greater debt to the Greek edition of the New Testament published by Desiderius Erasmus in 1516. Erasmus's landmark effort exemplified the Renaissance desire for purified classical learning as well as the religious reformer's desire for the living Word closest in form to what had been originally written. Erasmus's text paralleled the Vulgate. Luther, however, in order to stress the entire dependence of the sinner on divine mercy, translated this passage with an explicit "only": "So halten wyrs nu das der mensch gerechtfertiget werde on [ohne] zu thun der werck des gesetzs *alleyn* durch den glawben" (emphasis added).[20]

Luther the Translator could not, it seems, pass up the opportunity to render this passage in such a way as to satisfy Luther the Theologian. But was Luther's "alleyn" ("only") so obviously implicit in the Apostle's argument that it simply needed to be inserted; or was it an illegitimate intrusion of the translator's bias twisting the original into what Luther thought it had to mean? Such questions implicated the foundation of all Protestant efforts at making Scripture the supreme determination of faith and practice. The principle of biblical authority rang out clearly, but the practices of Bible translation and Bible interpretation were never so clearly dispositive.

The apparatus with which Luther surrounded his translation constituted a second hallmark of that famous work. The annotations he supplied for the text represented a striking contrast from the biblical texts Luther had earlier prepared for theological students at the University of Wittenberg. As Gerald Bruns and Jaroslav Pelikan have pointed out, Luther's decision to print a special edition of the Psalter for the students— with broad margins and enhanced empty space between lines—signaled

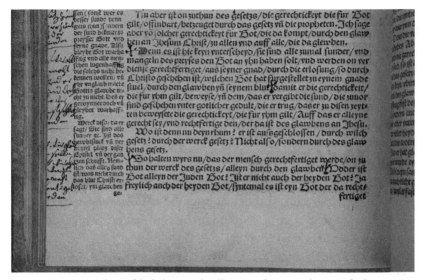

In 1522 Martin Luther added the word "alleyn" to his translation of what is now designated as Romans 3:28 ("justified...alone through faith"). This assist in clarifying what he considered the heart of the Christian gospel, along with the extensive explanatory notes he also provided, set a pattern that many published Bibles would later follow. (Courtesy of the American Bible Society Library)

his willingness to set aside the centuries of commentary that had usually garnished medieval theological texts. Those student worksheets seemed to suggest that the interpretation of the Bible could begin afresh, with what the students chose to pen in the margins counting as much as what honored figures of the past had said about a particular passage.[21] But now in 1522, Luther filled the slender margins alongside his translated text with quotations from what he considered pertinent Old Testament passages, as well as with explanations about what he felt the New Testament authors were trying to say.

Luther also supplied prefaces, first to the New Testament as a whole and then to each of the individual books. In the introductory preface Luther took pains to spell out what he considered the crucial message of the whole Bible. "Thus this gospel of God or New Testament," he wrote, was "a good story and report" that the apostles have given to the world. It tells of "a true David who strove with sin, death, and the devil, and overcame them, and thereby rescued all those who were captive in sin, afflicted with death, and overpowered by the devil." This message highlighted the way of salvation so that sinners, "without any merit of their own," could be made righteous and experience the peace with God that is given to all who "believe firmly and remain steadfast in faith."[22]

Even before he summarized the gospel message in this way, however, Luther explained why there needed to be a preface at all. His very first sentence echoed the profession of biblical authority he had made before the emperor: "It would be right and proper for this book to go forth without any prefaces or extraneous names attached and simply have its own say under its own name." Yet Luther did provide a preface because "many unfounded [*wilde*] interpretations and prefaces have scattered the thought of Christians to a point where no one any longer knows what is gospel or law, New Testament or Old." It was, therefore, a "necessity" for Luther to give some "notice . . . by which the ordinary man can be rescued from his former delusions, set on the right track, and taught what he is to look for in this book, so that he may not seek laws and commandments where he ought to be seeking the gospel and promises of God."[23]

Without a doubt, Luther intended the Bible to be the final judge for Christian teaching and Christian practice. It was not, however, a naked Bible, "the Bible alone," or *sola scriptura* in any simple sense that Luther offered to the world—despite his own strong insistence on that principle early in his reforming career.[24] This very first Protestant Bible translation mingled the ideal and the real as they would be consistently mingled in Protestant history, and nowhere more thoroughly than in American experience. The ideal was biblical authority alone; the real was a regular provision of assistance to understand the Bible appropriately.

The Bible Against Itself?

Three more developments in the first years of the Reformation are pertinent for the history of the Bible that eventually extended to North America. They show that the exultant liberation conveyed by an opened Bible could be matched by considerable confusion concerning what that open Bible said.

The first development concerns the pace of reform in Wittenberg. While Luther was hidden away in the Wartburg Castle, colleagues who shared his convictions got to work in Wittenberg. They were led by an older university professor and cleric, Andreas Bodenstein von Karlstadt, who almost immediately pushed change farther and faster than Luther thought wise. In short order Karlstadt came out against clerical celibacy, drastically simplified the ritual of the Mass, distributed the wine with the bread in his new *Gottesdienst*, credited the word of "prophets" who attacked the baptism of infants, dismissed the need for special learning to interpret Scripture, and urged the destruction of artistic images in Wittenberg churches. Luther and the Elector Frederick were aghast. To check what they saw not as reform but a rush into chaos, Frederick called Luther back from the Wartburg Castle to deliver a series of sermons during Lent. Dressed in his monastic habit, Luther defended the need to purify the church but also counseled restraint, patience, and calm.[25]

Once the prince and preacher had Karlstadt resuscitated, he continued in his rural parish to organize life around the Bible, preaching every day from the book of Acts and on Fridays from the Gospel of John, while also translating the Psalms into German for the purpose of congregational singing.[26] He also continued to stir up trouble by insisting that when Jesus told his disciples at the Last Supper, "This do in remembrance of me," he referred to the bread and the wine as only symbols of his saving work. This position Luther considered a grave attack on a fundamental aspect of Christian worship: the real presence of Christ in the sacrament. Moreover, Karlstadt also seemed to support the radicalism of Thomas Müntzer, a proponent of reform who spoke of himself as a prophet in the biblical sense and recommended violence for reforming the corruptions of Christendom. Karlstadt's association with Müntzer, closer in Luther's eyes than in actual fact, was the last straw. When the Elector Frederick decided to banish Karlstadt entirely from Saxony, Luther approved.

The second development also involved Luther, but outside of Wittenberg. Publication of Luther's writings fatally exacerbated a percolating tension between European landowners, including the church, and their peasants. To long-standing complaints about many oppressions, Luther seemed to offer a spiritual boost. In the words of one historian, the peasants thought "that Luther's teachings pointed out a way whereby the vested financial institutions of the church might be overthrown without forfeiting the spiritual benefits the church claimed to confer."[27]

So it came about in early 1525 when peasants of Memmingen in Swabia embarked upon direct action against their landlords, they stated their grievances with the kind of appeal to Scripture that everyone at the time recognized as distinctly "of Luther." To ensure that no one mistook their intentions, they published their twelve reasons for protesting, with biblical texts printed in the margins—only chapter references, but anticipating the chapter and verse citations that would adorn some later documents be published in Puritan New England.[28]

The peasants affirmed that their twelve protests were "all basically concerned with hearing the word of God and living according to it." Their "fervent prayer" was to "live according to [God's] word."[29] Then the document set out their goals: privilege to choose their own pastors, freedom from excessive tithes, an end to the slave-like encumbrances of peasant land ownership, access to communal forests for firewood, and so on. Along the way, they attacked "the custom for men to hold us as their own property," by claiming that "it agrees with Scripture that we be free and will to be so." The broadside concluded that "if one or more of the articles set forth here is not in agreement with the word of God (though we think this is not the case),... we shall withdraw such an article—after the matter is explained to us on the basis of Scripture."[30]

The peasants' obvious recourse to the kind of statements about Scripture that Luther had made at the Diet of Worms—as well as in many published works—naturally drew his attention. For Luther, to have attention drawn was to put pen in hand. Relative to the tone of other pamphlets in that era, his first response remained relatively moderate. It began with an expression of pleasure that the peasants were willing to be shown from Scripture their errors, since "it is indeed right and proper that no one's conscience should be instructed or corrected except by Holy Scripture." He then quoted the Latin Vulgate from Psalm 107:40 to warn landowners that "Effundit contemptum super principes" (God pours contempt on princes), as he also conceded to the peasants that when "princes and lords... forbid the preaching of the gospel and oppress the people unbearably [they] deserve to have God put them down from their thrones" (quoting Lk 1:52). But then the rest of the pamphlet became a stern rebuke warning peasants that rulers enjoyed a "divine right" to exercise that rule. Further, if peasants took the vengeance against unjust rulers into their hands that belonged to God alone (citing Rom 12:19), they would be "worse than heathen or Turks."[31]

Thereafter events careened ahead at such a ferocious pace that Luther's efforts at running commentary succeeded only in permanently damaging his reputation. In April 1525 on a journey through Thuringia, he saw some evidence of destruction caused by peasant militia-mobs, heard reports of more extensive damage, and expressed bewilderment that Frederick the Wise, then near death, took no action. The result was a second intervention. This furiously denunciatory tract, "Against the Robbing and Murdering Hordes of Peasants," has long been noted for its apocalyptic advice to landowners: "Let whoever can [,] stab, smite, slay.... If anyone thinks this is too harsh, let him remember that rebellion is intolerable and that the destruction of the world is to be expected every hour."[32]

In the short interval between the composition of this second pamphlet and its publication, rulers gathered their forces, destroyed the ragtag army of Thomas Münzer at Frankenhausen, and then began a reign of terror upon anyone with the least suspicion of having been involved.

The timing, which caused Luther's second screed to be read as unalloyed approval of this massacre, prompted yet his third pamphlet. Moderation had long since flown away when this pamphlet appeared in late 1525. It, along with the other two, were filled with scriptural quotations defending every one of Luther's judgments. In the third he professed that he did "not want to hear or know about mercy, but to be concerned only about what God's word requires." Yet not surprisingly, Luther's hearing ran along the lines of the conservative conception of God-ordained social order with which he had been raised and that he never thought to question. By the time he wrote this third pamphlet, he had begun to articulate what would become the traditional Lutheran understanding of Two Kingdoms as defining the proper relationships in Christendom: "The Scripture passages which speak of mercy apply to the Kingdom of God and to Christians, not to the kingdom of the world, for it is a Christian's duty not only to be merciful, but also to endure every kind of suffering—robbery, arson, murder, devil, and hell....But the kingdom of the world, which is nothing else than the servant of God's wrath upon the wicked and is a real precursor of hell and everlasting death, should not be merciful, but strict, severe, and wrathful in fulfilling its work and duty."[33] The quotations that immediately followed from Romans 13:3–4, Exodus 22:14, and Hebrews 10:28 may have struck Luther as biblical words ending discussion. But for many of his contemporaries, and most Bible-believers since, they did not.

As Luther experienced in the disputes with Karlstadt and then the peasants, biblical authority created, as well as resolved, problems. To announce "my conscience is captive to the Word of God" before the emperor in rebuke of church corruptions had been one challenge. To convince others, even those who shared his understanding of how God revealed divine mercy to humanity in Jesus Christ, represented another quite different challenge. Private understanding of Scripture had led on to public consequences; the transition was neither smooth nor uncontroversial.

The third development took place outside the Holy Roman Empire in Switzerland.[34] Reforming ideas advanced in Zurich under the leadership of Ulrich Zwingli in rough parallel to what was happening in Wittenberg.

Yet as in the Luther lands, political contests over authority to interpret the Bible continued alongside the liberating effect of Scripture appropriated afresh. Zwingli's biography shared much with Luther's, including inspiration by Erasmus's edition of the Greek New Testament, opposition to the indulgence traffic, bold preaching from the New Testament, and a dramatic experience of God's grace from his personal encounter with Scripture. In Zwingli's reforming efforts there was also a partnership with governing officials, in his case the town councils of Zurich.

Zwingli's battle cry echoed Luther's. When in 1523 he drew up a series of *Sixty-Seven Theses* to clarify obscured doctrines and reform corrupt practices, he affirmed "I have preached in the worthy city of Zurich these sixty-seven articles…on the basis of Scripture." He stood ready "to defend and vindicate these articles with Scripture." And he desired, "if I have not understood Scripture correctly," to be instructed, "but only from the same Scripture."[35] If, however, Luther had his Karlstadt, so Zwingli had his Anabaptists.

Zwingli's arguments convinced the Zurich town fathers to renounce their Catholic bishop and to reform their city's church order. Yet other reformers in Zurich, equal in zeal to Zwingli and eager with him to be guided by Scripture, interpreted the Bible differently. As they read the sacred book, they did not find any justification for a church to be supported by government, they did not see any instruction for Christians to wage war, and they did not believe any biblical passage taught that the state could punish deviance in religious beliefs. These erstwhile followers of Zwingli became the Anabaptists (or "re-baptizers") when they concluded that Scripture did not authorize the baptism of infants, but rather that baptism should be offered only to adults who made a personal profession of faith.

The Zurich council combated this biblical attack on Christendom even more harshly than Frederick of Saxony had dealt with Karlstadt. Felix Manz, once an ardent disciple of Zwingli, became the first Anabaptist martyr when he was executed by his fellow Zurich Protestants on 5 January 1527. The authorities fixed the mode of execution as drowning in Lake Zurich in order to mock his stance on baptism. A Christendom structure could still constrain a liberated Scripture, but what would happen when formal Christendom faded away?

Sola Scriptura *(The Bible Alone)*

Out of the Reformation came a sharpened focus on biblical authority— growing from a sharper sense of liberation found in Scripture and leading to sharper conflicts over interpreting the Bible. Implicated in the entire process was the Protestant desire to live by the Bible, or even by the Bible alone. Yet the appeal to Scripture as comprehensive authority enjoyed a well-established career long before Luther appeared on the scene. The phrase "Scripture alone" (*sola scriptura*), or its equivalents, had appeared often from the fourteenth century on among both supporters of church councils against the Roman curia and supporters of the curia against church councils. Pausing to sketch that history highlights not only some of the fine distinctions that complicated the original Protestant movements, but also those influences that continued into later Protestant history, especially in the United States.

Experts in pre-Reformation history have made helpful distinctions about what people meant when they announced their trust in Scripture.[36] As early as the fourteenth century, the notion of *sola scriptura* was already functioning in two ways. John Wycliffe, as the most famous example, excoriated England's institutional church for what he considered its sinful imposition of false teaching concerning the Lord's Supper and its blithe disregard of widespread corruption in the religious orders. As his standard for judgment, he appealed to *sola scriptura*, but understood in two different senses. Sometimes he used the phrase in what might be called "a catholic and traditional sense" as the main trajectory of scriptural interpretation to which early church fathers, popes, the ecumenical councils, bishops, theologians, and the lay faithful had all made important contributions.[37] In other words, he thought that a consensus of historical church teaching condemned dangerous innovations with respect to the Eucharist and corrupt degeneration among the religious orders. At other times Wycliffe seems to have used *sola scriptura* in what might be called "a literal sense."[38] Here he was willing, as one historian has put it, "to drive a coach and four through the testimony of any of these [other authorities] insofar as it [did] not harmonize with his own views; so that in a very true sense it can be said that he [did] not in fact accept Tradition."[39]

Martin Luther, Ulrich Zwingli, and others who dominated in the Christendoms set up by magisterial Protestants mostly used *sola scriptura* in the first sense, with a muted critical edge. After Luther's initial proclamation of scriptural authority against church corruption, which could sound very much like a fully "literal sense," he and the magisterial Protestants usually interpreted Scripture by what they considered a "traditional sense." As they restructured church authority in their individual regions, they accepted other authorities, most obviously coercive governmental power, but also a great deal of church tradition as a legitimate complement to ultimate biblical authority.

Catholic officials who gathered at Trent in the early 1540s to formulate a comprehensive guide for the faithful—and a comprehensive rebuke to Protestant error—also spoke on the status of Scripture. At one of their earliest sessions, they absolutely repudiated *sola scriptura* as a literal personal possession. They also moved farther in giving tradition more explicit authority than any Protestant could concede. Their decree from the fourth session in 1546 proclaimed that the Gospel, "before promised through the prophets in holy Scripture," had come to its full expression in "our Lord Jesus Christ." The "truth and discipline" of the Gospel, moreover, "are contained in the written books, and the unwritten traditions which, received by the Apostles from the mouth of Christ himself, or from the Apostles themselves, the Holy Ghost dictating, have come down even unto us."[40] As the formal Catholic response to Luther and other reformers, Trent proclaimed that the Church followed not "the Bible alone" but the Bible paired with equally authoritative church tradition.

Protestants, from the sixteenth century until very recently, have not been interested in nuanced interpretations of formal Catholic dogma. To them, *sola scriptura* stood courageously against what they could only view as Catholic traditionalism devouring the holy book. Yet among Protestants, the differences between the possible meanings of *sola scriptura* consistently spread controversy, and especially when the restraining authority of state power gave way. Since the Second Vatican Council, Catholics have expended great energy in refining the exact relationship between "the written book" and "the unwritten traditions," with consequences leading to productive and cooperative discussion with Protestants of the sort almost entirely unknown in the sixteenth century and for many centuries thereafter.

The Early Reformation and the American Future

The later history of the Bible in America grew directly from beginnings in the earliest years of the Protestant Reformation. On questions of principle, the Protestants who did so much to shape American civilization agreed with near unanimity that Scripture, as infallible divine revelation, should be the supreme authority for all important questions concerning God, the Christian faith, and life in this world. Intimately connected with this theological principle came a practical commitment to certain cultural practices. Protestants were always a word-oriented people both committed to publication and devoted to reading. On modes of interpretation, American Protestants followed ideals outlined by Luther and Zwingli in holding up personal engagement with Scripture as the key to experiencing new life in Christ and putting the church on the course it should go.

Yet the American Protestant experience eventually developed far beyond what Luther's generation practiced. Luther had the Elector, and Zwingli the city councils who policed how authoritative Scripture could be put to use. These early Protestant leaders continued to insist that even if the message of Scripture stood open for all who inquired, the training obtained in formal institutions of learning and guidance from certified experts in divinity were essential for understanding the Bible correctly. They hoped to purify Christian tradition, not throw it away. They were reformers, not radicals. They wanted Christendom renewed, not overthrown. To their Catholic opponents they might look like spiritual vandals destroying all in their path, but Protestants hailed them as spiritual physicians restoring a sickened society to health.

In some ways the same Bible and the same ideals for galvanizing its salvific message would continue on in American history, but in other ways things worked out differently because of how the landscape changed. In particular, by setting aside governmental coercion to enforce biblical interpretation, Americans attempted a new configuration for religion and society, which only a few of Europe's most advanced dissenters had envisioned.[41]

Lectures offered by G. W. F. Hegel in the 1820s offered surprising insight into this later history. For a savant much better known for abstract rather than concrete reasoning, Hegel spoke insightfully about some particulars of Western history. When he expatiated on the meaning of the Reformation, he emphasized "a fact of the weightiest import...the Bible has become the basis of the Christian church;...each individual enjoys the right of deriving instruction for himself from it...We see a vast change in the principle by which man's religious life is guided." Earlier in the same lectures Hegel had cast his eye westward to the spectacle of a society that combined republican distrust of concentrated power and Protestant trust in human religious creativity. His conclusion was that "America is therefore the land of the future where, in the ages that lie before us, the burden of the World's History shall reveal itself."[42]

Whether Hegel saw correctly the course of "World History," he did understand something about the change that experience in America worked on the European inheritance, and in particular on Protestant trust in the Bible alone, however configured. What he failed to note were the crucial events in England that paved the way for what eventually transpired in America.

2

From William Tyndale to the King James Version

IF MARTIN LUTHER'S initial appeal to Scripture planted the seed that eventually grew into the United States' Bible civilization, the flowering of that seed took place in England. Labors of William Tyndale that led in 1525 to the first Protestant-inspired English-language New Testament—and then continued through succeeding generations of translators to the Authorized Version in 1611—produced the biblical texts that decisively shaped the later history of North America. Yet just as important as the texts were the contexts surrounding the translations and their uses. Visceral spiritual hunger inspired the longing for a vernacular Bible, while deep-seated concern for the spiritual well-being of church and nation operated almost as strongly among those who tried to discipline, restrain, or guide that longing. Scripture as a contested doorway to heaven was always an equally controversial prop of social-political order. The Bible—read, in the words of Tyndale's translation, "tomake the[e] wyse vnto saluacion thorowe the fayth which ys in Christ Iesu"[1]—also served as a tool of social ordering eagerly deployed by monarchs and Parliament, reformers and reactionaries, prelates, populists, and partisans. Not incidentally, Scripture in an era of heightened religiosity also supplied the vocabulary of culture—language, literature, family relationships, the arts, even to some extent economics and science. What Christopher Hill once wrote about sixteenth- and seventeenth-century England spoke for conditions that also extended across the Atlantic: "The availability of the Bible in English...was a cultural revolution of unprecedented proportions, whose consequences are difficult to over-estimate....The words and themes of the Bible were familiar in popular usage, to an extent which demands an effort from us to understand."[2]

For the era when the Bible became an everyday cultural commodity in English life, nothing was more important than the ever-present assumptions

of Christendom. Americans, long habituated to separating the institutions of state and church, need a special reminder of this fundamental
fact. From time out of mind, Europeans had acted upon the premise that
while the eternal and the temporal might be distinguishable, they could
never be divided. A controversialist in the 1640s, when the British Isles
were filled with earnest debate on such matters, succinctly expressed this
common assumption: "Piety and policy, Church and State, prince and
priest are so nearly and naturally conjoined in a mutual interest that, like
to Hippocrates his twins, they rejoice and mourn, flourish and perish, live
and die together."[3] The dramatic changes occasioned by Protestant movements in the sixteenth century left Catholics contending with Reformers
and Protestants contending with each other. Yet except for a few extreme
sectarians, Protestants also continued to believe that religion and social
order depended on each other organically. The definition of Christendom
by Hugh McLeod (already cited in the Introduction) bears repeating in
order to underscore the frame that encompassed the history of the Bible
in English. Thus, Christendom meant "a society where there are close ties
between leaders of the church and secular elites; where the laws purport
to be based on Christian principles; where, apart from certain clearly defined outsider communities, everyone is assumed to be Christian; and
where Christianity provides a common language, shared alike by the de-
vout and the religiously lukewarm."[4] The Bible had always helped define
European Christendom, but now it did so even more thoroughly in the
Protestant lands where Scripture became the crucial weapon of self-de-
fense against Catholics powers loyal to Rome and for disciplining a properly Christian society.

The sketch of English history that follows by no means does justice to
a rich but complex story of competition and cooperation among translators, successes and failures of different translations, brutal partisanship
and magnanimous patronage, spiritual liberation and violent controversy.
It can, however, show that circumstances critical for America's history of
the Bible were set firmly in place before the first English colonists established a foothold in the New World—in particular, how the appearance of
Bibles in English responded to ardent spiritual desires while also fueling
those desires; how the religious story always involved broader ecclesiastical, social, and political stories; and how in the era after the beginning of
colonization, England took a path that the colonies followed only in part.
The difference for America was not any weakening of deference to Scripture
but the gradual transformation of Christendom.

William Tyndale as the Fountainhead

Printed Bibles in English began with William Tyndale, who was born in Gloucestershire sometime in the early 1490s and who throughout his life remained passionate about freeing Scripture to communicate the truth of the Christian gospel.[5] In 1530, Tyndale published a "Prologue" to his translation of the book of Genesis that likened the biblical text to a precious jewel that only became valuable when its possessor recognized the jewel's great worth. "It is not enough," he wrote, merely to possess the Bible, or even "to read and talk of it." The imperative thing was to "desire God, day and night instantly, to open our eyes and to make us understand and feel wherefore the scripture was given, that we may apply the medicine of the scripture every man to his own sores."[6] Tyndale might have been, as one well-qualified critic once concluded, "the best prose writer of his age," unrivaled "in economy, in lucidity, and above all in rhythmical vitality."[7] But the compelling reason his translation caught on and then survived to supply a great portion of the wording for all English versions through the King James Bible was spiritual. The fact, as David Norton put it, that "more of our English is ultimately learnt from Tyndale than from any other writer of English prose" is owing almost completely to the Bible-fixation of sixteenth-century England.[8] The most obvious testimony to Tyndale's enduring impact is the wealth of expressions from his translations that remain standard in English prose—as a small example only: alpha and omega, apple of his eye, beautiful, brokenhearted, busybody, castaway, cast the first stone, eye of a needle, fatted calf, fell flat on his face, harden his heart, housetop, infidel, pillar of salt, powers that be, rose-colored, scapegoat, sheep's clothing, signs of the times, sins of the fathers, sorcerer, stiff-necked, still as a stone, stumbling block, two-edged sword, uproar, viper.[9] These words and phrases became a fixed part of the language because great portions of the English public pored over successive biblical translations with a diligence unmatched for any other text in modern history.

Tyndale ardently hoped that an English-language Bible would promote what his fellow-reformer, the Cambridge priest Thomas Bilney, found when he studied newly published Greek and Latin editions of the New Testament. Of his experience in the 1520s, Bilney wrote he had not "heard speak of Jesus" until he studied Erasmus's Latin and Greek text. There, although he had purchased that edition solely because of its literary reputation, he was almost immediately transfixed by its spiritual message: "at the first reading...I chanced upon this sentence of St. Paul (O most sweet and comfortable sentence to my soul) in I Tim. i: 'It is a true saying and worthy of all men to be embraced that Christ Jesus came into the world to save sinners, of whom I am the chief and principal.'" By this biblical word, Bilney "through God's instruction and inward working" was "wounded with the guilt of my sins." Yet then from this text he experienced "a marvelous comfort and quietness, insomuch that my bruised bones leaped for joy."[10] Hugh Latimer, who would also become a reformer, spoke of Bilney as the one who prompted Latimer "to smell the word of God" and so also to forsake "the school doctors and all such fooleries."[11] Tyndale devoted himself to Bible translation so that such revelations and such renewals might become universal among those who knew only English. He would succeed beyond his fondest hope.

Like Latimer, Tyndale pursued reform with an open Bible in hand. This positive pursuit accompanied a negative certainty that the unreformed Catholic church stood in the way. Tyndale saw the corruption of that church first in its leaders' resistance to the translation of Scripture into vernacular languages and then in its heavy-handed regulation of the biblical texts that already existed. John Foxe, the Protestant martyrologist, once reported a conversation between Tyndale and "a learned man" who asserted that it was more important to understand the pope's "law" than "God's law." To which Tyndale replied with words that became a fixture of Protestant ideology: "I defy the Pope and all his laws...if God spare my life ere many years, I will cause a boy that driveth the plough, shall know more of the Scripture than thou dost."[12] From earliest days, and deep into American history, positive commitment to Scripture remained extreme because of extreme Protestant depictions of Catholicism as an anti-biblical religion.

Tyndale studied at Oxford before taking up his lifelong vocation as a translator. Like Bilney, he had also been much inspired by Erasmus's works, especially the Latin translation of the New Testament that Erasmus in 1516 published alongside the Greek original. What did not impress Tyndale was the array of medieval textbooks his teachers interposed between himself and the Scriptures. To promote the liberation he had experienced by going first to the Bible, Tyndale sought assistance for a translation project from the bishop of London, Cuthbert Tunstall. The bishop seemed a logical choice since he supported the new learning of the Renaissance and had befriended Erasmus during the latter's earlier sojourns in England. By the time Tyndale made his request, however, Tunstall had grown cautious.

Along with England's hierarchies in both church and state, he had been scandalized by Luther's protest to Charles V at Worms in 1521 and was already taking steps to stop the circulation of Luther's books in England. Tyndale, as someone obviously infected with the Lutheran virus, was suspect. Tunstall peremptorily refused his request, whereupon the scorned translator left for the Continent and took up the vagabond life he led for the rest of his days.

Cologne was the site of Tyndale's first attempt at publishing an English-language New Testament translated directly from the original Greek. The year was 1525. The preface to this effort carefully explained "the causes that moved me to translate." To Tyndale, a Bible in the vernacular was "light…shewed to them that walk in darkness, where they cannot but stumble, and where to stumble is the danger of eternal damnation."[13] This first English-language effort looked very much like Luther's German New Testament of 1522, including an adaptation of Luther's prefaces and marginal notes, along with type and page layouts also imitating what the German reformer published. But before this press run could be completed, local authorities hostile to Luther stopped the printing—though portions of the Gospel of Matthew, and perhaps of Mark, did make it back to England.

Nothing daunted, Tyndale repaired to Worms where in 1526 he completed a second New Testament translation. This one came without notes or preface; it was a pocket-sized octavo as would be all of Tyndale's subsequent publications. These were relatively inexpensive books to be used by any who could read. Very soon, printers in Antwerp were duplicating this edition and smuggling copies hidden in bales of cloth back to English and Scottish ports. Reprintings and corrected editions flowed thereafter in a continuous stream.

As Tyndale turned to translating the Old Testament Pentateuch, he took time out to write two other treatises that made the broader scope of his efforts as "cleare as cristall" (Tyndale, Rev 21:11). Both were published in 1528. The *Parable of the Wicked Mammon* expounded Jesus's story from Luke 16 that began in Tyndale's version, "And he sayd also vnto his disciples. Ther was a certayne rych man, which had a stewarde, that was acused vnto him, that he had wasted his goodes." And ended: "Ye can not serve God and mammon" (Tyndale, Lk 16:1–13). This book insisted that faith constituted the proper foundation of true Christianity, with good works a consequence of that faith, but not (as Tyndale interpreted Catholic teaching) a source of salvation themselves.

The strong anti-Catholicism of this work was exceeded only by the strong English patriotism of Tyndale's *The Obedience of a Christian Man*. Like his *Parable*, this tract defended scriptural authority as the church's indispensable guide, but it also advocated loyalty to the English crown in sharpest terms. It began with the same argument that, seven years later, John Calvin repeated in the first edition of his *Institutes of the Christian Religion*: the liberated Bible would bring the church badly needed reform, and rulers had nothing to fear since Bible-based reform was neither seditious nor treasonous. As Calvin would also argue, Tyndale maintained that only by freeing Scripture to remake the church could Henry VIII and other rulers be liberated from Roman corruption and enjoy the deference they deserved as "the powers that be...ordeyned of God" (Tyndale, Rom 13:1).[14]

Reactions to Tyndale's reforming efforts demonstrated the deep entanglement of Bible translation with the institutions of church and state. They showed how much efforts at reform implicated social order and civil peace. As soon as copies of Tyndale's first New Testament appeared in London in 1525, Bishop Tunstall excoriated them as "that pestiferous and most pernicious poison"; on 27 October 1526, he supervised the burning of Tyndale's translation at St. Paul's Church in London and then preached a sermon on the thousands of errors and the multiplied heresies in the book.[15]

In 1527, pressure from Bishop Tunstall and Cardinal Thomas Wolsey, the king's chancellor as well as the archbishop of York, led Thomas Bilney to renounce his adherence to Luther's biblical interpretations. Bilney, however, was so stricken in conscience by this renunciation that he eventually repented of his repentance. He then openly preached sermons advocating standard Lutheran themes and underscored his allegiance to the new teachings by presenting Tyndale's New Testament and his *Obedience of a Christian Man* to a prominent prioress. Whereupon he was rearrested, retried in a church court, convicted as a relapsed heretic, and handed over to state authorities who burned him at the stake in his native Norwich on 19 August 1531.[16] By that time, laypeople brought up before English tribunals were being regularly interrogated about their knowledge of Tyndale's *Obedience of a Christian Man*.

In 1529 Thomas More, who would later replace Thomas Wolsey as Henry's chancellor, received special permission from Bishop Tunstall to study banned books. The result was More's exasperated polemic, *A Dialogue Concerning Heresies*. It mounted a full-scale attack on Tyndale's New Testament as a diabolical effort scandalously deviating from the church's official Latin Vulgate and its strict English equivalents. When in 1531 Tyndale responded with *An Answer unto Sir Thomas More's Dialogue,* More rounded on Tyndale with a blast of nearly two thousand pages, *Confutation of Tyndale's Answer,* which reached a rarely duplicated plane of vituperation. Although More's tirade mostly defended the Catholic Church as the sole reliable authority for interpreting Scripture, it also paused frequently to explain how Tyndale's teaching imperiled political peace and social order. Attitudes toward spiritual reform and principles of social order remained indivisible.

For his part, Henry VIII eagerly participated in the era's religious controversies. In 1526 he published an English version of an earlier Latin denunciation of Martin Luther in which he charged that the German heretic had helped "one or two lewd persons born in this our realm [Tyndale and his assistant William Roye] for the translating of the New Testament into English."[17] Four years later, he issued a public proclamation that made possession of English Bible translations a crime; this edict took pains to denounce Tyndale's "pestiferous English books" as designed "to stir and incense [the people] to sedition."[18] Yet after his own break with Rome shortly thereafter, Henry's political interests led him to a different opinion. When Anne Boleyn, his new queen, gave Henry a copy of Tyndale's *Obedience of a Christian Man,* the monarch apparently praised this work as just the sort of book that all kings should be reading.[19]

Tyndale was cheered by such reports, but his own days were numbered. He hoped that by supporting Henry in the king's break with Rome he might one day be allowed to carry on his translating work in England, but it was not to be. In 1535 Tydnale was betrayed to the Catholic authorities in Antwerp who put him in prison. In October 1536, his keepers took him to a place of execution where he was strangled to death and his body burned. The assumptions of Christendom informed what were reportedly the Bible translator's final words: "Oh Lord, open the King of England's eyes."

From Tyndale to King James

The interweaving of religion and politics continued to mark the history of translation from the death of Tyndale to the production of the King James Bible. Shortly before Tyndale's execution, a fellow Protestant, Miles Coverdale, published the first complete Bible in English. Coverdale and his associates followed Tyndale closely where he had provided material, but offered their own translations from the Latin Vulgate for the parts of the Old Testament that Tyndale had not completed. Two years later in 1537 the first English Bible to obtain a royal license appeared under the name of an editor identified on the title page as "Thomas Matthew." But "Thomas Matthew" was actually John Rogers, one of Tyndale's assistants who used a pseudonym to protect himself in the event that the king changed his mind about allowing the translation to go forward. In 1539 the first complete Scripture to be widely distributed in England appeared as "The Great Bible," so called because, as a large folio edition, it weighed several pounds and required a substantial stand on which to rest. As one scholar has written, this translation represented "Coverdale's revision of John Rogers' revision of Tyndale's Bible, so far as Tyndale's Bible went."[20]

As a public event, three other things were noteworthy about the Great Bible.[21] First was the elaborately etched title page dominated by an image of Henry VIII shown handing copies of the Scriptures to Archbishop Thomas Cranmer and the vice-regent, Thomas Cromwell. Crowds of ordinary people appear at the bottom of the page shouting out "Vivat Rex" and "God save the king." The title page contained a crowded field of banners, all but "God save the king" in Latin and most quoting biblical passages that underscored the authority of kings to command the people.[22]

Second was a royal injunction to parish priests published alongside this Bible itself. It commanded that a copy be "set up in some convenient place within the said church that ye have cure of, whereas your parishioners may commodiously resort to the same and read it." But it also commanded that while priests were to encourage the reading and hearing of Scripture, they were also to urge hearers "to avoid all contention and altercation therein...and to refer the explication of obscure places to men of higher judgment in scripture."[23] Royal officials sensed correctly that contention over what the Bible said would follow wide access to the Scriptures as day follows night.

Third was the rapt enthusiasm that in many parishes greeted the public reading of the Bible in English. So great did this enthusiasm become that the king and the archbishop issued injunctions prohibiting public readings that disrupted sermons and warning against unauthorized expositions of Scripture.[24] Recent scholarship has shown that public rapture at hearing Scripture in the vernacular did not translate automatically into popular approval for all Protestant efforts.[25] Yet however the public excitement is interpreted, it did mean that the appearance of Scripture in English met a widespread longing in the populace.

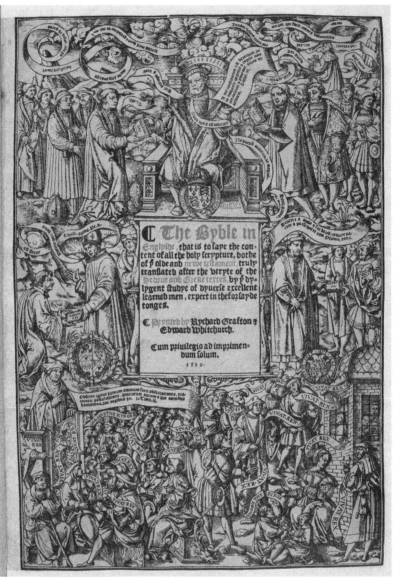

The "Great Bible" of 1539 was in fact *the* "Authorized Version," since it, and not the King James Version of 1611, received official recognition from the monarch. Its title page is noteworthy for the many individuals who are depicted as shouting "*vivat rex*" (long live the king!). (Courtesy of the American Bible Society Library)

The history of the Great Bible thus reveals that intense religious interest coexisted with extensive concern for social order and ecclesiastical discipline. This translation and all to come represented battles for the control of Christendom as well as provisions for spiritual life.

Plans for further Bible translation and distribution continued under Henry VIII's successor, his only legitimate son Edward VI (r. 1547–53). But this precocious Protestant was a sickly lad who survived only six years as monarch before succumbing at age fifteen to his many infirmities. Upon Edward's death, Bible production in England came to sudden halt because his successor and half-sister, Mary Tudor (1553–58), was a dedicated Catholic who repeated her father Henry VIII's early actions by banning the circulation of English-language Bibles.

Yet because Mary's harsh stand against Protestants drove many of their leaders into exile, her efforts led inadvertently to the sixteenth-century's best and most widely circulated English translation. This version was undertaken by Protestant leaders who gathered in the Geneva of John Calvin after fleeing from England. There they followed the lead of other exiled Protestants who used this strongly Reformed city as a safe haven for preparing vernacular Scriptures in several European languages. The New Testament by the English exiles appeared in 1557, the entire Bible in 1560. Almost immediately it became the dominant version. As the first complete English Bible to be translated entirely from the Scripture's original languages, it bore much evidence of expert scholarship. It was also unusually readable, in part because it incorporated so much of Tyndale's work. It was compact in size and economical in price. Although the translation's very extensive notes would later excite the wrath of King James I (r. 1603–25), most of these notes provided helpful linguistic and geographical advice that all readers appreciated. It was printed in a clear and distinct roman type. This combination of qualities made it the most important source, after Tyndale, for the King James translators. Later authorized as the Bible for Scottish Presbyterians, it would also be the Bible used by Shakespeare and the version quoted by the King James translators in their extensive Preface to the Reader. Later, it was also the first English language Bible brought to Virginia, Plymouth, and Massachusetts.

An important feature of the Geneva translation that exerted a powerful, if subliminal, effect on Bible reading throughout the English-speaking world was its division of the text into verses. While chapter divisions had been made centuries before, verse markers responded to the spread of print and the need of new Bible readers for a means of referencing what they had read. Polemics stimulated by the Reformation, where recourse to Scripture played a central role in the back-and-forth controversies of the era, heightened readiness for such an innovation. Versification in the Geneva Bible followed the Greek New Testament of Stephanus (Robert Estienne) that had appeared in Geneva in 1551, which itself followed a division of the Latin Vulgate appearing only a few decades earlier. The Geneva Bible of 1557 marked the first occasion that any European Scripture printed each verse beginning with its own line of print, even when the verse marker divided complete sentences.[26]

This new way of printing the Bible made its individual parts much more accessible. In modern terms, it represented a reader-friendly aid with a strong democratic effect. Now any literate English-reader could reference the sacred page with a facility once reserved to scholarly masters. Yet especially in an era also experiencing the first stirrings of modern scientific procedure committed to empirical investigation, the printing change, in the words of David Norton, "had a huge effect on the way translators and readers experienced the text." Norton, as the world's leading authority on the literary history of English-language Bibles, knows what he is talking about. Alongside the older habit of the continuous reading of complete narratives, prophetic pronouncements, and doctrinal or poetic expositions, readers now could also approach the text "in bits, each bit numbered and presented like a paragraph." Because of the numbering of verses, along with cross-references supplied by the Geneva translators, what Norton calls "concordant reading" became more common, with "a verse in one part of the Bible directing the reader not to its surrounding verses but to another some distance away."[27] For believers, the Bible had always been the Word of God written in human language. With enduring effect, versification tilted instincts about Scripture away from the human and toward the divine. It made it much easier to assemble proof-texts from throughout the sacred volume that the assembler could present as authentic divine teaching, despite the potential damage done to understanding the whole narratives, pronouncements, and expositions from which the verses came. The American history of Scripture, from first to last and with consequences that have never been sufficiently studied, is the history of a versified Bible.

After the Geneva Bible two more important translations greeted the public before the appearance of the KJV. In 1568 Anglican officials, responding to the popularity of the Geneva Bible and fortifying themselves against dissent from abroad, prepared another large folio edition that became

d Locuftes are falfe teachers, heretikes, and worldlie futtil Prelates, with Monkes, Freres, Cardinals, Patriarkes, Archebifhops, Bifhops, Doctors, Bafchelers & mafters which forfake Chrift to mainteine falfe doctrine.

e Falfe and deceiuable doctrine, which is pleafant to the flefh.

f That is, fecretly to perfecute and to fting with their taile as fcorpiōs do: fuche is the facion of the hypocrites.

Ifa.2,19.
hofe.10,8.
luk 23,30.
chap.6,16.
Wifd.16 9.

g For the falfe prophetes cā not deftroie the elect, but fuche as are or deined to perdicion.

h That is, the infideles whome Satan blindeth with the efficacie of error, 2 Thef 2,11

i Thogh the elect be hurt, yet they can nor perifh.

k The elect for a certeine fpace and at times are in troubles: for the grefhoppers

and the ayre were darkened by the fmoke of the pit.

3 And there came out of the fmoke **d** Locuftes vpon the earth, and vnto them was giuen **e** power, as the **f** fcorpions of the earth haue power.

4 And it was commanded them, that they fhulde not hurt the **g** graffe of the earth, nether anie grene thing, nether anie tree: but onely thofe **h** men which haue not the feale of God in their forheades.

5 And to them was commanded that they fhulde not **i** kil them, but that they fhulde be **k** vexed fiue moneths, and that their paine fhulde be as the paine that cometh of a **l** fcorpion, when he hathe ftung a mā.

6 *Therefore in thofe daies fhal men **m** feke death, and fhal not finde it, and fhal defire to dye, and death fhal flee from them.

7 *And the forme of the locuftes *was* like vnto **n** horfes prepared vnto battel, and on their heades *were* as it *were* **o** crownes, like vnto golde, and their faces **p** *were* like the faces of men.

8 And they had heere as the **q** heere of women, and their **r** teeth were as the teeth of lions.

9 And they had **f** habbergions, like to habbergions of yron: and the founde of their **t** wings *was* like the founde of charets when manie horfes runne vnto battel.

10 And they had tailes like vnto fcorpions, and there were **u** ftings in their tailes, & their power was to hurt mē fiue moneths.

11 And they haue a King ouer them, which is the **x** Angel of the bottomles pit, whofe name in Hebrewe *is*, **y** Abaddon, and in Greke he is named Apollyon.

17

18

19

20

21

The Geneva Bible of 1560 was the first in English to divide the text into numbered verses. Most of its notes merely conveyed helpful, but also innocuous, information. A few, however, like the words here for Revelation 9:3, played a significant role in King James I's desire to replace it with a new translation. (Courtesy of the American Bible Society Library) known as the "Bishops' Bible." This version was commissioned and edited by Matthew Parker, Elizabeth I's archbishop of Canterbury, who sought a theologically neutral text with minimal notes. While parish churches were encouraged to buy this version, its stilted prose and suspect scholarship kept it from becoming a serious rival to the Geneva Bible.

The last major translation before the KJV once again introduced foreign intrigue. It was the 1582 translation of the Latin Vulgate's New Testament prepared by scholars at the English Catholic College in Rheims, France. In 1610, this text would be joined by the Old Testament translated at Douai to make up the Douai-Rheims Bible that remains, after several revisions, a main English-language version for Catholics.[28] The language of this early Catholic translation reflected the Latinate character of the Vulgate, and it was not widely circulated at the time. Nonetheless, the KJV translators perused it carefully and borrowed several individual words from their Catholic contemporaries, including "Paraclete," "advent," "evangelise," and "concupiscence." It also supplied several phrases that became standard in English when they were used in the KJV, including "white as snow," "of making many books there is no end," "render unto Caesar the things that are Caesar's," and "see through a glass darkly."[29] In an age of fierce Catholic-Protestant disagreement, it was as unexpected as it was striking that the Protestant translators of the KJV went to school on this Catholic version.

The complicated textual history of the sixteenth century left puzzles that can still be noticed today. One is illustrated whenever Christian worshipers in traditional services recite together the Lord's Prayer from Matthew 6. Some will say "forgive us our debts, as we forgive our debtors"—they are following the KJV reading taken over from the 1535 translation by Miles Coverdale. But others will recite "forgive us our trespasses, as we forgive those who trespass against us," which was William Tyndale's rendering from the mid-1520s given worldwide currency by its preservation in the Anglican Book of Common Prayer. That puzzling variation should be a reminder that words on a page, while communicating something about their referents, also have a history.

The history of translation between Tyndale and King James underscores the depth of commitment that drove translators, helpers, and sometimes critics in their efforts to clarify what the Bible said. The marginalia that owners and readers penciled in the margins of a remarkably high percentage of sixteenth-century Bibles testified to the seriousness with which they read.[30]

It also reveals how many circumstances came together—political pressure, social demands, ripening scholarship, spiritual hunger, and expert translation—to create the world in which the King James translators got to work.

King James and His Bible

The circumstances that produced the King James Version anticipated much about the later history of the Bible in America, where the King James Version enjoyed such long preeminence. In retrospect, probably the most difficult thing for later readers to grasp is that while religion and language factored large in the process, the driving force behind James's sponsorship of a new translation was political.[31]

The Bishops' Bible of 1568 (rev. 1572) was not a distinguished translation, but only a few complained about its central place in most English churches. The Geneva Bible of 1560 enjoyed a much better reputation and, with its many notes, provided a more informative version that enjoyed great popularity among ardent Protestants and also many others. Its compact size, economical price, roman print, and all-around utility made it a genuine peoples' book. The grounding of all sixteenth-century translations of the New Testament and the Pentateuch in William Tyndale's reasonably accurate and beautifully phrased versions of the 1520s and 1530s ensured that these successor translations were both reliable and readable.

James nonetheless took the initiative to commission the leading lights in England's intellectual firmament to prepare a new translation. In doing so, he most wanted to assert his own authority. James VI had been crowned king of Scotland in 1567 when he was only thirteen months old. Through a perilous youth and then with steely determination after he obtained his majority, James stabilized the economic condition of his desperately poor land, held his own in tense theological debate with his Presbyterian tutors, and—most importantly—unified the intransigent factions that had made life impossible for his mother, Mary Queen of Scots.

Now as the newly crowned monarch of England, where the stakes were higher and the factions more powerful and almost as belligerent as in Scotland, James I employed all of his considerable wiles to secure his own rule and consolidate a realm in imminent danger of fracture. Commissioning the new translation was a stroke of genius.

When James succeeded to the throne, the Church of England was being torn apart by those who wanted to push reform farther (Puritans) and those who saw the church as a stabilizing force in the realm (bishops of the Church of England). Puritan advocates enjoyed their greatest appeal in midsize towns and among the rising middle classes. The bishops came forth as the main spokesmen for stability, order, and uniformity in both church and nation. England's Puritans hoped that the new king would favor their reforms, since they knew he had been tutored by leaders of the Church of Scotland whose views closely resembled their own. They did not realize that James had come to abominate his Presbyterian tutors as dangerous extremists who threatened the principle of kingly authority.

After the death of Queen Elizabeth in 1603, as James and his royal retinue headed south from Edinburgh to London, Puritan leaders presented him with a petition calling for a welter of church reforms. It became known as the Millenary Petition because it was signed by roughly one thousand Puritan or Puritan-leaning ministers. James, though not at all favorably disposed to what the Puritans demanded, did not want the church's bishops to think they could manipulate him for their own purposes. He, therefore, agreed to a conference that would allow the Puritans to advocate for their reforms while also giving the bishops a chance to defend their views. The conference convened early in 1604 at Hampton Court. One after another, James dismissed the Puritan proposals—for more congregational autonomy, for less ritual, for reforming the selection process of bishops, and many more. At one point, when yet another proposal to reform the bishops was advanced, James reportedly shouted, "No bishop, no king!" In other words, if you keep attacking my bishops, I will know that you are really attacking me.

Yet in reply to one—but only one—of the Puritans' proposals, James said "yes." It was their request for a new translation of the Bible. Although most of England's advanced reformers remained more than content with the Geneva Bible, they offered their proposal in hopes of producing a text that would be commonly received—and so strengthen Bible-reading in the populace at large. James immediately agreed, then authorized the recruitment of the country's best scholars for the project. He commissioned the archbishop of Canterbury to divide translating duties among teams in London, Oxford, and Cambridge. Seven years later the new English version appeared.

Everything in this new translation's physical presentation announced its status as a Bible of Christendom. An impressive title page opened the volume with images depicting the Trinity and several New Testament apostles arranged at the top of the page. Moses and Aaron, representing

Moses and Aaron, or what we would today style church and state, were the largest figures on the title page of the King James Bible in 1611. (Courtesy of the American Bible Society Library)

civil and religious authority, flanked the center section as the largest images. After the title page came an extensive note to the reader describing the effort to produce a new version as coming from "Zeal to promote the common good." Aside from an attack on the Church of Rome for requiring special licenses to access vernacular translations, most of this note dwelt on the spiritual significance of the Bible: "But now what piety without truth? What truth, what saving truth, without the word of God? What word of God whereof we may be sure, without the Scripture?"—followed by references to John 5:39, Isaiah 8:20, Acts 17:11 and 8:28–29, Matthew 22:29, Luke 24:25, and 2 Timothy 3:15. An obsequious dedication "To the Most High and Mighty Prince James" came next. It began by recalling the "great and manifold...blessings, most dread Sovereign, which Almighty God, the Father of all mercies, bestowed upon us the people of *England*, when first he sent Your Majesty's Royal Person to rule and reign over us." Then followed the table of contents, with the books of the Apocrypha separated out between the Old and New Testament lists, and finally "The First Book of Moses, Called Genesis."[32] The four elegant type faces used to produce the first edition bespoke learning, dignity, status, and authority.[33]

James's authorization of a translation was a shrewd move for several reasons, none of them narrowly religious. First, a respected Bible prepared for public reading would strengthen and unify the state church (thus, demonstrating the king's authority to his bishops). Second, a translation undertaken at the request of Puritans showed that they too might find a place in the king's church (even if James rejected all of their other proposals for reform). Third, a learned translation would advertise James's own considerable expertise as a scholar and lay theologian (in both Scotland and England, James worked on his own metrical translations of the Psalms direct from Hebrew). Fourth, and not least, a scriptural text that replaced the Geneva Bible would rid the realm of the Geneva notes that specified the circumstances under which subjects could disobey their monarchs.

Although most of the notes in the Geneva Bible were innocuous, a few looked like dynamite to a monarch extremely sensitive about the prerogatives of royal power. Explications like those for Revelation 9:3—which defined the "Locustes" of the passage as "suttil Prelates...Monkes, Freres [friars], Cardinals, Patriarkes, Archebishops"—may have struck James ambiguously.[34] As a Protestant he approved reproof of Rome, but as a leader defining his own authority as from God, he did not approve of any who doubted the principle of divine right. Beyond question he certainly abhorred the "argument" that the Geneva editors supplied to the book of Exodus: it explained the narrative of this book in terms that sensitive ears may have heard as commentary on current events: "the King and the country grudged and endevored bothe by tyrranie and cruel slavery to suppresse" God's people, against which Moses and the faithful resisted heroically.[35] Similarly offensive could appear the "argument" for the book of 1 Samuel that explained how, when the people of Israel asked for a king, God "gave them a tyrant and an hypocrite to rule over them, that they might learne, that the persone of a King is not sufficient to defend them, except God by his power preserve and kepe them."[36]

So it was that for reasons concerning neither the quality of existing translations nor the spiritual well-being of his realm as such, James ordered a new translation. As much as politics lay behind James's decision, it was not coincidental that the translators produced a literary masterpiece, for the king's royal self-interest matched the literary acumen of his translators. James, in other words, really did want a translation superior in scholarship and language to what had gone before. His desire was not simply political. Yet this desire meshed perfectly with his *need* for a text that undergirded the king's authority while unifying his people.

The King James Bible

The result was a text of Scripture that has been universally recognized as a literary masterpiece. Yet in its first decades, the KJV won out because Bible printing fell to a monopoly enterprise, and those who held the monopoly forcibly prevented the printing and distribution of other translations. Within a few decades, however, the economical beauty and balanced majesty of the prose became even more important than a printer's monopoly as reasons ensuring its extraordinary standing in English-speaking cultures. Only Jerome's Latin Vulgate and Luther's German translation have occupied anything like the massive cultural and religious presence of this particular translation.

Jonathan Swift in the early eighteenth century pioneered the praise for this translation that has never ceased. As someone who abominated the Geneva Bible for its rank Presbyterianism, this Anglo-Irishman praised the KJV, along with the Book of Common Prayer, for keeping alive the prose of the sixteenth century. His encomium ran, "No Translation our Country ever yet produced, hath come up to that of the Old and New Testament: And by the many beautiful Passages...I am persuaded that the Translators of the Bible were Masters of an English Style much fitter for that Work, than any we see in our present Writings, which I take to be owing to the Simplicity that runs through the whole."[37]

With Shakespeare as the only, even distant comparison, the King James translation provided prose and poetry as close to immortality as anything ever written in English.[38]

(Genesis 1:26–27) And God said, Let us make man in our image, after our likeness: and let them have dominion over the fish of the sea, and over the fowl of the air, and over the cattle, and over all the earth, and over every creeping thing that creepeth upon the earth.

So God created man in his own image, in the image of God created he him; male and female created he them.

(Ruth 1:16–17) And Ruth said, Intreat me not to leave thee, or to return from following after thee: for whither thou goest, I will go; and where thou lodgest, I will lodge: thy people shall be my people, and thy God my God.

Where thou diest, will I die, and there will I be buried: the Lord do so to me, and more also, if ought but death part thee and me.

(Psalm 23) The Lord is my shepherd; I shall not want.

He maketh me to lie down in green pastures: he leadeth me beside the still waters.

He restoreth my soul: he leadeth me in the paths of righteousness for his name's sake.

Yea, though I walk through the valley of the shadow of death, I will fear no evil: for thou art with me; thy rod and thy staff they comfort me.

Thou preparest a table before me in the presence of mine enemies: thou anointest my head with oil; my cup runneth over.

Surely goodness and mercy shall follow me all the days of my life: and I will dwell in the house of the Lord for ever.

(John 14:1–6) Let not your heart be troubled: ye believe in God, believe also in me.

In my Father's house are many mansions: if it were not so, I would have told you. I go to prepare a place for you.

And if I go and prepare a place for you, I will come again, and receive you unto myself; that where I am, there ye may be also.

And whither I go ye know, and the way ye know.

Thomas saith unto him, Lord, we know not wither thou goest; and how can we know the way?

Jesus saith unto him, I am the way, the truth, and the life: no man cometh unto the Father, but by me.

(1 Corinthians 13:1, 13) Though I speak with the tongues of men and of angels, and have not charity, I am become as sounding brass, or a tinkling cymbal....

And now abideth faith, hope, charity, these three; but the greatest of these is charity.

As indicated by the wealth of solid books and articles published to commemorate its quadricentennial in 2011, the KJV's literary excellent and cultural significance remain firmly fixed in modern consciousness.[39] The even greater wealth of not-so-solid writings offered its own kind of affirmation. More recently a survey in early 2014 of more than 1,500 scientifically selected Americans testified to the versions' staying power as a spiritual resource. The survey revealed that among the nearly half of Americans who remain readers of Scripture—and after decades of carefully prepared and well marketed alternative translations—fifty-five percent responded that the KJV remained their Bible of choice.[40]

Attending closely to the historical circumstances of the KJV's origins makes it easier to remember that it was prepared and has always been read within webs of power. A history structured by networks of conflict should not detract from the literary, cultural, or linguistic signification of the KJV, but it should make it impossible to forget the dense entanglement of the worldly with the supernal that shaped this history from Tyndale on.

It was not only that Tyndale's versions supplied so much of the later KJV text. It was not only that Bible translation, Bible distribution, and even Bible reading were regularly viewed as politically subversive acts. It was also that Tyndale, his fellow Protestant translators, and (in their own way) the Continental Catholic authorities who destroyed his earliest efforts and immolated him at the stake all agreed on one thing. Divine revelation in Scripture implicated matters of supreme importance; understanding that revelation correctly and putting it in the correct words under the right authority spelled life and death, now and for eternity. William Tyndale went to the stake only three decades before the birth of James I. A mere half century after Tyndale's execution, James's mother, Mary Queen of Scots, was charged with conspiring as a Roman Catholic to depose Elizabeth, the Protestant queen of England. This Elizabeth, daughter of Henry VIII and the executed Anne Boleyn, on her own death bed in 1603 passed over a host of near Catholic relatives to designate the Protestant James VI of Scotland her successor as England's monarch as James I. Earlier in 1586 she had reluctantly consented to the execution of Mary Queen of Scots. Between the time when King James authorized a new translation and it appeared, desperate Catholic conspirators attempted in November 1605 to blow up James and his Parliament. It was an age when Bible translation, Bible reading, and convictions about Scripture really mattered.

The elements that made up the English history of the Bible also began the American story. A powerful Protestant ideology constantly exalted the Scriptures as fundamental to spiritual liberation and uniquely authoritative for daily life. Whenever anything Catholic seemed to threaten, the invariable defense turned to Scripture. The Bible did, in fact, operate with unusual power to shape personal religion and community religious identity—even as it expanded its reach as an all-purpose resource for English-language culture. Once the translation wars of the sixteenth century gave way by the mid-seventeenth century to the hegemony of the King James Version, "the" Bible occupied central conceptual space for the entire civilization. Inevitable political entanglement came from the effort to exert (or sanction) public authority on the basis of what was known to be true according to the Scriptures.

This near-universal deference to Scripture overlay the near-universal assumption of Christendom. In England from the beginnings with Tyndale, the Bible for salvation and the Bible for church reform was also Scripture for the body politic. Within Christendom, strengthening the church and reforming the realm inevitably entailed large-scale political contests. The contests for control that have been sketched in this chapter for the sixteenth century, and that are outlined for the seventeenth in the following chapter, bequeathed the Bible to the American colonies. For a time the colonial story offered only variations on the homeland's experience of the Bible in Christendom. Soon, however, those variations developed a trajectory of their own. Eventually the American story would emerge into a new phase when Britain's establishmentarian Christendom did not survive the American War of Independence. But even with dramatic changes to the social and political framework, the American history of the Bible developed as a shoot off of English stock.

3

The English Bible in the Era
of Colonization

ENGLISH ADVENTURERS LANDED at Jamestown and began the colonization of Virginia in 1607, three years after James I agreed to prepare a new
translation of the Bible and four years before the King James Version
appeared. Wandering separatist Puritans (or Pilgrims) arrived at Plymouth
in 1620, five years before James's death and eleven years after they had left
England for Holland in an effort to organize a church according to standards they believed Scripture demanded. James's son, Charles I, who succeeded to the throne in 1625, showed even more determination than had his
father for compelling the Parliament and England's people to accept his
understanding of how a properly Christian nation should be governed. The
initial colonizing effort of Puritans to Massachusetts Bay in 1629 and 1630
coincided with the beginning of Charles I's effort to rule England by himself, after sending Parliament into permanent recess for (among other reasons) asserting a different understanding of what Scripture demanded for
the nation and its established church. In 1632 Charles I granted a charter to
Cecil Calvert, Second Lord (Baron) Baltimore, to found the colony of
Maryland where Catholics like Calvert would be free to settle; it was named
after Charles's queen, Henrietta Maria of France, whose open practice of
Catholic faith offended the strongly Protestant leaders of Parliament who
regarded Catholicism as flatly antithetical to what the Bible taught. England's
new-world colonies, in other words, came into existence when her citizens
simply took for granted the organic unity of government, church, and society, and when the Bible figured prominently in the apprehension of that
unity on both sides of the Atlantic. Much contention existed over how Scripture
should be put to use, but deference to its position of authority remained
universal.[1]

The political instincts, ideological assumptions, and religious convictions of seventeenth-century England were also the instincts, assumptions,

and convictions of the American colonists. The course of colonial history would begin to diverge from the course of English history only as the old-world inheritance evolved in response to new-world conditions. Because almost all of England's specific beliefs about the Bible and the various ways that the English put Scripture to use transferred to the New World, the history of America's engagement with Scripture began with English history.

The common starting point was explicit trust in the Bible as the essential guide to salvation and, therefore, the necessary corrective to the waywardness of late-medieval Catholicism. Not as explicit, though almost as widespread in both the Old World and the New, was the conviction that since the Bible opened the pathway to salvation, it also established guidelines for all else in life. Confidence in these explicit and implied verities, folded into the nearly universal assumption of a unified Christendom, came as English Protestant baggage to the New World.

Events in sixteenth- and seventeenth-century England, with significant contributions also from Scotland, shaped later American history because they placed Scripture at the center of religious, social, and cultural development. They were equally important for showing how the centering of Scripture developed in the colonies differently than in the mother country. In particular, those who tried hardest to make Scripture the detailed guide for all of life visibly and conspicuously failed in England. In the colonies the ones who made the same effort succeeded only in part, but with effects lasting for a very long time.

Two reasons explain the collapse of those strenuous efforts in England. One arose from the intensity of disagreements among Protestants who could unite in their complaints against Rome but not in finding alternatives to Rome. The other arose from the strength of Protestant factions that, while holding to Scripture as the key to salvation, also remained deeply committed to the traditions of England's comprehensive church-state settlement. These more traditional believers considered the Anglican establishment sufficient; they were always proportionately stronger in the mother country than in the colonies where those who advocated for comprehensive reform exerted more influence.

Scripture played a large role in all the great dramas of seventeenth-century British history: the conflict of Parliament and Puritans with Charles I, the civil wars of the 1640s (Parliament versus monarch and then England versus Scotland), the Commonwealth under the Lord Protector Oliver Cromwell, the Restoration of Charles II in 1660, and then the Revolution of 1688 that removed James II from the throne. The Bible in Protestant England and Scotland exerted a manifest force for spiritual liberation, but always functioning within the constraints of organic church-state establishments. During the civil wars and under Cromwell, those constraints were hotly contested; intermittently they also relaxed. The Restoration of 1660 signaled the nation's decision to reaffirm the main features of Christendom, with consequent restrictions on the liberty to proclaim, interpret, and apply Scripture. Debate would go on about what form of Christendom the nation should embrace, with England firmly Anglican and Scotland ultimately allowed to be Presbyterian. Negotiations also continued over how much toleration could be extended to the remnants of Puritan movements that had failed in their efforts to take over the established churches and then, after 1660, resisted the reimposed Anglican settlement. Negotiations toward the end of the seventeenth century explored whether it might be possible to tolerate Roman Catholics, though these moves heightened perennial anxiety about Catholic encroachments and so stimulated Protestants to hew closer to the Bible. After 1660, however, no serious efforts arose in England to reconstitute all of society on the basis of the Bible alone. In other words, biblicism faded. Instead, some of England's most innovative thinkers strove to devise formulas for political life that, while retaining considerable respect for Scripture, effectively subordinated the Bible as a guide for public order.

Colonial history developed differently. The factions in early-seventeenth-century English society that looked most expectantly to Scripture as a guide for all of life enjoyed greater strength in the colonies than in the mother country. In some of the colonies, those factions confronted less competition from advocates of competing beliefs about how to follow the Bible. Through much of the seventeenth century, traditions with a stronger commitment to "the Bible alone" remained strong. When in the late seventeenth century religious pluralism and alternative ways of relying on Scripture that challenged Christendom gained strength, the earlier biblicist tradition faded gradually. Yet in the colonies no debilitating civil wars contested these issues, and England's Restoration prompted only moderate changes. Attitudes toward the place of Scripture in public life underwent peaceful evolution rather than climactic rupture. The result was a surviving Bible-only tradition that could be revived by eighteenth-century developments and so survive as an influence in the new United States that arose after the Revolutionary War threw off the institutions of British Christendom.

That colonial story is the subject of chapters to come. This chapter treats English (and also Scottish) history of the sixteenth and seventeenth centuries. For later developments across the Atlantic, the English story explains the depth of American attachment to Scripture. It also shows why the collapse of efforts to create a Bible civilization in the tumultuous middle decades of the seventeenth century set England and Scotland on a different course from the colonies, which nonetheless remained strongly indebted to the mother country for their biblical heritage.

The Anti-Catholicism of English Protestantism

The Bible translations that accompanied colonists to America come out of an interwoven theological-political history. They also came with a strong Protestant tradition of vigorous anti-Catholicism. For centuries after the first colonization, positive belief that the Scriptures "are able to make thee wise unto salvation through faith which is in Christ Jesus" (2 Tim 3:15) would be matched by a negative conviction that Catholic corruptions of Scripture eviscerated true Christianity. This combination of foundational commitments—Scripture and salvation, Scripture and politics, Scripture and anti-Catholicism—grounded the Protestant Christian faith in England and Scotland. Even as the international history from Tyndale to the Great Bible to Geneva and finally to King James tracked the emergence of Scripture as the one essential English-language text, so also the development of an English doctrinal tradition defined an emerging understanding of how Scripture should function in a Protestant regime.

William Tyndale, who keyed efforts to translate the Bible, also militantly promoted strict adherence to Scripture in combination with fierce antagonism to Rome. As Karl Gunther has recently shown, Tyndale led several other radical evangelicals who from the start of the English Reformation pushed hard for a total restructuring of English church life on the basis of something very like "the Bible alone." With an abiding concern about the "papal" tendencies of the English state-church, these strict Protestants followed the arguments of Tyndale's *Obedience of a Christian Man* (1528) to outline, in Gunther's summary, "the biblical duties and responsibilities of all members of society toward each other."[2] So it was that in 1530 they republished an earlier sermon by John Colet that used Jesus's admonition in Matthew 20:25–28 ("whosoever wilbe chefe, let him be your servaunt," Tyndale, v. 27) to demand a complete overhaul of the episcopacy. In the same year Tyndale's *The practyse of Prelates* set up a strict biblical standard by detailing "what officers the apostles ordered in christes chirche & what their offices were to do." In 1534 the preacher and diplomat Robert Barnes urged in a "supplication" to Henry VIII that the English church be reformed according to the first chapter of the book of Titus where the Apostle Paul called for a "bishop" in every town. Late in Henry's reign as he turned against reform, successors to Tyndale and Barnes, both of whom by this time had been executed, again appealed to "the law of the gospel" to guide England away from Roman influences toward authentic Christian practice.[3]

Henry, along with his cautious archbishop of Canterbury, Thomas Cranmer, were not won over by these scripturally driven mandates for total reform. Yet despite turning from a radical course, the mainstream of English Protestantism still advanced strong biblical remedies for what they viewed as fatal papal diseases. The Anglicans' official doctrinal standard began life as the Forty-Two Articles, drafted by Cranmer under Edward VI (1552), but then appeared revised and reissued as the Thirty-Nine Articles under Queen Elizabeth.[4] Although the earlier version worried almost as much about Anabaptism as about Roman Catholicism, the later Elizabethan statement (Latin, 1563; English, 1571) concentrated on Rome as the great danger. The earlier Forty-Two Articles had taken pains to rebut interpretations of Scripture associated with Continental Anabaptists, some of whom had affirmed the sleep of souls after death, the salvation of all humanity, the release of believers from the requirements of God's law, and a millennial kingdom of a literal thousand years. A few worries about such notions survived in the Elizabethan formula; it rejected Anabaptist beliefs that sins after baptism could not be forgiven (#16), that warfare was ruled out for Christians (#37), and that oaths in court were improper (#39). But the revised Articles downplayed such concerns while emphasizing explicit objections to Rome. For the future course of both Britain and America, it was decisive that the Articles' positive statements claimed to follow the clear teachings of Scripture, while Catholic doctrines were condemned for violating explicit biblical teaching.

Positively, the Articles strongly affirmed "the sufficiency of the Holy Scripture for salvation" (#6) and mandated the use of the Nicene, Athanasian, and Apostles' creeds, "for they may be proved by most certain warrants of Holy Scripture" (#8). The Thirty-Nine Articles' moderately Calvinist affirmation of predestination was based on what is "generally set forth in Holy Scripture" and what "we have expressly declared unto us in the word of God" (#17). "Holy Scripture," Article 18 stipulated, "doth set out to us

only the name of Jesus Christ, whereby men must be saved." And so it
went throughout all of the Articles.

Their rebuff of Rome sometimes came indirectly, for example, in
Article 6 that defined the apocryphal books, affirmed with full authority by
the Council of Trent, as subordinate to the definitive sixty-six books of the
Protestant canon.[5] Article 15 proclaimed that only Christ was sinless,
which could be understood as a repudiation of Catholic beliefs about the
perfection of Mary. More frequently, the counter-Catholic claims were direct: medieval teaching about the "grace of congruity" was wrong (#13); the
Church of Rome, with all other Christian traditions, "hath erred, not only
in their living and manner of ceremonies, but also in matters of faith"
(#19); communicants should receive the wine as well as the bread in the
Lord's Supper (#30); the "sacrifices of masses...were blasphemous fables
and dangerous deceits" (#31); and priests could marry (#32).

As much as these Articles repudiated individual Catholic teachings
and practices, the document's strongest statements emphasized the Protestant conviction that blatant denial of scriptural teaching represented
Rome's most damaging error. Article 14 condemned the Catholic doctrine
of "supererogation," or the idea that humans could do good works increasing their merit before God, by quoting what "Christ saith plainly" in Luke
17:10. Article 22 attacked "the Romish doctrine concerning purgatory, par-
dons, worshiping and adoration, as well of images as of relics, and also
invocation of saints" as "grounded upon no warranty of Scripture, but
rather repugnant to the word of God." According to Article 28, the Catholic
doctrine of transubstantiation, which taught that the bread and wine of
communion became the sacramental flesh and blood of Christ, "is repugnant to the plain words of Scripture." And in a complex statement that was
meant to bolster the Anglican establishment while condemning Rome,
Article 20 declared that it was "not lawful for the church to ordain any
thing that is contrary to God's written word."

The doctrinal propositions of the Thirty-Nine Articles, though this document was far from the only significant Protestant creed, articulated a dogmatic foundation maintained by almost all Protestants for most of the next
four centuries: the foundational error that turned the Church of Rome
against God—that made it, according to many Protestants, Antichrist—
was its consistent, unconscionable, destructive, and deliberate violation of
the clear teaching of the Bible. The anti-Catholic animus so visible in colonial American history sprang from this fundamental proposition.

Yet in the context of the sixteenth century, these Articles were also both theologically moderate and strongly establishmentarian. While other Protestant confessions began by defining the supremacy of Scripture that rescued conscientious Bible-readers from the depredations of Rome, the first five of the English Articles affirmed propositions about the Trinity and the Incarnation of Christ held by virtually all Christians of that age, most assuredly including Catholics. The Articles were unmistakably anti-Roman, but their positive affirmations sought wider goals than just holding Catholicism at bay.

The prominent establishmentarianism of the Articles, which became a stone of offense for later Puritans, shows how thoroughly the imperatives of Christendom informed Anglican efforts to repair the errors of Rome. Articles 6 and 20 allowed the monarch considerable room to regulate England's external church life. Crucially in an environment where radicals advocated biblicism, Article 20 sided more with Martin Luther than with Ulrich Zwingli in treating the authority of the Bible as the *final* rather than as the *only* word on religious matters; that stance opened the way for other authorities like a state church to mandate details for putting authoritative Scripture to use. Article 37 did restrict the sovereign from exercising the clerical functions of preaching and administration of the sacraments, but it also proclaimed unambiguously the monarch's "chief power" to exercise the "chief government of all estates of this realm, whether they be ecclesiastical or civil." In 1801 the American Episcopal Church would delete this article as it adjusted to the new separation of church and state that prevailed in the young American republic.[6] By contrast, for England and Scotland, the ideal of a corporate state church unified institutionally under God long remained a presupposition of society, education, and culture as well as politics. This presupposition meant that all attention to Scripture, no matter how personal it might appear, also carried political implications. "Because church and state were one," Christopher Hill once wrote, "religion became politics, with the Bible as text book for both."[7]

English and Scottish Protestants spoke as one when they denounced Rome for perverting Scripture, sequestering the Bible from the laity, and substituting the fallible word of prelates, priests, and popes for the life-giving Word of God. They also spoke as one in trusting Scripture for personal spiritual direction and for the reform of church and nation. From the first, however, that unity splintered when Protestants specified positively what it meant for God's word to become "a lanterne vnto my fete, and a light vnto my path" (Geneva, Ps 119:105).

The Template of Biblical Authority

English history offered aggrieved reformers a cornucopia of opportunities to complain about violations of biblical standards perpetrated by political authorities. Those opportunities always led to demands for reform of church structure, customary practices, or ecclesiastical regulations according to the Word of God. For later American history it was crucial that the pressure behind biblical reform had been building in Britain for nearly three generations before colonization began. Just as important, the negative focus of that pressure (against Rome, against errors of the English state-church) had been much stronger than the positive pressure for any one set of reforms. If the appeal to Scripture as a guide for reform was nearly universal, voices diverged in stipulating the shape of biblical reform. The result was a powerful ideology of scriptural authority easily appropriated as an imperative for change, but much more difficult to focus on specific changes. Too many would-be reformers crowded too close to each other in too little space.

Reliance on Scripture nonetheless propelled every stage of English Protestant development from the age of Tyndale to the era of John Bunyan. The Bible as the engine of reform emerged unmistakably in official statements like the Thirty-Nine Articles, but it emerged even more powerfully in the movements that led to Puritanism, and that would exert a special influence in America. Christopher Goodman, one of the exiles under Mary Tudor who fled to Geneva, assisted there in preparing the Geneva translation. In 1558, he published a tract whose title revealed his fixation on Scripture but also the comprehensiveness of his biblical vision: *How Superior Powers Ought to be Obeyd of their subjects: and Wherin they may lawfully by Gods Worde be disobeyed and resisted. Wherin also is declared the cause of all this present miserie in England, and the onely way to remedy the same.*[8] Goodman defined carefully the discernment demanded in his title by beginning with Acts 4:19 and the reply of Peter and John to the Jewish authorities who had demanded that they stop preaching: "Whether it be right in the sight of God, to obey you rather than God, iudge ye" (Geneva).[9] Then in rapid fashion he deployed a slew of biblical examples to make his case: the story of the evil Doeg from 1 Samuel 22 who murdered Israel's priests; the actions of "cruell Herode" in slaying the babies at Bethlehem; the "wicked Jewes" who murdered the prophets and then Jesus; "furious Jesebel and her false Priestes and Prophetes"; and more. Goodman pounded on his main point, that Queen Mary could be resisted,

"Seeing...that kinges are institute to rule in Goddes feare and Lawes, as subjects and Sergeants to God, and not agaynste his Lawes"—but she and her councilors had forsaken their "dutie in defending Gods glorie and the Lawes committed to their charge." Those who opposed Mary, even "thoghe you had no man of power upon your parte," could do so boldly because "you...have the warrant of Godds worde upon your side." Goodman's standard leapt from the page: "what Moyses wryteth, or rather the Spirite of God by him."[10]

Goodman's evocative use of biblical examples to reform current practices verged close to what Puritans called "typology." Typology, or reading material in the New Testament as antitypes fulfilling Old Testament types, usually featured main points of Christian theology strictly considered. Yet the typological approach to Scripture did strongly encourage the exploitation of biblical examples, especially from the Old Testament, for contemporary instruction.[11]

Back in England, after the death of Mary and the succession of Elizabeth, the Presbyterian party led the way as the most ardent proponents of further reform. It sought to move the Church of England beyond simply replacing Catholicism toward what its advocates considered a more thoroughly biblical nation. In particular, they wanted to replace top-down church-rule by bishops with power derived from elders and ministers (= presbyters) in local churches and exercised through delegates sent from the churches to a national synod. One of the leading Presbyterian spokesmen, the Cambridge don William Fulke, in about 1577 wrote a carefully argued appeal for "the Discipline and Reformation of the Church of England."[12] Yet it revealed much about the tumults of the age that by the time Fulke's tract was published in 1584, he had begun to disassociate himself from the most determined Presbyterian reformers.

Nonetheless, Fulke's published work articulated a common argument. Its preface, amidst a flurry of references to the evil-doers who troubled Old Testament Israel, described the English church as threatened by "the famine of hearing the word of God preached." The nation desperately needed "that which at the least in the judgment of all true Christians hath no small probability (as we judge *necessity*) of truth out of the Scriptures." Along the way this tract evoked standard anti-Catholic themes by defining a local minister's proper "authority" as very different from "the pope and his usurped supremacy," which was "not only without the warrant of God's word, but clean contrary to it." As also conventional, this attack on the papacy moved easily to an attack on what the Presbyterians considered

Catholic elements lingering in the Church of England. The same biblical warrants "that have banished the pope" also condemned "all other usurped authority that is practiced in the church." For proof, the tract provided a catena of eight biblical citations. The conclusion of Fulke's appeal for greater church purity is worth quoting at length because it succinctly set out a biblicist template of the kind invoked by many others who sought reform of church and state, and on both sides of the Atlantic:

> Thus have we briefly set forth a form of reformation touching matters ecclesiastical...agreeable to the word of God, and as we are able to prove, consenting with the example of the primitive church, building *only* upon the most sure foundation of the canonical scriptures; but intending...hereafter to set forth the practice and consent of the godly fathers in their acts, counsels and writings, following the same rule and interpretation of the Scriptures that we have done.[13]

This pattern, once established, continued. Paired with instinctive, comprehensive, and often exhaustive appeal to Scripture as a general corrective (but especially against Catholic errors) came countless programmatic efforts aimed at reforming the church and the nation. Occasionally a full-orbed statement of principle would appear, but usually proposed reforms rested on a four-fold set of assumptions:

- The Bible was the source of purest truth.
- Catholicism was the source of foulest error.
- England, half-reformed, could easily slide back into pestilent Roman ways.
- Scrupulous attention to Scripture could purify church and nation.

This rubric functioned implicitly as much as it did explicitly, but each of its propositions enjoyed a deep resonance in the spiritual psyche of British Protestantism. Significantly, New England was settled by reformers whose views on such interpretive matters clustered toward the proposition that the Bible as supreme authority came close to meaning the Bible as only authority.

Tumultuous Times

Full statements of biblical principle as well as specific proposals for biblically guided reform unfolded against the backdrop of a tumultuous era. During the reign of James I (1603–25) the monarch kept a tight grip on the kingdom—despite protests by Puritans ardent for reform guided strictly by Scripture, and parliamentarians, like the jurist Edward Coke, who worried about the king's drift toward divine-right monarchy.

When James's son, Charles I, succeeded to the throne in 1625, England's competing Christendoms moved from low-level insurgency to open conflict. Early in his reign, Charles hinted at wanting to imitate the absolutist rule of the era's French monarchs and also relaxing England's strictures against Roman Catholics. These moves spurred a coalition between his parliamentary opponents, who feared the onset of despotism, and his Puritan opponents, who feared a retreat from the Reformation. After a decade of standoff beginning in 1630, unrest boiled over in Scotland, followed by civil war between king and Parliament in England. During that time the Massachusetts colony, begun in 1629/30, grew more secure and two new Puritan commonwealths, New Haven and Connecticut, were founded. In the early stages of Britain's armed struggle, reform-minded Protestants, aided by the Presbyterian Scots, strongly supported the armies of Parliament against the Royalists. But then, as the broad parliamentary-Puritan-Scottish alliance gained the upper hand, internal dissension rent the coalition. Emblematic of that division was Oliver Cromwell's 1650–51 conquest of Scotland, a nation that only shortly before had joined the Puritan-parliamentary coalition to fight against King Charles. English Presbyterians, English Congregationalists, English radicals, and Scottish Presbyterians could unite to oppose royal despotism, but when they turned to follow Scripture in refashioning Christendom, they ended by attacking each other.

By far the most important leader was Cromwell, the parliamentary general.[14] After defeating royal forces on the field of battle, he became England's effective ruler from 1649 until his death in 1658. Cromwell remains a controversial figure for pushing Parliament to execute the monarch in January 1649 and for his murderous reprisals against Catholic communities in Ireland. But Cromwell was also ahead of his times in believing that civil order did not require strict religious homogeneity. Thus, he legalized the readmission of Jews to England and also advocated a relatively broad religious toleration (though of course excluding Catholics). This program of toleration represented a weakening of assumptions about uniformity that had been axiomatic in traditional Christendom. In the public space opened by toleration, advocates for reform leapt at the chance to broadcast their views. Some used the opportunity to continue advocating for the one best way to purify the nation-and-church, but others made the innovative case that the time had come for full freedom of religion.

A panoply of dissenters took advantage of this unprecedented opportunity. A few already existing groups like the Baptists grew exponentially; some of the most extreme, like the Ranters and the Muggletonians, quickly passed from the scene. Others, like the Levellers, propounded radical ideas that would much later become mainstream. Still others, like the Society of Friends (Quakers), became permanent additions to the Protestant world. All of them, though in different ways, challenged the assumptions of Christendom that took for granted the intermingling of biblical precept and political comprehension.

In 1660, exhausted by intra-Protestant religious strife as well as by political division, England called Charles II, the son of Charles I, back from the Continent to restore the monarchy. Scotland too joined in the recall, with hopes that the restored sovereign would allow for the full-scale implementation of Presbyterian church order that a desperate Charles had promised to the Scots amid the confusion following his father's execution in 1649. That promise had led Scotland to break ranks with Cromwell, who engineered Charles I's execution, and thereby turned the Scottish-parliamentary alliance into an English-Scottish war. Once Charles II's throne was secure, however, he promptly forgot his earlier promise to the Scots, he implemented a fully reconstituted Anglican regime in England, and he tried to push Scotland toward an Episcopalian-type state church. Only after the Glorious Revolution of 1688 would Scotland gain the unencumbered right to constitute Presbyterianism as the national church.

For our purposes it is important to realize that the Restoration represented an extreme recoil in England from Puritanism and the radical movements that sprouted from Puritan stock. In particular, during the Restoration era most of England stopped trying to promote comprehensive reform according to the Word of God. Making Scripture central for totalizing visions of kingdom, church, and social order had proved simply too disorderly. The Bible would remain important for Britain, both church and nation, but claims to organize all of life by its teaching faded away.

To be sure, a few holdouts kept the faith, including Cromwellian republicans like the blind poet John Milton and pietists like the Bedford tinker, John Bunyan. Viewed in their own times, Milton's *Paradise Lost* (1667, 1674) and Bunyan's *Pilgrim Progress* (1678) can be read as works trying to revive the biblical spirituality that had been undercut when the Puritan vision of comprehensive scriptural reform collapsed. Other holdouts included the two thousand ministers ejected in 1662 from their livings as Anglican clergymen for refusing to swear allegiance to episcopal church order and strict observance of the Book of Common Prayer as mandated by a new Act of Uniformity. In Scotland, the most extreme holdouts defending comprehensive Presbyterianism as a scriptural necessity were the Covenanters who found themselves harried, harassed, and outlawed for sticking to their beliefs.

Thus, even as the Bible commonwealths of New England continued on with reasonably successful efforts to structure society by Scripture, and just before a different understanding of biblical imperatives inspired a new Quaker colony organized by William Penn, the dominant English influences in church and state backed away from the earlier Protestant goal of a thoroughly biblical civilization.

Classic Protestant Biblicism

Yet even as the tide of events pushed England away from reform inspired directly by Scripture, the ideal of a comprehensively biblical application to all of life remained very much alive. Among comparatively rare statements of Protestant principle during this period, the Westminster Confession of 1646 provided the gold standard. Parliament had called the Westminster Assembly into being three years earlier at an uncertain time when it was struggling to unite England's anti-monarchical forces while also enlisting Scotland in its war against the king. A parliamentary ordinance of 12 June 1643 expressly evoked both the Protestant ideal of reform by Scripture and the Christendom ideal of a comprehensive redirection of religious life: "such a government shall be settled in the Church as may be most agreeable to God's Holy Word, and most apt to procure and preserve the peace of the Church at home, and nearer agreement with the Church of Scotland, and other reformed churches abroad."[15] To take up the crucial task of formulating a doctrinal standard embodying these ideals, Parliament nominated thirty of its own members to serve with one hundred and thirty learned divines. The divines included four discernible parties: Five commissioners from Scotland advocated the Presbyterian system of church government that their nation had long sought. A minority contingent of Independents (or Congregationalists) spoke up for their vision of churches organized by local authority. A strong English majority leaned toward Presbyterianism, the dominant view in Parliament in 1643 when the commissioners were appointed. A few additional members held to the Erastian principle that Scripture authorized national governments to take the lead in telling churches what they could and could not do.

Soon after Parliament issued its commission, the assembly convened at Westminster Abbey, where it would hold over 1,100 sessions stretching into 1649. Their initial mandate charged the delegates to "give their advice and counsel" to Parliament concerning "the liturgy, discipline and government of the Church of England" according to what "shall be most agreeable to the Word of God."[16] Over the course of its existence—and working steadily amidst the military, political, and religious upsets of civil war—the Assembly produced a full-scale confession of faith, larger and shorter catechisms, a "Form of Presbyterian Church Government," and a "Directory of Public Worship" intended as a replacement for the Book of Common Prayer. Most of the Westminster divines, along with many in the Parliament of 1643, hoped that the Assembly's work would provide the comprehensive purification of church and nation that the most ardent reformers had long sought. In the end, however, this array of Bible-based formulas would never be implemented in England—and never fully implemented anywhere. Yet the documents, and especially the Confession itself, set forth the ideal of a Bible civilization with unmistakable clarity. For those who wrote it, but also for the many colonists who contended long after the Restoration for such a fully biblical approach to all of life, the Westminster Confession remained a lodestar.

It began with a memorably full chapter on "Holy Scripture." The opening paragraph of that first chapter has long served as an authoritative affirmation about the Bible for a wide range of Protestants, including both Presbyterians who embraced the entire Confession and many others who objected to some of its provisions:

> Although the light of nature and the works of creation and providence do so far manifest the goodness, wisdom, and power of God, as to leave men inexcusable, yet are they not sufficient to give that knowledge of God and of his will which is necessary unto salvation. Therefore it pleased the Lord, at sundry times, and in diverse manners, to reveal himself, and to declare that his will unto his church; and afterwards, for the better preserving and propagating of the truth, and for the more sure establishment and comfort of the church against the corruption of the flesh, and the malice of Satan and of the world, to commit the same wholly unto writing, which maketh the Holy Scripture to be most necessary; those former ways of God's revealing his will unto his people being now ceased. (I.1, p. 604)[17]

TO

The Right honorable the Lords and
Commons Aſſembled in PARLIAMENT.
The humble Advice of the Aſſembly of Divines
now, by Authority of *Parliament,* ſitting
at *WESTMINSTER.*

Concerning a Confeſſion of Faith.

CHAP. I.
Of the Holy Scripture.

Lthough the Light of Nature, and the works of Creation and Providence do ſo far manifeſt the Goodneſs, Wiſdom, and Power of God, as to leave men un-excuſable *a* ; yet are they not ſufficient to give that knowledg of God and of his Will, which is neceſſary unto ſalvation *b*. Therefore it pleaſed the Lord at ſundry times, and in divers man-ners, to reveal himſelf, and to declare that his Will unto his Church *c*; and afterwards for the better preſerving and propagating of the Truth, and for the more ſure e-ſtabliſhment and comfort of the Church againſt the corruption of the fleſh, and the malice of Satan and of the world, to commit the ſame wholly unto writing *d*; which maketh the Holy Scripture to be moſt neceſſa-ry *e*; thoſe former ways of Gods revealing his Will un-to his people, being now ceaſed *f*.

a Rom.1.14.
15.
Rom.1.19.20.
Pſa.19 1.2.3.
Rom 1.32.
with chap.2.1.
b 1 Cor. 1,21.
1 Cor.2 13.
14.
c Heb 1.1.
d Prov.22.19.
20,21
Luk. 1. 3. 4.
Rom. 15. 4.
Mat.4.4 7.10.
Iſai.8 19.20.
e 2 Tim.3.15.
2 Pet. 1. 19.
f Heb.1.1 2.

A 2   II. Under

When the Westminster Confession came from the press in 1646, readers immediately noted the strong statement of scriptural authority with which it began. Almost as obvious were the proof texts in the margin that the Westminster divines added at the behest of Parliament. (Used by permission of the Folger Shakespeare Library)

Comparing the Westminster Confession and the Anglican Thirty-Nine Articles reveals both continuities and discontinuities in how English understandings of Scripture had developed in the eighty-five years from the Elizabethan Thirty-Nine Articles to the English Civil War. Like the Articles, the Confession specified the sixty-six books of the Protestant Bible as authoritative Scripture. It also continued to assume the interconnections of Christendom, with magistrates given the power "to take order, that unity and peace be preserved in the church, that the truth of God be kept pure and entire, that all blasphemies and heresies be suppressed, all corruptions and abuses in worship and discipline prevented or reformed, and all the ordinances of God duly settled, administrated, and observed" (XXIII.3, p. 636). "The civil magistrate," in other words, was to exercise the authority that the Thirty-Nine Articles had given to "the King's [or Queen's] Majesty" (Article 37).

The authors of the Confession, however, obviously did intend it as an improvement over the Articles. Most prominently, the Confession and the other Westminster documents set out a detailed program for a Presbyterian church order. This program reorganized "Religious Worship and the Sabbath-day" (chap. XXI) while providing for a national church directed by "Synods and Councils" (chap. XXXI). Presbyterian worship and church order replaced the via media Anglicanism of the book of Common Prayer.

In all such reforms, the Presbyterians defined their path as the biblical path. Thus, "the acceptable way of worshiping the true God is instituted by himself, and so limited to his own revealed will, that he may not be worshiped according to the imaginations and devices of men, or the suggestions of Satan, under any visible representations or any other way not prescribed in the Holy Scripture" (XXI.1, p. 632). Similarly, local councils and the national synod had the right "ministerially to determine" controversies and to set rules for religious life "if consonant to the word of God." Such determinations, moreover, "are to be received with reverence and submission; not only for their agreement with the word, but also for the power whereby they are made, as being an ordinance of God appointed thereunto in his word" (XXXI.3, p. 645).

Other important differences with the Thirty-Nine Articles included the fact that the Confession was much longer. It provided a much more detailed account of the process by which God accomplished redemption, with fourteen separate chapters beginning with divine providence and extending to "the assurance of grace and salvation" (V–XVIII). Compared to the Thirty-Nine Articles, the Confession devoted less space to attacking Catholicism, though when its attention did turn toward Rome the judgment was severe: "There is no other Head of the church but the Lord Jesus Christ; nor can the pope of Rome, in any sense be head thereof; but is that Antichrist, that man of sin, and son of perdition, that exalteth himself, in the church against Christ, and all that is called God" (XXV.6, p. 639).

On Scripture itself, the Confession repeated much of the nuanced moderation found in the Articles. While the Confession affirmed that "the whole counsel of God" was either "set down in Scripture, or by good and necessary consequence may be deduced from Scripture," it also defined "the whole counsel of God" carefully as "all things necessary for his own glory, man's salvation, faith and life" (II.6, p. 607). It restricted what people could learn intuitively and universally from Scripture to "those things which are necessary to be known, believed, and observed for salvation" (I.7, p. 607). It also stated forthrightly that the Holy Spirit, rather than human reasoning, convinced people of the truths of Scripture (I.5., pp. 606–7) and that quite a few important matters were left to be resolved by "the light of nature and Christian prudence, according to the general rules of the word" (I.6, p. 607). The desire to follow Scripture was obviously foundational for the Confession, but the divines pursued that desire with considerable interpretive sophistication.

Yet a near-century of constantly repeated Protestant professions to live by the Bible, along with an immediate context marked by competing interpretations of scriptural reform, clearly left their mark on the Confession. Unlike the Thirty-Nine Articles, the Westminster divines set out their doctrine of Scripture before treating any other matter; that initial treatment on Scripture constituted by far the longest of the document's thirty-three chapters. Constant, if also conflicting, Protestant appeal to the Bible had made it imperative to state a doctrine of Scripture precisely. Simultaneously, however, the Confession reflected other Protestant principles as these too had been developing since the beginning of the Reformation. Particularly notable was its strong definition in chapter 20 "Of Christian Liberty, and Liberty of Conscience." After defining that liberty first in spiritual terms, as "freedom from the guilt of sin, the condemning wrath of God, the curse of the moral law" (XX.1, p. 630), the divines proceeded with the rousing declaration that "God alone is Lord of the conscience, and hath left it free from the doctrines and commandments of men, which are in any thing contrary to his word, or beside it, in matters of faith or worship" (XX.2, p. 631). Questions about how to determine what contradicted Scripture or what was extraneous to it remained hanging in the air. The divines, however, just as quickly condemned those who, "upon pretense of Christian liberty, shall oppose any lawful power, or the lawful exercise of it, whether it be civil or ecclesiastical" (XX.4, p. 631). Still, the imperative placed upon individuals to determine what the Bible demanded of them individually came through more clearly than anything contained in the Thirty-Nine Articles. Later in American history, liberty of conscience became a principle coordinate with, rather than subordinate to, the authority of Scripture.

The fate of the Westminster Confession after the divines finished their work spoke revealingly about the broader history of Scripture in the seventeenth century. First was the demand by Parliament, when it had received the Confession, that the divines provide each assertion of the document with biblical proof texts. This demand, which led to a thick apparatus of sidenotes supplying chapter and verse, demonstrated a traditional Protestant commitment to the authority of the Bible. It also testified to the influence of modern principles. The Parliament's charge was protodemocratic; it took for granted that if a teaching was to be accepted as scriptural it had to be demonstrated publicly so that anyone who could read the Bible would find it so for himself (judgment for herself would come much later). It reflected the weight of early modern science by showing how the versification of Scripture enabled Bible study to imitate the practice of empirical, inductive investigation. In the same way that natural philosophers (later to be known as "scientists") were making remarkable advances by collecting empirical facts about the discrete operations of nature, so too would theologians advance by collecting scriptural facts from throughout the entirety of the written word.

The Westminster divines, despite the modernity of their reforming zeal, had instinctively relied on their traditional authority as learned pastors in presenting their conclusions: deliverances from the nation's theological elite did not need proof texts, since their authority alone sufficed. By contrast, Parliament showed its modernity by insisting on documentation, keyed to exact biblical passages specified by chapter and verse, as proof for the doctrinal formulas advanced by the learned clergy.

In its charge, Parliament betrayed its assumption that Christian teaching should be communicated propositionally, in an analogy to the empirical deliverances that were transforming the study of nature. The Bible had always been viewed in multiple dimensions. But now the perception of Scripture as a reservoir of fact grew stronger at the expense of both medieval preferences that had regarded the Scriptures as a web of types, and the earliest Protestant vision that had regarded the Bible as a narrative of redemption. Scholars, with an eye toward the emergence of critical biblical scholarship that emerged in Europe before the end of the seventeenth century, have spoken of the "eclipse of biblical narrative" and the exchange of the traditional spiritual Bible for "a cultural Bible."[18] The move within English reforming Protestantism toward what might be call a "protoscientific Bible" paralleled these critical developments occurring at just about the same time.

The second telling fact about the history of the Westminster Confession was that despite its initial commission by Parliament and Parliament's evident interest displayed by the request for proof texts, the Confession never became the law of the land. By the time Parliament received the divines' work, its Presbyterian majority had alienated Oliver Cromwell's army with its dominant Independent (or Congregational) faction. The Confession's strong Presbyterianism did not please the increasingly influential voices who held that the Bible demanded congregational church organization. In addition, the imperative to define doctrine so as to enlist Presbyterian Scotland in the fight against the king had become moot, for in the years when the Assembly was finishing its work the Scots had become the enemies of Parliament. The eventual result was that Scotland, represented by only five commissioners in the Assembly, would adopt the Westminster Confession and its Presbyterian directories, but the English, despite enjoying a vast majority of the commissioners implemented only a few miscellaneous bits from the Westminster documents, and that for only a very brief period.

The fate of the Westminster Confession revealed as much as did its content. For England, the six years of the Assembly's life marked an important transition from biblical unity against royal prerogatives to biblical fragmentation in pursuit of reform. The same period witnessed the weakening of Christendom, which would be restored in England even as it continued to weaken in colonial America.

Protestant Biblical Diversity

The Protestants who could write with such confidence about the authority of Scripture in documents like the Westminster Confession experienced a crisis in the 1640s and 1650s. It came from the ironic fact that the biblical unity, manifest in protests against the lingering shadow of Rome, vanished when royal resistance disappeared. The crisis was not caused by any loss of trust in Scripture. With very rare exceptions, Britons continued to believe that the Bible communicated the Word of Life and that this communication comprehended social as well as personal existence.

Those beliefs rested on countless personal stories where lives had been redirected, illuminated, inspired, or rescued by the personal appropriation of biblical material. The biography of Oliver Cromwell offers one of the best examples because it was so representative of many of the leaders who came to Puritan New England as also of those who pushed for reform in Britain. Cromwell's biblicism is a well-known aspect of his military success. After the battle of Marston Moor on 2 July 1644, in which his cavalry had turned the tide of battle, Cromwell wrote to console a father whose son died fighting for Parliament. The mental framework, the tone, the phrasing, and often the very words spoke of his immersion in Scripture: "England and the Church of God hath had a great favour from the Lord in this great victory given unto us...God made [the opposing cavalry] as stubble to our swords [see Is 41:2, Joel 2:5]....[The son died] full of comfort [see 2 Cor 7:4]." Cromwell, who had himself earlier lost a son, encouraged his friend with the thought that "the Lord took him into the happiness we all pant after [see Ps 42:1] and live for." A year later, after the climactic battle of Naseby that sealed the defeat of the monarch, Cromwell wrote with a similar biblical inflection "I can say this of Naseby....When I saw the enemy draw up and march in gallant order towards us, and we a company of poor, ignorant men [see Acts 4:13], to seek how to order our battle,...I could not, riding alone about my business, but smile out to God in praises, in assurance of victory [see Heb 6:11], because God would, by things that are not, bring to naught things that are [quoting 1 Cor 1:28]. Of which, I had great assurance, and God did it."[19]

The biblicism of Cromwell's public career rested on a biblicism firmly in place well before he became a public figure. His conversion, though shadowed in uncertainty, probably occurred in the late 1620s, after he had married and taken on responsibilities as a landowner and father.[20] Yet once Cromwell entered into a life of self-conscious faith, it became almost impossible for him to write or speak without channeling the Bible. As an example, in October 1638, he wrote to a female in-law to explain how "God had mercy on me." The letter, as suggested by the following paragraph, was almost completely a biblical pastiche:

Yet to honour my God by declaring what He hath done for my soul, in this I am confident, and I will be so. Truly, then, this I find: that He giveth springs in a dry and barren wilderness where no water is [Ps 63:1]. I live (you know where) in Mesheck [Ps 120:5], which they say signifies *Prolonging*; in Kedar [Ps 120:5], which signifieth *Blackness*;

yet the Lord forsaketh me not. Though He do prolong, yet He will
(I trust) bring me to His tabernacle, to His resting-place [see Prov
24:5]. My soul is with the congregation of the firstborn, my body
rests in hope, and if here I may honour my God either by doing or
by suffering, I shall be most glad.[21]

Robert Paul, the most thorough student of Cromwell's religious life,
once analyzed a short, two-paragraph letter that Cromwell penned in
January 1636 about the provision of Puritan lectures in Cromwell's home
county. He found twelve scriptural references in a document "almost entirely couched in Biblical phrases…so interwoven as to make the task of
tracing some of them to any particular passage or version virtually impossible."[22] John Morrill has reached an even more definitive conclusion: "the
empowerment that came from being the instrument of God's will came
from a much more immediate interaction with the words of Scripture….
[I]n the end [he] found all his own messages in the Scriptures from his
own prayerful confrontation with it."[23] If the layman Cromwell might have
been unusual in the degree of his biblical usage, his immersion in the
Bible as the all-purpose guide for life, was entirely representative of his
age. As we will soon see, the same Scripture fixation evident as Cromwell
emerged as the leader of Puritan-parliamentary reform in England acted
just as powerfully for key figures trying to establish biblical commonwealths in the New World.

Not surprisingly, diverse appeals to Scripture featured large in the public history of the era. Almost as instinctively as seventeenth-century Britons
turned to the Bible for personal self-definition, so too did they move from
convictions about how the scriptural message quickened their own lives to
implementing that biblical understanding for the nation as a whole. If colonial history diverged in significant ways from what happened in the
homeland, this aspiration nonetheless loomed large on both sides of
the Atlantic.

Early in the conflict between king and Parliament, appeal to Scripture
functioned alongside other motivating concerns. In 1628, one of Charles
I's early directives aimed at securing his position as head of a unified
Church of England began by ascribing his own royal position to "God's
ordinance" and by asserting that the Thirty-Nine Articles "do contain the
true doctrine of the Church of England agreeable to God's Word." But
most of the declaration concerned the monarch's claim to act as "supreme
Governor of the Church of England."[24]

In response, a set of parliamentary resolutions from early 1629 took for granted that biblical truth had already been well established in the realm and so urged the king to exercise his authority appropriately. To the parliamentarians the great need was for the king to overcome "the Popish party" that had recently "disquieted" the church in Scotland; in Ireland, which "is now almost wholly overspread with Popery, swarming with friars, priests, and Jesuits, and other superstitious persons of all sorts"; and in England, in order to counteract "an extraordinary growth of Popery" and "the subtle and pernicious spreading of the Arminian faction."[25]

Yet conflict with the king and with the royal appointees whom Puritans and the Parliament regarded as secret papists only increased. As it did, direct appeals to govern by the norms of Scripture became ever more pronounced. When the Scots, offended by Charles I's efforts to impose episcopacy on their nation, signed a National Covenant in 1638, suspicion about the monarch's crypto-Catholic intentions fused with their biblicism into a white-hot appeal: "in special we detest and refuse the usurped authority of that Roman Antichrist upon the Scriptures of God, upon the Kirk, the civil magistrate, and consciences of men;...his erroneous doctrine against the sufficiency of the written Word...; his five bastard sacraments, with all his rites, ceremonies, and false doctrine, added to the ministration of the true sacraments, without the Word of God...."[26] Along with much political protest, Scotland's "humble petition" of December 1640, named after its proposals for Root and Branch reform (see Mal 4:1), asked Parliament to abolish England's current regime in order that "the government according to God's Word may be rightly placed amongst us." In the bill of particulars making up this petition, the Scots' harsh denunciations of Catholic practices and Anglican malfeasance were balanced by consistent appeals to Calvinist doctrines defined as "the truth of God" and complaints against regulations "withdrawing of people from reading, studying, and hearing the Word of God, and other good books."[27]

After the outbreak of full civil war and while the outcome hung in the balance, a new Solemn League and Covenant adopted by Parliament in September 1643 aimed to unify all the forces arrayed against the king. It began by evoking as one undivided entity the welfare of the kingdom, loyalty to the king, "one reformed religion...the glory of God, and the advancement of the kingdom of our Lord and Saviour Jesus Christ." Then it set out the highest goal binding the reforming interests of England and Scotland together as "the preservation of the reformed religion in the Church of Scotland, in doctrine, worship, discipline, and government, against our common enemies; the reformation of religion in the kingdoms of England and Ireland, in doctrine, worship, discipline, and government, according to the Word of God, and the example of the best reformed Churches."[28] Language with similar purpose appeared commonly in New England during these same years, where the same instinctive equation prevailed between Scripture as the source of salvation and Scripture as the norm for reformed Christendom.

This period of intense civil-religious strife provided the context for William Chillingworth's famous declaration concerning "the Bible as the only religion of Protestants," which was mentioned in the Introduction. Yet like so much else in the period, this memorable statement hid as much as it revealed. In 1637, the thirty-five year old Chillingworth, a protégé of Archbishop William Laud, had entered into serious literary combat with a Jesuit who contended that England's official religion led inevitably to heretical forms of Christianity.[29] Chillingworth, who had himself briefly converted to Catholicism before returning to stouthearted Anglican allegiance, begged to differ. He shared his religious position with members of The Great Tew Circle, so named after a private estate near Oxford where Anglican divines associated with Archbishop Laud gathered for discussion. Their position was latitudinarian, or oriented toward moderation informed by reason, and Arminian, or favoring human autonomy more than a Calvinist understanding of divine sovereignty. Yet from that standpoint, Chillingworth stood every bit opposed to Catholicism as Puritans were from their conservative Reformed position. And so Chillingworth deployed a full range of his era's standard anti-Catholic polemics to defend the assertion of his book's title, *The Religion of Protestants a Safe Way of Salvation*. Among his many arguments, Chillingworth's focus on Scripture stood out as preeminent. He contended that the religion of Protestants could not be defined by any particular individual or confession, "but that wherein they all agree, and which they all subscribe with a greater Harmony, as a perfect rule of their Faith and Actions." Then came his famous declaration: "The BIBLE, I say, THE BIBLE only is the Religion of Protestants!" He went on to explain that "Whatsoever else" Protestants may "believe besides it, and the plain, irrefragable, indubitable consequence of it, well may they hold it as a matter of Opinion, but as matter of Faith and Religion, neither can they with coherence to their own grounds believe it themselves, nor require the beliefe of it of others, without most high and most Schismaticall presumption."[30]

The ironies of Chillingworth's situation have been much less observed than his famous words have been quoted, for as a Laudian who used Scripture to define what "the religion of Protestants" entailed, Chillingworth himself was mercilessly assailed by Presbyterians, Baptists, and other reforming Protestants who opposed the Laudians, including Chillingworth, as nothing better than crypto-Romanists. Although Chillingworth lived long enough to write against Scottish Presbyterians and to enlist for King Charles I in the first phases of the English Civil War, he died in 1644 and so did not witness the full hurricane of reform that Puritan understandings of Scripture unleashed in England during the next decade and a half. Nor could he witness the Restoration of 1660 when the return of monarchy and an Anglican established church forever ended Puritan efforts to convert a partially reformed England into a full-blown Bible commonwealth. Nonetheless, his statement about "the BIBLE only" has long resonated as a capsule definition of core Protestant belief.

Difficulties in putting this ideal into practice were well illustrated by the attitudes of Richard Baxter, a prolific Puritan author positioned somewhere between the Presbyterians and the Congregationalists. In the early days of the English Civil War, Baxter won renown for his pastoral work in Kidderminster before he became a chaplain in Cromwell's army. As a chaplain with Cromwell, Baxter confronted challenges to the system of theology and church practice he taught as the only one expressly required by Scripture. To Baxter, it became particularly disconcerting when sectarians asserted their right to stand on Scripture in order to advocate doctrines repugnant to his beliefs. Baxter was especially struck by the Levellers he met in the army who attacked all forms of inherited hierarchy, whether in church or state, as contrary to biblical teaching. Their appeal to a direct, plain reading of Scripture reached its climax in the many pamphlets of Gerrard Winstanley who, as for example in 1650, used biblical authority to champion "This great Leveller, Christ our King of righteousness in us."[31] Baxter reacted with astonishment when these radicals "fiercely cried down our present Translation of the Scriptures, and debased their Authority, though they did not deny them to be Divine." The Levellers also "cried down all our Ministry, Episcopal, Presbyterian, and Independent; and all our Churches." What particularly galled Baxter was their stance in debate: "they allowed no argument from Scripture but what was brought in its express words."[32]

Baxter's quarrels with the Levellers sharpened his ability to define the biblical basis for his own position, but it did not yet undermine his confidence in the Scriptures as an absolute guide. Neither did it undermine his more general belief that Christendom—the entire society—could be ordered according to scriptural divine counsel. In 1659 during the short interval between Oliver Cromwell's death and the Restoration of the monarchy, Baxter published *A Holy Commonwealth, or Political Aphorisms, Opening the True Principles of Government* intended to encourage "sober Christians that long to see the Kingdoms of this world, become the Kingdom of the Lord, and of his Christ." In it Baxter defined "the Law of Nature, commonly called the Morall Law" that God gave to humans, alongside "a Law of Grace, and...many Positive Laws; and both sorts...contained in the holy Scriptures." These clear communications made it possible to establish a "Common-wealth" that honored God; therefore, "the more theocratical, or truly Divine any Government is, the better it is." Practically speaking, "in a true Theocracy, or Divine Common wealth, the Matter of the Church and Common-wealth should be altogether or almost the same."[33] Baxter would later repudiate the arguments of this treatise, after he suffered deprivation and imprisonment under the Restoration monarchy. But his forthright defense in 1659 of a single church-state union, even after the chaotic fortunes of the Civil War, showed how deeply engrained were the two main assertions of Puritan reform: the Bible proclaimed God's pattern for all of life; societies could and should be ordered comprehensively to follow that pattern.

Others, however, who experienced the same struggles to define and implement godly order, were no longer convinced. The proposed alternatives to these twin Puritan convictions varied dramatically, from strongly Christian efforts at finding a better way to honor the Scriptures to much less traditional alternatives that proposed secular substitutes for divine guidance. To mention only a few of these alternatives, as they were advanced in the ideologically charged crucible of the interregnum, is to understand how profoundly the events of that period shook traditional understanding of God's relationship to the political world.

Some believers maintained traditional trust in Scripture, but felt confirmed by the rancorous divisions of the time in their conviction that the systems of Christendom *opposed* Scripture.[34] They are treated in chapter 5. Others made different adjustments. In 1648 Anglicans, trying to persevere in the face of Cromwellian reforms, brought out the hitherto unpublished last part of Richard Hooker's *Ecclesiastical Polity*. In that work Hooker (d. 1600) had set out a conservative path toward the renewal of England's Christendom. Now in this newly published addendum readers could see how he championed reason and tradition as entirely proper means of fleshing out the general pattern for society that God had established in Scripture. In other words, the Bible was basic but not comprehensive: "As for the supreme power in ecclesiastical affairs," he averred, "the Word of God does nowhere appoint that all kings should have it, neither that any should not have it." Instead, "human right" was sufficient to show that "Christian Kings" should be given such power.[35] After the interregnum, Richard Baxter himself backed away from his earlier conclusions to propose that "mere Christianity" might draw together those whose biblical interpretations differed on secondary matters.[36]

Movement away from thorough reliance on the Bible also marked the era. Thomas Hobbes characteristically defined the strongest position. In a tract from 1651 on the "philosophical rudiments" of government, he thoroughly subordinated Scripture to concepts of "natural right" and "nature" as the crucial determinants for establishing order in society.[37] The very next year Robert Filmer, who would later become notorious for an all-out defense of divine-right monarchy in *Patriarchia* (1680), published an anticipation of his later contentions. It argued first negatively concerning scriptural authority: "I cannot find any place or text in the Bible where any power or commission is given to a people either to govern themselves, or to choose themselves governors, or to alter the manner of government at their pleasure." And then positively: "There is a ground in *nature* for monarchy."[38] James Harrington, after enduring the varied crises of the period, insisted that the way forward lay in more thoroughly republican government. His major statement appeared as *Oceana* in 1656, but three years later he continued by contending that Scripture could not be treated as handbook for government. He asked, "who imagines that the Romans governed by proof out of Scripture?" only then to point out that the apostle Peter urged believers to submit to "every ordinance of man" (1 Pet 2:13). To Harrington, it was clear that the apostle approved a Roman government that the Romans never justified by appealing to the Bible. He went on to point out that "The most frequent comparison of a commonwealth is to a ship; but who imagines that a ship ought not to be built according to the art of the shipwright, or governed unto the compass, unless these be proved out of Scriptures?"[39]

In a word, the jarring clash of principles that so thoroughly upset British public life in the two decades between 1640 and 1660 jolted many influential leaders away from the ideal of Christendom governed directly by the application of Scripture. The road to John Locke was open. Although Locke publically honored the Bible, he looked to nature for principles of religious tolerance and effective, peaceful government. That effort reflected a gradual move away from direct recourse to Scripture as a comprehensive guide for all of life.[40]

Colonial America would also come to embrace Locke, but more for his defense of natural rights than for his specific views on Scripture. Yet, significantly, the colonies had been spared the violent standoffs of the English Civil War. Their populations also included a greater proportion of leaders and common people who remained confident in their ability to discern and apply a biblical pattern for all of society.

Karl Marx once famously quipped that "Cromwell and the English people had borrowed speech, passions and illusions from the Old Testament. . . . When the bourgeois transformation had been accomplished, Locke supplanted Habakkuk."[41] For the British colonies and later American experience, it was not so much that Locke supplanted the biblical witness. It was rather that Locke and Habakkuk would advance together in shaping the public life of late-colonial America and then the early United States.

4

Colonial Christendom

THE HISTORY OF sixteenth- and seventeenth-century Britain is much more than just antiquarian background for considering the Bible in America. Many elements essential to the American story came as direct bequests of sixteenth-century English history, or of English history as it unfolded during the first years of colonization. At the foundation was the Protestant confidence that Scripture represented God's definitive communication to humankind and that this communication spoke directly, deeply, and distinctly to the most basic human needs. It followed naturally that divine revelation, so perfectly adapted to restore fellowship with God, possessed the same capacity to guide human beings in the exigencies of daily life. The negative reference, always hovering near the surface, contrasted the positive good that humble Christians took from Scripture with the cataclysmic damage that Rome caused by distorting the Bible.

Colonists also brought to America the physical Bibles produced in England. At first the Geneva Bible took precedence over the King James, but as in the mother country the latter soon won out over the former.[1] Although the presses in colonial America teemed with print dependent on Scripture, the actual production of Bibles remained a monopoly of the king's printers. Colonists would print the Bible in Algonquian and German, but not until the War of Independence rendered British copyrights irrelevant were English-language Bibles legally printed in America.[2] Portions of Scripture in Spanish, Latin, and native tongues existed wherever Catholic missionaries worked in New Spain and New France, including territory that would later be part of the United States. But the Bibles that dominated colonial history were English and Protestant.

Nor was it surprising that the British precedent of never-ending Protestant debate, controversy, disagreement, and contention over how best to use Scripture continued in the colonies. The first New Englanders shared the same commitment as their English Puritan confreres to structuring all of life according to the Scriptures. But because of their circumstances in the

New World, New England efforts to create societies normed by Scripture ended differently. This chapter outlines the well-known Bible fixation of the early American Puritans. Then follows a chapter on the colonists who shared the Puritans' biblicism but who stood with the age's small minority who considered the Bible antithetical to Christendom. Those holding this latter stance enjoyed greater freedom in the colonies to act on their objections, a freedom that over time contributed significantly to a distinctly American history.

American Puritan efforts to renew Christendom on the basis of "the Bible only" proved, in the end, no more successful than in the Old World. Yet they did not fail because of the internal conflicts that beset Cromwell's unsuccessful revolution or because of a coercive reimposition of comprehensive Anglican Christendom. America offered a plentitude of space that kept competing biblical visions at a distance from each other. Instead, the gradual evolution of Christendom under colonial conditions—the changing social and political contexts in which inherited convictions about Scripture developed—moved that story along.

Later chapters try to explain why colonists from late in the seventeenth century until the 1740s turned gradually away from biblicism while at the same time growing more attached to a British Christendom that featured anti-Catholic ideology along with a heightened sense of the empire's providential destiny (chaps. 6 and 9). It also details how the evangelical revivals of the mid-eighteenth century reawoke strongly biblicist impulses that, for a time, remained restricted to narrowly religious spheres (chaps. 7 and 8). By the time of the American Revolution, the colonies were adapting to a different set of circumstances than prevailed in Britain. Those colonial circumstances included both less and more direct appeal to Scripture in a pattern that would also characterize the new United States.

The Puritan vision of an entire society enticed (or coerced) into accepting the rule of the saints is the subject of this chapter. It ends by suggesting that although the pervasive biblicism of early New England eventually faded, central elements of that effort survived to influence later American history.[3]

The concentration on early New England in a book purportedly about "America" raises a perennial question: Does not such a concentration distort a reality in which Boston did not, in fact, speak for all colonial perceptions, actions, predispositions, and commitments? Of course. Yet especially for a history of the Bible, New England's general influence is hard to exaggerate. New England leaped far ahead of the rest of the colonies as a publishing dynamo, even as it led in the promotion of literacy and the provision of education at all levels and for all social classes. For the thirteen colonies to adopt themes of national election during the Revolutionary period, and eight decades later for southern states to convene special days of communal fasting and thanksgiving of the sort that had once been limited to New England, illustrate only two of the most obvious examples of how that region shaped "American" history.[4] When American publication of English-language Bibles began after the Revolution, New York and Philadelphia pushed past Boston as centers of the Bible trade. Yet what they did for the nation as a whole stood in direct lineage with what began for "America" in the Puritan colonies of New England.

The Foundation of Puritan Biblicism

This account of colonial history focuses on New England, and not Virginia, even though the Chesapeake colony began some years before permanent settlement occurred farther to the north. It is also true that early Virginia allowed a broad public authority for Scripture. In the colony's first code of laws, promulgated just before the publication of the KJV, deference to the Bible featured almost as prominently as it would in New England. This code began by directing authorities to "call upon their people to heare Sermons, as that also they diligently frequent Morning and Evening praier themselves." It required that "No man shall speake any word, or do any act, which may tend to the derision, or despight of Gods holy word upon paine of death." And it stipulated that the settlers not act "contrarie to the word of God" by disobeying magistrates.[5] Yet the elements that made New England such a hotbed of definitive Protestantism—and by extension a general tutor for the American nation—were much less salient in Virginia and then also later in Maryland.

Those elements included thriving printing presses, an active trade in books and pamphlets, early provision of schools from primary through college, a large number of educated clergy, and a populace constantly exposed to sermons based on the Scriptures. The Chesapeake, by contrast, sustained a much lower ideological temperature, while its book trade in the seventeenth century constituted, in the words of David Hall, "a history of absences and censorship."[6] Yet even there, as the circulation of books and habits of reading developed, the Bible was a main presence.[7] The contrast with Puritan New England must be stated carefully. The Church of England supplied Virginia with a tenacious church-state establishment; Maryland's singular history would reflect an enduring Roman Catholic influence as well as significant later contributions from state-church Anglicanism. But for a history of the Bible—as well as of books, learning, literature, education, and formal ideologies more generally—New England took the lead.

Puritanism in New England never represented a tightly organized phalanx with clear intentions and unambiguous accomplishments. Instead, settlers in the Puritan colonies (Plymouth 1620, Massachusetts 1629, Connecticut 1636, New Haven 1638) made up a fluid force field of convictions and aspirations. The convictions came from long-standing efforts to purify self, church, and society according to the will of God as recorded in Scripture. The aspiration was to complete the work of reformation that had been well begun in sixteenth-century England but then stalled under James I and Charles I. United as they were in their general goals for what they wanted to do, the settlers of New England nonetheless harbored significant differences among themselves—whether church reform should be Presbyterian, Congregational, or some hybrid of the two; whether it was necessary to separate totally from the Church of England; whether purity or comprehension should be the primary goal; and whether government should follow biblical chapter and verse or scriptural principles more generally. It is important to keep this Puritan plasticity in view. For the longer American story, however, it is even more important to remember the Puritan dependence on Scripture.

That dependence emerged unmistakably whenever Puritan leaders spoke of themselves and their enterprise. Utter reliance on the biblical word as the herald of salvation lay at the bottom. Puritans wanted to be guided by Scripture because in the Scriptures they discovered the source of life. Efforts to control others sprang naturally from the common social logic of the seventeenth century—the good for me as a person had to be the good for society as a whole. Although Puritans routinely practiced a level of coercion that modern democratic liberalism instinctively condemns, their attempts at social control (as also similar attempts from their Anglican competitors and Catholic antagonists) grew organically from conceptions of personal and communal well-being. For the Puritans, as often for the others, cynical exploitation of ideology remained extremely rare.

The case of Rev. Thomas Shepard (1605–49) illustrated a common path. In 1634 Shepard migrated with his family to Massachusetts where he immediately assumed a prominent role in the religious and political development of the colony. Shepard, quickly settled as minister in Newton (later renamed Cambridge), led the prosecution of Anne Hutchinson when she advocated what Massachusetts leaders considered dangerous disrespect for God's law. To them, Mrs. Hutchinson seemed to question the entire project of building a fully biblical Christendom.[8] Shepard's reputation as a sensitive guide to those who struggled with a wounded conscience was one of the reasons that the colony in 1636 located their college, soon to be known as Harvard College, in Cambridge.

In 1646, when Shepard neared the end of his relatively short life, he composed an autobiography for the benefit of his oldest son. He wanted that son, if Shepard did not live, to understand "God's great kindness" to him and so "to know and love the great and most high God, the God of his father." That autobiography detailed what Shepard described as a wayward and tormented youth decisively redirected by his conversion as an undergraduate at Cambridge's Emmanuel College. As with so many other Puritans, the crucial spiritual transaction came through the internalization of a biblical passage. For Shepard, it was the text of a sermon by John Preston, the much renowned Master of Emmanuel, on 1 Corinthians 1:30—"Christ is made unto us wisdom, righteousness, sanctification, and redemption." This encounter became the turning point of Shepard's life: "And when he had opened how all the good I had, all the redemption I had, it was from Jesus Christ, I did then began to prize him and he became very sweet unto me, although I had heard many a time Christ freely offered by his ministry if I would come in and receive him as Lord and Savior and Husband." If Shepard subsequently experienced "many fears and doubts," his life course was nonetheless set.[9]

It exaggerates only slightly to call that life course a biographical meditation upon Scripture. Michael McGiffert's edition of Shepard's autobiography and the one extant volume of his journal (Nov. 1640–Mar. 1644) details the intensely introspective character of Shepard's personal religious journey, along with efforts to provide spiritual assistance to others. McGiffert's index to the biblical references in these two short documents records Shepard's specific evocation of twenty separate biblical events or figures, especially the apostle Paul, and his quotation or citation from seventeen Old Testament books (with a profusion of references to the Psalms) and seventeen New Testament books (heavily weighted to the Gospel of John).[10] Shepard, like so many Puritans, lived in the Scriptures almost as much as he lived in his daily round.

Crucially, it was not just the pastors. Another document from Shepard testifies to the broad reach of Puritan biblicism. During the latter years of his ministry in Cambridge (1638–45), Shepard recorded the public confessions of fifty-one men and women who were admitted into the full fellowship of his church.[11] In the protocol that had quickly become standard in

New England, these testimonies were intended to show that God had done a work of grace in the applicant's life. Although the confessions reflected considerable individual difference—unlettered servants and common farmers offered statements with much less polish than learned college graduates—all hewed to the basic Puritan formula: early lives of spiritual rebellion (often specifying breach of the Sabbath, willful spiritual igno- rance, or general loose living), then spiritual conviction followed by an- guished cycles of alternating faith and doubt, and finally some measure of peaceful confidence in Christ. Even more prominent than this standard narrative template was a common reliance on Scripture for its vocabulary of personal transformation. Even granting Shepard's controlling influence on how the testimonies were written down, this selected slice of lay spirit- uality revealed a remarkably comprehensive spiritual biblicism.

Typical was the confession of Edward Hall, who was about thirty years old when Shepard recorded his testimony. The four-hundred-word state- ment began by referring to the impression made on Hall when a Puritan pastor in England preached on the hypocrisy of Israelites, described in Jeremiah 7:4, who vainly repeated their supposed loyalty to "the temple of the LORD." It ended with Hall's testimony that by "hearing the Lord was willing to take away his enmity, he by Revelation 22:17 was brought nearer to the Lord." In between, Hall cited or quoted five other biblical texts to describe his personal journey.[12]

Among the better educated, confessions resembled well-constructed treatises in existential theology. Nathaniel Eaton's statement contained scriptural reflections on losing his first love for God (Rev 2:4), but then recalling the faithfulness of God to his covenant promises (1 Sam 12:22) and trusting that "seeds cast upon me shall last unto eternal life" (echoing Mt 13:18–23; Mk 4:3–8; Lk 8:5–8).[13] It helps to keep professions of Puritan godliness in perspective to remember that Eaton is today remembered as the first president of Harvard College, who was dismissed after a short tenure for embezzling funds, abusing students, and beating a servant nearly to death. Another statement from the same social class came from Mary Angier Sparrowhawk, one of the gentry who provided key financial support in Massachusetts's early days. Her somewhat longer confession detailed a spiritual journey made up of ten different passages from the prophet Isaiah, along with nine other scriptural texts (three from the Old Testament, six from the New).[14]

The testimony of Jane Wilkinson Winship illustrates how often regular Puritan preaching made Scripture come alive for congregants. She related her story almost entirely in terms of what she had received from the pulpit, first in England and then in Massachusetts. "Hearing" Thomas Shepard explain the "terror to all [who] were out of Christ" was especially important, but this experience led on to "hearing" another minister explain Psalm 80 (absence of peace for those who were chastened by God), "hearing" an exposition of Isaiah 35:4 about the coming of the Lord, "hearing" of Christ as the antitype of the Old Testament's cities of refuge, "hearing humble yourself under God's hand [1 Pet 5:6] [and so] comforted"—in all, seventeen "hearings" as the framework for her confession.[15]

Most revealing were the testimonies of unlettered servants, for they probably absorbed Scripture without being able to read. A young woman identified only as "Katherine, Mrs. Russel's Maid," did not quote chapter and verse as most of the other confessors did. Yet as recorded in Shepard's notes, Katherine offered a striking account of how the Bible exposed her to harsh moral demands, but also to the ineffable love, of God:

> And so I sought the Lord in a way of humiliation, the name of the Lord is a strong tower [Prov 18:10]. And thought here the Lord might be found, and doubtful whether I had a call to come because I was to leave my friends. Hence I remembered that Scripture—I'll be with thee in the first waters [Isa 43:2]—and I knew I should be armed like Jacob in all straits to have a promise. And in our way when ready to be cast away, stand still and see salvation of God [Ex 14:13; 2 Chr 20:17], then heard Lord is my portion [Pss 73:26; 119:57; 142:5]....And hearing of coming to Christ and Christ will not cast away [Jn 6:37], which was a great lifting up of my heart to the Lord. And I heard though Judas forsook all, yet he had not Christ for his last end and that there I took my rest. As the rich man said—soul take thy rest [Lk 12:19]—so I found Christ to me.[16]

To one degree or another, the testimonies that Shepard recorded were, like Katherine's, informed by instinctive, heartfelt reliance on the sacred text: "the Scripture came oft to mind"; there arose "encouragements from other Scriptures"; "some Scriptures brought me to submit to the Lord"; "I found the word greatly working upon my heart"; I encountered "the revealed will of God in the word, the only rule of faith and manners"; "conscience did check me often and that Scripture appeared"; "one morning considering things James 4 came to mind"; the "Lord brought that to mind [a text from Mt 11]"; and on and on.[17] It was not just that such testimonies evidenced an extraordinary grasp of scriptural content. Even more, biblical passages clearly defined the critical decisions of life, sparked the most intense internal traumas, built the framework for self-definition, and brought the sweetest sense of hope. The testimonies Shepard recorded were doubtless unusual in their fervor—and their formulaic character is unmistakable—but they also unmistakably expressed the biblicist norm spread wide throughout the early Puritan colonies.

For the Leaders: Bradford and Winthrop

Two well-known documents from the two leading laymen of New England's early history highlight the shaping force that widespread reliance on Scripture exerted on the Puritan enterprise as a whole.

William Bradford served as governor of the Plymouth Colony for most of the years from the colony's founding in 1620 to his death in 1657. Historians now call the colonists who came with him to the Plymouth region congregational separatists.[18] They had followed their consciences, first in England and then in the Netherlands, as they sought to organize churches locally through the mutual covenanting of members (instead of hierarchically under the guidance of state-designated bishops or in regional fellowships led by state-sanctioned presbyters). Dependence on Scripture informed every aspect of their venture, even as it informed the private narrative that Bradford penned and that was eventually published in the nineteenth century as *Of Plymouth Plantation*. This meditation sought to document the ways of God with a community that had braved persecution in England and then the harsh realities of emigration in order to do what it felt Scripture required. Its grounding in the Bible was organic but can be discussed in terms of rhetoric, precepts, models, and self-definition.[19]

Bradford's rhetoric was biblical in the way he sometimes lapsed into the rhythms of Tyndale, the Geneva Bible (his personal text), or the new King James Version. For example, Bradford's narrative at many points imitated the staccato parataxis (i.e., short, successive declarative sentences) of the Gospel of Mark, as when he described the animus of the bishops' party against the godly during the reign of Queen Elizabeth:[20]

> and that it was most needful that the fundamental points of religion should be preached in those ignorant and superstitious times. And to win the weak and ignorant they might retain divers harmless ceremonies; and though it were to be wished that divers things were

reformed, yet this was not a season for it. And many the like to stop the mouths of the more godly, to bring them on to yield to one ceremony after another, and one corruption after another. (5)

More generally, the phraseology of Scripture so filled Bradford's mind that he deployed its phrases naturally in the normal flow of his own prose. Thus,

· "the first breaking out of the light of the gospel [2 Cor 4:4] in our honorable nation of England" (1)
· "the main truths of the gospel ... being watered in the blood of the martyrs [Rev 17:6] and blessed from heaven with a gracious increase" (2)
· "that old serpent [Rev 12:9] could not prevail by those fiery flames and other his cruel tragedies" (3)
· "the plague of England to this day, which are like the high places in Israel [Jer 32:35] which the prophet cried out against" (4)

... and so on.

Bradford's narrative also reflected biblical precepts as much as biblical phraseology. In large part that rhetoric flowed so easily because Bradford's community had organized its corporate existence by what it had heard in Scripture. His narrative did not repeat the extensive exegesis his revered pastor in the Old World, John Robinson, had published to defend the case for congregational church organization separated from the Church of England. But Bradford nonetheless referred constantly to the normative prescriptions of Scripture that the Plymouth separates always tried to follow. Their initial impetus, he explained, was the desire "to have the right worship of God and discipline of Christ established in the church, according to the simplicity of the gospel, without the mixture of men's inventions; and to have and to be ruled by the laws of God's Word, dispensed in those offices, and by those officers of Pastors, Teachers and Elders, etc. according to the Scriptures" (4). In England, the separatists boldly faced the threats of church officials for refusing to "become slaves to them and their popish trash, which have no ground in the Word of God, but are the relics of that man of sin [2 Thess 2:3]" (5–6). They rejoiced when "many became enlightened by the Word of God" (7) and when "the Lord" made it possible "to see further into things by the light of the Word of God" (7).

From attending so carefully to the Scriptures the separates, though harassed by a church establishment still infected with Catholic poison, felt that they were approaching a scriptural pattern for church life. The Bible, that is, supplied models as well as precepts and rhetoric. Looking back from about 1630, when he wrote the first part of his narrative, Bradford detailed the community's wanderings, first in England and then in the Netherlands, before they embarked for the New World. During at least some of their time in the Netherlands, Bradford felt that they had almost reached the ideal: so genuine were "the piety, the humble zeal and fervent love of this people … toward God and His ways," so "singlehearted … and sincere" was the people's affection for each other "that they came as near the primitive pattern of the first churches as any other church of these later times have done, according to their rank and quality" (19).

Imitation easily slid into identification. In Bradford's telling, the story of the Plymouth settlers became one with the story of God's protection of Israel and his care for the New Testament church. The "professors" who saw the need to carry reform further, "whose hearts the Lord had touched with heavenly zeal for His truth," took the step "as the Lord's free people" to enter "a covenant of the Lord" in order to form "a church estate, in the fellowship of the gospel, to walk in all His ways made known, or to be made known unto them, according to their best endeavours, whatsoever it should cost them, the Lord assisting them" (8). At one perilous point in the shipboard journey to the Netherlands, one of their vessels was caught in a dreadful storm. But as with the apostle Paul in the voyages described in the book of Acts, "when man's hope and help wholly failed, the Lord's power and mercy [Ps 59:16] appeared in their recovery" (14). Again, when the journey from the Netherlands to the New World was about to take place, their enemies slandered them "as the heathen historians did feign of Moses and the Israelites when they went out of Egypt" (20). As Bradford and his company followed the Word of God, the Pilgrims *became* the people of God.[21]

The sections of Bradford's narrative written after 1630 recorded his disappointment that the Plymouth settlers failed in their original goal to establish a thoroughly godly commonwealth. Disputes over land, several heinous murders, sharp business dealings, many sexual sins, and a general turn toward worldly preoccupations—all tempered the expectations that Bradford had entertained in the early pages of his memoir. Yet his facility for quoting Scripture, citing biblical precedents, and turning to the Bible for encouragement never faltered. A brief excursus on the unusual longevity of the Plymouth colonists who survived the first deadly winters included five biblical quotations and many references or allusions (364–66). But the hope that the biblical outline would actually be fulfilled, and fulfilled in the Plymouth colony, faded.

Bradford's writing, as a private document, did not exert a public influence. Instead, it indicated the depth at which orientation to Scripture
worked as the foundational referent for Bradford, as it did for other leaders of the colony who shared his convictions and the experiences through
which these convictions had borne them. Before the watching world, they
sought to create a Bible commonwealth, because the Bible had first reor-
dered their private lives.

A few details aside, the same orientation based in the same scriptural foundation undergirded the more extensive Puritan experiment in Massachusetts
Bay. For the ongoing importance of Scripture throughout American history, it
is crucial to remember not just the scriptural foundation but also the comprehensive aspiration of the New World's Bible commonwealths. Plymouth and
Massachusetts differed not so much in that aspiration—both sought a fully
Reformed society—but in the greater wealth, authority, education, political
will, and numbers that Massachusetts brought to the task. Until Plymouth's
incorporation into Massachusetts in 1691, it remained true to its separationist
principles that churches should not seek the support of governments. But cooperation between church and state for the purpose of organizing all of life
under God was still the goal.

In Massachusetts, John Winthrop exerted a guiding force comparable to
Bradford's in Plymouth. Almost as renowned as Bradford's *Of Plymouth
Plantation* has become the speech, or lay sermon, that Winthrop delivered
to the first main contingent of Massachusetts Puritans either as they set out
from England or perhaps during their voyage at sea. It is known by the title
added to the manuscript by a later hand, "Christian Charitie: A Modell
Hereof."[22] Like Bradford's narrative, it illustrates how deeply, comprehensively, and pervasively ran the biblicism of the Massachusetts enterprise. In
its relatively short compass, Winthrop cited chapter and verse thirty times
from six Old Testament and nine New Testament books. This short address
also contained more than sixty other biblical allusions or references.

Winthrop was forty-two years old when in 1630 he joined the migration of Puritans who left England in order to create a godly commonwealth
in the New World. Behind him lay a modest life of gentlemanly accom-
plishment in the Suffolk countryside and in the London legal world.
Ahead lay the wilderness, yet also a Puritan vision that had been frustrated
in England. This vision foresaw a complete social order where, as defined
by careful obedience to Scripture, fellowship with God and God's people
would be the controlling norm. For the nineteen years until his death,
Winthrop led Massachusetts as the key figure seeking to transform that

vision at least partially into reality. For most of those years he served as the colony's governor, an office filled by yearly elections; for all of those years he was the heart and soul of the Puritan enterprise.

As documented in detail by Francis Bremer's recent biography, the type of society that Winthrop tried to build in Puritan Massachusetts developed naturally from what he had experienced in Puritan Suffolk.[23] With short stints at Cambridge (for liberal arts and divinity) and London's Inns of Court (for law), Winthrop also sampled the book learning sought by progressive gentlemen of his day. But above all other interests, the Winthrop family pointed him toward the reform of the Anglican church and the pursuit of personal holiness.

In the Stour River Valley of Suffolk a determined, but also moderate, variety of Puritan reform enlisted the efforts of many families, including the Winthrops. This type of Puritanism featured eager cooperation between magistrates and ministers, a basic confidence in the precedents of English common law, an expectation that charity as defined by Scripture could create an entire social order founded on godliness, and a preference for loosely defined personal authority over narrowly codified legal prescription. Later, Winthrop sought to complete in Massachusetts what had begun in the Stour Valley as one of the most thoroughly, but also one of the most humanely, Puritan regions of England.

Biblical precepts guided his vision for the New World, a vision he expressed in scriptural terms and narrated with biblical phrases. It began by affirming that God had set human kind in ranks—some rich and eminent, others poor and dependent—so that in their diversity, people might realize they "have need of other[s], and from hence they might be all knit more nearly together in the Bond of brotherly affeccion [Rom 12:10]" (77). Then Winthrop explained that God had given "two rules whereby we are to walke one towards another: JUSTICE and MERCY" (77). He took particular pains to show that, while God demanded both justice and mercy in all dealings, it was particularly imperative for mercy to prevail "in the estate of regeneracy…[with] a difference betweene Christians and others…[and] especially to the household of faith [Gal 6:10]" (78). For example, lending without thought of repayment to poor Christian brothers, embracing danger for oneself in order to protect others as "in the primitive Churche" (82), and other acts of self-sacrifice were all part of what it meant to live mercifully. Throughout, Winthrop stressed again and again that he was speaking to "all true Christians…of one body in Christ…the body of Christ [1 Cor 12:27; Eph 4:15–16]" (84).

Based on his biblical exposition of justice and mercy, Winthrop declared that the colonists—as "being the body of Christ"—had to manifest love to one another (89). As he explained the nature of that love, he also explained the comprehensive nature of their enterprise: "for the worke wee have in hand, it is by a mutuall consent through a speciall overruleing providence, and a more than an ordinary approbation of the Churches of Christ to seeke out a place of Cohabitation and Consorteshipp under a due forme of Government both civill and ecclesiasticall" (90).

The Massachusetts Puritans had "entered into Covenant" with God for their colonizing project in the New World (91). This covenant existed between God and a church-state community of like-minded Puritan believers linked organically to other "Churches of Christ" that remained in the Old World. In Winthrop's view, the covenant for the Puritans was analogous to God's covenant with ancient Israel; first came spiritual and ecclesiastical implications, then, the legal and governmental.

Once the Puritan settlers understood their covenantal relationship with God, they could also understand the if-then contingencies of that relationship. If the Massachusetts settlers did not love each other and if they acted only to further their "carnall intencions," God would "surely breake out in wrathe against us" (92). By contrast, if the settlers "followe the Counsell of Micah, to doe Justly, to love mercy, to walke humbly with our God [Mic 6:8], . . . to abridge our selves of our superfluities, for the supply of others necessities, . . . [to] delight in eache other, make others Condicions our owne [,] rejoyce together, mourne together [1 Cor 12:26], labour, and suffer together, allwayes having before our eyes our Commission and Community in the worke" (92), then New England would prosper. Then God would make the Puritan effort "a prayse and a glory" (93).

Next came the well-known words: if the Puritans kept covenant by loving each other, then "men shall say of succeeding plantacions: the lord make it like that of New England: for wee must Consider that wee shall be as a Citty upon a Hill [Mt 5:14], the eies of all people are uppon us" (93). Immediately, however, Winthrop continued: but if "wee shall deale falsely with our god in this worke" the enemies of God would rejoice. Winthrop was more concerned for how the Puritan experiment would "shame the faces" of "all professours for Gods sake" than he was for any imagined national future for Massachusetts (or a future United States he could in no way imagine) (93). Yet a government ordered according to God's word was crucial for the enterprise to which they had committed themselves.

To the extent that the Massachusetts Puritans were concerned with "civill Government," they took for granted the type of church-state establishment common to Christendom, and so very different from the United States' later separation of church and state. New England would be a city on a hill much more as an experiment than as an example. If the experiment worked, God would be praised. If it did not, all of the godly in Europe, as well as in America, would be humiliated. The public norm that Winthrop strove to follow was the Bible, and the Bible understood as providing a blueprint for all of life.[24]

Because Winthrop's speech, like Bradford's memoir, was not published until long after his death, it must not be read as itself a direct, continuing influence on Massachusetts development. It was, rather, the forceful expression of an ideal for a Bible-centered Christendom. The first generations of Massachusetts leaders shared the ideal, if not necessarily Winthrop's exact phrasing. It was also shared in full measure by the founders of Connecticut (1636) and New Haven (1638) and in only slightly modified form by Bradford and the Plymouth Colony. For more than the next two centuries, many later Americans would also embrace the foundational orientation to Scripture that infused early Puritan life, even as that orientation did its work in the altered circumstances of American political and religious development.

In Print

The biblicism of New England ran deep and wide. If it never extended as comprehensively as the Puritans claimed, the Bible's presence was still singularly ubiquitous. The ubiquity began with printing, Bible-related items preeminent but extending much further to include the staples of private reading, the week-by-week structuring of community life, and the colonies' formal documentation of state and church organization. Historians have succeeded fairly well in recognizing the salient features of that story. But to see them summarized briefly and together should help depict the extraordinary reach of the Bible within Puritan New England, and then from New England throughout the colonies.

The recently published volume on the colonies in the landmark five-volume *History of the Book in America* documents this biblical presence thoroughly. It shows both that publishing in New England was far in advance of other colonial regions and that New England publishing rested on a scriptural foundation. Because of the monopoly enjoyed by the king's printers in Britain, colonists did not themselves produce Bibles. But the colonial book trade still disproportionately tilted toward other publications dependent on Scripture. The North American Imprints Program maintained by the American Antiquarian Society has identified 25,404 separate items published in the colonies between 1640 and 1790. Of that number, 53 percent came from New England (almost 37 percent from Massachusetts alone). Items printed for colonial governments made up the largest category of publications (28 percent of the total), but sermons, prayer books, hymnals, and psalmbooks together came next (16 percent). Massachusetts was the only colony where more sermons (2,067)—virtually all based on a scriptural text—were published than government items (1,931) and the colony where by far the most sermons were printed (65 percent of the colonial total). New England as a whole witnessed the publication of 3,200 sermons, prayerbooks, hymnals, and psalmbooks in this 150-year period.[25]

Among the most often reprinted works in colonial publishing history, religious texts based directly or indirectly on Scripture predominated. Only almanacs and a few basic school books enjoyed larger print runs than the most popular religious books—and almanacs regularly took for granted a pervasive knowledge of Scripture.[26] Those most reprinted titles included manuals of religious instruction like the *Shorter Catechism* of the Westminster Assembly or, from the 1740s, Martin Luther's *Small Catechism* in German; hymnbooks, with Isaac Watts's Christianized Psalm paraphrases a major presence from the late 1720s; individual sermons or sermon collections; and works related to well-known religious figures like George Whitefield's *Journals*.[27]

The most often reprinted book in the first century of American colonial publishing was also the first full book printed in the colonies. Including its many editions from Cambridge and Boston, *The Bay Psalm Book* appeared twenty-four different times from a variety of presses in the century from 1640 to 1740, and then another seven over the next fifty years.[28] Its publication in 1640 had been the first full book printed by the press that the early Puritan leaders had insisted on importing as soon as they could. The press was set up at Cambridge, in the precincts of Harvard College that had enrolled its first students only shortly before the book was published. The consistent reprinting—in large runs and in later revisions—of this metrical paraphrase of the Psalms meant that when New Englanders ventured beyond the Bible itself, their most consistent reading—and singing—was Scripture in another form. The paraphrased translation, made

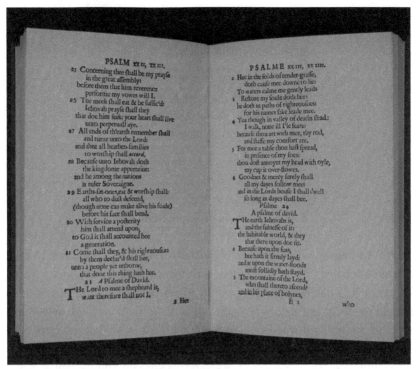

Literary scholars have not been impressed with the literary merits of the Bay Psalm Book, as at Psalm 23. But New Englanders, as well as readers from the other colonies and in England, made it one of the very best selling books of seventeenth and eighteenth centuries. (Courtesy of the American Bible Society Library)

directly from the Hebrew, was the work of three university-educated ministers, including Richard Mather, the first of that notable clerical clan, and John Eliot, who would later expend great labor in translating the Bible into Algonquian. The prosody of *The Bay Psalm Book* has often been criticized for its clunky style, but no one should question how deeply internalized its content became for a substantial part of the New England population over a substantial period of time.

> *Psalm 1. O Blessed man, that in the advice*
> *of wicked doeth not walk:*
> *nor stand in sinners way, nor sit*
> *in chayre of scornfull folk.*
> *But in the law of Iehovah*

is his longing delight:
and in his law doth meditate,
by day and eke by night.

Psalm 23. The Lord to mee a shepheard is,
want therefore shall not I.
Hee in the folds of tender-grasse,
doth cause mee downe to lie.

Psalm 100. Make yee a joyfull sounding noyse
unto Iehovah, all the earth:
Serve yee Iehovah with gladnes:
before his presence come with mirth.[29]

Not surprisingly, the "Preface" that Richard Mather penned for the book offered a detailed biblical exposition, with much citing of chapter and verse, concerning "what psalms are to be sung in churches," whether such psalms should be sung "in their owne words, or in such meter as English poetry is wont to run in," and whether they should be sung as a whole congregation or "by one man singing alone." To Mather and the other translators, it mattered little that "the verses are not always so smooth and elegant as some may desire or expect" since "God's Altar needs not our pollishings: Ex. 20."[30]

As wide as the distribution of imprints like the Bay Psalm Book that depended on Scripture reached, that distribution paled besides the much wider availability of the Bible itself. For the early Puritan generations, the texts brought along with the immigration or imported in consistently great quantities were central because "the Bible served as a manual of law, literature, history, and warfare, as well as a primer for reading and, of course, religion."[31] The "of course, religion" must be underscored. "No book was read more often or in so many different ways: privately in silence, aloud in households where the reading may sometimes have proceeded 'in course' through the Old and New Testaments, and in church services as the text for Sunday sermons."[32]

Spiritual instruction constituted the main reason for that constant use. In Scripture—as testified to in private diaries, public professions of faith, and retrospective reports of crises—the text "enabled people to 'see' themselves truly." It was "the gift of life."[33] Bibles, as a consequence, were the only books regularly appearing in wills as specially designated bequests. Inventories for probate showed that Bible was often the only book that a family owned.[34]

In Church

In early New England, the personal possession and private use of Scripture powerfully reinforced its iconic public status and its central place for defining community. And vice versa. From its origin, Puritanism presupposed that all practices of worship and church government had to enjoy an explicit scriptural mandate. Thus were banished statues, stained glass, organs, pictures, communion tables, kneeling benches, candles, and much else that had been customary in Anglican worship. Yet one exception stood out in their relentless effort to follow the Bible alone. The exception, not surprisingly, concerned the Scripture itself. From the earliest days in New England one colorful ornament not mandated in the Bible became a fixture in the Puritan meeting house. It was a cushion for the Scriptures.

In a book whose loving attention to detail has rarely been surpassed, Ola Winslow's *Meetinghouse Hill* described what the Puritan Bible cushion was like:

> Custom had early decreed that this cushion should be of green velvet or plush, with long tassels hanging from the corners. It sometimes took as much as four yards of velvet, ten yards of silk, and much [congregational] voting time to achieve this mark of prideful elegance, but eventually it was always achieved. Even the length and color of the tassels (should they or should they not match the velvet) were important enough to be mentioned in the minutes of the precinct meeting which finally took action toward such improvement.[35]

The central place of the physical Bible in Puritan meeting houses reflected its central place in Puritan worship. The ability to deliver regular sermons that opened the scriptural word gave Puritan clergy their special status. As Harry Stout put it in his definitive study of the subject, "the ministers' sermons were the only voice of authority that congregations were pledged to obey unconditionally." Yet because those sermons of necessity had to open the Scriptures, the Scriptures themselves exercised a check on the ministers. The authority they possessed came from "their specialized knowledge of the Scriptures and their ordination....The printed Bible was the bridge linking ministers to congregations." Because the laity also paid such close heed to the Bible, they "could participate in a common community of discourse." The scriptural expertise of ordinary people guaranteed the functioning of the New England Way: "Congregations were obliged not only to obey the voice of the sermon but also to read their Bibles and make sure their ministers held true to biblical doctrines."[36]

As illustrated from the testimonies collected by Thomas Shepard, the importance of the sermon only magnified the role of Scripture. For all of New England's colonial history, even after the expansion of book and newspaper publication, the overwhelmingly dominant form of formal linguistic communication for almost all New Englanders was the sermon—two discourses on Sunday every week extending for at least an hour each, with attendance required by law and enforced by strong cultural expectations, not to mention regular midweek sermons in the larger towns and a bevy of occasional sermons to mark special days of fasting or thanksgiving, the annual opening of the legislature, or the periodic assembling of local militias.

Because far more New Englanders attended church regularly than actually became members, many of those who reached a relatively old age would have heard as many as seven thousand different sermons over the course of their lives—in an age before radio, television, movies, and the Internet; during an era when newspapers were only just coming into existence; and while other public speeches remained few and far between. In Stout's words, "As the only event in public assembly that regularly brought the entire community together, it also represented the central ritual of social order and control."[37]

Significantly, the structure and content of weekly sermons remained remarkably stable from the 1630s into the Revolutionary period. In form, almost all sermons began with a short biblical passage followed by a brief effort to explain the text in its scriptural context along with a statement of the text's "doctrine." Then came extensive development of the doctrine, often in a set of enumerated "reasons." The discourse typically ended with "uses," or applications, when the minister spelled out implications of the divine message for children, youth, young married couples, parents, the aged, believers, those not yet professing faith, and so on.[38] This set pattern nonetheless allowed for considerable flexibility as ministers conveyed the results of their own scriptural study and addressed what they perceived as the spiritual needs of their congregations.[39] The one unvarying constant was their effort to drive home a message from the written word of God.

In substance, week-by-week Sunday sermons long continued to stress the main elements of Puritan spirituality. Traditional reliance on the Bible grounded a message of personal salvation by God's saving grace and a common set of injunctions about daily life directed toward the honor of God. Attention to the covenant along the lines of Winthrop's exposition in

"A Model of Christian Charity" commonly joined reflections on God's providential oversight of all daily events, personal relationships, and unexpected crises. Occasional sermons (election, fast, thanksgiving, militia) expanded themes of covenant and providence in order to explain how God was dealing with the colonies, the mother country, and the great struggle between the children of God (Protestants) and the servants of Antichrist (Catholics). The shifting relation between the basically spiritual message of weekly sermons and the political interpretations of occasional sermons influenced the general place of Scripture in late-colonial culture (see chaps. 9, 10, and 11). But the overarching reality did not change: sermons anchored New England's public life and Scripture anchored the sermons. As will became apparent in the pages that follow, New England's sermons mostly defined the genre for the other colonies as well.

In Society

The depth of Puritan biblicism distinguished New England from the many other Protestants of their era who also agreed with William Chillingworth that "the BIBLE, I say, THE BIBLE only is the Religion of Protestants!"[40] Protestants of every sort turned instinctively to Scripture for guidance, authority, direction, and self-definition, but on a comparative scale New Englanders did so more thoroughly. They really meant it.

As they set about building their outposts on the edge of the North American continent, the Puritans remained entirely typical of their age in what they assumed about the organic unity of society. In England they objected not to Anglican efforts at coordinating all public life, religious and political, but to how the king and archbishop went about that coordination. In New England they were determined to get it right. Their Christendom would be authentically biblical.

The Pilgrims who came to Plymouth worried more than other Puritans about the threat of political entanglements. Yet even they, when they drew up what came to be known as the Mayflower Compact, spoke of the "Civil Body Politic" they created as "undertaken for the Glory of God and advancement of the Christian faith and Honour of our King and Country."[41] John Winthrop was even more direct in his hope that Massachusetts Bay could construct "a due forme of Government both civill and ecclesiasticall."[42]

The biblicism of such aspirations reached its culmination in 1638 and 1639 when John Davenport took the lead in organizing the New Haven colony. Before coming to America, Davenport had been the minister of an

Anglican church in London and then of a congregationally organized
church of ex-pats in the Netherlands. His participation in a series of ecclesiastical disputes had convinced him that Scripture demanded a strictly
congregational church life. He was equally convinced that the Bible clearly
defined the straight and narrow path for political organization. The meeting
he chaired in 1639 to formalize government for the new colony on the
northern shore of Long Island Sound proceeded through a series of questions.[43] The first asked, "whether the scriptures do hold forth a perfect rule
for the direction and government of all men in all duties which they are to
perform to God and men, as well as in the government of families and
commonwealths as in matters of the church." When the assembled settlers agreed unanimously, Davenport asked if they were ready to confirm
an earlier pledge to be guided entirely by Scripture. Again there was common assent. Then the meeting moved to Davenport's explication of scriptural passages from Exodus 18, Deuteronomy 1 and 17, and 1 Corinthians
6 concerning how a genuine church should be founded. The historian
Francis Bremer has concluded that, although "the colony's legal structure
differed from that of other New England colonies in that scriptural law
was the explicit basis for decisions," yet this emphasis represented "more
a variation on common New England themes rather than a dramatic alternative to that of the other Bible Commonwealths."[44]

Given the detailed character of New Haven's scripturalism, it can be no
surprise that the colony adopted its legal code from a document originally
prepared for Massachusetts. It had been written by the Reverend John
Cotton when the magistrates of Massachusetts asked for a draft document
keyed to Scripture that could serve as the colony's fundamental law.[45] Cotton,
who had been a leading promoter of Puritanism in old-world Boston
(Lincolnshire), exercised leadership as soon as he arrived in the new-world
Boston. John Winthrop was reluctant to draw up a detailed law code, both
in order to keep as much flexibility as possible for the prerogative of magistrates and in order to attract as little attention as possible to the ways in
which Massachusetts deviated from customary English practice. Yet pressure from the middle ranks of Massachusetts freemen for a clearly stated
legal foundation prompted a series of efforts to comply. The Reverend
Cotton's was the first.

His document, drawn up in 1636, was eventually published six years
later in London as *An Abstract of the Lawes of New England*. For good reason,
John Winthrop styled Cotton's effort "a model of Moses his Judicials"
since from first to last it rested directly on the Bible.[46] The heavy reliance

on the Five Books of Moses, the Pentateuch, was evident from how its lines appeared on the page:

First, all Magistrates are to be chosen.

First, By the free Burgesses. Deut 1.13.

Secondly, Out of the free Burgesses. Deut 17.15.

Thirdly, Out of the ablest men and most approved amongst them. Ex 18.21.[47]

So it continued through fifteen tightly packed pages. The density of biblical citations thinned out in the code's sections on "commerce," "the rights of inheritance," and "the protection and provision of the countrey" (concerning the establishment and funding of militia units). But when it treated "crimes," biblical references crowded the margins thickly. As it had been in the Mosaic code, so it would be in Massachusetts: death was the stipulated penalty for blasphemy, idolatry, witchcraft, heresy, "wilfull perjury," "profaning the Lords day," betraying the country to Spain or France or Holland, "reviling of the Magistrates," rebellion (including rebellious children), murder, adultery, incest, "unnaturall filthinesse," "whoredome," "man-stealing," and bearing false witness—and all documented with references to specific Bible verses.[48]

In the end, Massachusetts never formally approved Cotton's *Abstract*, though it remained the legal foundation in New Haven until 1662 when that colony, punished for supporting Oliver Cromwell, was folded into Connecticut. Yet when Massachusetts did finally adopt a "Body of Liberties" in 1641, it retained much of the biblical orientation of Cotton's explicit attempt. This 1641 document, which enumerated the rights of citizens, began by guaranteeing that no legal action could be taken against anyone unless the violation transgressed a published law, "or in case of the defect of a law in any particular case by the word of God. And in Capitall cases, or in cases concerning dismembering or banishment [as punishments], according to that word to be judged by the Generall Court." This "Body of Liberties" also charged civil authorities "to see the peace, ordinances and Rules of Christ observed in every church according to his word. [S]o it be done in a Civill and not in an Ecclesiasticall way." It followed the pattern of Cotton's *Abstract* by detailing the biblical texts specifying punishments for each capital offense. The last major section, which treated "the Liberties the Lord Jesus hath given to the Churches," was replete with repeated evocations of "the rules of scripture," "the rules of his word," "the Institutions of the lord," and "the word of God."[49]

Meanwhile, on the ecclesiastical front, a similar effort advanced to affirm the biblical structure of New England's churches. It came in response to challenges on both sides of the Atlantic. The experiment of a full church order organized on congregational principles was basically succeeding in Plymouth, Massachusetts, Connecticut, and New Haven. But numerous tiffs over details and several major clashes over foundational difficulties led some influential voices to seek a clarification of congregational first principles. At the same time, the Presbyterian sentiments in Britain that were pushing forward the Westminster Assembly seemed to call for an explanation from New England as to why it remained attached to congregationalism.[50]

The upshot was an appeal in 1646 by several Massachusetts ministers to the colonial legislature that it convene a synod to address such questions definitively. Much debate followed—on whether magistrates could or should call such a meeting, on whether the call should be a command or an invitation, and on how strongly advisory the conclusions of a synod should be. Eventually in the spring of 1646 a summons invited churches to send ministers and other messengers to consider these matters. Further debate and low-level controversy followed, but after some fits and starts a synod convened; in late 1648 it delivered its conclusions. To indicate how close the New Englanders remained to their reforming brethren in Britain, it endorsed the Westminster Confession "for substance of doctrines"—except where Westminster dealt with church government. John Cotton provided a preface to explain this recommendation of the Westminster Confession but also why a careful statement of congregational convictions was necessary. Then came a sixteen-chapter exposition of those convictions. The entire document began by announcing "A Platform of Church Discipline gathered out of the Word of God: and agreed upon by the elders and messengers of the churches assembled in the Synod at Cambridge in New England." The exposition on church government proceeded under the same authority: "Of the form of Church-Government; and that it is one, immutable, and prescribed in the Word of God."[51]

The biblical warrant for congregationalism that authors of the Cambridge Platform provided deserves quotation at length. It demonstrates the confidence with which New England leaders read and applied the Scriptures:

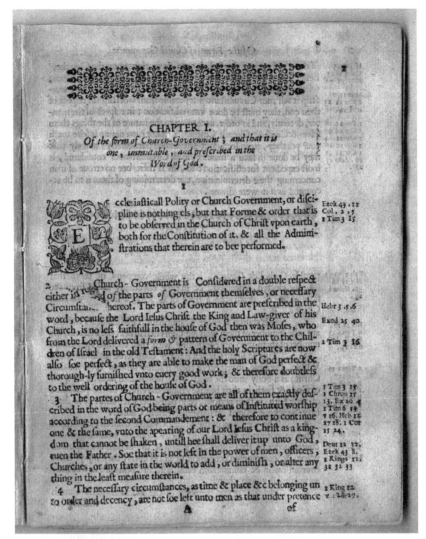

The Cambridge Platform of 1649, which justified Massachusetts's Congregational form of church government to skeptics in England, illustrated its dependence on Scripture with its liberal side notes documenting the Platform's reliance on biblical chapter and verse. (Courtesy of the American Antiquarian Society)

The parts of Government are prescribed in the word, because the Lord Iesus Christ the King and Law-giver of his Church [Heb 3, 5, 6 cited in margin], is no less faithful in the house of God [than] was Moses [Ex 25:40], who from the Lord delivered a *form & pattern of Government to the Children of Israel in the old Testament: And the holy Scriptures are now also soe perfect [2 Tim 3:16], as they are able to make the man of God perfect & thoroughly furnished unto every good work; and therefore doubtless to the well ordering of the house of God.[52]

The Platform stressed the autonomy of local congregations under Christ in matters of covenanting, defining and electing pastors and teachers, admitting members, and seeking counsel from other congregations. But it also affirmed that a congregational system "stands in no opposition to civil government of comon-welths, nor any intrencheth [subverts] the authority of Civil Magistrates in their jurisdictions." Magistrates were "to take care of matters of religion, &...improve his civil authority for the observing of the duties commanded in the first, as well as the observing of the duties commanded in the second table [of the Ten Commandments]." Believers did have the responsibility to form congregations even when governments stood in opposition. But the ideal existed when magistrates "restrained and punished by civil authority" idolatry, blasphemy, heresy, contempt of preaching, violations of the Lord's Day, and anything else that disturbed "the peaceable administration & exercise of the worship & holy things of God."[53] In other words, to follow the Bible meant finding one, and only one, scriptural pattern for the entire social order, including government.

To support its claims about proper church government and the proper relationship of congregational churches to civil authority, the Cambridge Platform followed the example of the augmented Westminster Confession and John Cotton's *Abstract of Lawes* by providing biblical proof texts in the margins of their document. For its thirty printed pages there were at least 443 such scriptural proofs. Although the references came from throughout the Bible, for most of the Platform the book of Acts and the New Testament epistles predominated. For the chapter on civil government, by contrast, the majority came from the Old Testament, especially 1 and 2 Kings, Ezra, Nehemiah, and Daniel. As with New England's legal system, so too its church life was to follow the Scriptures explicitly, extensively, and exhaustively.

* * * * *

Efforts of the early New England settlers to follow the Bible were definitely of their place and time. In New England they carried on the vision from old England that had inspired their fellows left behind. It was a new place where a much more expansive geography would eventually modify the immigrants' inherited instincts. But it would take time for the hard lesson to be learned that, even in a land without unreformed bishops, meddling monarchs, and an insensate populace, it was easier to envision a fully biblical society than actually to build one.

Intellectual movements of the seventeenth century, including rational disputing and the beginnings of what has come to be known as the scientific revolution, were also important. The prominence of proof texting—as featured so prominently in the Westminster Confession, John Cotton's *Abstract of Laws*, the Cambridge Platform, and even Massachusetts's 1641 *Body of Liberties*—spoke volumes. When William Tyndale translated narratives of salvation, it had taken considerable effort to break them into constituent pieces in order to argue doctrine or comment on the king's performance. By the 1630s and 1640s, with now eighty years of experience using bibles divided into discrete verses, Scripture was more easily enlisted for what might be called engineering projects—assembling constructs of doctrine, proposing improved plans for church formation, building models of political order. Along with the spread of literacy and the industry of printers, the ability to manipulate versified Bibles had a definite democratic effect. More and more individuals were able to read Scripture for themselves and put its teachings to use for more and more purposes. A democratized Scripture provided great energy for the Puritan experiment in New England, as indicated best by the critically important part that Bible-inspired laymen (and women) played in making the Puritan colonies go. The difficulty in holding a Bible commonwealth together, when so many of its citizens were reading the Bible and synthesizing its verses for themselves, would become clearer as time moved on.

The growing importance of a democratized Scripture, with verses open to all literate readers for their own moral or political purposes, did not mean that the Bible's liberating effects decreased. As suggested by the experience of John Winthrop, William Bradford, Thomas Shepard, the members of Shepard's Cambridge congregation—as well as by the content of many sermons—the Bible certainly remained a bridge of redemption stretching from the gracious forgiveness of God to the longings of needy sinners. But even as that centripetal effect of Bible-reading and Bible-hearing ensured the central place of Scripture in colonial life, the centrifugal forces of democratic access, printing expansion, versified rationality, and exegetical controversy also had their effect.

Early New England was a Puritan regime in the strict sense of the word. Its leaders in both church and state determined to purify the Christian inheritance they brought with them from the Old World to the New. The refiner's fire that would carry out this purification was the Bible. The fire burned brightly in the early decades of New England's history. It burned away much of the dross that remained from England's imperfect Reformation. But as events soon proved—in Massachusetts itself, and not long after in Pennsylvania—such a fire could not be kept from burning out of control and threatening to consume Christendom itself.

5

Beyond Christendom

THE HISTORY OF the Bible in America, exemplified most visibly by the dominance of the King James translation, grew organically from the history of the Bible in Britain. Also inherited from Britain came beliefs in Scripture as definitive divine revelation, appropriation of the Bible along strongly Protestant lines, ideals for society expressed in biblical images, identity shaped by conflation with biblical Israel, and contention over important public questions carried out through competitive biblical interpretations. In later eras, America and Britain would alike see doubters like Tom Paine, Thomas Huxley, and Robert Ingersoll, all of whom advanced attacks against Christianity based on their own thorough knowledge of Scripture. Catholics and Jews also experienced something similar in the two nations as they battled to carve out space for their own uses of Scripture against a jealous Protestant dominance. Yet for all these similarities, one major difference separated British from American experience. That difference concerned the relationship of the Bible to Christendom.

In England, Puritan biblicists worked hard to establish an alternative and (in their eyes) truly scriptural Christendom as a substitute for the Christendom embodied in the Elizabethan Settlement. The failure of that effort discredited the idea of comprehensive biblical reform; instead of a Bible Commonwealth, the Restoration of the monarchy in 1660 reinforced the ideal of Anglican Christendom. Increasingly from the latter part of the seventeenth century, that Anglican ideal became for its advocates a God-given means to stabilize the realm.[1] They did not pretend that this ideal necessarily replicated ultimate divine truth in every particular. More general stability, more generally accepted, was the goal. Of course many defenders of that stability also promoted devotion to Scripture, but stability remained the imperative thing. In the eighteenth century, leading reformers like John Wesley and George Whitefield would proclaim sharply defined biblical challenges to conventional British religion, but they too continued to accept the church-state establishment as the governing norm for national life.

Over these same decades, the most important proposals for comprehensive political reform in Britain did not look to the Bible for sanction. Robert Filmer offered a conservative monarchy. John Locke promoted liberal contract theory. Radical Whigs proposed an ideology keyed to the restraint of power. Filmer (as we read in chap. 3) took care to explain why his theory of top-down authority did not need explicit scriptural warrant; Locke always spoke respectfully of the Bible, even achieving renown for his paraphrases of Paul's epistles; and the widely read "Cato's Letters" of John Trenchard and Thomas Gordon from the early 1720s skillfully evoked Protestant biblical precedents when championing the need for "Real Whig" reforms. But unlike the Puritans, these reformers no longer turned first to the Scriptures as they advanced their plans for a healthy political order.[2]

It was different in the colonies. In America, the strongest early challenges to Christendom as established by Puritan biblicists came from other biblicists. They contended that Scripture opposed the very premise of Christendom. While those early challenges did not succeed, they did contribute to forces that eventually altered the New World's Bible Commonwealths. Crucially, the clash of alternative biblicisms took place without sidelining Scripture as a public force; indeed, the controversies may have stimulated a broader reliance on the Bible. By the early eighteenth century, the schemes that in England were being proposed as replacements for biblical politics also came to the colonies. Yet colonists who clung to the Christendom ideal, as well as those who repudiated it, perceived these reforms as complementing scriptural authority rather than supplanting it. Biblicism did weaken in the colonies from the middle of the seventeenth century to the middle of the eighteenth, but for different reasons and with different effects than in England (then "Britain" after the Union between Scotland and England in 1707).

This chapter first describes the main American challenges to Puritan biblicism, which were advanced by biblicists who were also Puritans. It then sketches other developments that from the mid-seventeenth century further undermined Christendom in the New World. Among these, the founding of Pennsylvania as a colony organized by Bible believers who did *not* pursue the Puritan Way loomed as particularly important. And so the overarching purpose here is to illuminate the background for eighteenth-century developments: first, how warfare pulled the colonies toward tighter integration into the British Empire, though without strengthening loyalty to its church-state establishment; second, how the revivals of the Great Awakening deepened attachment to Scripture; third, how by contrast Scripture's presence also thinned during the period of the Awakening when colonists accepted social, intellectual, and political conventions of the empire; and, finally, how the American War of Independence dealt a death blow to establishmentarian Christendom while at the same time freeing up a vigorous biblicism to exert far-ranging effects in the new United States. To oversimplify this story: where Britain retained Christendom by subordinating the Bible, America would unleash the Bible by overthrowing Christendom.

The Bible against Christendom

Early New England Puritans feared greatly that the mother country would frustrate the Bible Commonwealths of the New World just as it had crippled prospects for scriptural reform in the homeland. In their eyes, the tyrannical machinations of Charles I and the Romeward-leaning plots of Archbishop William Laud played Goliath to the scriptural truths that served Puritans as David's slingshot and five smooth stones. Complete reliance on a Bible freed at last from the toils of half-hearted reform inspired John Winthrop to proclaim the enormous potential of charity, Thomas Shepard to guide his congregants toward redemption, and John Cotton to assist the magistrates by preparing a legal code. They did not anticipate that the most immediate and most serious challenges to their enterprise would come from fellow Puritans who trusted Scripture as fervently as themselves.

When in the very first years of New England settlement Roger Williams and Anne Hutchinson deployed the Scriptures to attack the Massachusetts Bible Commonwealth, they extended to the New World a trajectory of anti-Christendom biblicism that extended back to the dawn of the Reformation.[3] If at first that trajectory represented a small minority in the colonies, the pedigree was still distinguished. Over the long term, this tradition would exert an influence, albeit from the fringes of colonial consciousness, in a way it did not in Britain.

Martin Luther, in his first enthusiasm after finding a scriptural balm for his troubled soul, began the tradition. In 1523 he published a treatise on the question of obeying secular authorities, one that strongly defended what Baptists would later call "soul competency." In his words, "God cannot and will not permit anyone but himself to rule over the soul." Furthermore, whenever secular authorities presumed to dictate to the individual Christian, "it encroaches upon God's government and only misleads souls and destroys them."[4] Luther's commitment in this early outburst to the priesthood of all believers seemed to spill over naturally into a claim about the superiority of that biblically guided priesthood over any earthly power. As we know, however, Luther quickly retreated from this position when he faced the need to structure a Protestant alternative to Catholic Christendom.

The Bible, of course, remained Luther's doorway to salvation, but the necessity to organize churches and define the proper relationship between church authority and secular authority required a uniform, enforceable code. The extensive historical literature that now exists for Europe's "confessional" era describes in great detail how Lutherans, Anglicans, and the Reformed worked out those arrangements and in so doing came to resemble Catholic regimes by enforcing standards for church life and society on all of the citizens within any particular polity. Religious competition now took place between national units, but not within. The Protestant Reformation did significantly alter how Christian teachings were understood; Protestant regimes also gave unquestioned preeminence to Scripture in guiding their efforts. But Christendom, now broken into competing units, remained the unquestioned norm.

Or nearly unquestioned. A few lonely voices took up Luther's early willingness to pit the scripturally guided individual conscience against the political uniformity of Christendom. Balthasar Hubmaier, one of the first Anabaptist leaders, left the Catholic priesthood after reading Luther, eventually becoming a follower of Ulrich Zwingli, and then Zwingli's opponent. Hubmaier's stand on Scripture alone led him to reject infant baptism (the linchpin of Christendom) and then to deny that governments enjoyed coercive authority over religious opinions (the engine of Christendom).[5] The first full statement of Anabaptist convictions, promulgated in 1527 at Schleitheim in the Swiss canton of Schaffhausen, stressed the contradiction that radical Protestants perceived between the heart of the scriptural message and the inherited practices of Christendom: "The sword [civil coercive authority] is ordained of God outside the perfection of Christ .... In the perfection of Christ ... only the ban is used for a warning and for the excommunication of the one who has sinned, without putting the flesh to death—simply the warning and the command to sin no more."[6]

This appeal to Scripture *against* Christendom moved into English-speaking orbits through a book published in 1553. The author was Sebastian Castellio, a former teacher in Calvin's Geneva who left that city after disputing with Calvin over a doctrinal question and then settled in Basel, where he prepared his own translations of the Bible in both Latin and French. The 1553 work, *Concerning Heretics: Whether They Are to be Persecuted and How They Are to be Treated*, represented what Diarmaid MacCulloch has called "a great leap of imagination," since it explained why absolute trust in the Bible should lead *away* from the integrated ideal of traditional European Christendom. Where the Scriptures were clear, Castellio reasoned, they did not need a government's authority, but only a population willing to read and heed. Where they were not clear, it was the responsibility of each individual believer to discern the meaning while acting charitably toward others who struggled with similar difficulties.[7] Castellio's work was translated into Dutch several different times; in that form it bolstered a strand of anti-Christendom reasoning that arrived in the Netherlands from England.

These English expats, from the most radical fringes of biblicist reform, agreed in finding Elizabethan religion a sorry half-way affair. They included followers of Henry Barrow (Barrowists), who left the Anglican church in protest during the 1580s; John Smyth, who abandoned the establishment after serving as an Anglican priest; and the separatist Puritans under John Robinson whose number included the dedicated lay memoirist William Bradford. All of these groups drew support for their biblicism from Dutch Mennonites, though none became thoroughly Anabaptist; neither could they unite among themselves on one particular form of separatist biblicism.

Among these reformers, the most enduring influences on questions of religion, politics, church, and society came from the nascent Baptist movement. John Murton, who as a youth had accompanied separates to the Netherlands, returned to England and became a leading Baptist spokesman. In 1620 his *Humble Supplication to the King's Majesty* spelled out reasons for rejecting a defense of church establishment that King James had offered to Parliament earlier that year. Murton's pamphlet, which was eventually published with an earlier protest he had made against persecution for cause of conscience, sharpened the arguments of those who had gone before. Unlike their earlier efforts, this work was destined for a consequential afterlife on both sides of the Atlantic.

The first chapter of Murton's *Supplication* began boldly: "The Rule of Faith is the Doctrine of the Holy Ghost contained in the Sacred Scriptures, and not any church, Council, Prince or Potentate, or any mortal man whatsoever." Then followed seventeen separate biblical passages, quoted by chapter and verse to explicate that statement. Then after quoting an early Protestant work ("The scriptures contain the principles of our faith, and shall we not believe them?"), Murton declared that "This, and much more, the learned Protestants have written, and sufficiently confirms, that no church nor man whatsoever may be the judge, rule, or umpire in such matters of faith, but only the holy scriptures; and whosoever teacheth and practiseth otherwise they must hold and maintain the Papist's creed." More scripture citations pointed to the only practical application that Murton thought these texts allowed: "The Interpreter of this Rule is the Scriptures, and Spirit of God in whomsoever"—followed by another flurry of chapter and verse citations, and so on for the rest of the pamphlet.[8]

Murton's strongly biblicist reasoning probably played some role in the passionate appeals that John Milton made for religious liberty during the Cromwellian years.[9] Without question, as we will see, it linked Murton's complaint against King James's England with Roger Williams's complaint against Puritan Massachusetts.

The little-noticed biblicism espoused in Murton's *Supplication* enjoyed a mostly fugitive existence until it emerged as a significant American influence during the second half of the eighteenth century. But when it did emerge, it helped push colonists toward a new conception of church and state. As "religious freedom" became the operative American norm, the Bible-against-Christendom legacy also influenced many of those who sought to reestablish a shaping Christian influence on society without recourse to the establishmentarian form of old-world Christendom. By contrast, in Milton's England, such appeals to the free rights of individual conscience were first drowned out by competition from Puritan biblicists who wanted to newmodel Christendom and then were overwhelmed by Royalists who successfully overcame Puritan efforts as they restored Anglican Christendom.

The Bible against Puritan Biblicism: Anne Hutchinson and Roger Williams

When in the mid-1630s, Anne Hutchinson and Roger Williams challenged Massachusetts's Bible Commonwealth, they recapitulated some of what English radicals brought back from Holland, even as they anticipated the debates among Bible-believers that soon overtook England in the Crom-wellian era. On the colonial side of the Atlantic, biblicist protests against Puritan Christendom succeeded no better than biblicist reforms proposed by English Puritans succeeded in establishing their vision of a biblicist English Christendom. Thus, Williams and Hutchinson exerted little direct influence as such on American convictions until much later— Williams in the 1770s, Hutchinson perhaps not until scholarship on her blossomed in the 1970s. Their protests nonetheless articulated the kind of biblicism that remained much more viable in the spacious colonial world than, after 1660, it did in England.

Roger Williams objected comprehensively to the principles that lead-ers of the Bay Colony defended as the Bible's mandate for their new land.[10] Before he came to the New World, Williams as an undergraduate at Cambridge and chaplain to a well-connected Puritan household had fully embraced the Puritan drive for reform. He had also worked for several years as an amanuensis for Edward Coke, the great champion of Parliament and the Common Law. When in the early 1630s Williams left England for Massachusetts in order to escape a crackdown on ministers who advo-cated Puritan opinions, he had been well trained in kicking against the pricks, both civil and ecclesiastical.

Between his arrival in February 1631 and his banishment in October 1635, Williams's stopping points in Boston, Salem, Plymouth, and then Salem again were marked by near-constant controversy. And understand-ably so. Williams insisted that true Christians should separate completely from all things Anglican, including maintaining any fellowship with those who only attended Anglican worship when back in England. He opposed Massachusetts's efforts to enforce morality through civil codes. He sup-ported cutting out the cross from the royal banner displayed at Salem. And he denied that supposedly "Christian" nations had any right to appropriate Indian lands. Most important, he backed all of these charges against the Bible Commonwealth with an insistent appeal to Scripture. Often he turned to Revelation 17 and interpreted the Great Whore of Babylon described in that passage as either Roman Catholicism or any aggrandizement of power similar to Rome's fatal defect. Only a few years after Massachusetts banished Williams for advocating such views, he put his protests into print. But before that published challenge appeared, the colony had to deal with Anne Hutchinson. In her mind, she was trying to improve the Puritan enterprise as a whole; to her opponents, she threatened its very existence.

Anne Marbury was born in 1591 to militantly Puritan parents. From them she acquired what the historian Michael Winship has described as a "formidable command of the Bible."[11] In England, Anne's family, including her husband, William Hutchinson, became firmly attached to the preaching of John Cotton of Boston in Lincolnshire. Cotton's winsome teaching proved especially compelling as it depicted the assurance of salvation a believer could receive through union with Christ and the testimony of the Holy Spirit. That preaching was thoroughly Puritan, even though it leaned against one of the conventions of Puritan pastoral counseling—the belief that examining one's own progress in godliness (that is, one's own sanctification) could provide firm assurance of salvation. Cotton de-emphasized that standard; at some stage in her spiritual pilgrimage Hutchinson abandoned it altogether. When Cotton in 1633 embarked for the freedom that Massachusetts was offering Puritans under duress, the Hutchinson family followed the very next year. Shortly after their arrival, Anne and her husband entered into full membership at the Boston church to which Cotton had been called as the teaching pastor.

Soon Anne's position as the wife of a prominent merchant, her many acts of kindness to the Boston population at large, and her special gifts as a counselor to women in childbirth made her a prominent figure in the young town. As she advanced in social standing, so too did she promote more boldly her understanding of how Christians received assurance of their salvation: it was by grace communicated through the Holy Spirit, not by obsessive inspection of the supposed sanctification of one's own life. Her presentation of this teaching obviously appealed to the growing numbers of men and women who gathered informally in her home, even as it alarmed some of the Puritan leaders. Ministers like the recently arrived Thomas Shepard and lay leaders like the always influential John Winthrop became apprehensive. They feared that she was leading others astray from the path of salvation. Crucially, they also worried about the entire future of the Puritan vision because of how Hutchinson attacked the good works (the marks of sanctification) required to maintain a godly Commonwealth. Her alternative understanding of salvation amounted to an assault on a crux of the Puritan Way: to question the connection between salvation and the good deeds required for a Reformed society would shake the spiritual basis for the entire enterprise. The upshot was a series of trials before civil and ecclesiastical courts, a tense period of near estrangement between the popular John Cotton and several of the colony's other powerful ministers, and great concern for the fate of Massachusetts.

Worry about the colony sprang directly from Anne Hutchinson's mastery of Scripture, which she quoted with a dexterity dismaying to her learned opponents. Already on her way to America she had frustrated a clergyman when Anne rebuked him with Jesus's words in a passage from John 16 (v. 12: "I have yet many things to say unto you, but ye cannot bear them now") that led on to words she treasured for their evocation of the Holy Spirit (v. 13: "Howbeit when he, the Spirit of truth, is come, he will guide you into all truth").[12] In Boston, it eventually become much worse when she routinely quoted Scripture to refute the clergy who tried to convince her that *theirs* was the proper biblical understanding.

Hutchinson's public trial before the church in Boston. which took place in March 1638, illustrated her skill and their befuddlement. The learned ministers conducting this process, as well as the biblically informed magistrates who pitched in during the proceedings, found it a disquieting experience. They presented their detailed indictment as resting in almost every instance on a specific biblical text that, according to these accusers, she had misread to maintain a theological error—for example, "That the Soules Ecclesiastes 3.18–21 of all men by Nature are mortal."[13] The sixteen specific charges represented a textual cannonade designed to blow her out of the water.

But Anne Hutchinson fired right back with an impressive mastery of the same Scripture she was charged with abusing. She began by referring to the provision concerning church discipline spelled out in Matthew 18:15–18 where Jesus calls for private counsel from "two or three witnesses" before any accusation of wrong doing could be brought to "the church." Hutchinson stood firm on the Bible: "By what Rule of the Word," she asked, was she now being publicly arraigned "before they had privately delt with me?" Then on the contested points themselves she responded to supposed breaches of biblical teaching with a full scale defense drawn exclusively from Scripture. Thus, she cited "Hebrews 4" and "Luke 19:1" to defend her understanding of what happens to body, soul, and spirit when a person dies. Later she fired off references to several passages before concluding "I meane what that Scripture meanes 1 Corinthians 4:16." Early in the trial she rebuffed a general reproach from her one-time mentor John Cotton by appealing to the highest authority: "I desire to hear God speak this and no man. Shew me whear thear is any Scripture to prove" what Cotton had claimed without biblical warrant.[14]

In the end, Anne Hutchinson was bludgeoned into silence and betrayed by her own exasperated claim at a late point in the proceedings that she received special messages from the Holy Spirit. Her earlier assertion about the Spirit's direct witness to salvation fit within the further reaches of standard Puritan teaching; her claim to direct divine communications pushed her beyond the pale. She was therefore excommunicated from the Boston church after the church trial and banished from Massachusetts Bay. Five years later she and several members of her family were caught up in a dispute with local Indians and massacred in what is now the borough of the Bronx in New York City. Massachusetts officials considered these murders the proper reward of a heretic, but these same leaders were destined to experience a continuing series of shocks involving even more contentions with fellow Bible-believers over how a Bible Commonwealth should interpret the Scriptures.

Roger Williams led the way. In his brief career in Plymouth and Massachusetts Bay, then as he tried to organize the colony of Rhode Island, and finally with books published in England, Williams mounted an all-out attack on the notion of a Bible Commonwealth. Crucially, his opposition was drawn almost entirely from Scripture. He thus fomented among colonists a battle over biblical interpretation similar to what developed in England after 1640. In fact, the literary slugfest between Williams and John Cotton, who shouldered the burden for Massachusetts, was little more than a prolific citation of Scripture combined with painstaking explications of individual texts. The main works were Williams's *Bloudy Tenent of Persecution for Cause of Conscience* (1644), Cotton's rebuttal, *The Bloudy Tenent, washed, And made white in the bloud of the Lambe* (1647), and Williams's rebuttal to this rebuttal, *The Bloudy Tenent yet More Bloudy* (1652), but these books also contained reprintings of previous exchanges. However the disputants stated their positions, all were exercises in exegesis.

Williams published the *Bloudy Tenent* in England while he was also trying to aid citizens uprooted by the civil war and working to secure a Parliamentary charter for Rhode Island. This signature effort opened by spelling out the propositions Williams wanted to defend: "First, that the blood of so many hundred thousand souls of Protestants and papists, spilled in the wars of present and former ages for their respective consciences, is not required nor accepted by Jesus Christ the Prince of Peace [quoting Isa 9:6]." Second came his claim that "pregnant scriptures and arguments" spoke against "the doctrine of persecution for cause of conscience" and overturned "the scriptures and objections" of Cotton, John Calvin, Theodore Beza, and others who in defending a unified Protestant Christendom also defended the use of force to constrain belief or practice.

His fifth assertion contended that "all civil states" should treat "civil" affairs only and therefore could never qualify as "judges, governors, or defenders of the spiritual, or Christian, state and worship." The seventh offered a particularly telling rebuke of the Puritan fondness for finding precedents of their own enterprise in the Old Testament: "the state of Israel, the kings and peoples thereof, in peace and war, is proved figurative and ceremonial, and no pattern nor precedent for any kingdom or civil state in the world to follow." Eighth was a proposition that could only have seemed counterintuitive in that era: "God requires not a uniformity of religion," but, instead, where such uniformity is enforced the result was inevitably "civil war, ravishing of conscience, persecution of Christ Jesus in his servants, and...the hypocrisy and destruction of millions of souls."[15] What Williams had earlier spoken in the colonies he now published in London.

So it continued throughout the whole text. Williams's book proper began with a barrage of scriptures that he took from "a witness to Jesus Christ, close prisoner in Newgate." This "witness" was John Murton, whose biblicist arguments against the state-church we have already sampled. In just the first six of these single-sentence paragraphs, Williams quoted or cited Proverbs. 11:14; Matthew 13:30 and 38; Matthew 15:14; Luke 9:54 and 56; 2 Timothy 2:24–26; Isaiah 2:4; Mark 4:3–4; and 2 Corinthians 10:4.[16] The barrage did not stop until the work itself came to the end, even when Williams included a letter from John Cotton that had earlier replied to some of his assertions. That letter itself had been mostly given over to Cotton's interpretation of Acts 13 (on persecution), 2 Corinthians 10 (on carnal versus spiritual warfare), and Matthew 13 (on the parable of the wheat and tares, which were not separated until the Final Judgment).[17] A modern editor has indexed the range of Williams's biblical citations in his *Bloudy Tenent*; they encompassed hundreds of texts drawn from twenty-six Old Testament books and twenty-four New (including citations from all but Philemon, 2 John, and 3 John).[18]

Williams's *Bloudy Tenent* appeared in London as only a single drop in the river of controversial publications flowing from English presses during the interregnum. It received little attention in the mother country; the effect in New England was equally negligible. Rhode Islanders stood with Williams when he opposed Massachusetts, Plymouth, and Connecticut, but they stood together on little else. The Puritan colonies retained enough control over their own destinies that they could simply brush aside Williams's outlandish radicalism. But if efforts by these colonies to establish a Bible-based social order survived Williams's assault as well as the melt-down of England's Puritan Revolution, Williams had made a point with a future. In Michael Winship's summary, Williams defined "Christendom" as "that part of the world where the bloody sword of the magistrate pol-luted the purity of the Christian spiritual swords of discipline and scrip-ture."[19] In time, a majority of Americans would come to agree with this conclusion, even if Williams himself was forgotten.

The decline of Christendom in the New World involved much else be-sides disagreement over scriptural interpretation. The practical realities of religious pluralism and the influence of ideologies indebted to the Enlightenment also played important parts in that development. Yet two differences from England remained crucial. First, the undermining of Puritan Christendom took place as a slow, evolutionary process that left much of the original impetus—to order all of life by the Word of God—in-tact. Second, much of that undermining came from figures who believed just as thoroughly in the Scriptures as the leaders of Puritan Christendom themselves.

Chipping Away at Christendom Built on the Bible

New England's Puritan Way, with its twin allegiance to biblicism and Christendom, survived the challenges from Anne Hutchinson and Roger Williams. Yet the difficulty of maintaining both the Protestant principle respecting Scripture and the Puritan vision of a unified Reformed social order only increased over time. When English tumults of the 1640s allowed the always simmering pot of religious agitation to boil over, New England worked hard to contain the spillage. On the one hand, disorderly times in the mother country seemed propitious for the Puritan colonies since they were left alone to do as they pleased. On the other hand, a pan-oply of fresh problems emerged. Within the framework of the era's most widely shared assumptions, the most serious problems were Bible-based objections to the New England Way. Thus, the new-world Congregationalists were stung when English and Scottish Presbyterians upbraided them for misapplying the guidance of Scripture in their colonial church-state estab-lishment (their response, as we have seen, was the Cambridge Platform of 1648). Radicals like Roger Williams, who used the Bible to argue against Christendom itself, were easier to handle because such proposals seemed so obviously berserk. It was even easier to manage the Quakers who came missionizing from England and from Rhode Island with a message about the God-given "Inner Light" that they claimed took precedence over even Scripture. When after repeated warnings, Massachusetts authorities in 1659 and 1661 executed four Quakers for persisting in that subversive teaching, observers in England criticized the severity, but not the logic, of those judicial actions. In the years before 1660—when the options on offer were a monarchial state-church for England and Ireland, a state-church establishment contested between Anglicans and Presbyterians in Scotland, and either Anglican or Congregational establishments in the colonies—the Quakers' boast about some kind of direct divine communication remained as politically threatening as it was theologically suspect.

Much changed, however, and fairly rapidly, after 1660. In England, agitation from non-Anglican Protestants continued to build toward the Revolution of 1688 and the new regime's Act of Toleration for Protestant Dissenters in 1689. In Scotland, "the killing times" (when agents of the monarchy mercilessly harried the most thorough Presbyterians) gave way after 1688 to the acceptance of a Presbyterian regime. In the colonies, the founding of Pennsylvania in 1681–82 foreshadowed possibilities for both Quaker respectability and orderly toleration.

For the New England colonies, however, the confessional regime yielded only gradually. Through the middle decades of the seventeenth century, the most serious challenge to the Protestant confessional state again came from otherwise sound Puritans. Particularly disturbing was the recurring doubt about whether Scripture mandated the baptism of infants that was standard among the era's Reformed Protestants. This challenge involved much more than a theological quibble since Puritans regarded baptism as a divinely given seal of the covenant, and therefore crucial for church covenants and the community's covenant with God as a whole. The inclusion of children in the body politic was nothing less than the foundation for Puritanism's entire covenantal edifice.

Early uneasiness about this practice could be finessed. Deborah Moody, the wealthy widow of a former Member of Parliament, was harassed by King Charles's officials, which prompted her migration to Massachusetts in the mid-1630s. Although she joined the Salem church, she also expressed her doubts about the validity of infant baptism, which led to a formal charge from colonial officials. After high-level consultations, she migrated in 1643 to Long Island where Dutch authorities were more tolerant.[20] Anne Eaton, the wife of the governor of New Haven colony, was more persistent. After she walked out of several worship services when infants were being offered for baptism, and after she engaged in several well-publicized quarrels with family members and servants, her New Haven church brought her up on formal charges. When she refused to repent of her errors, she was in 1644 excommunicated. Because Mrs. Eaton thereafter kept her opinions to herself, she was allowed to remain in the colony.[21]

The case of Henry Dunster struck closer to the bone. Dunster arrived in Massachusetts in 1640, the same year he was appointed the first president of Harvard College. When a decade or so later, he did not bring a newborn son to be baptized, investigations followed. Colonial officials, who had earlier labeled those who rejected infant baptism as "Incendiaries of Commonwealths," labored to change Dunster's mind. But he resisted, resigned his Harvard post, and left the Bay Colony to become the teacher of a church in Plymouth at Scituate.[22] If a colony organized according to the principles of the Word of God could not convince all of its citizens that their biblical interpretations were correct, at least in the first decades those dissenters could be shunted aside. That marginalization became harder as the decades passed.

Boston witnessed more signs of a changed landscape in April 1668 as another memorable controversy unfolded over the same controverted question of what baptism meant and who should be baptized. The event was a public disputation that pitted a team of ministers defending the New England Way against a group of Baptist laymen and the pastor who had risen from within their ranks.[23] This minister, Thomas Goold of Charlestown, had begun to doubt the biblical warrant of infant baptism in the mid-1650s. When in 1655 he refused to present a newborn daughter for baptism to the Charlestown church, he was examined, censured, and fined. Yet he persisted. By the early 1660s Goold was joined by several others of similar convictions; in 1665, nine of them established a church of their own after baptizing each other by immersion. Despite fines and brief imprisonment for Goold and two others, this Baptist congregation continued to grow. In an attempt to quell this upstart and publicly assert their own authority, the governor and assistants concluded that a public debate should be held in First Church, Boston.

Several reasons explain the reluctance of the Massachusetts authorities simply to banish the Baptists. They were peaceful and respected citizens who had won a fair measure of public support because of their orderly carriage. Moreover, King Charles and his agents had demanded that Massachusetts tolerate loyal Anglicans and loyal Quakers, insisting on this leniency first through strongly worded communications and then in

1664–65 by a royal commission. For their part, the Massachusetts Puritans had only recently concluded a long-drawn-out controversy over whether the grandchildren of church members could be baptized if their parents had never formally joined the church. The Half-Way Covenant of 1662 allowed for such baptisms, but also indirectly supported the Baptists by demonstrating how complicated it was to move from full reliance on the New Testament to an unambiguous position on who should be baptized, under what conditions, and when.

The public debate of April 1668 featured a high level of casuistry from both sides. Common to all, however, was an unremitting appeal to Scripture. The tone was set early on when Thomas Goold responded to an assertion from an establishment minister by declaring, "Many answers are given but no scripture given. If convincing arguments be laid[,] it [Scripture] is that which answers." Then, according to the transcript, "Holding up the bible in his hand he said: We have nothing to judge but this." His opponent's immediate response was "I will give you 2: scriptures."[24] And so it went, back and forth, for two full days:

> Let me give you 2: or 3: scriptures to show you.... We find there is a scripture.... It is not justifiable by the word of God.... Our baptizing of believers the scripture warrants.... according to rule of the gospel as the pattern laid down by Christ Jesus.... To any rule of Christ we are willing to submit.... Where is the rule of Christ that we must follow the churches here farther than they follow Christ?... he saw no warrant from it from the word of God.... The question is whether it is justifiable from the word of God.... let me propound 2: or 3: scriptures.... The order of the gospels requireth.... The apostle declares it.... you instanced King David. Whether will you parallel New Testament government with Old?... The scripture saith.... The Old Testament rules are not parallel to the rules of the gospel.... proved by these scriptures.... the open violation of the order of God's house is not justifiable by the word of God.... We must take the institutions of the gospel from Christ Jesus.... you come not up to the order of the gospel.[25]

Throughout, virtuosic quotation and insistent appeal to chapter and verse supported almost every intervention.

The upshot was anticlimactic. The Massachusetts General Court did rule that Goold and his chief associates had to be banished. But this decision prompted sixty-six other citizens, some of them prominent, to petition for a pardon. After briefly imprisoning Goold and one of his colleagues, the court allowed them to slip into semi-banishment on Noodles Island in Boston Harbor. For the next five years they remained on the island but with liberty to hold worship services for any who chose to row over for that purpose. The number of Baptist meetings continued to grow, despite official harassment. Goold came back to Boston from the island in 1674 and conducted church services in a private dwelling. Finally, in 1681, Massachusetts authorities allowed the Baptists to construct a meeting house.

The experience of the Baptists in Charlestown and Boston testified to the weakening of Puritan Christendom. One of the ministers who took part in the debate described this weakening precisely in a letter written shortly afterwards: the Baptists' "very principle of making infant Baptisme a nullity...doth make at once, all our churches & our religious, Civill state and polity, and all the officers & members thereof to be unbaptized, and to bee no Christians, & so our churches to bee no churches; & so we have no regular freemen." In his view, the consequences could not have been more devastating: "& so we have no regular power to choose Deputies for any Generall Courts, nor to chuse any Magistrates...all our holsom lawes & orders made a nullity; & that hedge is pulled downe, & all left open to state destroyers...so that our very fundaments of civil & social order, here in New England, are at once thereby...overturned."[26] The historian William McLoughlin put the situation in a forward-looking perspective: "What the Puritans foresaw, even if dimly, in the thrust of the principles advocated by the Baptists was the overthrow of the medieval ideal of the corporate Christian state and the substitution for it of a voluntaristic, pluralistic, individualistic, or atomistic social order. This, in their eyes was tantamount to anarchy."[27]

For later American history, a second consequence was just as important. The most effective assault on Puritan Christendom did not come from secular or monarchical forces. It came from fellow Puritans who believed in the Bible *almost* the same way that they did. Colonists would soon embrace John Locke and Real Whig political thought. They would even concede a place for Anglicans who hoped that some kind of English church-state establishment could be erected in the New World. Unlike the course of development in the mother country, however, the chief advocates for an alternative to a Bible commonwealth defended their own absolute loyalty to Scripture.

Biblicist Christendom under Siege

Before the end of the seventeenth century, the Puritans' biblicist Christendom suffered further debilitating reversals. Bloody warfare, political disappointment, and scholarly innovations combined in different ways to frustrate the vision of a liberated Scripture turning the kingdoms of this world into the Kingdom of the Lord. The effect did not displace the Bible, but it did undercut the deliberate use of Scripture for organizing the entire society.

Historians have properly treated the brutal Indian warfare of the mid-1670s, usually called King Philip's War, as the climax of enduring cross-cultural misunderstanding. A major part of that fatal disconnect concerned the Bible.[28] The few Puritans who tried seriously to bring the blessings of Christianity to Native Peoples had made Scripture the centerpiece of their efforts. John Eliot labored arduously to learn the Massachusett dialect of Algonquian, and then to prepare a translation of the Bible in that language. Above all, he hoped to bring salvation to the Indians, but not salvation alone. The "praying towns" he established for Indian converts represented a civic translation of the Christendom ideal into Algonquian every bit as much as the biblical text represented a literary translation. When in 1648 Eliot advocated the establishment of such towns, he foresaw them as places where believing Indians could have "the Word constantly taught, and government constantly exercised." After they were up and running, he wrote in 1673 that these new villages "are expressly conformed to the Scriptures."[29] In the interim, North America's first full translation of the Bible was printed in the Algonquian language during the years 1660 to 1663. The praying towns offered native believers the same privilege of structuring all of life by their newly translated Scriptures as the European settlers were attempting with Greek and Hebrew texts for ministers and the King James Bible in English for all.

King Philip's War began with the murder of an Indian convert, John Sassamon, who had become a particularly important assistant to John Eliot in his translating efforts, even though it grew from decades of English encroachment upon native lands and a long-standing clash of cultures. Between the outbreak of hostilities in June 1675 and the death of Metacom/ King Philip in August 1676, thousands perished among both Natives and colonists, and tremendous damage was sustained by both communities. Colonists bent on reprisal lashed out as viciously against the peaceful residents of Eliot's praying towns as against Native warriors. Eventually they banished the Christian Indians to Deer Island in Boston Harbor, an expulsion that ended Christendom for them. For their part, Indian combatants reciprocated by hurling slurs that disparaged God, Jesus, and other prominent features of Christianity. Natives took special pains to destroy Bibles and other Christian publications available in Algonquian. A contemporary account reported that a colonist under attack clutched his Bible to ward off danger, but with an ironic denouement: the Indians "deriding his groundless Apprehension, or Folly therein, rippe[d] him open and put his Bible in his belly."[30] But English militias also destroyed much Christian literature in the Indian language because of the sympathy it bespoke for Native culture. If this spasm of European-Indian violence took an immense toll in lives and property, it also effectively destroyed the Puritans' belief that their way of relying on Scripture could function for others as they hoped it would function for themselves.

The violent destruction of this colonial war played a part in further weakening the Bible Commonwealth because it rendered Massachusetts too feeble even to contemplate forcible resistance against changes in the colony's charter. In 1684, Charles II revoked the Massachusetts instrument of government as a culmination of long-standing efforts by England to standardize control over its colonies and a particular concern on the part of the king to ensure that Massachusetts not promote the kind of Puritanism that had troubled the nation under his father. In response, Massachusetts sent one of its leading clerics, Increase Mather, to England in order to preserve as much of the colony's original autonomy as possible. While Mather did succeed in securing some concessions, he failed to preserve the mechanisms that had made the original Bible Commonwealth work. In the new charter, the franchise was now tied to property, church membership no longer bestowed political privileges, and the governor no longer came from among the godly but was to be a crown appointment. In the words of Michael Winship, the failure of the new charter to retain the organic link between converted church members and the colony's elected political leaders meant the end of "the theocratic dream of Elizabethan puritans...of a religiously and morally cleansed Reformed Christian polity—one state, one church, one godly path to heaven."[31]

The intensive biblical labors of Mather's son, Cotton Mather, testified to further anxiety for Puritan biblicists. The younger Mather was a precocious student and, from 1688, the colleague-pastor with his father at Boston's Old North Meeting House. Mather remains notorious for his part in abetting the Salem Witch Trials of 1691–92, but in his own day he was better known as Massachusetts's leading preacher, theologian, and all-around intellectual.[32]

Of particular note for our purposes was Mather's exhaustive devotion to the Bible. In scores of published sermons, almost all of his numerous treatises, and supremely in the great bulk of his obsessively encyclopedic *Biblia Americana*, Mather put Scripture to work promoting the kind of godliness he felt a rapidly changing world required. In much of his engagement with Scripture, Mather could hardly be distinguished from contemporaries like the English Presbyterian Matthew Henry, author of the much-used *Exposition of All the Books of the Old and New Testament*, or his near-contemporary Jonathan Edwards who had only just begun his ministerial career when Mather died in 1728.[33] They and most other traditional Protestant clergy of the day used the Bible to proclaim the way of salvation, urge parishioners to live godly lives, and explain day-to-day phenomena in terms of divine revelation.

Mather, however, differed from other orthodox voices like Henry and Edwards in ways that highlighted new challenges for all biblicists, especially those who pursued a scriptural Christendom. The difference shows most clearly in Mather's *Biblia Americana*.[34] Mather began work on this mammoth project in the 1690s, combining elements of a biblical commentary with a Bible dictionary and a commonplace book for extracts from authorities on all matters scriptural. The project grew like Topsy, even after Mather's efforts in 1713 and 1714 failed to find a London or Scottish publisher, until it reached nearly 4,600 holograph pages and three million words. Only now, in the twenty-first century, is it on the way into print. This recent effort represents a great boon to those who study the intellectual history of Mather's era, since this one manuscript constitutes an intellectual map charting the flow of information from the ancient and contemporary European worlds to Mather's corner of North America. As he organized that flow, it is significant that Mather was not primarily interested in the theological or spiritual uses of Scripture that otherwise predominated in his era. Instead, as phrased authoritatively by one of Mather's modern editors, his main purpose was to "reconcile the flood of new, if not dangerous, discoveries in the natural sciences and philosophy, with conservative standards of interpretations."[35] Mather, in other words, was trying to keep up with Europe's expanding scholarship in philology, natural philosophy, and ancient history so that he could summarize (and neutralize) that scholarship for the public. Though only a colonist, he nonetheless very much wanted to take part in the rapidly expanding debates of the early Enlightenment period concerning religion, reason, and science. Thus, the *Biblia Americana* engaged scientific findings from Robert Hooke, Isaac Newton, Gottfried Leibniz, Robert Boyle, and Athanasius Kircher; it worked to reconcile scriptural history with the best historical accounts from Mather's contemporaries; and it paid direct attention to the leading European voices (Jean LeClerc, Richard Simon, Baruch Spinoza) who were advancing a modern form of biblical criticism.[36]

As one example of Mather's chief interests, his treatment of Jacob's encounter with the "man" in Genesis 32:24–32 made very little effort to draw out spiritual, typological, or ethical applications of this powerful but mysterious passage. Instead, Mather expatiated at length on how the story resembled a Roman legend about Jupiter wrestling with Hercules; on what meat without sinews meant in later Old Testament history; on whether the Jews should be named "Children of Israel" or "Sons of Israel"; and on what modern medical advances could explain about the nature of Jacob's lameness.[37] With such concerns uppermost, Mather clearly hoped to edify readers by answering critics, rather than by direct spiritual application.

Mather's *Biblia America* pointed toward the future of the Bible in America. In other spheres of his hyperactive life, Mather innovated along similar lines: he was willing to accept a greater measure of toleration for non-Puritans than his Massachusetts ancestors, and he pioneered in promoting voluntary instead of establishmentarian methods for accomplishing evangelical purposes.[38] In these tendencies, but above all in his new dedication to a critical defense of Scripture, he anticipated the American future.[39] That future would continue to witness a great dedication to biblicist principles. But it also included an increasing number of Protestants who did not rely on the structures of Christendom to accomplish their goals. In addition, it spoke for many who realized they might have to fight for biblical authority if the culture no longer accepted older assumptions about the divinity of Scripture.

For Protestant biblicists of all kinds the intellectual challenges of biblical criticism continued to grow from that time forward. Whether from populist skeptics like Tom Paine in the eighteenth century or the much-celebrated avatars of German higher criticism in the nineteenth, challenges multiplied against the implicit trust in Scripture that had once been common in the early modern world. Mather's concern to shore up what once had been taken widely for granted heralded a landmark transition that would effect the course of the Bible in U.S. history and ultimately contribute to the decline of the nation's Bible civilization. But that development runs far ahead of our story at this point.

Pennsylvania

Pennsylvania was at once entirely the same and completely different. Like the early settlers of New England, William Penn relied on Scripture explicitly to guide his experiment in the New World. Unlike the Puritans, Penn's reliance on Scripture pushed him beyond Christendom to something very close to a modern understanding of religious freedom. The Quaker faith to which Penn converted in 1667 broke from standard Protestant teaching by postulating an "Inner Light of Christ" ("synteresis" was Penn's word) through which God communicated by direct intuition to the human conscience.[40] The result would appear to be a subordination of Scripture as the norm for belief and practice. But for the early leaders of the Society of Friends—and for a substantial part of Quaker tradition thereafter—this result did not occur. Trust in the Bible, alongside confidence in the Inner Light, functioned as a key component of William Penn's reasoning as he defended his newfound faith through many publications in England and as he maneuvered through complicated negotiations with Charles II to secure a colony in America. Thus, the experiment in religious liberty that Penn attempted in his new colony was only slightly less a product of biblical reasoning than the colonial Christendom sought by the Puritans in New England.

Penn outlined the principles of post-Christendom Protestantism with special clarity in a 1670 tract published while he languished in prison. He had been confined for opposing Parliament's Conventicle Act that imposed draconian restrictions on public worship by non-Anglicans. In response, Penn offered *The Great Case of Liberty of Conscience.* It attacked the "imposition, restraint, and persecution for conscience sake" first as a logical invasion of God's prerogatives and then as a contradiction to the character of Christianity itself. Penn drew on a standard Protestant polemic when he associated the restrictive practices of Anglican Christendom with the worst of Roman Catholicism: "such magisterial determinations carry an evident claim to that infallibility, which Protestants have been hitherto been so jealous of owning, that, to avoid the Papists, they have denied it to all but God himself." Even more determinedly Protestant was his turn to detailed biblical citations to support his "great case." The third of the tract's short chapters quoted a parade of scriptures to prove that the Conventicle Act and all similar measures "oppose the plainest testimonies of divine writ that can be."[41]

After announcing this theme, Penn offered full quotation of fifteen texts in the King James Version: three from the Old Testament, seven from the gospels, and five from the New Testament epistles. Penn quoted some passages without comment and interspersed parenthetical glosses with others, as in his citation of 2 Corinthians 10:3: "'For though we walk in the flesh,' (that is, in the body, or visible world) 'we do not war after the flesh; for the weapons of our warfare are not carnal.' 2 Cor. x.3 (but fines and imprisonments are; and such use not the apostles' weapons that employ those.)". Penn concluded this biblical barrage by confessing he did not know whether "persecutors at any time read the scriptures," but with the certainty that those who put people in prison for following their distinctive forms of Protestant Christianity "practice as little of them [the Scriptures] as may be, who with so much delight reject them."[42]

The constitutional documents that Penn drew up to establish Pennsylvania reflected the same determination to protect the rights of conscience, but also the same determination to ground these rights in an express application of biblical teaching. Pennsylvania's Charter of Liberties and Frame of Government, promulgated in May 1682, thus first invoked "the great and wise God" who "made the world," but then immediately turned to Scripture—"the Apostle [Paul] teaches in divers of his epistles"—to explain why such a constitution was needed. Three passages, quoted loosely from Romans 4:15, 1 Timothy 1:9–10, and Romans 13:1–5, provided the warrant for "settl[ing] the divine right of government beyond exception." Penn showed that he was keeping abreast of the intense political discussions of his era by noting that Pennsylvania would benefit from combined monarchical, aristocratic, and democratic principles. But the Frame's key assertion was its provision of religious freedom of the sort that, with the exception of Rhode Island and the Netherlands, existed nowhere else in the world: "That all persons living in the province, who confess and acknowledge the one Almighty and eternal God, to be the Creator, Upholder and Ruler of the world; and that hold themselves obliged in conscience to live peaceably and justly in civil society, shall, in no ways, be molested or prejudiced for their religious persuasion, or practice, in matters of faith and worship, nor shall they be compelled, at any time, to frequent or maintain any religious worship, place or ministry whatever."[43]

Notwithstanding this bold declaration, traces of Christendom did remain. Immediately after Penn's assertion of religious freedom, the Frame went on to specify that "according to the good example of the primitive Christians," Pennsylvanians would on Sundays "abstain from their common daily labor" in order to "better dispose themselves to worship God according to their understandings."[44]

The same rejection of traditional Christendom combined with lingering remnants of the intermixed religious and public duties that Penn otherwise rejected also appeared in a further "act for freedom of conscience" from December of that same year, 1682. It too was a Protestant statement that featured deference to Scripture as an unquestioned axiom. This act repeated the claim that government was "a venerable ordinance of God"; it repeated that no person who acknowledged God "shall in any case be molested or prejudiced for his or her conscientious persuasion or practice." But it also repeated that Sunday should be kept as a day free of the "usual common toil and labor." This restriction ensured that the people might "dispose themselves to read the scriptures of truth at home or frequent such meetings of religious worship abroad as may best suit their respective persuasions." The act also imposed a five-shilling fine, or five-day imprisonment, for any who "shall speak loosely and profanely" about God, Christ, the Holy Spirit, "or the scriptures of truth."[45]

Pennsylvania, in short, would be a new type of colony, with (Rhode Island excepted) an unparalleled degree of religious liberty. Guided by his Quaker principles, Penn broke with powerful European assumptions that had prevailed for most of a millennium. His colony appealed to the Scriptures as legitimation for its existence, but it did not mandate a particular understanding of the Bible. It did not institutionalize formal legal ties between the dominant authority's scriptural interpretations and the colony's legal structure, nor did it coerce citizens to acknowledge the superior claim of Penn's own biblical interpretations. Compared to ideals of religious freedom that came later, Penn's experiment remained incomplete. But compared to the world he inhabited during the second half of the seventeenth century, it represented almost pure innovation.

The significance of the Pennsylvania experiment is difficult to grasp except against the English backdrop of the period. If creative thinkers like John Locke were proposing the radical solution of religious toleration as a recipe for social harmony, the clash of competing Christendoms still dominated English public life. Penn went much farther. He proclaimed a distinctly Protestant liberty of conscience for Pennsylvania, but nonetheless a liberty of conscience beyond anything that any British polity had yet attempted. Penn came close to attempting in practice what Sebastian Castellio, John Murton, and Roger Williams had propounded as theory. For the history of the Bible in what became the United States, it was of first importance that Penn carried out his experiment as an exercise in scriptural Christianity.

Crucial for Penn's experiment was the fact that Pennsylvania, on the basis of Penn's understanding of Scripture, all but abandoned establishmentarian Christendom. Pennsylvania's early efforts to enforce a Protestant observance of the Sabbath may appear as the most significant exception. Even as Penn set out deliberately to establish religious freedom, he continued to believe in standard Protestant teachings about the comprehensive authority of the Bible, and he also continued to believe in the comprehensive reach of scriptural teaching. Penn wanted the Bible to be appropriated individually, without coercion, but he still sought a comprehensively biblical civilization In fact, confidence in Scripture undergirded his attack on Christendom. The Bible—read, heard, and heeded without formal legal support—remained the truth, the pattern, and the grand narrative for all of life. This trust that Scripture could exert its divine power without legal reinforcement by Europe's traditional church-state arrangements explains much about later American history. Biblicism would continue, and even expand, its influence. Yet the conscious move beyond formal Christendom did not spell the end to efforts at shaping the entire society. The abandonment of church establishment would blind the main Protestant bodies to how much coercive force could be exerted informally through social pressures, even when the law decreed complete religious liberty. In line with what Penn initiated, Protestant biblicism remained a culture-shaping force long after William Penn's principles of religious liberty were accepted by the national body politic.

* * * * *

The biblicism of the Puritans has understandably received more attention than the biblicism of Quaker Pennsylvania. Yet for Penn and many Friends after him, the Inner Light of Christ gave a scripturally defined gift to be experienced alongside a fully functioning reliance on the Bible. In that spirit, influential Quakers continued to insist on the need to restrain the Inner Light within scriptural bounds. The controversial George Keith was expelled from the Philadelphia Yearly meeting in 1691 for making a strong appeal for such a biblical restraint, but his expulsion probably had more to do with offenses against Pennsylvania's political hierarchy than for theological reasons.[46] Later, in the decades surrounding the War of Independence, Quaker voices against slavery and Quaker voices supporting the new nation drew significantly on the Scriptures to advance their goals.[47] They continued, in other words, to employ a standard Protestant reliance on the Bible even as they maintained the distinctive Quaker teachings undergirding their commitment to religious liberty.

The contribution of colonial Pennsylvania to the early American history of the Bible reinforced what came out of New England with Roger Williams, Anne Hutchinson, and the Boston Baptists. Together they represented rejection of the deeply engrained European conviction that took the union of church and state for granted as essential for social well-being. By no means, however, did their stance entail rejection of the Protestant trust in Scripture that British establishmentarians also affirmed. These important colonial forces that moved against Christendom were not moving against the Bible. They were, instead, defining a way of depending on Scripture without Christendom. Puritan energy, ideology, publishing, social construction, and internal conflicts planted biblicism securely in American civilization. As that civilization developed, post-Puritan biblicism became even more important.

6

Empire, 1689–1763

THE PLACE ACCORDED to Scripture evolved significantly in the decades
that stretched from William Penn's Frame of Government (1682) and the
loss of the original Massachusetts Charter (1684) to the First Amendment
of the Constitution and its guarantee of national religious liberty (1791).
The evolutionary character of that development must be stressed. If Scripture remained an indispensable resource amid the tumultuous events of
this period, what did not take place was also important. No intra-Protestant
crisis occurred like the clash of competing biblicisms during the English
Puritan Revolution or the controversies that came later in the United States
over the Bible and slavery. Nor did critical questions about the character of
Scripture itself—like those arising in continental Europe from the early
eighteenth century or that arrived with full force in the United States after
the Civil War—significantly disturb the nearly universal deference to the
Bible that prevailed in colonial America and, after a short period of uncertainty, continued to mark the new United States. Noteworthy events and
circumstances did modify, expand, abridge, deepen, vivify, and restrict traditional Protestant practices. But the framework of Protestant trust in the
Bible—conventions, assumptions, principles, and practices—maintained
what had been inherited from earlier English history.

While chapters 10 and 11, devoted to the 1770s and 1780s, explore the
complicated place of Scripture during the era of the Revolution, this chapter and the next three are devoted to what happened before that dramatic
period. They highlight the imperial wars when Britannia, freedom, and
Protestantism (including the Bible) stood fast as an idealized unity over
against the vicious combination of France, tyranny, and Catholicism (portrayed as an anti-biblical religion). They treat the revivalism of the century's middle decades as reflecting but also propelling a refashioned religious
culture heading toward individualism, democracy, and a rejection of tradition.
They pause to reveal how the revival's stress on direct apprehension of

scriptural truths created for the first time a self-sustaining African American Christian tradition. They also ask how the process of Anglicization, which drew the colonies closer to British values even as it prepared the way for independence, both reinforced and restricted the public role of the Bible. The main question for this period is why the Bible came to mean more for African Americans, for women, and among the laity in general, while at the same time losing authority for trade and wealth-creation, slavery and race, formal intellectual life, and political ideology.

These chapters narrate a singularly American story. Commitment to Protestantism as a component part of British imperial ideology grew stronger, along with a concomitant intensification of anti-Catholicism. For this aspect of colonial history, the Bible served as a powerful emblem constantly deployed to reinforce the chosenness of Britain's empire under God (the subject of this chapter). Perhaps ironically, the more directly that Protestant self-consciousness contributed to British imperial identity, the more widely conventions of the empire took the place of direct guidance from Scripture (chap. 9).

A similar complexity attends expectations that colonists brought to the Bible. New England's legally enforced biblicism continued to fade. The alternative biblicism that opposed Christendom gradually became more prominent as some of its advocates allied biblical teaching with the age's more secular political theories that also attacked the hierarchies of establishmentarian Christendom. Revival measurably strengthened reliance on Scripture for personal spiritual liberation (chap. 7) and so indirectly secured a stronghold for biblicism in the culture at large. Informal Christendom, or expectations about the generally Protestant shape of society, remained vital but also loosely defined or dimly perceived. No one yet faced the question of how a Protestant social order might be preserved without a legally ordained establishment. But the elements that foregrounded that question in the new United States were coming into place in these decades before the new nation was born.

Outposts of Empire

From the widest perspective, empire defined public life in the American colonies from the 1680s through the 1760s. Of the many factors that went into the creation of an imperial British identity, Protestantism ranked among the most important. Throughout the reigns of the last Stuart monarchs—

William and Mary (1689–1702) and Anne (1702–14)—and then their successors from Hanoverian Germany—George I (1714–27), George II (1727–60), and George III (from 1760)—colonists were drawn increasingly into the nexus of values accompanying the extension of Britain's empire. Historians parse differently the relative weight that should be accorded to the material, political, cultural, religious, and ideological elements of that nexus. Linda Colley has been most pronounced in asserting that "Protestantism was the foundation that made the invention of Great Britain possible"—but she also recognizes the contribution of rising prosperity, military success against Catholic powers, and an ever-expanding empire. Boyd Schlenther has stressed "burgeoning commercial culture" as the driving force in the era's merger of religious, political, and mercantile values. To Jack P. Greene, an ideological ideal of "liberty was...the single most important element in defining a larger Imperial identity for Britain and the British Empire," but again interwoven with Protestantism, prosperity, trade, and military conflict. Patrick Griffin highlights the same range of "ideals that made Britons a distinctive and chosen people" in the wake of victory over France in the Seven Years' War. Increasingly throughout this period American colonists joined residents of the homeland to think of themselves, in the succinct phrase of David Armitage, as a "people Protestant, commercial, maritime and free."[1]

For a history of the Bible, the key is not the prioritization of influences, but the integration of Protestant beliefs, organizations, and activities within the dynamics of empire. Another perceptive historian has written, "Politics were intertwined with religion and religious identity on all levels of society, as all British Americans knew."[2] That integration assumed one shape for Presbyterians in Scotland and Anglicans throughout the rest of the British world, since their established status gave them a proprietary stake in military victory and commercial expansion. But the 1689 Toleration Act negotiated between Parliament and King William meant that Congregationalists, Baptists, Presbyterians—as well as Quakers, Unitarians, and others on the doctrinal fringes of orthodox Protestantism—could be imperialists too. Almost all Dissenting Protestants, in fact, became strong Whigs; in time they supported with equal zeal the Hanoverian Succession and an ideal of liberty. The Act of Union (1707), which created "Great Britain" out of Presbyterian Scotland and Anglican England, communicated a de facto acknowledgment of Protestant pluralism. Especially when imperial commerce brought prosperity, when cosmopolitan ideas gained traction in the provinces, and when warfare with Catholic powers threatened the enterprise, generic Protestantism became evermore integral for what it meant to be British.

Trust in Scripture, over against the supposed Catholic disdain for the Bible, was a prominent theme throughout the era. But for roughly the first half century after 1689, biblicism of the sort practiced by the Puritans and later by free-form Protestants in the early United States receded. Because the Protestant, free, and commercial empire dominated colonial consciousness so thoroughly, Scripture for imperial purposes functioned more as an implicit grounding of authority than a didactic source of instruction. Colonists deployed the vocabulary of the King James Version to proclaim "British liberty," the Bible's narrative of salvation provided a template for Britain's providential destiny, Scripture's moral precepts were championed by all classes (often with the honor bestowed by hypocritical observance), and the Bible remained ever-present for all private devotion and much public ritual. Colonists also continued to debate Protestantism's traditional differences over biblical interpretation, even as they grew dimly aware of the broader challenges to scriptural authority coming from Europe's advanced intellectual circles. Nonetheless, in the colonies Scripture remained as securely a foundation for Protestantism as Protestantism remained foundational for empire.

The Bible's ubiquity meant that its themes retained great potential for specifically religious purpose—as when passionate revivalists blew with startling effect upon the embers of widespread biblical knowledge. Yet the same ubiquity could also make the Scriptures fuel for fires of empire set ablaze by commercial prospects or military threats that had little to do with religion narrowly conceived.

For Britain it was not quite the same.[3] In the mother country, internal Protestant debates over scriptural teaching and tentative doubts about the traditional trust in Scripture possessed a political edge that was much less pronounced in the colonies. Christendom as embodied in the established Church of England remained central to daily life in that country's 10,000 parishes. As such, the King James Bible was unavoidably foundational to the Anglican creed (The Thirty-Nine Articles), Anglican ritual (the Book of Common Prayer), and Anglican theology (where everything had to be shown not to contradict the Bible).[4] The allegiance came down differently in Scotland, with an established Presbyterian church, and in Ireland, where an Anglican establishment tolerated a Presbyterian minority while trying to repress the Catholic majority. But these British regions also experienced tight religious-political connections.

In England's Christendom, protests against either Anglican interpretations of the Bible (made by Bible-believing Dissenters) or against the traditional trust in Scripture that Anglicans maintained (coming from
theological radicals) necessarily assumed a political character. The vaunted
via media of the Anglican established church, far from working as a
strategy for harmony, became to those who questioned any aspect of the
church-state regime what Ethan Shagan has called "a profoundly coercive
tool of social, religious, and political power."[5] Thus, when challenges opposed the establishment's use of Scripture—either against *how* the established church understood the Bible or *that* it continued its traditional trust
in Scripture—it inevitably entailed a protest against British Christendom.
So it was that Dissenters and free-thinkers were naturally attracted to radical, or extreme Whig, political ideologies that featured warnings against
the abuse of Anglican power, perceived vice corrupting leaders in church
and state, and obsessed about the fragility of liberty. As a consequence, the
protesting positions of biblical Dissent and radical free thought often
came close to each other. This elective affinity explains J. C. D. Clark's conclusion that in Britain "the radical critique was aimed mostly against what
society saw as its fundamental political ideology: Trinitarian Christianity,
as interpreted by the Church of England."[6]

The same radical Whig politics migrated to the colonies, but because
established Christendom was weakening rapidly on this side of the
Atlantic, radical doubts about centralized political authority did not so
easily become attacks on traditional religion. Colonists knew about Deist
works like Matthew Tindal's *Christianity as Old as the Creation: or, The
Gospel, a Republication of the Religion of Nature* (1730), which questioned
the unique character of the Bible. They were also aware of controversies
about biblical interpretation that attended the rise of Unitarian opinions
among English Presbyterians and Congregationalists. But because personal, corporate, and theological uses of Scripture did not align so closely
with attacks on (or defenses of) the establishment, the Bible itself was less
salient as an object of controversy. Instead, colonists into the Revolutionary
period were becoming more British without taking on board the British
link between radical politics and radical theology.

The enthronement of William and Mary in 1689 marked a key political
transition. Even through the colonies' earlier, more independent charters
were revoked or regularized, and even though royal officials directed colonial governments by inattention, colonial loyalty to the monarchy grew
steadily. A telling reassurance had been provided by the coronation procession

of William and Mary into Westminster Abbey, which for the first time featured a publicly displayed Bible (King James Version).[7] Two other actions
were even more significant. The new monarchs first dismantled the un-
wieldy Dominion of New England, which James II had created to amalga-
mate all colonies from New Jersey northward into a single administrative
unit. Second, their Act of Toleration gave legal standing to those in Britain
who stood closest in theology and historical experience to the main
churches in the colonies. Of superlative significance—William and Mary,
unlike the deposed James II, were not Catholics.[8]

In the colonies, the process of Anglicization (but without much of an
Anglican church) involved incremental political, economic, and religious
developments. A number of specific events like the 1707 Union between
England and Scotland also contributed. For at least some New Englanders,
this Union held out the hope that the Scots' firmly Calvinistic piety might
promote the cause of true religion in the broader British Empire—and so
encouraged a similar hope that their own piety might do the same. Later
in the mid-1740s, Jonathan Edwards would act on that hope by trying to
enlist Scotland for "concerts of prayer" aimed at the spiritual renewal of
the British Empire and beyond.[9]

Colonial economic developments moved in the same direction. The
growing capacity to produce raw materials for export, to assume a full partnership in the slave trade, to enrich themselves from commerce carried on
throughout the empire, and to purchase more finished products from
London and other British entrepôts—all signified growing colonial prosperity but also closer ties to the mother country.[10]

Transatlantic connections grew just as strong in the realm of ideas.
The widespread colonial adoption of Britain's advanced political thinking
will be a major theme in chapter 8. But the trajectory in political thought
was much the same for other intellectual domains. From the late seventeenth century, Harvard College structured most of its instruction around
texts from the mother country, as did William and Mary, Yale, and the
other colonial colleges that got under way in the next century. For all of
them the major textbooks came from English, or later Scottish, thinkers.[11]
The best theologians of the period, with Cotton Mather and Jonathan
Edwards in the lead, reserved their most strenuous efforts for addressing
doctrinal errors coming from Europe.[12] The colonies' natural philosophers
("scientists" in modern terminology) also oriented themselves toward the
homeland. Whether creative syntheses like Cotton Mather's *Christian
Philosopher* (1721), or reports on earthquakes (Harvard's John Winthrop)

and electricity (Benjamin Franklin), colonial savants directed their efforts primarily to British audiences.[13]

It was the same with religious life. The first decades of the eighteenth century did witness moves in the colonies toward what later became the separation of church and state. A more pluralistic religious environment developed especially in the middle colonies where Pennsylvania welcomed Protestants of many opinions, and also in New York, where a functional pluralism of churches overwhelmed intermittent efforts to set up an Anglican establishment. The midcentury revivals that we examine below also advanced habits of individual responsibility and institutional initiative of the sort that became much more common by the end of the century. Yet even as these developments moved the colonies away from European-style Christendom, other ties grew stronger with the motherland.

After the Bible, the sermons of John Tillotson were perhaps the most widely distributed works among colonial ministers and laity of the middle and upper educational strata.[14] Tillotson (1630–94), after early life in a Puritan family, became a distinguished Anglican cleric who published works against Roman Catholic doctrines and served as a trusted counselor to William and Mary before they named him in 1691 as their first archbishop of Canterbury. His sermons, published individually during his lifetime and then gathered into collections after his death, were safely orthodox but known most for their fluent prose, enlightened perspective, and reasonable tone. The appeal of these sermons mixed compelling content with metropolitan sophistication. Tillotson's productions did invariably begin with a biblical text, but their cachet came more from style than from dogma.

In 1745, at a time of heightened military crisis, a Philadelphia firm reprinted his sermon, "The Usefulness of Consideration in Order to Repentance." It began with a text from Deuteronomy (32:29: "O that they were Wise, that they understood this, that they would consider their latter End!"), which Tillotson developed by reprising Moses's reproof of the grumbling Children of Israel. His application began by stressing "That God doth really and heartily desire the Happiness of men, and to prevent their Misery and Ruin." It continued by emphasizing human agency as the reason for humans failing to realize this happiness: "You see what Account the Scripture plainly gives of this Matter; it rests upon the Wills of Men, and God hath not thought fit to force Happiness upon Men." The sermon then considered the necessity of contemplating the long-term consequences of human actions, consulting "the Law of [our] own Nature, or the Will of God revealed in Scripture," and taking regular opportunities to consider the course of one's own life. Tillotson quoted many scriptures to underscore his points, even as he paused to take a swipe at those who turn from God to seek "the favour and Assistance of the Idols and false Gods whom they worshipp'd, to the Patronage and Aid of the Virgin *Mary* and the Saints." In many ways the sermon represented a standard Protestant effort. Yet the eternal consequences of sin, the wrath of God at human sinfulness, the power of God in redirecting the human will, the necessity of Christ as mediator—these standard Reformation themes faded into the background.[15] In the colonies this example counted.

An even stronger influence from across the ocean reshaped public worship as the long-standing Puritan-Presbyterian prejudice against singing hymns not based directly on Scripture finally gave way. When Congregationalists, Presbyterians, Baptists, and sectarian colonists began to use hymns in church, those hymns came primarily from Isaac Watts (1673–1748). As an author, Watts, whose sermons, treatises, and textbooks were well known in the colonies, was a regular correspondent with leading ministers like Jonathan Edwards. But it was his hymns—published regularly in various colonial editions from 1720 and also imported in vast quantities—that taught Protestant congregations to sing. The hymns in his first recorded colonial publication (1720) included several that long remained American mainstays, including "Alas, and did my Saviour bleed"; "Come, we that love the Lord"; and "When I survey the wond'rous cross."[16] Significantly, in some of Watts's collections, like his *Psalms of David, Imitated in the Language of the New Testament*, for which Benjamin Franklin was one of the early colonial printers in 1729, Britishness stood out as more than just implicit. References to the tumult of the times, for example, was obvious in Watts's famous paraphrase of Psalm 90 ("Our God, our Help in Ages past, / Our Hope for Years to come"). This great hymn became immediately popular as a prayer for Dissenters undergoing uncertainty under the Anglican establishment, but then for all Britons imperiled in the 1710s by civil war and threats from abroad. Even more explicitly, Watts labeled his paraphrase of Psalm 75 "Power and Government from God alone," and then added a worship note: "Apply'd to the glorious Revolution by King *William*, or the happy Accession of King *George* to the Throne."[17] Scriptural themes, allusions, and quotations suffused Watts's nationalistic hymns, but only rarely did the Bible itself figure as the focus of song.

Above all, colonists were attached most securely to the mother country by the never-ending imperial conflicts that followed the "Glorious Revolution." King William's military victories over the deposed James II, with his French and Irish Catholic supporters, at the Siege of (London)Derry (1689) and the Battle of the Boyne (1690) confirmed a Protestant future for the whole empire. These victories joined themes of Whig liberty and Protestant anti-Catholicism to create a cohesive ideological juggernaut.

Warfare—against France's Indian allies, against French troops, more rarely against Spanish forces—remained an almost constant goad drawing provincials closer to the crown.[18] Nomenclature offers a clue. While in Europe the imperial wars were known for dynastic conflicts, in the colonies many of them carried the names of Britain's Protestant monarchs:

> 1689–97, King William's War (in Europe, War of the League
>   of Augsburg)
> 1702–13, Queen Anne's War (in Europe, War of Spanish Succession)
> 1722–25, Dummer's War (against French-backed Indians in
>   New England)
> 1739–42, The War of Jenkins' Ear (against the Spanish)
> 1744–48, King George's War (in Europe, War of Austrian Succession)
> 1754–63, The French and Indian War (in Europe, the Seven
>   Years' War)

New England, as the driver of colonial publishing and the refuge of those most ready to explain the workings of providence, took the lead in defining the colonies' Protestant British character.[19] But by the middle decades of the century, the notes sounded by New England's late-Puritans echoed almost as clearly throughout the entire colonial world. In that process, the Bible remained an ever-present medium for expressing the deepest colonial convictions, but it was a Bible for empire as much as the Bible for itself.

New England in the Lead

In a consistent pattern that would persist through the eighteenth century and beyond, the intermingled glories of Protestantism, Liberty, and Prosperity shone most brightly when they were thought to be under most severe threat. So it was in the years from 1714 to 1716 when the colonists witnessed the death of Queen Anne, the last of the Stuarts, and the tense maneuvering between the homeland's Whigs and Tories. In their eyes Whigs stood for the ongoing progress of liberty, Tories for a relapse back toward autocracy or even the pope. Colonists breathed a deep sigh of relief

when the Whigs emerged as the dominant faction—and so could sideline
Tory hankering to restore the line of James II, bypass the claim of James's
Catholic son (also James, but more often "the Old Pretender"), and bestow
the crown on the Protestant Elector George of Hanover. (The unappeased
defenders of the Stuart succession were known as "Jacobites" from the
Latin for James.) Yet colonists continued to worry about the threat posed
to all Protestant regimes by France's Sun King, Louis XIV. That anxiety
became focused when in September 1715 die-hard supporters of the Old
Pretender launched a rebellion in Scotland with tacit French support.
When Louis died in 1715, and when the Jacobite uprising petered out in
early 1716, all British Protestants rejoiced—including Britons in the
provinces.

Cotton Mather never entirely represented even all New England
opinion, but his acknowledged stature as the smartest divine in that
clergy-dominated region gave his many published words unusual visibility. At that imperial juncture the words came from a sermon preached
to celebrate the death of Louis XIV who, according to the discourse's subtitle, had attempted "to make the world a wilderness, and destroy the cities
thereof."[20] Mather's text was Haggai 2:6–7 ("I will shake the heavens...I
will shake all nations.") In the sermon he referred frequently, both directly
and through subtle allusions, to Louis's banishment of the Huguenots from
France, his sanction for persecution of Savoy Protestants, and his constant
plotting against Protestant Holland and Britain. As he did so, Mather emp-
tied his storehouse of invective on the "Tyrant...[and]...*Popish King*"; "the
Greatest *Adversary* of a Glorious *Christ*, and of real *Christianity*, that ever
was in the world!" and "the French *Molech*."[21] Mather did take time to explain the religious lessons that Bostonians should learn from God's removal
of Louis, and he paused to hope for the day when "the *Spirit of Persecution*
shall be *shaken* out of" Christendom altogether. But his main point was to
sing a "Hallelujah" at this "*Mighty Turn* to the Disadvantage of the
Antichristian Interest." On a positive note, the sermon ended with a prayer
for "GEORGE, Our most Rightful and Lawful King...and the whole
Protestant Interest."[22]

When news of the final defeat of the Jacobite rising arrived shortly
thereafter, Boston's only ministerial rival for Mather's preeminence used
the occasion to provide his view of current events. Benjamin Colman and
Cotton Mather had differed often in their competitive visions for New
England's future: Colman's Brattle Street Church aspired to dignified respectability, while Mather at Old North worked harder at seeking innovative

means to revive the spirituality of the founding generation. But concerning the place of the colonies in the empire, they sounded very much the same.[23]

In late 1716, after the Jacobite rebellion was decisively defeated, Colman preached a vigorous sermon of "Publick Thanksgiving, For the Suppression of the late Vile and Traiterous Rebellion in Great Britain."[24] He took as his text words of the Queen of Sheba from 1 Kings 10:9 uttered in praise to God for King Solomon ("Blessed be the Lord thy God, which delighted in thee, to set thee on the throne of Israel: because the Lord loved Israel for ever, therefore made he thee king, to do judgment and justice"). For Colman, the passage showed that "when God raises up a wise and good KING to do Judgment and Justice, it is a signal Expression of his delight in Him and of his love unto his People, for which they are highly Obliged to laud and praise him." Before addressing the late rebellion directly, he paused to sketch the ideal results that would prevail under a wise and just monarch: "Tranquility and Peace... Rights and Liberties... Vertue and Religion... [so that] the Kingdom grows Wise and Rich, Potent and Renowned."[25]

But then Colman left no doubt concerning the miscreants who had risen against Britain's God-given "*Protestant Prince*, endued with Wisdom and Justice." These evil doers fomented "Vile and Traiterous *Rebellions*"; rejected "Religion, Liberties and Laws"; embraced "Popery and Slavery"; and promoted "the blackest Treacheries, Perjuries, Hypocrisies and Mockery of God." Colman was stunned by the depth of their evil: "Can *Protestants* so prophanely forget their religion, and *Englishmen* so basely betray their Liberties?" He closed by thanking God that Boston's strongest supporters in Britain, the committee of Dissenting Protestant ministers, "stood firm to a man unto the Protestant Succession" and were "true in this day of tryal to *God*, their *King* and their *Country*"—and by quoting the passage from 1 Peter 2 that ends "Fear god: Honour the King."[26] For Benjamin Colman, the treason of the Jacobites represented a negative opportunity to highlight the splendors of Liberty, Prosperity, Virtue, and Peace—all of which the empire enjoyed under the Protestant Hanoverians. As with Mather, the Bible provided the bulk of Colman's rhetoric, but Scripture bore most powerfully when Colman used it describe the mercies of God in the triumph of George I.

The themes that Mather and Colman sounded as they viewed from afar the Jacobite rebellion of 1715 reappeared soon thereafter when simmering tensions with native Americans broke into open conflict on

Massachusetts's northern frontier.[27] Dummer's War of 1722–25, so named after the Massachusetts lieutenant-governor who managed the mobilization, pitched land-hungry New Englanders against the Wabanaki Indians and, most significantly, their Jesuit patron and mentor, Sebastien Rale. Rale, who had been missionizing among North American natives since arriving from France in 1689, would be killed by Massachusetts militia in August 1724. But his role as a French priest, whom New Englanders perceived as a prime spur of Indian violence, represented everything that this outpost of Britain's Protestant empire feared.

As sporadic bloodletting increased through three fighting seasons, New Englanders interpreted the conflict in by-then standard terms. The Indians, in Benjamin Colman's summary phrase, were "also papists and entirely frenchifyed." Cotton Mather linked the Indian attacks to the failed Jacobite rebellion as coordinated parts of a French papal plot. In support of that suspicion, the same issue of the *Boston Gazette* that carried news of Father Rale's death in August 1724 also reported that Jesuits in France were executing Protestants, taking Protestant children from their parents, and carrying out other atrocities as well.[28] The local war slipped easily into an international framework; it meant Protestant versus Catholic, Britain versus France, public liberty versus conspiratorial treason, Christian civilization versus papal-supported savagery.

But because this conflict brought violent death much closer to home than Jacobite or Jesuit plots across the Atlantic, the public deployment of Scripture became at once more sober and more traditional—more sober from the need to comfort those whose loved ones died in battle, more traditional because focusing on New England's communal sin as the provocation for God's punishment of his covenanted people.

Thus, in 1724 Cotton Mather turned to Exodus 15:25 in order to support the family of a militia captain killed in battle ("the Lord shewed him a tree, which when he had cast into the waters, the waters became sweet").[29] A year later another Massachusetts minister did the same by using texts from Exodus 17 (v. 14, "write this for a memorial in a book, and rehearse it in the ears of Joshua") and 2 Samuel 1 (v. 27, "How are the mighty fallen, and the weapons of war perished!") to memorialize militiamen killed in another confrontation with Indians.[30]

When ministers preached on the larger meaning of this Indian War, they referred to the pervasive international schemes of the Catholics, but, even more, they rehearsed traditional Puritan jeremiads that called the community as a whole to repentance. In 1722, Boston's Benjamin Wadsworth proclaimed "true piety" as "the best policy for times of war" as he expounded Deuteronomy 23:9 ("When the host goeth forth against thine enemies, then keep thee from every wicked thing").[31] The next year Solomon Stoddard spoke from the Connecticut River Valley to chastise New Englanders for failing to carry out serious evangelism among the Natives. He specified their failure with pointed comparisons: unlike the Lutheran pietists from Germany and Denmark who were at work in the Indian subcontinent, Britain's colonists were not preparing Indian-language translations of the Bible; unlike even Catholic priests they were not setting up churches among the natives. His text was Romans 8:19 ("For the earnest expectation of the creature waiteth for the manifesta-tion of the sons of God").[32] The jeremiads continued when soon there-after Thomas Foxcroft of Boston applied Jeremiah 44:10–11 to his own auditors and those who read his published sermon ("They are not hum-bled even unto this day....Therefore saith the Lord of hosts, the God of Israel: Behold, I will set my face against you for evil, and to cut off all Judah").[33]

The use of Scripture in these Puritan jeremiads paralleled the way it was being used to celebrate Britain's Protestant empire. In both cases, ministers opened the Bible to define a corporate ideal. Significantly, how-ever, when that ideal was Protestant Britain rather than the Bible com-monwealth, the sharp edges of Puritan biblicism dulled. It was no longer the Bible as only, or uniquely superior, authority, but the Bible enlisted for King and Country. Yet even as Scripture served the empire, it remained potent for comforting families experiencing existential crisis and calling New Englanders to repentance for their sins. Those personal applications kept the spiritual meanings of Scripture very much alive, awaiting only the engine of revival to once again empower "the Bible alone."

Throughout the Colonies

Revivals did arrive at scattered colonial locations in the 1730s, and with much broader effect in the next decade. As they did so, the history of the Bible became more complicated. At the same time that revivals drove colo-nists to deeper personal investment in Scripture, imperial conflicts also continued. As revival pushed toward biblicism, warfare undercut biblicism by featuring Scripture as a prop for the British Empire. Before turning to the revivals' effects on scriptural usage in chapter 7, it is important to ob-serve that during the imperial wars from the 1740s onwards, colonists in the South and mid-Atlantic joined New England to enlist Scripture for the Protestant Interest.

Many in the colonies experienced the mid-1740s as a special time of crisis. At the start of the decade, violent conflict with Spain (the War of Jenkins' Ear) had threatened the Carolinas and the new colony of Georgia. From 1744, another round of battle with France commenced. This one included a significant colonial theater when in 1745 New England militia and a British naval force overcame long odds to capture the great French fort at Louisbourg on Cape Breton Island at the mouth of the St. Lawrence River. Immediately thereafter, news reached the colonies of yet another armed attempt by the Stuart pretenders to take back the British throne, this one led by the grandson of James II, Bonnie Prince Charles. The unfolding of these international adventures took place just after the headiest days of revival in the colonies. The conflicts also brought forth—this time, throughout the colonies and not only in New England—renewed gratitude for the privilege of living in an empire blessed by providence.

In early 1746, when the fate of the Jacobite rising still hung in doubt, William Stith, chaplain to Virginia's House of Burgesses, preached a hard-hitting sermon that depicted in strongest terms the contrast between what provincial Britons enjoyed and what they feared in France, the papacy, the late James II, the Young Pretender, and the perverse idea of royal privilege. Stith's text, taken from Mark 12:17 ("Render to Caesar the things that are Caesar's, and to God the things that are God's"), occupied his attention briefly as he rapidly surveyed Jesus's conduct toward the civil rulers of his day.[34] But the sermon's main purpose lay elsewhere—specifically, to assail the "Tyranny and Slavery [established] by *Divine Right*"; to defend the "Expulsion of King *James II*" a half century before as "in truth, a Constitutional Act"; and to depict "the great Injury and Injustice of the present Invasion and Rebellion." Stith advanced "our Religion…being now founded in the Scriptures" as the great protection against "the present Attempt of a *Popish* Pretender against our gracious and most rightful King, and against our excellent Establishment in Church and State."[35] "*Papal Tyranny*" was the foe. Briton was "fairly rid of Popery and Slavery."[36] Thankfully, "we have a Protestant King; and what can we desire more? We have a King, that governs according to Law," who protects all his subjects against "the least Violation or Encroachment upon…Liberty, Property, or Religion."[37] For Stith, Britain's providentially guided history revealed a seamless interweaving of blessings: liberty preserved from tyranny and slavery in terms

defined by England's advanced political ideologues; a constitutional monarchy guided by laws protecting against arbitrary rule; and Protestantism
grounded in Scripture as opposed to papal injustice and a popish king.

The same themes resounded in celebratory sermons preached in 1745
and 1749 by Gilbert Tennent, a mid-colony Presbyterian renowned for his
revival preaching. Yet when he turned to world affairs, Tennent became
almost as ardent in support of George II's empire as of Jesus's kingdom.
After the reduction of Fort Louisbourg, Tennent hailed the result raptur-
ously: "hereby our Commerce is both protected and encreas'd, and a Barrier
fix'd which may be of great Service to prevent the Inroads of the *French* and
Indians, upon the *Eastern* Inhabitants of this Continent." This success in
northern North America seriously checked the imperial ambitions of Louis
XV, "a proud and potent Prince, who unweariedly labours to rob us of our
civil and religious Liberties, and bring us into the most wretched Vassalage
to arbitrary Power and Church Tyranny." Tennent's entire sermon was little
more than a biblical pastiche. Its title-page epigraph came from Psalm 98:1
("O sing unto the Lord a new song; for he hath done marvelous things: his
right hand, and his holy arm, hath gotten him the victory"), its text from
Psalm 99:1 ("The Lord reigneth; let the people tremble: he sitteth between
the cherubims; let the earth be moved"). Biblical similes abounded, for example "Surely the same superintending *Providence*, that directed the Arrow
to pierce between the Joynts of *Ahab's Harnace* [see 1 Kings 22:34], guided
the *Bombs* to the Annoyance of the *Island-Battery* [at Louisbourg]." And biblical quotations were sprinkled liberally throughout, as in the injunction
toward the end that wove together the sermon epigraph from Psalm 98
with phrases from Deuteronomy 33:29: "And therefore to him let us as-
cribe the Glory; *Whose right Hand and holy Arm hath given us the Victory,
and made us tread upon the High Places of our Enemies.*"[38] In the course of his
sermon, Tennent did urge his listeners to repent and trust Christ, but
imperial jubilation noticeably edged spiritual edification aside.

Four years later the royal governor of New Jersey, Jonathan Belcher,
asked Tennent to celebrate the end of King George's War with a sermon.
On this occasion the governor himself selected the texts, one from Psalm
65 (v. 1, "Praise waiteth for thee, O God, in Sion: and unto thee shall the
vow be performed"), and the other from Philippians 1 (v. 27, "Only let your
conversation be as it becometh the gospel of Christ"). His selection was itself notable as one of the rare occasions when the New Testament supplied
the scriptures for such a public event. For this sermon, the title epigraphs
from the Psalms stressed the obedience that God's people owed him in

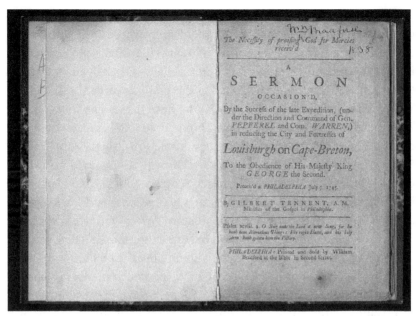

Psalm 98:1, which here adorns the title page of Gilbert Tennent's celebration of the colonial-British military victory over the French at Fort Louisbourg in 1745, appeared consistently as a text regularly deployed for imperial celebrations. (Courtesy of the Historical Society of Pennsylvania, LCP Api.745 B 7 [Am 1745 Ten])

response to his goodness (Ps 116:12, 14; Ps 50:23). Tennent's exposition of the passages chosen by the governor stressed fervently the great gratitude that citizens of New Jersey owed to God for Britain's success in the late war. Tennent did pause to say that the recently secured peace "was not attended with all the Advantages we could wish" (the Treaty of Aix-la-Chapelle had returned Louisbourg to the French). But the balance sheet remained clearly positive: Britain's ally Holland preserved, French power constrained, Britain's armies victorious "especially at the Battle of *Culloden*" (the final defeat of Bonnie Prince Charles), a new colony with prospects of prosperity in Nova Scotia, increased possibilities for trade, and enhanced protection from "the Ravages and Insults, of the *French* and the *Indians*."[39]

The sermon also became a primer in imperial Protestantism when it sketched Britain's history from the Glorious Revolution sixty years earlier, which had resulted in the "just and tender Regard" that George II displayed "to the Rights and Liberties of his Subjects." Similar praise arose for the monarch's unwillingness to "stretch...his Prerogative, to the prejudice of those wholesome Laws whereby it is reasonably limited." The contrast to what

prevailed before William assumed the throne was stark: "Evils...were fla-
grant in the tyrannical Reigns of the *Steward*-Family; whose violent Attachment
to *Popery*, and arbitrary Power...made the oppressed Nations groan, and their
illegal Government a Scourge to the Protestants in General, and a Curse to
GREAT-BRITAIN in Particular." But in the glorious reversal of 1688–89,
William "sav'd the oppressed *British* Nation from the terrible Inundation of
Popery, and Slavery, and guarded the Throne from a *Romish* race, in all succeeding Times." He guaranteed "our invaluable Priviledges, both Civil and
Sacred," especially "religious Liberty," which was "of greater Moment than
civil." He insured that "we have the sacred Scriptures put into our Hands, and
may worship God according to the Dictates of our Consciences." He rescued
all Britain from "the slavish Yoke of arbitrary Power." Thanks to victory in
battle sixty years later, George II powerfully sustained that sterling legacy.[40]

Tennent's sermon, which began with an appeal to thank God for his
general goodness, ended with a paean to the particular mercies celebrated
on that festive day. In a single sentence, Tennent blended devotion, empire,
Protestantism, militancy, and Whig political ideals with an enthusiasm
that merits quotation in full:

> What Words are big enough to express, or Colours strong enough
> to paint the Importance and Moment of that comprehensive and
> durable Blessing, which King WILLIAM the Third, brought to the
> Protestant Churches in general, and to the *British* Nations in par-
> ticular, by being (instrumentally) the Father and Founder of the
> present Happy and serene Succession in the illustrious House of
> *Hanover*, which (humanly speaking) is the principal Barrier of our
> Liberties, the Pillar of our Hopes, and Source of our Joys, as well as
> the Terror and Envy of our Enemies.[41]

Although the Scriptures filled this sermon to the brim, when Tennent
here celebrated the victories of empire, he was certainly not navigating by
"the Bible alone."

The next outbreak of imperial warfare generated much more of the
same. At the very time that revival impulses were deepening personal attachments to Scripture, military conflict once again turned
the Bible into a servant of empire. Several historians have expertly
detailed the mixture of Protestant fervor and imperial loyalty that became especially intense in New England during those next conflicts.
From the opening of the French and Indian War with skirmishes on

the Virginia frontier in 1754 to the Treaty of Paris in 1763, "in sermon after sermon [the New England clergy] lifted up the standard of British liberty against the aggressive tyranny of Roman Catholicism."[42] Yet as the much-noted sermons of Samuel Davies, a Virginia Presbyterian, indicate, this contrasting of "liberty" and "tyranny" extended far beyond New England.

Davies (1723–61), Delaware-born and a product of a Presbyterian academy in Pennsylvania, played the key role in winning civil rights for his fellow Presbyterians in staunchly Anglican Virginia.[43] He was also a moderate but determined promoter of the new style of revivalistic evangelicalism. His success in Virginia came in large part from Davies's ability to rally public support for battle against the French and their Indian allies. A remarkable series of sermons on special occasions during that war gave full scope to Davies's renowned oratory. They also demonstrated the continuing power of scriptural usage as Davies deployed the Bible to repel threats against Virginia in particular and Britain as a whole. The series began with three sermons from August 1755 in direct response to the defeat of General Braddock's regulars and the Virginia militia before Fort Duquesne.[44] It continued with a rousing recruiting sermon in May 1758,[45] and ended with a memorial sermon on the death of George II in January 1761.[46] The last was preached only three weeks before Davies's own untimely death at Princeton, where he had arrived to serve as president of the College of New Jersey less than two years before.

Davies's wartime sermons drove home the same evangelical imperatives that filled his week-by-week preaching: the need to confess sins before God, the eagerness of Christ to welcome repentant sinners, and the righteous standards that true believers should uphold in daily living. As Davies quoted, paraphrased, mimicked, and alluded to the Scriptures, he revealed a mind steeped in the Bible to a degree characteristic of his own time, but almost unfathomable in our own day. Yet most salient in these patriotic addresses, and by a long margin, were the identification of Virginia and Britain with Old Testament Israel, and the complete absorption of specifically Protestant theology into the ideals of British liberty.

The sermon texts all came from the Hebrew Scriptures that Davies immediately applied to current events: in August 1755, two sermons were based on Amos 3:1–6 ("Hear this word that the Lord hath spoken against you, O children of Israel…, You only have I known of all the families of the earth: therefore I will punish you for all your iniquities.") and one on Jeremiah 48:10 ("Cursed be he that doeth the work of the Lord deceitfully, and cursed be he that keepeth back his sword from blood"). Then in 1758, he preached from 2 Samuel 10:12 ("Be of good courage, and let us play the man for our people, and for the cities of our God: and the Lord do that which seemeth him good"). At the death of George II his text came from 2 Samuel 1:19 ("How are the mighty fallen!"). Proportions differed in the various sermons between Davies's description of the threat from terrestrial enemies and his focus on the repentance required to rescue God's people. But the elements stayed the same. Virginians were first inserted into the story of David fighting against the numerically superior Ammonites, beleaguered Israel oppressed by the Moabites, or into similar Old Testament narratives. Then they heard that turning to God offered the only hope of rescue. That rescue, in turn, secured treasures defined almost exclusively in terms of Whig political verities. Only once in these five sermons did Davies pause with a specific word focused on Scripture as such, when he reprimanded Virginians that among them "Cards [were more] in Use than the Bible." Scripture also came into the picture when Davies spelled out the larger meaning of the conflict: "greedy Vultures, *Indians*, Priests, Friers, and hungry *Gallic* Slaves" stood poised against "your Religion, the pure *Religion of Jesus*, streaming uncorrupted from the sacred Fountain of the Scriptures; the most excellent, rational and divine Religion that ever was made known to the Sons of Men."[47]

The rest was ardent imperial rhetoric. On the one side stood "the Spirit of Patriotism," "the best of Kings...[and] the inestimable Blessings of Liberty, *British Liberty*."[48] On the other were arrayed the hosts of darkness: "the *French*, those *eternal* Enemies of Liberty...the Power and Perfidy of *France*...merciless Savages...the horrid Arts of *Indian* and Popish Torture"; "infidious Barbarians...*Blood-thirsty Savages*...the hairy Scalps, clotted with Gore! the mangled Limbs! the ript-up Women! the Hearts and Bowels still palpitating with Life, smoking on the Ground!"; "*infernal Furies* in human Shape...arbitrary *Gallic* Power...Popish Slavery, Tyranny, and Massacre"; "the Oppression and Tyranny of arbitrary Power... the Chains of *French* Slavery."[49] Even if victory for France would lead to the imposition of Catholic theology and Catholic practices, Davies's foremost concern was the assault of barbarous papal savagery on British liberty.

His memorial sermon for George II began with a lament that recapitulated the virtues making him so beloved by his new-world subjects: "GEORGE, the Mighty, the Just, the Gentle, and the Wise; GEORGE, the Father of *Britain* and her Colonies, the Guardian of Laws and Liberty, the

Protector of the Oppressed, the Arbiter of *Europe*, the Terror of Tyrants and *France*; GEORGE, the Friend of Man, the Benefactor of Millions, IS NO MORE!"[50] This address, delivered so soon after the great British triumphs of the French and Indian War, served as flame to heat the crucible of patriotism. As with earlier conflicts, so this war also stoked the furnace that smelted together loyalty to Britain, the prosperity of her colonies, Whig ideals of liberty, and true religion defined in biblical terms. At the end of the last of these wars, what Patrick Griffin has called "the cult of the Crown" reached its apogee from Nova Scotia to the Caribbean.[51] Samuel Davies was only expressing the full measure of veneration found throughout the thirteen mainland colonies that would later become the United States.

The Imperial George Whitefield

That same mixture of Britain, liberty, and prosperity—expressed in the same strenuously biblical rhetoric—also came from outside the colonies in a remarkable document published by George Whitefield early in 1756.[52] As the next chapter on the colonial revivals indicates, Whitefield, the Grand Itinerant as he was known, remained the key personality in all phases of the Great Awakening's waxing and waning. For him to use Scripture in such a straightforwardly patriotic manner showed how securely the Bible that anchored evangelical convictions now also anchored British patriotism. Given his central role in colonial religious life, Whitefield's commentary on the imperial conflict probably meant more over the ocean than in his homeland.

Whitefield had returned to Britain from yet another journey to the colonies in mid-1755. In England, he heard of the British defeat at Fort Duquesne; he also witnessed firsthand the mobilization of Britain's army and navy against what appeared to be an imminent threat of French invasion. That threat prompted his intervention in early 1756 with a pamphlet reprinted seven times in that year, including one edition from Benjamin Franklin in Philadelphia. Ten years earlier, Whitefield had preached a memorable sermon in Philadelphia, "Britain's Mercies, and Britain's Duty," to celebrate the final defeat of Bonnie Prince Charles.[53] It had expressed heartfelt delight at the military outcome, but most of its content rehearsed Whitefield's standard themes as a revival preacher: Britain's sins, the need for repentance, and the restoring grace of Christ.[54] In 1756, Whitefield's title page for his *Address to Persons of All Denominations, Occasioned by the*

Alarm of an Intended Invasion came with an epigraph from Job 32:10, "I will also shew mine opinion."[55] This time his opinion was thoroughly imperial.

All of the standard elements of midcentury British ideology received a full airing, and, because this was Whitefield, with rhetorical flair. Four times he invoked "civil and religious liberties" as the inestimably valuable inheritance hanging in the balance.[56] Just as often he hymned "our dread and righteous Sovereign King *George*" as the defender of those liberties.[57] The enemy was as foul as George was fair. In condemnations that spoke of Whitefield's concern for the colonies, he twice excoriated the French under Louis XV for stirring up "savage *Indians*" to "horrid Butcheries, and cruel Murders committed on the Bodies of many of our Fellow-Subjects in *America*."[58] Throughout, Whitefield repeatedly underscored the malevolence of the Catholic religion that fueled the tyrannical aggressions of France and the bestiality of the Indians. After recounting the ruin delivered by "our Popish Adversaries," "a Popish Sword," "Popish Priests," and (remembering Mary Tudor) "a cruel Popish Queen," he asked whether "*Rome*, glutted, as it were, with Protestant Blood, will now rest satisfied."[59] The answer, with Charles Stuart (Bonnie Prince Charles a decade after 1745/46) poised to embark with invading enemy forces, was obvious: it would, in fact, be the ultimate divine judgment if "a *French* Army, accompanied with a Popish Pretender, and Thousands of *Romish* Priests, was suffered to invade, subdue, and destroy the Bodies and Substance, and, as the necessary Consequences of both these, to blind, deceive, and tyrannize over the Souls and Consciences of the People belonging to this *happy* Isle."[60]

For our purpose, the most important feature of Whitefield's fervent address was its comprehensively biblical framework. While the preacher-in-print did use biblical phrases on two or three occasions to implore his readers to repent and trust in God, much more frequently Scripture drove home his patriotic message. Thus, beleaguered Protestant Britain stood with God's faithful people in the Old Testament—with King David, Queen Esther, and Deborah the judge. The nation enjoyed the opportunity to repent and be spared, as had the Ninevites who responded to Jonah's preaching. They faced the threats of Ahab (an evil king in France), Ahithophal (an evil counselor), and Babel (total confusion).[61] Even more explicitly than had Gilbert Tennent or Samuel Davies, Whitefield identified the Scriptures directly as a bulwark in that day of trouble. "Sacred Story" offered "Proofs, that those that humble themselves shall in God's due Time be exalted." The record of the past could nerve a threatened people if "we consult that History of Histories, that too much neglected Book…emphatically call'd the *Scriptures*."[62] Yet very much

in the manner of the colonial patriots, Whitefield filled his address with biblical quotations, paraphrases, and allusions. These many quotations included
a famous imprecation from the song of Deborah and her fellow-judge Barak
after the Israelites had defeated a Canaanite army; it was a passage that
American patriots would also find irresistible some twenty years later: Judges
5:23 (with Whitefield's capitalization)—"Curse ye Meroz, curse ye bitterly the
Inhabitants thereof, because they came not to the Help of the Lord, to the
Help of the Lord against the Mighty."[63]

Unlike most of Whitefield's regular preaching, this address barely
mentioned Christ or the new birth. Instead, it devoted almost all energy to
defining and defending British liberty, even as it depicted evil as embodied in the imperial enemy. The tone of the whole was captured by a quotation from Exodus 15:3, with which Whitefield summarized the course of
history from ancient Israel to modern Britain: "if our Researches descend
forwards down to our own Annals, we shall be soon satisfied, that the
British Arms were never more formidable than when our Soldiers went
forth in the Strength of the Lord, and with a Bible in Hand, and a Sword
in the other, cheerfully fought under his Banner, who hath condescended
to stile himself *a Man of War*."[64]

At the very same time that Whitefield published this pamphlet, he was
caught up in a dispute with a London bishop that spotlighted the place of
Scripture in relation to imperial public life.[65] The dispute arose in February
1756 when Whitefield agreed to offer regular midweek sermons at a
Dissenting London chapel, for which a license had been obtained and
where Whitefield used the standard Anglican liturgy when he preached.
When the bishop forbade Whitefield to take up this assignment while
winking at ruffians who tried to break up these services violently,
Whitefield wrote a series of letters to the bishop that he eventually
published.[66]

More than his patriotic address, which during this controversy he also
forwarded to the bishop, these letters underscored Whitefield's labors for
the gospel—specifically the "good" accomplished through "this foolishness
of preaching" (quoting 1 Cor 1:21).[67] Yet just as prominent in Whitefield's
epistolary apology were the patriotic themes, including his great concern
for America, that infused his address. As only one of many such examples, at the conclusion of the longest letter he expressed a determination
to preach "especially at this juncture, when all our civil and religious liberties are as it were at stake." And he took pains to spell out the peril of
"this juncture": "if there were ten thousand sound preachers, and each

preacher had a thousand tongues, they could not well be too frequently employed in calling upon the inhabitants of *Great-Britain* to be upon their guard, against the cruel and malicious designs of *France*, of *Rome*, and of hell."[68]

For a history of Scripture, it is significant that these letters quoted, referenced, and paraphrased the Bible almost as much as had Whitefield's pamphlet.[69] The alignment of Scripture with British liberty and against Catholic France was unusual only because of the preacher's bravura rhetoric. More unusual—and foreshadowing what would come later in the colonies—was Whitefield's willingness to deploy a biblical arsenal *against* what he considered the abuses of Christendom. The notion that a biblical defense of British liberty might turn against Britain was all but unthinkable in the early stages of the Seven Years' War. Yet even more than his peers in the colonies, Whitefield's use of Scripture opened up that possibility. As probably the best known personage in all colonial history, and certainly one who saw more of the colonies personally than almost anyone else, these writings published first in London, also echoed loudly in America.

The Broader Landscape

Imperial warfare at midcentury featured the general salience of Scripture throughout the colonies, but also the conditions under which changes would take place after that fighting ceased. Two illustrations, neither from New England, fill out the story for this period—the first, illuminating something of the process that drew the colonies ever closer to the mother country; the second, again involving Whitefield, hinting at circumstances that would alter the dynamics of Scripture in colonial life.

Jonathan Belcher (1682–1757) rose from a wealthy merchant family in Boston to serve as royal governor of New Hampshire and Massachusetts Bay (1730–41) and then New Jersey (1747–58).[70] Belcher, a determined advocate for the merchant communities of Massachusetts and New Jersey, embodied the imperial commitments of his day. He gained office through his faithful support of the Hanover succession and Britain's leading Whig politicians. During his gubernatorial tenures, things sailed smoothly when he could balance the interests of merchants, landowners, and London's Board of Trade with solicitude for colonial political sensitivies. But difficulties multiplied when he could not keep these interests in balance. In New Jersey his greatest success came in uniting its contentious political factions to support the empire during the early years of the French and Indian War.

Religiously, Belcher was unusual as a royal governor for not belonging to the Church of England. Instead, he was known as a "Puritan" and a defender of traditional Congregational beliefs, though in the moderate shape promoted by his Boston friend Benjamin Colman.[71] Dissenting connections probably won his appointment as governor of New Jersey, for he was the candidate promoted effectively by the committee of London Nonconformist ministers whom Colman had praised for remaining steadfast during the 1715 Jacobite rebellion.[72] In New Jersey, Belcher stabilized the fledgling College of New Jersey (later Princeton), supported the religious purposes of its Presbyterian board of trustees, and at his death bequeathed to the college his extensive library. That he personally chose the texts for Gilbert Tennent's celebratory sermon of 1749 suggests the depth of his own biblically infused piety. At his funeral in 1757, he was eulogized by the Princeton president, Aaron Burr, as "truly exemplary in his Family, *reading the Scriptures* and *praying* with them as long as his Health and Strength would possibly admit."[73]

Beyond such conventional encomia, Belcher's religion appeared as more generally Protestant, Dissenting, and Whig than single-mindedly biblical. As evidence of his ideological priorities, the several proclamations he issued for days of thanksgiving and fasting while he was governor of Massachusetts contained the standard injunctions to repent of sin, petition God for the health of the royal family, and trust in Christ for salvation. A reliance on Scripture in these proclamations that included loose quotation was obvious, but detailed or specific references were absent.[74] Belcher was keeping alive the Bible as a powerful underlying current, but in his public service he appeared most visibly as, in the title of Burr's eulogy, "A Servant of God." Belcher's service to the king comported well with service to God, even though it was not a service defined by the biblicism characterizing the earlier Puritans.

Another measure of the temper of those times came from the early history of Georgia. When George II established this colony in 1732, its Protestant character was taken for granted, but neither the organizers nor the settlers sought anything like the explicitly biblical goals of early Massachusetts or early Pennsylvania. In the forefront, instead, were philanthropy, trade, and security. James Oglethorpe (1696–1785), the driving force behind the establishment of the colony, had gained renown for his military service on the Continent and for his sponsorship as an MP of prison reform. The Georgia colony fulfilled his plan to settle industrious debtors as a buffer in the region between South Carolina and Spanish Florida. Provision for clergy, a special invitation to Protestant refugees, and Oglethorpe's concern for Briton's disadvantaged classes bespoke his deep religious convictions. But the colony's preeminent purposes, after offering hope to impoverished Englishmen, were to "strengthen his Majesty's Colonies, and increase the Trade, Navigation and Wealth of his Majesty's Realms."[75] These words came from a 1742 defense of the colony in which its trustees rebutted charges of mismanagement and abuse published by disgruntled settlers the year before. That settlers' document complained that the original charter—no liquor, no Negro slaves, no legislature, no large estates, no clear land tenure—made it impossible for the colony to flourish.[76] The trustees replied that these regulations were necessary for the well-being of the former debtors—and that they also supported the mercantile and imperial purposes of the colony. The trustees' defense detailed Governor Oglethorpe's achievement in holding off military threats from Spanish Florida and his relative success in protecting the colony from depredations threatened by the French and their Indian allies.[77]

Although religion played a minor role in this particular battle of pamphlets, the colony's early history illustrated the challenges it posed to traditional Christendom in the colony's young life: Christendom, in fact, was declining; the imperial struggle against Catholic powers enjoyed taken-for-granted support, but space was also opening for a resurgence of Protestant biblicism. Observers from far and near noticed when Georgia accepted some of the Protestant refugees from Salzburg whom that city's Catholic archbishop expelled in 1732.[78] Oglethorpe also welcomed Moravian missionaries in the early days of the colony. Yet as routine for the period, the colony's tolerant religious policies still excluded Roman Catholics.

The contrasting Georgia careers of two early evangelical leaders offers telling insight into the character of eighteenth-century colonial Protestantism. In late 1735 John Wesley, already known as a "methodist" but not yet having undergone a decisive conversion experience, arrived in Georgia as a missionary sent out by the Anglican Society for the Promotion of Christian Knowledge (SPCK).[79] His efforts at ministry to European colonists and evangelism among the Indians failed spectacularly. Part of the reason was Wesley's unbending personality, but part came from his effort to transpose a full range of establishmentarian practices to this frontier. In their complaint from 1741, the disgruntled settlers included Wesley as one of their chief grievances. His intention, they claimed, was "to enslave our *Minds*, as a necessary Preparation for enslaving our *Bodies*." They resented his attempt to enforce "Attendances upon Prayers, Meetings and Sermons"; they recoiled when he discriminated against ("damned" was their word) non-Anglicans; and they thought he far over-stepped propriety by insisting upon "Confession, Pennance [*sic*], Mortifications." So exasperating did these protesters find Wesley that they eventually "came to look upon him as a *Roman Catholick*" and to accuse him of practicing "*Jesuitical* Arts." The way that imperial ideology was stirring together politics, religion, and military preparedness lay behind their charge that he was out "to break any Spirit of Liberty" and so demonstrate the "strict Connexion betwixt Popery and Slavery."[80] It may sound strange to think of John Wesley as a promoter of Roman Catholicism, but to the disgruntled Georgia settlers, that charge expressed their strong rejection of his efforts to discipline the colony with the standards of establishmentarian religion. In 1737 Wesley fled Georgia in disgrace; he had tried to bring what he considered true religion to the colony, but Georgians rebeled against what they perceived as the worst features of coercive Christendom.

Shortly thereafter, George Whitefield arrived in Savannah.[81] Although he came as a junior associate of John Wesley, and fully supporting Wesley's labors to revive the state of religion in Britain, he received a very different reception. While Whitefield's efforts to serve as a Church of England minister and to establish an orphanage encountered difficulties, Georgians still responded positively. Again, part was personality, for Whitefield had much less interest in micromanaging other peoples' lives than did Wesley. But part was also a difference in methods and goals. Whitefield's ministry featured preaching deliberately taking in all hearers; he made very little of traditional denominational boundaries; he concentrated on the new birth while paying scant attention to church forms; and the Bible occupied the center of his always dynamic sermons.

In his early Georgia career, Whitefield received unusually strong support from Josiah Smith, a Presbyterian minister in nearby South Carolina. Smith, a graduate of Harvard College, had been ordained in 1726 by Cotton Mather and Benjamin Colman, and then moved to establish his ministry in the southern colony. His tenure was marked by controversy with South Carolina's Anglican rectors, some of whom accused him of abusing the highly charged terms of "liberty" (as supposedly defining the Presbyterians) and "slavery" (as supposedly promoted by Anglicans). Upon Whitefield's arrival, Smith praised the young minister for stressing the sort of lively, personal faith that Smith himself had been trying to promote. The era's standard deference to empire—but also a newer willingness to exalt Scripture within the imperial context—shone forth in Smith's commendation of Whitefield as "a Gentleman of the *Establishment*," but also as one who supported his revivalistic practices "so well from *Scripture, Experience,* and the Articles of *his own church*."[82]

The early history of Georgia, as the last of the mainland Thirteen Colonies, was Protestant to the core. It was, moreover, a Protestantism enfolded within the purposes of the empire, but a Protestantism that would be energized not by the forms of church establishment but by the preaching of the Word. In the revival fires that spread throughout the colonies from the mid-1730s, Scripture burned unusually bright. The principal revivalists continued to believe that the British Empire represented the clearest public presence of God in the world, but their scriptural preaching—even more, the response of lay people to that preaching—marked a new era in the public history of the Bible.

7

Revival

BEGINNING IN 1739 and lasting for several years, colonial Americans experienced a series of religious revivals now known as the Great Awakening. A Philadelphia printer, writing later about the period when evangelical excitement was at its height, reported, "It seemed as if all the World were growing Religious; so that one could not walk thro' the Town in the Evening without Hearing Psalms sung in different Families of every Street."[1] Benjamin Franklin, who left this record—along with other printers in Boston, Philadelphia, and to a lesser extent elsewhere—managed a land-office business in religious pamphlets, sermons, broadsheets, and hymn books so long as revival fervor continued. According to the authoritative *History of the Book in America*, the print generated by the revivals in general—and in particular by the labors of the Grand Itinerant, George Whitefield—exceeded anything ever devoted to any public event in the colonies to that time. What James Green has written about one American region in this *History* obtained for all: "The Great Awakening caused a spike in all the activities of the book trades in the middle colonies. Book importation, wholesale and retail bookselling, the reprinting of English books, the publishing of new books written by Americans—all increased."[2] This intensive turn to religion affected colonial life comprehensively, not least in recourse to the Scriptures.

The public use of the Bible changed in the eighteenth century as Scripture escaped, or at least began to ignore, Christendom. That escape took place when new forms of more personally appropriated religion spread as a by-product of evangelical renewal. The Bible most obviously provided the jumping-off point for the revival sermons preached so memorably in so many places by Whitefield and his imitators. Most noticeably, the revivals' intensification of a personalized Protestant religion extended even farther the rhetorical preeminence of Scripture—phrases, allusions, cadences, and quotations from the King James Version—in all forms of colonial communication. Most enduringly, biblical narratives supplied a road map for individual

spiritual journeys that countless colonists undertook as they experienced the
new birth and dedicated themselves to God. Most importantly for our purposes, the manner in which Scripture came alive during the awakening
years significantly advanced the singularly American presence of the Bible
in public life.

It was not, however, that the Awakening sparked disagreements over
Scripture itself. For the most part, the revivals' colonial critics maintained
traditionally high views of the Bible, even as they complained that revival
undermined the good order of society. The leading revivalists, in their turn,
also maintained conventional views of Scripture, even as they innovated in
how they put the sacred text to use. The great shift of the mid-eighteenth
century concerned lay believers who appropriated Scripture for their own
purposes and under their own control. That development, through which
the communal Bible of Protestant Christendom became the personal Bible
of spiritually empowered individuals, redirected colonial culture.

The fullest denunciation of the revival fever sweeping over parts of New
England in the early 1740s came from Charles Chauncy, a young but already
respected Boston minister. Chauncy was disturbed by what he regarded as
doctrinal errors promoted by itinerating revivalists, with the charismatic
George Whitefield as chief offender. He also worried that those excesses
were defended by some of New England's settled clergy, including the
learned Jonathan Edwards. But most of all Chauncy was outraged at the
social consequences wrought by those who claimed to be advancing "a work
of the Spirit." One of his strongest criticisms, in a monster book of more than
four hundred pages from 1743, addressed the new voices crowding into
New England's public spaces. After a lengthy quotation from a seventeenth-
century English Puritan emphasizing the importance of clinging to "the
clear Word of Prophecy, the *Rule* and *Standard* of our *Faith* and *Duty*,"
Chauncy let fly. The revivals devastating New England were being advanced
by "so many *Exhorters*." When he elaborated on why these new voices posed
such a threat, he specified how revival undermined Christendom: "And I'm
really asham'd to say" that exhorters came from "*Men of all Occupations*,
who are vain enough to think themselves fit to be *Teachers* of others." Even
worse, "these Exhorters" included "*Babes in Age*, as well as *Understanding*.
They are *chiefly* indeed *young Persons*, sometimes *Lads*, or rather *Boys*: Nay,
Women and Girls; yea, *Negroes*, have taken upon themselves to do the business of *Preachers*."[3] The institutions of New England's church establishment, including learned ministers and traditional social hierarchy, trembled

under assault. For that assault, the liberation of Scripture from the restraints of Christendom provided a chief weapon.

Whether a single discernible colonial Great Awakening actually took place remains an interesting academic puzzle.[4] Beyond doubt, the evangelical religion spurred by local revivals from the 1730s on did represent a new stage in the evolution of British Christianity. Central to that evolution were the "boys," "women," and "Negroes" who took up "the Business of Preachers" by reading and proclaiming the Scriptures for themselves. From one angle, these new public actors only continued deeply engrained Protestant traditions by turning to the Bible as the one indispensable resource for edifying themselves and exhorting others. Yet from another angle, they departed from traditional Christendom as they read Scripture, pondered its meaning, and shared their interpretations without heeding the formal authorities that most Protestants had simply taken for granted since the Reformation. We return to the Connecticut farmer, Nathan Cole, to show how the personal appropriation of Scripture reoriented his life; here a manuscript memorandum penned around 1760 suggests the way that revival religion undercut Christendom structures. Cole titled it "An Appeal to the Bible." Its main concerns were not matters of Christian doctrine; instead, it railed against the union of church and state, against mandated tithes to support "hireling ministers" of the established church, and against pastors who gained their positions simply because they had been to college.[5] The Bible of an awakened Nathan Cole led him away from the constraints of Christendom.

Evangelical movements of the mid-eighteenth century were revivals in the strict sense of the word.[6] They did not create but rather revivified an inherited Protestant faith. They did not need to exalt Scripture as the ultimate religious authority, since supreme regard for the Bible had inspired Protestants for more than two centuries. They did not need to teach the basic content of the Scriptures, since the universal presence of the King James Bible had spread biblical literacy far and wide.[7] They did not need to invent an appeal for "true religion," as opposed to papal perversions or merely nominal church adherence, for those contrasts had been consistently exploited through the generations from Martin Luther on. Even the revivalists' strong emphasis on "the new birth"—so central in the preaching of George Whitefield and other popular itinerants—had been a main theme of English Puritanism from the late sixteenth century and European Pietists from the mid-seventeenth. The revivalists' stress on godly living did come with a stronger emphasis on the Holy Spirit's work in the individual; but even here, when awakeners spelled out their picture of an ideal Christian life, as in Jonathan Edwards's well-known *Treatise concerning Religious Affections*, their teaching also stressed the importance of regular, consistent good works.[8] In other words, the innovations of eighteenth-century evangelical revivalism lay mostly in the means by which its adherents brought traditional Protestantism back to life. In turn, that quickening significantly altered the course of Scripture in American history.

The Bible against Revivalism

The sharpest critics of the awakenings rarely spoke out against the authority of Scripture that the revivalists so obviously also embraced. Instead, they obsessed over revival "enthusiasm," particularly as they saw that enthusiasm wreaking havoc with settled ecclesiastical and social order. Critics, in fact, regularly complained that the *revivalists* abused, ignored, or turned against Scripture. One of the earliest denunciations of George Whitefield came from the Anglican Commissary in South Carolina, Alexander Garden, in a pair of sermons from 1740 based on Romans 8:16 ("The Spirit itself beareth witness with our spirit, that we are the children of God"). Garden charged Whitefield with "forsaking the *ordinary* Ways and Means of attaining the Knowledge of our Religious Duty, *viz.*, Natural *Reason* and the *written* Word of God" in favor of whims and fancies. In Garden's eyes, Whitefield too easily exchanged "the *standing* Oracles of God" for "the fancied *immediate* Revelations of his *Holy Spirit*."[9] Charles Chauncy's *Seasonable Thoughts* of 1743 catalogued at length what he considered runaway enthusiasm, but he also expended considerable effort to demonstrate that the "*Schism*, and *Confusion*, and other *evil Works*" were "not such…as the *Bible* knows anything of." For Chauncy, the "evil" that resulted could even be charged with undermining Protestantism; errors of the revivalists resembled nothing so much as the evils of "the Romish Communion" and the "*Passions*" inspired by "*Popish Priests*."[10]

Later, when excitements of the early 1740s had hardened into distinct pro- and anti-revival factions, the anti-revivalists repeatedly invoked Scripture to stay on the attack. Thus, in 1749 a Massachusetts minister who took exception to Jonathan Edwards's theological defense of the awakenings began his intervention with an appeal to the biblical standard: "Certain it is, that the Word of God…has either thro' the Weakness, Inattention, and Ignorance, or more criminal Designs of its Expositors.…in all Ages of the

World been wretchedly abused to serve the Purposes of Error, Superstition and Vice."[11] A year later, when revival partisans in a Connecticut church expelled their minister for lack of spiritual ardor, he made the same appeal. The ousted pastor's pamphlet began by affirming that he and his supporters "do really believe the Scriptures both of the Old and New-Testament to contain the Truth of God." Because in their view Connecticut's standing church order was "agreable to the Scriptures of Truth," they called the outcries that led to the minister's dismissal an appalling abuse.[12] The Bible—as such and for itself—was, therefore, never a central matter of contention in the years of revival.

Contention, rather, centered around the makeup of authentically scriptural religion in a Protestant social order. Anti-revival writings invariably featured complaints about the irrational or enthusiastic deployment of Scripture or, even more, about the disorder that irrational enthusiasm unleashed. New England, as the colonies' publishing hub with a strong continuing church-state establishment, supplied most of the complaints, but similar charges also arose wherever revival took hold.[13]

The very first complaint struck against the disruptions that revivals caused. Late in 1741 Charles Chauncy warned his parishioners against following the itinerant exhorters, since that mistake "may lead you to forsake your *own ministers* on the *Lord's day*, to the breaking in upon the good order of the *Town*." In July 1742, he rued the Awakening because "it has promoted faction and contention; filled the church oftentimes with confusion, and the state sometimes with general disorders."[14] The same year an anonymous pamphletereer complained about "the great Confusion in the Churches" when converts became "turbulent, and disorderly" toward their ministers and opposed "Order, Regularity, Decency, and such Things."[15] In Connecticut, Isaac Stiles used his election sermon of 1742 to warn the General Assembly against revivalist New Lights whose social excesses "have a very awful tendency to Undermine our Foundations, to Sap our Walls, to Bury us in a general Desolation, and lay our Jerusalem utterly Waste."[16] Then in 1743, Chauncy's *Seasonable Thoughts* took hundreds of pages to document ministerial authority undercut by enthusiasm, community order destroyed by excess, and general instability promoted by wayward itinerants. The physical layout of Chauncy's massive book testified to the cooperation between government and church that he saw as threatened by revival; it began with an eighteen-page subscriber list headed by the governors of Massachusetts, Connecticut, and Rhode Island, with two lieutenant governors of Massachusetts following close behind.[17]

Outside of New England, revivalists and their critics also took the authority of Scripture for granted, even as they clashed over ideals for religious practices. In early 1740 Gilbert Tennent of New Brunswick, New Jersey, delivered a notorious sermon in Nottingham, Pennsylvania. Its text was Mark 6:34 ("And Jesus, when he came out, saw much people, and was moved with compassion toward them, because they were as sheep not having a shepherd: and he began to teach them many things")—which Tennent directed against those "Caterpillars" who "labour to devour every green Thing."[18] The sermon's title, "The Danger of an Unconverted Ministry," spoke to the awakeners' conviction that conversion (the new birth) should count for much more than formal education or formal ministerial status.

In South Carolina, the brothers Hugh and Jonathan Bryan were converted under Whitefield's preaching and immediately became promoters of revived religion. Hugh Bryan soon became renowned for enthusiastic eccentricity, as when he tried to part the waters of a local river as Moses had parted the Red Sea. But the offense for which he was most strongly pilloried was social. As reported far and wide, Bryan became a threat when he "gather[ed] considerable Numbers of all sorts of People about him, specially Negroes."[19]

In Virginia, the efforts of Presbyterians who favored revival similarly troubled leaders of the colony's Anglican church-state public order. The Reverend Patrick Henry of Hanover, uncle of the famous patriot, wrote in 1745 that revivalists were dispatching poorly trained preachers into "all parts of America, to disturb the established Churches." These itinerants considered themselves qualified for such duty only by self-proclaimed "experiences of a word of grace in their hearts."[20] A few years later another Anglican, Charles Woodmason, reported from his outpost in the Carolina backcountry on the striking contrasts between the worship he practiced and the excesses he observed. On the one side were "Solemn, Grave, and Serious Sett Forms," on the other "Wild Extempore Jargon, nauseous to any chaste or refin'd Ear."[21] The concerns of these critics closely resembled what also disturbed their New England peers like Charles Chauncy: revival, including the revivalists' deployment of Scripture, imperiled the inherited forms of Protestant society.

Yet throughout the British colonies, revivalists drew upon the same Bible that was everywhere fixed as the Protestant standard. As their opponents perceived immediately, they preached with new emphases that elicited, or corresponded with, new effects among the laity. Those emphases and effects, rather than anything new about the doctrine of scriptural authority itself, acted as a solvent to loosen the embeddedness of Scripture in Christendom.

The Bible Preached for Revival

The scriptural focus of the revivals' leading preachers represented both convention and innovation. Conventional was their confidence in the Bible as God's perfectly revealed standard for faith and life. Jonathan Edwards, for example, held that Scripture should be "our guide in all things, in our thoughts of religion, and of ourselves."[22] His student and first biographer, Samuel Hopkins, defended his mentor by noting Edwards's fixation on the historic Protestant standard: he "studied the Bible more than all other Books, and more than most other Divines do.... He took his religious Principles from the Bible, and not from any Human System or Body of Divinity."[23] In Hopkins's rendering, Edwards was unusual in his day but only for the diligence of his biblical study, and for his many efforts to confirm crucial theological points through painstaking reasonable argument as well as exhaustive scriptural citation.[24]

George Whitefield, whose much-heralded and much-criticized itinerancy exemplified New Light religion, spoke frequently of Scripture as "the unerring rule of God."[25] In a sermon first published in 1740, he underscored his own bona fides for ministry with this conventionally Protestant proclamation: "If we once get above our Bibles and cease making the written word of God our sole rule both as to faith and practice, we shall soon lie open to all manner of delusion and be in great danger of making shipwreck of faith and a good conscience."[26] So much was standard Protestant teaching.

Innovations came with the revivalists' all-out promotion of personal religion. That emphasis predominated, almost to the exclusion of all else, in their preaching from Scripture, their teaching about Scripture, and their discourses infused with Scripture. George Whitefield, by always beginning sermons with a text and then offering at least brief attention to the historical and canonical settings of his chosen passage, repeated age-old Protestant practice. He became the public phenomenon of his age, not because he preached from the Scriptures but because of his virtuosity that turned every text into a moving appeal for the new birth.[27] Thus, on "Abraham Offering Up His Son Isaac" (from Gen 22:12): "let me exhort you to look to him whom you have pierced, and mourn."[28] On "Christ the

Believer's Husband" (from Isa 44:5): "But you are blind, and miserable, and naked; to whom then should you fly for succour, but to Jesus, who came to open the eyes of the blind, to seek and save the miserable and lost, and clothe the naked with his perfect and spotless righteousness."[29] Or again, on "The Duty of Searching the Scriptures" (from Jn 5:39): "First, Have always in view, the end for which the scriptures were written, to show us the way of salvation, by Jesus Christ."[30]

The most famous sermon in American history took the same form. It started conventionally with seven short paragraphs explaining the setting, context, and "doctrine" of a scriptural text, in this instance a fragment from Deuteronomy 32:35, "Their foot shall slide in due time." As was also conventional for the beginning of a sermon, Jonathan Edwards linked his text with other biblical passages reinforcing the meaning he wanted to emphasize—in this case references to Psalm 73:18–19 and other biblical passages with the phrases "slippery places" and "brought into desolation." Yet as all who have been asked to read Edwards's "Sinners in the Hands of an Angry God" realize, the conventional opening of this sermon led to a most unconventional appeal: "The bow of God's wrath is bent, and the arrow made ready on the string, and Justice bends the arrow at your heart, and strains the bow, and it is nothing but the mere pleasure of God, and that of an angry God, without any promise or obligation at all, that keeps the arrow one moment from being made drunk with your blood."[31]

Much more commonly, Edwards's sermons moved in a calmer direction, but still maintaining the conventional pattern of brief textual exposition followed by an extensive development of "doctrine" and concluding with "uses" drawn from the text. Jonathan Edwards first preached "Sinners in the Hands of an Angry God" to his home congregation in Northampton, Massachusetts, in June 1741; the next month he declaimed it again in nearby Enfield, Connecticut, where the sermon prompted the much-publicized reaction: in the words of one eyewitness, "a great moaning & crying out throughout ye whole House."[32] That same June, however, he also preached on Isaiah 27:13: "And it shall come to pass in that day, that the great trumpet shall be blown, and they shall come which were ready to perish in the land of Assyria, and the outcasts in the land of Egypt, and shall worship the LORD in the holy mount at Jerusalem." On that occasion he again linked his text with other biblical passages (Isa 24:21–23; 25:9; 26:1–2; 27:1–3, 12–13) before expounding a "doctrine" that culminated in a standard appeal. Yet this appeal, as existentially urgent as his application from Deuteronomy, touched an entirely different emotional register:

SINNERS

In the Hands of an

Angry GOD.

A SERMON

Preached at *Enfield, July* 8th 1 7 4 1.

At a Time of great Awakenings ; and attended with remarkable Impreſſions on many of the Hearers.

By *Jonathan Edwards*, A.M.

Paſtor of the Church of CHRIST in *Northampton*.

Amos ix. 2, 3. *Though they dig into Hell, thence ſhall mine Hand take them ; though they climb up to Heaven, thence will I bring them down And though they hide themſelves in the Top of Carmel, I will ſearch and take them out thence ; and though they be hid from my Sight in the Bottom of the Sea, thence I will command the Serpent, and he ſhall bite them,*

B O S T O N : Printed and Sold by S. KNEELAND and T. GREEN, in Queen-Street over againſt the Priſon. 1 7 4 1.

Jonathan Edwards's famous 1741 sermon, "Sinners in the Hands of an Angry God," took as its text Deuteronomy 32:35 ("Their foot shall slide in due time"). Readers of the sermon were prepared for what followed by the passage from Amos 9 that appeared on the title page. (Courtesy of the American Antiquarian Society)

Hearken, you poor discouraged souls, you that are ready to say that you are cast out of God's sight: yet let the joyful sound of this trumpet awaken your attention and encourage your heart to look towards God's holy temple. Look up, see the door that is opened in heaven, the door of mercy and of hope. See the pleasant light that shines forth from that door. 'Tis the light of the new Jerusalem; 'tis the light of the glory of God and the Lamb. Thither you are invited to enter; the way is open. The root and the offspring of David, the bright [and morning star], says, Come; and the Spirit and the Sender says, Come; and whosoever will, let him come [quoting Rev 22:16–17].[33]

Responses have not been recorded to this sermon, but its depiction of a loving Savior eager to dispense mercy was responsible, along with "hell-fire-and-brimstone," for the Awakening's striking effects.

Throughout the English-speaking world, awakeners of less renown than Whitefield or Edwards were preaching the same way, often with the same results. And such preoccupations were by no means limited to New England. In 1744 Samuel Blair, a Presbyterian minister from southeastern Pennsylvania who conducted the academy that Samuel Davies attended, penned an account of events in his region from four years before "when the God of Salvation was pleased to visit us with the blessed Effusions of his Holy Spirit in an eminent manner." Blair described succinctly the preaching style that was changing the shape of public religion: "I endeavour'd, as the Lord enabled me, to open up and prove from his Word, the Truths which I judged most necessary for such as were in that State to know and believe in order to their Conviction and Conversion." He then reported on the re-action when he preached on Matthew 6:33 ("Seek ye first the Kingdom of God, and his righteousness"): "I came to press the Injunction of the Text upon the Unconverted and Ungodly.... This Consideration seem'd to come and cut like a Sword upon several in the Congregation, so that while I was speaking upon it they could no longer contain, but burst out in the most bitter Mourning." As Blair reported, his biblical exposition had the desired effect: "I treated much on the Way of a Sinner's closing with CHRIST by Faith, and obtaining a right Peace to an awakened wounded Conscience."[34]

Biblical texts like Matthew 6:33 were hardly new in Protestant circles, and the revivalists' doctrine of conversion was likewise familiar in at least many precincts. But their all-out concentration on the personal need met by a personal Savior resounded with unprecedented force. Of course, much else contributed besides new emphases in biblical preaching. The historian Jack Greene once explained "the widespread appeal of evangelical religion represented by those revivals" as a result of inherited religious forms failing "to meet the spiritual needs of colonial populations" and newer practices providing a "more emotionally satisfying form of religious belief that emphasized the importance of conversion, the centrality of the individual in the conversion experience, and the primacy of religious beliefs in daily life."[35] Family tensions, economic change, political uncertainty, imperial warfare, unsettling migrations, and much else shaped the emerging evangelical religion.[36] Yet whether explained in broad social terms or by the specific dynamics of spiritual renewal, the new evangelical style gave the Bible a striking personal salience wherever that style took effect.

This personal salience, moreover, pruned as it nurtured. Above all else, that pruning directly affected the structures of Christendom in which Protestant dedication to Scripture had so long nested. The challenge to those structures came as an implicit byproduct whenever revivalists linked the power of a biblical message to the inward work of the Holy Spirit rather than to any outward religious duty. Jonathan Dickinson, the intellectual leader of mid-colony Presbyterians who in 1747 would be recruited as the first president of the College of New Jersey (later Princeton), spelled out that crucial connection in several notable sermons. In 1740 he preached to his Newark congregation on Romans 8:16, "The Spirit itself beareth witness with our Spirit, that we are the Children of God." His theme was "the witness of the Spirit...On Occasion of the wonderful Progress of converting Grace in these Parts." As Dickinson explained the operations of grace, "if the Spirit of God carry on his work," the Spirit would convict unbelievers of their sin, underscore the great patience of God in not sending them to the hell they deserve, and bring them to trust only in divine "Grace and Mercy" for salvation.[37] A year later he expanded upon the Scripture-Spirit connection at greater length: "the principal Method, by which this great Change [conversion] is wrought in the Heart of a Sinner by the Spirit of God, is *his giving him a realizing View of the great Truths revealed in the Word of God, and enabling him to see Things as they are.*"[38] Not formal doctrinal teaching, not deference to learned ministers, not membership in a duly constituted church—but personal illumination of scriptural truth brought the Spirit's life-transforming work.

If the marginalization of inherited forms remained implicit for the leading revivalists, it was still ever present. George Whitefield again took the lead. In 1739, he responded to an all-out attack delivered by Joseph

Trapp, a London Anglican with high-church convictions and fashionable connections, who charged that Whitefield and his ilk reprised the threat of fanatical Puritans from the mid-seventeenth century.[39] Whitefield offered a characteristic response. He first defended his status as a duly authorized clergyman of the Anglican establishment by referring to the church's written standards, all themselves summaries of scriptural teaching. But then he exalted the work of the Spirit over *any* church tradition: "I am a friend," he said, to the Anglican Thirty-Nine Articles, "to her homilies . . . to her liturgy . . . but I do not confine the Spirit of God there; for I say it again, I love all that love the Lord Jesus Christ and esteem him my brother, my friend, my spouse; aye, my very soul is knit to that person."[40]

Admirers of Whitefield often made the same distinction between his formal status and his effective work. When in 1740 Josiah Smith of South Carolina rushed to Whitefield's defense, he acknowledged the preacher's casualness about form but contended that this attitude was largely irrelevant: "What is there in [Whitefield's preaching], but what is perfectly agreeable to *Scripture*! How can we be *led by the Spirit* or have Joy in the Holy Ghost, without some sensible Perception of it! . . . He is not bigoted to the *Modalities* and lesser *Rites* and *Forms* of Religion." Smith went on to say that Whitefield, rather, properly stressed the essentials of faith, not secondary concerns of "Meats and Drinks" (as Smith quoted from Heb 9:10).[41]

Protestant Christendom had always exalted the Scriptures as the supreme guide to properly ordered religion as well as public order in general. Now during the revivals the sermons of Awakeners pushed Protestantism's traditional reliance on the Bible in two directions that took on much greater force. First was the all-or-nothing application of a scriptural message to individual hearts and minds, and with almost no other concern. Empowerment of those who received this message—including "young Persons, sometimes Lads, or rather Boys: Nay, Women and Girls, yea Negroes," in Charles Chauncy's shocked phrases[42]—meant that Scripture resonated more powerfully "from below."

A second related effect touched one of the key assumptions long taken for granted by Protestant regimes on the Continent, in England and Scotland, and throughout most of the colonies. This assumption took for granted that formally structured church establishments—along with the history, tradition, and deference to the formally constituted authorities intrinsic to establishments—provided the best means for communicating the life-giving truths of Scripture. Most of those who led the colonial revivals did not so much challenge that assumption as simply ignore it. The direct challenges came from laymen and laywomen who subverted the assumption with dramatic effect.[43]

The Bible Practiced

"The laity," in the perceptive observation of Harry Stout, became "the real winners" in the debates sparked by the midcentury revivals. Weighty traditions had made Protestant clergymen the crucial spokesmen for God and to God. In the revivals, empowerment bestowed on laymen—and, remarkably, laywomen as well—meant that ministerial authority increasingly depended on "the trust and voluntary support of their congregations."[44] Direct engagement with the Scriptures provided the crucially important source of this new lay empowerment. As never before, the eighteenth-century revivals brought together the classical Protestant doctrines of *sola scriptura* and the priesthood of all believers. The result was explosive. Leaders of the Protestant establishments had proclaimed this universal priesthood, but by giving institutionally licensed experts the responsibility for interpreting the Bible, they severely restricted the exercise of a common priesthood. When those restrictions melted away in the heat of evangelical revival, it became a much-debated question whether the new situation improved Christian faith or strengthened Christian influences. For better and for worse, though, the crucial first step occurred when laywomen and laymen acted upon what they heard revivalists proclaim about the liberating work of the Spirit through the Word.

Revivalists everywhere held out the prospect that when individuals took Scripture to heart, as spelled out by Samuel Blair and Jonathan Dickinson, conversion and serious Christian life followed. Proof positive for this confidence came from the regular results of revival preaching. Multiplied experience built the great confidence of evangelicals in their message. In 1740 a young Mohegan, Samson Occom, attended revival preaching near his home in New London, Connecticut, that prompted seriousness about his own sinfulness and then a classic evangelical conversion: "when I was 17 years of age I had, as I trust, a Discovery of the way of Salvation through Jesus Christ and was enabled to put my trust in him alone for Life & Salvation. From this time the Distress and burden of my mind was removed, and I found Serenity and Pleasure of Soul in Serving God. By this time I just began to read in the New Testament without Spelling, and I had a Stronger Desire Still to Learn to read the word of God."[45] The next year, in nearby Norwich, another young man, Isaac Backus, whom we will meet again as the dynamic leader of late-colonial Baptists, also heeded revival preaching from his own pastor and was converted in much the same way: "[W]hile I was mowing in the fields" on August 24, 1741, Backus was touched by the Holy Spirit and so "enabled by divine light to see the perfect righteousness of Christ and the freshness and riches of His grace.... The Word of God and the promise of His grace appeared firmer than a rock."[46]

Across the border in Newport, Rhode Island, at about the same time, a young woman named Susanna Anthony endured torments from what she described as "horrid blasphemies" put in her mind by the devil—until she took to heart sermons based on Hebrews 7 (v. 25, "Wherefore, he is able also to save them to the uttermost that come into God by him [Christ]") and Colossians 3 (v. 11, "Where there is neither Greek nor Jew...but Christ is all, and in all"). Whereupon she reported, "the Spirit of God...[did] powerfully apply these truths to my soul. Thus, thus, infinitely lovely did Christ appear to me."[47] Occom, Backus, Anthony, and many others who passed through similar experiences later underwent reversals, doubts, and intense discouragements—about which evangelicals spoke far less than about the joys of conversion. Yet awakened religion really did bring biblical words alive and really did communicate the life-redirecting power of the Holy Spirit to great numbers in many locations and with lasting effect.

The evangelical religion that spread in the wake of revival renewed a well-trod Protestant path. Since the days of Martin Luther, Thomas Bilney, and William Tyndale, life-transforming personal appropriation of biblical texts had characterized the most active and often most influential Protestant movements. In the mid-eighteenth century the potent combination of Word and Spirit resulted in new effects against the background of new circumstances.

The eighteenth-century emergence of the modern "individual" was a product of wide ranging economic, social, political, and intellectual changes that sometimes created great uncertainties for traditional Christian faith.[48] Yet the evangelical religion promoted by revival also did its part to differentiate individuals from inherited forms, customs, habits, and hierarchies. Significantly, the disturbance to traditional Christianity promoted by the new evangelicalism came primarily from the historical Protestant insistence on the comprehensive authority of Scripture. Three biographical sketches of lay individuals transformed by evangelical religion can suggest how the revivals' traditional Protestant reliance on Scripture led these converts, and many others with similar experiences, out beyond traditional

Christendom toward new appropriations of biblical faith in both private and public life.

Beyond Christendom

On one of George Whitefield's first colonial tours, the parents of a fifteen-year-old Marylander named Herman Husband (1724–95) took him to hear the already famous preacher. Arriving before Whitefield began his sermon, Husband heard others talking about the young sensation: "what does this Man preach? any thing that is New?... No, nothing but what you may read every Day in your Bible." When, however, Whitefield began expounding his text from Matthew 25:1–13 (the parable of the wise and foolish virgins), Husband found that this ordinary passage created an extraordinary impression.[49] As he put it, "the Spirit of God witnessed to me" and Husband became "now fully convinced that this was the Way to Happiness to yield Obedience to Christ in me." As was customary, Husband subsequently underwent a long spiritual struggle during which he continued "searching the Scriptures after these things," even as "at other times I have felt the Spirit of God work so irresistibly, that I have wondered all the World was not converted."[50] Eventually Husband grew settled in evangelical faith.

But the story does not end there. Shortly after hearing Whitefield preach, Husband forsook the Anglican Church of his youth for Presbyterians who favored the revival—who, that is, stood by the written Word but also looked for strong inner stirrings from the Holy Spirit. After a few more years, Husband joined the Quakers who favored the witness of the Spirit over even the Bible itself. In the 1760s, Husband moved to North Carolina where he became one of the leading Regulators who protested what they saw as the tyrannical government of that colony. The route from earnest hearer of the Word to earnest advocate of democratic rights was not necessarily typical, but Husband's independence of mind—in politics as well as religion—characterized more than a few who appropriated the Bible's message of salvation for themselves.[51]

Less overtly political, but even more subversive of established Protestant forms, was the life of Sarah Osborn (1714–96), a decades-long friend of Susanna Anthony in Newport, Rhode Island. The unusually extensive documentary record that Osborn left has provided the sources for Catherine Brekus's splendid recent book on the rise of evangelical Christianity in colonial America.[52] In 1743—after Whitefield, other itinerants, and some local clergy had promoted revival in Newport—Sarah Osborn, then nearly thirty years old, penned a record of her spiritual journey. Her first decisive turn to God had, in fact, occurred some years before the new evangelicalism spread, but it occurred in typical evangelical fashion. After a clash with her parents and disturbing thoughts of suicide, a scriptural word brought inward resolution: "while in the utmost Hurry, anguish, and distress, these words [from Jas 4:8] come to me with great power, 'resist the devil and he will flee from you. Draw nigh to God and he will draw nigh to you.'" The powerful result (indicated by the way she quoted "come" in the present tense, though describing an experience more than a decade before) was cathartic: "Oh! how then did I fall down prostrate on the floor and adore the infinite goodness of a compassionate God."[53]

Sarah Osborn's course was far from smooth after this early rescue, for she later experienced the early death of her first husband, recurring economic distress, repeated physical ills, and ongoing spiritual struggles. Throughout her eventful life the Scriptures remained a constant companion, sometimes confronting her with the severity of God and her own unworthiness, but more often bestowing a sense of divine mercy and redemption in Christ. The faith that sustained her was, from one angle, traditional; for example, her image of a loving God was patriarchal—even as her friend, he was also the Lord, a King, and Conqueror.[54] Less traditional was her attitude toward Scripture, in Catherine Brekus's words: "Sarah almost always portrayed God in masculine terms as a father, but she occasionally used feminine imagery when writing about Scripture, imaging God's word as a mother that nourished and comforted her."[55]

Sarah Osborn immersed herself so thoroughly in the King James Bible that hardly a sentence passed in her memoir, extensive diaries, many letters, and one published writing (*The Nature, Certainty, and Evidence of True Christianity*, 1755) without a scriptural phrase, allusion, or reference. Her manuscript memoir of 1743 described the decisive days in late 1737 when she received full assurance of acceptance by God. The key was the scriptural word she found in Isaiah 54:4–5 after in desperation she opened the Bible at random: "For thou shalt forget the shame of thy youth, and shalt not remember the reproach of thy widowhood any more. For thy Maker is thine husband, the Lord of Hosts is his name, and thy Redeemer the Holy One of Israel; The God of the whole earth shall he be called."[56] Later, in 1742, she experienced the same kind of reassurance when she again turned randomly to the Scriptures for guidance on whether to marry an older widower who sought her hand in marriage: "the very instant while I was pleading, these words with amazing power and sweetness set home upon my soul: Go forward, Fear not, for I am with thee."[57] Whereupon she opened her Bible at random and found these very words in Exodus 14:15. She was, in ideal Protestant terms, a woman almost completely of the Book.

The biblical framing of Sarah Osborn's life became never more evident, and never more poignant, than when she recorded the death of her only son, Samuel, who passed away as an eleven-year-old in 1744. When she first learned that Samuel, who had been sent out as an apprentice, lay desperately ill, Sarah immediately thought of scriptures that described Hezekiah in the Old Testament and Epaphroditus in the New Testament as "sick unto death." As she rode to the place where he was confined, a wealth of passages ran through her mind: from Psalm 50 (v. 15, "call upon me in the day of trouble, and I will hear thee"); Psalm 34 (v. 6, "This poor man cried, and the LORD heard him; and saved him out of all his troubles"); 2 Peter 1 (v. 4, concerning God's "exceeding great and precious promises" to save humans from sin); Genesis 32 (God's pledge to save Jacob in time of trouble); and Psalm 86 (vv. 5–7, "For thou, Lord, art good, and ready to forgive: and plenteous in mercy unto all them that call upon thee.... In the day of trouble I will call upon thee; for thou wilt answer me"). When Sarah arrived at his bedside, she once again "dedicated" her son to God as the biblical Hannah had dedicated her child Samuel (1 Sam 1).[58] As Sarah's son declined, she called to mind the story of the woman of Canaan who pled with Jesus to save her daughter (Mt 15:22), the thief on the cross who asked Jesus to remember him "when thou comest into thy kingdom" (Lk 23:42), and, again, of Jacob who wrestled all night with God until he received a divine blessing (Gen 32).[59] At the moment of Samuel's death, she echoed the words of Psalm 71 by recording, "God was pleased to give such evidence of his love that my mouth was filled with praises" (cf. v. 8). Then, in what Catherine Brekus describes as "an almost mystical encounter," Sarah spoke to herself in these words: "Lord, I adore thee as my all. I rejoice in thee as my only portion [see Ps 9:2]. Lord, if I have thee, I have enough. Though all the streams were cut off, yet the fountain remains; I cannot be poor. Whom have I in heaven but thee? And there is none on earth I desire besides thee. Though my flesh and my heart fail; yet God is the strength of my heart and my portion forever [Ps 73:25–26]. Blessed God, though death separate from all things here below, It cannot separate between thee and me [echoing Rom 8:35]."[60] Whatever an observer of modern sympathies might think about Sarah's reaction to the death of her son, there can be no question that in her hour of deepest distress these biblical words became both a message from God and the very presence of God.

As an account of personal faith sustained by a thorough internalization of Scripture, Sarah Osborn's life course was unusual for being so fully recorded. Yet that life also came up to the ideal that Protestant spokesmen had long envisioned for personal growth-in-grace. Significantly, for Sarah Osborn this biblical fixation did not remain only private.

Others took special note of Osborn's life because her biblical faith inspired actions making her one of Newport's most influential citizens. Personal devotion to Scripture resulted in public effects. Soon after her decisive conversion, she began ministrations to Newport's poor for which she, along with Susanna Anthony and a few other pious women, became renowned. Soon she was also conducting a school for younger children. Then, during another revival outbreak in the mid-1760s, she began to host meetings in her home for prayer, hymns, and Bible study. For weeks she functioned as the key promoter of the city's most important awakening of the century. Here is Catherine Brekus's summary: "To handle the throng, she arranges for different groups to meet on different nights of the week: white boys, young men, 'neighbor's daughters,' and 'Ethiopians' join her family for worship on Sundays; Baptist men gather on Mondays [in this Congregationalist's house]; blacks on Tuesdays; the women's society during their traditional time on Thursdays; and Baptist women on Fridays. Since she is reluctant to pray aloud in front of adult white men, she asks her husband, Henry, to pray with them instead."[61] New Englanders with long memories recalled the unsettling conflicts when Anne Hutchinson held such home meetings in Boston slightly more than a century earlier. Osborn took greater care to observe at least some of the proprieties, but her meetings still broke Christendom norms in multiple ways: a woman was hosting men; slaves and freed African Americans enjoyed equal status to whites; the privacy of a home assumed public functions.

Then in 1768, when the minister of Sarah's First Church was dismissed for habitual drunkenness, she and Susanna Anthony emerged as the informal, but no less real, guides for the congregation. Sarah ratified the dismissal of a pastor who had once been a trusted confidant; in the interim, without a pastor, Sarah's house served as the church's spiritual headquarters; and with Anthony, Sarah lent decisive support to the choice of Samuel Hopkins as the new minister, even though many in the Newport church strongly opposed this colleague and student of Jonathan Edwards.[62] Without thrusting herself forward, without setting out to disturb traditional decorum, and without ever enjoying formal civic privileges like the right to vote on the selection of a pastor, Sarah Osborn, by dint of her spiritual status, nonetheless became the acknowledged leader of Newport's Christian community.[63] For that unsought role, her mastery of the Bible—or, as she would have put it, the Scriptures' mastery of her—provided the indispensable basis.

Sarah Osborn's reliance on a personal, existential Bible undercut the patriarchal, ecclesiastical, clerical features of traditional Christendom indirectly and almost inadvertently. For other converts coming out of the revival, the challenge to Christendom was more direct.

Nathan Cole enjoys an iconic status in the history of the colonial Great Awakening because of his much reprinted account of George Whitefield's appearance at Middletown, Connecticut, on 23 October 1740. This breathless narrative describes how Cole and his wife dashed many miles after receiving a late announcement of Whitefield's preaching appointment until they saw a "Cloud or fogg [of dust] rising" and a "low rumbling thunder" created by eager citizens racing to Middletown. When they arrived they were smitten by Whitefield who, according to Cole, "Lookt almost angelical: a young, Slim, slender youth before some thousands of people with a bold undaunted Countenance." The report is just as famous for describing how Whitefield's sermon gave Cole "a heart Wound" and convinced him "that my righteousness would not save me."[64] Yet the memoir with this graphic rendition was only part of a lengthy manuscript not published in full until in 1976, when Michael Crawford expertly annotated the entire document.[65] That full publication illuminates the long-term effects of evangelical revival every bit as clearly as it did the dramatic presence of the young Whitefield. Crucial to the memoir as a whole was the sanction that Nathan Cole's personal appropriation of Scripture gave him to break loose from the historical constraints of Protestant Christendom.

According to the memoir, written in 1765, Cole's moving reaction to Whitefield's preaching did not lead to immediate conversion. Instead, Cole underwent nearly two years of intense spiritual wrestling, consumed by the fear that "I was not Elected, and that god made some for heaven and me for hell."[66] His turmoil came to an end on a day when, after being confined to bed because of anxious depression, God appeared to him in a vision to assert his divine prerogative, quoting Romans 9:21, to redeem or condemn as he pleased. As soon as Cole assented in "my Soul" to God's sovereignty, the vision departed and Cole experienced great relief. Immediately he "was filled with a pineing [sic] desire to see Christs own words in the bible." Whereupon he opened to John 15 and read "if ye love me keep my Commandments and then says he this is my Commandment that ye love one another."⁶⁷ The electric effect paralleled what Martin Luther had experienced some 230 years before when a similar "evangelical breakthrough" set his mind racing throughout the Bible: "I saw the whole train of Scriptures all in a Connection, and I believe I felt just as the Apostles felt the truth of the word when they writ it, every leaf line and letter smiled in my face; I got the bible under my Chin and hugged it; it was sweet and lovely; the word was nigh me in my hand [echoing Deut 30:14], then I began to pray and to praise God." As he went on to convey the effects of this transformation, Cole evoked still other scriptures: Canticles (Song of Solomon) 5:16 ("he was altogether—lovely"); Luke 18:22 ("forsake all and follow Christ"); and 1 John 3:20 ("For God is greater than my heart").⁶⁸

Within three months, a similar scriptural encounter confirmed this experience. After borrowing all the books he "could find on the nature of Conversion, and with the bible they all built me up more and more," he had a vision while in his fields "as if I really saw the gate of heaven by an Eye of faith." The vision, which solidified his understanding of "free Grace" and "Christs Righteousness," became for him "the sealings of the Holy Ghost." As Cole continued the narrative of his spiritual journey, he filled it with references to biblical figures: Heman (Ps 116:3), David (Pss 22:14; 119:120), the Sons of Anak (Deut 9:2–4), Ichabod (1 Sam 4:21), Nebuchadnezzar (Dan 4:33–37).⁶⁹ Through numerous personal and family trials that followed, he returned constantly to Scripture as his guide. Several times he even referred to how "my heart and Soul eats Gods word."⁷⁰

Cole was not just an awakened, converted believer. He was an awakened, converted believer who stood on Scripture as his rock. Whatever might be thrown against that rock, his hold on the Bible remained firm— even when opponents vigorously defended the social structures that earlier Protestants had considered the essence of Christian faith.

The Bible that opened the gates of paradise for Cole became his sword of the Spirit against forces defending traditional Protestant order. In the late 1740s Cole left the Saybrook Congregational church, where he had been a member for almost fifteen years, because that church allowed unconverted people to take the Lord's Supper. His conclusion—that "the Old Standing Churches were not in a gospel order"—rested on a passage from Psalm 50 (v. 16) where "the Lord says to the wicked what hast thou to do to take my Covenant into thy mouth?"⁷¹ Because he could no longer regard his old congregation as "a Gospel church, or Christs spouse, Christs bride [Rev 21:2], Christs beloved one, Or Christs garden well enclosed [Canticles 4:12]," he left to join a Separatist fellowship. After this departure, Cole quarreled with town authorities over paying the stipulated taxes that supported the established Congregational Church—"to pay rates to the hireling Ministers," with a reference to John 10:12–13, was how he put it. These rates, according to Cole, were "not according to Gods law."[72] When called before town officials, he "gave my reasons supported by Scripture."[73] The Separatist congregation that he joined in Middletown met his approval because it "was following the foot steps of the flock in the bible."[74]

One final element in Cole's narrative bears on the argument of chapter 8. When the French and Indian War came to an end in 1763, Connecticut's economy fell on hard times because agricultural production, stimulated by war demand, flooded the market and drove prices down. Cole read the resulting economic disaster, with many law suits and much recrimination of neighbor against neighbor, as "a dreadful Storm of vengeance on the Land" from God.[75] The relevant point for a public history of the Bible is that Cole's heartfelt immersion in Scripture led him to intensely biblical analysis of his personal spiritual life, the religious health of churches, and the workings of providence in society. It did not prompt him to search the Scriptures for wisdom to explain the causes, effects, or moral implications of colonial economic life. The Bible for Cole penetrated deeply, but also narrowly.

For Herman Husband, Sarah Osborn, and Nathan Cole, the Scriptures brought new birth and sustained a new life. They and others like them experienced extraordinary depths of Christian understanding and extraordinary heights of spiritual self-confidence—all mediated by their intense engagement with Scripture. For Sarah Osborn, this biblical spiritual empowerment moved beyond Christendom almost inadvertently; for Husband and Cole the move was more deliberate. For many in their generation, there would be no going back.

Qualifications

This shift in biblical usage does, however, have to be stated carefully. In England a parallel evangelical upsurge also challenged Christendom, but less thoroughly, less successfully, and with less long-term influence. Outcries against evangelicals in Britain, like the 1754 attack from the bishop of Exeter, George Lavington, denounced the same sort of social (and, of course, religious) disorder that opponents of revival like Charles Chauncy emphasized in the colonies.[76] When revivalists stressed God's free grace and championed the Spirit's work in the heart as more important than formal church observance, the defenders of Anglican Christendom took offense. As summarized by a fine recent study of the Hanoverian parish, "Evangelicals seemed to be sapping the theological outworks of the social order so painfully built up by the post-Restoration Church, encouraging the poor and ignorant not merely to disregard their duty and the example of their betters but to social insubordination and perhaps even worse."[77] Yet in the mother country, the structures of Christendom remained more resilient than their counterparts in the New World. In America, a political revolution with an innovative provision for the separation of church and state would complete the dramatic reduction of formal Christendom beyond what to this day has still not happened in Britain. For the history of the Bible in America, the revivals represented a decisive step in that direction. Yet caution is needed not to make a complex story too simple.

In a first instance, the colonists' break with Christendom took time to develop. The most prominent colonial revivalists—Jonathan Edwards, Gilbert Tennent, Jonathan Dickinson, George Whitefield—like their counterparts in England (John Wesley, Whitefield), Wales (Daniel Rowland, Whitefield), and Scotland (William McCulloch, John McLaurin, Whitefield), were all official ministers of established or quasi-established churches. As such, if implications in their preaching undercut the structural order of established Protestantism, they at most neglected rather than challenged the assumptions of Christendom. Such radical challenges did come from the likes of James Davenport, Elisha Paine, and Isaac Backus, but it took time for those challenges to become the rule rather than the exception.

James Davenport's unremitting attack on the established Congregational churches of Connecticut culminated in a riotous burning of theological books on 6 March 1743 in New London, Connecticut.[78] Davenport's public ministry from 1741 to the time of that climactic event, after which he repented of his folly, rested as much on his own sense of divine commissioning as on a narrow appeal to Scripture. When his supporters were brought before New London magistrates to answer for their deeds, they defended their actions by "what they then judged in their consciences *Duty* and agreeable to the word of God, Acts 19, 19" (a passage where converts at Ephesus publicly burned books of "curious arts").[79] But Davenport himself preached under the impression that he had been, as a nineteenth-century chronicler reported, "sent hither with a message from God." Condemnation of these rash acts, moreover, was led by the pro-revival New Lights of New London who, in the words of the same source, "took reason and discretion for their guides and interpreted more soberly the suggestions of conscience and the commands of Scripture."[80] A gathering of ministers, with New Lights prominent, chose Jonathan Edwards to preach a sermon in order to censure Davenport's enthusiasm.[81] Even if some of Davenport's followers used Scripture to defend their rejection of inherited Protestant forms, they enjoyed little support at that early moment in American revival history.

Elisha Paine of Windham County, Connecticut, fared only slightly better when his revival experiences pushed him toward radical separation from the colony's established church. In 1745 the Windham County ministerial association published a documentary record of their dealings with Paine, a well-respected lawyer who under revival impulses had turned to itinerant preaching. Their account began by praising the "Divine Grace" that had brought spiritual refreshment to the land, but they turned quickly to condemn the way that Separates like Paine had gone astray in setting up churches outside the establishment. Most of the errors they specified involved breaches of inherited practices. The Separates, that is, went too far when they trusted "their own inward Feelings" to identify true ministers of the gospel, when they regarded "an inward Motion of the Spirit" as a sufficient call to the ministry, when they claimed that "Lay-preaching and Exhorting" were more godly than the preaching of duly ordained ministers, and when they concluded that "GOD disowns the Ministry and Churches in this Land, and the Ordinances as administered in them."[82]

But this documentary record also included a short letter written by Paine in 1744 that, unlike Davenport's approach, leaned heavily and explicitly on Scripture to argue that churches should be made up only of the self-consciously redeemed (like Separate fellowships) rather than tolerate a mixture of those who did and did not profess saving faith (like the established churches). Paine's fusillade of references—to passages from four Old Testament books and twelve from the New—ended by likening the established ministers to "the Romish church" and challenging them to "find one Scripture to warrant your Opinion."[83] The ministers responded by claiming that Paine was relying on "special Impulses of the Holy Ghost" and by quoting one of the texts most often cited by defenders of traditional church order, 1 Corinthians 7:24: "Brethren, let every Man, wherein he is called, therein abide with God."[84] In 1744, Paine's use of Scripture against the establishment had not yet decisively triumphed over the use of Scripture to support the establishment.

Within a decade, however, Paine's reasoning was clearly gaining ground, especially in circles increasingly frustrated with the mechanics of church establishment. Isaac Backus, who would move from his initial position as a Separate to become the acknowledged leader of the Baptists in New England, published in 1754 his first of many works. It justified ordination to the ministry on the basis of "the special influences of the Holy Spirit."[85] Backus's calm presentation of biblical evidence for his argument marked a notable advance over the frenzied dissents of the early revival period. At the very start he made his key contrast explicit. His negative reference spoke against those who made "a wrong use of the practice of the godly in past ages." Such unwarranted deference to tradition created "a great hindrance to men's receiving truth." He went on to explain: "How common is it for men to say that this or that is contrary to what our fathers held, and so reject it, as if they were our rule." Positively, he held out a biblical antidote for the inherited poison: "If we do not vary from the Scriptures we are safe and happy."[86] In Backus's view, if a call to the ministry led to genuine conversions, promoted godly living, and encouraged faithful Christian witness, then those fruits demonstrated that the call came from God. Opinions that relied on Scripture to abrogate settled church traditions were not completely ascendant when Backus published this tract, but they were clearly becoming more respectable.

Long into the national period, there would be Protestants devoted to Scripture who, like the most prominent revivalists and the Windham County ministerial association, did not object to settled Protestant traditions or who actively defended at least some of those traditions as completely biblical. Their number, however, would continue to shrink as the number of those, like Isaac Backus, who viewed the Bible as overthrowing those traditions, continued to grow.

The Challenge to Christendom

It is important to emphasize that the trajectory represented by Backus shook the frameworks within which most Protestants had long appropriated the Bible. Controversies of the mid-eighteenth century featured, on the one side, Scripture plus traditional order plus a sense of Christendom imperiled, and on the other, Scripture plus the Holy Spirit plus a rejection (or ignoring) of Christendom. Revival pushed colonial regimes with established churches toward a fork in the road: either abandon the inherited structures of Christendom in order to enjoy personal experience of divine grace, or resist claims concerning that personal manifestation in order to preserve a unified, sanctified society. In all colonial regions, the revivals built momentum for choosing against Christendom. Yet regional differences remained important.

In New England, Puritans had taken from Scripture the covenants by which they structured their personal, church, and political lives. When Christendom began to fade, the sense of standing in covenantal relationship with God remained strong, but that allegiance was easily transferred from the godly community of the spiritually elect to new political entities constituted to defend virtue and liberty. In the Southern colonies, Anglicans had found support in Scripture for Britain's Protestant empire. When Christendom began to fade, the sense of divine national purpose remained strong, but transferred from the mother country to the new American nation. In the middle colonies where varieties of dissenting Protestantism had prevented established churches from taking root, the revivals of the mid-eighteenth century encouraged entrepreneurial habits prompting voluntary organization from below. This turn to voluntarism perfected the instruments that after the Revolution created the new nation's Bible civilization, which flourished for half a century or more and survives in fragments to the present. In all regions, the Bible—which before the awakenings had provided normative guidance for personal and corporate life—retained a much venerated source of authority but now within new social and political contexts. As hinted in this chapter and developed more completely in the next, the loosening from Protestant Christendom meant most to populations that Western Christendom had brutalized or enslaved. But the extraction affected all strata of colonial society.

The Bible and Populism

The Awakening's populist approach to biblical interpretation also became more influential in succeeding decades. During the revivals the Bible most often came alive when ordinary laypeople appropriated it in straightforward, direct, and commonsensical terms. Historically, the Scriptures that guided Protestant nations had been expounded through formal confessions, church-sanctioned preaching, and inherited hermeneutical conventions. In the heat of revival, those molds melted away.

Wherever evangelical religion advanced most forcefully, structured use of Scripture retreated. George Whitefield's preaching often took place out of doors or in public spaces unconstrained by formal ecclesiastical architecture. Whitefield preached wherever he found an audience, almost entirely heedless of inherited church orders. For their part, dedicated Bible readers like Sarah Osborn and Herman Husband did not let their lay status hinder them from exercising their own judgment about whether to observe or ignore settled institutional forms. Elisha Paine, Isaac Backus, and a growing number like them spoke up boldly because of the scriptural message they found for themselves, not because anyone in authority gave them permission to speak.

Ironies certainly attended this populist surge. Whitefield, the evangelist who most powerfully communicated the biblically themed message of personal liberation in Christ, also casually accepted Christendom's practice of slavery. Early in his career he used the pages of Benjamin Franklin's *Pennsylvania Gazette* to severely chastise, with characteristic verve, Southern slave owners for how they mistreated their bondsmen and bondswomen.[87] But Whitefield never attacked the system itself; soon, as a part of the effort to make an economic go of his Georgia orphanage, he lobbied vigorously to lift the ban on slavery that this last of the Thirteen Colonies had included in its founding charter.[88] Nonetheless, as a preacher Whitefield's sermons focused so exclusively on the new birth—and displayed so little interest in social structures—that his own defense of slave-trading imperial Christendom hardly mattered to those who responded to that preaching.

In addition, pubic arguments that appealed to biblical chapter and verse received a great boost in the Awakening. By the mid-eighteenth century, the proof-texting habit was a conventional feature of all forms of Protestant discourse and among all classes of society. The impulse that had taken root in the seventeenth century, when Parliament required the framers of the Westminster Confession (1646) to provide proof texts for their document and when John Cotton and Roger Williams hurled biblical thunderbolts at each other, now came fully into its own. Public appeals to specific texts sprang ever more confidently from traditional trust in the Bible's supreme authority.

Spreading literacy, widespread access to King James bibles, strengthened habits of personal Bible-reading, rapt attention to preaching—all made it possible for laypeople to speak routinely of "the texts" (Susanna Anthony), "searching the Scriptures" (Herman Husband), "these words" (Sarah Osborn), "according to God's law" (Nathan Cole), or "one Scripture to warrant" (Elisha Paine). Beyond simply the Scriptures as foundational authority, these lay Bible-readers now exercised an effective capacity for self-assertion—because they had mastered the commonly accepted system of biblical reference.

The revivalists' emphasis on personal appropriation liberated Scripture for individual use, but it also bled over into much greater openness to other sorts of divine revelation, including dreams, visions, and direct messages from God. The revivals' critics had reason to worry. They saw clearly that when ordinary believers used the Bible to escape the inherited structures of Christendom, they sometimes relied on other unstructured authorities as well. Popular preachers who emphasized the personal, existential experience of conversion did not intend to promote antinomianism or a free-for-all of religious authority. But rank enthusiasts like James Davenport and a wider circle that grew confident of more modest communications from the Holy Spirit certainly exploited the weakening of Christendom. The visions of Nathan Cole and the near mysticism of Sarah Osborn much reduced their need for outside authorities to direct their lives.

In the American setting, trust in the Bible would prove much more secure than the restraints of Christendom. But when formal Christendom collapsed in the Revolutionary period, it also meant that questions about the possibility of present-day revelations—either complementing the Scriptures or adding to them—came vibrantly alive.[89] That result depended on sustained belief in the Bible as divine revelation, but it also reflected a range of new possibilities arising with the decoupling of Scripture from traditional Protestant establishments.

In short, the revivals' effect in freeing up Scripture—and especially freeing it for much wider lay appropriation—was one of the most significant developments of the mid-eighteenth century. We examine in chapter 8 the effect of that liberation for the most marginal populations in the colonies. That effect touched them only because it was extended to all.

Imperial Warfare Alongside Revival

For the middle decades of the century, it is an oversimplification to speak of different "Bibles," since the ubiquity of the King James Version insured that when colonists evoked this sacred text for one purpose, it invariably affected how they used it for others.[90] Yet as an oversimplification, it is still possible to distinguish what might be called a Bible of Christendom, a Bible of personal existential faith, and an imperial Bible. The Bible of Christendom entailed traditional Protestant teaching about the life-giving character of scriptural faith, but it also deliberately embedded that teaching within inherited political and social structures. During the heyday of European Christendom, some biblicists, like the Puritans, sought self-consciously to apply scriptural principles to all domains of life. Most Protestants, by contrast, simply took for granted that the Scriptures and the inherited Protestant regimes supported each other.

Those who came to trust in an existential Bible shared the convictions of Protestant Christendom concerning Scripture as foundational for faith and life. But over the course of the eighteenth century, more and more such Bible-believers came to the conclusion that Protestant Christendom had betrayed this spiritual foundation by allowing religion to become nominal, formal, stagnant, and impersonal. Awakeners in the 1730s and 1740s dedicated themselves to preaching biblical truths in order to inspire lively, active, and personal faith. Whether inadvertently or with direct intent, their turn to Scripture entailed a turn away from Christendom.

The imperial Bible, as the sacred book of an expanding Protestant Britain, often represented a simple extension of the Christendom Bible. In that sense the imperial Bible supported Christendom by standing for Protestant virtue and British liberty in the struggle against papal vice and French tyranny. Preaching infused with Scripture also linked those ideological convictions to the prospect of prosperity and the need for military security. Although this Bible easily drifted from the narrowly religious emphases of traditional Protestant faith, it could take on a distinctly spiritual force, especially when Jeremiahs like Cotton Mather and Benjamin Colman, or awakeners like Gilbert Tennent and Samuel Davies, proclaimed that repentance for personal sins and faith in a personal Savior offered the surest protection against Indian, French, and Roman Catholic enemies.

Yet the imperial Bible could also be read, preached, and meditated upon with other effects. By giving a scriptural sanction to ideals of liberty and virtue against the French, it anticipated a soon-coming day when Scripture would sanction ideals of liberty and virtue against the British. When that day arrived, the imperial Scripture ironically became an antidote to the poison of Christendom.

For the long-term, it is hardly possible to exaggerate the importance of what occurred in the middle decades of the eighteenth century. The revivals' undermining of Christendom strongly shaped the way the Bible would be read by all Americans until the middle of the nineteenth century and for many to this day. The decline of Protestant Christendom also had the revolutionary effect of liberating Scripture for populations exploited, enslaved, or marginalized by the very structures of Christendom. But when colonists sanctioned the structures of empire with Scripture and when colonial opinion turned against Christendom, the combination also narrowed the range of life circumstances for which Protestants had earlier sought didactic guidance from Scripture.

Because the Awakening energized religion at roughly the same time that the empire came under dire threat, the Bible for persons could also be the Bible for Britain. This religious-political relationship soon evolved when the personal Bible was taken up into the Whig political ideology that supplanted British imperial ideology.

When revivalists encouraged a personal Bible while ignoring or assaulting Christendom, they also pushed colonists toward biblicism. This movement toward biblicism was anticipated by their heightened reliance on Scripture, personally appropriated, and by their increased willingness to disregard traditional, structural, and deferential interpretations of Scripture. The move toward biblicism also advanced when the revivalists implicitly sanctioned populist interpretations and a plain reading oriented toward chapter-and-verse proof texting. The more such reliance on Scripture grew and the more that Christendom faded, the more likely it became for believers like Nathan Cole to understand reliance on Scripture as reliance on "the Bible strictly alone."

Yet even as the revivalists undercut Christendom as a controlling context for interpreting the Bible, revival leaders also fully enlisted the Bible for empire. When George Whitefield, Gilbert Tennent, Samuel Davies, and other prominent evangelicals ardently preached the new birth and almost as ardently preached the empire, they set the stage for the confluence of a personal Bible with an imperial Bible to evolve into the confluence of a personal Bible with a national Bible.

8

Deepened

IMPERIAL WARFARE AND revival excitement accentuated, but also complicated, the place of Scripture in colonial life during the mid-eighteenth century. To combat what they perceived as mortal threats from the empire's enemies, colonial Britons exploited fully the Bible's storehouse of charged providential rhetoric. Those threats—French papal tyranny and Indian papal barbarism—seemed aimed at everything they held sacred. The King James Version, which monopolized the vocabulary of the sacred for the entire eighteenth century, supplied the narratives, the metaphors, and the very words to name the poison and identify the antidote.

Scripture worked to a different end in the revivals. The imperatives that evangelists proclaimed to crowds out of doors, as well as inside the churches, exploited Scripture more intensely than did the era's patriotic discourse. While the revival message was never entirely apolitical, the tyranny it decried defined not national enslavement but the individual's bondage to sin. Liberation from *that* tyranny required humble souls who would hear, honor, and heed the Word.

Contrasting application of "the curse of Meroz" from Judges 5:23 offers a striking illustration of the difference. Fifteen years before George Whitefield in 1756 evoked this passage to rally Britons throughout the empire against the French, it had served Jonathan Edwards as a sermon text.[1] When he expounded this passage, Edwards did not even mention military enemies. Instead, as he sensed the intensity of revival ebbing in his Northampton congregation, he applied the text to strictly spiritual purposes: the "Canaanites [are] types of the spiritual enemies of the church. Deborah [is] a type of the church, Barak a type of the ministry." His "doctrine" was just as innocent of politics: "When God remarkably appears in a great work for his church and against his enemies, it is a most dangerous thing for any of his professing people to lie still and not to put to an helping hand."[2] The contrast between Whitefield and Edwards lay not in their turn to Scripture but in what they took from the individual text to which they turned.

For a history of the Bible, the combination of empire and revival pushed in two quite different directions, yet both growing from the centrality of Scripture in British Christendom. On the one side, the Bible energized revival themes that jerked individuals out of conventional existence. On the other, biblical support for a free and Protestant empire embedded Scripture even more firmly into a British culture already thoroughly permeated with Scripture. In this trajectory, the Bible supported not just freedom but British freedom; it upheld the reality of Providence not in the abstract but in the outworking of God's care for Britain; it underscored an image of well-being that took for granted the commercial prosperity of Britain. In other words, when British Christendom came under threat, the result for Scripture was domestication. The assumption grew more self evident that what Britain required the Bible supplied—but also conversely, that what the Bible required Britain supplied.

With one very important twist. Imperial warfare certainly made the colonists more intensely British. But to be British in the colonies entailed a different relationship between ideals and institutions than prevailed in Britain. The historian J. C. D. Clark has shown that for most Britons of this era especially, national self-identity involved some level of acceptance of a national church—as well as the alignment of this establishment with ideals of liberty, Protestantism, and prosperity.[3] Some in the colonies also viewed those ideals as necessarily bound up with comprehensive church institutions, though more of them favored a Puritan establishment than the Anglican. Still, more simply paid less attention to whether those same ideals required an established church. By midcentury a few were even asking if Anglican prerogatives might actually be undermining the ideals of liberty, Protestantism, and prosperity.[4] For a history of the Bible, the crucial development was a *stronger* bond with the ideals of British Christendom, but also a weaker tie between the ideal of liberty and the mother country's ecclesiastical embodiment of that ideal.

So it was that the Bible, considered from an imperial perspective, became *thinner* in the colonies as it was simply taken for granted that British ideals represented practices and convictions sanctioned by Scripture. In chapters 10 and 11, we see this conflation of Scripture with British values continuing through the Revolutionary era, but with biblical backing for ideals of liberty coming to oppose what patriots considered British tyranny. In chapter 9, the focus will turn to spheres where no overt clashes occurred, but where, instead, colonial thinking simply took for granted conventional British values about race, the intellect, political principles, and commercial life. For these spheres, at least some earlier colonists had self-consciously studied the Bible for detailed Christian instruction—sometimes even in a biblicist fashion. At midcentury, by contrast, conventions of British Christendom, refined in the furnace of war, defined the conventions of colonial scriptural usage.

This chapter treats the other significant development of the mid-eighteenth century that set a different course for the Bible. And this side of the story follows the course of Scripture when it was unleashed as an instrument of personal redemption. The structures of Protestant Christendom had traditionally served to mediate between individuals and the sacred text. Clearly, Scripture required personal appropriation, but just as clearly it had functioned to sanction church establishment, social ranking, and the privileges of education. Personal reliance on the Bible, in other words, had long been embedded in social structures that were understood as no less scriptural.

As chapter 7 showed, revival preaching did not usually attack these Christendom structures directly, though with radicals like James Davenport an exception and Baptists like Isaac Backus moderate in dissent. Implicitly, however, the intensely personal application of a biblical message offering individual salvation worked corrosively against Christendom. Even when ardent preachers of the New Birth reminded hearers that they were delivering a strictly spiritual message—with no necessary implications for the inherited structures of Christendom—auditors easily missed that reminder if the main message took hold. We have already seen hints of this result for Sarah Osborn, Herman Husband, Nathan Cole, and others.

To indicate further how revival religion drove the message of the Bible *deeper*—and also with scant consideration of Christendom—this chapter focuses on the population that Christendom had enslaved. African Americans were slow to accept Christian teachings for themselves until the era of the Great Awakening. Much else was involved when at first a trickle, and then a steady stream, of black converts embraced Christianity. Yet one factor that fairly shouts from the public record left by slaves and former slaves was the forceful salience of Scripture—but now operating by itself, largely separate from the structures of Christendom. For this population, revivalistic evangelicalism, with an all-or-nothing concentration on the New Birth, led to that *deeper* influence for Scripture at midcentury and beyond. Once loosened from the mediation of Christendom, the Bible produced striking, even revolutionary, results for those on the social margins whom Christendom, empire, and much of organized Protestantism had silenced or simply ignored.

The complexity of this era comes from the fact that the Bible—in support of British Christendom and the Bible apart from the structures of Christendom—became increasingly important at the same time. For some, the mediation of Christendom between Scripture and individuals grew stronger, for others much weaker, and for still others both stronger and weaker at the same time. Thus, even as colonists implicitly took for granted the biblical character of British commerce, racial definitions, political principles, and practices of the intellect, some were also being spiritually transfixed by an explicit—and potentially disruptive—biblical message. The pairing of the Bible for empire and the Bible for personal renewal continued to shape the history of Scripture in the Revolutionary era and long thereafter.

Deeper

A number of outstanding historical studies have explained why the Great Awakening represented a religious watershed for African Americans.[5] In the Southern colonies, where most enslaved persons lived, a sharp contrast separated early efforts by Anglican parish clergy from the later work of revivalists. Thomas Bray, the colonial representative of the bishop of London in Maryland during the first years of the eighteenth century, had led the effort to reach enslaved blacks. Two organizations linked to those attempts—the Society for the Propagation of the Gospel in Foreign Parts (SPG) and the Associates of Dr. Bray—recruited a number of dedicated clergymen who, along with their parish duties, sought to Christianize the slaves. Results were negligible. In the words of Sylvia Frey and Betty Wood, authors of the most comprehensive account, "the vast majority of bond-people found little in Anglicanism with which they could or wished to identify."[6] The contrast with what came later was dramatic. Janet Cornelius in another fine study states, "the most powerful and long-lasting result of the Great Awakening...was its impact in extending religious enthusiasm to the lower classes, including free blacks and slaves."[7]

Many reasons explained this sharp difference. For our purposes, it is most significant that ministers with the SPG communicated the gospel as an integral part of inherited British Christendom, while the revivalists did not.

Thus, Anglican ministers like Francis Le Jau, who worked sacrificially among South Carolina slaves in the first years of the eighteenth century, found his labors consistently blocked by planters who feared that converted slaves would agitate for their freedom. Slave owners in general worried about any religious activity—indeed, *any* activity—that undermined principles of hierarchy, questioned settled social orders, or altered the ecclesiastical structures that they, as vestrymen, dominated. When revivalists in the mold of George Whitefield appeared, they operated with considerable freedom over against slave masters because their financial support did not come from the planters. Moreover, awakening preachers showed scant respect for social hierarchies and regularly transgressed traditional social boundaries. The revivalists—all "methodists" to one degree or another—also favored an ecclesiastical structure made up of local small groups and lay leadership instead of formally defined church orders.

These differences extended into many spheres of life. The older pattern featured catechesis aimed at the comprehension of Christian truths; the newer sought conversion emphasizing Christian experience.[8] Anglican parish clergy frowned on enthusiasm and tried to extirpate all religious practices that looked even remotely African. Revivalists allowed for enthusiasm, if they did not promote it directly. In addition, they were not troubled if the dreams, visions, and voices inspired by fervent preaching resembled features of African primal religion. Anglican worship took place in thoughtfully designed and well-constructed chapels, while most revival preaching occurred out-of-doors or in humble lay structures.[9] While the religion of the Great Awakening did not for the most part attack racial stereotypes, it also did not display the "pervasive racism" that characterized plantation religion.[10] It paid more attention to females, casually mixed the races in public assemblies, and occasionally led to something like black-white friendships.

Above all, revival religion provided open access to a scriptural message of personal redemption—and, consequently, open access to Scripture itself. In the summary of Vincent Carretta, "During the Great Awakening, conversion was linked with the ability to read the bible for oneself. Conversion of the poor led to efforts to teach basic literacy skills to the poor, black or white."[11]

The most important evidence supporting this conclusion came from African Americans themselves, but brief attention to reactions from whites can underscore the importance of this breakthrough. Anglican reports on dealings with slaves consistently expressed worry about the slaves who could read. Francis Le Jau, who tried hard to provide teaching in basic Christianity, turned to oral as opposed to written instruction after a disquieting episode in 1710. This incident concerned the reverend's star pupil, "the best scholar of all the Negroes in my parish and a very sober and honest Liver." Soon this scholar-reader extracted apocalyptic passages from the Old Testament book of Joel that led to trouble: "He told his master abruptly there would be a dismal time and the Moon would be turned into Blood [quoting Joel 2:31], and there would be dearth of darkness and went away." In consequence of such experiences, Le Jau scaled back his teaching efforts with the conclusion, "it had been better if…those that run into the Search after Curious matter had never seen a Book."[12] During slave uprisings, either rumored or actual, in Virginia (1731) and South Carolina (1739), scriptural themes in the rhetoric of rebels led the dominant white society to retreat even farther from promoting slave literacy of any kind.[13] Through such experiences, the Bible in these British colonies became ever more tightly bound to the structures of Christendom.

With the coming of revival, attitudes changed. The most successful preachers to slaves, as well as to free blacks and Native Americans, were not abolitionists. None of the major revivalists attacked slavery; as noted, Whitefield eventually became a strong defender of the institution. Yet in their preaching they urged those responding to their Scripture-anchored sermons to read the Bible themselves. It made no difference who those converts were. After enthusiastic forms of Christianity had taken secure root, a Presbyterian colleague of Samuel Davies in Virginia reported with pleasure that in the three Hanover County churches he oversaw, "hundreds of *Negroes* beside *white* people can read and spell, who a few years since did not Know one letter." This pastor, John Todd, went on to say that "The poor Slaves are now commonly engaged in learning to read, some of them can read the Bible.…The sacred hours of the Sabbath, that used to be spent in frolicking, dancing, and other profane courses, are now employed in attending upon public ordinances, in learning to read at home, or in praying together, and singing the praises of God and the Lamb."[14]

Even if Todd exaggerated, the contrast between worrying about slave literacy and promoting it signified a momentous alteration in the relationship of Scripture to traditional social order. Moreover, the most important evidence of this change came from what African Americans said themselves. Publications by colonial blacks began only in the year 1760, in the midst of an empire caught up in war fever. When slaves and ex-slaves took advantage of print, however, they testified to the effects of a very different fever.

The Biblical Black Atlantic

First came two short works from individuals both named Hammon, but apparently unrelated. Briton Hammon, the slave of a Massachusetts military officer, in 1747 took to sea with his master's permission for a routine commercial voyage to the Caribbean. Foul weather intervened on the return trip, however, and Hammon's vessel ran aground off the coast of Florida. Whereupon he was captured by Indians, then escaped to a Spanish ship that took him to Cuba, where he was imprisoned before he escaped again, this time to a British naval vessel, on which he served on the Atlantic and in British waters until, after thirteen perilous years, he was reunited with his master in Massachusetts who rejoiced in seeing Hammon "like one arose from the Dead."[15]

The narrative Hammon published about his trials adopted a strongly pious tone, with frequent references to "the kind Providence of a good GOD for my Preservation," "the Providence of God [who] order'd" his rescue from near death, and the "Divine Goodness" by which he had been "miraculously preserved, and delivered out of many Dangers."[16] The concluding paragraph of this fourteen-page pamphlet, which provides all of the known information about Briton Hammon, expressed a deep Christian faith but did so with a remarkable mastery of biblical narrative, references, and phrasing. Without further evidence, it cannot be known how much help Hammon had in preparing this publication, but his conclusion deserves to be quoted in order to show how Hammon interwove the scriptural story of the boy-shepherd David and the gospel account of Jesus exorcising the Gaderene demoniac with carefully selected quotations from two different Psalms:

> And now, That in the Providence of that GOD, who delivered his Servant David out of the Paw of the Lion and out of the Paw of the Bear, [1 Sam 17:37] I am freed from a long and dreadful Captivity, among worse Savages than they; And am return'd to my own Native Land, to Shew how Great Things the Lord hath done for Me; [Mk 5:19] I would call upon all Men, and Say, O Magnifie the Lord with Me, and let us Exalt his Name together! [Ps 34:3]—O that Men would Praise the Lord for His Goodness, and for his Wonderful Works to the Children of Men! [Ps 107:8, 15, 21, 31][17]

In this first-ever published work from an African American or African Briton, the author's faith drew directly on the Scriptures—but not a Bible cushioned within the superstructure of Christendom.

The same biblical orientation marked the next African American publication, an eighty-eight-line poem dated from Christmas Day 1760, by Jupiter Hammon, an enslaved man on Long Island. This Hammon (1711–

ca. 1806) had been a Bible reader at least since 1733, when he purchased a text for himself from his master.[18] His broadside of 1760 began with the word "salvation," which was then repeated twenty more times in the poem, and with a direct evocation of Scripture specifying the origin, nature, and availability of that salvation:

> *Salvation comes by Jesus Christ alone,*
> * The only Son of God;*
> *Redemption now to every one,*
> * That love his holy Word.*[19]

In the poem there followed a few more direct references to Scripture: for example, "We cry as Sinners to the Lord, / Salvation to obtain; / It is firmly fixt his holy Word, / *Ye shall not cry in vain.*"

Even more, it overflowed with scriptural phrases employed to describe the gift of salvation that supplied the poem with its grand theme: "Lord unto whom now shall we go" (paraphrasing Jn 6:68); "Ho! every one that hunger hath" (echoing Isa 55:1); "Salvation be thy leading Staff" (alluding to Ps 23:4); "Our hearts and Souls do meet again, / To magnify thy Name" (echoing Ps 34:3); and "Now Glory be to God on High" (derived from Lk 2:14).[20] Yet as with Briton Hammon's narrative, Jupiter Hammon's poem kept its focus tightly on the salvific message derived from the Scriptures, rather than anything imperial, military, cultural, or political.

Eighteen years later Hammon published another broadside poem, this one to honor a former slave whose publications had gained much wider recognition than Hammon's own efforts. Yet the poem's title, its themes, and its layout on the page all bespoke the same nexus of Bible, person, and Christian salvation as found in his "Evening Thought" from 1760.

This later poem appeared as "An Address to Miss Phillis Wheatly [*sic*], Ethiopian Poetess, in Boston, who came from Africa at eight years of age, and soon became acquainted with the gospel of Jesus Christ."[21] Its first stanza announced the theme that the remaining twenty stanzas unfolded:

> *O Come you pious youth! adore*
> * The wisdom of thy God,*
> *In bringing thee from distant shore,*
> * To learn his holy word.*

HARTFORD, August 4, 1778.

AN ADDRESS to Miss PHILLIS WHEATLY, Ethiopian Po-
etefs, in Boston, who came from Africa at eight years of age, and
soon became acquainted with the gospel of Jesus Christ.

Miss WHEATLY; pray give me leave to expres as follows:

1.
O Come you pious youth! adore
The wisdom of thy God,
In bringing thee from distant shore,
To learn his holy word.

2.
Thou mightst been left behind,
Amidst a dark abode;
God's tender mercy still combin'd,
Thou hast the holy word.

Psal. cxxxvi. 1, 2, 3.

3.
Fair wisdom's ways are paths of peace,
And they that walk therein,
Shall reap the joys that never cease,
And Christ shall be their king.

Psal. i 1, 2, 3.
Prov. iii. 7.

4.
God's tender mercy brought thee here;
Tost o'er the raging main;
In Christian faith thou hast a share,
Worth all the gold of Spain.

Psal. ciii. 1, 2, 3, 4.

5.
While thousands tossed by the sea,
And others settled down,
God's tender mercy set thee free,
From dangers still unknown.

Death.

6.
That thou a pattern still might be,
To youth of Boston town,
The blessed Jesus set thee free,
From every sinful wound.

2 Cor. v. 10.

7.
The blessed Jesus, who came down,
Unvail'd his sacred face,
To cleanse the soul of every wound,
And give repenting grace.

Rom. v. 21.

8.
That we poor sinners may obtain
The pardon of our sin;
Dear blessed Jesus now constrain,
And bring us flocking in.

Psal. xxxiv. 6, 7, 8.

9.
Come you, Phillis, now aspire,
And seek the living God,
So step by step thou mayst go higher,
Till perfect in the word.

Matth. vii. 7, 8.

10.
While thousands mov'd to distant shore,
And others left behind,
The blessed Jesus still adore,
Implant this in thy mind.

Psal. lxxxix. 1.

11.
Thou hast left the heathen shore,
Thro' mercy of the Lord;

Psal. xxxiv. 1, 2, 3.

Among the heathen live no more,
Come magnify thy God.

12.
I pray the living God may be,
The shepherd of thy soul;
His tender mercies still are free,
His mysteries to us fold.

Psal. lxxx. 1, 2, 3.

13.
Thou, Phillis, when thou hunger hast,
Or pantest for thy God;
Jesus Christ is thy relief,
Thou hast the holy word.

Psal. xliii. 1, 2, 3.

14.
The bounteous mercies of the Lord,
Are bid beyond the sky,
And holy souls that love his word,
Shall taste them when they die.

Psal. xvi. 10, 11.

15.
These bounteous mercies are from God,
The merits of his Son;
The humble soul that loves his word,
He chooses for his own.

Psal. xxxiv 15.

16.
Come, dear Phillis, be advis'd,
To drink Samaria's flood;
There nothing is that shall suffice,
But Christ's redeming blood.

John iv. 13 14.

17.
While thousands muse with earthly toys,
And range about the street,
Dear Phillis, seek for heaven's joys,
Where we do hope to meet.

Matth. vi. 33.

18.
When God shall send his summons down,
And number saints together,
Blest angels chant, (triumphant found)
Come live with me for ever.

Psal. cxvi. 15.

19.
The humble soul shall fly to God,
And leave the things of time,
Start forth as 'twere at the first word,
To taste things more divine.

Mat. v. 3, 8.

20.
Behold! the soul shall waft away,
Whene'er we come to die,
And leave its cottage made of clay,
In twinkling of an eye.

Cor. xv. 51, 52, 53.

21.
Now glory be to the Most High,
United praises given,
By all on earth, incessantly,
And all the host of heav'n.

Psal. cl. 6.

Composed by JUPITER HAMMON, a Negro Man belonging to Mr. JOSEPH LLOYD, of Queen's Village,
on Long-Island, now in Hartford.

* * * The above lines are published by the Author, and a number of his friends, who desire to join with him in their best
regards to Miss WHEATLY.

Jupiter Hammon's "Address" to Phillis Wheatley from 1778 illustrates both
the literary skill of this African American slave and his thorough familiarity
with Scripture. (Courtesy of the Connecticut Historical Society)

That theme was the Christian redemption Wheatley experienced as a result of her forced migration to Boston as a child: "That thou a pattern still might be, / To youth of Boston town, / The blessed Jesus set thee free, / From every sinful wound."

On the page, the format of this poem stood out, resembling the layout that Cotton Mather had employed when he supplied a specific reference to biblical chapter and verse to each section of his proposed laws for early Massachusetts. So Jupiter Hammon in his poem to Phillis Wheatley glossed each stanza with a scriptural reference, as for the first, Ecclesiastes 12:1 ("Remember now thy Creator in the days of thy youth").[22] By 1778, Phillis Wheatley's poems had ranged far beyond the drama of salvation, narrowly construed. But because her broader poetic efforts nonetheless regularly featured the same elements that Hammon stressed, those efforts also underscored the relationships rooted in Scripture that infused this celebratory broadside.

For his part, only a few years later Hammon published a pamphlet of advice "to the Negroes in the State of New-York." The scripture on its title page came from Acts 10:34–35: "Of a truth I perceive that God is no respecter of persons: But in every Nation, he that feareth him and worketh righteousness, is accepted with him." That passage gave Hammon the license to say explicitly what had been implicit in his poems: "If there was no Bible, it would be no matter whether you could read or not.... In the bible God has told us every thing it is necessary we should know, in order to be happy here and hereafter.... [The Bible] tells us that those who do repent, and believe, and are friends to Christ, shall have many trials and sufferings in this world, but that they shall be happy forever, after death, and reign with Christ to all eternity."[23]

The Wheatley Exception

Phillis Wheatley has rightly taken her place as the most prominent African American writer in the Revolutionary period.[24] As an author she shared with all other publishing African Americans and African Britons of her age an intense reliance on Scripture. Yet she was also the only black author who employed Scripture for self-consciously imperial purposes in the manner of her white contemporaries. Her life, therefore, illustrates both the deeper and thinner biblical presence of this era.

In 1761, as a girl of about eight years of age recently snatched from Ghana or Gambia, Phillis was purchased by John Wheatley, a prosperous Boston merchant. Wheatley and his wife Susanna were members of the New South Congregational Church, where Susanna avidly supported the labors of George Whitefield. The itinerant evangelist may have received hospitality in the Wheatley home during the years that Phillis served the family. For her part, the young enslaved girl immediately displayed unusual intellectual capacities, which the Wheatleys encouraged. The Bible featured prominently in her rapid learning curve but in a context significantly different from all other contemporary black authors. When in 1773 the collection of poems that secured her reputation appeared in London, John Wheatley prefaced the work with a letter testifying that these writings represented authentic productions from Phillis's own hand. He did so by documenting her early mastery of the Scriptures: "Without any Assistance from School Education, and by only what she was taught in the Family, she, in sixteen Months Time from her arrival, attained the English Language, to which she was an utter Stranger before, to such a Degree, as to read any, the most difficult Parts of the Sacred Writings, to the great Astonishment of all who heard her."[25]

Also prefaced to this volume was a notice signed by eighteen notable Bostonians, placed prominently "to assure the World" that the poems were actually "written by Phillis, a young Negro Girl, who was but a few Years since, brought an uncultivated Barbarian from *Africa*, and has ever since been, and now is, under the Disadvantage of serving as a Slave in a Family in this Town."[26] The attestation spoke not only to the authenticity of Phillis's poems but also to her singular position as a black woman recognized and approved by high ranks of late-colonial New England Christendom. The eighteen men who signed the testimonial included the Massachusetts governor and lieutenant-governor, Thomas Hutchinson and Andrew Oliver; nine leading merchants including Harrison Gray and John Hancock; along with seven well-known ministers, including Whitefield's leading opponent, Charles Chauncey, and two of New England's few Congregational ministers to become Loyalists during the Revolution, Mather Byles and Ebenezer Pemberton.[27] The verses making up the book, so authenticated, showed as did Phillis's other writings both her immersion in Scripture and her standing within the structures of Britain's imperial Christendom. For black authors of the period it was a unique combination.

Phillis published her first poem in 1767, a contribution to the *Newport Mercury*, which in the style of Alexander Pope deployed iambic rhyming couplets to celebrate the rescue of a storm-tossed ship voyaging from Boston to Nantucket.[28] It ended with two pious lines, but devoid of specific biblical reference:

> *Blest Soul, which sees the Day while Light doth shine,*
> *To guide his Steps to trace the Mark divine.*[29]

The poem that catapulted her to international renown was similar in its formal classicism, similar in its direct reference to events in the wider imperial world, but more directly biblical in its metaphors and allusions. This poem, an elegy on the death of George Whitefield, appeared shortly after the revivalist's death in September 1770. As it happened, the month before he died Whitefield had preached four times in Boston's Old South Church, where Phillis would be baptized a year later and where she may have heard the renowned revivalist.[30] Phillis's evocation of the departed preacher used biblical terms to highlight the liberating power of Christian redemption—in this case, with special reference to the meaning of that redemption for the enslaved. The combination of Scripture, liberation, and redemption for any and all constituted the heart of the poem:

> *He offer'd THAT he did himself receive,*
> *A greater gift not GOD himself can give:*
> *He urg'd the need of HIM to every one;*
> *It was no less than GOD's co-equal SON!*
> *Take HIM ye wretched for your good;*
> *Take HIM ye starving souls to be your food. [Isa 55:1]*
> *Ye thirsty, come to his life giving stream; [Jn 4:10]*
> *Ye Preachers, take him for your joyful theme:*
> *Take HIM, "my dear Americans," he said,*
> *Be your complaints in his kind bosom laid:*
> *Take HIM ye Africans, he longs for you;*
> *Impartial SAVIOUR, is his title due;*
> *If you will chuse to walk in grace's road,*
> *You should be sons, and kings, and priests to GOD. [Rev 1:6]*[31]

In revisions for her London collection of 1773, *Poems on Various Subjects, Religious and Moral,* Wheatley added more biblical allusions. They included references to Whitefield as "the prophet in his towering flight" (cf. Elijah, 2 Kings 2:11) and how "he has wrestled with his God by night" (cf. Jacob, Gen 32:24–32).[32]

The easy familiarity with Scripture evident in this elegy for Whitefield characterized all of Phillis Wheatley's writing, but with a significant difference from the period's other black authors. She became a literary sensation in both New England and England because as an untutored slave she displayed mastery of classical allusions and followed the fashionable poetic conventions of her age. For his poems, Jupiter Hammon employed the populist ballad form—well known in hymnody as "Common Meter (CM)," of which Isaac Watts was the nonpareil master. In her poems, Phillis aimed higher. Thus, her celebrated 1773 book began with an address "To Maecenas," a classical reference to the patron in ancient Rome of Horace and Virgil and, by extension, a salute to this book's dedicatee, the Countess of Huntingdon:

> MAECENAS, you, beneath the myrtle shade,
> Read o'er what poets sung, and shepherds play'd.
> What felt those poets but you feel the same?
> Does not your soul possess the sacred flame?[33]

Within the conventions of such high-art verse, Phillis found full scope for scriptural reference. Her book's longest poem, "Goliath of Gath," came with a biblical reference as subtitle: "1 Sam. Chap. xvii." It retold the famous story of the young shepherd David, called from his sheep to rescue Israel, but did so with self-conscious artistry:

> And now the youth the forceful pebble flung,
> Philistia trembled as it whizz'd along:
> In his dread forehead, where the helmet ends,
> Just o'er the brows the well-aim'd stone descends,
> It pierc'd the skull, and shatter'd all the brain,
> Prone on his face he tumbled to the plain.[34]

Other poems were almost as full of biblical quotation or allusion, like a meditation titled "Isaiah lxiii.1–8" that featured Christ speaking as the fulfillment of prophetic words from the Old Testament:

> "Mine was the act," th'Almighty Saviour said,
> And shook the dazzling glories of his head,
> "When all forsook I trod the press alone, [Isa 63:3a, 6a]
> And conquer'd by omnipotence my own;
> For man's release sustain'd the pond'rous load,
> For man the wrath of an immortal God: [Isa 63:3b]
> To execute th'Eternal's dread command
> My soul I sacrfic'd with willing hand."[35]

Yet most of the poems in this first-ever book by an African American (and, with Sarah Osborn's, one of the very first published by a colonial woman), though set consistently in a Christian frame of reference, did not feature Scripture itself. Even the most directly religious, including an interpretation of her enslavement as providential, were as much theological as directly biblical:

> 'TWAS mercy brought me from my Pagan land,
> Taught my benighted soul to understand
> That there's a God, that there's a Saviour too:
> Once I redemption neither sought nor knew.
> Some view our sable race with scornful eye,
> "Their colour is a diabolic die."
> Remember, Christians, Negroes, black as Cain, [Gen 4:8–16]
> May be refin'd, and join th'angelic train.[36]

Phillis Wheatley's voice was distinctive as "a young Negro girl" of obvious piety. Yet it was also distinctive for its self-conscious positioning within an imperial frame. The original version of her elegy for Whitefield praised him for taking up the cause of the colonies during the French and Indian War, while adding to his advocacy for them during the Stamp Act Crisis of 1765. She also wrote often with the establishment in view. Besides the dedication of her London book to the Countess of Huntingdon, that volume included poems for the Earl of Dartmouth, secretary of state for the colonies, and for several "Gentlemen and Ladies" among Boston's elite. Her poem, "To the KING's Most Excellent Majesty" provided a footnote for the lines—"Midst the remembrance of thy favours past / The meanest peasants most admire the last"—in order to specify "the Repeal of the Stamp Act" as the last and greatest of George III's gifts to the colony.[37]

Only a few years later, as another indication for how easily colonists could transform a sanctified British Empire into a sanctified new nation, Phillis penned memorial poems to honor patriot military leaders and "His Excellency George Washington."[38] At the conclusion of the Revolutionary War, she also published an encomium to "Liberty and Peace" that hailed the patriotic triumph with the same ideological conventions espoused by many of her American peers. It included these lines of thanksgiving to Louis XVI for sending the French fleet to aid the patriots' effort:

> The generous Prince th'impending vengeance eyes,
> Sees the fierce Wrong, and to the rescue flies.

*Perish that Thirst of boundless Power, that drew
On Albions Head the Curse to Tyrants due.*[39]

For Phillis Wheatley, an ability to deploy the Bible's resources in verse confirmed her abilities as a real poet. Her fame as an author began with her
elegy to Whitefield, the key figure in the evangelical revival, even as her
poems included many references to the spiritual redemption wrought by
the gospel message that Whitefield preached. But, unlike the published
writings of other black authors, Wheatley's also celebrated the high offi-
cialdom of imperial Britain, and then the new nation. Many of her poems
memorialized significant events in the political sphere. All of her verse
resembled in form the fashionable literature of the age. It was a marvel for
a young black woman to publish well-crafted poems; the themes of her
poetry, however ably expressed, were conventional.[40]

The More Common Pattern

The other black voices that addressed the public sounded much more like
the two Hammons than Phillis Wheatley. For Wheatley, the ability to read the
Bible confirmed her right to be heard; for the others, hearing or reading
Scripture accomplished its own purpose.

In 1772, James Albert Ukawsaw Gronniosaw published in England a
narrative of his life dedicated, like Phillis Wheatley's volume, to the Countess
of Huntingdon. The Countess' well-known patronage of George Whitefield
drew African writers like iron filings to a magnet. For Gronniosaw, Scripture
as vivified in the revival made the pivot propelling his story.

Gronniosaw's *Narrative* appeared with an Old Testament text prominent on the title page: "I will bring the Blind by a Way that they know not,
I will lead them in paths that they have not known: I will make darkness
light before them and crooked things straight. These things will I do unto
them and not forsake them. Isaiah. xlii.16."[41] His story was sadly familiar—
captured in Africa, shipped to Barbados, sold to an American—until a minister heard of Gronniosaw's casual talk about God and devils in his fumbling
attempts to speak English. The minister was Theodore Frelinghuysen of
New Brunswick, New Jersey, an ally of Whitefield and the leading early promoter of revival in the middle colonies. The date was somewhere in the
early 1740s. Intrigued by what he saw as spiritual precocity, Frelinghuysen
purchased Gronniosaw and then patiently instructed his new slave in
the rudiments of Christianity: "he took great pains with me, and made me

A

NARRATIVE

OF THE

Moſt Remarkable Particulars

IN THE

LIFE

OF

James Albert Ukawſaw Gronñioſaw,

An *African* Prince,

Written by HIMSELF.

I will bring the Blind by a Way that they know not,
I will lead them in Paths that they have not known :
I will make Darkneſs Light before them, and crook-
ed Things ſtraight. Theſe Things will I do unto
them, and not forſake them, ISAI. xlii. 16.

BATH Printed ;

NEWPORT, RHODE-ISLAND : Reprinted and Sold by
S. SOUTHWICK, in Queen-Street, 1774.

The text that James Gronniosaw placed on the title page of his 1774 narrative exemplified the hope that many African American Christians of the period found in the promises of Scripture. (Courtesy of the American Antiquarian Society) understand that he pray'd to God, who liv'd in Heaven; that He was my Father and BEST Friend." When Gronniosaw responded that there must be some mistake, since his father—his mother and sister too—lived far away in "Bournou," and that he desperately wanted to see them again, Frelinghuysen wept and tried to explain the Christian concept of the universal Fatherhood of God. A period of great emotional turmoil followed, which was much exacerbated when Gronniosaw heard his master preach from Revelation 1:7 ("Behold, he cometh in the clouds; and every eye shall see him and they also that pierc'd him") and Hebrews 12:14 ("follow peace with all men, and holiness, without which no man shall see the Lord"). His unease intensified when Frelinghuysen gave him a copy of Richard Baxter's seventeenth-century classic, *A Call to the Unconverted*. But then, in standard evangelical fashion, resolution came through a text: "in the midst of my distress, these words were brought home upon my mind, '*Behold the Lamb of God.*' [Jn 1:29] I was something comforted at this, and began to grow easier and wished for day that I might find these words in my bible."[42]

Gronniosaw's spiritual and physical struggles did not end with this evangelical breakthrough, even though shortly after his vision of the Lamb he received "full assurance" of the forgiveness of his sins when "this text of scripture came full upon my mind. 'And I will make an everlasting covenant with them, that I will not turn away from them, to do them good; but I will put my fear in their hearts that they shall not depart from me' [Jer 32:40]."[43] Before Frelinghuysen died in 1748, he gave Gronniosaw his freedom. Yet many difficulties followed as Gronniosaw struggled to find a livelihood, then secured transport to England, and turned up unannounced at George Whitefield's doorstep. From Whitefield and his allies he received considerable help, but other Englishmen provided even more deceit and exploitation. Shortly before publishing his 1772 narrative, Gronniosaw and the wife he met in England had found reasonably secure accommodations. And so he ended his account: "As Pilgrims, and very poor pilgrims, we are travelling through many difficulties toward our HEAVENLY HOME, and waiting patiently for his gracious call, when the LORD shall deliver us out of the evils of this present world [echoing Gal 1:4] and bring us to the EVERLASTING GLORIES of the world to come. To HIM be PRAISE for EVER and EVER. Amen."[44]

Scripture occupied a similar place in the narrative of John Marrant, which was published in 1785, also in England, but with most of its details concerning events in the colonies during the late 1760s and 1770s.[45] Marrant was born a free black in New York but spent most of his early years in

Georgia and South Carolina, where his eventful life involved family disputes, captivity by Indians, threats from wild animals, brutality from slave masters, and more. The structure of his narrative indicated the proportionate value Marrant placed on the experiences of his life. The Revolutionary War, which he called the "American troubles," received less than one sentence.[46] Page after page, by contrast, detailed his conversion, his spiritual ups and downs, his prayers, his teaching of others to pray and read the Bible, and his visions of God.

Marrant's conversion began when he happened into a Charleston meetinghouse where an aged George Whitefield was preaching during his last American tour,: "I was pushing the people to make room...just as Mr. Whitefield was naming his text, and looking round, as I thought, directly upon me, and pointing with his finger, he uttered these words, 'PREPARE TO MEET THY GOD, O ISRAEL.' [Am 4:12] The Lord accompanied the word with such power, that I was struck to the ground, and lay both speechless and senseless near half an hour." Thereafter followed intense engagement with the Bible. Sometimes the engagement was talismanic, as when the daughter of a hostile Indian "King" took Marrant's Bible from his hand "and having opened it, she kissed it, and seemed much delighted with it." At other times it was textual, as when he taught slave children to recite the Lord's Prayer.[47] Compared to the unfolding crises of empire, the Bible's ancient narratives loomed much larger. As an example, when his Indian captors were preparing to burn him alive, "I fell down upon my knees, and mentioned to the Lord his delivering of the three children in the fiery furnace, [Dan 3] and of Daniel in the Lion's den, [Dan 6:24–28] and had close communion with God."[48]

As Marrant brought his narrative to a close, he reported that, having been recently ordained as a chaplain in the Countess of Huntingdon's Connexion, he was on the way to Nova Scotia for service as a missionary. Presumably he was intending to work with the former slaves, including David George (next paragraphs), who had been taken to that loyal colony by their British liberators during the last days of the Revolutionary War. Marrant's title page included texts from Psalm 110:3 ("Thy people shall be willing in the day of thy power") and Psalm 96:3 ("Declare his wonders among all people").[49] His narrative closed with Isaac Watts's paraphrase of Psalm 107.

As with the books from James Gronniosaw and John Marrant, David George's autobiographical account featured Scripture working apart from most of the structures of traditional Protestant society. Like them, George appropriated the Bible in the course of escaping the restrictions with which

British Christendom, undergirded by a different kind of support from Scripture, surrounded his life. Unlike them, and also Phillis Wheatley, George did not enjoy personal contact with George Whitefield, though a variation on Whitefield's type of religion proved decisive for him as well.

The remarkable life of David George began around 1743 when he was born as a slave in Sussex County, Virginia. A half-century later he dictated a narrative of his life to two British Baptist pastors who then published it in the London *Baptist Annual Register* for 1790–93.[50] When he made this record, George was visiting England from Sierra Leone, where he served as pastor of the first Baptist church established in Africa and also functioned as a leader of the North American immigrant community recently planted in that region. Most members of this community were former slaves like himself who had been manumitted by the British during the War of Independence and then transplanted to Nova Scotia. George was the key black figure in Nova Scotia who accepted the offer of the Sierra Leone Company to make another, even more arduous migration across the Atlantic. With his patrons, George and the other African Canadians hoped to establish a colony that could undermine the slave trade while creating a model civilization for those rescued from the trade. The Sierra Leone Company was a British philanthropy created with considerable Quaker support by well-positioned members of the Church of England, many of whom had been touched by currents of evangelical renewal similar to those that eventually reached into the slave-holding colonies of North America. While also indebted to revivalistic evangelical religion, George, however, rarely conformed to the expectations of his Anglican collaborators.

In South Carolina, Nova Scotia, and Sierra Leone, George received various forms of support from individuals with a stake in the Christian heritage of Protestant Britain. While still a slave, he had been given instruction in the faith and then baptized by a Connecticut Baptist minister who itinerated in the South. He had been delivered from slavery by British military officials who viewed the American rebellion as a threat to orderly Christian civilization. British officials provided assistance in setting up new communities for black Loyalists in Nova Scotia, although that assistance never overcame the racist actions and attitudes of the area's whites. Despite that prejudice, George and other former slaves did enjoy enough liberty to establish a small network of self-governing black churches in the British colony. Those churches, in turn, became the chief recruitment sites when leaders of the Sierra Leone Company, inspired by explicitly Christian motives, explained their vision of a new colony in West Africa. Yet although the structures of British Christendom did much to accommodate George and his fellow Georgian-Canadian-West Africans, these black Loyalist-migrants remained apart.

Their way of engaging Scripture illustrated a prominent feature of that distinctiveness. Directly for white colonial preachers and Anglican philanthropists—as well as indirectly for Loyalist opponents of the American Revolution—the Bible served as a resource for strengthening Christendom. William Wilberforce, the anti-slavery crusader and supporter of the Sierra Leone venture, published in 1797 a much-noticed appeal for his fellow Britons to actually live as the Christians they claimed to be. All but the first edition of his ardent book carried a text immediately below the title: "Search the Scriptures!—John 5:39."[51] Most of Wilberforce's Bible-saturated book offered spiritual remedies for spiritual ills, but toward the end it also gestured significantly toward the body politic: "If indeed, through the blessing of Providence, a principle of true Religion [which he had defined in biblical terms] should in any considerable degree gain ground, there is no estimating the effects on public morals, and the consequent influence on our political welfare." By contrast, if irreligion advanced to the extent that England lost "our church establishment," then "no prudent man dares hastily pronounce how far its destruction might not greatly endanger our civil institutions."[52] Wilberforce's jeremiad followed a well-worn path as it emphasized the capacity of lively biblical faith to renew the individual, the family, and the local fellowship—but also, as a natural consequence, the entire nation.

David George did not repudiate that familiar logic; he may, in fact, have embraced it himself. But the chief concern of his narrative lay elsewhere. Scripture figured in what he explained to the British pastors almost exclusively as a message of inward spiritual liberation. As a youth he had occasionally attended "the English church," an Anglican chapel near his home, but in George's words, "he did not fear hell, was without knowledge." What did impress him at that stage of his young life was the brutality of enslavement, often directed at himself; "the greatest grief...was to see them whip my mother, and to hear her, on her knees, begging for mercy."[53]

At about age nineteen in 1762, George ran away. After narrow escapes as he moved southward, he was eventually captured by Indians and then sold to a considerate master near Silver Bluff, South Carolina. There about a decade later, when "a man of my own color, named Cyrus" warned him that if he did not change his ways, he would "never see the face of God in Glory," George grew spiritually serious: "I saw myself [as] a mass of sin. I could not read, and had no scriptures. I did not think of Adam and Eve's sin, but I was sin." Soon thereafter he experienced a classical evangelical conversion: "I saw that I could not be saved by any of my own doings, but that it must be by God's mercy—that my sins had crucified Christ; and now the Lord took away my distress." Then he heard a black preacher, George Liele, who would later found Baptist churches in Savannah and Jamaica. Liele's text confirmed George in his faith: "His sermon was very suitable, on 'Come unto me all ye that labour, and are heavy laden, and I will give you rest' [Mt 11:28]." Almost immediately George himself "began to exhort...and learned to sing" the hymns of Isaac Watts. When politics intruded—"the American war was coming on" was his laconic phrase—George took much more notice of personal than of imperial implications. Because masters did not want blacks to learn about British intentions to free loyal slaves, they no longer allowed white preachers to conduct services; for George this became his moment: "I had the whole management, and used to preach among them myself." Then and only then did he find opportunity to learn to read, a process that led him back to the confirmation of his spiritual liberty: "The reading so ran in my mind, that I think I learned in my sleep as really as when I was awake; and I can now read the Bible, so that what I have in my heart, I can see again in the Scriptures."[54]

From that point George preached regularly, first as strife intensified between patriots and Loyalists, then when he and hundreds of former slaves were carried to Nova Scotia, and, after the passage of some years, as he led the expedition to Sierra Leone. This preaching invariably took the standard Protestant pattern of expositing or exhorting from a text of Scripture. After returning to Sierra Leone from England, for example, he wrote to one of the British Baptists who had recorded his personal narrative that he had preached on John 20:28 ("My Lord and my God"), and "the meeting was joyful."[55]

One further incident in Sierra Leone sheds more light on the varied understandings of Scripture among proponents of revived religion. In April 1797, George and the governor of the colony, who was appointed by the evangelicals in England, engaged in extensive debate about the conduct of George's congregation. The governor, Zachary Macaulay, had concluded that the African Canadians of Sierra Leone were antinomians, or at the least lax about living morally disciplined lives. George responded that such concerns deserved less attention than what he considered the more important matter of the New Birth that secured redemption. According to the governor's extensive notes of their debate, both agreed at the outset that "the rule of our faith and practice" had to be "the written word [i.e., the Bible]." Yet while George held out for the importance of "the spirit within" and the "inward feelings" experienced by believers, Macaulay insisted that proper Christianity "involved a turning from sin to holiness, and that every other evidence was vain" regardless of where it came from.[56] The dispute touched upon important theological issues concerning conversion in relation to sanctified living. But for our purposes, the crux lay with the different uses of Scripture. For the governor, the Bible properly understood supported godly civilization; for George, the Bible properly understood guided the godly person. Neither denied the other's emphasis, but the ranking of priorities was important.

For David George, as also for James Gronniosaw and John Marrant, expressive religious experience, depicted almost entirely in the literal terms of Scripture, provided an anchor in the perilous seas of life. The same intense focus on the biblical message of personal redemption had been expressed on a smaller scale in the earlier testimonies of Jupiter Hammon and Briton Hammon. It would also be found in the more substantial works published in the 1780s by Quobna Ottobah Cugoano (also know as John Stuart) and Olaudah Equiano. Although these pathbreaking books dealt only indirectly with life in the American colonies, the testimonies they offered spoke for growing numbers of African-descended individuals throughout the Atlantic world. The story was becoming familiar: enslavement and racial prejudice, religious despair and rescue, conversion and personal empowerment—and throughout, a profoundly comprehensive reliance on Scripture as opening the pathway to salvation before God and dignity of self in the world. Cugoano and Equiano belong in an American story only tangentially, but the burden of what they published still illuminates what other African-descended believers experienced who lived all or most of their lives in the colonies.

The Interesting Narrative of the Life of Olaudah Equiano, or Gustavus Vassa, the African, Written by Himself, appeared in 1789.[57] It was soon recognized as a compelling story of degrading enslavement overcome by personal pluck, British liberty (however grudging), and divine Providence. Recent investigations have cast doubt on Equiano's account of birth and kidnapping in what is now southeastern Nigeria (he may have been born in South Carolina[58]), but they have also confirmed the major points of the life he recorded—service as a slave on a British merchant ship, purchase of his own freedom, continued employment as a sailor plying routes into the Mediterranean as well as the Caribbean and the colonies, participation as a slave overseer in an abortive scheme for a Central American plantation, and then deepening involvement in efforts to combat the slave trade and establish the Sierra Leone colony.

For our purposes, the paradigmatic character of Equiano's *Narrative* extended also to its deep immersion in Scripture. The words immediately following the book's title supplied a text: "Behold, God is my salvation; I will trust, and not be afraid, for the Lord Jehovah is my strength and my song; he also is become my salvation. / And in that day shall ye say, Praise the Lord, call upon his name, declare his doings among the people. Isa[iah] xii.2.4."[59] In the *Narrative*'s penultimate sentence another text summarizes the lessons Equiano wanted readers to take away from his life: "After all, what makes any event important, unless by its observation we become better and wiser, and learn 'to do justly, to love mercy, and to walk humbly before God!'" [Mic 6:8][60] In between came a fusillade of scriptural quotations and allusions, accompanied by multiplied references to Equiano's purchase of, reading in, discussions about, and pondering on—the Bible.[61] In the course of his narrative, Equiano cited chapter and verse, quoted, or directly echoed at least one hundred different passages of Scripture—over forty from at least fifteen different Old Testament books, over fifty from at least eighteen from the New Testament.[62] When on the sixth of October 1774, he received full assurance of faith, Equiano described that experience with a pastiche of scriptures, some of which he identified, others simply quoted. A portion of this record conveys the flavor of the whole.

> In the evening of the same day, as I was reading and meditating on the fourth chapter of the Acts, twelfth verse ["Neither is there salvation in any other: for there is none other name under heaven given among men, whereby we must be saved"], under the solemn apprehension of eternity,...in this deep consternation the Lord was pleased to break in upon my soul with his bright beams of heavenly light; and in an instant, as it were, removing the veil, and letting light into a dark place, Isa[iah] xxv. 7. I saw clearly, with the eye of faith, the crucified Saviour bleeding on the cross on Mount Calvary: the Scriptures became an unsealed book, I saw myself a condemned criminal under the law, which came with its full force to my conscience, and when "the commandment came sin revived and I died." [Romans 7:9] I saw the Lord Jesus Christ in his humiliation, loaded and bearing my reproach, sin, and shame. I then clearly perceived, that by the deed of the law no flesh living could be justified. [echoing Rom 3:20] I was then convinced, that by the first Adam sin came, and by the second Adam (the Lord Jesus Christ) all that are saved must be made alive. [alluding to Rom 5:12–15] It was given me

at that time to know what it was to be born again., John iii. 5. ["Jesus answered, Verily, verily, I say unto thee, Except a man be born of water and of the Spirit, he cannot enter into the kingdom of God"].[63]

The biblical religion that Equiano embraced—or, as he would have said, embraced him—did not differ materially from what others caught up in the eighteenth-century evangelical revivals experienced. If there was a difference, it lay in the nearly total application of Scripture to the liberating effect of the Christian gospel for the individual person. Equiano did indeed express a hope toward the end of the *Narrative* that the British Parliament would outlaw the slave trade: "May Heaven make the British senators the dispersers of light, liberty, and science, to the uttermost parts of the earth: then will be glory to God on the highest, on the earth peace, and good-will to men."[64] [echoing Lk 2:14] But as is obvious, even this casual detour into affairs of state merely extended the biblical frame of Equiano's thinking a step or two beyond the personal. A more typical passage came when, at an earlier stage in his life, Equiano earnestly sought an answer to his spiritual longings by "frequenting the neighbouring churches" in London. But, he reported, "I really found more heart-felt relief in reading my bible at home than in attending the church."[65] The institutions of Christendom did little or nothing for him. From first to last, the *Interesting Narrative* remained a story of divine rescue. It was the Bible for persons, even from among the most despised category of human beings, that drove the story. The Bible for empire, the Bible for political order, the Bible for intellectual exertion— these uses of Scripture were all but irrelevant.

The same concentration characterized the other major publication by an African during this period. Quobna Cugoano was born in Ghana, captured as a youth, subjected to plantation life in Grenada, and then as a fifteen-year-old manumitted in 1772 after being taken to Britain. In 1787 he published the first full-scale attack on the slave trade by an African-born writer. This forceful work of 150 pages advanced a panoply of arguments, almost all of which either drew directly on Scripture or were delivered in what Vincent Carretta calls "Cugoano's pseudobiblical diction."[66] The striking passage in which Cugoano explained his debt to Scripture is worth quoting at length, since it offered an explicit statement of the sentiments held by almost all of the other early writers in the black Atlantic world:

[O]ne great duty I owe to Almighty God...that, although I have been brought away from my native country, in that torrent of robbery and wickedness, thanks be to God for his good providence towards me; I have both obtained liberty, and acquired the great advantages of some little learning, in being able to read and write, and, what is still infinitely of greater advantage, I trust, to know something of *HIM who is that God whose providence rules over all*.... But, above all, what I have obtained from the Lord God of Hosts, the God of the Christians! is that divine revelation of the only true God, and the Saviour of men, what a treasure of wisdom and blessings are involved? How wonderful is the divine goodness displayed in those invaluable books the Old and New Testaments, that inestimable compilation of books, the Bible? And, O what a treasure to have, and one of the greatest advantages to be able to read therein, and a divine blessing to understand![67]

Cugoano used his scripturally-grounded arguments to promote public policy, but public policy construed for explicitly Christian purposes: "We would wish to have the grandeur and fame of the British Empire to extend far and wide; and the glory and honor of God to be promoted by it, and the interest of Christianity set forth among all the nations wherever its influence and power can extend; but not to be supported by the insidious pirates, depredators, murderers and slave-holders."[68] To anticipate the themes of the next chapter, the tragedy of Cugoano's biblical reasoning lay in its inability to undermine the taken-for-granted commerce in human beings that Protestant societies promoted, even as they prided themselves on loyalty to Scripture. Whatever such loyalty to Scripture meant, it took endless political horse-trading (Britain) and massive military effort (the United States) to reform the structures of Britain's formal Christendom and America's informal Christendom in order to end the slavery that Cugoano's reading of Scripture so sharply attacked.

Taking Stock

It is important to stress how thoroughly the first writers of the black Atlantic foregrounded the Bible as they presented themselves to the reading public. Vincent Carretta, who has done more than any scholar to publicize these authors, perceptively linked their reliance on Scripture to their own spiritual autobiographies: "For most of the Black writers, Protestant Christianity with its emphasis on direct knowledge of the bible was the primary motive for literacy. Virtually all the Afro-British publications in prose took the form of spiritual autobiographies that trace the transition from pagan beliefs to the Christianity shared with the authors' British readers."[69] These black authors also shared with some other Anglo-Americans a concentrated form of the evangelical religion that famous revivalists preached and many ordinary believers practiced. This religion grew organically from older Protestant forms but took shape with distinctive new emphases on conversion, self-reflection, and personal spiritual empowerment. If evangelical revival characteristically leaned toward a religion of "the Bible alone," African American and African British evangelical religion went farther. Phillis Wheatley was a partial exception. For the rest, it was "the Bible alone" with a vengeance. Yet this biblicism from the heart and for the heart differed from the Puritan biblicism of an earlier era because it did not seek to organize all of a community's existence according to scriptural principles. For white adherents, intense evangelical religion became quasi-political when they found themselves chafing at the structures of Christendom. The even more intensely Bible-only faith of black authors slipped easily into public anti-slavery. Otherwise, as the Bible quickened and expressed deeper personal faith, spiritual biblicism did not become social, cultural, or political biblicism. Instead, as chapter 9 indicates, as the Bible was becoming more powerful for persons touched by the revival, it also became less salient for important features of the broader society.

Two legacies of revivalist personal biblicism were especially important for the long term. First, for African Americans it established a trajectory of biblical practice that functioned with almost no opportunity for exercising power in public. Among the early black authors, only Phillis Wheatley, Cugoano, and Equiano received noteworthy attention, but they remained much more curiosities than influences. Scripture, nonetheless, had taken root in previously rocky soil. In African American communities the deep appropriation of the Bible would continue, despite the pressures exerted upon those communities by a national culture that while honoring the Scriptures dishonored its black population.[70]

Second, if personal, spiritual biblicism exerted scant political influence in the early blaze of revival, it still renewed a potent strand of Protestant scriptural tradition. The many lay believers, whose quickened response to the revival message constituted the Great Awakening, hoped that vivified personal faith would somehow renew Christianity in Christendom. But their chief concern remained the awakening of persons, families, congregations, and localities. They did not devote energy to exploiting biblicism either for or against Christendom. For them, it was "the Bible alone," not in the biblicist sense of trying to organize all of a community's existence according to scriptural principles, but as a pillar of fire guiding them through an otherwise pathless wilderness. Yet when the new United States repudiated the British form of Christendom as hopelessly corrupt and then struggled to find new means for connecting private Christianity to public well-being, the revivalists' style of all-out reliance on Scripture was at hand to suggest biblicist strategies for infusing the political with the personal.

Coda: Revival, the Bible, and Native Americans

For native Americans, the story was only partially similar. The religious intensity of the Great Awakening did bring Scripture alive in a new way for some American Indians. But what the historian Linford Fisher has aptly described as "the ambiguity and open-endedness" of colonial religious practice had characterized Native engagement with Scripture long before the 1740s—and would continue to do so long thereafter as well.[71] Native experience resembled African American experience in the impetus given to Christianity by the revival; the difference lay in the relatively intact Indian cultures that had been mediating the appropriation of Scripture well before the revivals began.[72]

The Bible certainly did play a memorable role for the best known Indian convert of the Awakening. As noted, Samson Occom in 1741 was a Connecticut youth when James Davenport and other itinerants "began to visit us and Preach the Word of God." Occom would go on to a much-heralded career as a preacher to whites and Indians, an educator, and (eventually) a negotiator mediating between New Englanders and Natives at the time of the American Revolution. Yet that career also witnessed a number of betrayals, disappointments, and reversals from colonial colleagues who had also been inspired by the evangelical revival.[73]

Occom's attachment to Scripture was not, however, a new thing for Native Christians. Although Indian warriors during King Phillip's War went out of their way to destroy copies of the Algonquian-language bibles translated by John Eliot, other Natives remained serious readers of that text even after the devastating assaults on Native communities during that war. Marginalia from many Indian hands in extant copies of the Algonquian Bible testify not to any simple acceptance of Eliot's Puritanism but to patient Indian attention to the Bible on their own terms.[74] Similarly, among the Wampanoag of Martha's Vineyard, successful evangelistic efforts by the Mayhew family, which also dated from the seventeenth century, resulted in much serious use of Scripture by Natives—but again on their own terms. David Silverman has shown that Wampanoag Christianity began and remained a primarily oral faith, with Native ministers memorizing and quoting the Bible while downplaying the standard white reverence for the printed text.[75] These patterns were well established before the new religious excitement occasioned by George Whitefield and his collaborators.

Revival certainly did spark fresh interest in Scripture among at least some Indians, as for the Pequots of Connecticut who in 1742 petitioned that colony's General Court: "Our knowledge is but very little, but we want to learn to read the Bible and to have our Children learn to read it too, & thereby learn to know more of the Great God & what he would have us do in this world that we may live with him in the next."[76] This interest in Scripture, as Linford Fisher has carefully summarized, represented a response to revival: "The boisterous singing, extemporaneous preaching, explicit licensing of individual ecstatic religious experience, and overall framing of anti-authoritarianism in favor of individual expression and religious authority are part of what gave the revivals such traction among Indians and whites alike."[77]

Yet for Indians, preexisting accommodations between traditional and English cultures continued to shape responses to revival. For many Native believers, the heightened evangelical emphasis on the Bible acted as a supplement to dreams, visions, trances and other traditional means of divine contact.[78] The Moravian mission to western Massachusetts illustrated the synergies at work. As Rachel Wheeler has shown, Christianization of Mohicans advanced rapidly in the early 1740s, when converts exchanged their Native names for names from the Bible: Johannes, Abraham, Jonathan, Isaac, Joshua. More than other Europeans, the Moravians encouraged Natives to take up active responsibilities as soon as possible. The result was forceful preaching by a number of Indians, but Indians who successfully translated what they learned from the missionaries into the cultural idiom of their own people. As Wheeler explains one subtle adjustment, "Mohican preachers seemed not to have used the Moravian rhetoric of being washed and purified by the blood of the Savior but emphasized instead the power of the Savior to protect individuals from harm and exorcise bad spirits."[79]

Along with African Americans, Christian Indians touched by revival religion also became more self-conscious hearers and doers of the Word. They too experienced a deeper attachment to Scripture. They too found little attraction in the structures of European Christendom. And they too synthesized the revival emphases with aspects of traditional Indian practice, as blacks did with traditional African practices. Yet contrasting cultural experience also differentiated Native Americans from African Americans. Indians usually retained their own languages, older communal structures, and some self-consciousness about life before the arrival of Europeans. The results over time were distinctly Native internalizations of Christianity, including the place of Scripture, along with synthetic relationships between Native religions and the religions of colonial societies. African American Christianity also displayed features strikingly at odds with mainstream culture. Yet because enslavement was more destructive of African cultures and forced blacks into tighter contact with whites, African American Christianity would present the strongest example of "the Bible alone," functioning as it also did rhetorically in the dominant culture, while also contradicting how the dominant culture relied on "the Bible alone" to reinforce the slave system.

* * * * *

For a history of the Bible in America, African American and Native experiences provide an essential counterpoint to what occurred in white communities. For the most part, and in almost all venues, the deeper attraction of "the Bible alone" that evangelical revival promoted among blacks and Indians did not visibly alter the shape of colonial, and then national, public life. In the dominant society, those who also professed allegiance to "the Bible alone" remained much closer to the levers of cultural authority. The Bible in Native and African American communities would, thus, seem to have less importance for a public history of Scripture. That impression is a mistake. The importance lies in how the biblical presence among the powerless could illuminate the scriptural course among the powerful. African Americans, whose engagement with Scripture drew more directly on the message of white revivalists than was the case for Natives, provided an especially important mirror to the wider society. Their attachment to "the Bible alone" established a strong alternative perspective for understanding what the revivalists' "Bible only" meant for the public character of colonial history.

9

Thinned or Absorbed

ANYTHING BUT "THE Bible alone" characterized the approach of even believing colonists to many spheres of life in the mid- to late-eighteenth century. To be sure, revivalistic evangelical religion did promote something resembling biblicism for the purposes of spiritual life: the extraordinary scriptural mastery of lay evangelicals like Sarah Osborn and David George revealed even more of what such biblicism could mean than did the steady scriptural drumbeat of sermons from famous preachers like George Whitefield. This "biblicism for the spiritual" also occasionally expanded into a biblicism directed at church practices, as when Nathan Cole followed what he considered scriptural mandates to leave the established Congregational church and join the Separates.

Less frequently the revivals' fixation on Scripture could extend even farther. As detailed in chapters 10 and 11, biblical quotations and allusions flew thick and fast in the era's heated political atmosphere. Yet much of that Scripture remained at the service of principles with a more secular origin. Biblical language continued to enjoy very wide currency but as a supple vehicle easily enlisted to sanctify many other entities—physical nature, human reason, sentiment, progress, or the imperiled rights of freeborn Englishmen. Yet occasionally disputants did ground public arguments more explicitly on positive scriptural teaching. In 1773, for example, the Massachusetts Baptist, Isaac Backus, issued "An Appeal to the Public for Religious Liberty." This political intervention did not rest on Lockean natural rights (as had become customary for American patriots) or on sacred traditions of hierarchy (the standard platform for Loyalists). Instead, it began specifically with biblical instruction—from an inscription on the title page quoting Galatians 5:13 ("Brethren, ye have been called unto Liberty; only use not Liberty for an occasion to the Flesh, but by love serve one another") and extending in early paragraphs to numerous texts affirming the sinful bent of humans in all relationships, including government. From that starting point, Backus then went on to combine biblical proof texting with reasoning from political principles to make his case against the ecclesiastical establishment that maintained civil penalties for Backus's Massachusetts co-religionists.[1]

By the middle of the century, however, it had become increasingly rare for others to attempt what Backus carried out in his "Appeal"—that is, to self-consciously anchor arguments concerning political questions explicitly or exclusively in the Bible. More frequently, as in political discourse or exercises in natural and moral philosophy, scriptural language enhanced positions that had become conventional for other than narrowly religious reasons. For additional spheres, overt attention to Scripture was notable mostly by its absence.

This chapter highlights four of the domains in late-colonial life where the Bible, though manifestly still present, did not function as a teaching authority. For the operations of economic life and for considerations of slavery and race, the biblical presence thinned so as almost to disappear. For formal philosophy, both natural and moral, and for political thought, the Bible remained an obvious presence, but it functioned more as priest to sanction other authorities than as prophet to guide them. This process represented absorption.

In these four domains, the broadening enterprises of the Protestant British empire dominated more and more colonial instincts, yet with an ironic consequence. The foundational profession of Reformation Protestantism to rely on Scripture before—or even apart from—other authorities faded as Protestant self-identification strengthened. But because this fading took place while the Bible, in line with traditional Protestant ideology, remained salient in other aspects of colonial life, the position of Scripture grew increasingly fissile. For what followed in American history, it would become significant that these developments occurred on the eve of the political crisis that sent Americans of all sorts in search of solid authorities for personal, communal, and political life.

Before surveying these four venues, preliminary words are in order for two larger questions. What causal hypothesis might explain this bifurcated pattern? How should it be evaluated with moral criteria?

If I am right that Scripture's role as an explicit source of authority thinned or was absorbed as the eighteenth century unfolded, the most important reason had to be tighter integration of the colonies into the British empire and broadened colonial participation in the Enlightenment (however difficult it is to define exact parameters for "the Enlightenment"). The imperial wars described in chapter 6, and the strengthening commercial ties that are sketched in this chapter, drew colonists closer to the conventional thought processes as well as the physical structures of empire. In addition, the instincts of the Enlightenment, though manifest in great variety, nonetheless featured a broader reliance on empirical method, personal experience, the affections, nature, and reason that edged aside the single-minded reliance on Scripture characteristic of some earlier Protestants.

The situation in the mid-eighteenth century differed considerably from what it once had been for a portion of British Protestantism earlier and what it would become for some American Protestants later. English Puritans applied Scripture with great assurance to many spheres of life when British Christendom frustrated Puritan efforts at further reform in English church and society. In the face of that opposition, the biblicism of Puritan spirituality expanded into a biblicism attempting the reform of all Christendom. Puritans in New England succeeded for a time in efforts to construct a total society on the basis of biblical exegesis. Separation by an ocean enabled them to carry out the total reform of Christendom that their colleagues in England at first could not (because of royal opposition) and then would not (because of intra-Puritan fractures in the Cromwellian period). For Puritans on both sides of the Atlantic, biblicism affected much more than just spiritual and ecclesiastical life because they were competing for the control of Christendom (England) or trying to set up a Christendom rightly ordered by Puritan principles (New England).

Later, after the War of Independence brought an end to formal British Christendom in America, direct appeal to Scripture (often in the form of biblicism) once again expanded, but under a different set of circumstances. Now it was the absence of Britain's ancestral structures combined with grave uncertainties about the American future that prompted some believers to push their spiritual confidence in Scripture outwards toward social and political applications. Those activists did not seek to replicate Britain's church establishment but to shape the new nation by voluntary means.[2] If those efforts achieved only partial success, they did exert enough influence to attract the attention of foreign observers like Alexis de Tocqueville (positively) and Mrs. Frances Trollope (negatively).[3]

A rough generalization would seem to cover developments from late sixteenth-century England to the early-nineteenth-century United States: when the relationship between (on the one side) individual believers and local believing communities and (on the other) the broader social order was contested or unsettled, traditional Protestant reliance on Scripture moved toward "the Bible only" stance of biblicism and toward efforts at applying explicitly biblical teaching to the social order. By contrast, when that relationship seemed settled and secure, there existed a lessened tendency to expand specific scriptural teaching from the personal to the public. Under such circumstances, the Bible could still remain prominent but as a force strengthening, sanctifying, or illustrating broadly accepted social values, not as their immediate source.

If this generalization is even partially correct, it explains much about colonial life in the middle decades of the eighteenth century. Because the colonies were functioning more comprehensively within the expanding British Empire, the conventions of British Christendom could also be more simply taken for granted, even among those who remained determinedly Protestant. Scripture continued as a highly visible component of British self-consciousness, but few turned to the Bible for first-order guidance on social and political questions. Public expressions on these questions certainly reflected the "package" of British Christendom, including the exaltation of Scripture, but not much reference to the Bible as a source of detailed instruction.

Moral evaluation of such broad developments is even more precarious than determining historical causes and effects. In Protestant terms, it is a good thing when more people pay more attention to Scripture. Yet even in those terms, it is not universally true that more Scripture equals more godliness or a healthier society. The eighteenth-century revivals did mark genuine progress when they succeeded in bringing the Bible to life among populations where it had become a nominal presence or had never before taken hold. Yet calmly considered, it is obvious that Bible-fixated revival religion also led to a number of serious problems. Of these, hubris about one's own understanding of Scripture ranked among the worst since it could result in enthusiasm that fractured communities, divided churches, fueled censorious backbiting, and obscured otherwise pressing moral difficulties.

From the angle of the eighteenth-century Enlightenment, a similar ambiguity prevails. For strictly social purposes, when more individuals exercised the right of private judgment in the interpretation of Scripture, it led to stronger checks against the corruptions of hierarchy and expanded opportunities for democratic human flourishing. Yet the same expansion of Protestant-inflected individualism could also promote excess. The hyper anti-Catholicism widespread during the years of imperial warfare, with the consequent demonization of French and Indian opponents, was one example. Another was the frenzy that sometimes overtook the expression of political grievances when holy writ sanctified the conclusions of political reasoning.

For the eighteenth century as a whole, the relationships described in this chapter did represent secularization. But whether that secularization defined a path of religious declension (with religion simply losing out to anti-religious forces) or healthy cooperation between a slightly receding biblical focus and a rapidly expanding turn to empire, reason, and nature, it is difficult to say. There may be moral "lessons" to be drawn from a history of the Bible in public life during this period, but for both modern believers and modern secularists it is imperative that these lessons be drawn with great care.

The surveys that follow depend upon the impressive scholarship of others. That scholarship, however, speaks almost unanimously to the fact that as American colonists became more self-consciously British, they exerted less effort to reason directly from Scripture about the circumstances of their lives. Compared to earlier and later periods of Protestant history, the Bible in the age of empire may not have receded in visibility, but it did recede as a specific guide to public issues.

Thinned: Economic Life

Throughout the history of Christianity, there had always existed a measure of self-conscious theological attention to economic practices and economic structures. It could hardly have been otherwise, given the prominence of scriptural instruction concerning wealth. The Old Testament Pentateuch features detailed Mosaic instruction about many economic questions, while the Psalms regularly link godliness to prosperity and the prophets just as regularly pronounce judgment on economic oppression. The New Testament provides, if anything, even more precepts explaining the moral meaning of money: from Jesus's warning, "woe unto you that are rich," (Lk 6:24) to apostolic observations about money as "the root of all evil" (1 Tim 6:10) and injunctions about being "content with such things as ye have" (Heb 13:5). From the earliest church fathers, considerations of such texts resulted in ongoing efforts to formulate church teaching concerning private property, just prices in trade, and the obligations of charity. Based on statements from Deuteronomy (23:20), the Psalm 15 (v. 5), and the Gospel of Luke (6:35), which censured lending money at interest, usury in particular was almost universally condemned as a blatant evil. During the Reformation, the great rift between Protestants and Catholics did not for the most part extend to economics. If Protestant complaints against Rome emphasized how avarice had corrupted the church, Catholic reformers took special care to address such corruptions. And if John Calvin innovated by cautiously approving loans at 5 percent, though hedged with stiff warnings against greed and many injunctions to charitable altruism, Martin Luther remained adamantly opposed.[4]

Puritan reformers in England, and then in New England, stood with inherited theological traditions in denouncing usury and, more generally, condemning the credit practices demanded by the era's cutting-edge merchants. The Geneva Bible expressed these views in its gloss on the concession of Deuteronomy 23:20 ("unto a stranger thou maiest lend upon usury"). Its notes explained that this instruction only allowed usury "for a time for the hardness of their heart."[5] In general, the mind-set brought to the New World in the seventeenth century featured a hierarchy of authority in which biblical theology stood uppermost. The colonists by no means despised trade nor questioned rights of private property. But in the words of Mark Valeri's authoritative account of the era's religious-economic connections, "they relied on a discourse of Scripture and Reformed doctrine that rarely accommodated the language of market exchange....They thought that their task was to teach merchants the grammar of faith, not to conform their speech to the rules of commerce."[6]

So it was that in 1639, the leading Boston merchant Robert Keayne could be arraigned by the Massachusetts General Court and censured by Boston's First Church for violating biblical prohibitions against profiteering, price-gauging, and market manipulation.[7] In John Winthrop's journal, the lay governor expressed entire approval when the Reverend John Cotton publicly condemned Keayne's business practices, including usury.[8] Keayne, himself an earnest church member, offered in defense that he was only following the standard procedures of England's best merchants. Cotton, with broad support from the community, challenged those procedures with specific arguments drawn from a wide array of scriptures. The two important points are that in early New England, as the most intensely ideological colonial region, biblical reasoning extended self-consciously to economic life, and economic life was subject to explicit moral discipline.

From the mid-seventeenth century, this biblicist concern began to shift away from theological prescriptions toward a vision of New England's economic life contributing to the empire as part of a grand divine plan. The next generation, at the end of the seventeenth century and beginning of the eighteenth, moved still farther in the direction of accepting the British empire's expanding market practices as ordained by God; this movement coincided with an even higher sense of God's providential direction of the entire imperial project.

An illustration of how much changed over the course of the century came in a work published by Cotton Mather in 1699 that reported the deliberations of Boston area ministers on thirty cases of conscience. One of them responded to the question, "What Loan of Money upon USURY may be Practised?" The answer showed how far the ground had shifted from the era of Cotton and Winthrop. Mather did take care to adduce biblical passages that in his view allowed for lending of money at interest, like Jesus's parable of the talents from Matthew 25:14–30. Yet most of the answer explained why "there is every sort of *Law*, except the *Popish*, to Justifie a regulated *Usury*." Against official Catholic teaching, which stood firm against usury, Mather cited a variety of "laws" (equity, parity, charity) allowing for the practice. Yet first in Mather's list was "the Law of *Necessity* and *Utility*," since "*Humane Society*, as now circumstanced, would sink if all *Usury* were Impracticable."[9] The practicalities of Boston's connections with London, Glasgow, and the Caribbean now loomed large.

The Bible of course remained relevant for Mather and his associates, but they now read its teachings as aligned with, rather than disciplining, the imperial economy. By the time they sanctioned a "regulated usury"—that is, after the tumults of the Cromwellian era, the monarchical Revolution of 1688, and the loss of the original Massachusetts charter; and as conflict with Catholic France intensified—the mercantile pull of the imperial center on its outlying colonies had considerably increased.

From the late seventeenth century, the English (soon to be British) economy displayed a growing degree of purposeful organization.[10] What had once been scattered and piecemeal now came to exhibit a new degree of centralization with London merchants and money men as the key centralizing figures. The establishment of the Bank of England in 1694 heralded the central role that expanding credit, heightened tax revenue, and government-merchant cooperation would play in the expanding empire. Navigation Acts from Parliament soon followed, which tasked the Royal Navy with protecting British international trade. As early as the Treaty of Utrecht (1713), which we have seen was celebrated in the colonies as a God-blessed triumph of Protestant virtue over Catholic perfidy, Britain emerged, in Patrick O'Brien's phrase, as "the leading naval and military power in Europe and as a mercantile and industrializing economy on its

way towards dominance in supplying services, shipping, credit, insur-
ance, and distribution, as well as manufactured commodities to global
markets." The rapid rise of tax revenues over the course of the eighteenth
century enabled a great expansion of military infrastructure to protect trade
routes, colonies, and markets throughout the entire world, while government debt undergirded the maritime enterprise. The transformation of the
British economy into a powerful international force depended on a number
of physical and social factors: an island protected by oceanic barriers, the
beginnings of industrialization, agricultural surpluses, enterprising merchants, organized credit, and expanding colonial markets. It also depended
on what O'Brien calls a "supportive public consensus" which included "traditional religious and deferential predispositions."[11]

In the colonies, that support grew ever stronger as key leaders linked
the economic fate of the empire to the designs of providence. The adjustment to circumstances articulated by Cotton Mather in 1699 went even
farther during his latter years as he and his colleagues came to view the
expanding British market system as divinely sanctioned. To influential
ministers like Boston's Benjamin Colman, that system followed divine
dictates as a "Law of Nature" equivalent to how up-to-date contemporaries
were interpreting physical nature in the wake of Sir Isaac Newton's labors.

For Colman, biblical guidelines still mattered for economic questions,
but in the same fashion as we have seen, they mattered for his assessment
of imperial conflict.[12] Just as Colman "improved" the military expansion of
Britain's empire to promote godly ends, so he described the profits from
imperial trade as an opportunity for good deeds. As opposed to earlier
periods, Colman now simply took for granted the workings of modern
market systems, as also the need to defend the empire. Scripture spoke to
how the fruits of trade should be used, not to the trading system itself.

So it was with his sermon preached in multiple parts in 1725 and 1726,
but published only in 1736, with the title, "The Merchandise of a People
Holiness to the Lord." Publication came in the latter year expressly for what
its title page described as "A Thank-Offering to God for repeated surprising
Bounties from London for Uses of *Piety* and *Charity*." These bounties had
been sent by Samuel Holden, to whom the publication was dedicated.
Holden's family had welcomed Colman during a much earlier visit to
London, after which Holden himself had gone on to a noteworthy career as
Russian merchant, governor of the Bank of England, and prominent
spokesman for Britain's Dissenting churches.[13] Colman, with long-standing

connections to leading English Dissenters, thanked Holden for his general openhandedness, but especially for his generosity to Harvard College. The sermon, which featured a quotation from 2 Corinthians 9:9 on the title page ("He hath dispersed abroad, he hath given to the Poor, his Righteousness remaineth for ever"), took its text from Isaiah 23:18 ("And her Merchandise, and her Hire shall be holiness to the LORD"). From his exposition of the judgment pronounced by the prophet on the merchant city of Tyre, Colman instructed his New England audience that if they came to enjoy a "rich and opulent state," they should use those riches *religiously, to the Honour of God and in his Service.* If they did treat their wealth in this way, then New England's prosperity would also become "Holiness to the Lord."[14]

Colman also went on to pronounce a benediction on the expansion of Britain's imperial economy: "we know, that *Christianity* has been greatly serv'd by Trade and *Merchandise*, by means whereof a great Part of the world has been *gospelised*. For the knowledge of Christ has been *propagated* by Trade far and near."[15] In his telling, the merchants who attended Colman's Boston church had taken prominent roles in a divine drama.

As illustrated by Colman's sermon, and explained in Mark Valeri's magisterial book, the relationship of Scripture to New England's economic life did not represent secularization in any straightforward sense. Rather than commercial and consumerist values simply crowding out religious convictions, self-conscious religious reasoning engaged intimately at each stage with New Englanders' market practices. For the first generation, religion acted directly to chastise merchants for sins of avarice; for the second and third generations, religion continued to caution merchants about economic excesses, but even as pastors turned to explaining how economic cooperation in the empire served first New England's social order and then all Britons; for the fourth generation, religion declared that the market practices of an integrated "empire of goods" were ordained by God as part of his creation of the world.[16]

Significantly, Valeri shows that the revivals of the 1740s did not upset the consensus that viewed British trade as a divine provision. The Awakening dramatically intensified the application of scriptural precepts to personal spiritual life and strengthened concerns about using wealth inappropriately. But it did not renew the earlier Puritan effort to think self-consciously about economic matters in biblical terms.[17] While the revivals divided New England into competing theological camps, evangelicals and liberals united in their continued embrace of the integrated imperial market. In

Valeri's phrase, "pious merchants understood their spiritual duty to reside in the cultivation of reasonable moral sentiments in the midst of a market run by natural principles."[18]

New England, with its numerous publishing ministers, explained most elaborately how scriptural usage could function in support of imperial conventions for trade, wealth, and money. But a similar process, in which explicitly scriptural economics gave way to what Cotton Mather styled "the law of necessity and utility," was also at work elsewhere. Katherine Carté Engel's study of eighteenth-century Bethlehem, Pennsylvania, parallels the account that Valeri has provided for New England.[19] Founded in 1741 as an outpost of the international Moravian movement, Bethlehem was a far-western settlement of the renewed Unity of the Brethren headquartered at the Saxon landed estate of Count Nikolaus Ludwig von Zinzendorf, the energetic head of the movement. The particular distinction of the Moravians was their undivided dedication to missionary service that, unlike other Protestant efforts of the era, subordinated national and economic considerations to religious purposes. Central to this enterprise was the Moravians' creativity in financing their missionary ventures.

At its origin, Bethlehem organized itself as a "pilgrim community" dedicated to mission. Its founders created a corporate entity known as "the Oeconomy" that acquired property, established businesses, assigned workers, and negotiated with outside interests. In the process, the Pennsylvania Moravians engaged in many of the same economic activities as their colonial peers but with a significant difference. Their business dealings primarily supported missionary outreach to other European settlers, to Native Americans, and to the enslaved populations of the West Indies. In its first decades, great fluidity attended these activities, with a large percentage of Bethlehem's millers, storekeepers, tanners, and weavers going off for short- or long-term stints as missionaries themselves and with economic decisions regularly subordinated to the missionary cause. Although the Moravians did not promote distinct economic practices, they did regulate the era's usual economic activities by the careful moral standards of their evangelical community and for the purpose of supporting missionaries. Into the 1760s the synergy between the Moravians' functioning as missionary pilgrims and Bethlehem's organization as a community economic enterprise achieved remarkable results. Even with their strong ties to Germany, the colonial Moravians were among the colonies' most attractive evangelical movements, and their missionary work among the Indians was far more successful than comparable attempts by other Protestants.[20]

After the first decades, however, changes multiplied. The death of Zinzendorf in 1760 left the whole Moravian movement beset by a huge debt that this farsighted but detail-challenged visionary left behind. The end of the Oeconomy under the Moravians' new leadership in 1762 began a clear separation between religious and economic purposes. The Seven Years' War, with attacks on the Moravian's Indian converts by marauding Pennsylvanians (the Paxton Boys) dealt their religious goals a severe blow. Shortly thereafter the War of Independence created fresh difficulties for a movement that included many pacifists who remained grateful to the British Parliament for earlier legal recognition.[21] The result by 1800 was a Moravian Bethlehem that remained prosperous and intensely religious, but that no longer attempted to govern economic life by explicit religious principles.

In the majority of the American colonies, which lacked the intense zeal of the late-Puritans of New England or the Moravians of Bethlehem, it was even less complicated simply to accept the regular workings of the imperial economy as the unquestioned status quo. That acceptance did not necessarily entail scandalous immorality or even ethically questionable practices. It did mean that however much the Bible might be quickening spiritual life, regulating attitudes toward wealth, or sanctifying public pronouncements rhetorically, it was not being consulted to direct, discipline, or regulate the developing imperial economy.

Thinned: Race and Slavery

The history of biblical engagement with slavery and the race-specific enslavement of Africans unfolded differently but with a similar result. Reaching into the eighteenth century, Puritans and, to a lesser extent, other British and colonial Protestants did try to reason from Scripture about economic life, with those attempts gradually dying out to near extinction. Likewise for race and slavery, the biblicist drive of the Puritans resulted in some specifically scriptural consideration to about 1700. Yet from that point and for the next seventy years, rarely did even the most ardently Protestant colonists acknowledge that the Bible could speak definitely about slavery and race. Instead, conventional wisdom preempted biblical reasoning as it did for considerations about the imperial economy. With the exception of isolated interventions from Philadelphia-area Quakers, specifically biblical attention to slavery and race reappeared only in the early 1770s. Eventually, and as a difference from the consideration of economic issues, the fraying imperial relationship stimulated passionate scriptural controversy about slavery—though less about race—that would continue for a very long time. But for most of the eighteenth century, the Bible on such matters was a thinning presence.[22]

The Puritan effort to establish Massachusetts Bay on scriptural foundations had extended to a consideration of enslavement.[23] As noted, the colony's "Body of Liberties" from 1641 provided a legal code that self-consciously deferred to "the word of God."[24] At the time of its promulgation, forms of servitude pointing toward slavery were developing in the colonies, but not yet the complete identification of Africans as the only possible slaves. Not surprisingly, when it took up the subject, the Massachusetts statutes referred indirectly to the Old Testament legislation in Leviticus 25:39–46 and Deuteronomy 20:10–11, which had regulated the conditions under which Israelites could enslave enemies captured in warfare: "There shall never be any bond slaverie, villianage or Captivitie amongst us unles it be lawfull Captives taken in just warres, and such strangers as willing selle themselves or are sold to us. And these shall have all the liberties and Christian usages which the law of god established in Israell concerning such persons doeth morally require."[25]

This biblicist push survived for at least the next two generations. At the turn of the eighteenth century, Cotton Mather and Samuel Willard stood in the forefront of Boston's ministerial elite, by which time African slavery had become solidly institutionalized in the Bay Colony. Both Mather and Willard published sermons stressing that the "Word of God," as Willard phrased it, required "a Duty of Love" to even "the poorest Slave."[26] Several of Mather's many publications expanded on this theme. In 1696 he preached a sermon based on the "servants obey your masters" texts of the New Testament. But on the title page he also inscribed a strong statement from Joel 2:29 concerning the privileged state of bondspeople, eschatologically considered: "Also upon the SERVANTS, & upon the HANDMAIDS in those Days, will I Pour out my Spirit."[27]

A decade later Mather became more specific in a tract enjoining masters to work for the conversion of their slaves. The force of convention was evident as Mather passed over the mechanics of enslavement, slave trading, and perpetual bondage with a quick nod to divine sovereignty: "It is come to pass by the *Providence* of God, without which there comes nothing to pass, that Poor NEGROES are cast upon your Government and Protection." Nonetheless, the texts he placed on his title page announced the theme of familial solicitude that the discourse then demanded of Boston's slaveowners: Joshua 24:15 ("As for me, and my House, we will Serve the LORD") and Psalm 68:31 ("Ethiopia shall soon Stretch out her Hands unto God").[28]

In between these two Mather publications came the most deliberate late-Puritan effort to bring slavery squarely under the aegis of biblical direction. Conventional wisdom had become strong enough to keep Samuel Sewall from biblical considerations of race; yet his brief pamphlet from 1700 proved that Puritan professions about heeding the Scripture comprehensively were not mere sounding brass or tinkling cymbal.

Sewall, a wealthy Boston merchant and respected magistrate, figures significantly in Mark Valeri's account of New England economic life as one of the last Boston merchants trying to discipline trade by explicit scriptural warrants.[29] Shortly before Sewall published what he thought Scripture required with respect to slavery, he had followed his sense of what the Bible demanded of public officials by offering a public apology in Samuel Willard's Third Church for the "sin" occasioned by his service as one of the judges at the Salem Witch Trials.[30] Now in 1700, he was reading the works of an English Puritan who expounded on sin as equivalent to slavery even as an influx of African captives poured into Boston, and another merchant enlisted his aid to secure the manumission of a black man and his wife who claimed to be enslaved illegally.[31]

The result was *The Selling of Joseph*, a tract of about 1,900 words that deployed fourteen scriptures specified by chapter and verse to answer a pressing question: "The Numerousness of Slaves as this day in the Province, and the Uneasiness of them under their Slavery, hath put many upon thinking whether the Foundation of it be firmly and well laid; so as to sustain the Vast Weight that is built upon it."[32] To Sewall the answer could not have been clearer. God had condemned man-stealing (Ex 21:16); the so-called Curse of Ham from Genesis 9:25–27 had nothing to do with contemporary "Blackamores"; the fact that Abraham owned "servants" did not justify modern slavery; Old Testament Israel was "forbidden the buying and selling one another for Slaves. Levit[icus] 25:39–46; Jer[emiah] 34:8–22"; and precepts from the gospels (Mt 5:43–44, Jn 13:34) allowed for only one conclusion: "These Ethiopians, black as they are; seeing they are the Sons and Daughters of the First Adam, the Brethren and Sisters of the Last ADAM [Jesus], and the Offspring of GOD; They ought to be treated with a Respect agreeable [to that status]."

Only when Sewall considered whether Massachusetts could sustain a large black population did he let up on his Bible thumping. In a paragraph beginning "And all things considered," he explained, without any scriptural reference, why "there is such a disparity in their Conditions, Colour & Hair, that they can never embody with us, and grow up into orderly Families, to the Peopling of the Land: but still remain in our Body Politick as a kind of extravasat Blood." Race, as opposed to slavery, had become for Sewall a subject of conventional wisdom.

Yet if Sewall's effort sustained, at least partially, the Puritan aspiration to guide practical affairs by biblical teaching, his protest against slavery was stillborn. A response published almost immediately by John Saffin, with whom Sewall was then disputing on several matters, seized the biblical high ground.[33] Saffin pointed out that the Old Testament had clearly allowed Israelites to perpetually enslave non-Hebrews, along with their children. In fact, contended Saffin, if Sewall insisted on eliminating slavery, he would demonstrate his contempt for all the decrees with which God had ordered human society. Moreover, Sewall himself had conceded that Africans did not belong as free citizens in a European colony like Massachusetts. Even more important than Saffin's arguments was the simple weight of convention. Saffin offered the kind of biblical and cultural defenses of slavery that would become commonplace from the 1770s on. But until that time, few whites entertained the notion that Scripture provided any particular guidance for the system of race-specific slavery that was becoming entrenched throughout the colonies.

The exceptions came from Quakers who, even as they took their place in Pennsylvania as pillars of established order, still retained something of their earlier capacity to question the assumptions of British Christendom.[34] In 1688 four Friends in Germantown, Pennsylvania, probably influenced by their nonresistant Mennonite heritage, petitioned the Philadelphia Yearly Meeting against slavery, but their petition was tabled and remained unremarked until well into the nineteenth century. Several times over the next few years the Chester Monthly Meeting asked the Philadelphia Yearly Meeting to take a stand against slavery, which the latter did finally in 1719 when it joined the London Yearly Meeting in agreeing to sanction members who imported slaves. Public agitation specifically against slave-holding emerged later from two Friends born in England, Ralph Sandiford and Benjamin Lay, both of whom ended up in Philadelphia where they railed against their fellow Quakers for accumulating wealth on the back of enslaved Africans. In 1729 Sandiford convinced Benjamin Franklin to publish his *Brief Examination of the Practice of the Times* that drew promiscuously on many authorities, including Scripture, to chastise the Philadelphia Meeting for tolerating the institution in its midst.

Shortly thereafter Lay, a hunchbacked sailor, small-time entrepreneur, and repentant former slave-owner arrived in Philadelphia from Barbados. When Sandiford was disfellowshipped by his Quaker meeting for disturbing the peace, Lay stood by him faithfully. His own animus against slavery drove him to resurrect scripts from the Quaker's earlier disruptive heritage. One of his several dramatic stunts took him into a Quaker worship service out-fitted in a military uniform, including a sword. With this sword he made a great show of stabbing a folio meant to represent the Bible. When the poke-berry juice with which Lay had filled a bladder hidden inside the folio exploded in a shower of blood-red liquid, he had made his point. But the Philadelphia Quakers were offended more than convinced. A meandering screed against "slave keeping," which Benjamin Franklin had published for Lay in 1737, berated Friends for what he called "the greatest" of "the world's Corruptions...that ever the Devil brought into the church in America." The Philadelphia Quakers found Lay's eccentricities an easy excuse for ignoring his protests. If non-Quakers paid any attention, they would have been put off by his appeal to "the counsel and direction of the Holy Spirit," which Lay claimed as a stronger warrant for his anti-slavery activism than even the Scriptures.[35]

Considerably different in tone and eventual effect was the intervention of John Woolman, a Quaker of gentle spirit whose publications on the sub-ject eschewed the confrontational style that had rendered Sandiford and Lay ineffective. Woolman's 1754 *Some Considerations on the Keeping of Negroes* also differed from those earlier tracts since it, along with supporting publi-cations by fellow-Quaker Anthony Benezet, eventually contributed to a much wider controversy on the scriptural justification for and against slavery.

From the mid-1740s, Woolman traveled widely as a minister autho-rized by the Burlington (New Jersey) meeting, located across the Delaware River from Philadelphia.[36] These journeys eventually took him into Maryland and Virginia where firsthand contact with these slave colonies turned his earlier distaste into determined opposition. The pamphlet he finally published in 1754 certainly drew freely on the era's intellectual fash-ions. It showed, for instance, Woolman's familiarity with the language of the moderate Enlightenment, including several references to "Natural Affection," "Instinct," and "Offices of Reason."[37] It repeated the mantra, "civil and religious Liberties," that so many of his Whig contemporaries also invoked. It also called on Scripture to affirm the sense of colonial chosenness that England's Puritan heritage had contributed to the whole empire: "He that sleeps not by Day nor Night [see Ps 121:3–4], hath watched over us, and kept us as the Apple of his Eye [Ps 17:8]."[38]

Yet the heart of Woolman's argument lay elsewhere. From first to last, the pamphlet asked readers to embrace with existential seriousness a vision of Christianity drawn directly from the Scriptures. Like so many who would later approach questions of slavery with Bible in hand, Woolman paged freely through both testaments for support. Unlike most of the later arguments, which appealed to specific texts for specific justifications or condemnations, Woolman offered a synthetic, conceptual, but still intensely biblical statement.

He began by noting how "Ties of Nature" led to "Natural Affection" that promoted "Self Love" of one's own family, tribe, and nation. So far so good. But then Woolman left no doubt about his opposition to the social and economic effects upon Africans when those natural sentiments exceeded their bounds. His argument deserves full quotation in order to show its explicitly biblical foundation:

> Thus Natural Affection appears to be a Branch of Self-Love, good in the Animal Race, in us likewise, with proper Limitations; but otherwise is productive of Evil, by exciting Desires to promote some by Means prejudicial to others.
>
> Our Blessed Saviour seems to give a Check to this irregular Fondness in Nature, and, at the same Time, a President [precedent] for us: *Who is my Mother, and who are my Brethren?* Thereby intimating, that the earthly Ties of Relationship, are, comparatively, inconsiderable to such who, thro' a steady Course of Obedience, have come to the happy Experience of the Spirit of God bearing witness with their Spirits that they are his Children [Rom 8:16]:—*And he stretched forth his Hands towards his Disciples, and said, Behold my Mother and my Brethren: For whosoever shall do the will of my Father which is in Heaven* (arrives at the more noble Part of true Relationship) *the same is my Brother, and sister, and Mother,* Mat[thew]. xii. 48.[39]

Woolman went on to cite many passages that in his view demanded that those who claimed the Christian faith had to treat all human beings as family members worthy of the same love and respect that parents devote to their children. To that end he enlisted Yahweh's reminder to Israel about the dignity of other peoples (Isa 65:5); similar reminders about Israel's own status as strangers in Egypt (Deut 10:19, Ex 23:9); the story from the book of Acts about Cornelius who, though a Gentile, was welcomed into the family of faith (Acts 10); and God's specification of "Loving Kindness" as the fullest definition of his character (Jer 9:24).[40] Throughout, Woolman sought to move readers from a broad consideration of Christianity to a life consistent with its character: "If we, by the Operation of the Spirit of Christ, become Heirs with him in the Kingdom of his Father," and so are liberated from "the alluring counterfeit Joys of this World," then it will be impossible "for the Sake of earthly Riches" to "deprive ... Fellow Creatures of the Sweetness of Freedom" or to "neglect using proper Means, for their Acquaintance with the Holy Scriptures, and the Advantage of true Religion."[41]

Although Woolman never mentioned the words "slave" or "slavery," he clearly intended to move far, far beyond the bounds of conventional British norms—on race as well as slavery. Even if almost all of Protestant British Christendom simply took the traffic in Africans for granted, this Quaker would not. Protestants who were not Friends worried that the Quaker commitment to the Inner Light undercut their reliance on Scripture. In this instance, Woolman and not the doubters showed how upsetting a reliance on *sola scriptura* could be when shorn of Christendom conventions.[42]

The circumstances in which Woolman published his 1754 tract were important. Warfare pitting the English colonists against mostly the Native allies of the French fatally disrupted Pennsylvania's experiment in government by pacifists. Outlying settlers clamored for military protection. Aggrieved frontiersmen threatened violence against all Natives, including Indians who had converted to Christianity and lived in Moravian villages. Non-Quaker mediators like Benjamin Franklin maneuvered to keep the peace but also to break the hold of the Quaker rulers. In response, Pennsylvania's Quakers fragmented into factions and withdrew from political leadership of the colony.[43]

The military crisis that confronted Pennsylvania's ruling Quakers stimulated self-examination, reconsiderations, and a search for authentic first principles. Out of that crucible, fired by war, came John Woolman's elixir for the disease of slavery. The same set of conditions lay behind an expansion of Woolman's appeal by fellow-Quaker Anthony Benezet in his 1759 *Observations on the Inslaving, Importing and Purchasing of Negroes*. It too was written against the background of the imperial call to arms that worked like an earthquake among Philadelphia Quakers; it too echoed Woolman's anti-slave manifesto in even stronger terms, as "the absolute Necessity of Self-Denial, renouncing the World, and true Charity for all such as sincerely Desire to be our blessed Saviour's Disciples."[44]

For the rest of the colonies, the French and Indian War represented a military and economic crisis rather than a moral crisis. As such, it reinforced loyalty to the Protestant British Empire while focusing religious reflection on the destructive perfidy of Roman Catholicism. It would take

the next military crisis, in the 1770s, to bring slavery into public consciousness as the French and Indian War had done for Quakers.

Why did it take most of the eighteenth century for colonial Protestants
to consult their highest spiritual authority about this social-economic-
moral relationship that affected all aspects of colonial life? A most succinct answer came from John Newton, the redeemed slave captain who
lived long enough to ponder why so many years passed after his conversion before he gave up his slave-trading career and came to see its pernicious character. In a work published in 1788, with a quotation on the title
page following John Woolman's lead (Mt 7:12, "All things whatsoever ye
would that men should do to you, do ye even so to them; for this is the law
and the prophets"), Newton answered: "The Slave Trade was always un-
justifiable; but inattention and interest prevented, for a time, the evil from
being perceived."[45] In other words, the weight of convention combined
with the allure of profit overcame whatever imperatives might have arisen
from a more attentive reading of the Bible.

The So-Called Curse of Ham

A brief reception history of "the Curse of Ham" illustrates starkly the
damage that "inattention and interest" did to the integrity of Bible-exalting
Protestantism, as well as the moral health of British and colonial societies.[46] That history underscores the respect that Scripture continued to
enjoy throughout this period, but it also reveals the relative ease with
which European conventional wisdom could poison the Protestant profession to be guided by Scripture. The biblical account in Genesis 9:18–27
unfolds the last act in the drama of the Great Flood that destroyed all
humans except Noah and his family. It depicts Ham, the son of Noah,
viewing his father fall into a drunken stupor but doing nothing about it
except to inform his brothers Shem and Japheth. When Noah awakens he
pronounces a malediction (v. 25): "Cursed be Canaan; a servant of servants
shall he be unto his brethren." The critical point is that Canaan was only
one of Ham's four sons and that serious Bible commentators, both ancient
and modern, have read this curse as applying to the Hebrews long-ago
occupation of the Land of Canaan described in the book of Joshua. Yet in
the early modern period, "Canaan" somehow became "Ham" in popular
readings of this text, and the focus shifted to Ham's other sons (like Cush)
who were taken to be the progenitors of black Africans. These transformations occurred from the late fifteenth century when a small army of learned

commentators, zealous Protestant preachers, and academic charlatans created the image of "Ham" as a black, hypersexualized African destined by God for perpetual enslavement.

Modern scholarship has decisively refuted two persistent claims for the Curse of Ham: that it came from Jewish exegetes and that medieval Christians had interpreted Ham as African.[47] Instead, while early Christian interpreters, like Augustine, did view the curse of Genesis 9:25 as linking slavery to the sin of the enslaved, and while in the European Middle Ages Ham was regularly described as the ancestor of serfs, nothing before the late fifteenth century anticipated the later Curse of Ham. This deception started with a clever forger, John Annius of Viterbo, who in 1498 published a much reprinted work titled *Commentaries...on Works of Various Authors Discussing Antiquities*. This book was written to provide historical support for claims by the papacy to Italian land and hereditary nobility. Annius's effort was breathtaking in its audacity. To explain how sin reentered the world after the Flood, he has Ham expose Noah's nakedness and castrate him with a spell. With this move Annius explained the mystery of the Genesis text, which narrates a heavy curse for a seemingly trivial offense. But then he also went on to identify Ham with figures in Persian and Greek mythology notorious for their wild immoralities and to suggest that licentious Ham may have been exiled to Africa.

Slavery entered this interpretive tradition in the sixteenth century when England hustled to catch up with Spain and Portugal, which had already established colonial outposts in Africa, and as Protestant interpreters continued to stress that Noah's curse justified the enslavement of Ham's descendents. In the 1540s, the English reformers Hugh Latimer and John Hooper pushed interpretation along by preaching about Noah's curse of *Ham* (not Canaan as in the text). Then, gradually, in Whitford's artful phrase, "the homiletical loss of Canaan" became "the textual loss of Canaan."[48] In the annotations of popular Protestant Bibles, that transformation could be presented as settled opinion, for example in how the Geneva Bible (1560) followed what had appeared earlier in Coverdale's Bible (1535): Noah "pronounceth as a Prophet the curse of God, against all those, that honour not their parents: for Ham and his posteritie were accursed.... [Servant means] a most vile slave."[49] A popular travel narrative by George Best in 1578, which ironically treated the Inuit of Hudson's Bay with considerable charity, emphasized connections among Africa, blackness, and the curse. By the early seventeenth century widely used lexicons commonly referred to this curse as falling on Ham and were also beginning to link Ham with blackness, licentiousness, and Africa. In 1680, the English scholar Morgan Godwyn protested against using the Curse of Ham as justification for enslaving Africans, an opinion that was repeated by Cotton Mather and in the anti-slave protests from Samuel Sewall and Pennsylvania Quakers.[50]

Yet despite a nearly unanimous verdict from those who carefully studied the question, a prominent English bishop, Thomas Newton, could publish in the 1750s a much-admired exposition of biblical prophecy that twisted a number of individual arguments into a definitive conclusion: the received text ("cursed be Canaan") was actually a corruption of the authentic original ("cursed be Ham the father of Canaan"). With Newton, the chain of emendations, fabrications, deceptions, and eisegesis that transformed a cryptic ancient text into a modern mandate for black-only slavery reached its culmination. The consequence could be viewed in John Brown's ironically titled *Self-Interpreting Bible* (1778) where the editor told readers how they should interpret Genesis 9: "For about four thousand years past the bulk of Africans have been abandoned of Heaven to the most gross ignorance, rigid slavery, stupid idolatry, and savage barbarity."[51]

The astonishing popular persistence of "the Curse of Ham" testified eloquently to the enduring power of Scripture. Its reappearance in so many venues, as a taken-for-granted interpretative conclusion, also demonstrated how instinctively the culture deferred to Scripture. Yet it also revealed the difficulty that Protestants experienced in practicing their own profession to be guided primarily or solely by Scripture. Whatever the Bible per se taught, stock usage and cultural assumptions about what the Bible simply *had* to teach were stronger. The reception history of this passage shows how easily contemporary conventions, no matter how insubstantially grounded or simply fraudulent, could replace careful, judicious, and responsible biblical interpretation. "The curse of Ham" revealed this Protestant principle, embraced to secure the truth about God and humanity, trivialized to support falsehoods about the human condition.

* * * * *

As either a resource not consulted for formal teaching or a background presence reinforcing cultural stereotypes, the Bible thinned as white colonists in the eighteenth century pondered issues of slavery and race. This thinning contrasted sharply with the parallel history of deepening as some African Americans found a powerful liberating message in the sacred volume. The counterpoint of biblically encased cultural racism and biblically inspired personal empowerment illuminated the complex history of

British Protestantism even as it anticipated the no-less-complex unfolding of early American history.

This complexity involved a still deeper biblical complication. In Scripture, the many passages that mention, regulate, or reference slavery are matched by an almost complete absence of passages keyed to race in its modern meanings. As Colin Kidd has accurately written, "The Bible itself is largely colour-blind: racial differences rarely surface in its narratives."[52] Yet in eighteenth-century America, where "slaves" had come to mean "Africans," and vice versa, this basic difference in biblical treatments received virtually no attention. That lack of discrimination contributed an even deeper complexity to eighteenth-century developments as well as to the momentous conflicts that emerged from the colonial period to profoundly trouble the new nation.

Absorbed: Natural and Moral Philosophy

For formal intellectual life, the Bible did not so much thin as it was absorbed. Because the eighteenth century witnessed a self-conscious assertion of British *Protestant* identity, the Bible naturally continued as a prominent feature of almost all intellectual life. Yet it did so with references to Scripture absorbed into, or rendered relative to, reasoning drawn from reason, nature, or human nature. Sometimes that blending was self-consciously substantial, with the Bible supplying precepts joined to principles from these other authorities; at other times it was only rhetorical, with biblical citations garnishing arguments derived primarily from those sources. Yet although colonists remained still confidently Protestant, they nonetheless drifted away from tight scriptural fixation, whether as biblicist or a more general adherence.[53]

A number of historians have, with slightly different interpretive judgments, described eighteenth-century intellectual history as a mixture of Enlightenment and traditional Christian values. Based on careful research they depict an American Enlightenment that did not draw a sharp distinction between human learning or the fruits of science and traditional Christianity. The American colonial situation thus differed considerably from what scholars like Peter Gay and Jonathan Israel have written about Europe.[54] The historians of early America have convincingly documented, not a standoff between divine revelation versus human reason, human experience, and the human understanding of nature but accommodations, however awkward, between the Bible and this-worldly sources of authority.

Henry May's still definitive *The Enlightenment in America* put it most carefully. After defining the Enlightenment as belief that "the present age is more enlightened than the past; and...that we understand nature and man best through the use of our natural faculties," May narrated a history where Protestant convictions functioned as "matrix, rival, ally, and enemy" alongside the principles of Enlightenment.[55] May's account featured an especially helpful differentiation among a Moderate (or Rational) Enlightenment represented by Isaac Newton and John Locke, which colonists respected; a Skeptical Enlightenment (Voltaire) and a Revolutionary Enlightenment (Rousseau and William Godwin), which they rejected; and a Didactic Enlightenment heavily indebted to Scottish commonsense philosophers, which they embraced. This differentiation among European influences explains why eighteenth-century Americans could seem so much of, and also so much opposed to, "the" Enlightenment.

The conclusions of other historians dovetail neatly with May's account. To Donald H. Meyer the intellectual history of the century climaxed with a War of Independence that created a new nation where "the principles of the Enlightenment were shown to be in harmony with those of true religion, sound morality, and sane political thinking."[56] In her study of Enlightenment currents in Philadelphia, Nina Reid-Maroney nicely phrased the contrast she saw between the American and European contexts: "The intellectual history of the Philadelphia circle is not about the effort to 'rationalize' things spiritual; rather it is about the effort to sanctify things rational."[57] Robert Ferguson, with a focus on literature, brought his assessment back to the subject of this book. He first underscored that the stress on personal experience promoted by evangelical revivals proceeded in step with a humanistic stress on nonreligious aspects of life: "As revitalization assures the continuing power of religion in American thought, so a growing humanism furnishes more and more common ground for the mix of theology and Enlightenment ideology." But then he also specified how the individual appropriation of Scripture could strengthen prominent Enlightenment traits. Ferguson linked the revivals' emphasis on personal Bible reading to political dispositions, but his analysis describes other intellectual domains as well: "The duty of reading the Bible on one's own—the Bible as the supreme guide in communal life, as the only true source of the connection between divine and human history, as the personal property of every true believer in the pious act of interpretation—appears to have been especially crucial in the evolution of a language of dissent."[58]

In a word, colonial intellectual life became more directly focused on nature, human experience, and human society (and so in that sense, more secular) at the same time that it maintained a broad deference to Scripture within an ongoing assertion of Protestant identity. E. Brooks Holifield's definitive study of early American theology described this confluence as "the quest for theological rationality" and "an understanding of reason in religion that can best be designated as 'evidential'." Holifield goes on to show that "natural theology," or the effort to demonstrate the existence of God from strictly natural sources, "assumed unprecedented importance during the eighteenth century."[59] With European thinkers, Americans too expressed much greater confidence in reason, intuitive human experience, and empirical explorations of nature. But unlike much advanced European thought, the American pattern featured a process of addition, rather than subtraction.

Illustrating with only a few examples from natural and moral theology cannot provide comprehensive demonstration. But it can indicate that the deeply researched conclusions reached by other scholars concerning the Enlightenment and religion hold also for the history of the Bible.

For natural philosophy, later to become "physical science," colonists joined their European peers in deeper commitment to empirical investigation as the essential pathway for understanding nature. Cotton Mather's *The Christian Philosopher* of 1721 had been a landmark; it was published to show how nature displayed the goodness of God, but its method rested unambiguously on close attention to the physical world.[60] When colonists rejected one Scripture-themed scientific approach from England, they continued in Mather's path. That is, they paid scant attention to the biblicist efforts of John Hutchinson (1674–1737), a Yorkshire Anglican who, because he felt that Isaac Newton's science led to atheistic materialism, developed a picture of nature from the text of the Old Testament, hyperliteralistically interpreted.[61] Where Americans did take notice of Hutchinson, it was to disregard his proposal. Stephen Sewall, who in 1765 became Harvard's first Hancock Professor of Hebrew, dismissed Hutchinson's effort out of hand.[62] So also did John Witherspoon in the lectures on moral philosophy he delivered from 1768 to undergraduates at the College of New Jersey at Princeton. Witherspoon told the students that "The Hutchinsonians ... insist that not only all moral, but also all natural knowledge comes from revelation, the true system of the world, true chronology, all human arts, etc." To Witherspoon this approach was nonsense. Instead, he told students why it was imperative to understand nature and the human mind on the basis of human investigation. Yet he also took care to explain why such efforts would harmonize with what believers found in the Bible: "I am of the opinion that the whole Scripture is perfectly agreeable to sound philosophy; yet certainly it was not intended to teach us every thing."[63] Study of Scripture and observation of nature complemented each other; in this period the latter gained in cachet while the former steadily receded.

Typical for this period were the labors of Ebenezer Kinnersley, a self-taught Baptist from Philadelphia, and John Winthrop, a Harvard professor of mathematics and natural philosophy. Neither followed the biblicist course of John Hutchinson. Instead, both demonstrated in their work a knowledgeable commitment to Scripture, even as they drew their conclusions about nature from direct observations rather than biblical deductions. In so doing, they demonstrated by their particular efforts what historians of the American Enlightenment have described in general.

Ebenezer Kinnersley first came to public attention as a young Baptist minister in Philadelphia who objected to how leaders in his denomination abetted the enthusiasm of the Great Awakening.[64] To Kinnersley, preaching that warned "prophane, unrepentant Sinners of their awful and tremendous Danger" became objectionable when ministers preached with "Enthusiastic Ravings."[65] The intra-Baptist quarrel, thus begun, simmered for several years, with a final flurry of polemical publications in 1746 and 1747. For our purposes, the key feature of Kinnersley's Baptist history was his strong reliance on Scripture as a standard by which to upbraid his erring brethren. Thus, in a 1746 complaint against several decisions by the Philadelphia Baptist Association concerning ordination and women's public duties, he placed a biblical text prominently on the title page (Job 32:17: "I said, I will answer also my Part, I also will shew mine Opinion") and then built his argument around dozens of biblical quotations and citations. He closed this polemic by concluding, "I can find no Scripture Warrant" for the association's decisions.[66]

The timing of this polemic is intriguing since, just as he was engaging in this last Baptist dispute, he had also begun to work on electrical experiments as an apprentice for the publisher of the *Pennsylvania Gazette* who had opened the pages of his newspaper to some, though not the most intemperate, of Kinnersley's attack on his denominational opponents. That publisher, Benjamin Franklin, would win enduring fame for his life-threatening research with lightning. But Ebenezer Kinnersley, as the Whitefield of Electricity, became the public voice who thrilled audiences throughout the colonies with dramatic and up-to-date electrical demonstrations. In 1764

Kinnersley, who had become the professor of English and Oratory at the College of Philadelphia, published an outline of two lectures he had delivered on many occasions. They described in brief the experiments he had been conducting in order to explore "that curious and entertaining Branch of Natural Philosophy, called Electricity." A paragraph published on its own page as a preface to this work showed clearly that Kinnersley perceived no divergence between his earlier life as a Bible-quoting Baptist and his more recent experience as a natural philosopher. As he explained, his course of experiments involved "Knowledge of Nature" and so "tends to enlarge the human Mind, and give us more noble, more grand and exalted Ideas of the Author of Nature." To end this prefatory statement, Kinnersley added a quotation from Psalm 111:2: "The Works of the Lord are great, and sought out of all them that have Pleasure therein."[67]

Kinnersley's contemporary as a natural philosopher, John Winthrop, displayed the same confidence in scientific investigation and the same ease when aligning the results of such investigation with Scripture.[68] Winthrop's pedigree was as elite as Kinnersley's was humble. From 1739 this descendent and namesake of Massachusetts's first governor served as Hollis Professor of Mathematics and Natural and Experimental Philosophy at Harvard, where he won renown for lectures on the calculus, electricity, and his own astronomical researches. His relevance for illustrating a common colonial attitude toward Enlightenment science in relationship to Scripture came from the way he responded to a severe earthquake in November 1755, which greatly disturbed the whole New England region. Winthrop, though conceding that such natural phenomena served a "grand moral purpose," nonetheless objected strenuously when a Boston minister described the earthquake as caused directly by God as punishment for sin—and as a rebuke to the hubris displayed when citizens erected lightning rods to control nature.[69]

By contrast, Winthrop explained the earthquake as a result of natural causes. In a carefully worded lecture delivered in the Harvard chapel, he canvassed reports of earlier earthquakes, detailed the effects of New England's recent shock, and cited the best contemporary thinking (with lengthy quotations from Isaac Newton) about the physical origin of quakes.[70] His conclusion scorned the notion that earthquakes "were *nothing but scourges* in the hand of the Almighty," even as it affirmed the basic principles of the era's standard natural theology: "For . . . I make no doubt, that the laws of nature were established, and that the operations of nature are conducted with a view, *ultimately*, to *moral* purposes; and that here is the most perfect coincidence at all times, between GOD's government of the *natural* and of the *moral* world." Yet for himself, he was content to "consider the subject, only in the relation which it bears to *natural philosophy*." He ended the lecture proper, before a technical appendix, with two quotations from Isaiah 28:29: "How 'wonderful in counsel,' how 'excellent in working' is that Being, who can bring good out of the greatest evils; and can answer intentions, the most widely differing, by one and the same dispensation of His providence!"[71]

The Bible for the natural philosophy of Kinnersley and Winthrop was not irrelevant. It was rather an adjunct, a supplement, or a framing presence for what could be discovered by paying direct attention to nature itself.

The situation was much the same for moral philosophy, which comprehended what would later emerge as psychology, anthropology, sociology, and political science. The Anglican Samuel Johnson of New York, the pro-revivalist Congregationalist Jonathan Edwards, and the anti-revivalist Congregationalist Thomas Clapp of Yale represented an older approach where reasoning about human nature proceeded first from theological premises to conclusions about human experience.[72] The "new moral philosophy" moved the other way. Francis Hutcheson of Glasgow, whose formulas concerning commonsense moral reasoning and the innate human conscience as providing universal ethical principles, exerted a particularly strong influence in the colonies.[73] Introspection combined with attention to the mental experience of other people began the path of discovery. The colonies' leading moral philosophers after Johnson and Edwards followed the Scottish pattern. They included Francis Allison at what would become the University of Pennsylvania, several savants at Harvard, and Witherspoon at Princeton, but also numerous lawyers, pastors, and other colonists familiar with contemporary British currents of thought.

Despite significant differences in conclusions about what could be discovered from attention to human instincts and experiences, the conclusions took the same shape. Independent attention to human nature led to results that could then be harmonized with what the various Protestant traditions drew from Scripture. Witherspoon's lectures were paradigmatic. They began with his admission that earlier generations had found moral philosophy suspect because of its independence from Scripture. Witherspoon countered that he did "not know any thing that serves more for the support of religion than to see from the different and opposite systems of philosophers, that there is nothing certain in their schemes, but what is coincident with the word of God."[74] He would, thus, maintain a traditional Protestant deference to the Bible but carry out his investigations of human morality, the mind, and social order through natural means.

Colonial intellectual life remained provincial in the sense that Americans who reflected on general questions of nature, human nature, or social order took their bearings from European authors. Yet as colonists adapted the thinking of selected Europeans for their own purposes, that thinking represented something distinct. For a history of the Bible, it is significant that the colonies rarely witnessed the deliberate setting aside of Scripture as outmoded, deceptive, or merely human, which had already taken place on the Continent with figures like Spinoza and in England with Deists like John Toland—and that would appear in the United States by the end of the century in the deliberately heterodox works of Ethan Allen and the later Tom Paine.[75] Yet because of where figures like Kinnersley, Winthrop, and Witherspoon led, the dismissive attitudes toward Scripture that did finally appear after Independence gained much less traction than they enjoyed in Europe. From a different perspective, however, it was also true that the Protestant profession to be guided primarily by Scripture remained for fundamental intellectual questions more a rhetorical statement than a substantive platform.

Absorbed: Political Thinking

Colonial political reasoning represented yet another instance that explains why in the same era when revivalism dramatically focused attention on Scripture, other developments blurred its presence. By midcentury a mixture of Lockean and Real Whig principles oriented the thinking of most Americans as they contemplated the fortunes of Europe's competing nation states or worried about the distribution of power within the British Empire.[76] From Locke, the combination drew an articulate definition of natural rights and explained the freedom of individuals by reference to a primordial state of nature. From the radical Whig or republican tradition, it took an ideal of social well-being supported by freely exercised altruistic virtue, but constantly imperiled by the mutually reinforcing evils of political corruption and aristocratic tyranny. This composite political philosophy, which grew in strength from late in the previous century to widespread acceptance by the end of the French and Indian War (1763), operated more diffusely than the principles of Scottish ethical reasoning. Nonetheless, it represented a "new political philosophy" that resonated in the colonies even more powerfully than the "new moral philosophy." Like natural and moral philosophy, it too came to expression for the colonists as a partner of biblical usage rather than an opponent.

Three political statements from midcentury illustrate variations that remained expressly biblical, even as they received their distinctive thrust from the era's commonplace political principles. Of all forms of colonial thought, political reasoning most obviously preserved a biblical vocabulary but also most deeply absorbed the era's political certainties. Close attention to these midcentury expressions also prepares the way for the singular place of Scripture in the Revolutionary era, which we take up in the next chapters.

Elisha Williams's 1744 protest against restrictive actions by the Connecticut legislature has long been noticed as a noteworthy early expression of Lockean political principle.[77] By the time he published his manifesto, this well-connected fifty-year-old from a New England First Family had already served as a clergyman, Yale tutor, Connecticut judge, and Connecticut legislator. The next year he would accompany New England troops against the French fort at Louisbourg. An act by the Connecticut assembly in 1742, which severely restricted the activities of itinerant preachers, promoted this pamphlet, whose title page spelled out the argument unambiguously: *The Essential Rights and Liberties of Protestants: A Seasonable Plea for the Liberty of Conscience, and the Right of Private Judgment, in Matters of Religion, Without any Controul from human Authority.* The title page also presented the author's pseudonym, "a Lover of Truth and Liberty," or Philalethes, along with what served as, in effect, its text, Matthew 22:21 ("Render...unto Caesar the things, which are Caesar's; and unto God, the things that are God's").

Williams's effort offered an early illustration of what became a common colonial pattern. It drew principles from Protestantism's biblical (and anti-Catholic) traditions into tight conjunction with principles from contemporary political theory. In this case, the Protestant legacy appeared as a favored quotation from Galatians 5:1—"stand fast in the liberty wherewith Christ has hath made us free"—, while the politics came from "the celebrated Lock...the celebrated Mr. Lock...Mr. Lock in his *Treatise of Government*...the great Mr. Lock."[78] Although it is possible to interpret Williams's pamphlet in different ways, for my purposes it represented a fusion of Protestant and liberal reasoning, with the latter supplying the comprehensive framework and the former providing a heartfelt invocation of Scripture to fill out the liberal frame. For Williams and the many colonists who followed in his train, the Bible remained much more than a rhetorical gloss. Yet as shown particularly by the limited range of biblical texts adduced throughout the pamphlet, Williams's intervention reflected first contemporary political convictions, then standard Protestant principles allied with those convictions, and (not inconsequentially, but still third), actual instruction from biblical narratives or precepts. As such, the Bible remained more conspicuous than for contemporary considerations of economics, race, and slavery, but nonetheless a receding presence.

Williams began by posing his question: what was "the extent of the civil magistrate's power respecting religion"? His answer articulated what sounded like a Protestant first principle: "the sacred scriptures are the alone rule of faith and practice to a Christian." But immediately he moved to the crux of his argument: "therefore...every Christian has a right of judgment for himself what he is to believe and practice in religion." When he then affirmed "the great importance...to the Christian...to his standing fast in that liberty wherewith Christ has made him free," readers could wonder whether "liberty" or "Christ" would dominate the exposition. But not for long: "I shall first, briefly consider the *Origin and End of Civil Government....* Reason teaches us that all men are naturally equal in respect of jurisdiction or dominion one over another."[79] The Lockean center of gravity became unmistakable as the pamphlet repeatedly exalted "natural liberty," along with a chain of argument built from links of "unalienable right," "an original right of the humane nature," "rights of conscience," and "sacred rights of conscience."[80] The evils bound by this chain loomed no less definite: "notoriously unjust laws" that led to "tyranny" and claims "of *power* inconsistent with this right" of private judgment that slid inevitably into "a state of slavery."[81]

The Bible, to be sure, was never far away. Repeatedly Williams spelled out the implications of his argument with phrases like "a Christian's *natural and unalienable right of private judgment* in matters of religion."[82] But actual attention to what a believer found in Scripture when exercising private judgment came in only three places. Early in the pamphlet he paused to reference some of the classical texts teaching the inspiration of Scripture (2 Tim 3:15–16, Jn 20:31, 1 Jn 5:13). To these he added texts that in his view limited the authority of church officers to religious rather than civil matters (Mal 2:7, 1 Thess 5:21, 1 Jn 4:1, 1 Cor 10:15). Then, after a detailed argument against church establishments of any kind, including the establishments of New England, the pamphlet offered its most extension exegetical section. In it Williams took pains to define the limits of Hebrews 13:17 ("obey them that have the rule over us") and Romans 13:1 (in his paraphrase, "be

subject to the higher Powers, for that the Powers that be, are of God"). His
conclusion, for both religious and civil authorities, was no surprise: "Their
power is a limited one; and therefore the obedience is a limited obedience."[83] Later in the pamphlet Williams devoted a substantial paragraph to
a number of "freedom" texts from the New Testament, including 2
Corinthians 3:17 ("where the Spirit of the Lord is, there is Liberty") and the
reminder from Matthew 23:8 (only "one is your Master, even Christ").[84]

These expository sections carried considerable force, but they took their
place in a discourse dominated by Williams's Lockean philosophy and his
practical attack on the Connecticut legislature. Anti-Catholicism also contributed a steady background drumbeat, including the claim that "by his
very principles [the papist] is an enemy or traytor to a Protestant state; and
strictly speaking popery is so far from deserving the name of religion, that
it is rather a conspiracy against it, against the reason, liberties, and peace of
mankind; the visible head thereof the pope being in truth the vice-gerent
[sic] of the Devil, Rev. 13.2."[85] The triumphs of British liberty also featured
significantly, from "the priviledges of an Englishman contained in Magna
Carta" to "the late great deliverer (William IIId. of happy memory)" who
freed "the British nation from popery and slavery."[86] And never far away
was the Protestant banner of *sola scriptura*. These other forces certainly
contributed to Williams's conclusion, a paragraph-by-paragraph refutation
of the Connecticut legislation against itinerancy. Yet the engine that, before
all, propelled this attack was a deep commitment to natural right as the
best defense against civil and ecclesiastical tyranny. The Bible, for Elisha
Williams, added real strength to his contentions, but in so doing also gave
way as the primary engine in his presentation.

A brace of sermons by Thomas Prince of Boston from the second half
of 1746 illustrates another pattern for how Scripture could be aligned with
conventional public wisdom. In Prince's case, the same fusion of biblical
and political principles that drove Williams's 1744 discourse took a subordinate place alongside a more intensive effort to link older Protestant conventions with the more recent amalgam of Locke and republicanism. Both
of Prince's efforts were thanksgiving sermons: the first on 14 August to
celebrate the victory of George II's troops over the Jacobite army at Culloden
in Scotland, the second on 27 November to praise God for the numerous
British victories of the past year. Prince in 1746 was the much-respected
minister of Boston's Old South Church, a scholar and preacher of wide
interests who had supported the colonial Great Awakening and who, with

his son, Thomas Prince Jr., had for two years edited a magazine, *The Christian History*, chronicling the progress of revival throughout the empire.[87]

In these two sermons from 1746 Prince updated traditional Protestant themes of divine providence, anti-Catholicism, and national election in order to explain the deeper significance of contemporary events. His use of the Bible was almost exclusively typological. The interpretive strategy that usually linked the Old Testament to Christian spiritual truths now enlisted for the empire. What Israel had once been under God as type, so as antitype Britain had become. Scripture, drawn overwhelmingly from the Old Testament, taught God's universal sovereignty over all things, the dangerous evils of Catholicism, and the fact that since Israel had turned away from Jesus Christ, "God has had in some Country or other, a peculiar People owning his Revelation and their covenant Engagement with him."[88]

In both sermons Prince announced scriptural themes at the outset, then spent the great bulk of each discourse (roughly 90 percent of the published pages) describing current events, before closing each address with flurry of biblical quotations. The August sermon on Culloden featured Exodus 15:1, 6–7 on the title page ("I will sing unto the Lord, for he hath triumphed gloriously:...Thy right hand, O LORD, hath dashed in pieces the enemy.") and then presented Prince's text from Ezra 9:13–14 ("And after all that is come upon us for our evil deeds,...seeing that thou our God hast punished us less than our iniquities deserve,...should we again break thy commandments,....") After very brief attention to that text, most of the sermon expatiated on "how exceeding applicable are the same Histories and Reasonings to the *British* Nations and their depending *Colonies*."[89] Then in his "improvement," Paine quoted several Old Testament passages (Judg 15:18, Ps 18:1ff., 1 Chr 11:14, Ps 47) in order to pose a rhetorical question: "must we not freely own that the same glorious God is *our's* in *Covenant* by the most open and continual Possessions and Engagements?"[90] A peroration offered the only references to the New Testament in the entire sermon, as he evoked several passages from the book of Revelation (including 12:10: "And I heard a loud voice saying in heaven, Now is come salvation, and strength, and the kingdom of our God, and the power of his Christ: for the accuser of our brethren is cast down..."). That evocation referred specifically to "the final Judgment of the papal Empire."[91]

The November sermon, which celebrated not only Culloden but the New Englanders' victory at Louisbourg and several British triumphs on the continent, drew exclusively from the Old Testament. It's title page quoted Jeremiah 14:8 ("O the Hope of Israel, the Saviour thereof in Time of Trouble!"), Psalm 120:1 ("In my Distress I cried unto the Lord, and He heard me"), and Psalm 105:5 ("Remember his marvelous Works that He hath done"). The sermon's text came from Exodus 14:13 ("Stand still, and see the Salvation of the LORD"), which he applied "in our considering the wonderful Salvations God has wrought for the whole *British Empire* with his *Allies* in general, and for these her *Northern Colonies* in special, in the *Year past.*"[92] The "dangers" of the present day he described with language from the Psalms.[93] The "salvation" God worked for his people took visible shape in the various British triumphs. The sermon closed with a fusillade of Old Testament texts praising God's redemptive sovereignty.

Prince brought his typological understanding of Britain as an elect nation into a modern frame by conjoining the older Protestant themes with the newer political certainties. The marriage of Charles I to "a *French Papist*" had been "the pernicious Fountain" leading to the deadly combination of "Popery, Slavery, and Destruction" that sought to "ruin...the Protestant interest" and "destroy...the very essential Ends of Government." By contrast, under its last four Protestant monarchs, Britain had "enjoyed such Civil and Religious Liberty, Trade, Wealth and Prosperity, as they never knew before."[94] Similarly, in his November 1746 effort, a typical paragraph on France's military efforts featured a mingled vocabulary of "the popish Spirit," "cruel," "Liberties," and "absolute Slaves."[95]

The Bible for Prince clearly retained great authority. Yet his strict adherence to typology meant that Scripture functioned almost entirely to energize Prince's understanding of how divine providence had disposed recent events to bless Protestant Britain. As a result, the sermons offered virtually no instruction drawn directly from biblical narratives or biblical precepts.

Jonathan Mayhew's famous denunciation of "Unlimited Submission and Non-Resistance" from January 1749/50 differed greatly from Prince's discourse.[96] The sermon proper took dead aim at what Mayhew considered the increasing menace of Anglican aggression that each year more ardently celebrated King Charles I as a sainted martyr. Charles's death on the scaffold exactly one century earlier served Mayhew as the occasion for his sermon. The published version featured almost forty pages of tightly reasoned exposition on Romans 13:1–7. This classic Pauline text had long provided grist for Christian thinking about civil life, as it had for Elisha Williams in his pamphlet. Unlike Williams's concentration on natural rights philosophy and Prince's recourse to typology, however, Mayhew lingered for substantial consideration of the text itself. Yet the four-page

T Wallcut (handwritten)

A
DISCOURSE
CONCERNING
Unlimited Submiſſion
AND
Non-Reſiſtance
TO THE
HIGHER POWERS:
With ſome REFLECTIONS on the RESISTANCE made to
King CHARLES I.
AND ON THE
Anniverſary of his Death :

In which the MYSTERIOUS Doctrine of that Prince's
Saintſhip and Martyrdom is UNRIDDLED :

The Subſtance of which was delivered in a SERMON preached in
the Weſt Meeting-Houſe in *Boſton* the LORD's DAY after the
30th of *January,* 1749 | 50.

Publiſhed at the Requeſt of the Hearers.

By JONATHAN MAYHEW, A. M.
Paſtor of the Weſt Church in *Boſton.*

Fear GOD, *honor the King.*   Saint PAUL.
He that ruleth over Men, muſt be juſt, ruling in the Fear of GOD.
                                   Prophet SAMUEL.
*I have ſaid, ye are Gods— but ye ſhall die like Men, and fail like
one of the PRINCES.*   King DAVID.

Quid memorem infandas cædes ? quid facta TYRANNI
Effera ? Dii CAPITI ipſius GENERIQUE reſervent—
Necnon Threïcius *longa cum veſte* SACERDOS
Obloquitur——   *Rom. Vat. Prin.*

BOSTON, Printed and Sold by D. FOWLE in Queen ſtreet ;
and by D. GOOKIN over-againſt the South-Meeting-Houſe. 1750.

Jonathan Mayhew's celebration of the 100th anniversary of the execution of
King Charles I let him explain, and at great length, why the admonition to
honor "the powers that be" from Romans 13 did not apply to a monarch who
broke trust with his people. Mayhew's blend of Scripture and Roman ideology, as exemplified by quotations from the Old Testament and from Virgil
on his title page, marked an early example of the Christian Whig ideology
that grew in strength from that time forward. (Courtesy of the American
Antiquarian Society)

preface that preceded the sermon and the fifteen-page history lesson that followed also revealed that this effort closely resembled what Williams and Prince had published. Much more extensive attention to the Bible as a teaching authority nevertheless yielded a similar result: Scripture clothed what opposition politics created.

Mayhew's preface indicated the shape of exposition to come. It offered a defense against the charge that he was "preaching politics, instead of Christ" by reference to 2 Timothy 3:16 (though identified in his footnote as 2 Pet 3:16) and its teaching that "all scripture—is profitable for doctrine, for reproof, for *Correction*, for instruction in righteousness." What Mayhew wanted to correct was "the *slavish* doctrine of passive obedience and non-resistance" that high-church Tory Anglicans had been promoting since the Restoration of 1660. He hoped his sermon would protect his auditors and readers from "the iron scepter of tyranny...civil tyranny...ecclesiastical tyranny" that were leading inevitably to "*ignorance* and *brutality*." To keep Boston from the clutches of "The kingdom of Antichrist," which had taken root long before in "Italy" and now "has...overspread and *darkened* the greatest part of *Christendom*," Mayhew knew the time had come to draw a line. His sermon drew it between "Liberty, the BIBLE and Common Sense, in opposition to Tyranny, PRIEST-CRAFT and Non-sense."[97]

The sermon itself featured careful attention to the flow of argument in Romans 13, with some quoting of supporting Scriptures and even more patient responding to possible objections against his interpretation. If his conclusion was never in doubt, it still rested on painstaking argumentation: yes, the apostle clearly taught subjection to rulers, but that teaching was "of such a nature, as to conclude only in favour of submission to such rulers as he himself describes; i.e. such as rule for the good of society.... Common tyrants, and public oppressors, are not intitled to obedience from their subjects, by virtue of any thing here laid down by the inspired apostle."[98]

When biblical exposition stopped and the historical lesson began, Mayhew's strong anti-Catholicism emerged, and with vigor. The problems leading to Charles I's execution began when "he married a *french Catholic*." The clearest lesson from the history of his reign was that "*Cromwell* [Oliver] and his adherents were not, properly speaking, guilty of *rebellion*; because he, whom they beheaded was not, properly speaking, *their king*; but a *lawless tyrant*."[99]

Besides Mayhew's skillful exposition of Scripture in favor of a Whig understanding of English history, one other feature of his sermon illustrated regular colonial usage. When Mayhew attended to Romans 13, the

Bible functioned as a direct authority for moral instruction. When, however, Mayhew expounded on history or political precepts, Scripture shifted to a merely ancillary function. "Civil tyranny," for example, always began small, "like 'the drop of a bucket'" (with a footnote to Isa 11:15, though the phrase is actually from Isa 40:15). Again, the Antichrist who came out of Rome resembled "the kingdom of heaven" in only one particular; it began "as a 'grain of mustard seed'" (footnote to Mt 13:31).[100] Rather than teaching from Scripture, these biblical quotations lent a sanctified aura to arguments coming from elsewhere. Well before Mayhew and well after, Scripture maintained its great vitality in the colonies through the potent, but also indiscriminate, combination of direct authoritative teaching and incidental evocative rhetoric.

* * * * *

These three examples from New England (1744, 1746, 1749/50) were not necessarily representative of general political reasoning in the colonies at that time. With a tradition of highly politicized public interventions, as well as deep familiarity with Scripture and nearly instant access to the printing press, New England moved well ahead of the other colonies. Yet the biblical patterns these sermons represented would continue, with only a few additions and alterations, to dominate the fervent deployment of Scripture that so thoroughly filled public space in the Revolutionary era. There would be Thomas Prince's biblical reasoning by type and antitype that treated the colonies as a new Israel; Elisha Williams's amalgamation of Protestant principle and political precept (usually patriotic Whig, less often Loyalist) with only occasional exploration of actual scriptural teaching; and Jonathan Mayhew's elaborate biblical exposition brought to the service of communally sanctioned political convictions. The kind of study described in the book of Acts for the Bereans (who "searched the scriptures daily, whether these things were so," Acts 17:11) was not entirely absent. But it did become increasingly rare.

From their past, American colonists of the eighteenth century had inherited a variety of ways to enliven the scriptural principle of Protestantism. The convictions they professed, especially when Protestants criticized one another or Catholics or the workings of Christendom, ran toward biblicism. In a few circumstances—as for early New England Puritanism, the Puritan's internal critics, and the religion promoted by revival—biblicism actually guided what people tried to do. More commonly, biblicism as a weapon for criticism became, for guidance, a more flexible Bible in combination with other authorities. The combinations could be acknowledged or unacknowledged, dominant or recessive, through academic construction or sermonic declamation. This chapter has sketched the nature of those combinations for economic life, race and slavery, moral and natural philosophy, and politics. It points to the conclusion that for roughly the first two-thirds of the century, Protestants—without yielding on the principle of *sola scriptura*—nonetheless put Scripture to use without thinking explicitly about its relation to other authorities, as a recessive influence, and primarily through sermons. The exceptions, which were not trivial, included Bible usage coming out of the awakenings and for black Americans.

These broad trends coincided with a continued weakening of the British Christendom that had contextualized the place of Scripture from time out of mind. Even as the impact of Scripture deepened as a result of the revivals, it was also thinned because of the general needs of empire (trade) and the instincts of tribal identity (race), or absorbed by the concerns of formal thought (intellectual life) and the contingencies of nascent imperial conflict (political thought). The way was thus prepared for a revolution in biblical usage that paralleled the political Revolution, when American independence threw over inherited British Christendom as well as the rule of king and parliament.

10

Revolutionary Rhetoric

DURING THE MIDDLE decades of the eighteenth century the Bible became both more salient (through revival) and less prominent (for considerations of race, slavery, politics, and economic life). Similarly, in the succeeding Revolutionary years, even as Scripture expanded its presence as a didactic spiritual authority, it also came to function more routinely as rhetorical support for political positions only casually attached to direct scriptural teaching. Considered broadly, the era's political crises certainly heightened the visibility of the Bible; not since the first generation of Puritan settlement would Scripture be so often cited, so passionately evoked, and so publicly disputed. Yet examined more particularly, it is obvious that in the heated contentions of this tumultuous era the Bible functioned publicly in almost contradictory ways. Although evocation of Scripture in whatever manner might be thought to produce an undifferentiated aura of divine sanction, even casual attention to the era's sermons, speeches, pamphlets, treatises, and official government statements reveals substantial differences that can be arranged on a spectrum with at least tolerable clarity separating the various uses.[1]

At one end was the Bible purely as rhetoric. Rhetorical usage did not necessarily entail an absence of religious sincerity, since behind the rhetoric might also stand positive convictions with some connection to didactic scriptural teaching. But when public voices in this era drew on the Bible as Thomas Prince had earlier done to nerve New Englanders for battle against Catholic France, they were not aiming to convince or to propose a course of action; instead, they intended like Prince to clothe political convictions in the armor of righteousness.[2] The Protestant inheritance as a whole, along with the deep cultural embeddedness of the King James Version, ensured that the Bible as rhetorical model and omnipresent literary resource informed a vast range of public expressions. For what came later in American history, it was significant that a massive baptism of the patriot cause dominated the era's rhetorical deployment of Scripture.

On the opposite end of the spectrum appeared the strictly instructional, where public voices turned to Scripture for its own spiritual or ethical teaching. Due to the intensely political atmosphere of the day, it was rare when public references to the Bible were not connected to some consideration of rights, virtue, liberty, tyranny, order, or God's providential disposal of events. It should, therefore, come as no surprise that during the 1770s the publication of Bible-based works aimed specifically at religious edification declined precipitously, while the number of published sermons and other Bible-influenced works serving political purposes rose dramatically.[3] Among the authors who did seek direct biblical guidance, Christian pacifists stood out by invoking the sacred page to defend positions that had been derived originally from Scripture.

In between appeared innumerable mixtures of rhetoric and instruction, of direct appeals to scriptural principles alongside reasoning from other sources. Sermons and treatises from both patriots and Loyalists provided the most obvious as well as the most numerous examples of such mixtures. For patriots, the Bible simply spilled over with teaching that condemned conspiratorial tyranny and justified defense of civil and religious liberty. Among Loyalists it was almost as obvious that Scripture commanded respect for inherited order and deference to God-ordained authority. The Loyalist Bible lay within traditional Christendom, the patriot Bible reflected contemporary Whig ideals. As these spokesmen put the Bible to use, they followed the path of Elisha Williams's earlier interweaving of Locke and Protestant Dissent; like him they joined into a single unit strands of authority from Scripture and regnant political ideologies.[4]

For the public presence of Scripture in this era, controversy over two other questions, indirectly but powerfully related to what became the War of American independence, also stimulated pronouncements that mingled biblical and other-than-biblical reasoning. First were contentions over the Church of England's desire to install a bishop in the colonies, contentions that involved sharply polemical writing on both sides of the Atlantic from midcentury into the 1770s.[5] Second was the controversy that flared in the early 1770s over the legitimacy of slavery, which also engaged disputants throughout the Atlantic world.[6] While the political conflicts of the era clearly influenced public expressions on these two matters, those who wrote about them routinely turned more directly to Scripture as they defended their conclusions. Many of these publications, thus, resembled the form of Jonathan Mayhew's 1750 sermon commemorating the execution of Charles I.[7] Extrabiblical purpose may have been obvious, but whatever the political end in view, it did not crowd out extensive scriptural instruction or turn biblical exposition into a merely rhetorical exercise.

This chapter first explores the rare instances when disputants made a didactic scriptural appeal, not intending to influence the era's political outcomes but to reassert underlying positions they had earlier staked out in the Bible. The bulk of the chapter then documents the profuse rhetorical deployment of Scripture, which has been the subject of considerable historical attention.[8] Chapter 11 canvasses the middle range of biblical usage where scriptural argument appeared in conjunction with forthright political expression: concerning bishops, among patriots, among loyalists, in controversy over Tom Paine's *Common Sense*, and concerning slavery. Besides illuminating the public place of Scripture in the Revolutionary era, this history directly anticipates what came later in the early history of the United States. For the future, the combined force of two Revolutionary-era developments exerted an extraordinary influence: arguments pushed patriotic Americans toward biblicism, and Scripture's rhetorical presence bulked ever larger in public life.

Scripture in Support of Scripture

The most obvious use of the Bible as a direct source of straightforward instruction came from pacifists provoked by the outbreak of hostilities to defend their entire way of life. In colonial America the failure to replicate the rigorous uniformity of European Christendom created a religious pluralism most unusual for eighteenth-century Western societies. By 1770, non-Congregational Protestants in New England and non-Anglican Protestants in the South had secured a relatively full measure of toleration, while in the middle colonies practical religious freedom prevailed for all Protestants— and even eased the way for Catholics and Jews. Catholics in Maryland remained legally disadvantaged but functionally free. For pacifist minorities that had been marginalized or actively persecuted in Europe, this colonial religious pluralism was a great relief. The flourishing of Quakers in Pennsylvania and elsewhere, along with the refuge found by central European sectarians in Pennsylvania, Delaware, North Carolina, and beyond—Mennonites, Brethren (Dunkers), and Moravians—meant that these pacifists faced a sharp dilemma when political tension escalated into open warfare.[9]

Direct appeals to Scripture resulted when authorities (almost all on the patriot side) demanded that pacifists join their cause by actually enlisting, providing alternative service, or paying for military substitutes. When sufficient numbers of sufficiently influential citizens existed in one locale, as Quakers in the Philadelphia area or Mennonites in the Shenandoah Valley of Virginia, negotiations usually ended in compromises to protect both the dissidents' convictions and the authorities' need for recruits, supplies, and money. Yet sometimes in those areas—and even more where isolated pacifist communities lacked political or social influence—spokesmen had to defend their position explicitly.

So it was in November 1775 when Mennonites and Brethren in Pennsylvania published a brief response to laws from the new state legislature that had begun to function independently of Great Britain. After thanking the assembly for exempting conscientious objectors from direct military service, the petitioners quoted Matthew 25:37 as expressing their dedication whenever possible "to feed the hungry and give the thirsty drink." Further quotation followed from well-known passages when they expressed their desire to follow "Christ's command to Peter, to pay the tribute, that we may offend no man [Mt 17:27]; and so we are willing to pay taxes, 'and to render unto Caesar those things that are Caesar's, and to God those things that are God's' [Mt 22:21]"—and all part of a profession "to be subject to the higher powers [Rom 13:1]."[10]

If such professions satisfied the leaders of the new state, they did not protect all who shared these convictions. Near Easton, Pennsylvania, in the summer of 1778 a dozen Mennonite families, who had refused the loyalty oath demanded by local patriots, were ordered to leave the state within thirty days—but not before an auction sold off their household goods, grain, farm equipment, and more in order to pay the fines also levied by local authorities. Bystanders took special note that the confiscation included their "Bibles and books."[11]

Less accommodating circumstances could stimulate lengthier and stiffer responses, as from the petitioners for three Quakers who had been imprisoned in Massachusetts for not securing military substitutes. These Friends refused to participate in "the Unnatural War Subsisting Between Great Britton and the American Colonies"—in fact, "in any Warrs Whatever"— because such participation was "Contrary to the Precepts of Christ as Sett Forth in many Places in the New Testament." Their petition supplied a barrage of biblical quotations, each accompanied by a specific explanation for how warfare violated scriptural injunctions: that Christ had enjoined his followers to "'Love our Enemies'" [Mt 5:44]; that the Apostle Paul had taught "we Warr not after the Flesh &... fight not with flesh & Blood"

[2 Cor 10:3; Eph 6:12]; that he declared "the Weapons of Our Warfare are not Carnal but Spiritual" [2 Cor 10:4]; that the Apostle James taught explicitly "that Warrs & Strifes Came from the Lust which was in the members of Carnal men" [Jas 4:1]; and that Christ taught "his Kingdom is not of this world and therefore that his Servants Shall not fight" [Jn 18:36]. The conclusion, which again rested firmly on the Bible, spoke with the directness for which Friends were notorious: "Therefore Those that fight are not his Disciples nor Servants and many other Passages which are Omitted."[12]

Anthony Benezet, as he had already done on the question of slavery, appealed directly to the Scriptures in the era's most forceful defense of Quaker pacifism. In 1778, he published two works with similar titles that left no doubt about his understanding of the scriptural mandate. The first, a four-page pamphlet titled "Serious Reflections," quoted several other authorities in an effort to wake Americans from "the insensibility that so generally prevails." To drive home what he most wanted to say, he quoted five biblical passages by chapter and verse, including Matthew 5:44 ("Love your Enemies"), Matthew 5:9 ("Blessed are the Peace-makers"), and James 4:1 ("From whence come Wars and Fightings").[13] The second work, "Serious Considerations on Several Important Subjects," devoted thirteen pages to slavery, in which Scripture was prominent; seven pages against drink, in which an appeal to Scripture was mostly absent; and twenty-eight pages on warfare, again relentlessly biblical. This section featured quotations and other scriptural allusions that for Benezet made warfare illicit; he also paused to refute biblical interpretations that others were using to justify military struggle. Full quotation of this pamphlet's first paragraph suggests his nearly complete immersion in the sacred text:

Christ our Lord, to whom every knee must bow, and every tongue confess [Phil 2:10–11], either in mercy or in judgment, came down from his father's glory, took upon him our nature and suffered death for us [see Phil 2:8], to restore to us that first life of meekness, purity and love, that being dead to sin, we should live unto righteousness [1 Pet 2:24]. Leaving us an example, saith the Apostle, that we should follow his steps [see Phil 2:5]. He positively enjoins us, to love our enemies, to bless them that curse us; to do good to those that hate us, and pray for them which despitefully use us and persecute us [Mt 5:44]. A new commandment, saith our blessed Saviour, I give unto you, that ye love one another, as I have loved you

[Jn 13:34]. The meek, the merciful and the pure in heart are by him pronounced to be the particular objects of divine regard [see Mt 5:5, 7, 8]. These are the watch words of Christianity to all the true followers of Christ.[14]

Immediately, Benezet then turned, "on the other hand," to demonstrate—pausing for quotation from one or two other authors but always coming back to pound the Scriptures—how warfare manifestly violated all that the Bible revealed about the deity as a "God of Love."[15]

Although the Pennsylvania Mennonites, Massachusetts Quakers, and Anthony Benezet leaned with all their weight on the scriptural testimony that almost all other colonists also professed to follow, neither the message they took from the Bible nor their style of direct reliance on Scripture made much of a difference in Revolutionary America. Scripture was too securely embedded in the convictions sanctioning or resisting revolt—it had functioned too long as a force embedded in those convictions—for the pacifists' appeal to displace long-standing conventions of interpretation. Yet however little noticed, these pacifist professions cast their mite into the treasury of American opinion. With their direct appeal to the Bible alone, they too strengthened the biblicism that was expanding incrementally during these years.

Rhetoric: Examples, Analogies, Parallels

The ever-memorable conclusion of Patrick Henry's oration to the Virginia delegates gathered at St. John's Church, Richmond (23 March 1775), as they considered whether to join Massachusetts in the fight against Parliament, is etched deep in national mythology: "give me liberty or give me death." Few, however, have attended to the words that came before, where Daniel Dreisbach has recently identified at least ten distinct biblical echoes in the twenty clipped sentences that preceded that famous declaration. These included a direct quotation from Ecclesiastes 9:11—"the battle, sir, is not to the strong alone"—and a form of words drawn from Genesis 17:4 and Joshua 24:15 to frame the oration's stirring climax: "I know not what course others may take; but as for me, give me liberty or give me death!"[16]

It was much the same when Samuel Adams, Boston's foremost Son of Liberty, addressed the Continental Congress in late September 1777. Only shortly before, this much depleted body had fled to York, Pennsylvania, after the British had occupied Philadelphia. When Adams rose in an effort to nerve his discouraged colleagues, his oratory, like Henry's, bore the stamp of biblical originals:

> Let us awaken then, and evince a different spirit,—a spirit that shall inspire the people…to persevere in this glorious struggle, until their rights and liberties shall be established on a rock [see Mt 7:25].…We have appealed to Heaven for the justice of our cause, and in Heaven we have placed our trust. Numerous have been the manifestations of God's providence in sustaining us. In the gloomy period of adversity [echoing Eccl 7:14], we have had "our cloud by day and pillar of fire by night" [quoting Ex 13:21–22]. We have been reduced to distress, and the arm of Omnipotence [echoing Pss 44:3; and 136:12] has raised us up. Let us still rely in humble confidence on Him who is mighty to save [quoting Isa 63:1]. Good tidings [see Lk 2:10 and many other passages] will soon arrive. We shall never be abandoned by Heaven while we act worthy of its aid and protection.[17]

As it happened, good tidings soon thereafter arrived, with news the next month of the military victory at Saratoga that began to turn the tide.

As for Patrick Henry and Samuel Adams, so also for many others. The Bible occupied a prominent place in the language of Revolution—usually not, however, for exposition or instruction but rather for the rhetorical evocation of a sacred sanction:

· For John Adams in his *Dissertation on the Canon and Feudal Law*, published in response to the Stamp Tax of 1765, when in describing the tendency of monarchs and priests to abuse their power, he drew on a biblical vocabulary that Protestants had long used to denounce the pope and to anticipate the end of time—that tendency Adams personified as "the man of sin [2 Thess 2:3], the whore of Babylon [see Rev 17:5], the mystery of iniquity [2 Thess 2:7]";[18]
· For the many political and military leaders who from the time of the Stamp Act controversy forward called their political or military foes "the devil" or spoke of their opponents' "diabolical" schemes;[19]
· For Benjamin Franklin and Thomas Jefferson when in 1776 they proposed images for the new nation's official seal depicting the Israelites' safe crossing of the Red Sea and the same pillar of cloud and pillar of fire that Samuel Adams later invoked;[20]

Benjamin Franklin's explanation for the design he proposed as the seal of the United Colonies illustrated the great power that scriptural narrative enjoyed in the Revolutionary period: "Moses standing on the Shore, and extending his Hand over the Sea, thereby causing the same to overwhelm Pharaoh who is sitting in an open Chariot, a Crown on his Head and a Sword in his Hand. Rays from a Pillar of Fire in the Clouds reaching Moses, to express that he acts by Command of the Deity."

- For the prominent Philadelphia physician and signer of the Declaration of Independence, Benjamin Rush, who in 1778 expressed the opinion to Patrick Henry that although the nation had passed through the Red Sea, it still faced "a dreary wilderness" requiring "a Moses or a Joshua" to be raised up "on our behalf, before we reach the promised land;"[21]
- For the exhortation to Continental troops on July 4, 1779, which quoted Psalm 22:4–5 ("Our fathers trusted and the Lord did deliver them; they cried unto Him and were delivered; they trusted in Him and were not confounded"), in order to inspire the soldiers setting out to destroy Iroquois villages and fields in retribution for the Natives' alliance with the British;[22]

- For George Washington in the hundreds of biblical expressions with which he peppered his published and unpublished words;[23]
- For Mercy Otis Warren who in verse described Britain's commercial empire as a "Pharaoh" who "Plagu'd Israel's race, and tax'd them by a law, / Demanding brick, when destitute of straw";[24]

...and for many, many more.

For Henry, Adams, and the others, Scripture supplied an inexhaustible treasury of words, phrases, apothegms, images, sayings, maxims, and aphorisms for public speech.[25] All such expressions denoted something specific about events in their own time. But they also did more—by intimating a close connection between ancient biblical narratives and a modern national story, by taking for granted that speakers could clearly discern how the biblical "then" related to the contemporary "now," and by connoting a special divine sanction for their enterprises.

The Clergy

As much as laymen and women expressed these intimations, assumptions, and connotations, their clerical contemporaries deployed them much more extensively. For ministers in Revolutionary America the same patterns prevailed that had marked the Puritan use of Scripture.[26] Rarely did they depict the patriot cause as a direct antitype fulfilling a biblical type; typology, strictly considered, remained a method for linking Old Testament passages with their Christian realization in the New. Nonetheless, the constant use of exemplary analogical parallels, along with deductive reasoning that relied on a biblical premise, could in practice function much like the identification of type and antitype.

James Byrd's recent examination of biblical texts associated with eighteenth-century military conflicts provides exhaustive documentation of the Revolutionary era's extraordinarily rich sermonic backdrop that ministers provided for the Revolution. His sample of 17,148 citations from 543 sources covers primarily the last four decades of the century, but with a heavy concentration on the 1770s and early 1780s. Although the authors whose works he canvassed came predominately from New England, he found enough samples from other regions to show that New England stood out for intensity and volume, but not for its scriptural frame of reference. As among the laity, the ministers also relied much more on analogy, example, and parallel experience than they did on direct didactic instruction.[27]

A clear majority of the era's most-often referenced texts spotlighted Old Testament events or pronouncements that speakers applied to the American situation. Not surprisingly, chapters 14 and 15 from the book of Exodus, with their account of the Hebrews' deliverance from Egypt and the miraculous parting of the Red Sea, ranked very near the top of most-cited biblical stories. From these chapters, preachers frequently returned to one particular affirmation from the song of "Moses and the children of Israel" as they praised God, who "hath triumphed gloriously: the horse and his rider hath he thrown into the sea" (Ex 15:1). That passage also included a much-cited declaration that "the LORD is a man of war" (Ex 15:3).[28] Almost as popular was the story from Judges, chapters 4 and 5, of the prophets Deborah and Barak who rallied Israel to fight against oppressing Canaanites. From this narrative preachers drew particular attention to the heroine Jael, who acted on her own initiative to drive a nail through the head of the Canaanite captain Sisera; they also returned repeatedly to the curse pronounced on the men of Meroz "because they came not to the help of the LORD, to the help of the LORD against the mighty" (5:23).[29] Another favorite came from 1 Kings 12, where Rehoboam, the wayward son of King Solomon, began his reign by telling the children of Israel, "my father also chastised you with whips, but I will chastise you with scorpions. Wherefore the king hearkened not unto the people" (12:14–15).[30] When Byrd catalogued entire biblical books, he found that more preaching took off from the Psalms than any place in Scripture, with David's thanksgiving for the Lord's rescue of Israel (Ps 124) a particular favorite.[31]

The one New Testament text that regularly sparked rhetorical pyrotechnics came from Galatians 5:1 ("Stand fast therefore in the liberty wherewith Christ hath made us free, and be not entangled again with the yoke of bondage"). Occasionally, ministers might pause actually to exegete this text; much more frequently it served only as a springboard for exhortations to persevere against Parliamentary tyranny.[32]

It is important to note that amid this tidal wave of biblical rhetoric, Revolutionary-era ministers also sustained a steady flow of straightforward biblical exposition. As described in chapter 11, didactic teaching from Scripture played an important role in justifying actions and sustaining public morale. Yet such exposition took a definite second place to the overwhelming application by analogy, models, parallels, exempla, and metaphors.

It is also important to realize that Loyalists could put the Bible to use in similar fashion. An interesting example unfolded at Wallingford, Connecticut, on a fast day decreed by the colony's new Revolutionary government for 20 July 1775. Samuel Andrews, a missionary of the Anglican's Society for the Propagation of the Gospel (SPG), addressed his congregation from Amos 5:21, "I hate, I despise your feast days, and I will not smell in your solemn assemblies." Evidence from the printed version of this sermon shows that it featured extensive exposition, drawn from this passage and several others, to proclaim that true repentance meant a flight from personal evils, including the evil of slave-holding. Yet not surprisingly, Andrews also found it necessary to add a preliminary "Advertisement to the Reader" in order to allay the suspicion that "the text was chosen in contempt of the late Continental Fast, & that the Chooser was unfriendly to his country." Whether or not Andrews did have that subversive intention, his final thoughts on God's guidance for ancient Israel turned to the present crisis: "should we not then examine, whether our resentments may not have carried us, even too far, at least in some things? whether the laws of God will fully justify, the whole mode of our proceedings?...I am not so much afraid of the power of England, as I am of the sins of America."[33] If in Andrews's mind instruction from Scripture had been his goal, others concluded that he was using the Bible by analogy to criticize the patriots' move toward revolt.

After hostilities had broken out, the rector of New York City's Trinity Church, Charles Inglis, preached a sermon to encourage Americans who had enlisted to fight for Britain. Inglis, to whom we return for the standards he believed Scripture mandated for the larger political sphere, in this instance also spent much time expositing guidance for soldiers from Luke 3:14, "And the soldiers likewise demanded of him [John the Baptist]—And what shall we do? And he said unto them, Do Violence to no Man, neither accuse any falsely, but be content with your Wages." Yet when Inglis came to describe "contentment," he put the Bible to use, not for straightforward exposition, but in the deductive manner that was so common with patriots: "A discontented Mind is never at Rest....O how melancholy an Instance of this Truth, does this wretched Country afford at present! Where a Land of Peace and Plenty—a Land distinguished above any other by its Civil and Religious Privileges, is turned into a Field of Blood." Inglis also displayed his skill with scriptural phraseology by echoing Luke 4:18 as he reminded these Loyalists that "you have taken up the Sword that those who are Captives, for Conscience, sake may be set at Liberty, and that the Prisoner may go free."[34] As the examples from Andrews and Inglis suggest, however, the Loyalists usually lacked the flare for analogizing ancient Israel that patriotic ministers mastered.

A rapid survey of a handful of publications from a smaller handful of New England ministers cannot describe the skill of such preachers in detail, but it can indicate the general pattern of biblical application that having been built up over many years came to full expression in the Revolutionary crisis. As the extensive investigations of James Byrd and others have documented, the examples that follow were entirely representative of the New England public sphere and substantially representative of patriotic sermonizing as a whole.

The snapshots that follow—from 1755 to 1778—highlight the elements of a powerful sermonic ideology. Five propositions built the ideological infrastructure:

(1) The political community could be addressed in the same biblical terms as used to address the church.
(2) The history of ancient Israel provided a master narrative whose elements illuminated the patriots' contemporary cause.
(3) The covenant promises of Scripture applied just as much to the American colonies fighting for their lives against Britain as to Old Testament Israel fighting against Philistia, Assyria, or Babylon.
(4) Scripture, understood aright, demonstrated the apocalyptic evil of Roman Catholicism and the duty of Protestants to contest the temporal representatives of that evil, increasingly designated as the British Parliament.
(5) Scriptural terms defining Christian liberty and the tyranny of sin described also the civil situation that political Whigs viewed as menaced by the tyranny of political foes, first France and then Britain.[35]

Significantly, these propositions bore the stamp of the colonists' Christendom heritage. At the same time that they felt increasingly threatened by what they considered the oppressive venality of Parliament, the biblical terms in which they expressed their resistance took for granted the interweaving of civil and ecclesiastical spheres. Instincts of Christendom, thus, propelled the arguments that would soon bring an end in America to Britain's formal Christendom.

To begin this parade of examples, a sermon from 1755 offers a reminder that public biblical religion in the Revolutionary era descended directly from public religion during the French and Indian War. Solomon Williams, the minister in Lebanon, Connecticut, and a cousin of Jonathan Edwards, preached on Psalm 20:5 to a militia company being assembled to take part in the attack on the French fortress at Louisbourg. His text ("We will Rejoice in thy Salvation, and in the name of GOD we will set up our banners") afforded Williams the opportunity to speak of the soldiers' civil and religious lives as a unified whole. They were fighting to support "the interests of the Redeemer's Kingdom, the interest of the Churches of Christ in New England, and of all *English America*." Since victory by France and the pope would lead to "our Souls enslaved," the soldiers could go to battle with the assurance that "when you Fight, those you Fight with, are the Enemies of Christ." Only at the very end did Williams exhort his hearers, in the standard pattern of a traditional jeremiad, to repent of their own sins as their part of the heavenly bargain.[36]

The next year, George Beckwith based his Connecticut election sermon on Romans 8:31 ("If God be for us, who can be against us?"). Even as Beckwith exulted in the British victory over the "Fortress of Cape-Breton" at Louisbourg, the outcome of the struggle with France still remained in doubt. His message offered primarily reassurance: "God is for *his People*, as he is in Covenant with them, & so engaged to them and for them, as he condescends to dwell among them, and take them under his special Care and Protection." To the colonial representatives assuming their duties at the start of a legislative season, Beckwith specified the special blessing Connecticut enjoyed with church and government cooperating together, in his words, "by the Agency, & Conduct of Moses and Aaron, whom he appointed over them in their respective Orders to lead, and guide *his People*, in the ways of Duty and Safety."[37]

When the tide of battle had definitely turned, ministers again drew on Old Testament narratives to express their thanksgiving for the British triumph of Quebec. In the course of a sermon with the Song of Moses as his text from Exodus 15:2, Solomon Williams in 1760 demonstrated "how our Relations to God resemble those of the Israelites" and, consequently, why "our Obligations and Engagements are similar."[38] The Massachusetts election sermon of that year offered Samuel Dunbar the chance to show how a text from 2 Chronicles (15:1–2, "And the spirit of God came upon Azariah…And he went to meet Asa, and said unto him…The LORD is with you, while ye be with him") could be applied directly to Massachusetts. With the same reference to "his people" that Connecticut's George Beckwith had evoked earlier, Dunbar explained how Israel's history applied directly to Massachusetts: "Their covenant relation to God constitutes them his peculiar people." He also reiterated the transaction standard in the jeremiad tradition, though gently: "The promise of God has ever made good to his people: they ever found that, when they were with God in the way of duty, God was with them in the way of providential mercy."[39]

In 1761, Ezra Stiles preached a much-noticed sermon on the potential of a more self-conscious unity among all the Congregational churches of New England, to which we return shortly for its expository content. In the course of this sermon, Stiles lingered at length to drive home teaching from the Apostle Paul in Philippians 3:16 ("Nevertheless, whereto we have already attained, let us walk by the same Rule, let us mind the same thing"). But the sermon also afforded an opportunity to rehearse local history, which led him to aver that "In more things than one, that of exile, our New England churches may resemble God's antient chosen people." With this parallel firmly fixed, Stiles went on to urge that "the great errand into America never be forgotten." His means for securing that memory was to make children "well acquainted among other parts of sacred history, with the history of the Hebrew nation; in which they will see examples of public reward and public chastisement of providence in a very striking light."[40] As the handling of these texts illustrates, already in the years from 1755 to 1761 the analogy between Israel as a political society and New England as a church-state union had become conventional wisdom.

Colonial resistance to the Stamp Tax that followed the war inflamed the public sphere. After protests, riots, tense standoffs with agents designated to collect the tax, and fevered communication across the Atlantic, relief was palpable when Parliament rescinded the tax. In Boston, two of the city's leading ministers preached celebratory sermons, both launched from Old Testament texts, though with no exposition of those passages. On 23 May 1766, Jonathan Mayhew turned to Psalm 124:7–8: "Our soul is escaped as a bird from the snare of the fowler: the snare is broken, and we are escaped. Our help is in the name of the LORD, who made heaven and earth." His discourse, "the snare broken," began with a fulsome dedication to William Pitt, whom colonists saw as their Parliamentary savior, and then began to exposit the recent events that occasioned the discourse: "The late gracious appearance of divine providence for us, in the day of our trouble" was so great as to call forth this thanksgiving sermon.[41] Two months later on 24 July, Charles Chauncy preached on "good news from a far country." His text came from Proverbs 25:25: "As cold waters to a thirsty soul, so is good news from a far country." Again, no exposition of the text followed but rather a recital of recent events combined with praise to God for his "allwise over-ruling-wise influence, that a SPIRIT was raised in all the Colonies nobly to assert their freedom as men, and English-born subjects."[42] With Mayhew, Chauncy did not need to explain how and why he used the Bible as he did. Both could simply rely on the interweaving of narratives—biblical history and New England's history—that had long prevailed in their region.

Three months after the so-called Boston Massacre of 5 March 1770, Chauncy was once again asked to speak for Massachusetts with a sermon. The request came after the royal governor had removed the colony's General Court to Cambridge from its usual meeting site in Boston. This time Chauncy chose Psalm 22:4 as his text: "Our fathers trusted in thee; they trusted, and thou didst deliver them." As he spoke, Chauncy lingered longer with his text in order to demonstrate how much the ancient story of God's people had anticipated what Massachusetts was experiencing. A longer quotation can show how completely he and most of his audience made this identification:

> My text, though thus primarily directed to the Jews to engage their trust in God…is yet applicable to other people, under like circumstances; and may obviously be accommodated to the people of God in this land. Perhaps, there are no people, now dwelling on the face of the earth, who may, with greater pertinencey, adopt the language of King *David*, and say, "our fathers trusted in thee; they trusted, and thou didst deliver them."…As they [our ancestors] trusted in God, he made way for their deliverance from this tyranny, by bringing them over to this then desolate land, with CHARTER-RIGHTS, but intitling them to distinguishing liberties and privileges, both civil and religious…. The deliverance of our forefathers from tyranny and oppression, by bringing them over to this distant region, is not unlike his carrying his Israel of old thro' the red sea to the promised land of rest.[43]

New England preachers differed in how much Christianity they mixed into their historical accounts of "God's people" in the New World. Most included at least some injunctions to put faith in Christ or live by standards of virtue outlined in the New Testament. When in April 1773 Benjamin Trumbull of North Haven, Connecticut, preached at the annual meeting of New Haven's "freemen," he emphasized the Christian character of his colony's governing arrangements. Yet his sermon unfolded mostly as an extended analogy of Israel's history. The text came from Exodus 1:8, "Now there arose up a new king over Egypt, which knew not

Joseph," with a predictable application to the Parliamentary strangers who abused the colonies as Pharaoh had abused the children of Israel. A Christian element returned when Trumbull proposed that good rulers, in contrast to Parliament, were "Men who love their country—love the churches of our LORD JESUS CHRIST—and for their brethren and companions' sakes will seek the peace and prosperity of Jerusalem, and 'because of the House of the LORD our God, will seek HER GOOD' (Psal. 122:7, 8, 9)." In turn, the freemen, as the responsible citizens of New Haven, were charged to remember that "you are acting for your neighbours, your friends, yea, your brethren not barely for the ties of nature, but by the more sacred bonds of our COMMON CHRISTIANITY."[44] A thoroughly Christianized social order, though aspiring to Christian virtues, naturally drew its instructions from Hebrew originals.

The outbreak of open conflict only reinforced the long-standing application of biblical tropes, models, and parallels to current events. Again, however, with variations. The jeremiad template, with its emphasis on the need for colonists to repent of their sins in order to restore God's favor, came back more strongly as warfare took lives, shook the economy, and disrupted daily life. John Devotion's extraordinary performance at the annual Connecticut election sermon of 1777 exploited his text from Isaiah 8:13 ("Sanctify the LORD of hosts") in that standard pattern. It concentrated on the need for Connecticut's citizens to promote "vital piety, a sacred regard to justice, mercy, humility, fidelity, and sanctity" as "the readiest way to an honourable and safe issue, of a war that threatens the very being of a state." Yet still this mandate for the preacher rested on an Old Testament narrative: "Through undeserved mercy, God's conduct has hitherto been, toward us, as it was toward Israel, in the days of Jehoahaz; when they were oppressed by Hazael king of Syria; 'And the Lord was gracious to them...because of his covenant with Abraham' [2 Kings 8:8—13:23]." Although Devotion began his sermon by explaining that it would not be a political discourse, he nonetheless ended it with an anthem specially composed for the occasion. He titled it "Independence"; inevitably it was peppered with scriptural allusions, for example: "As of many waters [Rev 14:2], / Trust ye the Lord Jehovah, / Make him your help and shield [Ps 33:20]."[45]

When in 1778 Boston's leading minister was asked to deliver a Thursday lecture-sermon, Charles Chauncy concentrated much more on chastising American patriots for their sins than he had done in the sermons we noticed from 1766 and 1770. According to Chauncy, the military struggle against parliamentary oppression was bringing out the worst in the patriots.

He asked rhetorically, was "our land...ever in a more corrupt and degenerate state?" And his bill of particulars ran on and on: "oppression... extravagance, intemperance and lewdness...sabbaths...profaned...sanctuary...polluted...horrid cursing and swearing." Chauncy, as it turns out, was most exercised by the economic sins of runaway inflation; at considerable length, he stressed the special impact of these evils on *"salary-men,* and particularly *the Clergy."* Inevitably, for his jeremiad Chauncy turned again to Old Testament Israel, in this case the story from the book of Joshua about Achan who had violated the Lord's command by taking spoil from the destruction of Jericho and hiding it in his tent: "Thus saith the LORD God of Israel, There is an accursed thing in the midst of thee, O Israel: thou canst not stand before thine enemies, until ye take away the accursed thing from among you" (Josh 7:13). In Chauncy's treatment, this passage meant that if Massachusetts and the Continental Congress did not stabilize the currency, their struggle against Parliamentary tyranny might collapse. After he recounted many instances of God's providence working on behalf of the American forces, he concluded that the Bible could not be clearer: Israel's history showed that when it broke covenant, it could not stand before its enemies; God deals with "other people, as he dealt with Israel."[46]

Several scholars have pointed out that patriots outside of New England did not identify their cause with God's chosen people of the Old Testament as tightly as did Chauncy. Yet thanks to James Byrd's exhaustive research, it is evident that the biblical usage so common in New England prevailed elsewhere to a considerable degree as well. Thus, several sermons printed in Philadelphia during this period explained the struggle with Britain in terms of Egyptian evil and the rescue of Israel through the miraculous parting of the Red Sea.[47] Printed sermons featuring Deborah and the Curse of Meroz came from New York, Charleston, Philadelphia, and Lancaster, Pennsylvania, as well as from Boston and New Haven.[48] The life of David, and more generally inspiration from the Psalms, informed more than one printed discourse from New York and several from Pennsylvania.[49] Presses in New York, Pennsylvania, and North Carolina disseminated numerous ministerial reflections that described the fate of America with passages from the book of Revelation.[50]

For assessing the ubiquitous biblical rhetoric of the period, other distinctions besides geography are also important. Some New England ministers actually played down the covenantal status of their own region. In particular, students of Jonathan Edwards were as likely to view God's covenant as extending moral law and potential righteousness to all humankind rather than to any modern national unit.[51] Again, Baptists throughout the colonies often applied biblical themes of covenant to individual believers and the churches gathered by the converted, instead of to society at large.[52] Over the course of the war, some patriotic recourse to Scripture also followed the arc of Charles Chauncy's sermons in shifting from a fevered, Manichaen account of virtuous colonial Good versus corrupt parliamentary Evil to a more sober indictment of patriotic as well as parliamentary sins.[53]

Most importantly, much sermonizing as well as much private recourse to Scripture continued to emphasize personal redemption, holy living, and the life of faith.[54] However much political upheaval intruded into the lives of David George in Savannah, Sarah Osborn in Newport, Methodists tiptoeing gingerly between competing loyalties in the middle colonies, or Shakers and Freewill Baptists on the New England frontier, the Bible remained for these and many others primarily a spiritual resource and only incidentally a political manual.[55]

Yet necessary qualifications having been made, there can be no doubt about the tremendous stimulus that the Revolutionary War gave to biblical rhetoric. That stimulus worked in many guises—as a literary resource universally accessible in the phrases of the King James Version, a vocabulary of divine presence to sanctify military conflict, a repository of morally charged examples, a treasury of tropes to encourage or admonish in the face of uncertainty, and a narrative written expressly for a people in covenant with God. A rhetorical presence already without rival in colonial America extended its reach even farther.

Revolutionary Argument

AS THE BIBLE extended its already pervasive rhetorical presence in Revolutionary America, its place as a teaching authority also expanded. Direct appeal to the Bible for specific instruction in these years had the significant effect of effacing the instincts of British Christendom, especially the instinct that Scripture needed to be apprehended within an establishmentarian framework. Colonial experience had already weakened that instinct. Anglicanism had always been much stronger as an ideal in London and Canterbury than as a reality in the Thirteen Colonies; the divine-right Presbyterianism so dear to the Scots gained barely a toehold in the religious pluralism of the middle colonies; New England's Congregational establishment had always been defended with a Dissenting exaltation of *sola scriptura*; in the rest of the colonies, sectarian Christians carried that same reverence for Scripture into an attack on all church-state impositions; and as the eighteenth century wore on, more and more colonists elided their Christian convictions with political principles intensely distrustful of any top-down exercise of authority, including the authority of inherited religious establishments.

In these circumstances, direct appeals to the Bible carried a double significance. Most obvious was the effect of such appeals for the questions under immediate consideration—for example, whether the colonies needed bishops, whether war for independence could be justified, or whether God sanctioned the enslavement of Africans. Less obvious was the effect of such appeals on assumptions about Scripture itself. James Bradley, a historian of eighteenth-century England, has made an observation about Dissenters there during the Revolutionary period that also illuminates the American situation. He notes that while almost all English Protestants agreed that Scripture should be revered as the highest authority, this profession "had a keener edge in the mouths of Nonconformists" because it expressed their rejection of inherited establishmentarian authority and their reliance on a right of private biblical interpretation. When some of these Nonconformists protested against Parliament's actions in the colonies, they acted consistently "with their doctrine of the church," since for them "the formal principle of authority was located outside of the institution of the Established Church and above the state."[1] So it was also in the colonies, except with a much weaker establishmentarian counterbalance. As a result, colonial appeals to the Bible—on any matter—tilted against the traditions of Christendom or simply disregarded them. As they did so, these appeals prepared the way for an untried type of religious existence: Christianity without formal Christendom. How this experiment might function would take many decades to work out, but public biblical arguments against Anglican institutions, especially against Anglican bishops, marked an important early stage in what eventually became the United States' incorporation of the right of private judgment into constitutional religious freedom.

Argument over Bishops

Colonial fear about local bishops, which intensified during the 1750s and 1760s, enjoyed a long history. As early as 1687, during an earlier period of imperial conflict, Increase Mather had published a tract against the incursion of Anglicans into New England. Its title anticipated the scriptural standard that such arguments almost always advanced: *A Testimony Against Several Prophane and Superstitious Customs Now Practiced by some in New-England, the Evil Whereof is Evinced from the Holy Scriptures, and from the Writings both of Ancient and Modern Divines.*[2] Thereafter, resentment at what many colonists perceived as Anglican encroachments simmered steadily. When simmering turned to boil during the Stamp Act crisis, the intensity of the debate spoke to its pertinence. Patricia Bonomi has supplied a helpful reminder: the controversy over bishops "easily consumed as much paper as the Stamp Act dispute, and probably exceeded it over the long run since the question of episcopacy was debated periodically from at least 1702 onward."[3]

Jonathan Mayhew's inflammatory sermon of 1749 that lionized the executioners of Charles I had articulated the oppositional or Whig political ideology forever wedded to colonial worry about bishops.[4] Almost all colonial Anglicans wanted two things: ministerial candidates ordained without the dangerous and expensive journey across the ocean that was required for the laying on of a bishop's hands, and local ecclesiastical coordination without cumbersome reliance on the bishop of London. A smaller, but significant, number nurtured the hope that a local Episcopal presence could administer an antidote of hierarchical authority to the poisons of sectarian disorder. By contrast, colonists who were not Anglicans (and many who were) feared that bishops inevitably entailed unchecked, corrupting power poised as a deadly threat to civil and religious liberty. In the increasingly heated debates between proponents of those opposing views, scriptural defenses and attacks came repeatedly to the fore, but always in conjunction with broader political commitments.

Controversy on this question received a significant stimulus from the address that Ezra Stiles delivered in April 1760 to the Congregational clergy of Rhode Island. When published the next year, his *Discourse on the Christian Union* accomplished three things: it appealed forcefully for stronger bonds among all the Congregational and Presbyterian clergy in the colonies; it fused radical Whig and Dissenting Protestant principles in a manner that would become increasingly powerful; and it outlined the basic case against colonial bishops, or indeed bishops as such.

As we saw in chapter 9, this substantial work began with extensive biblical exposition, six packed pages on Stiles's text from Philippians 3:16: "Let us walk by the same rule, let us mind the same thing." Then Stiles set out an extensive catalogue of agreed-upon convictions that Calvinist ministers throughout the colonies already held in common—like belief in God, original sin, and justification by grace through faith. That list featured prominently "the belief of the inspiration of the scriptures" as "an authentic and the only infallible account of the whole system of revelation made from Time to Time to mankind."[5] In the more than one hundred pages that followed, Stiles repeatedly enlisted biblical passages to support his arguments; the barrage of didactic Scripture evoked for teaching slackened only when he began his extensive recital of New England's history fashioned as a parallel to the history of ancient Israel. Throughout the entire work, Stiles's determined reliance on Scripture also functioned as a Whig protest against illegitimate authority. The union was seamless, as in these expressions from a single paragraph: "the scriptures as infallible rule...we shall stand fast in the liberty wherewith the gospel has made us free...the right of conscience and private judgment is unalienable...it is truly the interest of all mankind to unite themselves into one body, for the liberty, free exercise and unmolested enjoyment of this right, especially in religion." In his enthusiasm, Stiles also showed once again how easily the Protestant turn to Scripture as a critical instrument could became a statement of biblicism: "God be thanked we are not embarrassed with subscriptions and oaths to uninspired rules for defining truth, in this land of liberty, where the SCRIPTURES are professedly our ONLY RULE."[6]

As the controversy over a colonial bishop intensified, detailed biblical exposition regularly gave way to simple political denunciation. Yet not always. Only shortly after Stiles published his *Discourse*, a Congregationalist minister from Stamford, Connecticut, Noah Welles, produced a study that went far beyond Stiles in laying out a scriptural mandate for ordaining ministers in the Congregational or Presbyterian fashion (through local councils) and *not* as the Anglicans (through bishops). Welles's title page made room for 1 Timothy 4:14, the only place in the KJV that uses the *p*-word: "The Gift…which was given thee,…with the laying on of hands of the Presbytery." Short quotations from Jerome and Thomas Cranmer followed the Timothy quotation, attesting that the early church had used the terms "presbyter" and "bishop" interchangeably. The pamphlet itself began with extensive exposition of 2 Corinthians 10:8—"For though I should boast somewhat more of our authority (which the LORD hath given us for edification, and not for your destruction) I should not be ashamed." Welles then quoted or cited scores of biblical references—all but one or two from the New Testament, many from the Pastoral Epistles of 1 Timothy, 2 Timothy, and Titus. When Welles cited extrabiblical authorities, he quoted ancient church fathers and Anglican clergy not as independent voices but because they confirmed Welles's interpretation of the relevant scriptural passages. In the midst of this appeal to chapter and verse, Welles paused to state his foundational principle. That statement is worth quoting, because the shape of his reasoning would reappear consistently for more than the next century in debates over a wide range of public issues—and continue to resonate to this day among communities self-defined by their reliance on Scripture.

> Now, as the Christian ministry is an office of divine institution, appointed by Jesus Christ, the greatest head and king of his church, it hence follows, that his word contained in the scriptures, is the only sure rule, by which pretensions of any to this office can fairly be tried, and their ministerial authority established and proved.
>
> If therefore, I can make it appear, that the ministers of our churches, are endued with the qualifications which the scriptures require;—that they are called to the work, according to the scripture pattern and direction, and are regularly set apart to it, and invested with the powers of it, agreeable to the direction and example left us

by Christ and his apostles; the consequence, I think will be undeniable, that they are regular gospel ministers, and possessed of complete authority to act as such.[7]

With such a definite standard supported by such extensive scriptural demonstration, it is little wonder that opponents of a colonial bishop took for granted that they enjoyed the biblical high ground.

That could be the reason why many of those who spoke out against a colonial bishop rarely did more than gesture toward Scripture—for example, Jonathan Mayhew in the several extensive tracts in which he attacked the SPG for abandoning evangelization of natives in order to lead astray the residents of New England cities. In one such response to a critic from 1764 he spent almost all of his energy excoriating England's bishops for participating in "every scheme for promoting tyranny and bondage." In the sort of paragraph by paragraph refutation that must have been as satisfying to write as it is now tedious to read, Mayhew also stressed how close Anglicanism came to the corruptions of Catholicism. His only reference to the Bible responded to his opponent's claim that Anglicans followed the "scripture rule" of proceeding decently and in order (1 Cor 14:40): "As to the *scripture rule* which the gentleman speaks of, respecting *decency and order*, if forms of prayer may be supposed to come under it, so as to be *needful for the observance thereof*, why may not the sign of the cross also?...Where will people stop in introducing their own inventions, in this lax way of expounding scripture rules?"[8]

It was the same for William Livingstone, a New York attorney and the leading publicist for advanced political views in the middle colonies. He had emerged in the 1750s by using Dissenting Protestant and Whig principles to attack plans for a publicly funded Anglican college in that city.[9] When in the next decade Livingston entered the lists against Anglican schemes for a colonial bishop, he extended the strongly republican arguments of his early polemics. To allow such an office in America meant inevitably that the colonists would soon be forced to make "an implicit submission to ecclesiastico-political power arbitrarily assumed, and tyrannically exercised." Livingstone still could make a biblical claim when responding to charges that the Congregational and Presbyterian clergy of the colonies had abandoned the "native religion" of the first settlers: they still "to this day," he affirmed, "teach and inculcate them [the doctrines of the Thirty-Nine Articles] in the same scriptural and unadulterated sense, in which they were believed, taught and inculcated at the time of the reformation."[10]

But such references appeared rarely. If for disputants like Mayhew and Livingston, the Bible as such occupied only an incidental place in their polemics, others like Stiles and Welles had already done a thorough job at demonstrating, at least to their anti-episcopal satisfaction, the rock-solid biblical support for their position.

But what of the Anglicans who also professed to follow biblical guidance and who were not shy about putting their arguments before the public? The crucial observation about their extensive polemics is not that they lacked either the willingness or the expertise to argue from the Scriptures. It is, rather, that these defenders of a colonial bishop nested their biblical arguments in a broader defense of church establishment, Anglican ordination, and the weight of history. In short, they offered the Bible-of-Christendom against the colonists' Bible-as-republican-witness.

Advocates for a bishop in the colonies included several capable authors who eagerly took up the biblical challenge. Jeremiah Leaming, an SPG missionary in Norwalk, Connecticut, published probably the most thorough of such works in 1766. In his sights were Noah Welles's 1763 vindication of ordination by presbyteries and a Dudleian Lecture at Harvard by Charles Chauncy with the same general thesis.[11] Even a hardcore biblicist would have been pressed to fault Leaming's procedure. After beginning with the requisite scriptural quotations on his title page, Leaming pointed out that Dissenters differed widely among themselves on how they interpreted the sacred book, and then he raised his standard: "Let us then take the scripture for our rule, which is the only sure guide" and so seek "a right understanding of the scriptures" for what to conclude about "apostles, presbyters, and deacons."[12] In a work almost as densely packed with biblical references as Welles's defense of Presbyterian ordination, he called leaders functioning like modern Anglican bishops an "incontestable scripture fact"; he claimed that "the universal facts of the primitive church" affirmed what Leaming concluded about the New Testament; and he called the New Testament account of Paul's commissioning of Timothy and his address to the elders of Ephesus "the direct proof for episcopacy that I have...taken from the facts recorded in the sacred Volume."[13] Although Leaming also added an appendix appealing to historical testimony from the early church, the Reformation, and the history of England, his effort rested from first to last on biblical exposition. Its tone is conveyed by the scorn he heaped on Charles Chauncy who, in recounting the history of New England's churches, had evoked Galatians 5:1—as Leaming quoted Chauncy, "May they ever stand fast in this liberty, wherewith he who is head over all things has made us free." "Where," responded the indignant Anglican, "does he find in scripture This [Chauncy's defense of ordination by local church councils] to be declared a part of Christian liberty?" In reality, Leaming protested, New England's ordinations rested "not upon *scripture*, but upon the *law of the province*, which declares who shall be the patrons, in each parish, to chose the minister."[14]

Leaming's thorough study seems not to have made much of an impression; it certainly has dropped almost completely out of sight, even in the best historical accounts.[15] By contrast, Thomas Bradbury Chandler's 1767 *Appeal to the Public in Behalf of the Church of England in America* drew considerable fire when it first appeared and has continued to register as the most able presentation of the Anglican position.[16] Chandler, the SPG rector of St. John's Church, Elizabethtown, New Jersey, enjoyed the patronage of Samuel Johnson, who as a famous convert to Anglicanism, learned moral philosopher, and president of King's College (later Columbia) in New York City, had himself long campaigned for a colonial bishop. Chandler began his full-scale defense with a "sketch" of the biblical "Arguments in favor of Episcopacy" and an explanation of what Scripture taught about "Government, Ordination, and Confirmation." Although with less attention to detail than Jeremiah Leaming, Chandler still provided extensive demonstration from "the Writings of the Apostles, and the *Canonical Records* of their Proceedings."[17] When he turned to practicalities, he insisted that colonial bishops would exercise only spiritual and administrative authority—without positions in government, without enforced tithes, without future "Augmentation of their Power."[18]

Yet if Chandler's *Appeal* directly evoked Scripture and directly confronted fears of episcopal oppression, his arguments seemed deliberately designed to stoke colonial apprehensions, beginning with the work's flowery dedication to the "Lord Archbishop of Canterbury."[19] Chandler interwove his scriptural appeals with even more appeals to ancient and modern church authorities, not in Noah Welles's fashion to confirm a biblical conclusion but as authorities in their own right. Moreover, as the climax of his tract, Chandler expatiated at length on the natural affinity linking episcopacy, monarchy, and loyalty to Britain. The contrasting instincts of the "rigid Republican" he portrayed as inimical to the crown specifically and to Britain in general. Whatever credit Chandler gained by his not inconsiderable recourse to the Bible, he lost by clothing that appeal in Tory garb.

Others who took the side of Leaming and Chandler argued much more like Jonathan Mayhew and William Livingston, that is, getting right to the political payoff without addressing questions of scriptural principle. In 1763, East Apthorp, an aggressive Anglican missionary charged with reshaping the epicenter of New England elite opinion in Cambridge, Massachusetts, devoted a complete published defense of the SPG to demonstrating that the current practice of the SPG really did "conform to the design of their incorporation" and to "the CHARTER, granted by King William III, in MDCCI."[20] The same year a veteran Boston Anglican, Henry Caner, responded to Jonathan Mayhew's attacks on the SPG more calmly, but still by featuring an exposition of the SPG charter without meaningful reference to Scripture. Caner did pause to ask his colonial opponents why they seemed so unconcerned about Mayhew's heterodox theological opinions, like his denial of the full deity of Jesus Christ. In recounting these errors, Caner specified "how easy" it had been for Mayhew "to discard even the sacred canon of scripture itself."[21] Yet neither in spotlighting these doctrinal errors nor in refuting Mayhew's challenge to the SPG did Caner reason directly from the Bible.

In sum, when assessing the verse-to-verse combat that contributed to public confrontation on the question of a bishop for the colonies, it is difficult to see a clear victory for either camp. Both those who favored bishops and those who did not could mount sophisticated biblical arguments. Instead, the crucial difference lay in the frameworks surrounding biblical usage. To evoke nomenclature from an earlier era, "the Bishops' Bible" underscored the time-honored principles of English Protestant Christendom. In opposition, "the Anti-Bishops Bible" reinforced more recent ideologies of power, corruption, and liberty. The thesis of Carl Bridenbaugh's study of the conflict bears repeating: "It is indeed high time that we repossess the important historical truth that religion was a fundamental cause of the American Revolution."[22] Yet by examining the way Scripture in particular defined this conflict, it is possible to say more: not just that "religion" factored large in the American Revolution, but that the War of Independence represented the struggle of Scripture incarnate as a weapon of the establishment contesting Scripture incarnate as a Whig weapon.

Argument from Patriots

Biblical phrases, biblical examples, biblical parallels, biblical models—all pervaded the discourse of colonial patriots as they first protested British policies and then took up arms. The regular pattern took the form of citing an event in Old Testament history that illuminated contemporary developments. Direct appeals to biblical precepts, doctrine, or ethical injunctions—that is, to scriptural teaching that required a specific response of obedience—were rare. Yet sometimes the common practice featuring Old Testament examples could be developed into didactic exposition, especially when ministers defended the conflict with Britain as a "just war."[23] Patriot spokesmen also sometimes moved painstakingly from exegeting a scriptural passage to making a truth claim on the basis of that passage and then applying that truth as authoritative guidance. In this section, we examine three such efforts that, while evoking Scripture rhetorically, also developed chains of biblical reasoning aiming at authoritative instruction. These sermons all made extensive reference to incidents from ancient Hebrew history, but, significantly, they did not apply the tropes of "chosen nation" or "covenanted people" to the patriot cause. They show, in other words, that biblical framing of the conflict with Britain rested on much more than the New England Puritan legacy.

The first of these sermons, though delivered in Boston, came from an English Baptist who had only recently arrived in America. John Allen's English experience included a short pastorate in London where he had defended "the rights of the people" in the controversy that witnessed the expulsion of radical John Wilkes from Parliament. In America he expanded upon the meaning of "rights" with "An Oration Upon the Beauties of Liberty" that was preached first in December 1772 and then distributed widely in multiple printed editions. So much noticed was the published version of Allen's tract that scholars have called him "New England's Tom Paine."[24]

Allen's sermon illustrated how an Old Testament example could be brokered into a full-scale call to arms. His text from Micah 7:3 may have seemed at first chosen for its sheer incomprehensibility: "That they may do evil with both hands, earnestly, the Prince asketh, and the Judge asketh for a reward; and the great Man, he uttereth his mischievous desire: So they wrap it up."[25] But because the book of Micah opens by locating the prophet in the reign of Israel's wicked King Ahaz, whose malefactions are described at length in 2 Chronicles 28, Allen had found a word for his times. At the very outset he stated forthrightly how he would be treating this text: "it was the dark time with the nation [Israel]…when Micah appeared…as a prophet of the Lord and a son of liberty.…Is not the day of the watchmen of America come, who watch for the rights of the people, as the centinels of the land, to defend them from every invasion of power and destruction?" After announcing that "it is…plain that a craving, absolute prince, is a great distress to a people," Allen embarked upon a phrase-by-phrase exposition followed by application.[26]

> Text: "the Judge asketh for a reward." Application: if the colonies' magistrates are appointed and paid by the Crown, "then you may easily judge whose servants and slaves you are to be."[27]
>
> Text: "that they may do evil with both hands." Application: "This shews that an arbitrary dispotic power is the ruin of a nation."[28]
>
> Text: "the great man uttereth his mischievous desires." Application: "it is no rebellion to oppose any king, ministry, or governor, that destroys by violence or authority whatever, the rights of the people."[29]
>
> Text: "and so they wrap it up." Application: If Parliament can unilaterally impose duties on tea, imports, and clearances, then it may tax "every acre of land you enjoy...every apple tree you rear...every barrel of cyder you make...every pair of shoes you wear...the light of the morning...the sun, that a kind heaven gives you."[30]

John Allen's explanation for how the prophet Micah's commentary on the reign of Ahaz pertained to American colonists under George III displayed a certain measure of creativity. Yet because of how closely his sermon fit—and also propelled—a "language of liberty," its creative exposition became for at least some colonists biblical illumination for their generation.[31]

John Witherspoon, president of the College of New Jersey at Princeton, delivered a more restrained, more deliberately theological sermon in May 1776, less than three weeks before he signed the Declaration of Independence as one of New Jersey's delegates to the Continental Congress. Eight years earlier Witherspoon had come from Scotland to Princeton, where he immediately engineered an effective renewal of this Presbyterian-led institution that had suffered the untimely death of its first five presidents. As with Allen's flamboyant effort, Witherspoon's careful address made a real difference in moving public opinion to support the cause for which as a Signer he would dedicate his life, fortune, and sacred honor.[32]

Witherspoon preached this sermon on a Fast Day appointed by the Continental Congress to pray for the future of "the United Colonies." This traditional New England exercise, now extended to all thirteen colonies, allowed Witherspoon to express political views he had heretofore not addressed from the pulpit. It also gave him an occasion for making a powerful theological statement based on Psalm 76:10, "Surely the Wrath of Man shall praise thee: the remainder of wrath shalt thou restrain." Four

For the Revd. Mr. Smith of. Weymouth

John Adams

No. 10

The Dominion of Providence over the Pas-
fions of Men.

A

SERMON

PREACHED

At PRINCETON,

On the 17th of MAY, 1776.

BEING

The GENERAL FAST appointed by the CONGRESS
through the UNITED COLONIES.

TO WHICH IS ADDED,

An ADDRESS to the NATIVES of SCOTLAND residing in
AMERICA.

By *JOHN WITHERSPOON*, D. D.

PRESIDENT OF THE COLLEGE OF NEW-JERSEY.

PHILADELPHIA:

PRINTED AND SOLD BY R. AITKEN, PRINTER AND
BOOKSELLER, OPPOSITE THE LONDON COFFEE-
HOUSE, FRONT-STREET.
M.DCC.LXXVI.

1776

Unlike many of the printed sermons of his era, John Witherspoon's influential 1776 appeal for resistance to Britain appeared with a relatively uncluttered
title page. In this case, he reproduced the words of his text from Psalm 76:10
but no supplementary passages. (Courtesy of the American Antiquarian Society)

things are most impressive about Witherspoon's exposition of the "doctrine" he derived from this text, "that all the disorderly passions of men,
whether exposing the innocent to private injury, or whether they are the
arrows of divine judgment in public calamity, shall, in the end, be to the
praise of God."[33] First was extensive biblical exposition of a doctrine of
divine providence. Second came his identification of the "wrath" of his text
with political oppression. Third was application of that identification to
the American situation. Fourth were closing exhortations that urged his
auditors (or readers) to advance in faith and virtue.

More than half of the sermon treated theological foundations. From
Witherspoon's reading of the biblical history of salvation, as well as from
his interpretation of more recent history, he proclaimed that God consistently turned human evil to his own glorious purposes. So it had been time
after time after time: in humankind's original Fall, which led to God's provision of salvation; in the death of Christ, which secured that redemption;
in the Protestant Reformation, where "nothing contributed more to facili-
tate" the renewal of true religion "than the violence of its persecutors";
in the English Civil War where God guided Oliver Cromwell and John
Hamden through unexpected circumstances to bring "the tyrant to
the block"; and in North America when "violent persecution" by leaders of
the Church of England had propelled the settlement of New England.[34]
The conclusion from Scripture and history could only be that God frustrated the plans of the wicked for the praise of his name and the good of
his people.

The crucial move from ancient Israel to contemporary events came
after Witherspoon identified the "wrath" of his text as an attack on Israel
by the marauding Sennacherib, king of Assyria (described in Isa 36). That
identification allowed him to apply his text to the colonies' current situation marked by "the ambition of mistaken princes, the cunning and cru-
elty of oppressive and corrupt ministers, and even the inhumanity of
brutal soldiers." It is a curious fact, though not relevant to Witherspoon's
effort, that modern translations sometimes make God, rather than a human
agent, the wrathful one of Psalm 76:10.[35] More to the historical point,
Witherspoon admitted in passing that the occasion for his text was "probably the unsuccessful assault of Jerusalem, by the army of Sennacherib."[36]
This "probably" seems not to have been much noted at the time, but it
does cast at least a shadow of a doubt on the pertinence of Witherspoon's
text to the American situation in May 1776.

Once having identified "wrath," Witherspoon boldly applied his text. At a time when "our civil and religious liberties" were imperiled by Parliament's desire for "unlimited dominion," the colonies faced "the fatal consequence of unlimited submission." Witherspoon conceded that Britain may not have intended great evil for the colonies, but because its leaders were fallible humans, "for these colonies to depend wholly upon the legislature of Great-Britain, would be like many other oppressive connexions, injury to the master, and ruin to the slave."[37]

In his closing exhortations, Witherspoon turned from the evil of the British to a challenge for the colonists. Now he spoke as a Christian republican. For God to turn aside Britain's wrath, it was necessary for Americans to abandon "profligacy and corruption of manners," embrace "true and undefiled religion," and oppose "profanity and immorality of every kind." Especially society's leaders—"magistrates, ministers, parents, heads of families"—must lead the way in practicing industry, fleeing idleness, and promoting "frugality."[38] He closed by praying "that in America true religion and civil liberty may be inseparable."[39]

It was a powerful sermon delivered with broad and deep attention to Scripture. Its thoughtful and deliberate unfolding contrasted markedly with John Allen's hasty exegesis. Yet were not Witherspoon's exposition so firmly embedded in a Whig perception of the political crisis, it is not obvious that its teaching would have seemed as responsibly biblical as Witherspoon's many grateful readers considered it to be.

Unlike Allen and Witherspoon who drew their sermons from Old Testament examples, patriot preachers very occasionally spoke directly from New Testament scriptures for the purpose of providing straightforward, didactic instruction. One such occasion came on the last day of 1775 in a sermon to Virginia's Anglican clergy assembled in Williamsburg. The preacher was David Griffith, rector of Shelburne parish in Loudoun County. His text from Romans 13:1–2 could have been perceived as risky, since it was also much favored by Loyalists: "THE POWERS THAT BE, are ordained of God. Whosoever, therefore, resisted the power, resisteth the ordinance of God." But Griffith, as he explained in his published preface, had chosen it deliberately in order "to reconcile seeming contradictions; to make self evident truths (flowing from the attributes of God, and loudly proclaimed by nature) agree with some plain declarations of scripture."[40] It was a calm, deliberate performance, which, though clearly intending to support the colonies, drew more comprehensively from Scripture and depended less completely on Whig ideology than had Jonathan Mayhew's exposition of the same text in 1749.[41]

Griffith began by arguing that human happiness depended on a well-ordered society and "a due submission to wise and equitable laws." This proposition he found not only in nature but also from reflecting on "the intensions of God" who appointed temporal rulers for "the advancement of general happiness."[42] Multiple biblical examples served Griffith as proof: Genesis 41 (where God supplied Joseph as a just ruler for Egypt), Deuteronomy 16:18–20 (where God ordered Moses to appoint judges), Deuteronomy 17:18 (where God set out standards of justice for Israel's king), the histories of King Saul and King David from 1 and 2 Samuel (where God blessed Saul and David when they pursued righteousness, but took the kingdom from Saul when he did not), and 2 Chronicles 9:8 (where the queen of Sheba praised Solomon for the justice of his realm). Yet despite this clear picture, according to Griffith, some in the recent past had turned aside from Scripture to construct a doctrine of passive obedience—"that, though rulers are bound to govern according to the immutable laws of equity, yet an obligation lies on Christians to pay an exact obedience to *all their commands*: That no abuse of power will justify disobedience; and however contrary their laws may be to the benevolent designs of the creator, that Christians are bound to observe them with the most strict conformity." If, however, these "advocates for despotism and an implicit obedience" relied on Romans 13 for support, they made a grievous error. Griffith's thesis articulated carefully the reason for their mistake: "God requires obedience from his people, to all laws that are equitable...he expects them to be obedient to magistrates and rulers, when *their commands* do not contradict *his own*."[43]

Once again, Griffith turned to exposition rather than bluster to make his case. No evidence suggested that God condemned Israel for "murmuring" against Pharaoh's unjust rule.[44] More to the point, the book of Acts was filled with instances where the very apostle who penned the book of Romans himself disobeyed rulers, insisted on his rights as a Roman citizen, and called out magistrates who violated strict standards of justice (from Acts 16, 22, 25, and more). Thus, whatever one would make of Romans 13, it could not be interpreted to teach that Christians "were to obey implicitly, every dictate of power, however unjust and oppressive, and however contrary to the divine will and intentions."[45]

Then Griffith took up another much-favored Loyalist text, this one from 1 Peter 2. The injunctions there "to submit to every ordinance of man" needed to be interpreted in light of Acts 5 where John joined Peter in saying they had to obey God rather than man. His conclusion, after extensive scriptural demonstration, addressed the recent efforts by Parliament to establish new guidelines for the colonies. Nothing in Scripture, according to the preacher, could support a posture of passive obedience when the "lives and property" of Americans "are at the ABSOLUTE DISPOSAL of the king and his subjects in England," or could in any way justify a principle that the "legislature of Great Britain is right to make laws, binding on America, IN ALL CASES WHATSOEVER." In resisting such claims, the colonists only affirmed "those rights which God has appointed them and the laws confirmed."[46]

Griffith's almost last word added ancient anti-Catholicism into his biblical defense of the colonies: "In my opinion, the doctrine of transubstantiation is not a greater absurdity than the notion of America's being represented in the British parliament." Against such parliamentary overreach stood "The voice of God, of truth, of justice, of humanity."[47]

Patriotic sermons supporting independence would have been more impressive as biblical instruction if they had followed David Griffith's thoughtfully constructed arguments rather than John Allen's flights of fancy. John Witherspoon's reliance on an Old Testament precedent that "probably" supported colonial resistance undercut the force of his biblical reasoning only slightly. Clearly, however, in the context of the times, exegetical precision was not required in order to enlist the Bible for the patriot cause.

Argument from Loyalists

The challenge for Loyalists lay in overcoming the patriot monopoly of the Bible. Patriotic biblical exposition dominated the Revolutionary era because of how thoroughly the Protestant ideal of supreme trust in Scripture had been woven into the Whig vision of liberty threatened by corrupt conspiracies. It also carried the day, at least in part, because of patriot effectiveness in silencing opposing biblical opinions.

The life of Jonathan Boucher, rector of Queen Anne's parish near Annapolis, Maryland, and an Anglican connected to the colony's leading families, illustrated the challenges faced by those who wanted to present an alternative interpretation of Scripture.[48] In July 1775, Boucher prepared a sermon that he hoped would bring rebelling Marylanders to their senses. The first Sunday he tried to deliver it, however, he was prevented from ascending the pulpit by a melee that almost resulted in gunfire (Boucher had come to church armed with a loaded pistol, as had many of his patriot parishioners). The next Sunday, 27 July 1775, he succeeded in delivering the sermon but only after shouting down the opposition. That sermon, augmented by extensive footnotes and perhaps somewhat expanded, was published twenty-two years later.[49]

One of the footnotes added for publication explained that Boucher intended his discourse "in answer" to a sermon preached earlier in July by Jacob Duché, an Anglican colleague, before "the First Battalion of the City and Liberties of Philadelphia."[50] Boucher chose as his text the same passage from which Duché had preached, Galatians 5:1—"Stand fast, therefore, in the Liberty wherewith Christ hath made us free."

In his address, Duché had paused to explain that bondage "to the arbitrary power of sin" was the very worst thing imaginable. Yet he expanded more time and energy discoursing on "civil liberty," which he called "as much the gift of God in Christ Jesus" as spiritual freedom, and in arguing against the notion that the biblical injunction from 1 Peter 2:13 ("submit to every ordinance of man for the Lord's sake") required submission "to the unrighteous ordinances of unrighteous men." As Duché's last word, he left an unfinished sentence, which did not require divine wisdom to complete: should it come to pass that "Britain or rather some degenerate sons of Britain, and enemies to our common Liberty, still persist in embracing a DELUSION, and believing a lie—if the sword is still unsheathed against us, and SUBMIT or PERISH is the sanguinary decree.... "[51]

The more than two decades it took Boucher to shepherd his own sermon into print did nothing to dampen his fury at Duché's exposition. Even before coming to his text, he cited another passage as providing "as direct and clear a commission for a Christian minister's preaching on politics...as can be produced for our preaching at all on any subject."[52] And then he let fly. As a basic expository requirement that Duché had violated, Boucher defined the need "to know the circumstances of the writer, and his end and aim in writing." After carrying out that discipline himself, he insisted that Paul in Galatians 5 had only "Jewish zealots" in view. Hence, "the liberty inculcated in the Scriptures (and which alone the Apostle had in view in this text) is wholly of the spiritual or religious kind."[53]

Then in a virtuoso display supporting this exegetical conclusion, Boucher called upon Plato, Cicero, ancient history more generally, John Locke, and Bishop Butler to urge that "liberty is not the setting at nought and despising established laws." In this fusillade, Scripture was never far behind. The Church of England, he reminded his readers, "in perfect conformity with the doctrine here inculcated" in Galatians 5, taught through her catechism that the Fifth Commandment (children obey your parents) entailed "the congenial duty of *honouring the king and all that are put in authority under him.*" The Bible could even instruct through its silences, since "mankind are no where in the Scriptures commanded to resist authority"; rather they were required to be in subjection *"for the Lord's sake"* (quoting 1 Pet 2:13). Finally, after adding an exposition of Matthew 22:21 (*"render unto Caesar the things that are Caesar's"*) and further attacking Duché's work, Boucher ended by quoting the entirety of 1 Peter 2:13–17, with its summary injunction, "Fear God. Honour the King."[54]

Positive arguments from Loyalists followed the course of Boucher's 1775 sermon. They were straightforward in exactly the way that (one might think) would appeal to Protestants who set great store in the Scriptures as their chief guide. The passages that came to the fore were entirely predictable: as in Boucher's sermon, "render unto Caesar" (Mt 22:21 and parallels in the other gospels) and 1 Peter 2:17 ("Fear God. Honour the King"); along with Romans 13:1–2 ("The powers that be are ordained of God. Whosoever therefore resisteth the power, resisteth the ordinance of God") and 1 Timothy 2:1–2 ("I exhort...that, first of all, supplications, prayers, intercessions, and giving of thanks, be made for all men; For kings, and all that are in authority; that we may lead a quiet and peaceable life in all godliness and honesty"). Loyalist interpreters also patiently developed what they obviously thought was a powerful appeal to context—that these biblical teachings arose at a time when the Roman yoke bore down upon early Christians much more grievously than ever Parliament's missteps oppressed the colonies.

In an effort to recommend such biblical guidance, Charles Inglis of New York delivered several memorable pulpit performances during the course of the conflict. His 1777 sermon to Loyalist militiamen, which we noted in chapter 10 for its rhetorical verve, mostly expounded his text from Luke 3:14, with its admonition from John the Baptist that soldiers should do their work justly and without violence.[55] Yet as he provided this instruction about soldierly duty, he could not refrain from characterizing the Loyalists' opponents. His reminder to the soldiers that "by this Injunction, all Violence to a Superior, or Disobedience to his Commands, is also forbidden" led him to add that, "the Want of Subordination and Discipline among our infatuated Adversaries, affords you one very great Advantage over them. Their wild Principles naturally lead to these and other Disorders."[56]

Later in this sermon, Inglis wandered off text in the manner of so many of his patriot peers. The "honourable" and "necessary Cause" for which the militia fought was "the Cause of Truth against Falsehood—of Loyalty against Rebellion—of legal Government against Usurpation—of Constitutional Freedom against Tyranny—in short, it is the Cause of human Happiness, the Happiness of Millions, against Outrage and Oppression." When he returned to biblical instruction, he poured special scorn on those who claimed religious sanction for fighting against the King: "turning Faith into Faction, and the Gospel of Peace, into an Engine of War and Sedition. We dare not thus prevaricate or trifle with the living God; or handle his Word deceitfully." Again he averred that "we have the express Declarations of his own unerring Word" that God favored Loyalist principles.[57] And so in closing he invoked the timeless words of Jesus from Luke 4:18 to reassure his congregation that "You have taken up the Sword that those who are Captives, for Conscience, sake may be set at Liberty, and that the Prisoner may go free."[58]

Three years later Inglis set out his most complete appeal to Scripture in a sermon preached at two different New York Anglican chapels on 30 January 1780.[59] As Jonathan Mayhew had done in his much publicized sermon from 1749 on this same anniversary date for the execution of Charles I, Inglis worked a reading of history into his reading of Scripture. Now reversing Mayhew's judgments, Inglis asked listeners to consider how that earlier "Failure" to honor God and the monarch "did once involve our Nation in all the Horrors of Rebellion and Civil War.... the Phrenzy of Enthusiasm, and Republican Ambition."[60] But mostly he turned to the Scriptures: Proverbs 24:21–22 ("fear thou the Lord and the king"); "render unto Caesar" (Mt 22:21; Mk 12:17; Lk 20:25); the Apostle Peter exhorting to "mutual Love and Submission to Government, 'for the Lord's Sake'" (1 Pet 2:13); the Apostle Paul in Romans 13; and exhortations from the Old and New Testaments to pray for the king (1 Tim 2:1–3; Prov. 8:15).[61] Inglis's amazement that others could read the Scriptures differently is worth quoting at length since he dramatically contradicted what so many patriots saw so clearly when they appealed to the Bible:

But that professing Christians, who really believe in a divine Revelation, and acknowledge its Authority—that they should be the Dupes of such Men—that they should make no Conscience of dishonouring the King, and rebelling against him—that they should knowingly trample on the Law of God, and act as if no such Law existed—that instead of obeying this Law, they should be Trumpeters of Sedition and Rebellion: This is astonishing indeed![62]

On what he obviously considered this firm biblical basis, Inglis then presented variations on his theme: the earliest Christians were exemplary in the honor they paid to Roman officials; learned historical voices like Tertullian and Hugo Grotius agreed with the Loyalist interpretation of 1 Timothy; and considerations of both reason and the welfare of society pointed in the same direction.[63] Most egregiously in his view, the patriots betrayed centuries of Protestant history, and so revealed their perfidy, by allying themselves with France, "the Popish, inveterate Enemies of our Nation…a Power which has extinguished Liberty, and extirpated the Protestant Religion from all its Dominions."[64] Nothing more could be said except to evoke a kind of reverse jeremiad by reminding those who were throwing over the king of "the frequent Denunciations in [God's] Word, against sinful Nations,"[65]

Inglis's painstaking exposition of passages drawn from throughout the Bible made as strong a scriptural case as possible for abandoning rebellion and preserving loyalty to Britain. But to no avail. Against lonely voices like the New York rector, the patriot biblical chorus was louder, its advocates more numerous, its emotional appeal stronger, its historical depiction more persuasive, its ideological fit tighter, and its political righteousness more intuitive. Loyalist biblical reasoning might impress Britain's Native allies, like Joseph Brandt and Little Abraham, but it had almost no effect at the centers of colonial power.[66]

Patriot biblical exposition was also better enforced. Boucher, who earlier in his Maryland career had stood up for the liberties of Catholics against intense colonial prejudice needed someone in the Revolutionary era to stand up for him. The difficulties he encountered in publishing his sermon on Galatians 5 reflected the broadly successful efforts of patriots at controlling public communication. John Witherspoon, as only one other example, played an active role in disgracing the printers Benjamin Towne (Philadelphia) and James Rivington (New York) for putting their presses at the disposal of Loyalist authors when the British occupied their cities. Until "the moral authority of the Revolution" could be established, such strong arm tactics helped clarify what the Bible really meant.[67]

Argument Between Tom Paine and His Foes

The masterful propaganda of Tom Paine's *Common Sense* sparked the most dramatic controversy over Scripture in the entire Revolutionary period. Long before the appearance of this tract, published to great effect in January

1776, the nearly universal veneration of the King James Version alongside New England's self-identification with ancient Israel had made the Old Testament a potent source of political principle. Yet earlier configurations of the analogy between the Hebrews and New England (or the colonies as a whole) had routinely taken for granted limited monarchy as an accepted component of a well-ordered government.[68] Tom Paine's straightforward appeal to the Bible took dead aim at that assumption. His relatively short pamphlet, which demanded a total break with Britain, canvassed several topics: the British constitution, current events that had led to the outbreak of military hostilities, possible allies for the combatants, and the colonies' fiscal capabilities. But Paine delivered his most passionate polemic in a section titled "On Monarchy and Hereditary Succession." It amounted to little more than a Bible lesson.

A burst of superb recent scholarship has documented the genealogy of Paine's appeal to Scripture as well as the broad influence it exerted on colonists hesitant to break with the mother country.[69] Paine's incendiary contention that the great problem with British rule lay not with Parliament's blunders or incidental mistakes in colonial administration, but with the institution of monarchy itself, decisively moved colonial public opinion. Paine rested that contention solidly on Scripture, evoked both generally but also with specific reference to multiple texts from both Testaments. On the considerable line of rabbinic and English republican interpretation that lay behind Paine's deployment of this particular argument, he years later told John Adams that "he had taken his Ideas in that part [of *Common Sense*] from Milton."[70] A handful of colonists had earlier floated the notion that the "Hebrew republic" of the Old Testament in effect ruled out monarchy as a God-approved form of government.[71] But Paine's effort—with its riveting prose, extraordinary dissemination, and dramatic effect in persuading the colonies to fight—propelled scriptural argumentation into the center of Revolutionary consciousness.[72]

Not surprisingly, defenders of the crown took great offense. The most capable of such replies offered point-by-point refutations of Paine's biblical exposition. To sketch Paine's eight specific assertions, alongside his opponents rebuttals, illuminates how deeply a contest over biblical interpretation entered into the national founding. It also anticipates the kind of biblical argumentation that would continue to mark public life in the new American nation for a long time to come.

Two Anglican clergymen offered the most substantial refutations, the first in a series of letters by William Smith, provost of the University of

Pennsylvania, published in the *Pennsylvania Ledger* and several other colonial newspapers in March and April 1776.[73] Smith, a veteran public advocate for colonial bishops, had nonetheless also criticized Parliament for mistreating the colonies; he indicated his own self-understanding as a political liberal by publishing on Paine under the revered name of Cato, the ancient Roman renowned by Whigs for his incorruptibility. The second detailed response appeared shortly thereafter in a pamphlet from Philadelphia with "strictures" against *Common Sense* from "an American."[74] This anonymous author was Charles Inglis, at that time assistant rector at Trinity Church in New York City, whom we have encountered already as an active Anglican publicist. Like Smith, Inglis carefully distanced his stance from positions held by divine-right Tories and also freely employed a moderate language of Whig rights and liberties, even as he defended loyalty to Britain.[75]

Paine's recourse to Scripture included four general assertions, three brief exegetical moments, and one extended exposition. The assurance with which he enlisted the Bible to demonstrate the irredeemable evil of monarchy was matched only by the assurance with which Smith and Inglis replied to demonstrate its complete propriety.

As his knock-out blow against monarchy, Paine offered a long discussion of 1 Samuel 8, which narrates God's chastisement of Israel for demanding a king. Before that extended onslaught, however, he engaged in serious biblical sparring. (#1) "Scripture chronology" showed that "in the early age of the world...there were no kings." Humanity was thrown "into confusion" only when monarchs appeared on the scene.[76] (#2) "Heathens" were responsible for introducing the world to monarchy, "the most prosperous invention the Devil ever set on foot for the promotion of idolatry."[77] (#3) Until the ancient Hebrews entertained the "national delusion" that they needed a king, Israel functioned under "a kind of republic administered by a judge and the elders of the tribes," which demonstrated that "the Almighty, ever jealous of his honour," disapproved of kingship usurping "the prerogatives of heaven."[78]

Wrong, wrong, wrong, chorused Paine's critics. (Rebutting #1) As Inglis read "scripture chronology and scripture history," violence abounded in the world "long before we hear a syllable about kings." Moreover, the biblical account in early Genesis (chap. 14) of the virtuous Melchizedek, king of Salem, demonstrated that monarchs existed very early on and that they could act with perfect righteousness.[79] (Rebutting #2) Inglis turned aside Paine's second claim with scornful laughter: if kingship did come from

"Heathens," so also did "Greek and Latin—[and] smoking tobacco; and yet I can dip into Homer and Virgil, or enjoy my pipe, with great composure of conscience."[80] (Rebutting #3) Against the idea that Israel's history before the coronation of King Saul proved that God favored "a kind of republic," William Smith countered with his understanding of the Bible as a whole and gospel quotations from Jesus in particular: "There is no particular denounciation of God's displeasure against any FORM whether MONAR-CHIAL or DEMOCRATICAL."[81] As Smith and Inglis turned to the sacred page, they discovered a very different world than Paine described.

The argumentation in *Common Sense* sharpened as Paine turned to individual texts. (#4) When Jesus, as recorded in the Synoptic Gospels, proclaimed "render unto Caesar the things that are Caesar's," Paine contended that he was articulating "the scriptural doctrine of courts" and not implying any approval of monarchy, since under the Roman occupation Jews lacked rulers of them own.[82] (#5) Likewise, when the Bible described David "as a man after God's own heart," it signified his personal standing before the Lord rather than a "notice of him *officially as a king.*"[83] (#6) Even better for Paine's purposes was the account of Gideon, the judge, who after he had rescued Israel from the Midianites (Judg 6–8) and the people begged him to become their king, "in the piety of his soul replied...THE LORD SHALL RULE OVER YOU." Accordingly, "words need not be more explicit" to indicate the evil of even the idea of a king.[84]

Once again: wrong, wrong, wrong. (Rebutting #4) Jesus, according to Inglis, explained to his Jewish interlocutors that since they were using Caesar's money, they should respect Caesar's rule. He was telling them only that "whatever is by custom, law, or otherwise, justly due to sovereigns, should be punctually paid, whether it be tribute, obedience, honour, etc."[85] (Rebutting #5) Smith found Paine's account of David absurd. Not only had "the lord...commanded him [David] to be Captain over his people" (quoting 1 Sam 13:14), but the Apostle Paul in summarizing the history of Israel had affirmed that God himself had "raised up unto them David to be their King" (quoting Acts 13:22).[86] (Rebutting #6) Gideon's rejection of the crown, according to Inglis, showed only that God might so act "on...particular occasions, and for some peculiar reasons; and yet our government by Kings at this time, may be as acceptable to the Almighty, as any other governments."[87]

These preliminaries only prepared the way for Paine's pièce d'résistance. (#7) In an exposition of roughly seven hundred words, Paine quoted and commented on verses 5–20 of 1 Samuel 8.[88] The crux came in the categorical

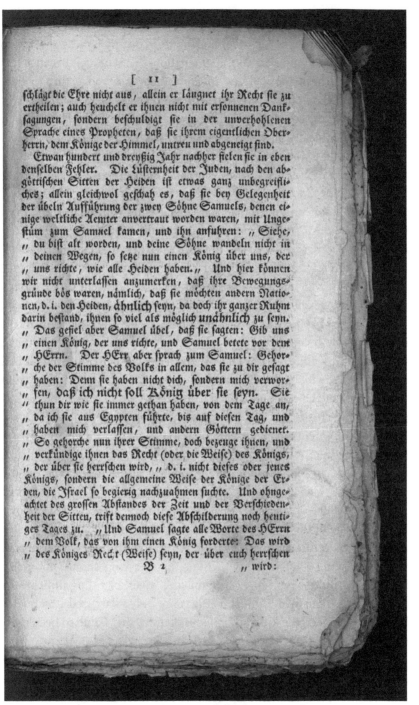

schlägt die Ehre nicht aus, allein er läugnet ihr Recht sie zu
ertheilen; auch heuchelt er ihnen nicht mit ersonnenen Dank-
sagungen, sondern beschuldigt sie in der unverhohlenen
Sprache eines Propheten, daß sie ihrem eigentlichen Ober-
herrn, dem Könige der Himmel, untreu und abgeneigt sind.

Etwan hundert und dreyßig Jahr nachher fielen sie in eben
denselben Fehler. Die Lüsternheit der Juden, nach den ab-
göttischen Sitten der Heiden ist etwas ganz unbegreifli-
ches; allein gleichwol geschah es, daß sie bey Gelegenheit
der übeln Aufführung der zwey Söhne Samuels, denen ei-
nige weltliche Aemter anvertraut worden waren, mit Unge-
stüm zum Samuel kamen, und ihn anfuhren: „ Siehe,
„ du bist alt worden, und deine Söhne wandeln nicht in
„ deinen Wegen, so setze nun einen König über uns, der
„ uns richte, wie alle Heiden haben.„ Und hier können
wir nicht unterlassen anzumerken, daß ihre Bewegungs-
gründe bös waren, nämlich, daß sie möchten andern Natio-
nen, d. i. den Heiden, ähnlich seyn, da doch ihr ganzer Ruhm
darin bestand, ihnen so viel als möglich unähnlich zu seyn.
„ Das gefiel aber Samuel übel, daß sie sagten: Gib uns
„ einen König, der uns richte, und Samuel betete vor dem
„ HErrn. Der HErr aber sprach zum Samuel: Gehor-
„ che der Stimme des Volks in allem, das sie zu dir gesagt
„ haben: Denn sie haben nicht dich, sondern mich verwor-
„ fen, daß ich nicht soll König über sie seyn. Sie
„ thun dir wie sie es immer gethan haben, von dem Tage an,
„ da ich sie aus Egypten führte, bis auf diesen Tag, und
„ haben mich verlassen, und andern Göttern gedienet.
„ So gehorche nun ihrer Stimme, doch bezeuge ihnen, und
„ verkündige ihnen das Recht (oder die Weise) des Königs,
„ der über sie herrschen wird, „ d. i. nicht dieses oder jenes
Königs, sondern die allgemeine Weise der Könige der Er-
den, die Israel so begierig nachzuahmen suchte. Und ohnge-
achtet des grossen Abstandes der Zeit und der Verschieden-
heit der Sitten, trift dennoch diese Abschilderung noch heuti-
ges Tages zu. „ Und Samuel sagte alle Worte des HErrn
„ dem Volk, das von ihm einen König forderte: Das wird
„ des Königes Recht (Weise) seyn, der über euch herrschen

B 2   „ wird:

This section from a 1776 German translation of Tom Paine's "Common Sense" used Martin Luther's last revision of his German Bible to present the passage from 1 Samuel 8 that Paine discussed at length from the King James Version in his English original. (Courtesy of Special Collections & Archives, Trexler Library, Muhlenberg College) rejection by the prophet Samuel and by the Lord of Israel's request to "make us a king to judge us like all the nations" (1 Sam 8:5). Because this request "displeased Samuel" (v. 6) and since God spoke through the prophet to declare "they have rejected me, that I should not reign over them" (v. 7), Paine could exult in asking what could be more obvious than this unmistakable divine disapproval of monarchy?

The answer, to Smith and Inglis, was "almost everything." (Rebutting #7) In exasperation they could not contain themselves—Smith for more than three thousand words, Inglis at even greater length. The bulk of Smith's rejoinder contended that God's displeasure with Israel came from the Hebrews' desire for a king who ruled in the manner of neighboring monarchs; for these kings, "ARBITRARY WILL stood in the place of Law."[89] In this argument, Smith put his Whig bona fides on display by indicating how much he thought a constitutional monarchy differed from arbitrary, unchecked kingship. To Inglis it was the same, since he "took this whole passage [to be] a description of the eastern despotic monarchs"; it could hardly be confused as a blanket rejection of monarchy.[90] Inglis went farther by pointing out that the divine displeasure with Israel had nothing to do with governmental principles, but stemmed rather from "the *manner* of their asking a King…in a *disregard* of the venerable old prophet—but chiefly in a *neglect of the directions* above mentioned."[91]

Those "directions" to which Inglis referred came in a lengthy quotation from Deuteronomy 17:14–20 with which Inglis had begun his biblical counterattack. In the common understanding of the day, Deuteronomy was thought to have been written before 1 Samuel, which to Inglis meant a great deal since it revealed Yahweh's approval of a king for Israel long before the age of the prophet Samuel. The Deuteronomy passage relates that God would himself install a monarch in the future day when Israel asked for a king—but with instructions that the king should not abuse his trust by multiplying horses, multiplying wives, or ruling unjustly. In other words, Inglis had found a text that not only relativized 1 Samuel 8 but also sanctioned the kind of limited monarchy that Paine so heedlessly rejected.[92]

Once Paine's foes began with other biblical testimony, there was no stopping them. Inglis went on to quote twelve different passages that he felt refuted Paine's already shaky conclusions from 1 Samuel 8—including seven from the Old Testament (like Eccl 10:20, "Curse not the King, no, not in any thought") and five from the New (including the Loyalist favorite from 1 Pet 2 that ends with v. 17, "Fear God, Honour the King").[93] Without any duplication from Inglis's list, Smith provided chapter and verse for four additional passages that indicated God's approval of monarchy.[94] Whatever the quality of their biblical exegesis, the quantity of their scriptural references vastly exceeded Paine's.

Finally, (#8) Paine's last biblical sally raised an intriguing theological issue that his opponents did not touch. He claimed that for the notion of hereditary succession, "no parallel" existed "in or out of scripture, but the doctrine of original sin, which supposes the free will of all men lost in Adam." If, however, the passing on of kingship from parent to child paralleled only the disaster that fell on the human race because of Adam's primal sin, then, in Paine's phrases, "Dishonourable rank! Inglorious connection!"[95] Neither Smith nor Inglis engaged Paine on this issue. The once-sturdy Reformation doctrine of imputation, or vicarious crediting, of Adam's guilt to all humankind (as well as the crediting of Christ's righteousness to believers) had become increasingly controversial over the course of the eighteenth century. Devotees of Reason decried it as immoral, while even New England's self-conscious Calvinists in the generation after Jonathan Edwards had begun to modify their understanding of this doctrine. Anglicans in an era dominated by reasonable latitudinarian theology would not have been strong defenders of this ancient teaching, which may explain why Paine's opponents left his last biblical gambit alone.[96]

For Paine's foes it mattered little that they had left one stone unturned. In William Smith's summary opinion, "there never was a greater perversion of Scripture."[97] Inglis declared that Paine so clearly violated "the genuine testimony of Scripture," that he would have to "renounce my bible, if I believe[d] this republican."[98] But Paine, a brilliant phrase-maker who had mastered Protestant ideology with its atavistic anti-Catholicism, carried the day with a dramatic conclusion to his exposition of 1 Samuel 8:

> These portions of scripture are direct and positive. They admit of no equivocal construction. That the Almighty hath here entered his protest against monarchial government is true, or the scripture is false. And a man hath good reason to believe that there is as much of king-craft as priest-craft in withholding the scripture from the public in Popish countries. For monarchy in every instance is the Popery of government.[99]

* * * * *

Examined in the cold light of formal discourse, there could be no doubt about the outcome of this exegetical duel. Where Paine universalized a single moment in Israel's ancient history into a principle binding on all times and places, his opponents scoured the entire Bible to show that God in fact approved a limited monarchy—or at least showed no preference for any particular form of government. Yet in very late colonial America— nine months after Lexington and Concord, seven months after the British assault on Breed's or Bunker Hill in Boston—inflamed passion burned brighter than cold intellectual discourse.

In point of fact, this particular conflict reinforces the general truism that when Scripture comes into a fight that is already under way, it becomes all but impossible for the Bible to exercise an objective, unprejudiced authority. The impact of Paine's tract also testified that his way of relating Old Testament history to the late-eighteenth century enjoyed purchase not only in New England but throughout the colonies. If ten editions of *Common Sense* were printed in New England before 1776 ran its course, another eight, including one German translation, came from presses in New York and Philadelphia.[100] Rebuttals to Paine, including those by Smith and Inglis, also appeared in multiple printings—but not nearly so many and from far fewer sites.[101] A fevered colonial climate brought alive the political relevance of Old Testament Israel not only for New England, but for the rest of colonial America as well.

Paine's appeal to Scripture also confirmed a mode of argument that, far from unknown before his time, became even more important in the new American nation. As he explained the meaning of the relevant biblical passages, Paine referred to no learned authorities, he disdained contextual considerations, and he wrote with passionate effect for all and sundry—in a word, he let the King James Version speak, as it were, for itself. In decades to come, this way of enlisting Scripture for public debate would reappear consistently—on temperance, foreign relations, economic prosperity and decline, race, and (preeminently) slavery. William Smith recognized shrewdly that in this "country," by which he probably meant only the colonies, "(God be thanked) the Scriptures are read and regarded with that reverence which is due to a revelation from Heaven."[102] Smith, however, did not reckon with a "country" in which democratic interpretive practice would become as strong as in the new United States.

Whether Paine's appeal to Scripture was a complete exercise in cynicism remains an intriguing, but not particularly relevant, question. In the much later conversation that John Adams reported, Adams told Paine that "his reasoning from the Old Testament was ridiculous, and I could hardly think him sincere." In reply, Paine reportedly "expressed a hatred of the Old Testament and indeed of the Bible at large, which surprised me."

Whether Adams remembered correctly, or perhaps credited Paine with opinions he developed later in publishing *The Age of Reason* (1794, 1795), does not affect the role that scriptural evocation played in the effectiveness of Paine's pamphlet.[103] Instead, the prominence of that evocation reinforces what most students have claimed for the presence of Scripture in Revolutionary America, phrased in this instance by a student of Paine's rhetorical world: "biblical mythology penetrated deeply, and in ways that have not been studied, into ostensibly secular revolutionary discourse.... Recovering the role that the Hebrew Republic played in the early 1776 debate is just a first step toward a fuller understanding of how the scriptures shaped revolutionary America."[104]

Argument Over Slavery

After remaining nearly silent on slavery for more than two generations, the Bible once again began to speak in the early years of the Revolutionary crisis. A concern taken up by only a few Quakers now drew the attention of the Sons of Liberty. As Christopher Brown has demonstrated in his masterful book on the rise of abolitionism in the British Empire: "the colonial revolt against British rule touched off a revolution in the public conversation about human bondage."[105]

The chronology of this other revolution merits close attention. Between the so-called Boston Massacre of 1770 and the so-called Boston Tea Party of 1773 came the Somerset decision of 1772. This judgment by Lord Mansfield of the King's Bench Court that English common law could not support the existence of slavery on English soil ignited the intense public debate—legal, social, economic, ethical, and religious—that would end in Britain with Parliament's abolition of slavery in 1833. That same debate would wax and wane in the colonies and the new United States into the early 1830s, after which it only waxed, until the Civil War led to the constitutional amendments that likewise spelled the end to the institution. On both sides of the Atlantic, the crises of empire stimulated controversy over slavery. Again to quote Christopher Brown's lapidary summary, "The propriety of enslaving Africans began to matter to the colonists only in the 1760s and 1770s, as patriots articulated their reasons for resisting British authority, when Revolutionary ideology gave the institution of chattel slavery an unexpected and unintended pertinence."[106]

The imperial fracture defined the wider context in which Protestants in Britain and the colonies returned to the Scriptures for explicit moral guidance on slavery. For a few who had been shaped by the colonial revivals, new attention to slavery flowed also from evangelical imperatives. Significantly, however, the return of scriptural attention to the question of human bondage led to strongly contradictory conclusions. Nor did the imperial crisis stimulate a corresponding attention to biblical teaching on racial difference. Conventions about the latter remained for the most part firmly in place.

In 1772 Thomas Thompson, an Anglican missionary with experience in West Africa, the West Indies, and New Jersey, opened this phase of public controversy with a work titled *The African Trade for Negro Slaves, Shewn to be Consistent with Principles of Humanity, and with the Laws of Revealed Religion*. Published in England, where Thompson had finally settled, this work cited Leviticus 25:39–55 as what he considered a conclusive last word. The permission in that passage for Israel perpetually to enslave "the heathen that are round about you" (25:44), along with attendant rules for regulating the bondsmen and bondswomen, seemed definitive. The ability to quote gave Thompson his assurance that, in the summary of David Brion Davis, "any practice so clearly and positively sanctioned by God could not be inconsistent with natural law."[107]

Immediate rebuttals from England and America demonstrated that scriptural authority still mattered, even as they showed that practices of slavery so firmly established under the conventions of a Protestant and liberty-affirming empire would be difficult to eliminate using Protestant and liberty-affirming arguments. These first rebuttals included an immediate response from the reforming Philadelphia physician Benjamin Rush, *An Address to the Inhabitants of the British Settlements in America, upon Slave-Keeping* (1773), and then two impassioned works from the key spark of British abolitionism, Granville Sharp, *An Essay on Slavery, Proving From Scripture its Inconsistency with Humanity and Religion* (1773), and only three years later *The Just Limitation of Slavery in the Laws of God, Compared with the Unbounded Claims of the African Traders and British American Slaveholders* (1776).

Sharp's 1773 pamphlet was published first in New Jersey where he observed with favor that new legislation in this province was hastening the end of the institution. His pamphlet opened with Psalm 9:9 on its title page: "The Lord also will be a Refuge for the Oppressed—a Refuge in Time of Trouble." Then followed much on "Liberty," the Somerset decision, Britain's common law, "universal *moral laws*, and those of *natural equity*," "*universal benevolence*"—but most of all the Scriptures.[108] After appealing for "a careful and attentive perusal of the Sacred Writings," he explained why the Leviticus passage cited by Thompson should be regarded as only local, why it did not apply for more than one generation, and why it had nothing to do with Africans. Most importantly, he claimed that the Old Testament provision for slavery had been "certainly annulled, or rather *superseded*...by the more perfect doctrines of *universal benevolence*" taught by Christ himself, who "came not to destroy, but to fulfil the law," including the law as adumbrated in Leviticus itself, 19:18: "thou shalt love thy neighbour as thyself."[109] Buttressed by a hail of supporting quotations (from Prov 14:34, Hab 1:13, Mt 7:12, Lk 4:18, Acts 8:27, Acts 10:34, Philem, 1 Cor 7:22, and more), Sharp rested his case firmly on the Sacred Text.

Rush, who did not offer as much exegesis as Sharp, rested his anti-slave animus more directly on political reasoning rather than on general humanitarianism. Yet Rush too shared fully the conviction that appeals to Scripture on behalf of slavery abused nature and offended God. In a work that defended the intellectual capacities of Africans, attacked the notion that colonial agriculture required slavery, stressed the inhuman cruelties of slave life, and defined practical steps to eliminate the institution, Rush did not neglect scriptural argument. If Old Testament patriarchs did keep slaves, so also did they practice polygamy, but the New Testament spoke as sharply against the one as the other. Moreover, permission to enslave surrounding nations reflected only God's desire to preserve the purity of the Jewish people as a vehicle for the coming Messiah. Still, the Old Testament contained many hints about the illegitimate character of the institution, like the Jubilee liberation promised every seven years to Hebrews in bonds, which pointed directly to "the Gospel, the Design of which was to abolish all distinctions of name and country."[110] Rush's summary is worth quoting because of how much it anticipated so many anti-slave writings from later in United States history:

> Although [Christ] does not call upon masters to emancipate their slaves, or slaves to assert that Liberty wherewith God and Nature had made them free [see Gal 5:1], yet there is scarcely a parable or a sermon in the whole history of his life, but what contains the strongest arguments against Slavery. Every prohibition of Covetousness—Intemperance—Pride—Uncleanness—Theft—and Murder, which he delivered,—every lesson of meekness, humility, forbearance, Charity, Self-denial, and brotherly love, which he taught, are leveled

against this evil;—for Slavery, while it includes all the former Vices, necessarily excludes the practice of all the latter Virtues, both from the Master and the Slave.[111]

Like Sharp, Rush wove together his biblical conclusions with appeals drawn from the zeitgeist, in his case with a definite Whig flavor: "Ye men of SENSE and VIRTUE—Ye ADVOCATES for American Liberty, rouse up and espouse the cause of Humanity and general Liberty."[112]

The almost immediate rejoinder to Rush's rebuttal to Thompson also came embedded in broader concerns, in this case the good name of British planters in the Caribbean. The author was Richard Nisbet, an Englishmen trained in law and theology who had lived in Nevis and St. Kitts before relocating to Philadelphia.[113] Against Rush and like-minded idealists, Nisbet described slavery in the West Indies as mild, he pointed out that Caucasians could not work in the conditions demanded by Caribbean agriculture, and he demonstrated at length the importance of the institution for the whole British economy. But before expatiating on those arguments, Nisbet took pains to show that "the scriptures, instead of forbidding it [slavery], declare it lawful."[114] As proof, he first quoted extensively from Old Testament passages that either directly sanctioned the enslavement of non-Hebrews (Lev 25:44–46) or showed God setting down guidelines for the treatment of slaves (Ex 21:4–6, 20, 22; Deut 15:16–17; Ex 21:16; Deut 24:7). Concerning the New Testament, Nisbet began by noting "the remarkable boldness" of Christ and his apostles in speaking to so many of life's foundational questions. The inevitable conclusion followed: "the Addresser [i.e., Rush] is so wicked as to accuse our Saviour of the meanest dissimulation" by failing to mention slavery simply because it was allowed under Roman law. Rather than an argument against slavery, such misreadings of Scripture revealed that "this Gentleman, attempting to be religious, becomes blasphemous."[115] In the same way that Rush's appeal to the general sense of Scripture anticipated many later anti-slave arguments, so too Nisbet's reliance on direct quotations from the Old Testament and strategic exploitation of silence in the New Testament paved the way for very much that also followed.

By 1773, one year after the Somerset decision in England, the Bible on slavery was no longer thinning as a public presence. The vigor with which Thompson and Nisbet advanced a biblical justification for slavery created an even more obvious interpretive clash than the biblical arguments being offered for and against independence. In the immediate war years, however, it seemed as if the tide of publicity on slavery was moving just as definitely against the institution as the biblical-political tide was moving toward independence.

During the war years, scriptural reasoning mounted up against slavery from many sides and with several admixtures of contemporary ideology. When Benjamin Rush responded to Nisbet's attack on his initial pamphlet, he cited the testimony of "Reason and Humanity" against slavery, while also spending considerable effort in a point-by-point refutation of Nisbet's account of Caribbean conditions and Britain's economy. Yet he also paused to scorn those who would "set up a few detached Texts of Scripture against the whole Tenor of the Jewish Law." As in his first tract, Rush underscored the progression of revelation, with the Hebrews' "an Eye for an Eye" superseded by the Christian command "not to resist Evil, but to him that smiteth on the right cheek, to turn the other also" (eliding Mt 5:39 and Lk 6:29).[116]

Anthony Benezet also returned to the fray with the same 1778 work in which he denounced warfare as a complete evil. His wide-ranging brief included a quotation from the preface of the Declaration of Independence to contend that "nothing can more clearly and positively militate against the slavery of the Negroes"; passionate ethical advocacy on behalf of "the blood of the innocent"; and long quotations from ship captains and others with firsthand evidence of what slavery actually entailed.[117] Yet Benezet's appeal to Scripture remained paramount. That appeal included several Old Testament imperatives "to relieve the oppressed; to plead for the fatherless" (Isa 1:17), but also an extended exposition of a literal jeremiad. The text was Jeremiah 34:8–17, which described the Lord's retribution when Judah promised to free their slaves but then reneged "in proclaiming liberty every one to his brother" (v. 17). In similar manner, God now threatened "judgment" upon the colonies who in their own time and place "falsified their covenant."[118]

By the time Benezet's tract was published, the anti-slave forces had been joined by several theological heirs of Jonathan Edwards who introduced a new element into the abolitionist campaign. That element, in the summary of James Essig, described "slavery as an emblem of colonial iniquity."[119] Samuel Hopkins, Sarah Osborn's minister in Newport, Rhode Island, who had been Edwards's closest student, proposed several schemes with his local colleague, Ezra Stiles, to emancipate slaves and recruit them for missionary work in Africa. In 1776, and very much with the military conflict in view, he also published a forceful anti-slave work that proclaimed "the duty and interest of the American people to emancipate all their African slaves." Emancipatory texts from Proverbs 31:9 and Luke 6:31 featured prominently on the title page. While this effort did not engage extensively in exegetical details, it did note that slavery contradicted "the whole divine revelation."[120] In a most unusual declaration by a New Englander in that crisis hour, Hopkins *denied* that the colonies (or Britain) enjoyed a special place in God's eyes, since "this distinction [of Israel] is now at an end, and all nations are put upon a level." Yet Hopkins did not require the presupposition of a special national covenant to chastise patriots for their political hypocrisy: "behold the *sons of liberty*, oppressing and tyrannizing over many thousands of poor blacks, who have as good a claim to liberty as themselves." Nor was he reluctant to preach like Jeremiah as he warned that failure to act against slavery would "bring down the righteous vengeance of heaven on our heads."[121] Infusing all of this evangelical's treatment of the patriots' most debilitating moral failure lay a firm conviction that biblical religion demanded benevolence that could not tolerate slavery.

Similar protests based on similar premises arose also from the margins of colonial society. In Boston, the Somerset decision inspired a contingent of slaves to petition the royal governor and colonial legislature to end a practice that they described as clearly opposed to natural law, Britain's common law, and natural rights. Their petition closed with a scriptural declaration: "we have a Father in Heaven, and we are determined...to keep all his Commandments."[122] Likewise in the nascent Methodist movement, key leaders in that still tiny group resolved on biblical grounds to translate John Wesley's published opposition to slavery into a practical guideline for their efforts.[123] One of those leaders, Francis Asbury, was sequestered in Delaware in June 1778—because the Methodists' position in the Church of England made them suspect as Loyalists—when he noted that "the more pious part of the people called Quakers, are exerting themselves for the liberation of the slaves." To Asbury, this effort manifested "a very laudable design; and what the Methodists must come to."[124] Two years later a conference of Methodist itinerants meeting in Baltimore urged their fellows to work for emancipation as a requirement of "pure religion."[125]

Yet abolitionists did not have the field to themselves. In late 1780 and early 1781, the *New Jersey Gazette* in Trenton published a series of nine essays debating the morality of slavery where, in the summary of Jonathan Sassi, "the Bible occupied a central place."[126] Alongside appeals to Whig principles, pragmatic economic considerations, and racist assumptions about the dangers of a free black population, contest over chapters and verses filled the page. Emancipationists quoted Deuteronomy 7:26 to describe slavery as "a cursed thing," invoked the Apostle Paul's exaltation of freedom in Galatians 5:1, and presented the Golden Rule of Matthew 7:12 as a dispositive denunciation of the institution. Their opponents hurled back a different interpretation of "whatsoever ye would that men should do to you, do ye even so to them": Christ's words could only mean that slave owners should treat slaves the way they would wish to be treated if they found themselves in bondage. Defenders of the institution also cited or quoted what had fast become the standard litany: Abraham's ownership of slaves (Gen 17:23); divine permission to enslave non-Hebrews (Lev 25:45–46); Mosaic guidelines for formalizing lifelong bondage (Ex 21:6, Deut 15:17); and New Testament injunctions for slaves to obey their masters "in the Lord" (1 Cor 7:20–21, Eph 6:5–8, Philem 15).

As the published controversies that mushroomed from the early 1770s made clear, the colonial crisis of independence sparked also the American crisis of slavery. A Whig discourse fixated on liberty joined Quaker philanthropy, Calvinist benevolence, Enlightenment humanitarianism, and an appeal to English common law in propelling emancipationist reform—but also in generating principled and pragmatic defenses of the institution. The Bible featured as a prominent weapon for both attack and defense. Beyond the simple fact that revolutionary agitation heightened the salience of Scripture, the character of that salience contributed significantly to what came to pass in the new nation. Americans valued the Bible that was so securely joined to the cause of national liberty for both the letter of its individual passages and the spirit of its overarching gospel message. It oversimplifies, though not by much, to say that the great biblical contest dominating the next eighty years would be whether letter or spirit prevailed.

Taking Stock

Beginning almost a century ago with Alice Baldwin, historians have been demonstrating the strong religious contributions to the American Revolution, and even more specifically the importance of Scripture in that era. As Baldwin summarized her pioneering work, for New England's leading public spokesmen "the most common source was the Bible.... Indeed there was never a principle derived from more secular reading that was not strengthened and sanctified by the Scriptures."[127] Baldwin's later research, along with the labors of many others, has shown that the biblical presence outside of New England, while marked by fewer analogies between ancient Israel and God's contemporary "people," was almost as pervasive.[128] Since the 1970s, a tide of scholarship has demonstrated the tight bond between the patriots' Whig principles and the application of the Old Testament to their situation, while the recent surge of painstakingly researched publications has only sharpened awareness of how much reliance on Hebraic scripturalism contributed directly to Revolutionary ideology. Scholarship on Loyalists and pacifists has not expanded in the same way, but the record of representative figures like Charles Inglis and Anthony Benezet shows that they too exhibited a similar reliance on Scripture. In sum, there are today no reasonable grounds for doubting James Byrd's claim that "the Revolution may be the most important event in American history, and the Bible was arguably its most influential book."[129]

Yet once having established Scripture's ubiquitous rhetorical presence, its unique status as a teaching authority, and its substantial contribution to the ideology of independence, serious interpretive questions remain that contemporary contentions over "Christian America" or "the godless Constitution" obscure almost completely.[130] Biblical narratives and individual texts from both Testaments gave all colonists a vocabulary for depicting absolute rights and wrongs—in social and public spheres as well as for individuals and domestic circles. These narratives, much personal meditation, and a long Protestant tradition of pulpit exposition supplied a language that for many colonists expressed their deepest personal experience of divine condemnation and gracious redemption. When such believers, but also those without these specifically Christian experiences, turned to consider public actions, actors, crises, dilemmas, controversies, and conundrums, it was inevitable that they would perceive them within a biblical frame of reference.

As even casual attention to public debates of the era indicates, however, the pervasive presence of Scripture by no means guaranteed that convictions defended with biblical argument and expressed in biblical language would produce biblical agreement. So it was that this era reprised the persistent Protestant dilemma of supreme trust in Scripture accompanied by divergent interpretations of Scripture.

The biblical history of the period also demonstrates that a public sphere infused with Scripture would not necessarily produce moral integrity instead of moral hypocrisy. Emancipationists in Britain, along with more than a few colonists, were deeply troubled by patriots eagerly exploiting Scripture to defend a liberty threatened by no more than ill-considered Parliamentary blunders while tolerating a devastating system of actual enslavement resting on completely unbiblical assumptions about racial difference. Some observers might even conclude that patriotic actions understood as reenactments of ancient biblical history could produce *more* self-serving violence, self-righteousness bigotry, and conspiratorial panic than the charity, self-sacrifice, and trust in providence that much of the Bible seems to enjoin on those who would follow its teaching.

Ellis Sandoz begins his excellent anthology of eighteenth-century political sermons with the statement that "Religion gave birth to America . . . all of our writers agree that political liberty and religious truth are vitally intertwined."[131] Yet one of his most interesting selections strikingly underscores the complexity required to evaluate the intertwining of religious and political convictions. This work from 1776 by John Fletcher, John Wesley's most learned lieutenant in England, put Scripture to use in a fiercely Loyalist fashion. As he chastised patriots for their hypocrisy concerning slavery and as he defended the basic integrity of the British monarchy, he deployed the Bible with the same virtuosity as did Jonathan Mayhew, John Witherspoon, or David Griffith. There was the same rhetorical creativity ("*Certain sons of Belial* [Judg 19:22], belonging to the city of Boston, beset a ship in the night"), the same expertise with analogies (a story from Judg 20:23–26 about civil war in ancient Israel told Fletcher that God blessed those who put down rebellions), and the same ability to exposit direct biblical teaching (predictably in this case from the Loyalists' favorite texts in Rom 13 and 1 Pet 2).[132]

From Fletcher's example, it is evident that the mere presence of a biblical frame of reference could not guarantee that those who operated within that frame acted with what either believers or unbelievers might describe as virtuous action. Fletcher may not have been correct in how he put Scripture to use, but he was relying on the Bible just as completely as those who used it to defend the American cause.

Unlike culture-war publicists, careful historians rarely venture too far beyond painstaking explorations of empirical cause and effect into the perilous terrain of moral judgment. One exception, however, appears in a thoroughly researched recent study on the religious convictions of the founding generation. This opinion is categorical: "The Bible mentions rebellion 131 times, and every reference is condemnatory or negative. The American Founding era preachers desperately wanted, however, to justify a rebellion," and so they "deftly ignored or reinterpreted problem passages of Scripture."[133] More often, those who document the importance of religion in Revolutionary America remain content with historical conclusions, or they express moral judgments cautiously, as in this aside from Thomas Kidd's generally celebratory account of the nation's founding: "More problematically,... the framing of the war as the action of Providence could make it difficult for American leaders to maintain a critical perspective on the war or its tactics."[134]

If moral judgments about the use of Scripture in the Revolutionary era entail significant ethical and theological ambiguity, historical analysis yields firmer conclusions derived from the unfolding of events. First, because the American War of Independence succeeded, the fusion of its Whig ideology with scriptural examples expanded the rhetorical presence of Scripture in American society. The new nation conceived in liberty had a biblical midwife who remained seriously invested in the young child's life.

Second, that same Whig-biblical confluence substantially detached Scripture from its British setting. Because the Revolution was fueled by an ideology of suspicion—especially against the hereditary hierarchies of church and government—American reliance on Scripture broke at least partially free from the hierarchical usages of English Christendom. To be sure, deeply engrained Protestant instincts along with universal reliance on the KJV kept the new nation closer to British traditions than ardent patriots realized, but a significant breach had nonetheless taken place.

Third, Revolutionary ideology eased the way for an upsurge of biblicism, the attempt to believe and act on the basis of "the Bible alone" that always attended the Protestant exaltation of scriptural authority. The Whig fear of corruption flowing from traditional centers of power cut cultural channels amenable to the instincts of biblicism. If inherited deference to the king and an aristocratic Parliament endangered civic health, so also did deference to learned authorities and denominational traditions threaten access to the Word of Life.

Finally, in the debates over colonial bishops and slavery that accompanied political controversy, controversialists regularly appealed more directly and didactically to the Scriptures than in the era's political controversies. Those appeals prepared the way for other direct appeals to the biblical text that also strengthened the impulse of biblicism.

For these reasons, the American Revolution shaped the future history of the Bible as much as the British Protestant history of the Bible shaped the Revolution. Use of Scripture in the Revolutionary era—as both expanded presence and specific guide—left an enduring mark on the history of the United States.

Conclusion

THE PROMINENCE OF Protestantism in early American experience is sufficient warrant for attempting a history of the Bible. From the early sixteenth century, Protestants ceaselessly repeated the refrain that Scripture revealed God's truth uniquely, and in such a way that people of ordinary intelligence could grasp its meaning and have that meaning direct their lives. This conviction became particularly strong in England and Scotland during the Reformation era, as testified by the contentious history of Bible translations from the time of William Tyndale through the Geneva Bible to the ultimate provision of the King James Version. During that period and subsequently, those who viewed themselves as particularly dedicated to God's Word—those who *were in fact* particularly dedicated—affirmed aggressively that they followed Scripture as their primary, or even as their only, guide. From that number came the Puritan founders of New England but also the furious critics of institutional Puritanism like Roger Williams and, with a more moderate program, William Penn and the Quaker founders of Pennsylvania. Ardent Protestants of all persuasions viewed the Bible as a fulcrum placed outside the world; hearing and heeding the Scriptures harnessed energy that could lever lost souls into fellowship with God and (perhaps) move the world.

If actual practice never fully measured up—if the application of scriptural truth never worked as successfully as Protestant theology claimed it should—the consequences were still breathtaking. The English-language world came to reflect a permanent scripturalization. Especially after the King James Version secured its monopoly among publishers and its hegemony among readers, that one Bible translation impressed itself on English and Scottish cultures profoundly—vocabulary, rhetorical styles, coded meanings of great affect, and an ever-present potential for sanctifying actions of almost any kind.

In this book we have observed the Bible as an engine of spiritual transformation in the lives of Martin Luther, Thomas Bilney, the named and unnamed citizens of early New Haven, Sarah Osborne, Nathan Cole, Jupiter

Hammon, and many more. Such transformations did not translate directly into social influence, but their consistent reappearance amounted to a personal deep structure variously shaping the surface structure of public life.

Throughout the colonial period the Bible sanctified all manner of public speech. Often that sanctification occurred as ministers preached sermons based on a biblical text and filled with biblical quotations, but intending to interpret current events. Sometimes it occurred when lay men or women read the circumstances of their lives with the Scriptures in hand. Once the Bible had achieved a place of honored distinction for selves and society, it became a lens through which believers perceived the eternal significance of temporal events, but also a torch that shone its illuminating rays on those events.

From the mid-sixteenth century on, an open Bible also served English, British, and colonial Protestants as an emblem of civil and religious liberty. A closed Bible, or even a violated Bible, stood foremost among the evils ascribed to the papacy, Catholic Spain, and Catholic France. In broader historical perspective, that judgment missed the mark. The Bible did remain a crucial feature of Catholic Christianity, if enfolded in a religious framework that Protestants disdained. Whatever the strictly empirical reality, Protestants looked on Scripture as a zealous sentry policing the great gulf that divided Western Christianity.

Close attention to actual uses of Scripture shows that the Bible never functioned as a God-given fulcrum outside of space and time. Everything scriptural was always completely cultural. Yet this modern understanding must not blind observers in our own day to how powerfully Scripture could *act* in culture. Scripture, which meant so much as a symbol for deep Protestant-Catholic differences, resonated in a great range of literary and rhetorical expressions, even as it participated in public activities of many kinds. Influences flew back and forth within the cultural landscape, but in many circumstances and at many times the flow moved as strongly from texts of Scripture outward as in the other direction.[1] Such a multifaceted presence demands assessment from many angles. If the distinction between historical and moral analysis oversimplifies lived reality, that distinction may still serve a heuristic purpose.

Historical Conclusions

A series of contrasts can summarize the developments examined in this book. These contrasts reveal how traditional Protestant dependence on

Scripture took shape, evolved, influenced, and was influenced by a history rooted in the Old World but producing unexpected fruit in the New.

Because the early generations of Europeans in North America adhered to forms of magisterial, establishmentarian Protestantism, the Bible must be understood first as a mainstay of Christendom. Yet almost from the start the colonies also became home to a few Protestants who believed that faithfulness to Scripture demanded opposition to Christendom. This stance, although entirely marginal in the seventeenth century, gained considerable momentum from the mid-eighteenth century on. To complicate an already conflicted Protestant trajectory, over the course of the latter century more and more colonists came to distrust the state-church structures of inherited British Christendom for political reasons, yet while also expecting to maintain the chief features of a Protestant culture through informal means. The Bible in the colonies defined a history of Christendom versus anti-Christendom, and then of formal versus informal public Protestantism.

A second contrast is obvious from even casual attention to how those who drew on Scripture actually put it to use. On many occasions colonists turned to the Bible as a didactic authority with the straightforward desire to be taught from its narratives, precepts, poetry, parables, and doctrines. Even more frequently colonists drew on Scripture rhetorically—not exactly to *discern* the will of God but more to *enlist* God's word on behalf of causes that may or may not have been directly taught from the sacred text.

Reasoning aimed at instruction witnessed a related contrast. Public figures often taught from the Bible by analogy, by relating an event in Scripture to a contemporary development illuminated by the ancient prototype. As the historian John Coffey has noted, strong evidence for the influence of Puritan New England appeared in sermons throughout the colonies during the Revolutionary period, which "were preached almost exclusively from Old Testament texts and propounded Hebraic tropes of election, covenant, and jeremiad."[2] By contrast, inductive teaching reasoned from precepts directly: early Puritans turned to Scripture for guidance in specifying which crimes they should treat as capital offenses; Roger Williams believed that the Golden Rule condemned Massachusetts's appropriation of Indian lands; William Penn held that Jesus's command to turn the other check ruled out coercive state violence; Jonathan Mayhew and David Griffith exegeted Romans 13 to explain why God did not require obedience to a tyrant; Charles Inglis exegeted the same passage to explain why George III was not a tyrant. For colonial history, it is a challenge to

discern how analogy, inductive instruction, and their many mixtures produced what kind of results under which kind of circumstances.

Another contrast marked the general Protestant effort to be guided by
the Bible. *Sola scriptura* remained an effective rallying cry, usually as criticism of positions held by others, but sometimes as a program for positive
action. Later observers can see more clearly than persons in the period
when other factors besides "the Bible alone" directed the deployment of
Scripture. We cannot, however, assess with clarity the motives of those
who made that claim—cynicism, naïveté, or utter sincerity were only
some of the possibilities. Claims to steer by "the Bible alone," however,
hardly exhausted the kinds of guidance sought from Scripture. Most
Protestants in most circumstances readily accepted other authorities, with
the only qualification that these others should be harmonized with overt
biblical guidance. Patriots questioned the Whig-Scripture confluence as
rarely as Loyalists queried the happy union of Scripture and monarchy. In
short, to be "guided by Scripture" informed multiple responses to biblical
authority.

Social class provides a last contrast, obvious in part because of our age's
interpretive fixations but also because a few colonial voices also practiced
something like a social hermeneutic. The use of the Bible to enforce or
attack governmental, ecclesiastical, or racial hierarchies provided the
clearest instances of this contrast. An observation that Abraham Lincoln
once made about scriptural defenses of slavery provides a poignant example. He imagined a slave owner who "sits in the shade, with gloves on
his hands, and subsists on the bread that [his slave] is earning in the
burning sun." If, Lincoln went on, the slave owner comes to the conclusion that God wills for slavery to continue, he remains seated in comfort.
But if he concludes that God wants slaves to be freed, then he must "walk
out of the shade, throw off his gloves, and delve for his own bread." Lincoln
answered his own question even as he posed it: Will the slave owner "be
actuated by that perfect impartiality, which has ever been considered most
favorable to correct decisions?"[3]

It was the same in the colonial period: the slave-owner who perceived
no biblical prohibition against the slave system from which he profited
may in fact have embraced a scriptural message of salvation for reasons
having nothing to do with profits from slavery. Nonetheless, it is easier to
conclude that the slave who drew a message of salvation from Scripture,
despite others' reliance on the Bible to defend slavery, embraced that message for reasons having little to do with this-worldly exercises of power. It

was natural for those who were spiritually quickened by biblical narratives of salvation to seek in Scripture a comprehensive guide for life—pertaining to themselves but also to others. Once such guidance intermingled with capacities for coercion, however, it becomes more difficult to assess the mixture of possible motives for using Scripture to serve public purposes.

Whatever one thinks about the wisdom or folly of so much attention to the Bible—or about the consequences for American national development flowing from that attention—it should be possible to recognize that a history of Scripture in colonial public life must assess these cultural tectonics: the Bible for and against Christendom, the Bible for teaching and the Bible for sanctifying, teaching from Scripture via analogy and teaching via didactic exposition, "the Bible alone" and the Bible leagued with other authorities, the Bible for those with power and those without. Yet obviously for all highly charged subjects like the Christian Scriptures, close attention to historical developments cannot rest with merely historical conclusions.

Moral Assessment

Confident authors have spelled out what they make of the sort of history this book relates. One school, made up of those who believe in Scripture as divine revelation, have concluded that since the colonists and then patriots fixated on Scripture, Americans in our own day should accept their interpretations of the Bible as from God. With New England in the lead, many Americans believed that the British Empire (and then the emerging United States) replicated the history of ancient Israel almost as antitype fulfills type. Accordingly, colonial Americans and then U.S. citizens did enjoy a special, even a unique, convenantal relationship with God.[4]

Another, more diverse school, whose members also believe in Scripture as divine revelation, understand prominent aspects of America history as flatly contradicting the clear instructions of Scripture. In their eyes, that contradiction might involve warmongering, where the Bible urges believers to follow the Prince of Peace.[5] It might involve the destruction wreaked on Natives, where the Bible demands treatment of all humans according to the Golden Rule.[6] Or it might point to the hypocrisy of a mania for liberty coexisting alongside vigorous promotion of slavery—when the Bible manifestly denounces such moral malfeasance.[7]

These two schools, despite contradictory readings of American history, rely on Scripture in a similar fashion—as itself the readiest standard for adjudicating past deployment of the Bible. Both, as a consequence, differ dramatically from standard secular interpretations that, if they note the presence of Scripture at all, have difficulty incorporating that presence into covering interpretations.

Still other historians have plied their trade neither by ignoring the presence of Scripture nor by trying to provide an explicitly biblical interpretation of events. This book reflects a deep debt to many such authors, including Carl Bridenbaugh, Catherine Brekus, Christopher Brown, Jane Calvert, David Brion Davis, Thomas Kidd, Harry Stout, Michael Winship, Edmund S. Morgan, Mark Valeri, and many more. Whatever their personal beliefs about God and divine revelation, they have interpreted the past in terms, at least partially as the historical actors understood their own experience, before also bringing their own standards to bear. The advantage that the best work of these historians enjoys over what might be called dogmatic religious or dogmatic secular interpretations is to allow earlier Americans a voice alongside the historians' own judgments.

From this history of the Bible in early American history, the moral judgment that makes most sense to me rests on a difference between Scripture for oneself and Scripture for others. In other words, I find persuasive Abraham Lincoln's recording of difference between scriptural adherence with social power and scriptural adherence bereft of such power. The Bible applied to oneself, as so powerfully in the cases of Sarah Osborn or Jupiter Hammon, should make later observers pause before seeking some more basic explanation than what these figures offered for their own experience. By contrast, where Bible-believers applied their scriptural interpretations to direct the lives of others, more questions about motives and actions must arise. Sincerity, integrity, and altruism may indeed lie behind efforts at making others follow one's own understanding of Scripture, but the evaluation of evidence in such cases becomes much more difficult.

Considered in broadest compass, I believe that professions to follow Scripture imparted commendable ethical seriousness to much of colonial life. More important, engaging the Bible did actually draw many people into life-giving fellowship with God and turn their lives outward, at least in some measure, toward self-sacrificing service to others. At the same time, I also believe that powerful traditions of Protestant biblical interpretation misled many colonists into thinking that Britain, or the colonies, enjoyed a special divine calling much more than casually analogous to the calling of biblical Israel. Further, dangerously mistaken interpretation of Scripture undercut the charity that the Bible enjoins toward foes, sanctioned murderous assaults on the sort of marginal people for which Scriptures requires special consideration, justified a system of racial slavery with no biblical warrant, and short-circuited the capacity for self-criticism that Scripture everywhere demands of God's elect people. Since this combination of moral judgments prevents simple affirmations or denunciations of colonial history, I am much less concerned that others share my evaluations than that they examine actually occurring events carefully before rendering their own judgments.

Looking Back, Looking Ahead

For a history of the Bible, the most important changes in the transit from Europe to America involved modes of appeal to Scripture and the contexts within which those appeals took place. In that transit, biblicism, or the profession to live by "the Bible alone," took on new force. In colonial America, the relative weakness of institutional Christendom opened more opportunities for all forms of scriptural reliance. Yet especially when Whig political principles made headway, they undercut many of the traditional buffers that in Britain kept biblicism in check.

Later, in the transition from Revolution to new nation, the Bible's presence became as fluid as it was manifest. Biblicism had grown stronger because of how revival quickened the personal force of some scriptural themes; but biblicism in the 1780s was not yet the active force for directing public policy that it had been with the Puritans who cited chapter and verse to renovate the details of government. Almost all Americans were turning against institutional Christendom in its British form; very soon the new nation, followed by the states, would complete the separation of church institutions from governmental structures. Still, many Americans—at different social levels and for different motives—felt strongly the need for guidance, wisdom, justice, morality, discipline, and perspective as they attempted to construct a civilization for the new country. Few put it in these terms, but the entire nation had become Rhode Island. Many looked to Scripture to sustain a comprehensively Christian society, but without state-church establishments.

After the tumults of imperial warfare, revival, and Revolution, citizens in the new United States—including revivalist evangelicals, anti-revival traditionalists, theological liberals, deists, and African American believers—remained fixated on the Bible, but they were also much freer to make of it what each one would. For religion, the new nation seemed to offer a

tabula rasa where a Bible-based Protestantism, republican Whig principles, and common sense moral philosophy had become more secure than
any particular *use* or *interpretation* of Scripture.[8]

The Bible remained centrally important for the religion of numerous
citizens, and the number of such citizens soon rose rapidly. The agenda
for the future posed this question: What would such ones do with the
biblical inheritance of Protestantism—and the ever-present possibility of
biblicism—when it was left to voluntary organizations instead of governments to construct the social order? Hints of answers can be glimpsed in
several snapshots from the immediate aftermath of the successful War of
Independence.

The Massachusetts Constitution of 1780 indicated how firmly the
instincts of Christendom remained in that new state. Patriots like Sam
Adams and John Adams took the lead in throwing off the corruptions of
British rule, but for them the republican fear of concentrated power did
not yet extend to Massachusetts's own church-state establishment. They
intended their new state constitution to provide a full measure of religious
toleration, but they could not bring themselves to give up Christendom:

> As the happiness of a people, and the good order and preservation
> of civil government, essentially depend upon piety, religion, and
> morality; and as these cannot be generally diffused through a com-
> munity but by the institution of the public worship of God, and of
> the public instructions in piety, religion, and morality: Therefore, to
> promote their happiness, and to secure the good order and preser-
> vation of their government, the people of this commonwealth have
> a right to invest their legislature with power to authorize and re-
> quire, and the legislature shall, from time to time, authorize and
> require, the several towns, parishes, precincts, and other bodies
> politic, or religious societies, to make suitable provision, at their
> own expense, for the institution of the public worship of God, and
> for the support and maintenance of public Protestant teachers of
> piety, religion, and morality, in all cases where such provision shall
> not be made voluntarily.[9]

An action by the Confederation Congress in 1782 also testified to the
lingering instincts of Christendom. On the twelfth of September, Congress
approved a resolution from a committee that included John Witherspoon to
authorize an American printing of the Bible. Robert Aitken, a Scottish-born

Philadelphia printer, had undertaken this project "at a time when from the circumstances of the war an English edition of the bible could not be imported." Among many other changes wrought by the conflict, the monopoly held by the king's printers for publishing the KJV no longer extended to an independent United States. Aitken showed the kind of initiative with Scripture that would soon characterize the entire national population. Yet old habits died hard. And so a Congressional committee recommended Aitken's work, subject to vetting by the Presbyterian and Episcopal chaplains of the Congress (George Duffield and William White). When the chaplains reported that Aitken's newly printed Bible was "executed with great accuracy as to the sense, and with as few grammatical and typographical errors as could be expected in an undertaking of such magnitude," the Congress approved "the pious and laudable undertaking of Mr. Aitkin [*sic*], as subservient to the interest of religion as well as an instance of the progress of arts in this country," and authorized Aitken "to publish this commendation in the manner he shall think proper."[10] The notion that printing and distributing bibles required governmental approval looked backwards at a time when much else in America was moving into an unknown future.

That future, however, rarely involved any lessening of respect for the Bible. As an important example, Ezra Stiles, the president of Yale College whom we have seen leading the fight against an Anglican bishop for the colonies, indicated in 1783 how easy it would to transform belief in the biblical chosenness of imperial Britain to the new United States. In the annual election sermon for the Connecticut legislature on May 8 of that year he chose as his text Deuteronomy 26:19. "And to make thee high above all nations, which he hath made in praise, and in name, and in honor; and that thou mayest be an holy people unto the Lord thy God." When Stiles applied this biblical promise to current events, he foresaw the day, within two hundred years, when the population of the new United States might exceed even the population of China: "If this prove a future fact, how applicable would be the text, when the Lord shall have made his american Israel, *high above all nations which he hath made*, in numbers, *and in praise, and in name, and in honor!*" Stiles then asked his auditors if that prediction sounded "visionary." He answered his own question by stating that it was no more visionary than thinking that the 20,000 original New Englander settlers might by the early 1780s have become nearly a million strong—or that, in a supposition, Catholics would soon experience "the certain downfall of the pontificate"[11]

THE

HOLY BIBLE,

Containing the OLD and NEW

TESTAMENTS:

Newly tranflated out of the

ORIGINAL TONGUES;

And with the former

TRANSLATIONS

Diligently compared and revifed.

PHILADELPHIA:

PRINTED AND SOLD BY R. AITKEN, AT POPE'S
HEAD, THREE DOORS ABOVE THE COFFEE
HOUSE, IN MARKET STREET.
M.DCC.LXXXII.

After securing a commendation from the Continental Congress, Thomas
Aitken in 1782 published the first complete English-language Bible in the
New World. (Courtesy of Wheaton College [IL] Special Collections, Buswell
Memorial Library)

Stiles's enthusiasm for the new nation's prospects knew no bounds: "How wonderful the revolutions, the events of providence! We live in an age of wonders." He was especially impressed by the way American experience had recapitulated the ancient Hebrew search for leadership. He noted that after the Battle of Bunker Hill, "Congress put at the head of this spirited army, the only man, on whom the eyes of all israel were placed." As a result, all the world could recognize the greatness of George Washington and acknowledge "that this american Joshua was raised up by God, and *divinely formed* by a peculiar influence of the Sovereign of the Universe, for the great work of leading the armies of this american Joseph (now separated from his brethren), and conducting this people through the severe, the arduous conflict, to liberty and independence."[12]

On 7 May 1783, one day before Stiles's stem-winding sermon before the Connecticut legislature, Francis Asbury turned to Scripture for a very different purpose. Asbury, one of the workers whom John Wesley had dispatched to the colonies to spread the Methodist message of scriptural holiness, was convening a much humbler conference than the gathering that witnessed Stiles's feted address. The record he left of this meeting nonetheless spoke to realities that would eventually shape the future of Scripture in the United States as much as Stiles's ideologically charged address. As Asbury wrote from Petersburg, Virginia, "Our conference began at this place. Some young laborers were taken in to assist in spreading the Gospel, which greatly prospers in the north. We all agreed in the spirit of African liberty, and strong testimonies were borne in its favour in our love feast; our affairs were conducted in love."[13] This early American testimony against slavery grew from what Asbury, as guided by John Wesley, felt the Bible commanded. Although that testimony would eventually fade as the Methodist movement began its remarkable rise, the stimulation of biblical religion "from below" would inspire multitudes of ordinary people to live by what they considered scriptural imperatives.

A year and a half later, James Madison marshaled all of his political wisdom with all of his political wiles for a project fundamental to creating what in his mind a free society should be. The mobilization took place against a bill proposed in the Virginia legislature by Patrick Henry that, as for postwar Massachusetts, would have continued Virginia's tax support for organized religion—though allowing all citizens to designate the particular churches for receiving this ecclesiastical tax. Madison, in his desire to secure full religious liberty for Virginians, strongly opposed Henry's proposal. His point of attack was the stipulation in Henry's bill that the tax money would go to "Christian teachers." In notes prepared for a speech he delivered on 23 December or 24 December 1784, Madison drew his weightiest arguments from the history of biblical interpretation. Who could determine, he wrote in notes prepared for this speech, "What is Christianity?" Then came a lengthy series of questions arising directly out of the post-Reformation history of conflict over scriptural interpretation: "What edition [of the Bible to be used]? Septuagint, or vulgate? What copy—what translation?...What books canonical, what apocryphal? the papists holding to the former what protestants the latter, the Lutherans the latter what other protestants & papists the former." And so it continued as he asked who would determine how to interpret the Bible, what doctrines were essential for Christianity, how to distinguish between "orthodoxy" and "heresy," and more.[14] Questions may be raised about whether Madison was speaking cynically—as someone who had given up on biblical revelation—or was channeling the arguments of biblicists who opposed Christendom. His well-documented sympathy for the Baptists whom Virginian Anglicans had persecuted, and later cooperation with these same anti-Christendom biblicists, suggests that he sensed how biblical arguments against establishment could carry equal or more force than Enlightenment arguments. Whatever his motivations, Madison's strategy worked, and the Virginia house did not approve Henry's bill.[15]

Thirteen months later that same body approved the Virginia Statute for Religious Freedom that Thomas Jefferson had drafted nearly a decade before. Its bold declaration decisively destroyed the key institutional foundation of formal Christendom:

> Whereas Almighty God hath created the mind free; that all attempts to influence it by temporal punishments, or burthens, or by civil incapacitations, tend only to beget habits of hypocrisy and meanness, and are a departure from the plan of the holy author of our religion, who being lord both of body and mind, yet chose not to propagate it by coercions on either, as was his Almighty power to do...
>
> Be it enacted by the General Assembly, that no man shall be compelled to frequent or support any religious worship, place, or ministry whatsoever, nor shall be enforced, restrained, molested, or burthened in his body or goods, nor shall otherwise suffer, on account of his religious opinions or belief; but that all men shall be free to profess, and by argument to maintain, their opinions in matters of religion, and that the same shall in no wise diminish, enlarge, or affect their civil capacities.[16]

Supported by its own interpretation of biblical accounts describing the "Lord...of body and mind," this landmark statute created a free space in which to promote biblical teaching voluntarily—or, if one chose, to turn completely away from the Bible. With the First Amendment to the Constitution of 1791, the Virginia statute's provision for full religious freedom also became national law ("Congress shall make no law respecting an establishment of religion, or prohibiting the free exercise thereof"). Soon, though not immediately, it was accepted by all of the states, with Massachusetts the last in 1833. So was set the American course without formal Christendom.

Intra-Christian, and especially intra-Protestant, controversies over how to interpret the Bible contributed substantially to rejecting the unchecked, coercive power that citizens of the new nation feared in state-church establishments. But what would be the fate of the Bible after dispensing with formal Christendom? An answer to that question could be discerned by attending once again to Francis Asbury, and at the very same time that James Madison gathered his anti-Christendom arguments to scuttle Patrick Henry's proposal for a modified church establishment.

In late November and early December 1784 Francis Asbury recorded a journey toward Baltimore whence he had called his associates for the purpose of setting up a Methodist Episcopal Church for the United States institutionally separated from the British movement. Asbury's account of that journey indicates why the Bible would dramatically expand some aspects of its influence in a post-Christendom United States.[17]

On Tuesday, November 30, Asbury preached to a small gathering in rural Maryland on "That we may have boldness in the day of judgment [1 Jn 4:17]." On that same day, he also recorded a conversation with a local bookseller named Mason Locke Weems. Weems, who had recently become one of the first ministers ordained in the new nation's re-formed Anglican communion, now called the Protestant Episcopal Church in the United States of America, discussed with Asbury questions of church organization by bishops (the Methodists would follow this same pattern). Weems later became famous for fabricating the story of a young George Washington chopping down a cherry tree and admitting to the misdeed because "I cannot tell a lie." For our story, he is much more important as an enterprising, and very successful, seller of books. Less than twenty years later, Weems wrote from the Virginia countryside to his publisher in Philadelphia about the success he was enjoying in retailing different editions of the King James Bible: "I tell you this is the very season and age of the Bible. Bible Dictionaries, Bible tales, Bible stories—Bibles plain or paraphrased, Carey's Bibles, Collin's Bibles, Clarke's Bibles, Kimptor's Bibles, no matter what or whose, all, all, will go down—so wide is the crater of public appetite at this time."[18] As he penned those words, that public appetite was being stoked by a great influx of converts to populist evangelical churches, with the Methodists in the lead.

On Saturday 4 December 1784, Asbury recorded that he "preached on Mark xiv, 29, 30, with freedom [But Peter said unto him, Although all shall be offended, yet will I not. and Jesus saith unto him, Verily I say unto thee, That this day, even in this night, before the cock crow twice, thou shalt deny me thrice]." Then on Sunday the twelfth he "enlarged on" the text, "Blessed are the pure in heart [Mt 5:8]." On Tuesday he rendezvoused with Dr. Thomas Coke, whom Wesley had sent from England with his blessing for an American Methodist church. At Abingdon, Maryland, Asbury reported that Coke expounded on "He that hath the Son hath life [1 Jn 5:12]." The next day, "Dr. Coke preached a great sermon on, 'He that loveth father or mother more than me,' etc. [Mt 10:37]." From 18 December Asbury and Coke began their careful preparations for the conference that would confirm the two of them as bishops of the American Methodist church, a meeting that convened almost exactly when Madison arose to oppose Patrick Henry's bill.

Colonial American history as it culminated in the American Revolution provides the necessary background for understanding why the United States threw off formal Christendom. The journal of Francis Asbury hints at why that abandonment could lead to a deeper and broader social influence of Scripture, advanced through voluntary means, than had ever occurred under the constraints of Britain's formal Christendom. Yet one of the most striking features of the record left by Asbury was his nearly complete indifference to political matters—with opposition to slavery as the only significant exception. Another notable aspect of the journal was its focus on biblical redemption, a message that resonated powerfully among individuals whose intensive private faith would one day produce inevitable, if unpredictable, public effects.

* * * * *

Ἐν ἀρχῇ ἦν ὁ λόγος. The Gospel of John opens with this enigmatic but powerful affirmation: "In the beginning was the *logos*, the Word." Use of this single term *logos* in only this one gospel is richly varied. In the immediate context of its initial expression, God's "word" is Jesus Christ, the one through whom "all things were made" (Jn 1:3) and who now had become "flesh and dwelt among us" in order to reveal God's "glory as the only be-gotten of the Father" (1:14). But later in the gospel the *logos* is also the whole body of teaching that Jesus expounded along with his life as the perfect exemplar of that teaching. Jesus called upon his disciples to "continue in my word" (8:31), which would enable them to "know the truth" that "shall make you free" (8:32). By contrast, those who reject "my words" will in the last day be judged by "the word that I have spoken" (12:48). In yet another instance, Jesus equates "the word of God" with what is "written in your law" and with "scripture [that] cannot be broken" (10:34–35). In John's Gospel, "the word of God" is a person, the entirety of life-course direction, and a definitive written record of divine revelation.

In the beginning of European-American history, "the word of God," considered from this-worldly perspectives, denoted a similarly diverse range of meanings. The Bible of Christendom arrived in the New World as the Scripture of state-church Christianity, even as the spaciousness of that world opened up room for Bible-believers opposed to Christendom. The imperial Bible gained great strength over the course of the eighteenth century, alongside growing strength for a Bible of personal faith. For colonial attitudes toward Scripture, sometimes it was "the Bible alone," much more often the Bible with other implicit or explicit authorities.

The Bible functioned in this period as a powerful source of guidance for individuals and communities. It also functioned as a rich treasury of tropes, models, types, examples, and precepts in service to principles that did not rise from its pages. Although Scripture provided language and a model for constructing the image of a modern nation in covenant with God, it provided no direct teaching to support the widespread belief that the British Empire (and then the new United States) enjoyed a chosen status parallel to ancient Israel. It was similar for general intellectual life and specific conceptions of politics; the Scriptures might sanctify but they did not directly teach. For economic questions, the Bible faded as a direct influence, even as it only began to emerge as a teaching authority on questions related to race and slavery. Yet even as conventional wisdom edged aside direct scriptural instruction on some particulars, revival intensified the grip of the Bible on many lives. A widespread longing for moral order, even after throwing off church-state establishments, also fueled a turn to Scripture for guidance.

In the beginning was the Word. After independence came heroic efforts to build a Bible civilization. The extent to which those efforts partially succeeded and eventually failed is a subject that requires its own exploration.

Notes

INTRODUCTION

Complete publishing information is found in the bibliography.

1. See 262, 280, 291, 294–95, 304–5, 317.
2. Especially informative studies have recently documented the deep contentions over the United States' informal Christendom in the nineteenth century, including Green, *The Second Disestablishment*; Sehat, *The Myth of American Freedom*; Porterfield, *Conceived in Doubt*; Green, *The Bible, the School, and the Constitution*; Schlereth, *An Age of Infidels*; Den Hartog, *Patriotism and Piety*; and Haselby, *The Origins of American Religious Nationalism*. Most of these studies rely in considerable measure on Hatch, *The Democratization of American Christianity*.
3. McLeod, *The Religious Crisis of the 1960s*, 18.
4. *Confessions of St. Augustine*, 118.
5. "Biblicism, n.," OED Online, December 2014 (accessed 20 Jan. 2015); Carlyle, *The Life of John Sterling*, 224.
6. In the later decades of the nineteenth century, "the biblicist" was also an expression designating those with a general trust in scriptural authority; for examples, see Livingstone, *Dealing with Darwin*, 180, 191.
7. Marsden, *Fundamentalism and American Culture*, 224.
8. See especially Bozeman, *To Live Ancient Lives*; Hughes, *The American Quest for the Primitive Church*; and for colonial history, Hutchins, *Inventing Eden*.
9. In recent decades several social scientists have taken pains to define a range of related practices they also call biblicism. Compared to these detailed studies, my use of the word is simpler. I take biblicism to mean a principle of authority (supreme trust in Scripture) combined with a principle of criticism (distrust to some significant degree of other forms of authority). Social scientists who stress biblicism as a negative principle include Malley, *How the Bible Works…Evangelical Biblicism*, 17–21; Bielo, *Words Upon the Word*, 52–55; and Smith, *The Bible Made Impossible*,

3–6, 180–83. For use of the term in a more neutral sense, see Malley, "Understanding the Bible's Influence," in *The Social Life of Scriptures*, ed. Bielo, 194 (biblicism here as "the complex of ideas and practices that surround the Bible").

10. Chillingworth, *The religion of protestants*, 375.

11. For an up-to-date consideration of the extensive literature on "confessionalization," see Gregory, *The Unintended Reformation*, 149–60 and passim.

12. See the "spiritual" authors anthologized in Williams, *Spiritual and Anabaptist Writers*.

13. Winship, *Godly Republicanism*, 3.

14. Frye, *The Great Code*, 206.

15. A solid treatment that explains parallel Catholic and Protestant histories in Britain and America is Daniell, *The Bible in English*.

16. For one of the most revealing of such studies, see Thuesen, *In Discordance with the Scriptures*.

17. One of the best accounts is Gutjahr, *An American Bible*.

18. Metzger, introduction to *New Testament with Psalms and Proverbs*, New Revised Standard Version, ix.

19. Miller, "The Garden of Eden and the Deacon's Meadow," 54.

20. Quoted biblical material from the sources follows the capitalization, punctuation, and spelling of the originals. Other scriptural material is taken from *The Bible: Authorized King James Version with Apocrypha*, ed. Robert Carroll and Stephen Pricket, Oxford World Classics.

21. See 266–69.

PRELUDE

1. Comprehensive treatment of the late fifteenth and early sixteenth centuries is found in *Handbook of European History, 1400–1600*. For a readable summary, see the early chapters of MacCulloch, *The Reformation*.

2. *The Libro de las profecías of Christopher Columbus*, trans. and ed. West and Kling. For directing my interest in Columbus, I am grateful to Sarah Costa (neé Jackman), "Eschatology and Exploration: Rethinking the Historical Columbus."

3. "Scripture Index," in *Libro de las profecías*, 274.

4. *Libro de las profecías*, 101, 103, 105 (Columbus counted the books in the then-standard Vulgate canon). Bible translations for Columbus and, below, Las Casas are from the Douay-Rheims-Challoner version, long the standard translation for English-speaking Catholics. See 61, for the influence of that translation on the KJV.

5. Fernández-Armesto, *Columbus*, 91. For helpful context on the *Libro de las profecías*, see Fernández-Armesto, *Columbus*, 157–59.

6. Lupas, *A Light to the Nations*, 46, 44. For the whole note, trans. Lupas, see 44–48 ("Appendix").

7. A thorough introduction along with the text is found in *Bartolomé de las Casas: The Only Way*, ed. Parish, trans. Sullivan, S.J.

8. *Bartolomé de las Casas*, 68. Editor Parish supplied chapter and verse references for Las Casas's scriptural quotations, but since versification had not yet occurred, he did not cite texts by verse numbers.

9. Ibid., 71.

10. For an important contemporary account, see Acosta, *Natural and Moral History of the Indies*; and for a superb recent history, MacCormack, *On the Wings of Time*.

11. I have relied on Wright, *Early Bibles of America*, 304–12; Alonso, "La Biblia en el Nuevo Mundo"; Daniell, *The Bible in English*, 396–97; Lori Anne Ferrell, *The Bible and the People*, 101–5; Pastena, *Protestant Empire*, 61; and Prien, *Christianity in Latin America*, 92–103, 209–10.

12. An image appears in Ferrell, *Bible and People*, 102.

13. Quoted in Alonso, "La Biblia," 26 ("no apruebo la opinión de los que dicen que los idiotas no leyesen las divinas letras en la lengua que el vulgo usa, porque Jesu Christo lo que quiere es que sus secretos muy largamente se divulguen").

14. Pope Paul III, *Sublimis Dei*, 29 May 1537, Papal Encyclicals on Line, available at www.papalencyclicals.net/Paul03/p3subli.htm (accessed 25 January 2015).

15. Alonso, "La Biblia," 26.

16. See Pardo, *The Origins of Mexican Catholicism*.

17. Prien, *Christianity in Latin America*, 209n40. In 1602 Cipriano de Valera prepared a revised edition of Reina's work, which formed the basis for the Reina-Valera translation that with additional revisions remains a popular Spanish-language version to this day.

18. Prien, *Christianity*, 209.

19. *Jesuit Relations and Allied Documents*, 15:165.

20. Fischer, *Champlain's Dream*, 57, 513.

21. See Anderson, *The Death and Afterlife of the North American Martyrs*.

CHAPTER 1

1. Reliable general introductions, representing a variety of perspectives, include Bossy, *Christianity in the West, 1400–1700*; Dickens and Tonkin, *The Reformation in Historical Thought*; Lindberg, *The European Reformations*; Fernández-Armesto and Wilson, *Reformations…1500–2000*; and MacCulloch, *The Reformation: A History*.

2. "Ninety-Five Theses, 1517," trans. C. M. Jacobs and Harold J. Grimm, in *Luther's Works*, 31:25. For Grimm's historical introduction, see *LW*, 31:19–23. *Luther's Works* will be cited hereafter as *LW*.

3. "Ninety-Five Theses," 31 (no. 62), 30 (no. 53), 25 (no. 1), 27 (no. 18).

4. "Lectures on Galatians, 1519: Chapters 1–6," trans. Richard Jungkuntz, in *LW*, 27:325. As yet, the text was not divided into verses. For dating these lectures, see Grimm, "Introduction," *LW*, 27:x.

5. "Lectures on Galatians," 326.

6. "Proceedings at Augsburg 1518," trans. Harold J. Grimm, in *LW*, 31:263.

7. Ibid., 265.

8. Ibid., 270–74.

9. Ibid., 265–76.

10. Ibid., 270, 271, 272.

11. "Preface to the Complete Edition of Latin Writings 1545," trans. Lewis W. Spitz, in *LW*, 34: 336. Quotations in this and the next paragraphs are from 336–37.

12. "Luther at the Diet of Worms, 1521," trans. Roger A. Hornsby, in *LW*, 32: 101–31.

13. Ibid., 111.

14. Ibid., 112.

15. Ibid., 113. The official was Johann Eck, but not the famous Eck with whom Luther had earlier carried on a momentous theological debate.

16. Ibid., 114n.

17. Volz et al., "Continental Versions to ca. 1600," in *Cambridge History of the Bible*, 3:94–140.

18. *The New Testament Translated by William Tyndale 1534*, 323, and 323n.

19. *Novum Testamentum Latine*, 410.

20. *Facsimiles of Early Luther Bibles*, vol. 2, *Romans*, 10.

21. Bruns, *Hermeneutics Ancient and Modern*, 139–40, as quoted in Pelikan, *The Reformation of the Bible: The Bible of the Reformation*, 28–29.

22. "Preface to the New Testament," trans. Charles M. Jacobs and E. Theodore Bachmann, in *LW*, 35:358.

23. Ibid., 357.

24. On the importance of those early professions, from which Luther backed away but others did not forget, see chap. 5, 127–28.

25. Bainton, *Here I Stand*, 199–201, 204; MacCulloch, *The Reformation*, 137–38; and Sider, *Andreas Bodenstein von Karlstadt*.

26. Sider, *Karlstadt*, 189.

27. Robert C. Schultz, "Introduction" to "Luther's Admonition to Peace," in *LW*, 46:5.

28. On versification, see 58–59.

29. Quoted in Schultz, "Introduction," 9.

30. Quoted in ibid., 12, 15–16.

31. "Admonition to Peace: A Reply to the Twelve Articles of the Peasants in Swabia," trans. Schultz and Charles M. Jacobs, in *LW*, 46: 17, 19, 23, 25, 27.

32. "Against the Robbing and Murdering Hordes of Peasants," trans. Schultz and Charles M. Jacobs, in *LW*, 46: 54–55.

33. "An Open Letter on the Harsh Book Against the Peasants," trans. Schultz and Jacobs, in *LW*, 46: 66, 70.

34. Authoritative on this controversy is Williams, *The Radical Reformation*, 89–101, 118–34, 137–46.

35. "The Sixty-Seven Articles of Ulrich Zwingli (1523)," in *Confessions and Catechisms of the Reformation*, ed. Noll, 39.

36. On this earlier history I have benefited especially from Hurley, *Scriptura Sola: Wyclif and his Critics*; Oberman, *The Harvest of Medieval Theology*, esp. 371–98; Berkouwer, *Holy Scripture*; Doyle, "William Woodford on Scripture and

Tradition," in *Studia Historico-Ecclesiastica*, 481–502; Mathisen, *The Shape of Sola Scriptura*; and McGrath, *Historical Theology*, 151–52.

37. The phrase is from Doyle, "Woodford," 502.
38. Ibid.
39. Hurley, *Scriptura Sola*, 25. For Wycliffe's own reference to *"sola scriptura,"* see *John Wyclif On the Truth of Holy Scripture*, 80; translating *John Wyclif's De Veritate Sacrae Scripturae.*
40. Fourth Session, April 1546, from the London 1848 translation by James Waterworth.
41. The historical transition that occupies the rest of this book has been set out succinctly in Hatch, *"Sola Scriptura* and *Novus Ordo Seclorum,"* in Hatch and Noll, *The Bible in America*, 59–78.
42. Hegel, *Philosophy of History*, 436, 104.

CHAPTER 2

1. 2 Timothy 3:16, in *The New Testament Translated by William Tyndale 1534.* For later citations from this source (designated as Tyndale), verse numbers are supplied, although they would not appear in English-language Bibles until well after Tyndale's death.
2. Hill, *The English Bible and the Seventeenth-Century Revolution*, 11, 31.
3. John Maxwell, *Sacro-Sancta Regum Majestas* (1644), in *Divine Right and Monarchy*, ed. Wootton, 63.
4. McLeod, *The Religious Crisis of the 1960s*, 18.
5. On Tyndale, see esp. Daniell, *William Tyndale*; and for a synopsis, Daniell, *The Bible in English*, 133–59.
6. C. S. Lewis, *The Literary Impact of the Authorized Version*, 13.
7. Norton, *A History of the Bible as Literature*, 1:85–86.
8. This compilation is from Malless and McQuain, *Coined by God: Words and Phrases that First Appear in the English Translations of the Bible*, passim; and Crystal, *Begat: The King James Bible and the English Language*, esp. 263–97.
9. Rupp, *Studies in the Making of the English Protestant Tradition*, 23, quoting John Foxe's *Acts and Monuments.*
10. Quoted in Rupp, *English Protestant Tradition*, 22.
11. Quoted in Daniell, *Bible in English*, 142.
12. Tyndale, "A Pathway into the Holy Scripture" (1525), in *Doctrinal Treatises and Introductions*, 7n1 ("moved me"), 7 ("light").
13. Calvin, "Prefatory Address to King Francis I of France," *Institutes of the Christian Religion*, 1:9–31.
14. Daniell, *Bible in English*, 144.
15. Rupp, *English Protestant Tradition*, 27–31.
16. Quoted in Daniell, *Bible in English*, 163.
17. Pelikan, *Creeds and Confessions*, 2:604 (with the whole confession, 601–49). Further quotations are identified by chapter, paragraph, and page number in Pelikan's *Creeds and Confessions.*

18. Quoted in ibid., 158.

19. Quoted in ibid., 147.

20. Bruce, *The English Bible*, 70.

21. It, rather than the King James Bible, was the only English translation ever "authorized" for use in the realm, despite the common reference to the KJV as the Authorized Version.

22. Daniell, *Bible in English*, 205–8.

23. Quoted in Bruce, *English Bible*, 68.

24. Ibid., 68–69.

25. See especially Duffy, *The Stripping of the Altars*.

26. Daniell, *Bible in English*, 274–75.

27. Norton, *The King James Bible: A Short History*, 21.

28. After Richard Challoner's revision of the this translation (1749, 1751), the standard English-language Bible for Roman Catholics has been known as the Douay-Rheims-Challoner version.

29. Crystal, *Begat*, 263–97 passim; Norton, *King James Bible: Short History*, 32.

30. See Sherman, "'The Book Thus Put in Every Vulgar Hand,'" in Saenger and Van Kampen, *The Bible as Book*, 125–33.

31. I have relied on Norton, *Bible as Literature*, vol. 1; Daniell, *Bible in English*; Bruce, *English Bible*; along with the popular, but reliable, Nicolson, *God's Secretaries*; and Bobrick, *Wide as the Waters: The Story of the English Bible*. The quadricentennial in 2011 yielded a bounteous crop, with especially helpful contributions from Norton, *King James Bible: Short History*; Campbell, *Bible, 1611–2011*; and a surprisingly good DVD, "KJB: The Book that Changed the World," presented by John Rhys-Davies, produced by Norman Stone.

32. *The Bible: Authorized King James Version*, ed. Carroll and Prickett, lii (title page), liii ("Zeal"), lv (on Scripture), lxxxi (dedication).

33. On the physical presentation and social meaning of those type faces, see Paul Gutjahr, "The Letter(s) of the Law: Four Centuries of Typography in the King James Bible," in *Illuminating Letters*, 18–23.

34. *The Geneva Bible: A Facsimile of the 1560 Edition*, New Testament, 118.

35. Ibid., 24 (Old Testament).

36. Ibid., 121 (Old Testament).

37. Swift from 1712, quoted in Campbell, *Bible, 1611–2011*, 144.

38. The passages that follow are taken from *The Bible*, ed. Carroll and Prickett.

39. In the wealth of publications in 2011, two of the best were Hamlin and Jones, eds., *The King James Bible after 400 Years*; and Jeffrey, ed., *The King James Bible and the World It Made*.

40. "The Bible in American Life," The Center for the Study of Religion and American Culture, Indiana University-Purdue University Indianapolis, report released 6 March 2014.

CHAPTER 3

1. For orientation to the themes of this chapter, unusually helpful works have been provided by Collinson, *The Elizabeth Puritan Movement*; Collinson, *The Religion of Protestants...1559–1625*; Knoppers, ed., *Puritanism and Its Discontents*; Green, *Print and Protestantism in Early Modern England*; Coffey and Lim, eds., *The Cambridge Companion to Puritanism*; Coffey, *Exodus and Liberation*, 25–55; and Gunther, *Reformation Unbound...1525–1590*.

2. Gunther, *Reformation Unbound*, 22.

3. Ibid., 21 (Colet), 26 (Tyndale), 30 (Barnes), 58 (law of the gospel).

4. The Articles are quoted here from the 1571 English version, as found in Pelikan and Hotchkiss, *Creeds and Confessions of Faith in the Christian Tradition*, 2:526–40. Useful guides include Cummings, *The Book of Common Prayer: The Texts*; and Jacobs, *The Book of Common Prayer A Biography*. The paragraphs that follow draw from the introduction to the Articles provided in Noll, ed., *Confessions and Catechisms of the Reformation*, 211–13.

5. Yet it is noteworthy that almost all early English Bibles, including the Geneva and the King James, printed the apocryphal or deuterocanonical books along with the Old and New Testaments.

6. It severely abbreviated the original Article to read only "The power of the civil magistrate extendeth to all men, as well clergy as laity, in all things temporal; but hath no authority in things purely spiritual...." See Pelikan, *Creeds and Confessions*, 2:558–59n4.

7. Hill, *The English Bible and the Seventeenth-Century Revolution*, 51.

8. Goodman, "Resistance to Tyrants," in Morgan, *Puritan Political Ideas*, 1.

9. The Geneva Bible's note on the Jewish officials mentioned in this passage offered a laconic denunciation: "They prefer...their autoritie to the ordinance of God." *The Geneva Bible: A Facsimile of the 1560 Edition*, New Testament, 56.

10. Goodman, "Resistance to Tyrants," in Morgan, *Puritan Political Ideas*, 5–9.

11. On the difference between typology and a wide array of exemplary uses, see Holifield, *Era of Persuasion...1521–1680*, 45–48.

12. The full title was *A Brief and Plain Declaration Concerning the Desires of All Those Faithful Ministers that Have and Do Seek for the Discipline and Reformation of the Church of England*, in Trinterud, *Elizabethan Puritanism*, 231–301.

13. Ibid., 240 (preface), 273–74 (anti-Catholic), 300 (conclusion). Emphasis on "only" added.

14. Up-to-date consideration is provided by Worden, *God's Instruments: Political Conduct in the England of Oliver Cromwell*.

15. Quoted in the excellent study by Paul, *The Assembly of the Lord*, 69.

16. Quoted in ibid.

17. Pelikan, _Creeds and Confessions_, 2:604 (with the whole confession, 601–49). Further quotations from the Westminster Confession are identified by chapter, paragraph, and page number in Pelikan's _Creeds and Confessions_.

18. Frei, _The Eclipse of Biblical Narrative_; Sheehan, _The Enlightenment Bible_.

19. Quoted in Firth, _Oliver Cromwell and the Rule of the Puritans in England_, 106–7, 123.

20. See Paul, _The Lord Protector . . . Oliver Cromwell_, 35.

21. Quoted in ibid., 36.

22. Paul, _Lord Protector_, 399; with the entire analysis, 397–400.

23. Morrill, "A Liberation Theology?" in Knoppers, _Puritanism and Its Discontents_, 39. Morrill's account of Cromwell's biblicism, 39–41 and 48n28, analyzes the same letter that Robert Paul quoted and finds even more scriptural quotations or paraphrases than I identify.

24. "The King's Declaration Prefixed to the Articles of Religion," in Gardiner, _The Constitutional Documents of the Puritan Revolution, 1625–1660_, 75.

25. "Resolutions of Religion Drawn by a Sub-Committee of the House of Commons," in Gardiner, _Constitutional Documents_, 77–82; quotations, 78–79.

26. "The Scottish National Covenant," in Gardiner, _Constitutional Documents_, 124–34; quotations, 125.

27. "The Root and Branch Petition," in Gardiner, _Constitutional Documents_, 137–44, quotations, 138–39.

28. "The Solemn League and Covenant," in Gardiner, _Constitutional Documents_, 267–71; quotations, 267–68.

29. Solid background on Chillingworth is found in Shapiro, _Probability and Certainty in Seventeenth-Century England_, 78–82; and Reedy, _The Bible and Reason:_ 10–11 and passim.

30. Chillingworth, _The religion of protestants a safe way to salvation_, 375–76.

31. Winstanley, "A New-Years Gift," in Wootton, _Divine Right and Monarchy_, 333.

32. _Rel. Baxteriana_, I.i., 53–54, (par. 77) as quoted in Paul, _Assembly of the Lord_, 48n96.

33. Baxter, _A Holy Commonwealth_ (1659), 1, 62, 63, 123, 129.

34. Their lineage is outlined carefully in Miller, _The Religious Roots of the First Amendment_.

35. Hooker, _Of the Lawes of Ecclessiasticall Politie_, in Wootton, _Divine Right and Monarchy_, 223.

36. See Keble, "C. S. Lewis, Richard Baxter, and 'Mere Christianity,'" 27–44.

37. Hobbes, "Philosophicall Rudiments Concerning Government and Society," in Wootton, _Divine Right and Monarchy_, 450.

38. Filmer, _Observations upon Aristotle's Politiques_, in Wootton, _Divine Right and Monarchy_, 111 (my emphasis on "nature").

39. Harrington, "The Art of Lawgiving," in Wootton, _Divine Right and Monarchy_, 408.

40. For a sampling of the large literature on debated questions about Locke, divine revelation, and principles of natural reason, see Miller, _Religious Roots and the First Amendment_, 63–90 (Locke favorable to Scripture); Rahe, _Republics Ancient and Modern_, 298–310 (Locke opposed to Scripture); Zuckert, "National Rights

and Protestant Rights," in *Protestantism and the American Founding*, 42–44 (Locke indifferent to Scripture); and Wolterstorff, "Locke's Philosophy of Religion," in *The Cambridge Companion to Locke*, 172–98 (Locke favoring reason over revelation).

41. Marx, *18th Brumaire of Louis Bonaparte* (1852), as quoted in Hill, *English Bible*, 40.

CHAPTER 4

1. For political dimensions of that winning out, see Stout, "Word and Order in Colonial New England," in Hatch and Noll, *The Bible in America*, 3–18; and the helpful revisions concerning the ongoing importance of the Geneva Bible for the colonies in Van Engen, "Origins and Last Farewells: Bible Wars, Textual Form, and the Making of American History."

2. See Cogley, *John Eliot's Mission to the Indians*; on the German Bibles in Luther's translation from the press of Christopher Saur in Germantown, Pennsylvania, see Roeber, "German and Dutch Books and Printing," in Amory and Hall, *History of the Book: Colonial*, 302. For the one illegal printing of the Bible in eighteenth-century Boston, see Amory, "The New England Book Trade, 1713–1790," in Amory and Hall, *History of the Book: Colonial*, 327–28.

3. For the great importance of establishmentarian thinking for all the colonies throughout the entire colonial period, see Gregory, "'Establishment' and 'Dissent' in British North America," in *British North America in the Seventeenth and Eighteenth Centuries*, 136–69.

4. On national chosenness, see chaps. 10 and 11. On sites of Bible publication in the early national period, see Hills, *The English Bible in America: A Bibliography...1777–1957*, 1–84. For later special commemorative days, see Stout and Grasso, "Civil War, Religion, and Communications," in *Religion and the Civil War*, 313–59.

5. "Articles, Laws, and Orders, Divine, Politic, and Martial for the Colony in Virginia" (1610–11), in Lutz, *Colonial Origins of the American Constitution*, 315–18 (articles 1, 5, and 13).

6. Hall, "The Chesapeake in the Seventeenth Century," in Amory and Hall, *History of the Book: Colonial*, 55.

7. Ibid., 66, 68–69, 73–74.

8. For more of her story, see 131–34.

9. Shepard, *God's Plot...the Autobiography and Journal of Thomas Shepard*, ed. McGiffert, 33, 45.

10. Ibid., 243–44.

11. Shepard, *Thomas Shepard's Confessions*, ed. Selement and Wooley.

12. Ibid., 33–34.

13. Ibid., 57.

14. Ibid., 67–69.

15. Ibid., 148–49.

16. Ibid., 100–101.
17. Ibid., 33, 67, 68, 87, 157, 167, 174, 177.
18. An up-to-date account is Winship, *Godly Republicanism*.
19. The paragraphs that follow take examples from only the first four chapters of Bradford's memoir, but they are representative of much that followed. Quotations are from Bradford, *Of Plymouth Plantation, 1620–1647*, ed. Morison, intro. Murphy, with page references in parentheses to this edition.
20. For the wide-ranging influence of biblical parataxis, see Alter, *Pen of Iron: American Prose and the King James Bible*, passim.
21. See Gordis, *Opening Scripture*, 107: Bradford's narrative "testifies not to a desire to supplant the biblical text with his own history, but rather to an impulse to link his own history typologically to the biblical one."
22. Winthrop, "A Model of Christian Charity," in Morgan, *Puritan Political Ideas*. All quotations are from this meticulously edited printing of Winthrop's draft manuscript and are indicated by page numbers in parentheses.
23. Bremer, *John Winthrop*, which is the source for the details about Winthrop's life that follow. Edmund S. Morgan's much shorter study remains a model of historical insight, *The Puritan Dilemma: A Life of John Winthrop*.
24. For solid historical accounts showing why Winthrop's speech must be read as a particularly Puritan effort defined by Puritan aspirations of the 1630s and not as anticipating an exceptionalist history for the United States, see Bremer, *John Winthrop*, 174–81; Van Engen, "Origins and Lost Farewells"; Richard M. Gamble, *In Search of the City on a Hill*; and especially Bozeman, *To Live Ancient Lives*, 90–119, esp. 95: Winthrop's words "would appear to be not only the most quoted but also the least understood in the Puritan literature." For a fuller discussion of national exceptionalism, which relies heavily on Morgan, Bremer, and Bozeman, see Noll, "'Wee shall be as a citty upon a hill.'"
25. Amory, "Appendix One: A Note on Statistics," in Amory and Hall, *History of the Book: Colonial*, 511.
26. Tomlin, *A Divinity for All Persuasions: Almanacs and Early American Religious Life*, esp. 8–88, 93–97.
27. Hall and Martin, "Appendix Two: A Note on Popular and Durable Authors and Titles," in Amory and Hall, *History of the Book: Colonial*, 519–21.
28. For a good introduction, see Miller and Johnson, *The Puritans*, 2:555–56.
29. Bay Psalm Book, *The Whole Book of Psalmes Faithfully Translated into English Metre*, unnumbered pages.
30. Ibid., [ii], [xiv]. The auction at Sotheby's in New York on 26 November 2013 of a first edition of the Bay Psalm Book for $14,165,000 indicated an enduring fascination for the antiquity, if not necessarily the biblicism, of the early Puritans.
31. Amory, "Printing and Bookselling in New England, 1638–1713," in Amory and Hall, *History of the Book: Colonial*, 109.
32. Hall, "Readers and Writers in Early New England," in Amory and Hall, *History of the Book: Colonial*, 123.

33. Ibid., 123, 124.
34. Ibid., 124.
35. Winslow, *Meetinghouse Hill*, 59.
36. Stout, *The New England Soul*, 19.
37. Ibid., 3.
38. Ibid., 31–33.
39. For a convincing explanation of that flexibility, see Gordis, *Opening Scripture*, 31–33.
40. On Chillingworth, see 93–94.
41. Bradford, *Of Plymouth Plantation*, 83–84.
42. Winthrop, "Model of Christian Charity," in Morgan, *Puritan Political Ideas*, 90.
43. Quotations that follow, along with detailed contexts, are from Bremer, *Building a New Jerusalem: John Davenport*, 181–82.
44. Bremer, *First Founders*, 157.
45. For a thorough treatment of this document, see Wolosky, "Bible Republicanism: John Cotton's 'Moses His Judicials' and American Hebraism."
46. Winthrop, *The Journal of John Winthrop, 1630–1649*, ed. Dunn and Yeandle, 107.
47. Cotton, *An Abstract of the Lawes of New England, As they are now established* (1642), 1. Deut 1:13: "Take you wise men, and understanding, and known among your tribes, and I will make them rulers over you." Deut 17:15: "Thou shalt in any wise set him king over thee, whom the Lord they God shall choose: one from among thy brethren shalt thou set king over thee: thou mayest not set a stranger over thee, which is not thy brother." Ex 18:21: "Moreover thou shalt provide out of all the people able men, such as fear God, men of truth, hating covetousness; and place such over them, to be rulers of thousands, and rulers of hundreds, rulers of fifties, and rulers of tens."
48. Cotton, *An Abstract of the Lawes of New England*, 10–11.
49. "The Massachusetts Body of Liberties" (1641), in Morgan, *Puritan Political Ideas*, 179, 190, 197–99 (crimes), 199–201 (churches).
50. For a full account of these developments along with authoritatively edited documents, see the classical work by Walker, *The Creeds and Platforms of Congregationalism*. For excellent treatment of contextual questions, see Bremer, *John Winthrop*; and Winship, *Godly Republicanism*.
51. *The Cambridge Platform*, in Walker, *Creeds and Platforms*, 195, 194, 203.
52. Ibid., 203.
53. Ibid., 235, 236, 237.

CHAPTER 5

1. See especially Clarke, *English Society, 1660–1832*; Julian Hoppit, *A Land of Liberty? England, 1689–1727*, 207–41; Hempton, *Religion and Political Culture in Britain and Ireland*, 1–24; and Strong, *Anglicanism and the British Empire, ca. 1700–1850*, 1–117.

2. A solid survey is Zuckert, *Natural Rights and the New Republicanism.*

3. The rest of this section relies heavily on the genealogy provided in N. Miller, *The Religious Roots of the First Amendment.*

4. Luther, "Temporal Authority; To What Extent it Should be Obeyed" (1523), in *LW*, 45:105.

5. See Miller, *Religious Roots*, 27–29; and G. Williams, *The Radical Reformation*, 64–67.

6. "The Schleitheim Confession" (1527), in Noll, *Confessions and Catechisms of the Reformation*, 54.

7. MacCulloch, *The Reformation*, 654. See also Miller, *Religious Roots*, 29–32; Williams, *Radical Reformation*, 623–30; and Castellio's *Concerning Heretics*, ed. Bainton.

8. Murton, *An Humble Supplication to the King's Majesty*, bound with *Persecution for Religion Judged and Condemned*, 60, 62, 63 (entire pamphlet, 58–82).

9. Miller, *Religious Roots*, 37, 41.

10. Particularly helpful accounts are Morgan, *Roger Williams, the Church and the State*; Gaustad, *Liberty of Conscience: Roger Williams*; and for the broader context of the 1630s, Winship, *Godly Republicanism.*

11. Winship, *Making Heretics…Massachusetts, 1636–1641*, 37. My account of Hutchinson's life follows Winship's fine study closely.

12. See Winship, *Making Heretics*, 41, for this dispute.

13. "A Report of the Trial of Mrs. Ann [*sic*] Hutchinson before the Church in Boston, March, 1638," in *The Antinomian Controversy, 1636–1638*, ed. Hall, 351. This book provides a very full context for Hutchinson's entire American career.

14. Quotations from Hall, *Antinomian Controversy*, 352–54, 361, 355.

15. R. Williams, *The Bloudy Tenent of Persecution for Cause of Conscience*, ed. Groves, 3.

16. Ibid., 11–12.

17. Ibid., 19–27.

18. Ibid., 277–83.

19. Winship, *Godly Republicanism*, 212.

20. For a sketch, see Bremer, *First Founders*, 91–93.

21. Ibid., 93–98.

22. Morison, *Harvard College: The Seventeenth Century*, 1:305–14. "Incendiaries" came from a Massachusetts law of 1644; Morison, *Harvard College*, 306.

23. An unusually useful article is McLoughlin and Davidson, "The Baptist Debate of April 14–15, 1668." For informative treatment of this incident, see also Hall, *Worlds of Wonder, Days of Judgment*, 63–68.

24. McLoughlin and Davidson, "Baptist Debate," 111.

25. Ibid., 112–31 passim.

26. *Massachusetts Historical Society Collections*, 4th ser., 8 (1868), 292, as quoted in McLoughlin and Davidson, "Baptist Debate," 104.

27. McLoughlin and Davidson, "Baptist Debate," 101. For similar use of Scripture by another Baptist that likewise undermined Puritan Christendom, see *Baptist Piety: The Last Will and Testament of Obadiah Holmes*, ed. Gaustad, esp. 29–30, 86, 89.

28. My account relies especially on Cogley, *John Eliot's Mission to the Indians*; and the early pages of Fisher, *The Indian Great Awakening*.

29. Quoted in Cogley, *John Eliot's Mission*, 65, 115.

30. Nathaniel Saltonstall, *A New and Further Narrative of the State of New-England* (London, 1676), as quoted in Lepore, *The Name of War: King Philip's War*, 105.

31. Winship, *Making Heretics*, 246.

32. For a recent and well-informed introduction, see Rick Kennedy, *The First American Evangelical: A Short Life of Cotton Mather*.

33. For a comparison treating the approaches to Scripture by Mather, Henry, and Edwards, see Noll, "Jonathan Edwards' Use of the Bible: A Case Study (Genesis 32:22–32) with Comparisons."

34. Excellent treatment of the broader contexts for this work is found in Smolinski and Stievermann, *America's First Bible Commentary*. A superb account of the work itself is Smolinski, "Editor's Introduction," *Cotton Mather. Biblia Americana*, vol. 1: *Genesis*, xvii–ccx.

35. Smolinski, *Biblia Americana: Genesis*, 269n1.

36. Smolinski, *Biblia Americana: Genesis*, passim; and *Biblia Americana*, vol. 3: *Joshua–2 Chronicles*, ed. Minkema, passim. The threatening character of those innovations for someone like Mather is well explored in Sheehan, *The Enlightenment Bible*; Legaspi, *The Death of Scripture and the Rise of Biblical Studies*; and Turner, *Philology*, 58–61, 73–80, 112–17, 210–29, and 357–68.

37. Mather, *Biblia Americana: Genesis*, 1050–54.

38. Kennedy, *First American Evangelical*, building on Lovelace, *The American Pietism of Cotton Mather*.

39. The modern character of Mather's apologetics are well explained and illustrated in Cotton Mather, *The Christian Philosopher* (1721), ed. Solberg.

40. For a clear introduction to synteresis, see Calvert, *Quaker Constitutionalism and the Political Thought of John Dickinson*, 68–70. For Penn's place in the anti-Christendom tradition, see Miller, *Religious* Roots, 54–63.

41. William Penn, *The Great Case of Conscience* (1670), from *The Sacred Rights of Conscience*, ed. Dreisbach and Hall, 42, 44, 45.

42. Ibid., 46.

43. "A Charter of Liberties and France of Government of the Province of Pennsylvania," in Lutz, *Colonial Origins of the American Constitution*, 272, 285.

44. Ibid., 286.

45. "An Act of Freedom of Conscience" (December 7, 1682), in Lutz, *Colonial Origins*, 287, 289.

46. See Calvert, *Quaker Constitutionalism*, 122–25; and Butler, "Gospel Order Improved: The Keithian Schism and the Exercise of Quaker Ministerial Authority in Pennsylvania."

47. See in chaps. 9 and 11 on Quakers John Woolman, *Some Considerations...*, and Anthony Benezet, *Observations on the Inslaving* and *Serious Considerations*, 249–51.

1. Colley, *Britons: Forging the Nation, 1707–1837*, 54; Schlenther, "Religious Faith and Commercial Empire," in *The Oxford History of the British Empire: Eighteenth Century*, 128; Greene, "Empire and Identity from the Glorious Revolution to the American Revolution," in *Oxford History of the British Empire: Eighteenth Century*, 208; Griffin, *America's Revolution*, 3; Armitage, *The Ideological Origins of the British Empire*, 8.

2. Brendan McConville, *The King's Three Faces...1688–1776*, 7.

3. The next two paragraphs express differences with Clark's *The Language of Liberty: Political Discourse and Social Dynamics in the Anglo-American World*, which depicted the colonies as experiencing almost the same connections between radical politics and radical theology that his other works have described for Britain. Yet this account is also strongly indebted to the crucially important insights of Clark's *English Society, 1688–1832*, 1st ed. (1985), for example, 277: "The ubiquitous agency of the State was the Church,...impinging on the daily concerns of the great majority, supporting its black-coated army of a clerical intelligentsia, bidding for a monopoly of education, piety and political acceptability."

4. Different religious-political dynamics existed for Scotland and Protestant Ireland, but the same range of political-religious intersections within the context of Christendom. For one forceful account, see Connolly, *Religion, Law and Power... Protestant Ireland, 1660–1760*.

5. Shagan, *The Rule of Moderation...in Early Modern England*, 3.

6. Clark, *English Society*, 278.

7. Colley, *Britons*, 47.

8. For the growing colonial affection for monarchy as well as the intensifying fear of Catholicism, see McConville, *King's Three Faces*, 7, 112–19, and passim.

9. See especially Mailer on these hopes: "Anglo-Scottish Union and John Witherspoon's American Revolution," 709–46 (739 on Edwards).

10. See especially Breen, "An Empire of Goods: The Anglicization of Colonial America, 1690–1776"; and Breen, *The Marketplace of Revolution*.

11. Fiering, *Moral Philosophy at Seventeenth-Century Harvard*; and Flower and Murphy, *A History of Philosophy in America*, vol. 1.

12. See on Mather's *Biblia Americana* in chap. 5, 143–44; and on Edwards, Brown, *Jonathan Edwards and the Bible*.

13. On these figures, see 257–59.

14. For the popularity of Tillotson, see May and Lundberg, "The Enlightened Reader in America."

15. Tillotson, *The Usefulness of Consideration in Order to Repentance*, 6, 8, 11, 18.

16. Watts, *Hymns and Sacred Songs*. On the colonial popularity of Watts, see Hall, "Readers and Writers in Early New England," in Amory and Hall, *History of the Book: Colonial*, 126; and on the enduring popularity of these particular hymns,

Marini, "American Protestant Hymn Project... Most Frequently Printed Hymns, 1737–1960," in *Wonderful Words of Life*, 253.

17. Watts, *The Psalms of David, imitated in the language of the New Testament*, 182, 154. John Wesley later revised Watts's filiopietistic "Our God" to a more generically human "O God." For expert commentary, see Stackhouse, "Hymnody and Politics," in *Wonderful Words of Life*, 44–52.

18. Among many other accounts, see McConville, *King's Three Faces*; T. S. Kidd, *The Protestant Interest*; Colley, *Britons*; Noll, *America's God: From Jonathan Edwards to Abraham Lincoln*, 78–82; Berens, *Providence and Patriotism...1640–1815*; and Hatch, *The Sacred Cause of Liberty*.

19. See especially Kidd, *Protestant Interest*.

20. Mather, *Shaking Dispensations* (1715).

21. Ibid., 2, 42, 45.

22. Ibid., 46, 48, 45, 48.

23. On Colman, I am much indebted to William (Billy) Smith, "A Heavenly Correspondence: Benjamin Colman's Epistolary World and the Dissenting Interest."

24. Colman, *A Sermon Preached* (1716). On this specific sermon, see Kidd, *Protestant Interest*, 38–39; and on Colman's general positioning of Brattle Street as a loyal outpost of empire, Kidd, *Protestant Interest*, 34–44.

25. Colman, *Sermon Preached*, 6, 23.

26. Ibid., 24–28. Not surprisingly, this passage from 1 Peter 2 became prominent once again in the 1770s; see on Loyalist sermons that employed this passage, 302–3, 305, 312, 323.

27. This section relies heavily on Kidd, *Protestant Interest*, 91–114.

28. Kidd, *Protestant Interest*, 103 (Colman), 108 (Mather); and for the *Gazette*, T. S. Kidd, "'Let Hell and Rome Do Their Worst': World News, Anti-Catholicism, and International Protestantism in Early-Eighteenth Century Boston," 274.

29. Mather, *Edulcorator: A brief essay on the Waters of Marah sweeten. With a remarkable relation of the Dep[l]orable Occasion afforded for it, in the premature death of Captain Josiah Winslow* (1725).

30. Thomas Symmes, *Historical Memoirs of the Late Fight at Piggwacket, with a sermon occasioned by the fall of the brave Capt. John Lovewell* (1725).

31. Benjamin Wadsworth, *True Piety the Policy for Times of War* (1722).

32. Stoddard, *Question whether God is not angry with the country for doing so little towards the conversion of the Indians*,10 (on the other Bible translations).

33. Foxcroft, *God's Grace Set Against an Incorrigible People* (1724).

34. Stith, *A Sermon, Preached before the General Assembly, at Williamsburg* (1746); for context, see Morgan, *American Slavery, American Freedom: The Ordeal of Colonial Virginia*, 370–72.

35. Stith, *Sermon*, 4 ("Divine Right"), 21–22 for the other quotations.

36. Ibid., 24, 28.

37. Ibid., 28.

38. Tennent, *The Necessity of Praising God for Mercies Receiv'd: A Sermon occasion'd by the success of the late Expedition... in reducing the City and Fortresses of Louisburgh on Cape-Breton* (1745), 36–38 (quotations).

39. Tennent, *A Sermon...for a Provincial Thanksgiving* (1749), 23–24.

40. Ibid., 22–24.

41. Ibid., 24.

42. Hatch, *Sacred Cause of Liberty*, 49, with 21–54 more generally on the imperial conflicts. See also Stout, *The New England Soul*, 233–55.

43. For background, see Pilcher, *Samuel Davies*; and Noll, "Samuel Davies," *American National Biography*.

44. First to be preached, though published after the third sermon, were Davies, *Virginia's Danger and Remedy: Two Discourses occasioned by the severe drought in sundry parts of the country; and the defeat of General Braddock* (1756). The third sermon was *Religion and Patriotism the Constituents of a Good Soldier* (1755).

45. Davies, *A Sermon preached to the militia of Hanover country* (1759).

46. Davies, *A Sermon...on the death of his late Majesty, King George II* (1761).

47. Davies, *Religion and Patriotism*, 19, 13.

48. Ibid., 5, 13.

49. Ibid., 3, 4, 5, 13.

50. Davies, *A Sermon on the Death of King George*, 3.

51. Griffin, *America's Revolution*, 43; see also McConville, *King's Three Faces*, 111–12.

52. For recognizing the importance of this document, I am indebted to Choi, "George Whitefield, the Imperial Itinerant," 210–32.

53. Whitefield, *Britain's Mercies, and Britain's Duty represented in a sermon... Occasioned by the suppression of the late unnatural rebellion* (1746).

54. The sermon text from the 1746 sermon came from Psalm 105:45, "That they might observe His Statutes and keep His Laws"; Whitefield, *Britain's Mercies*, 3.

55. Whitefield, *An Address... Occasioned by the Alarm of an Intended Invasion* (1756).

56. Ibid., 7, 9, 11 (twice).

57. Ibid., 11, with other such ascriptions on that page, also 3, 4.

58. Ibid., 13, also 5.

59. Ibid., 3, 4, 13 (priests, queen), 14.

60. Ibid., 10.

61. Ibid., 3–6. Ahithophal was the counselor in 2 Samuel 15–17 who gave Absalom the advice that led to his death in battle with armies loyal to Absalom's father, King David.

62. Ibid., 5, 7.

63. Ibid., 9. See on the use of this text in the Revolutionary period, 280, 287.

64. Ibid., 7. For the importance of the "Man of War" reference from Exodus 15:3 during the American Revolution, see 280.

65. For a full context, see Choi, "George Whitefield, Imperial Itinerant," 224–30.

66. The bishop was Zachary Pearce, recently transferred from the sea of Bangor to become the dean of Westminster; Whitefield addressed him throughout as the "Bishop of Bangor," perhaps to suggest that a newcomer to London had little

right to restrict what Whitefield had been doing under various arrangements for almost twenty years. See Whitefield to the bishop, 2 Feb., 16 Feb., 23 Feb., 20 March, 25 March, 1756, in *Works of Whitefield*, 3:157, 159–64, 165, 166–67, 168–70.

67. *Works of Whitefield*, 3:165 (on sending the bishop his patriotic pamphlet), and 160–61 ("foolishness of preaching").

68. *Works of Whitefield*, 3:164 (letter of 16 Feb. 1756).

69. As an example, the first letter of 2 February invoked the example of Jesus, "who in the days of his flesh taught all that were willing to hear, *on a mount, in a ship,* or, *by the sea-side,* and who after his ascension, commanded us by his Apostle, to be 'instant in season and out of season'" (quoting 2 Tim 4:2); *Works of Whitefield*, 3:157 (letter of 2 Feb. 1756).

70. Schutz, "Jonathan Belcher," *American National Biography*; for Belcher's affectionate attachment to the monarchy, see McConville, *King's Three Faces*, 65, 133–34.

71. On the Colman-Belcher connection, see Valeri, *Heavenly Merchandize: How Religion Shaped Commerce in Puritan America*, 180.

72. Wertenbaker, *Princeton, 1746–1896*, 25–26.

73. Burr, *A Servant of God Dismissed from Labour to Rest* (1757), 17.

74. Belcher, "By His Excellency Jonathan Belcher...Proclamation for a Publick Thanksgiving," *New-England Weekly Journal*, 2 Nov. 1730, 1; *By His Excellency Jonathan Belcher...A Proclamation for a Publick Fast* (1735). The latter broadside included the phrase "humbling themselves under the mighty hand of God" (echoing 1 Pet 5:6) but most noticeable were the bold letters proclaiming "GOD save the KING."

75. *An Account, Shewing the Progress of the Colony of Georgia in America* (1742), in *Tracts and Other Papers*, ed. Force, 1 (separately paginated).

76. *A True and Historical Narrative of the Colony of George, in America* (1741), in Force, *Tracts and Other Papers.*

77. *An Account* (1742), 21, 50–51 (Spain), 45–46 (France).

78. Ward, *The Protestant Evangelical Awakening*, 6–7 and passim.

79. For full context, see Hammond, *John Wesley in America.*

80. *A True and Historical Narrative* (1741), 29–31.

81. See Choi, "George Whitefield, Imperial Itinerant," 57–61.

82. Little, "The Origins of Southern Evangelicalism: Revivalism in South Carolina, 1700–1740," 795 ("slavery" and "tyranny"), 808 (last quotation).

CHAPTER 7

1. *The Autobiography of Benjamin Franklin*, 131.

2. J. N. Green, "Part One: English Books and Printing in the Age of Franklin," in Amory and Hall, *History of the Book: Colonial*, 261.

3. Chauncy, *Seasonable Thoughts on the state of religion in New-England* (1743), 221 (Puritan John Flavel identified), 226 (quotation); material on a proper "work of the Spirit" fills the first pages of the book.

4. The question has been well posed in best provocateur fashion by Butler, "Enthusiasm Described and Decried: The Great Awakening as Interpretive Fiction"; but answered positively and with discrimination by Michael J. Crawford, *Seasons of Grace: Colonial New England's Revival Tradition*; Lambert, *Inventing "The Great Awakening"*; and T. S. Kidd, *The Great Awakening: The Roots of Evangelical Christianity in Colonial America*.

5. Crawford, "The Spiritual Travels of Nathan Cole," 91n5.

6. A perceptive recent account that takes in all of the colonies and extends from the 1730s into the 1770s is Kidd, *Great Awakening: Roots*. This chapter has also benefited greatly from Gaustad, *The Great Awakening in New England*; Stout, *The New England Soul*, 184–211 ("Awakening") and 212–32 ("A New Balance"); Ward, *The Protestant Evangelical Awakening*; and especially from three excellent documentary collections that have pointed me to a wealth of relevant sources: Heimert and Miller, eds., *The Great Awakening: Documents*; Bushman, ed., *The Great Awakening: Documents*; and Kidd, ed. *The Great Awakening: A Brief History with Documents* (2008). My treatment also draws on Noll, *The Rise of Evangelicalism*, 76–135.

7. For the broad Christianization of British society *before* the revivals, see Hempton, *Religion and Political Culture in Britain and Ireland*, 15–18, 124–26; and Hempton, *Methodism: Empire of the Spirit*, 18–19.

8. The last and most secure "sign" of true godliness was, according to Edwards, that it had its "exercise and fruit in Christian Practice"; *A Treatise Concerning Religious Affections in Three Parts* (1746), in *Works of Edwards*, 2:383.

9. Garden, *Regeneration ... Being the Substance of Two Sermons ... Occasioned by some erroneous notions of certain men who call themselves Methodists* (1740), 1.

10. Chauncy, *Seasonable Thoughts*, 321, 325.

11. Lemuel Briant, *The Absurdity and Blasphemy of Deprecating Moral Virtue* (1749), 6.

12. John Bass, *A True Narrative of an Unhappy Contention in the Church at Ashford* (1751), 5.

13. In a still helpful study, "The Conservative Attitude toward the Great Awakening," Labaree detailed seven characteristics that opponents of revivals attacked; five of them dealt with challenges to the inherited structures of Christendom: itinerant preaching, lay exhortation, revivalistic censoriousness, disruption of church unity and discipline, and distractions of the laity from their secular callings.

14. Chauncy, *The Gifts of the Spirit to Ministers* (1742), 35; Chauncy, *Enthusiasm described and caution'd against* (1742), 15.

15. From a pamphlet published anonymously in Glasgow (by A.M., perhaps Charles Chauncy), *The State of Religion in New England* (1742), as found in Kidd, *Great Awakening: Documents*, 96.

16. Stiles, *A Prospect of the City of Jerusalem* (1742), 45.

17. Chauncy, *Seasonable Thoughts*, [xxxi–xlviii].

18. Tennent, *The Danger of an Unconverted Ministry* (1740), 3.

19. From *Boston Post Boy*, 3 May 1742, as found in Kidd, *Great Awakening: Documents*, 116.

20. Henry to William Dawson, 23 Feb. 1745, William Dawson Papers, Library of Congress, in Kidd, *Great Awakening: Documents*, 236.

21. Hooker, ed., *The Carolina Backcountry on the Eve of the Revolution: The Journal and Other Writings of Charles Woodmason*, 101.

22. Edwards, *Religious Affections*, 438.

23. Hopkins, *The Life and Character of the Reverend Mr. Jonathan Edwards* (1765), 40–41.

24. For an argument that Edwards should be regarded as more a Bible student than philosopher, ethicist, aesthetician, or even theologian, see McClymond and McDermott, *The Theology of Jonathan Edwards*, 135–36, 159–61, 169–80.

25. For a summary, see Gatiss, "Introduction," *The Sermons of George Whitefield*, 1:29–31.

26. Whitefield, "Walking with God" (1740), in *Works*, 5:27.

27. On the dramatic effects of Whitefield's concentration on the new birth, see Tracy, *The Great Awakening*, 139; and Stout, *The Divine Dramatist: George Whitefield and the Rise of Modern Evangelicalism*, 191.

28. Whitefield, "Abraham's Offering Up His Son Isaac" (1742), in *Works*, 5:49.

29. Whitefield, "On Christ the Believer's Husband" (1747), in *Works*, 5:196.

30. Whitefield, "The Duty of Searching the Scriptures" (1739), in *Works*, 6:82.

31. Edwards, "Sinners in the Hands of an Angry God," (1741), in *Works of Edwards*, 22: 404–5 (additional texts), 411 (quotation).

32. Quoting the Rev. Stephen Williams, in introduction to ibid., 400.

33. Edwards, "The Blowing of the Great Trumpet" (1741), in *Works of Edwards*, 22:438–40 (exposition), 446 (exhortation).

34. Blair, *A Short and Faithful Narrative, of the late remarakable [sic] revival of religion* (1744), 10–11, 12, 14–15, 19.

35. Greene, *Pursuits of Happiness*, 202–3.

36. The difficulties in assigning causes and effects for the Awakening are discussed in Noll, *The Rise of Evangelicalism*, 136–54.

37. Dickinson, *The Witness of the Spirit* (1740), title page, 8.

38. Dickinson, *The True Scripture-Doctrine Concerning Some Important Points of Christian Faith* (1741), 137.

39. Trapp, *The Nature, Folly, Sin, and Danger of being Righteous over-much; with a particular View to … certain Modern Enthusiasts*.

40. Whitefield, "The Folly and Danger of Not Being Righteous Enough" (1739), in *Works*, 5:131.

41. Smith, *The Character, Preaching, &c. of … George Whitefield* (1740), 9, 15.

42. See 357n3.

43. This colonial history bears out the insight of W. R. Ward, who defined the essence of early evangelicalism as resistance to assimilation by formal structures of power; Ward, *The Protestant Evangelical Awakening*.

44. Stout, *Divine Dramatist*, 211.

45. W. D. Love, *Samson Occam and the Christian Indians of New England* (1899), in Kidd, *Great Awakening: Documents*, 65, 67.

46. Backus manuscripts, in McLoughlin, ed., *Isaac Backus on Church, State, and Calvinism*, 2.

47. Samuel Hopkins, ed., *The Life and Character of Miss Susanna Anthony* (1799), 18 (blasphemies), 30–31 (texts and their effect).

48. On the confluence of revivalist and Enlightenment sources for the new sense of the Protestant individual, see Brekus, *Sarah Osborn's World*, 8–11 and passim; and Bebbington, *Evangelicalism in Modern Britain*, 50–69.

49. This sermon was probably "The Wise and Foolish Virgins" (1739), in Whitefield, *Works*, 5:373–91.

50. Husband, *Some Remarks on Religion, with the Author's Experience in Pursuit Thereof... Being the Real Truth of What Happened. Simply Delivered, without the Help of School-Words, or Dress of Learning* (1761), as found in Heimert and Miller, *Great Awakening*, 638–39, 642 (Spirit of God).

51. More on Husband can be found in Heimert, *Religion and the American Mind*, 43, 381; and Juster, "The Evangelical Ascendancy in Revolutionary America," 408–9.

52. Brekus, *Sarah Osborn's World*. All quotations from Osborn that follow are from this book.

53. Ibid., 67.

54. Ibid., 68.

55. Ibid., 68–69.

56. Ibid., 116. This passage provided also the text for one of George Whitefield's most memorable sermons, preached on a communion Sunday in the long twilight at Cambuslang, Scotland, on 11 July 1742 to upwards of 30,000 hushed listeners; see Noll, *The Rise of Evangelicalism*, 112–13.

57. Brekus, *Sarah Osborn*, 131.

58. Ibid., 142–43.

59. Ibid., 150.

60. Ibid., 153.

61. Ibid., 249.

62. Ibid., 275–80.

63. Not incidentally, it would be Samuel Hopkins who, after careful editing of passages deemed too enthusiastic, published some of Sarah's manuscripts after her death; Hopkins, *Memoirs of the Life of Mrs. Sarah Osborn* (1799).

64. Crawford, "The Spiritual Travels of Nathan Cole," 93.

65. Crawford, "Spiritual Travels," 89–126. All quotations from Cole are from this publication.

66. Ibid., 94.

67. Ibid., 96–97. Cole here conflates John 15:12 with John 14:15.

68. Ibid., 96 (Canticles), 97 (Luke, 1 John).

69. Ibid., 99–100.

70. Ibid., 113.

71. Ibid., 103.
72. Ibid., 108.
73. Ibid., 109.
74. Ibid., 117.
75. Ibid., 123.
76. Lavington, *The Enthusiasm of Methodism and Papists Compared* (1754).
77. M. Smith, "The Hanoverian Parish: Towards a New Agenda," 102.
78. See especially Stout and Onuf, "James Davenport and the Great Awakening in New London."
79. Quoted in Caulkins, *History of New London, Connecticut*, 456.
80. Caulkins, *History*, 454, 455.
81. Marsden, *Jonathan Edwards*, 275–76.
82. *A Letter from the Associated Ministers of the County of Windham* (1745), 3, 5–6. For helpful context, see Heimert and Miller, eds., *Great Awakening*, 399–400.
83. Included in *Letter from the Associated Ministers*, 10.
84. *Letter from the Associated Ministers*, 15.
85. Backus, *All true Ministers of the Gospel, are called into that Work by the special Influences of the Holy Spirit: A Discourse Shewing the Nature and Necessity of an Internal Call to Preach the Everlasting Gospel* (1754); in McLoughlin, ed., *Isaac Backus on Church, State, and Calvinism*, 65–128.
86. Ibid., 71, 72.
87. "A Letter from the Rev. Mr. George Whitefield to the Inhabitants of Maryland, Virginia, North and South Carolina," *Pennsylvania Gazette*, 17 April 1740.
88. For the full story, see Choi, "George Whitefield, the Imperial Itinerant," 157–209.
89. See especially Holland, *Sacred Borders: Continuing Revelation and Canonical Restraint in Early America*.
90. As an illustration of the parallel movement of Enlightenment philology and evangelical revival, the text of the King James Bible was fixed, in both senses of the terms, shortly after the public career of George Whitefield began when Benjamin Blayney of Oxford collated and regularized the thousands of variations that had appeared in printings of the King James Version; see Norton, *A Textual History of the King James Bible*, 103–14.

CHAPTER 8

1. For Whitefield, see 171. Jonathan Edwards, "The Curse of Meroz" (1741), in *Works of Edwards*, 22:490–508.
2. *Works of Edwards*, 22:501, 494.
3. Clark, *English Society, 1660–1832*, 2nd ed.
4. See 290–94.
5. As among the most important, see Raboteau, *Slave Religion*, 96–133; Sobel, *The World They Made Together: Black and White Values in Eighteenth-Century Virginia*, 178–87; Cornelius, *"When I Can Read My Title Clear": Literacy, Slavery, and Religion in the*

Antebellum South, 11–22; Carretta, ed., "Introduction," *Unchained Voices: An Anthology of Black Authors in the English-Speaking World*, 1–14; Frey and Wood, *Come Shouting to Zion: African American Protestantism in the African South and British Caribbean*, 63–99; Kidd, *Great Awakening: Roots*, 213–33; and Glasson, *Mastering Christianity: Missionary Anglicanism and Slavery in the Atlantic World*, 75–138.

6. Frey and Wood, *Come Shouting to Zion*, 75.

7. Cornelius, *When I Can Read My Title Clear*, 19.

8. See esp. Raboteau, *Slave Religion*, 132–33.

9. See esp. Sobel, *The World They Made Together*, 180–81.

10. Frey and Wood, *Come Shouting to Zion*, 77.

11. Carretta, ed., *Unchained Voices*, 19.

12. Quotations from Glasson, *Mastering Christianity*, 107, 109.

13. Frey and Wood, *Come Shouting to Zion*, 69–71.

14. Quoted in Sobel, *The World They Made Together*, 184.

15. *A Narrative of the Uncommon Sufferings, and Surprizing Deliverance of Briton Hammon, A Negro Man* (1760), 13. A reprinting of this document with helpful notes is found in Carretta, *Unchained Voices*, 20–25.

16. Hammon, *Narrative*, 3, 7, 14.

17. Ibid., 14.

18. Carretta, ed., *Phillis Wheatley: Complete Writings*, 201.

19. *An Evening Thought: Salvation by Christ, with Penetential Cries: Composed by Jupiter Hammon, a Negro belonging to Mr. Lloyd of Queen's-Village, on Long-Island, the 25th of December, 1760* (1760). Carefully annotated reprintings of this broadside are found in Carretta, *Wheatley Complete Writings*, 202–4; and Carretta, *Unchained Voices*, 26–28.

20. "Glory be to God on High" began a 1739 hymn by Charles Wesley, which was widely known in the colonies as no. 63 in George Whitefield, *A Collection of Hymns for Social Worship*, 52–53, which paraphrased the *Gloria in Excelsis* from the Book of Common Prayer, which was itself a paraphrase of the angelic song recorded in Luke 2:14.

21. A line at the foot of the broadside identified the author: "Composed by JUPITER HAMMON, a Negro Man belonging to Mr. Joseph Lloyd, of Queen's Village, on Long-Island, now in Hartford." (1778) This poem is reprinted in Carretta, *Wheatley Complete Writings*, 204–7.

22. The gloss for the fifth stanza, which describes the perils of the middle passage, substituted the single word "death" for a biblical reference. Of the 21 texts Hammon cited, 12 were from the Psalms, 2 from elsewhere in the Old Testament, and 7 from the New Testament.

23. Hammon, *An Address to the Negroes in the State of New-York* (1787), 15–16.

24. I have drawn on Richards, "Phillis Wheatley and Literary Americanization"; Carretta, *Phillis Wheatley: Biography of a Genius in Bondage*; and esp. Carretta, *Wheatley Complete Writings*.

25. Wheatley, *Poems on Various Subjects Religious and Moral* (1773), in Carretta, *Wheatley Complete Writings*, 7.

26. Ibid., 8.

27. On the identity of these Loyalists, see Noll, *Christians in the American Revolution*, 121.

28. The poem may have been published with the assistance of Sarah Osborn; see Carretta, *Phillis Wheatley*, 65.

29. "On Messrs Hussey and Coffin," in Carretta, *Wheatley Complete Writings*, 74.

30. Carretta, *Wheatley Complete Writings*, xiv; Carretta, *Phillis Wheatley*, 34.

31. "An Elegiac Poem, On…Whitefield"; these are lines 31–44 in the 62-line original of the poem published in Boston in 1770; in Carretta, *Wheatley Complete Writings*, 114. In the 1773 version published in England, this section is slightly abridged as lines 25–37 of a 47-line poem; in *Poems on Various Subjects*, in Carretta, *Wheatley Complete Writings*, 15–16.

32. *Poems on Various Subjects*, in Carretta, *Wheatley Complete Writings*, 15.

33. "To Maecenas," in ibid., 9.

34. "Goliath of Gath," in ibid., 24.

35. "Isaiah lxxx. 1–8," in ibid., 33–34.

36. "On being brought from AFRICA to AMERICA," in ibid., 13.

37. "To the KING's Most Excellent Majesty," in ibid., 12–13.

38. "To His Excellency General Washington" (1776), "On the Capture of General Lee" (1776), "On the Death of General Wooster" (1776), in Carretta, *Wheatley Complete Writings*, 88–90, 90–92, 92–94.

39. "Liberty and Peace" (1784), in Carretta, *Wheatley Complete Writings*, 101.

40. An extract from a letter written by Wheatley to Samsom Occom, published in 1774, was different; in it she spoke out boldly against slavery as an offense against the "love of Freedom" that God had "implanted" in all humans. She established this opinion on the basis of the Exodus narrative from the Old Testament. See Carretta, *Wheatley Complete Writings*, 152–53.

41. *A Narrative of the Most Remarkable Particulars in the Life of James Albert Ukawsaw Gronniosaw, An African Prince, as Related by Himself* (1772), in Carretta, *Unchained Voices*, 32–58. Carretta's notes offer major assistance for understanding this work. Biblical quotations here follow Gronniosaw's text; they differ slightly from standard KJV readings, particularly the capitalization.

42. Gronniosaw, *Narrative*, 39–41.

43. Ibid., 42.

44. Ibid., 53.

45. *A Narrative of the Lord's Wonderful Dealings with John Marrant a Black, (Now going to Preach the Gospel in Nova-Scotia)* (1785), in Brooks and Saillant, *Face Zion Forward*, 47–75. As the helpful introduction by Brooks and Saillant explains, this edition almost certainly came closer to what Marrant wanted to communicate than earlier and later editions, where some incidents of violence and racism

were suppressed; Introduction, 39. The editors also underscore the unusual importance of Scripture for black authors, since "allusions to the Bible were probably meant to be bursting with significance to black readers as well as appealing to white readers"; Introduction, 38.

46. Marrant, *Narrative*, in Brooks and Saillant, *Face Zion Forward*, 68.

47. Ibid., 51, 62, 68.

48. Ibid., 61.

49. Ibid., 47.

50. *The Baptist Annual Register, for 1790, 1791, 1792, and Part of 1793*, ed. John Rippon (London, [1793]), 473–83. Because of the very helpful annotations, I have used the text of George's narrative as found in Gordon, *From Slavery to Freedom: The Life of David George*, "Appendix A," 168–83. On the importance of George as a Loyalist and pioneer settler in Sierra Leone, see Schama, *Rough Crossings: Britain, the Slaves and the American Revolution*; and Jasanoff, *Liberty's Exiles: American Loyalists in the Revolutionary World*, xii–xiii, 46–50, and passim.

51. Wilberforce, *A Practical View of the Prevailing Religion System of Professed Christians . . . Contrasted with Real Christianity* (1797).

52. Ibid., 410–12. As a guide to this work, I have benefited from Belmonte, ed., Wilberforce's *A Practical View of Christianity*.

53. *From Slavery to Freedom: Life of David George*, 169.

54. Ibid., 171–73.

55. Ibid., 199.

56. Gordon, *From Slavery to Freedom*, 143. This debate is treated in Noll, *America's God*, 148–49.

57. Vincent Carretta has supplied a carefully annotated modern printing of this book's ninth edition, the last that the author personally revised: *Olaudah Equiano: The Interesting Narrative and Other Writings*. Expert context is offered by Carretta, *Equiano, the African*; and Johnson, "Colonialism, Biblical World-Making, and Temporalities in Equiano's Interesting Narrative." On Equiano in the wider history of Scripture, see Wimbush, *White Men's Magic: Scripturalization as Slavery*.

58. For a balanced discussion, see Carretta, *Equiano, the African*, xiv–xviii.

59. Equiano, *Interesting Narrative* (ed. Carretta), 4.

60. Ibid., 236.

61. For some of those references, see ibid., 118 ("I had eleven bits of my own; and my friendly captain lent me five bits more, with which I bought a Bible"); 181 ("the only comfort I then experienced was in reading the Holy Scriptures"); 182 ("I had a great desire to read the Bible the whole day at home"); 191 ("now the Bible was my only companion and comfort"); and 200 ("On those occasions I used to produce my bible, and shewed him in what points his church erred"). Equiano only sometimes capitalized "the Bible." The conclusion of Vincent Wimbush is apt: "The black struggle for survival, freedom, and acquisition of power are understood by Equiano to turn around awareness of and response to the dominant culture's fetishizing of the book, the Bible." *White Man's Magic*, 19.

62. Many of these references are specified in the notes to Carretta's edition of the book; I would like to thank my wife, Maggie, for discovering quite a few more.

63. Equiano, *Interesting Narrative*, 189–90.

64. Ibid., 233.

65. Ibid., 178.

66. Carretta, ed., *Unchained Voices*, 180n2.

67. Quobna Ottobah Cugoano, *Thoughts and Sentiments on the Evil and Wicked Traffic of the Slavery ad Commerce of the Human Species* (London, 1787), in Carretta, *Unchained Voices*, 151.

68. Ibid., 177.

69. Carretta, "Introduction," *Unchained Voices*, 9.

70. A recent survey indicates that, among major U.S. demographic groups, African Americans report the highest rates of regular Bible reading. "The Bible in American Life," The Center for the Study of Religion and American Culture, Indiana University Purdue University Indianapolis.

71. Fisher, "Native Americans, Conversion, and Christian Practice in Colonial New England," 119. The following paragraphs are heavily indebted to Fisher's *The Indian Great Awakening*.

72. Helpful studies, besides Fisher, *Indian Great Awakening*, that include attention to the effects of revival religion among Native Americans include Kidd, *Great Awakening: Roots*, 206–12; Silvervman, *Faith and Boundaries: Colonists, Christianity, and Community among the Wampanoag Indians of Martha's Vineyard*; Pointer, *Encounters of the Spirit: Native Americans and European Colonial Religion*; and Wheeler, *To Live Upon Hope: Mohicans and Missionaries in the Eighteenth-Century Northeast*.

73. Fisher, *Indian Great Awakening*, 157–58; Kidd, *Great Awakening: Roots*, 209–11.

74. Goddard and Bragon have documented eight such well-marked copies of Eliot's translation; *Native Writing in Massachusett, Part 1*, 374–465.

75. Silverman, *Faith and Boundaries*, 70.

76. Quoted in Fisher, *Indian Great Awakening*, 73.

77. Fisher, *Indian Great Awakening*, 83.

78. Ibid., 130.

79. Wheeler, *To Live Upon Hope*, 126, with a broader discussion, 117–18, 124–30.

CHAPTER 9

1. In defining the basis for his argument at the start of his tract, Backus quoted or referenced 1 Timothy 6:6, 9; Genesis 4:19; Genesis 6:13, 15; Genesis 8:21; Ecclesiastes 7:29; 1 Peter 2:11; and James 1:14–15. *Appeal to the Public for Religious Liberty, Against the Oppressions of the Present Day* (1773), in McLoughlin, ed., *Isaac Backus on Church, State, and Calvinism*, 308–11.

2. This effort, which I hope to explore in the book to come on the nineteenth century, has received careful treatment from a range of scholars, including Hatch,

The Democratization of American Christianity; Young, *Bearing Witness against Sin: The Evangelical Birth of the American Social Movement*; Wood, *Empire of Liberty*; and Porterfield, *Conceived in Doubt: Religion and Politics in the New American Nation*.

3. Tocqueville, *Democracy in America* (1835, 1840); Trollope, *Domestic Manners of the Americans* (1832).

4. There are good brief discussions in Graham, *The Constructive Revolutionary: John Calvin and his Socio-Economic Impact*, 90–94; Bouwsma, *John Calvin*, 198, 202–3; Bainton, *Here I Stand: A Life of Martin Luther*, 183–84; Kolb, *Martin Luther*, 184–85; and for general economic considerations Benedict, *Christ's Churches Purely Reformed: A Social History of Calvinism*, 537–42.

5. *The Geneva Bible: A Facsimile of the 1560 Edition*, 91; for full context, see Valeri, *Heavenly Merchandize: How Religion Shaped Commerce in Puritan America*, 32–33.

6. Valeri, *Heavenly Merchandize*, 2.

7. This paragraph relies on Valeri, *Heavenly Merchandize*, 37–39, 62–73, which documents in rich detail "a relentless confrontation between disciplinary ideals and commercial autonomy" (62). The degree to which Keane's case illustrated Puritan expressions of biblical primitivism, even more than Calvinist theology, is nicely argued by Masui, "Reconsidering Calvinist Ethics in the Massachusetts Bay: Robert Keayne, 'The Last Will and Testament' (1653)."

8. *The Journal of John Winthrop, 1630–1649*, ed. Dunn and Yeandle, 163–67.

9. Mather, *Thirty Important Cases Resolved with Evidence of Scripture and Reason* (1699), 49–52. See Valeri, *Heavenly Merchandize*, 154–55.

10. Helpful surveys include O'Brien, "Inseparable Connections: Trade, Economy, Fiscal State, and the Expansion of Empire, 1688-1815," in *The Oxford History of the British Empire: The Eighteenth Century*, 28–52; Hoppit, *A Land of Liberty? England 1689–1727*, 313–23 (esp. tables, 320); and Langford, *A Polite and Commercial People: England 1727–1783*, 167–82 (esp. table, 169).

11. O'Brien, "Inseparable Connections," 65, 68, 70.

12. See 159–60.

13. Price, "Holden, Samuel (1674/5–1740)," *Oxford Dictionary of National Biography*.

14. Colman, *The Merchandise of a People Holiness to the Lord* (1736), i–iv (dedication to Holden), 1–11 (exposition on Tyre), 6 (quotation). See Valeri, *Heavenly Merchandize*, 243.

15. Colman, *The Merchandise*, 10–11.

16. For the phrase, see T. H. Breen, "An Empire of Goods: the Anglicization of Colonial America, 1690–1776."

17. For the same pattern at the same time in England, with keen personal religion leading to greater scruples about the use of wealth—but with minimal attention to the means of wealth creation—, see Kadane, *The Watchful Clothier: The Life of an Eighteenth-Century Protestant Capitalist*.

18. Valeri, *Heavenly Merchandize*, 234, with general attention to the period of the Great Awakening, 234–49. See also Valeri, "Jonathan Edwards, the Edwardians, and the Sacred Cause of Free Trade," in *Jonathan Edwards at Home and Abroad*, 85–100.

19. The following three paragraphs rely on Engel, *Religion and Profit: Moravians in Early America*.

20. For another instance of the Moravians' better relations with Native communities, see Wheeler, *To Live Upon Hope: Mohicans and Missionaries in the Eighteenth-Century Northeast*.

21. For how patriots disrupted the economic lives of pacifist Moravians, see Fox, *Sweet Land of Liberty: The Ordeal of the American Revolution in Northampton County, Pennsylvania*.

22. From an immense literature, I have benefited most from Davis, *The Problem of Slavery in Western Culture*, esp. 291–390; Essig, *The Bonds of Wickedness: American Evangelicals Against Slavery*, 3–25; Davis, *The Problem of Slavery in the Age of Revolution, 1770–1823*, esp. 523–56; Fredrickson, *Racism: A Short History*; Brown, *Moral Capital: Foundations of British Abolitionism*; Davis, *Inhuman Bondage: The Rise and Fall of Slavery in the New World*; and C. Kidd, *The Forging of Races: Race and Scripture in the Protestant Atlantic World, 1600–2000*.

23. I have been guided to the material described in the next paragraphs by Cameron, "The Puritan Origins of Black Abolitionism in Massachusetts"; and Cameron, *To Plead Our Own Cause: African Americans in Massachusetts and the Making of the Antislavery Movement*, 8–28.

24. "The Massachusetts Body of Liberties" (1641), in Morgan, *Puritan Political Ideas, 1558–1794*, 179.

25. Ibid., 196.

26. Willard, *A Compleat Body of Divinity* (1726), 614. These lectures date from the 1690s.

27. Mather, *A Good Master Well Served…on the Properties and Practices of a Good Servant in Every Kind of Servitude* (1696), 3–4 (for the scriptures from Titus 2:9–10, 1 Tim 6:1–2, Eph 6:5–8, Col 3:22–25, and 1 Pet 2:18).

28. Mather, *The Negro Christianized* (1706), 3 (on providence).

29. Valeri, *Heavenly Merchandize*, 168–77. A readable popular introduction is provided by Laplante, *The Life and Repentance of Samuel Sewall*.

30. *The Diary of Samuel Sewall, 1674–1729* (14 January 1697), ed. Thomas, 1:367.

31. For context, see Davis, *Slavery in Western Culture*, 341–48; and Peterson, "The Selling of Joseph: Bostonians, Antislavery, and the Protestant International, 1689–1733."

32. This and the quotations to follow are from Sewall, *The Selling of Joseph* (1700), 1–3.

33. On Saffin and his response, see Davis, *Slavery in Western Culture*, 345–46.

34. For these Quaker exceptions, see Davis, *Slavery in Western Culture*, 306–25; and Slaughter, *The Beautiful Soul of John Woolman*, 107–17.
35. Benjamin Lay, *All slave-keepers that keep the innocent in bondage, apostates pretending to lay claim to the pure & holy Christian religion* (1737), 7, 8.
36. Helpful background on his traveling is found in Slaughter, *Beautiful Soul*, 126–42.
37. Woolman, *Some Considerations on the Keeping of Negroes* (1754), i–ii.
38. Ibid., 19, 18.
39. Ibid., ii.
40. Ibid., 4 (Isa), 8 (Deut, Ex), 4 (Cornelius), 22 (Jeremiah).
41. Ibid., 21.
42. Quaker exaltation of Scripture was often much firmer than outsiders realized. See, as an example, the professions by Pennsylvanian John Dickinson, raised a Friend and always close to Quaker circles, who affirmed that the Bible revealed "*Inestimable Truth!*" and was, in fact, "the most republican Book that was ever written." See Calvert, *Quaker Constitutionalism and the Political Thought of John Dickinson*, 284.
43. For this story keyed to the enduring influence of a Quaker political style, see Calvert, *Quaker Constitutionalism*, 177–89. On the general stimulus that war provided for such anti-slave activity, see also Erben, *A Harmony of the Spirits: Translation and the Language of Community in Early Pennsylvania*, 270–71.
44. Benezet, *Observations on the Inslaving, Importing and Purchasing of Negroes* (1759), quotation from title page. Reading this pamphlet moved John Wesley to declare modern African slavery "the sum of all villainies," which then predisposed him to discount the American patriots' claim to be "enslaved" by Parliament. See Rack, *Reasonable Enthusiast: John Wesley and the Rise of Methodism*, 362, 377.
45. Newton, *Thoughts upon the African Slave Trade* (1788), 6.
46. Among many excellent treatments, see Fredrickson, *Racism*, 43–46; Davis, *Inhuman Bondage*, 64–68; and C. Kidd, *Forging of Races*, passim. The paragraphs that follow rely especially on Whitford, *The Curse of Ham in the Early Modern Era*.
47. See especially Whitford, *Curse of Ham*, 19–42.
48. Ibid., 90.
49. *The Geneva Bible: A Facsimile of the 1560 Edition*, 5.
50. See Mather, *Biblia Americana: Genesis*, 672: "The Curse upon *Cham* [Ham], does it not Justify our Enslaving the *Negro's*, wherever we can find them?...The whole Family of *Cham* was not concern'd in that *Curse*....The *Negroes* are not the Posterity of *Canaan*."
51. Quoted in Whitford, *Curse of Ham*, 172.
52. C. Kidd, *Forging of Races*, 3.
53. The argument in this section and the next on political thought parallels a similar account of intellectual fusion that I offered for theology, ethical reasoning, and political thought in *America's God*, 53–113. That account provided reasonably full documentation, with the section on ethical reasoning especially indebted to

Norman Fiering's description of "the new moral philosophy" (*Jonathan Edwards's Moral Thought and its British Context*) and on "Christian republicanism" drawing crucial insights from the work of Jonathan Clark (*The Language of Liberty, 1660–1832*).

54. Gay, *The Enlightenment: An Interpretation*; Israel, *Radical Enlightenment*.

55. May, *The Enlightenment in America*, xiv, xiii.

56. Meyer, *The Democratic Enlightenment*, xxvi.

57. Reid-Maroney, *Philadelphia's Enlightenment*, xii.

58. Ferguson, *The American Enlightenment, 1750–1820*, 54, 46.

59. Holifield, *Theology in America…from the Age of the Puritans to the Civil War*, 5.

60. See especially Solberg's introduction and notes to Cotton Mather, *The Christian Philosopher*.

61. For Hutchinson's deep commitments to Anglican Christendom as a reason predisposing colonials against his views, see Noll, "Science, Theology, and Society: From Cotton Mather to William Jennings Bryan," in *Evangelicals and Science in Historical Perspective*, 105–8.

62. See Siegel, "Professor Stephen Sewall and the Transformation of Hebrew at Harvard," in Goldman, *Hebrew and the Bible in America: The First Two Centuries*, 234.

63. *An Annotated Edition of Lectures on Moral Philosophy by John Witherspoon*, ed. Scott, 65 (see for another rejection of Hutchinson, 98, with helpful commentary by Scott, 68, 100).

64. My account relies on Reid-Maroney, *Philadelphia's Enlightenment*, 52–53, 56–60; Lemay, *Ebenezer Kinnersley: Franklin's Friend*; and Lemay, "Ebenezer Kinnersley," *ANB*.

65. From 1740, quoted in Lemay, *Kinnersley*, 20.

66. Kinnersley, *A Letter to the Reverend the Ministers of the Baptist Congregations* (1746/47), 23. Kinnersley's biblical arguments supported his anti-revivalist commitment to traditional ecclesiastical order, since he contended that the Scriptures prohibited non-ordained men from preaching and likewise prohibited women from voting in church elections.

67. Kinnersley, *A Course of Experiments, in that Curious and Entertaining Branch of Natural Philosophy, Called Electricity* (1764), 2.

68. For orientation, see Bernhard, "John Winthrop," *ANB*. Winthrop's theological orthodoxy is the subject of Graham, "The Scientific Piety of John Winthrop of Harvard"; the widespread New England response to the 1755 earthquake is treated in Clark, "Science, Reason, and an Angry God: The Literature of an Earthquake."

69. Quotation from Winthrop to Ezra Stiles, 17 April 1756; in Bernhard, "Winthrop."

70. Winthrop, *A Lecture on Earthquakes* (1755), 20–21 (quotations from Newton).

71. Ibid., 29, 31.

72. On the efforts of these figures, see Noll, *America's God*, 99–102, 482–83n31.

73. For a succinct summary, Mark Valeri, "Francis Hutcheson," in Elliot, *Colonial Writers, 1735–1781*, 310–17. Hutcheson's usefulness for the colonies is described in Noll, *America's God*, 97–101, 107–13.

74. Witherspoon, *Lectures on Moral Philosophy* (ed. Scott), 64.

75. That process is well described in Sheehan, *The Enlightenment Bible*; Legaspi, *The Death of Scripture and the Rise of Biblical Studies*; and Turner, *Philology*, 58–61, 73–80, 112–17, 210–29, 357–68.

76. One accounting of a massive bibliography is found in Noll, *America's God*, 447–51.

77. Although my interpretation of Williams's tract differs somewhat from that provided by Nicholas Miller, I am much indebted to him for orientation and guidance on this important work; see Miller, *The Religious Roots of the First Amendment: Dissenting Protestants and the Separation of Church and State*, 94–113.

78. Williams, *Essential Rights and Liberties* (1744), in Sandoz, *Political Sermons of the Founding Era, 1730–1805*, 55, 57, 58, 59, 83.

79. Ibid., 55–56.

80. Ibid., on natural liberty (59, 60, 60–61, 61), "unalienable right" (61), "humane nature" (61), "conscience" (61), and "sacred rights" (73).

81. Ibid., 83, 95.

82. Ibid., 85.

83. Ibid., 80, with 77–81 for full consideration of these texts.

84. Ibid., 86–87.

85. Ibid., 93, with other anti-Catholic statements on 62, 65, 75, 83, 91.

86. Ibid., 110, 96.

87. See Kenneth Minkema, "Thomas Prince," *ANB*.

88. Prince, *The Salvation of God in 1746...Wherein the most remarkable Salvations of the year past, both in Europe and North-America...are briefly considered* (1746), 10.

89. Prince, *A Sermon...Being the Day of General Thanksgiving for the great deliverance of the British Nations by the glorious and happy Victory near Culloden* (1746), 6.

90. Prince, *Sermon for Culloden*, 35.

91. Ibid., 37.

92. Prince, *Salvation in 1746*, 10.

93. Ibid., 24–25 (Psalms 142, 143, 83).

94. Prince, *Sermon for Culloden*, 8–10.

95. Prince, *Salvation in 1746*, 17.

96. Mayhew, *A Discourse Concerning Unlimited Submission and Non-Resistance to the Higher Powers: with some reflections on the resistance made to King Charles I and on the anniversary of his death* (1750). The title page included three Bible verses— "Fear GOD, honor the King. Saint Paul [actually from 1 Pet 2:17] He that ruleth over Men, must be just, ruling in the Fear of GOD. Prophet Samuel [2 Sam 23:3] I have said, ye are Gods—but ye shall die like Men, and fall like one of the PRINCES. King David [Ps 82:6–7]." In addition, as an indication of Mayhew's commitment to classical republican ideals, there were also words from the *Aeneid*

that quoted Virgil on "insandas caedes" (bloody barbarities) and "facta TYRANNI effera" (the tyrant's awful deeds).

97. Ibid., [i–iii, unnumbered preface].

98. Ibid., 28–29.

99. Ibid., 41, 48.

100. Ibid., [ii] and [iii] of the unnumbered preface.

CHAPTER 10

1. Chapters 10 and 11 offer a welcome opportunity to take up questions I canvassed some time ago, throughout *Christians in the American Revolution*; and more specifically in "The Bible in Revolutionary America," in *The Bible in American Law, Politics, and Political Rhetoric*, 39–60. Although I was surprised upon re-reading to discover how much I still agree with my earlier self, it is also a privilege to acknowledge how much I have benefited from several studies that, amid much other solid scholarship, appeared after *Christians in the American Revolution* came out: especially Lutz, "The Relative Influence of European Writers on Late Eighteenth-Century American Political Thought"; Endy, "Just War, Holy War, and Millennialism in Revolutionary America"; Stout, *The New England Soul*, 259–311; Sandoz, ed., *Political Sermons of the American Founding Era*; T. S. Kidd, *God of Liberty: A Religious History of the American Revolution*; Byrd, *Sacred Scripture, Sacred War: The Bible and the American Revolution*; Coffey, *Exodus and Deliverance: Deliverance Politics from John Calvin to Martin Luther King, Jr.*, 56–78; and Dreisbach, "The Bible and the Political Culture of the American Founding," in Dreisbach and Hall, *Faith and the Founders of the American Republic*, 144–73.

2. On Prince, see 264–66.

3. See Stout, *New England Soul*, 270–71, 285, 379n8; and on the plummeting number of specifically religious publications in the 1770s, Noll, *America's God*, 163.

4. On Williams, see 262–64.

5. The essential study remains Bridenbaugh, *Mitre and Sceptre: Transatlantic Faiths, Ideas, Personalities, and Politics, 1689–1775*. An excellent update is found in Bonomi, *Under the Cope of Heaven: Religion, Society, and Politics in Colonial America*, 199–209.

6. The crucial studies are Davis, *The Problem of Slavery in the Age of Revolution, 1770–1823*; and Brown, *Moral Capital; Foundations of British Abolitionism*.

7. On Mayhew's sermon, see 266–69.

8. See especially Lutz, "Relative Influence of European Writers"; Byrd, *Sacred Scripture*; and Dreisbach, "Bible and the Political Culture."

9. For comprehensive surveys, the latter with many representative documents, see Brock, *Pacifism in the United States: From the Colonial Era to the First World War*, 133–321; and MacMaster, Horst, and Ulle, *Conscience in Crisis: Mennonite and Other Peace Charles in America, 1739–1789*.

10. "Preparing for the Revolution," *Mennonite Historical Bulletin*, July 1974, 6–7.

11. Brock, *Pacifism in the United States*, 263. For the full context, see Fox, *Sweet Land of Liberty: The Ordeal of the American Revolution in Northampton County, Pennsylvania*.

12. Quoted in Mekeel, "New England Quakers and Military Service in the American Revolution," in Brinton, *Children of Light*, 258–59.

13. Benezet, *Serious Reflections, affectionately recommended…particularly those who Mourn and Lament on account of the Calamities which attend us* (1778), 1–4.

14. Benezet, *Serious Considerations on Several Important Subjects; viz. On War and its Inconsistency with the Gospel. Observations on Slavery. And Remarks on the Nature and bad Effects of Spirituous Liquors* (1778), 2.

15. Benezet, *Serious Considerations*.

16. See Ecclesiastes 9:11 ("I returned, and saw under the sun, that the race is not to the swift, nor the battle to the strong"); Genesis 17:3–4 ("God talked with [Abram], saying, As for me, behold, my covenant is with thee"); Joshua 24:15 ("choose you this day whom ye will serve;…but as for me and my house, we will serve the Lord"); Dreisbach, "The Bible and the American Founding," 157. Henry's speech was written down later by some of those who heard it: William Wirt Henry, *Patrick Henry*, 1:262–66; T. S. Kidd, *Patrick Henry*, 98–100; and Cohen, "The 'Liberty or Death' Speech: A Note on Religion and Revolutionary Rhetoric," 702–17, esp. 705: in this speech Henry was "both a radical and a sermonizer."

17. Wells, *The Life and Public Services of Samuel Adams*, 2:491–93. For context, see Stoll, *Samuel Adams*, 4.

18. Adams, *A Dissertation on the Canon and Feudal Law* (1765), in Thompson, *The Revolutionary Writings of John Adams*, 25.

19. See Middlekauf, *The Glorious Cause: The American Revolution, 1763–1789*, 106, 129, 135, 162, 222, 318.

20. See Davis, *Religion and the Continental Congress, 1774–1789*, 138–40: "That two non-Puritan intellectual statesmen…would so readily adopt the analogy [of Israel and the United States] to permanently symbolize the nation's birth and destiny is proof enough of [the analogy's] influence on the American mind" (140).

21. Rush to Henry, 12 Jan. 1778, *Letters of Benjamin Rush*, ed. Butterfield, 1:182. On this deliverance motif during the Revolutionary era, see especially Coffey, *Exodus and Liberation*, 70.

22. Kidd, *God of Liberty*, 115–16.

23. Dreisbach, "The Bible and the American Founding," 155; Lillback, *George Washington's Sacred Fire*, Appendix 2: "Representative Biblical Quotations and Allusions Used by George Washington," 739–60.

24. Warren, "To the Hon. J. Winthrop, Esq." (who in 1774 voted to suspend commerce with Britain), in *Poems, Dramatic and Miscellaneous* (1790), 209. See Coffey, *Exodus and Liberation*, 68.

25. Many more instances are documented in Hutson, *The Founders on Religion*.

26. On Puritan usage, see 73, 107.

27. See Byrd, *Sacred Scripture*, 170 ("Most Cited Biblical Chapters . . . in the Revolutionary Era, 1763–1800").

28. Ibid., 45–71.

29. Ibid., 73–93. The Curse of Meroz featured prominently in Alan Heimert's account of how sermonic tropes developed in the colonial Great Awakening survived to shape the revolt against Britain; Heimert, *Religion and the American Mind*, 332–34, 501–6.

30. Byrd, *Sacred Scripture*, 112–14.

31. Ibid., 94–110.

32. Ibid., 129–36.

33. Andrews, *A Discourse Shewing the Necessity of Joining Internal Repentance with the External Profession of it* (1775), 14 (slave-holding), iii (advertisement), 16, 18. For Andrews's context, see Calhoon and Chopra, "Religion and the Loyalists," in Dreisbach and Hall, *Faith and the Founders*, 107.

34. Inglis, *The Christian Soldier's Duty Briefly Delineated* (1777), 13, 19. On the patriots' fondness for these deliverance motifs, see Coffey, *Exodus and Liberation*, 66–75.

35. For the "Christian republicanism" that resulted from that conflation, see Noll, *America's God*, 73–92.

36. S. Williams, *The Duty of Christian Soldiers, when Called to War, to Undertake it in the Name of God* (1755), 18, 24, 28, 30–32 (jeremiad). The text was Ps 20:5.

37. Beckwith, *That People a Safe, and happy People, who have God for, and among them* (1756), 25 (Cape-Breton) 16 (covenant), 25 (Moses and Aaron).

38. S. Williams, *The Relations of God's People to him . . . With a special View to New-England, and the rest of the British Subjects in America . . . On Occasion of the Smiles of Heaven to the British Arms in America* (1760), 14–15. For Exodus 15:1–2, see 280.

39. Dunbar, *The Presence of God with his People, their only Safety and Happiness* (1760), 19, 21.

40. Stiles, *A Discourse on the Christian Union* (1761), 108, 116–17.

41. Mayhew, *The Snare Broken, A Thanksgiving Discourse* (1766), 1.

42. Chauncy, *A Discourse on "the good News from a far Country"* (1766), 27. Chauncy's discourse did contain one section that turned to Scripture for explicit instruction: in an effort to dampen the levellerism, which Boston elites felt the Stamp Act agitation may have unleashed, he paused for an expanded gloss on 1 Timothy 2:1–2 ("I exhort therefore, that . . . prayers . . . be made for all men; For kings, and for all that are in authority") and 1 Peter 2:17 ("Honour all men. . . . Honour the king"), which he elided as "'pray for Kings, and all that are in subordinate authority under them' and to 'honour and obey them in the Lord'" (30).

43. Chauncy, *Trust in GOD, the Duty of a People in a Day of Trouble . . . . At the request of a great number of Gentlemen, friends to the LIBERTIE of North-America* (1770), 6, 13.

44. Trumbull, *A Discourse, Delivered at the Anniversary Meeting of the Freemen of the Town of New-Haven* (1773), 33 (with Psalm reference supplied by Trumbull), 36.

45. Devotion, *The Duty and Interest of a People to Sanctify the Lord of Hosts* (1777), 20, 36, 39, with 8n explaining that he would "handle the subject theologically, not politically."

46. Chauncy, *The Accursed Thing must be taken away from among a People, if they would reasonably hope to stand before their enemies* (1778), 13, 18, 14.

47. Byrd, *Sacred Scripture*, 196–98.

48. Ibid., 204, 206–7.

49. Ibid., 209, 211–13.

50. Ibid., 224, 226–28.

51. See Grasso, *A Speaking Aristocracy: Transforming Public Discourse in Eighteenth-Century Connecticut*, 71–73 and passim; Valeri, "The New Divinity and the Revolution," 751; and more generally McDermott, *One Holy and Happy Society: The Public Theology of Jonathan Edwards*.

52. See Holifield, *Theology in America*, 276.

53. See Bloch, *Visionary Republic: Millennial Themes in American Thought, 1756–1800*, chap. 4, "The Revolutionary Millennialism of the 1770s"; and Bloch, "Religion and Ideological Change in the American Revolution," in *Religion and American Politics*, 54–59.

54. See especially Stout, *New England Soul*, 268–71.

55. See Gordon, *From Slavery to Freedom: The Life of David George*, 30–39; Brekus, *Sarah Osborn's World*, 289–315; T. S. Kidd, *Great Awakening: Roots*, 308–20; along with Marini, *Radical Sects of Revolutionary New England*; and *The Journal and Letters of Francis Asbury*, ed. Clark, 1:291–345.

CHAPTER 11

1. Bradley, *Religion, Revolution, and English Radicalism: Non-conformity in Eighteenth-Century Politics and Society*, 135–36.

2. For context, see Bell, *A War of Religion: Dissenters, Anglicans, and the American Revolution*, 10.

3. Bonomi, *Under the Cope of Heaven: Religion, Society, and Politics in Colonial America*, 199.

4. On Mayhew's sermon, see 266–69.

5. Stiles, *A Discourse of the Christian Union* (1761), 28; the exegesis of Philippians 3:16 is found on 3–8.

6. Ibid., 28, 30.

7. Welles, *The Divine Right of Presbyterian Ordination Asserted, and the Ministerial Authority...in the established Churches of New England vindicated* (1763), 11–12.

8. Mayhew, *Remarks on an Anonymous Tract...on the Charter and Conduct of the Society for the Propagation of the Gospel in Foreign Parts* (1764), 12, 26. John Adams reasoned similarly in 1765 when he paid brief attention to New England churches founded with a desire to follow Scripture more closely, but then showed much

greater concern that pulpits "resound with the doctrines and sentiments of religious liberty"; Adams, *A Dissertation on the Canon and Feudal Law* (1765), in *The Revolutionary Writings of John Adams*, ed. Thompson, 25, 33.

9. For insightful treatment of the role of scripture for Livingstone, see Miller, *The Religious Roots of the First Amendment*, 114–32; and more generally on his opposition to a colonial bishop, Mulder, "William Livingston: Propagandist against Episcopacy," 96–100.

10. Livingstone, *A Letter to the Right Reverend Father in God, John, Lord Bishop of Landaff; occasioned by some passages in his Lordship's Sermon... in which the American Colonies are loaded with great and undeserved Reproach* (1768), 13, 10.

11. See on Welles, 292–93; and Chauncy, *The Validity of Presbyterian Ordination Asserted* (1762).

12. Leaming, *A Defence of the Episcopal Government of the Church* (1766), 9–10. The title page quoted Revelation 2:2 ("Thou hast tried them which say that are Apostles, and are not") and 1 Corinthians 12:28–29 ("GOD hath set some in his Church, first Apostles, secondly Prophets, thirdly Teachers. Are all Apostles? Are all Prophets? Are all Teachers?").

13. Leaming, *A Defence*, 5 ("incontestable" and reference to church fathers), 48.

14. Ibid., 16. Leaming's dedication to scriptural argument continued even after Britain's defeat in the Revolutionary War. Many years later, as the rector of an Episcopal church in Stratford, Connecticut, he reiterated his biblical case for episcopacy in *Dissertations upon Various Subjects* (1788 and 1789).

15. For example, Bridenbaugh seems to know this work only through a secondary source; see *Mitre and Sceptre*, 249–50.

16. See, most recently, Rohrer, *Jacob Green's Revolution*, 146–49.

17. Chandler, *An Appeal to the Public, in Behalf of the Church of England in America* (1767), 3; 3–12 ("sketch"), 13–25 ("Government, Ordination, and Confirmation").

18. Ibid., 109.

19. It was against a tract by the archbishop that William Livingstone had written; see 293–94.

20. Apthorp, *Considerations on the Institutions and Conduct of the Society for the Propagation of the Gospel* (1763), 7, 9.

21. Caner, *A Candid Examination of Dr. Mayhew's Observations on the Charter and Conduct of the Society for the Propagation of the Gospel* (1763), 79. The same strategy marked the first published work by Charles Inglis of New York, who on other occasions showed considerable skill in using the Bible as a teaching authority. See Inglis, *A Vindication of The Bishop of Landaff's Sermon... from Gross Misrepresentations and abusive reflections* (1768).

22. Bridenbaugh, *Mitre and Sceptre*, xiv. Similar conclusions are developed in Clark, *The Language of Liberty, 1660–1832*, 257–82.

23. This important point is well argued in Endy, "Just War, Holy War, and Millennialism in Revolutionary America," 4, 7, 12–13.

24. For this background, see Bumsted and Clark, "New England's Tom Paine: John Allen and the Spirit of Liberty."
25. Allen, *An Oration Upon the Beauties of Liberty, Or the Essential Rights of the Americans* (1773), in Sandoz, *Political Sermons*, 305–25. Modern translations would have made Allen's intentions more obvious, as from the New International Version: "Both hands are skilled in doing evil; the ruler demands gifts, the judge accepts bribes, the powerful dictate what they desire—they all conspire together."
26. Allen, *An Oration*, 315–16, 317.
27. Ibid., 318–19.
28. Ibid., 321.
29. Ibid., 323.
30. Ibid., 324.
31. See Clark, *The Language of Liberty*, 380, for a discussion of Allen's American publications.
32. Witherspoon, *The Dominion of Providence over the Passions of Men. A Sermon Preached at Princeton...to which is added An Address to the Natives of Scotland residing in America* (1776), in Sandoz, *Political Sermons*, 531–58. For Witherspoon's call to Princeton and his early labors there, see Noll, *Princeton and the Republic, 1768–1822*, 16–27. On the importance of the address to Scottish immigrants in the context of Witherspoon's aspirations for a renewal of religion in Scotland, England, and America, see Mailer, "Anglo-Scottish Union and John Witherspoon's American Revolution."
33. Witherspoon, *Dominion of Providence*, 534.
34. Ibid., 542–44.
35. While most modern translations parallel the KJV that Witherspoon used, the New International Version reads, "Surely your wrath against men brings you praise, and the survivors of your wrath are restrained."
36. Witherspoon, *Dominion of Providence*, 535, 539.
37. Ibid., 549–50.
38. Ibid., 553–56.
39. Ibid., 558.
40. Griffith, *Passive Obedience Considered*, 4.
41. On Mayhew's earlier effort, see 266–69.
42. Griffith, *Passive Obedience Considered*, 6, 7.
43. Ibid., 6–9 (examples), 9 (abuse of power), 10 (advocates for despotism), 11 (thesis).
44. Ibid., 14.
45. Ibid., 17.
46. Ibid., 21 (all quotations).
47. Ibid., 22, 23.
48. For a good summary of Boucher's life and a précis of his thought, see Calhoon, *The Loyalists in Revolutionary America*, 218–33.

49. Boucher, *A View of the Causes and Consequences of the American Revolution: in Thirteen Discourses* (1797), 495–560 ("Discourse XII: On Civil Liberty; Passive Obedience, and Non-Resistance").

50. Boucher, "On Civil Liberty," 495n; Duché, *The Duty of Standing Fast in our Spiritual and Temporal Liberties* (1775), with the "Battalion" identified on the title page.

51. Duché, *Duty of Standing Fast*, 7, 10, 13, 18. Yet after this sermon and after serving as the first chaplain of the Continental Congress, Duché returned to the side of the British; see Byrd, *Sacred Scripture*, 130.

52. Boucher, "On Civil Liberty," 498; that passage was Titus 3:1, "Put them in mind to be subject to principalities and powers, to obey magistrates, and to be ready to every good work."

53. Ibid., 502, 506.

54. Ibid., 509 ("liberty"), 529–30 ("Fifth Commandment"), 533–34 (silences), 538 ("render unto Caesar"), 544 (attacks), 560 (1 Pet 2).

55. Inglis also leaned on this text as "a full Answer to the crude Notions of those who assert the Unlawfulness of War, or of bearing Arms, on any Occasion," in *Christian Soldier's Duty*, 6–7.

56. Inglis, *Christian Soldier's Duty*, 11–12.

57. Ibid., 17.

58. Ibid., 19.

59. Inglis, *The Duty of Honouring the King... Being the Anniversary of the Martyrdom of King Charles I* (1780).

60. Ibid., 6; and 24, for how the execution of Charles I led to "absolute Tyranny... Abject Slavery" and the like. On Mayhew's sermon, see 266–69.

61. Inglis, *The Duty of Honouring*, 5, 6, 10 (Peter and Paul), 13.

62. Ibid., 16.

63. Ibid., 15, 18–19, 20.

64. Ibid., 26.

65. Ibid., 31.

66. Calhoon and Chopra, "Religion and the Loyalists," in Dreisbach and Hall, *Faith and the Founders of the American Republic*, 105; and Fitz, "'Suspected on Both Sides': Little Abraham, Iroquois Neutrality, and the American Revolution."

67. See Barnes and Calhoon, "Moral Allegiance: John Witherspoon and Loyalist Recantation," 273–83 ("moral authority," 282).

68. For example, Charles Chauncy, in Massachusetts's election sermon of 1747 preached on 2 Samuel 23:3 ("The God of Israel said... he that ruleth over men must be just, ruling in the fear of God"). In applying that text to the British Empire, he reflected conventional wisdom: "If the prerogatives of the King are sacred, so also are the rights of Lords and Commons." Chauncy, *Civil Magistrates Must Be Just, Ruling in the Fear of God* (1747), in Sandoz, *Political Sermons*, 147.

69. See Nelson, "'Talmudic Commonwealthmen' and the Rise of Republican Exclusivism"; Perl-Rosenthal, "The 'divine right of republics': Hebraic Republicanism and the Debate over Kingless Government in Revolutionary America"; Nelson, *The Hebrew Republic: Jewish Sources and the Transformation of European Political Thought*, 53, 165n104; Eran Shalev, *American Zion: The Old Testament as a Political Text from the Revolution to the Civil War*, 29, 44, 60; Nelson, "Hebraism and the Republican Turn of 1776: A Contemporary Account of the Debate over *Common Sense*"; and Byrd, *Sacred Scripture*, 71, 202n81, 215n48, 216n49.

70. *Diary and Autobiography of John Adams*, ed. Butterfield, 3:333. On those interpretations, see especially Nelson, "Talmudic Commonwealthmen"; and Nelson, *Hebrew Republic*.

71. Byrd, *Sacred Scripture*, 202–3n81, identifies three such efforts from New England and one from Philadelphia, all published in 1775: Dan Foster, *A Short Essay on Civil Government* (1775), 3–5; Gad Hitchcock, *A Sermon Preached at Plymouth, December 22d, 1774* (1775), 22–23; Samuel Langdon, *Government Corrupted by Vice, and Recovered by Righteousness* (1775), 11–12; and John Joachim Zubly, *The Law of Liberty. A Sermon on American Affairs, Preached at the Opening of the Provincial Congress of Georgia* (1775), 30–31. On Langdon's effort, see Stout, *The New England Soul*, 293–95, 303–5.

72. A solid brief description of the impact of *Common Sense*, from among many such accounts, is provided by Middlekauf, *The Glorious Cause: The American Revolution, 1763–1789*, 317–20.

73. Most relevant for our purposes are W. Smith, "To the People of Pennsylvania, Letter V" and "To the People of Pennsylvania, Letter VI," *Pennsylvania Ledger*, 30 Mar. 1776, 2–3; 13 Apr. 1776, 1, 4. On Smith, see Bridenbaugh, *Mitre and Scepter*, 210, 300–301; Calhoon, *Loyalists*, 148–52; and Perl-Rosenthal, "Hebraic Republicanism," 557–59.

74. An American [Charles Inglis], *The True Interest of America Impartially Stated, in Certain Strictures on a Pamphlet Intitled COMMON SENSE* (1776). On Inglis, see Chopra, *Unnatural Rebellion: Loyalists in New York City During the Revolution*, 3, 44, 81–86; Jasanoff, *Liberty's Exiles: American Loyalists in the Revolutionary World*, 29–36; and Perl-Rosenthal, "Hebraic Republicanism," 556–57.

75. One of the other most extensive rebuttals badly misread the colonial veneration for the Old Testament when it dismissed Paine's appeal to Scripture as irrelevant, since the Jews were a "contemptible race, more barbarous than our savages" and since the "Gospel Dispensation" had made political matters of no concern to Christians who should be contemplating with "only celestial objects"; Candidus [James Chalmers], *Plain Truth; Addressed to the Inhabitants of America, containing, remarks on a late pamphlet, entitled Common Sense. Wherein are shewn, that . . . Permanent Liberty and True Happiness, can only be obtained by Reconciliation with that Kingdom* (1776), 5–6. Yet printed as an addendum to Chalmers's long pamphlet, a short anonymous tract by "Rationalis," appearing without a title, did

engage Paine's biblical arguments. For context on Chalmers and "Rationalis," see Calhoon, *Loyalists*, 205–6; and Perl-Rosenthal, "Hebraic Republicanism," 555–56, 559.

76. Paine, *Common Sense*, quoted here from a superb recent edition, *Selected Writings of Thomas Paine*, ed. Shapiro and Calvert, 13.

77. Ibid.

78. Ibid.

79. Inglis, *True Interest*, 22–23.

80. Ibid., 23.

81. W. Smith, "Letter VI," 4. "Rationalis," likewise, rebutted Paine by asserting "there be no natural or divine law for any form of government"; see n75.

82. Paine, *Common Sense*, 13.

83. Ibid., 15.

84. Ibid., 14. Paine quoted Judges 8:23.

85. Inglis, *True Interest*, 26.

86. Smith, "Letter VI," 4.

87. Inglis, *True Interest*, 25.

88. Paine, *Common Sense*, 14–16.

89. W. Smith, "Letter VI," 1.

90. Inglis, *True Interest*, 29.

91. Ibid., 28.

92. Ibid., 27–28.

93. The other texts in his parade were 1 Samuel 26:9; Proverbs 8:15; Proverbs 24:21; Isaiah 49:23; Daniel 1:21; Daniel 4:25; Romans 13; 1 Timothy 2:1–2; 1 Peter 2:9–10; and Jude 8–9. Inglis, *True Interest*, 31–32.

94. W. Smith, "Letter VI," 4 (2 Sam 5:10–12; 1 Kings 8:16; Ps 78:70–72; and Ps 89: 20, 28). Rationalis (n75), 73–74, added several more (Prov 8:16; 1 Sam 8:4,7; 1 Sam 10:25; 1 Sam 11:1–15; and 1 Sam 12:13).

95. Paine, *Common Sense*, 17.

96. On these developments, see Holifield, *Theology in America*, 130–31, 144; and Noll, *America's God*, 134–35.

97. W. Smith, "Letter V," 2.

98. Inglis, *True Interest*, 33.

99. Paine, *Common Sense*, 15–16.

100. World Cat, <www.worldcat.org> (accessed 11 November 2014); Early American Imprints,<www.readex.com/content/early-american-imprints-series-1-evans-1639-1800> (accessed 11 November 2014). See also Nelson, "Hebraism and the Republican Turn of 1776," for the reach of Paine's biblical argument into Virginia.

101. World Cat; Early American Imprints.

102. W. Smith, "Letter VI," 1.

103. *Diary and Autobiography of Adams*, 333. See *Diary*, 330–31, for Adams's further disgust at Paine's use of Scripture. For the claim that Paine developed his

negative views on Scripture later, see Perl-Rosenthal, "Hebraic Republicanism," 552, 553n25. For the suggestion that Paine's pamphlet may not have been quite as influential as usually credited in American founding mythology, see Clark, "Thomas Paine: The English Dimension," in *Selected Writings*, 588–89.

104. Perl-Rosenthal, "Hebriac Republicanism," 563–64.

105. Brown, *Moral Capital; Foundations of British Abolitionism*, 105.

106. Ibid.

107. Davis, *The Problem of Slavery in the Age of Revolution, 1770–1823*, 532.

108. Sharp, *An Essay on Slavery, Proving From Scripture its Inconsistency with Humanity and Religion* (1772), 18 (moral laws), 23 (universal benevolence).

109. Ibid., x, 20.

110. Rush, *An Address to the Inhabitants of the British Settlements in America, upon Slave-Keeping* (1773), 9–10 (polygamy, slavery), 12 (quotation).

111. Ibid., 12–13.

112. Ibid., 28.

113. On Nisbet and his pamphlet, see Davis, *Slavery in the Age of Revolution*, 535–36.

114. Nisbet, *Slavery Not Forbidden by Scripture: or a Defense of the West-India Planters, from the Aspersions Thrown Out Against Them, by the Author of a Pamphlet, Entitled "An Address..."* (1773), 3.

115. Ibid., 8.

116. Rush, *A Vindication of the Address...in Answer to a Pamphlet Entitled, "Slavery Not Forbidden by Scripture"* (1773; printed with 2nd ed. of Rush's original *Address*, but separately paginated), 5, 7, 9.

117. Benezet, *Serious Considerations*, 28, 39, 32–34 (ship captains).

118. Ibid., 30 (Isa), 31–32 (Jer). Benezet hardly thought it was necessary "to repeat what has been so fully declared...of the inconsistence of slavery with every right of mankind, with every feeling of humanity, and every precept of Christianity...[and] with the welfare, peace and prosperity of every country, in proportion as [slavery] prevails" (32).

119. Essig, *The Bonds of Wickedness: American Evangelicals Against Slavery, 1770–1808*, 20. Alongside Essig's solid treatment on the anti-slavery convictions of these Edwardseans, see also Davis, *Problem of Slavery*, 291–95; Noll, *Christians in the American Revolution*, 92–102; Brown, *Moral Capital*, 178; and Rohrer, *Jacob Green*, 209–18.

120. Hopkins, *A Dialogue Concerning the Slavery of the Africans, Showing it to be the Duty and Interest of the American States to Emancipate All Their African Slaves...Dedicated to the Honourable the Continental Congress* (1776), 18. In a later work, Hopkins spent some time rebutting pro-slavery use of Leviticus 25 and the New Testament book of Philemon, but even then drew most heavily on his sense of the entire drift of Scripture: *A Discourse upon the Slave Trade, and the Slavery of Africans* (1793).

121. Hopkins, *Dialogue*, 21, 30, 49.

122. Petition dated 1773, quoted in Malcolm, "Slavery in Massachusetts and the American Revolution," 424.
123. See Wesley, *Thoughts upon Slavery* (1774).
124. *The Journal and Letters of Francis Asbury*, ed. Clark, 1:273–74.
125. Mathews, *Slavery and Methodism*, 8.
126. Sassi, "Religion, Race, and the Founders," in Dreisbach and Hall, *Faith and the Founders*, 186. The rest of this paragraph relies on Sassi, 186–88. For the role of Jacob Green's Edwardsean anti-slave agitation in perhaps sparking this dispute, see Rohrer, *Jacob Green*, 213.
127. Baldwin, *The New England Clergy and the American Revolution*, 7.
128. Baldwin, "Sowers of Sedition: The Political Theories of Some of the New Light Presbyterian Clergy of Virginia and North Carolina."
129. Byrd, *Sacred Scripture*, 164.
130. Daniel Dreisbach is convincing that "believers and skeptics alike made use of the Bible. Along with Christianity in general, the Bible informed their views of human nature, social order, political authority, civic obligations, and other ideas essential to organizing a stable and prosperous civil polity"; Dreisbach, "The Bible and the Political Culture of the American Founding," in *Faith and the Founders*, 164. Yet *how* informed, *how* made use, and to *what* end remain questions that careful documentation of the presence of Scripture cannot fully answer.
131. Sandoz, "Foreword," *Political Sermons*, xiv.
132. Fletcher, *The Bible and the Sword: or the Appointment of the General Fast Vindicated: In an Address to the Common People* (London, 1776), in Sandoz, *Political Sermons*, 570, 571, 574.
133. Frazer, *The Religious Beliefs of America's Founders*, 102.
134. T. S. Kidd, *God of Liberty*, 128.

CONCLUSION

1. As a theological footnote, classical Protestant doctrine, along with the teaching of other major Christian traditions, holds that the reality of Christ's Incarnation conveys the understanding that God has always acted completely within, as well as completely transcending, culture.
2. Coffey, *Exodus and Deliverance*, 67.
3. "Fragment on Pro-slavery Theology," dated with some uncertainty 1 Oct. 1858, *The Collected Works of Abraham Lincoln*, ed. Basler, 3:204–5.
4. As one best-selling example, see Marshall and Manuel, *The Light and the Glory, 1492–1793: God's Plan for America*.
5. Juhnke and Hunter, *The Missing Peace: The Search for Nonviolent Alternatives in United States History*.
6. Such a perspective informs Smith, Lalitha, and Hawk, eds., *Evangelical Postcolonial Conversations*.

7. See esp. Keillor, *This Rebellious House: American History and the Truth of Christianity.*

8. A few sections of this book have drawn on some of the same sources that informed my earlier study, *America's God: From Jonathan Edwards to Abraham Lincoln.* Yet here the story has a different end point. Where in the earlier work I described a "synthesis... of evangelical Protestant religion, republican political ideology, and commonsense moral reasoning" (9) as thoroughly integrated, and also unusually influential through the first decades of the nineteenth century, this book ends with a more complicated picture for Scripture, since trajectories of biblical usage were moving in different directions at the same time.

9. "Massachusetts Constitution (1780)," in Dreisbach and Hall, *The Sacred Rights of Consience: Selected Readings on Religious Liberty and Church-State Relations in the American Founding,* 244.

10. Facsimile of the Congressional Journal for 12 Sept. 1782, in Dreisbach and Hall, *Sacred Rights,* 232–33.

11. Stiles, *The United States Elevated to Glory and Honor,* 36 (capitalization [sic]).

12. Ibid., 37 (capitalization [sic]).

13. *The Journal and Letters of Francis Asbury,* ed. Clark, 1:441.

14. Madison's Notes for Debates on the General Assessment Bill... 23–24 Dec. 1784, <founders.archives.gov/documents/Madison/01-08-02-0104-0002> (accessed 22 Jan. 2015).

15. For a thorough discussion of the speech and its contexts, see Miller, *The Religious Roots of the First Amendment,* 144–51.

16. "A Bill for Establishing Religious Freedom, Virginia (1779 and 1786)," in Dreisbach and Hall, *Sacred Rights of Conscience,* 250–51.

17. Quotations that follow are from *Journal and Letters of Asbury,* 1:473–74.

18. Quoted by Wills, "Mason Weems, Bibliopolist," 68.

Bibliography: Primary Sources

This section of the bibliography includes modern editions, edited collections, and complete works found in those collections.

A Letter from the Associated Ministers of the County of Windham. Boston: J. Draper, 1745.

A True and Historical Narrative of the Colony of George, in America. Charlestown: P. Timothy, 1741.

Acosta, José de. *Natural and Moral History of the Indies.* Edited by Jane E. Mangan, translated by Frances López-Morillas. Durham, NC: Duke University Press, 2002.

Adams, John. *Diary and Autobiography of John Adams,* 3 vols. Edited by L. H. Butterfield. Cambridge, MA: Harvard University Press, 1961.

Adams, John. *The Revolutionary Writings of John Adams.* Edited by C. Bradley Thompson. Indianapolis, IN: Liberty Fund, 2000.

Allen, John. *An Oration Upon the Beauties of Liberty, Or the Essential Rights of the Americans,* 3rd corrected ed. New London: T. Green, 1773. (Also in Sandoz, *Political Sermons,* 305–25.)

An Account, Shewing the Progress of the Colony of Georgia in America, from it's First Establishment. Published per Order of the Honorable the Trustees. Annapolis, MD: Jonas Green, 1742.

Andrews, Samuel. *A Discourse Shewing the Necessity of Joining Internal Repentance with the External Profession of it.* New Haven, CT: Thomas and Samuel Green, 1775.

Apthorp, East. *Considerations on the Institutions and Conduct of the Society for the Propagation of the Gospel in Foreign Parts.* Boston: Green & Russell, 1763.

Asbury, Francis. *The Journal and Letters of Francis Asbury,* 3 vols. Edited by Elmer T. Clark. Nashville, TN: Abingdon, 1958.

Augustine of Hippo. *The Confessions of St. Augustine.* Translated by Rex Warner. New York: New American Library, 1963.

Backus, Isaac. *All true Ministers of the Gospel, are called into that Work by the special Influences of the Holy Spirit: A Discourse Shewing the Nature and Necessity of an*

Internal Call to Preach the Everlasting Gospel. Also Marks by which Christ's Ministers may be known from others, and Answers to sundry Objections. Boston: Fowle, 1754. (Also in McLoughlin, ed., *Isaac Backus*, 65–128.)

Backus, Isaac. *Appeal to the Public for Religious Liberty, Against the Oppressions of the Present Day.* Boston: John Boyle, 1773. (Also in McLoughlin, ed., *Isaac Backus*, 303–44.)

Bass, John. *A True Narrative of an Unhappy Contention in the Church at Ashford.* Boston: D. Gookin, 1751.

Baxter, Richard. *A Holy Commonwealth* (1659). Edited by William Lamont. New York: Cambridge University Press, 1994.

Bay Psalm Book. *The Whole Book of Psalmes Faithfully Translated into English Metre.* Cambridge, MA: Stephen Day, 1640.

Beckwith, George. *That People a Safe, and happy People, who have God for, and among them.* New London, CT: T. Green, 1756.

Belcher, Jonathan. *By His Excellency Jonathan Belcher . . . A Proclamation for a Publick Fast.* Boston: John Draper, 1735.

Belcher, Jonathan. "By His Excellency Jonathan Belcher . . . Proclamation for a Publick Thanksgiving," *The New-England Weekly Journal*, 2 Nov. 1730, 1.

Benezet, Anthony. *Observations on the Inslaving, Importing and Purchasing of Negroes.* Germantown: Christopher Sower, 1759.

Benezet, Anthony. *Serious Considerations on Several Important Subjects; viz. On War and its Inconsistency with the Gospel. Observations on Slavery. And Remarks on the Nature and bad Effects of Spirituous Liquors.* Philadelphia: Joseph Crukshank, 1778.

Benezet, Anthony. *Serious Reflections, affectionately recommended to the Well-disposed of every Religious Denomination, particularly those who Mourn and Lament on account of the Calamities which attend us.* Philadelphia: n.p., 1778.

Blair, Samuel. *A Short and Faithful Narrative, of the late remarakable [sic] revival of religion in the congregation of New-Londonderry, and other parts of Pennsylvania.* Philadelphia: William Bradford "at Sign of the Bible in Second-Street," 1744.

Boucher, Jonathan. "Discourse XII: On Civil Liberty; Passive Obedience, and Non-Resistance." In *A View of the Causes and Consequences of the American Revolution in Thirteen Discourses*, 495–560. London: G. G. and J. Robinson, 1797.

Bradford, William. *Of Plymouth Plantation, 1620–1647.* Edited by Samuel Eliot Morison. Introduction by Francis Murphy. New York: Modern Library, 1981.

Briant, Lemuel. *The Absurdity and Blasphemy of Deprecating Moral Virtue.* Boston: J. Green, 1749.

Brooks, Joanna, and John Saillant, eds. *"Face Zion Forward": First Writings of the Black Atlantic, 1785–1798.* Boston: Northeastern University Press, 2002.

Burr, Aaron. *A Servant of God Dismissed from Labour to Rest: A Funeral Sermon, Preached at the Interment of his Late Excellency, Jonathan Belcher, Esq.* New York: Hugh Gaine, 1757.

Bushman, Richard L., ed. *The Great Awakening: Documents on the Revival of Religion, 1740–1745.* New York: Atheneum, 1970.

Calvin, John. "Prefatory Address to King Francis I of France." In *Institutes of the Christian Religion*, 2 vols. Edited by John T. McNeill. Translated by Ford Lewis Battles, 1:9–31. Philadelphia: Westminster, 1960.

Caner, Henry. *A Candid Examination of Dr. Mayhew's Observations on the Charter and Conduct of the Society for the Propagation of the Gospel in Foreign Parts.* Boston: Thomas and John Fleet, 1763.

Carretta, Vincent, ed. *Phillis Wheatley: Complete Writings.* New York: Penguin, 2001.

Caretta, Vincent, ed. *Unchained Voices: An Anthology of Black Authors in the English-Speaking World of the Eighteenth Century.* Lexington: University Press of Kentucky, 1996.

Castellio, Sebastian. *Concerning Heretics* (1554). Edited by Roland Bainton. New York: Columbia University Press, 1935.

Chalmers, James [Candidus]. *Plain Truth; Addressed to the Inhabitants of America, containing, remarks on a late pamphlet, entitled Common Sense. Wherein are shewn, that … Permanent Liberty and True Happiness, can only be obtained by Reconciliation with that Kingdom.* Philadelphia: R. Bell, 1776.

Chandler, Thomas Bradbury. *An Appeal to the Public, in Behalf of the Church of England in America.* New York: James Parker, 1767.

Chauncy, Charles. *The Accursed Thing must be taken away from among a People, if they would reasonably hope to stand before their enemies.* Thomas & John Fleet, 1778.

Chauncy, Charles. *Civil Magistrates Must Be Just, Ruling in the Fear of God.* Boston: House of Representatives, 1747. (Also in Sandoz, *Political Sermons*, 137–78.)

Chauncy, Charles. *A Discourse on "the good News from a far Country."* Boston: Kneeland and Adams, 1766.

Chauncy, Charles. *Enthusiasm described and caution'd against.* Boston: J. Draper, 1742.

Chauncy, Charles. *The Gifts of the Spirit to Ministers.* Boston: Rogers & Fowle, 1742.

Chauncy, Charles. *Seasonable Thoughts on the state of religion in New-England. … Faithfully pointing out the things of a bad and dangerous tendency, in the late, and present, religious appearance.* Boston: G. Rogers, J. Fowle, and D. Fowle, 1743.

Chauncy, Charles. *Trust in GOD, the Duty of a People in a Day of Trouble. A Sermon Preached, May 30th, 1770. At the request of a great number of Gentlemen, friends to the LIBERTIE of North-America.* Boston: Daniel Kneeland, 1770.

Chauncy, Charles. *The Validity of Presbyterian Ordination Asserted and Maintained … the anniversary Dudleian-lecture.* Boston: Richard Draper, 1762.

Chillingworth, William. *The religion of protestants a safe way to salvation. Or an answer to a booke entitled Mercy and truth, or, Charity maintain'd by Catholiques, which pretends to prove the contrary.* Oxford: Leonard Lichfield, 1638.

Colman, Benjamin. *The Merchandise of a People Holiness to the Lord.* Boston: J. Draper, 1736.

Colman, Benjamin. *A Sermon Preached in Boston.* Boston: T. Fleet and T. Crump, 1716.

Columbus, Christopher. *The Libro de las profecías of Christopher Columbus.* Translated and edited by Delno C. West and August Kling. Gainesville: University of Florida Press, 1991.

Cotton, John. *An Abstract of the Lawes of New England, As they are now established.* London: F. Coules and W. Leyat, 1642.

Davies, Samuel. *Religion and Patriotism the Constituents of a Good Soldier: A sermon preached to Captain Overton's Independant [sic] Company of Volunteers, raised in Hanover county, Virginia, August 17, 1755.* Philadelphia: James Chattin, 1755.

Davies, Samuel. *A Sermon delivered at Nassau-Hall, January 14, 1761, on the death of his late Majesty, King George II.* New York: J. Parker; Philadelphia: William Bradford; and Boston: R. Draper and Z. Fowle, 1761.

Davies, Samuel. *A Sermon preached to the militia of Hanover country, in Virginia, at a general muster, May 8, 1758.* London: James Parker; and Boston: Z. Fowle and S. Draper, 1759.

Davies, Samuel. *Virginia's Danger and Remedy: Two Discourses occasioned by the severe drought in sundry parts of the country; and the defeat of General Braddock.* Williamsburg, VA: William Hunter, 1756.

Devotion, John. *The Duty and Interest of a People to Sanctify the Lord of Hosts.* Hartford, CT: Eben. Watson, 1777.

Dickinson, Jonathan. *The True Scripture-Doctrine Concerning Some Important Points of Christian Faith.* Boston: G. Rogers, 1741.

Dickinson, Jonathan. *The Witness of the Spirit.* Boston: S. Kneeland and T. Green, 1740.

Dreisbach, Daniel L., and Mark David Hall, eds. *The Sacred Rights of Conscience: Selected Readings on Religious Liberty and Church-State Relations in the American Founding.* Indianapolis, IN: Liberty Fund, 2009.

Duché, Jacob. *The Duty of Standing Fast in our Spiritual and Temporal Liberties, a Sermon.* Philadelphia: James Humphreys, 1775.

Dunbar, Samuel. *The Presence of God with his People, their only Safety and Happiness.* Boston: S. Kneeland, 1760.

Edwards, Jonathan. *The Works of Jonathan Edwards.* Vol. 2, *A Treatise Concerning Religious Affections in Three Parts.* Edited by John E. Smith. New Haven, CT: Yale University Press, 1959.

Edwards, Jonathan. *The Works of Jonathan Edwards.* Vol. 22, *Sermons and Discourses, 1739–1742.* Edited by Harry S. Stout, Nathan O. Hatch, and Kyle P. Farley. New Haven, CT: Yale University Press, 2003.

Equiano, Olaudah. *The Interesting Narrative and Other Writings,* 2nd ed. Edited by Vincent Caretta. New York: Penguin, 2003.

Fletcher, John. *The Bible and the Sword: or the Appointment of the General Fast Vindicated: In an Address to the Common People.* London: R. Hawes, 1776. (Also in Sandoz, *Political Sermons,* 559–78.)

Force, Peter, ed. *Tracts and Other Papers, Relating Principally to the Origin, Settlement, and Progress of the Colonies in North America.* Vol. 1. Washington: n.p., 1836.

Foster, Dan. *A Short Essay on Civil Government.* Hartford, CT: Eben. Watson, 1775.

Foxcroft, Thomas. *God's Grace Set Against an Incorrigible People: A Sermon preach'd at the publick lecture in Boston, Thursday, July 30, 1724.* Boston; B. Green, 1724.

Franklin, Benjamin. *The Autobiography of Benjamin Franklin*. Boston: Houghton Mifflin, 1917.

Garden, Alexander. *Regeneration... Being the Substance of Two Sermons... Occasioned by some erroneous notions of certain men who call themselves Methodists*. Charlestown, SC: Peter Timothy, 1740.

Gardiner, Samuel Rawson, ed. *The Constitutional Documents of the Puritan Revolution, 1625–1660*. Oxford: Clarendon Press, 1899.

Geneva Bible. *A Facsimile of the 1560 Edition*. Edited by Lloyd E. Berry. Madison: University of Wisconsin Press, 1969.

Goodman, Christopher. *How Superior Powers Ought to be Obeyd of their subjects: and Wherin they may lawfully by Gods Worde be disobeyed and resisted. Wherin also is declared the cause of all this present miserie in England, and the onely way to remedy the same* (1558). In Morgan, *Puritan Political Ideas*, 1–14.

Griffith, David. *Passive Obedience Considered: In a sermon preached at Williamsburg, December 31st, 1775*. Williamsburg: Alexander Purdie, [1776].

Gronniosaw, James Albert Ukawsaw. *A Narrative of the Most Remarkable Particulars in the Life of James Albert Ukawsaw Gronniosaw, An African Prince, as Related by Himself* (1772). In Carretta, *Unchained Voices*, 32–58.

Hall, David D., ed. *The Antinomian Controversy, 1636–1638: A Documentary History*, 2nd ed. Durham, NC: Duke University Press, 1990.

Hammon, Briton. *A Narrative of the Uncommon Sufferings, and Surprizing Deliverance of Briton Hammon, A Negro Man,—Servant to General Winslow, of Marshfield, in New-England*. Boston: Green & Russell, 1760. (Also in Carretta, ed., *Unchained Voices*, 20–25.)

Hammon, Jupiter. *An Address to Miss Phillis Wheatley*. [Hartford]: n.p, 1778. (Also in Carretta, ed., *Phillis Wheatley: Complete Writings*, 204–7).

Hammon, Jupiter. *An Address to the Negroes in the State of New-York*. New York: Carroll and Patterson, 1787.

Hammon, Jupiter. *An Evening Thought: Salvation by Christ, with Penetential Cries: Composed by Jupiter Hammon, a Negro belonging to Mr. Lloyd of Queen's-Village, on Long-Island, the 25th of December, 1760*. N.p.: n.p., 1760. (Also in Carretta, ed., *Unchained Voices*, 26–28.)

Hegel, Georg Wilhelm Friedrich., *Philosophy of History*. Translated by John Sibree. Kitchner, Ont.: Batoche Books, 2001 (orig. 1857).

Heimert, Alan, and Perry Miller, eds. *The Great Awakening: Documents Illustrating the Crisis and Its Consequences*. Indianapolis, IN: Bobbs-Merrill, 1967.

Hitchcock, Gad. *A Sermon Preached at Plymouth, December 22d, 1774*. Boston, 1775.

Holmes, Obadiah. *Baptist Piety: The Last Will and Testament of Obadiah Holmes*. Edited by Edwin S. Gaustad. Grand Rapids, MI: Eerdmans, 1978.

Hopkins, Samuel. *A Dialogue Concerning the Slavery of the Africans, Showing it to be the Duty and Interest of the American States to Emancipate All Their African Slaves... Dedicated to the Honoirable the Continental Congress*. Norwich, CT: Judah P. Spooner, 1776.

Hopkins, Samuel. *Discourse upon the Slave Trade, and the Slavery of Africans.* Providence, RI: J. Carter, 1793.

Hopkins, Samuel. *The Life and Character of Miss Susanna Anthony...Consisting Chiefly in Extracts from her Writings, with Some Brief Observations on Them.* Hartford, CT: Hudson & Goodwin, 1799.

Hopkins, Samuel. *The Life and Character of the Reverend Mr. Jonathan Edwards.* Boston: S. Kneeland, 1765.

Hopkins, Samuel. *Memoirs of the Life of Mrs. Sarah Osborn.* Worcester, MA: Leonard Worcester, 1799.

Hutson, James H., ed. *The Founders on Religion: A Book of Quotations.* Princeton, NJ: Princeton University Press, 2006.

Inglis, Charles. *The Christian Soldier's Duty Briefly Delineated.* New York: Hugh Gaine, 1777.

Inglis, Charles. *The Duty of Honouring the King, Explained and Recommended in a Sermon, Preached...on Sunday, January 30, 1780; Being the Anniversary of the Martyrdom of King Charles I.* New York: Hugh Gaine, 1780.

Inglis, Charles [An American]. *The True Interest of America Impartially Stated, in Certain Strictures on a Pamphlet Intitled COMMON SENSE.* Philadelphia: James Humphreys, 1776.

Inglis, Charles. *A Vindication of The Bishop of Landaff's Sermon from the Gross Misrepresentations and abusive reflections, contained in Mr. William Livingston's Letter to his Lordship: with some additional observations on certain passages in Dr. Chauncey's [sic] Remarks, etc.* New York: J. Holt, 1768.

Jesuit Relations and Allied Documents. Vol. 15, *Hurons and Quebec, 1638–1639.* Edited by Reuben G. Thwaites. Cleveland, OH: Burrows Brothers, 1898.

Kidd, Thomas S., ed. *The Great Awakening: A Brief History with Documents.* Boston: Bedford/St. Martin's, 2008.

King James Version. *The Bible: Authorized King James Version with Apocrypha.* 1611. Oxford World Classics. Edited by Robert Carroll and Stephen Prickett. New York: Oxford University Press, 1997.

Kinnersley, Ebenezer. *A Course of Experiments, in that Curious and Entertaining Branch of Natural Philosophy, Called Electricity; Accompanied with Explanatory Lectures: in which Electricity and Lightning will be proved to be the same Thing.* Philadelphia: A. Armbruster, 1764.

Kinnersley, Ebenezer. *A Letter to the Reverend the Ministers of the Baptist Congregations, in Pennsylvania, and the New-Jerseys.* Philadelphia: W. Bradford, 1746/47.

Langdon, Samuel. *Government Corrupted by Vice, and Recovered by Righteousness.* Watertown, CT: Benjamin Edes, 1775.

Las Casas, Bartolomé. *The Only Way.* Edited by Helen Rand Parish. Translated by Francis Patrick Sullivan, S.J. New York: Paulist, 1992.

Lavington, George. *The Enthusiasm of Methodism and Papists Compared in Three Parts.* London: J. & P. Knapton, 1754.

Lay, Benjamin Lay, *All slave-keepers that keep the innocent in bondage, apostates pretending to lay claim to the pure & holy Christian religion; of what congregation so ever, but especially in their ministers, by whose examples the filthy leprosy and apostasy is spread far and near; it is a notorious sin . . . a practice so gross & hurtful to religion, and destructive to government, beyond what words can set forth.* Philadelphia: Benjamin Franklin, 1737.

Leaming, Jeremiah. *A Defence of the Episcopal Government of the Church: Containing Remarks on two late, noted sermons on Presbyterian Ordination.* New York: John Holt, 1766.

Leaming, Jeremiah. *Dissertations upon Various Subjects.* New Haven, CT: T. & S. Green, 1788; Portsmouth: John Melcher, 1789.

Lincoln, Abraham. "Fragment on Pro-slavery Theology," dated with some uncertainty 1 Oct. 1858. In *The Collected Works of Abraham Lincoln.* Vol. 3, edited by Roy P. Basler, 204–5. New Brunswick, NJ: Rutgers University Press, 1953.

Livingstone, William. *A Letter to the Right Reverend Father in God, John, Lord Bishop of Landaff; occasioned by some passages in his Lordship's Sermon . . . in which the American Colonies are loaded with great and undeserved Reproach.* New York: Garrat Noel, 1768.

Luther, Martin. *Facsimiles of Early Luther Bibles.* Vol. 2, *Romans*, edited by Kenneth A. Strand. Belford, UK: Ann Arbor Publishers, 1972.

Luther, Martin. *Luther's Works* (American Edition). 55 vols. Edited by Jaroslav Pelikan and Hartmut T. Lehmann. St. Louis, MO: Concordia; and Philadelphia: Muhlenberg/Fortress, 1955–86.

Luther, Martin. *Luther's Works.* Vol. 27, *Lectures on Galatians . . . 1535[and] . . . 1519.* Edited by Jaroslav Pelikan. Saint Louis, MO: Concordia, 1964.

Luther, Martin. *Luther's Works.* Vol. 31, *Career of the Reformer* . Edited by Harold J. Grimm. Philadelphia: Fortress, 1957.

Luther, Martin. *Luther's Works.* Vol. 32, *Career of the Reformer II.* Edited by George W. Forell. Philadelphia: Fortress, 1958.

Luther, Martin. *Luther's Works.* Vol. 34, *Career of the Reformer IV.* Edited by Lewis W. Spitz. Philadelphia: Muhlenberg, 1960.

Luther, Martin. *Luther's Works.* Vol. 35, *Word and Sacrament I.* Edited by Theodore E. Bachmann. Philadelphia: Fortress, 1960.

Luther, Martin. *Luther's Works.* Vol. 45, *Christian in Society II.* Edited by Walther I. Brandt. Philadelphia: Fortress, 1962.

Luther, Martin. *Luther's Works.* Vol. 46, *The Christian in Society III.* Edited by Robert C. Schultz. Philadelphia: Fortress, 1967.

Lutz, Donald S., ed. *Colonial Origins of the American Constitution.* Indianapolis, IN: Liberty Fund, 1998.

Madison, James. Madison's Notes for Debates on the General Assessment Bill . . . 23–24 Dec. 1784. Available at <founders.archives.gov/documents/Madison/01-08-02-0104-0002> (accessed 22 Jan. 2015).

Marrant, John. *A Narrative of the Lord's Wonderful Dealings with John Marrant a Black, (Now going to Preach the Gospel in Nova-Scotia) Born in New-York, in North-America, Taken down from his own Relation. Arranged, Corrected, and Published By the Rev. Mr. Aldridge. The fourth Edition, Enlarged by Mr. Marrant, and Printed (with Permission) for his Sole Benefit, with Notes Explanatory* (1785). In Brooks and Saillant, *Face Zion Forward*, 47–75.

Mather, Cotton. *Biblia Americana*. Vol. 1, *Genesis*. Edited by Reiner Smolinski. Tübingen: Mohr Siebeck; Grand Rapids, MI: Baker, 2010.

Mather, Cotton. *Biblia Americana*. Vol. 3, *Joshua–2 Chronicles*. Edited by Kenneth P. Minkema. Tübingen: Mohr Siebeck; and Grand Rapids, MI: Baker, 2013.

Mather, Cotton. *The Christian Philosopher* (1721). Edited by Winton U. Solberg. Urbana: University of Illinois Press, 1994.

Mather, Cotton. *Edulcorator: A brief essay on the Waters of Marah sweeten. With a remarkable relation of the Dep[l]orable Occasion afforded for it, in the premature death of Captain Josiah Winslow, who with several of his company sacrificed his life in the service of his country; engaging an army of Indians, May 1, 1724.* Boston: B. Green, 1725.

Mather, Cotton. *A Good Master Well Served: A Brief Discourse on the Properties and Practices of a Good Servant in Every Kind of Servitude.* Boston: B. Green and J. Allen, 1696.

Mather, Cotton. *The Negro Christianized: An Essay to Excite and Assist that Good Work, the Instruction of Negro Servants in Christianity.* Boston: B. Green, 1706.

Mather, Cotton. *Shaking Dispensations. An essay upon the mighty shakes, which the hand of heaven, hath given and is giving, to the world.* Boston: B. Green, 1715.

Mather, Cotton. *Thirty Important Cases Resolved with Evidence of Scripture and Reason.* Boston: Bartholomew, Green, and John Allen, 1699.

Mayhew, Jonathan. *A Discourse Concerning Unlimited Submission and Non-Resistance to the Higher Powers: with some reflections on the resistance made to King Charles I and on the anniversary of his death: in the mysterious doctrine of the Prince's saintship and martyrdom is unriddled.* Boston: D. Fowle and D. Gookin, 1750.

Mayhew, Jonathan. *Remarks on an Anonymous Tract, entitled an Answer to Dr. Mayhew's Observations on the Charter and Conduct of the Society for the Propagation of the Gospel in Foreign Parts.* Boston: R. & S. Draper, 1764.

Mayhew, Jonathan. *The Snare Broken, A Thanksgiving Discourse.* Boston: R. & S. Draper, 1766.

McLoughlin, William G. ed. *Isaac Backus on Church, State, and Calvinism: Pamphlets, 1754–1789.* Cambridge, MA: Harvard University Press, 1968.

Miller, Perry, and Thomas H. Johnson, eds. *The Puritans: A Sourcebook of Their Writings.* 2 vols. Rev. ed. New York: Harper & Row, 1963.

Morgan, Edmund S., ed. *Puritan Political Ideas.* Indianapolis, IN: Bobbs-Merrill, 1965.

Murton, John. *An Humble Supplication to the King's Majesty*, bound with *Persecution for Religion Judged and Condemned, First Published in London, in the Year 1615*, 4th ed. Edited by Joseph Ivimey, 58–82. London: Wightman and Cramp, 1827.

Newton, John. *Thoughts upon the African Slave Trade*. London: J. Buckland, 1788.

Nisbet, Richard. *Slavery Not Forbidden by Scripture: or a Defense of the West-India Planters, from the Aspersions Thrown Out Against Them, by the Author of a Pamphlet, Entitled "An Address...."* Philadelphia: n.p., 1773.

Noll, Mark A., ed. *Confessions and Catechisms of the Reformation*. Vancouver: Regent College Publishing, 2004 (orig. 1991).

Novum Testamentum Latine, ed. Fridericus Brandscheid. Friburg: Herder, 1901.

Paine, Thomas. *Selected Writings of Thomas Paine*. Edited by Ian Shapiro and Jane E. Calvert. New Haven, CT: Yale University Press, 2014.

Paul III, Pope. "Sublimis Dei," 29 May 1537, Papal Encyclicals on Line. Available at <www.papalencyclicals.net/Paulo3/p3subli.html> (accessed 25 January 2015).

Pelikan, Jaroslav, and Valerie Hotchkiss, eds. *Creeds and Confessions of Faith in the Christian Tradition*. Vol. 2, *The Reformation Era*. New Haven, CT: Yale University Press, 2003.

Prince, Thomas. *The Salvation of God in 1746... Wherein the most remarkable Salvations of the year past, both in Europe and North-America, as far as they are come to our knowledge, are briefly considered*. Boston: D. Henchman, 1746.

Prince, Thomas. *A Sermon... Being the Day of General Thanksgiving for the great deliverance of the British Nations by the glorious and happy Victory near Culloden*. Boston: D. Henchman, 1746.

"Rationalis." Untitled tract againt Tom Paine's *Common Sense*, bound with Chalmers, *Plain Truth*.

Rush, Benjamin. *An Address to the Inhabitants of the British Settlements in America, upon Slave-Keeping*. Philadelphia: John Dunlap, 1773.

Rush, Benjamin. *Letters of Benjamin Rush*. 2 vols. Edited by L. H. Butterfield. Princeton, NJ: Princeton University Press, 1951.

Rush, Benjamin. *A Vindication of the Address... in Answer to a Pamphlet Entitled, "Slavery Not Forbidden by Scripture."* Philadelphia: John Dunlap, 1773.

Sandiford, Benjamin. *Brief Examination of the Practice of the Times*, Philadelphia: Benjamin Franklin, 1729.

Sandoz, Ellis, ed. *Political Sermons of the American Founding Era, 1730–1805*. Indianapolis, IN: Liberty Press, 1991.

Sewall, Samuel. *The Diary of Samuel Sewall, 1674–1729*, 2 vols. Edited by M. Halsey Thomas. New York: Farrar, Straus and Giroux, 1973.

Sewall, Samuel. *The Selling of Joseph: A Memorial*. Boston: Bartholomew Green and John Allen, 1700.

Shepard, Thomas. *God's Plot: The Paradoxes of Puritan Piety, Being the Autobiography and Journal of Thomas Shepard*. Edited by Michael McGiffert. Amherst: University of Massachusetts Press, 1972.

Shepard, Thomas. *Thomas Shepard's Confessions* (Publications of the Colonial Society of Massachusetts, vol. 58). Edited by George Selement and Bruce C. Woolley. Boston: The Society, 1981.

Smith, Josiah. *The Character, Preaching, &c. of the Reverend Mr. George Whitefield, Impartially Represented and Supported.* Boston: G. Rogers, 1740.

Smith, William. "To the People of Pennsylvania, Letter V." *Pennsylvania Ledger,* 30 March 1776, 2–3.

Smith, William. "To the People of Pennsylvania, Letter VI." *Pennsylvania Ledger,* 13 Apr. 1776, 1, 4.

Stiles, Ezra. *A Discourse on the Christian Union.* Boston: Edes and Gill, 1761.

Stiles, Ezra. *The United States Elevated to Glory and Honor. A Sermon, preached...at Hartford, at the anniversary election. May 8th, 1783.* New Haven, CT: Thomas & Samuel Green, 1783.

Stiles, Isaac. *A Prospect of the City of Jerusalem.* New London: T. Green, 1742.

Stith, William. *A Sermon, Preached before the General Assembly, at Williamsburg, March 2, 1745–6.* Williamsburg, VA: William Parker, 1746.

Stoddard, Solomon. *Question whether God is not angry with the country for doing so little towards the conversion of the Indians?* Boston: B. Green, 1723.

Symmes, Thomas. *Historical Memoirs of the Late Fight at Piggwacket, with a sermon occasioned by the fall of the brave Capt. John Lovewell and several of his valiant company, in the late heroic action there.* Boston: B. Green, 1725.

Tennent, Gilbert. *The Danger of an Unconverted Ministry.* Philadelphia: Benjamin Franklin, 1740.

Tennent, Gilbert. *The Necessity of Praising God for Mercies Receiv'd: A Sermon occasion'd by the success of the late Expedition...in reducing the City and Fortresses of Louisburgh on Cape-Breton...preach'd at Philadelphia July 7, 1745.* Philadelphia: William Bradford, 1745.

Tennent, Gilbert. *A Sermon preach'd at Burlington in New Jersey, November 23, 1749. Being the day appointed by his Excellency the Governor...for a Provincial Thanksgiving. Before the Governor and others upon Texts chosen by his Excellency.* Philadelphia: W. Bradford, 1749.

Tillotson, John. *The Usefulness of Consideration in Order to Repentance: A Sermon.* Philadelphia: William Bradford, 1745.

Tocqueville, Alexis de. *Democracy in America* (1835, 1840), 4 vols. Edited Eduardo Nolla. Translated by James T. Schleifer. Indianapolis, IN: Liberty Fund, 2010.

Trapp, Joseph. *The Nature, Folly, Sin, and Danger of being Righteous over-much; with a particular View to the Doctrines and Practices of certain Modern Enthusiasts.* London: S. Austen "at the Angel and Bible," 1739.

Trinterud, Leonard J., ed. *Elizabethan Puritanism.* New York: Oxford University Press, 1971.

Trollope, *Domestic Manners of the Americans.* 1832, Oxford World Classics. Edited by Elsie B. Miche. New York: Oxford University Press, 2014.

Trumbull, Benjamin. *A Discourse, Delivered at the Anniversary Meeting of the Freemen of the Town of New-Haven.* New Haven, CT: Thomas & Samuel Green, 1773.

Tyndale, William. *Doctrinal Treatises and Introductions to Different Portions of the Holy Scriptures* (Parker Society Edition). Edited by Henry Walter: Cambridge University Press, 1848.

Tyndale, William. *The New Testament Translated by William Tyndale 1534.* Edited by N. Hardy Wallis. Cambridge: Cambridge University Press, 1938.

Wadsworth, Benjamin. *True Piety the Policy for Times of War: A sermon preached at Boston-Lecture on August 16, 1722, soon after a declaration of war, against the Eastern Indians and Rebels.* Boston: B. Greene, 1722.

Walker, Williston, ed. *The Creeds and Platforms of Congregationalism.* Introduction by Douglas Horton. Philadelphia: Pilgrim, 1960 (orig. 1893).

Warren, Mercy Otis. *Poems, Dramatic and Miscellaneous.* Boston: Thomas and Andrews, 1790.

Watts, Isaac. *Hymns and Sacred Songs,* 7th ed. [Boston]: n.p., 1720.

Watts, Isaac. *The Psalms of David, imitated in the language of the New Testament, and apply'd to the Christian state and worship.* Philadelphia: Benjamin Franklin and Hugh Meredith, 1729.

Welles, Noah. *The Divine Right of Presbyterian Ordination Asserted, and the Ministerial Authority, claimed and exercised in the established Churches of New England vindicated and proved.* New York: John Holt, 1763.

Wesley, John *Thoughts upon Slavery.* London: R. Hawes, 1774.

Wheatley, Phillis. *Complete Writings.* Edited by Vincent Carretta. New York: Penguin, 2001.

Wheatley, Phillis. *Poems on Various Subjects Religious and Moral.* London: A. Bell, 1773. (Also included in Carretta, ed., *Phillis Wheatley: Complete Writings,* 1–65.)

Whitefield, George. "Abraham's Offering Up His Son Isaac" (1742). In Works, 5:38–51.

Whitefield, George. *An Address to Persons of All Denominations, Occasioned by the Alarm of an Intended Invasion.* Philadelphia: B. Franklin & D. Hall, 1756.

Whitefield, George. *Britain's Mercies, and Britain's Duty represented in a sermon preached at the new-building in Philadelphia, on Sunday August 24, 1746. Occasioned by the suppression of the late unnatural rebellion.* Philadelphia: Wm. Bradford, 1746.

Whitefield, George. *A Collection of Hymns for Social Worship.* London: William Strahan, 1753.

Whitefield, George. "The Duty of Searching the Scriptures" (1739). In *Works,* 6:79–88.

Whitefield, George. "A Letter from the Rev. Mr. George Whitefield to the Inhabitants of Maryland, Virginia, North and South Carolina." *Pennsylvania Gazette,* 17 April 1740.

Whitefield, George. Letters to Bishop Zachary Pierce, February/March 1756. In *Works* 3:157, 159–64, 165, 166–67, 168–70.

Whitefield, George. "On Christ the Believer's Husband" (1747). In *Works,* 5:171–96.

Whitefield, George. "Walking with God" (1740). In *Works,* 5:21–37.

Whitefield, George. *The Works of the Reverend George Whitefield, M.A.* 7 vols. Edited by John Gillies. London: Edward & Charles Dilly, 1771–1772.

Wilberforce, William. *A Practical View of the Prevailing Religion System of Professed Christians, in the Higher, and Middle Classes in this Country, Contrasted with Real Christianity,* 2nd ed. London: T. Cadeel, Jr., and W. Davies, 1797.

Willard, Samuel. *A Compleat Body of Divinity in Two Hundred and Fifty Expository Lectures.* Boston: Green, Kneeland, and Eliot, 1726.

Williams, Elisha. *The Essential Rights and Liberties of Protestants: A Seasonable Plea for the Liberty of Conscience, and the Right of Private Judgment, in Matters of Religion, Without any Controul from human Authority.* Boston: S. Kneeland and T. Green, 1744. (Also in Sandoz, *Political Sermons,* 51–118.)

Williams, George H., ed. *Spiritual and Anabaptist Writers: Documents Illustrative of the Radical Reformation.* Philadelphia: Westminster, 1957.

Williams, Roger. *The Bloudy Tenent of Persecution for Cause of Conscience* (1644). Edited by Richard Groves. Macon, GA: Mercer University Press, 2001.

Williams, Solomon. *The Duty of Christian Soldiers, when Called to War, to Undertake it in the Name of God.* New London, CT: T. & J. Green, 1755.

Williams, Solomon. *The Relations of God's People to him . . . With a special View to New-England, and the rest of the British Subjects in America. A Thanksgiving Sermon, On Occasion of the Smiles of Heaven to the British Arms in America, particularly the Reduction of Quebec.* New London, CT: Timothy Green, 1760.

Winthrop, John (1587–1649). *The Journal of John Winthrop, 1630–1649.* Edited by Richard S. Dunn and Laetitia Yeandle. Abridged ed. Cambridge, MA: Harvard University Press, 1996.

Winthrop, John (1714–1779). *A Lecture on Earthquakes; Read in the Chapel of Harvard-College . . . November 26th 1755.* Boston: Edes & Gill, 1755.

Witherspoon, John. *An Annotated Edition of Lectures on Moral Philosophy by John Witherspoon.* Edited by Jack Scott. Newark: University of Delaware Press, 1982.

Witherspoon, John. *The Dominion of Providence over the Passions of Men. A Sermon Preached at Princeton . . . to which is added An Address to the Natives of Scotland residing in America.* Philadelphia: R. Aitken. (Also in Sandoz, *Political Sermons,* 529–58.)

Woodmason, Charles. *The Carolina Backcountry on the Eve of the Revolution: The Journal and Other Writings of Charles Woodmason, Anglican Itinerant.* Edited by Richard J. Hooker. Chapel Hill: University of North Carolina Press, 1953.

Woolman, John. *Some Considerations on the Keeping of Negroes. Recommended to the Professors of Christianity of Every Denomination.* Philadelphia: James Chattin, 1754.

Wootton, David, ed. *Divine Right and Monarchy: An Anthology of Political Writing in Stuart England.* New York: Penguin, 1986.

Wycliffe, John. *John Wyclif On the Truth of Holy Scripture.* Edited and translated by Ian Christopher Levy. Kalamazoo, MI: TEAMS by Medieval Institute Publications, 2001.

Wycliffe, John. *John Wyclif's De Veritate Sacrae Scripturae Now First Edited from the Manuscripts with Critical and Historical Notes.* Edited by Rudolf Buddensieg. London: Wyclif Society, 1905.

Zubly, John Joachim. *The Law of Liberty. A Sermon on American Affairs, Preached at the Opening of the Provincial Congress of Georgia.* Philadelphia: Henry Miller, 1775.

Bibliography: Secondary Sources

Alonso, Vital. "La Biblia en el Nuevo Mundo." *Revista Bíblica* 30/31 (1988): 125–33.

Alter, Robert. *Pen of Iron: American Prose and the King James Bible*. Princeton, NJ: Princeton University Press, 2010.

American National Biography, 24 vols. Edited by John A. Garraty and Mark C. Carnes. New York: Oxford University Press, 1999.

Amory, Hugh, and David D. Hall, eds. *A History of the Book in America*. Vol 1, *The Colonial Book in the Atlantic World*. Chapel Hill: University of North Carolina Press, 2007.

Amory, Hugh. "Appendix One: A Note on Statistics." In Amory and Hall, *History of the Book*, 504–18.

Amory, Hugh. "The New England Book Trade, 1713–1790." In Amory and Hall, *History of the Book*, 314–46.

Amory, Hugh. "Printing and Bookselling in New England, 1638–1713." In Amory and Hall, *History of the Book*, 83–116.

Anderson, Emma. *The Death and Afterlife of the North American Martyrs*. Cambridge, MA: Harvard University Press, 2013.

Armitage, David. *The Ideological Origins of the British Empire*. New York: Cambridge University Press, 2000.

Bailyn, Bernard. *The Ideological Origins of the American Revolution*. Cambridge, MA: Harvard University Press, 1967.

Bainton, Roland H. *Here I Stand: A Life of Martin Luther*. Nashville, TN: Abingdon, 1950.

Baldwin, Alice. *The New England Clergy and the American Revolution*. Durham, NC: Duke University Press, 1928.

Baldwin, Alice. "Sowers of Sedition: The Political Theories of Some of the New Light Presbyterian Clergy of Virginia and North Carolina." *William and Mary Quarterly* 5 (Jan. 1948): 52–76.

Barnes, Timothy, and Robert Calhoon. "Moral Allegiance: John Witherspoon and Loyalist Recantation." *American Presbyterians* 63 (1985): 273–83.

Bebbington, D. W. *Evangelicalism in Modern Britain: A History from the 1730s to the 1980s.* London: Unwin Hyman, 1989.

Bell, James B. *A War of Religion: Dissenters, Anglicans, and the American Revolution.* New York: Palgrave Macmillan, 2008.

Belmonte, Kevin Charles. Introduction to *A Practical View of Christianity*, by William Wilberforce. Peabody, MA: Hendrickson, 1996.

Benedict, Philip. *Christ's Churches Purely Reformed: A Social History of Calvinism.* New Haven, CT: Yale University Press, 2002.

Berens, John F. *Providence and Patriotism in Early America, 1640–1815.* Charlottesville: University Press of Virginia, 1978.

Berkouwer, G. C. *Holy Scripture.* Grand Rapids: Eerdmans, 1975.

Bernhard, Winfred E. A. "John Winthrop (1714–79)." In *American National Biography*, 23:666–68.

"Bible in America, The." The Center for the Study of Religion and American Culture, Indiana University Purdue University Indianapolis, available at raac.iupui.edu/files/2713/9413/8354/Bible_in_American_Life_Report_March_6_2014.pdf (accessed 2 March 2015).

Bielo, James S. *Words Upon the Word: An Ethnography of Evangelical Group Bible Study.* New York: New York University Press, 2009.

Bloch, Ruth. "Religion and Ideological Change in the American Revolution" In *Religion and American Politics: From the Colonial Period to the Present*, edited by Mark A. Noll and Luke E. Harlow, 47–64. 2nd. ed. New York: Oxford University Press, 2007.

Bloch, Ruth. *Visionary Republic: Millennial Themes in American Thought, 1756–1800.* New York: Cambridge University Press, 1985.

Bobrick, Benson. *Wide as the Waters: The Story of the English Bible and the Revolution It Inspired.* New York: Simon & Schuster, 2001.

Bonomi, Patricia U. *Under the Cope of Heaven: Religion, Society, and Politics in Colonial America.* 2nd ed. New York: Oxford University Press, 2003.

Bossy, John. *Christianity in the West, 1400–1700.* New York: Oxford University Press, 1985.

Bouwsma, William J. *John Calvin: A Sixteenth Century Portrait.* New York: Oxford University Press, 1988.

Bozeman, Theodore Dwight. *To Live Ancient Lives: The Primitivist Dimension in Puritanism.* Chapel Hill: University of North Carolina Press, 1988.

Bradley, James E. *Religion, Revolution, and English Radicalism: Non-conformity in Eighteenth-Century Politics and Society.* New York: Cambridge University Press, 1990.

Breen, T. H. "An Empire of Goods: The Anglicization of Colonial America, 1690–1776." *Journal of British Studies* 25 (1986): 467–99.

Breen, T. H. *The Marketplace of Revolution: How Consumer Politics Shaped American Independence.* New York: Oxford, 2004.

Brekus, Catherine A. *Sarah Osborn's World: The Rise of Evangelical Christianity in Early America.* New Haven, CT: Yale University Press, 2013.

Bremer, Francis J. *Building a New Jerusalem: John Davenport, a Puritan in Three Worlds*. New Haven, CT: Yale University Press, 2012.

Bremer, Francis J. *First Founders: American Puritans and Puritanism in an Atlantic World*. Durham: University of New Hampshire Press, 2012.

Bremer, Francis J. *John Winthrop: America's Forgotten Founding Father*. New York: Oxford University Press, 2003.

Bridenbaugh, Carl. *Mitre and Sceptre: Transatlantic Faiths, Ideas, Personalities, and Politics, 1689–1775*. New York: Oxford University Press, 1962.

Brock, Peter. *Pacifism in the United States: From the Colonial Era to the First World War*. Princeton, NJ: Princeton University Press, 1968.

Brown, Christopher Leslie. *Moral Capital; Foundations of British Abolitionism*. Chapel Hill: University of North Carolina Press, 2006.

Brown, Robert E. *Jonathan Edwards and the Bible*. Bloomington: University of Indiana Press, 2002.

Bruce, F. F. *The English Bible: A History of Translations from the Earliest English Versions to the New English Bible*. New York: Oxford University Press, 1970.

Bruns, Gerald L. *Hermeneutics Ancient and Modern*. New Haven, CT: Yale University Press, 1992.

Bumsted, John M., and Charles E. Clark. "New England's Tom Paine: John Allen and the Spirit of Liberty." *William and Mary Quarterly* 21 (Oct. 1964): 561–70.

Butler, Jon. "Enthusiasm Described and Decried: The Great Awakening as Interpretive Fiction." *William and Mary Quarterly* 69 (Sept. 1982): 305–25.

Butler, Jon. "Gospel Order Improved: The Keithian Schism and the Exercise of Quaker Ministerial Authority in Pennsylvania." *William and Mary Quarterly* 31 (1974): 431–52.

Byrd, James P., *Sacred Scripture, Sacred War: The Bible and the American Revolution*. New York: Oxford University Press, 2013.

Calhoon, Robert M. *The Loyalists in Revolutionary America, 1760–1781*. New York: Harcourt, Brace, Jovanovich, 1973.

Calhoon, Robert M., and Ruma Chopra. "Religion and the Loyalists." In Dreisbach and Hall, *Faith and the Founders*, 101–19.

Calvert, Jane E. *Quaker Constitutionalism and the Political Thought of John Dickinson*. New York: Cambridge University Press, 2009.

Cameron, Christopher. *To Plead Our Own Cause: African Americans in Massachusetts and the Making of the Antislavery Movement*. Kent, OH: Kent State University Press, 2014.

Cameron, Christopher. "The Puritan Origins of Black Abolitionism in Massachusetts." *Historical Journal of Massachusetts* 39 (2011): 79–107.

Campbell, Gordon. *Bible, 1611–2011: The Story of the King James Version*. New York: Oxford University Press, 2010.

Carretta, Vincent. *Equiano, the African: Biography of a Self-Made Man*. New York: Penguin, 2005.

Carretta, Vincent. *Phillis Wheatley: Biography of a Genius in Bondage*. Athens: University of Georgia Press, 2011.

Caulkins, Frances Manwaring. *History of New London, Connecticut,…1612 to 1850*. New London: H. D. Utley, 1895.

Choi, Peter Y. "George Whitefield, the Imperial Itinerant: Religion, Economics, and Politics in the Era of the Great Awakening." PhD diss., University of Notre Dame, 2014.

Chopra, Ruma. *Unnatural Rebellion: Loyalists in New York City During the Revolution*. Charlottesville: University of Virginia Press, 2011.

Clark, Charles E. "Science, Reason, and an Angry God: The Literature of an Earthquake." *New England Quarterly* 38 (1965): 340–62.

Clark, J. C. D. *English Society, 1688–1832*. New York: Cambridge University Press, 1985.

Clark, J. C. D. *English Society, 1660–1832*, 2nd ed. New York: Cambridge University Press, 2000.

Clark, J. C. D. *The Language of Liberty: Political Discourse and Social Dynamics in the Anglo-American World*. New York: Cambridge University Press, 1994.

Clark, J. C. D. "Thomas Paine: The English Dimension." In *Selected Writings of Thomas Paine*, edited by Ian Shapiro and Jane E. Calvert, 579–610. New Haven, CT: Yale University Press, 2014.

Coffey, John. *Exodus and Deliverance: Deliverance Politics from John Calvin to Martin Luther King Jr*. New York: Oxford University Press, 2014.

Coffey, John, and Paul C. Lim, eds. *The Cambridge Companion to Puritanism*. New York: Cambridge University Press, 2008.

Cogley, Richard W. *John Eliot's Mission to the Indians before King Philip's War*. Cambridge, MA: Harvard University Press, 1999.

Cohen, Charles L. "The 'Liberty or Death' Speech: A Note on Religion and Revolutionary Rhetoric." *William and Mary Quarterly* 38 (Oct. 1981), 702–17.

Colley, Linda. *Britons: Forging the Nation, 1707–1837*. New Haven, CT: Yale University Press, 1992.

Collinson, Patrick. *The Elizabethan Puritan Movement*. Oxford: Clarendon Press, 1990 (orig. 1967).

Collinson, Patrick. *The Religion of Protestants: The Church in English Society, 1559–1625*. New York: Oxford University Press, 1982.

Connolly, Sean. *Religion, Law and Power: The Making of Protestant Ireland, 1660–1760*. Oxford: Clarendon Press, 1992.

Corenlius, Janet Duitsman. *"When I Can Read My Title Clear": Literacy, Slavery, and Religion in the Antebellum South*. Columbia: University of South Carolina Press, 1991.

Costa (neé Jackman), Sara. "Eschatology and Exploration: Rethinking the Historical Columbus." B.A. thesis, University of Chicago, 2008.

Crawford, Michael J. *Seasons of Grace: Colonial New England's Revival Tradition in British Context*. New York: Oxford University Press, 1991.

Crawford, Michael J. "The Spiritual Travels of Nathan Cole." *William and Mary Quarterly* 33 (Jan. 1976), 89–126.

Crystal, David. *Begat: The King James Bible and the English Language*. New York: Oxford University Press, 2010.

Cummings, Brian. *The Book of Common Prayer: The Texts of 1549, 1559, and 1662*. Oxford: Oxford University Press, 2011.

Daniell, David. *The Bible in English*. New Haven, CT: Yale University Press, 2003.

Daniell, David. *William Tyndale: A Biography*. New Haven, CT: Yale University Press, 1994.

Davis, David Brion. *Inhuman Bondage: The Rise and Fall of Slavery in the New World*. New York: Oxford University Press, 2006.

Davis, David Brion. *The Problem of Slavery in the Age of Revolution, 1770–1823*. 2nd ed. New York: Oxford University Press, 1999.

Davis, David Brion. *The Problem of Slavery in Western Culture*. Ithaca: Cornell University Press, 1966.

Davis, Derek H. *Religion and the Continental Congress, 1774–1789: Contributions to Original Intent*. New York: Oxford University Press, 2000.

Den Hartog, Jonathan. *Patriotism and Piety: Federalist Politics and Religious Struggle in the New American Nation*. Charlottesville: University of Virginia Press, 2015.

Dickens, A. G., and John M. Tonkin. *The Reformation in Historical Thought*. Cambridge, MA: Harvard University Press, 1985.

Doyle, Eric, O.F.M. "William Woodford on Scripture and Tradition." In *Studia Historico-Ecclesiastica: Festgabe für Prof. Luchesius G. Spätling O.F.M.*, edited by Isaac Vázquez O.F.M., 481–502. Rome: Pontificium Athenaeum Antonianum, 1977.

Dreisbach, Donald L. "The Bible and the Political Culture of the American Founding." In Dreisbach and Hall, *Faith and the Founders*, 144–73.

Dreisbach, Daniel L., and Mark David Hall, eds. *Faith and the Founders of the American Republic*. New York: Oxford University Press, 2014.

Duffy, Eamon. *The Stripping of the Altars: Traditional Religion in England, 1400–1580*. New Haven, CT: Yale University Press, 1992.

Endy, Melvin B., Jr. "Just War, Holy War, and Millennialism in Revolutionary America." *William and Mary Quarterly* 42 (1985): 3–25.

Engel, Katherine Carté. *Religion and Profit: Moravians in Early America*. Philadelphia: University of Pennsylvania Press, 2009.

Erben, Patrick M. *A Harmony of the Spirits: Translation and the Language of Community in Early Pennsylvania*. Chapel Hill: University of North Carolina Press, 2012.

Essig, James D. *The Bonds of Wickedness: American Evangelicals Against Slavery, 1770–1808*. Philadelphia: Temple University Press, 1982.

Ferguson, Robert A. *The American Enlightenment, 1750–1820*. Cambridge, MA: Harvard University Press, 1997.

Fernández-Armesto, Felipe. *Columbus*. New York: Oxford University Press, 1991.

Fernández-Armesto, Felipe, and Derek Wilson. *Reformations: A Radical Interpretation of Christianity and the World, 1500–2000*. New York: Scribner, 1997.

Ferrell, Lori Anne. *The Bible and the People*. New Haven, CT: Yale University Press, 2008.

Fiering, Norman. *Jonathan Edwards's Moral Thought and Its British Context*. Chapel Hill: University of North Carolina Press, 1981.

Fiering, Norman. *Moral Philosophy at Seventeenth-Century Harvard*. Chapel Hill: University of North Carolina Press, 1981.

Firth, Charles. *Oliver Cromwell and the Rule of the Puritans in England*. London: Oxford University Press, 1953 (orig. 1900).

Fischer, David Hackett. *Champlain's Dream*. New York: Simon & Schuster, 2008.

Fisher, Linford. "Native Americans, Conversion, and Christian Practice in Colonial New England, 1640–1730." *Harvard Theological Review* 102 (2009): 101–24.

Fisher, Linford D. *The Indian Great Awakening: Religion and the Shaping of Native Cultures in Early America*. New York: Oxford University Press, 2012.

Fitz, Caitlin A. "'Suspected on Both Sides': Little Abraham, Iroquois Neutrality, and the American Revolution." *Journal of the Early Republic* 28 (Fall 2008): 299–336.

Flower, Elizabeth, and Murray G. Murphy. *A History of Philosophy in America*, 2 vols. New York: Capricorn, 1977.

Fox, Francis S. *Sweet Land of Liberty: The Ordeal of the American Revolution in Northampton County, Pennsylvania*. State College: Penn State University Press, 2000.

Frazer, Gregg L. *The Religious Beliefs of America's Founders: Reason, Revelation, and Revolution*. Lawrence: University Press of Kansas, 2012.

Fredrickson, George M. *Racism: A Short History*. Princeton, NJ: Princeton University Press, 2002.

Frei, Hans. *The Eclipse of Biblical Narrative*. New Haven, CT: Yale University Press, 1974.

Frey, Sylvia R., and Betty Wood. *Come Shouting to Zion: African American Protestantism in the African South and British Caribbean to 1830*. Chapel Hill: University of North Carolina Press, 1998.

Frye, Northrop. *The Great Code: The Bible and Literature*. New York: Harcourt Brace Jovanovich, 1982.

Gamble, Richard M. *In Search of the City on a Hill: The Making and Unmaking of an American Myth*. New York: Bloomsbury, 2012.

Gatiss, Lee. Introduction to *The Sermons of George Whitefield*, 2 vols. Wheaton, IL: Crossway, 2012.

Gaustad, Edwin S. *The Great Awakening in New England*. New York: Harper, 1957.

Gaustad, Edwin S. *Liberty of Conscience: Roger Williams in America*. Grand Rapids, MI: Eerdmans, 1991.

Gay, Peter. *The Enlightenment: An Interpretation*, 2 vols. New York: Knopf, 1963.

Greenslade, S. L. *The Cambridge History of the Bible*. Vol. 3, *The West from the Reformation to the Present Day*. New York: Cambridge University Press, 1963.

Gleason, Travis. *Mastering Christianity: Missionary Anglicanism and Slavery in the Atlantic World*. New York: Oxford University Press, 2012.

Goddard, Ives, and Kathleen Bragon. *Native Writing in Massachusetts*, Part 1. Philadelphia: American Philosophical Society, 1988.

Goldenberg, David M. *The Curse of Ham: Race and Slavery in Early Judaism, Christianity, and Islam*. Princeton, NJ: Princeton University Press, 2003.

Goldman, Shalom. *God's Sacred Tongue: Hebrew and the American Imagination*. Chapel Hill: University of North Carolina Press, 2004.

Gordis, Lisa M. *Opening Scripture: Bible Reading and Interpretive Authority in Puritan New England*. Chicago: University of Chicago Press, 2003.

Gordon, Grant. *From Slavery to Freedom: The Life of David George, Pioneer Black Baptist Minister* (Baptist Heritage in Atlantic Canada). Hantsport, Nova Scotia: Lancelot, 1992.

Graham, Fred. *The Constructive Revolutionary: John Calvin and his Socio-Economic Impact*. Atlanta: John Knox, 1971.

Graham, Louis. "The Scientific Piety of John Winthrop of Harvard." *New England Quarterly* 46 (1973): 112–18.

Grasso, Christopher. *A Speaking Aristocracy: Transforming Public Discourse in Eighteenth-Century Connecticut*. Chapel Hill: University of North Carolina Press, 1999.

Green, Ian. *Print and Protestantism in Early Modern England*. New York: Oxford University Press, 2000.

Green, James N. "Part One: English Books and Printing in the Age of Franklin." In Amory and Hall, *History of the Book*, 248–97.

Green, Steven K. *The Bible, the School, and the Constitution: The Clash that Shaped Modern Church-State Doctrine*. New York: Oxford University Press, 2012.

Green, Steven K. *The Second Disestablishment: Church and State in Nineteenth-Century America*. New York: Oxford University Press, 2010.

Greene, Jack P. "Empire and Identity from the Glorious Revolution to the American Revolution." In *Oxford History of the British Empire*. Vol. 2, edited by P. J. Marshall, 208–30. New York: Oxford University Press, 1998.

Greene, Jack P., ed. *Pursuits of Happiness: The Social Development of Early Modern British Colonies and the Formation of American Culture*. Chapel Hill: University of North Carolina Press, 1988.

Gregory, Brad. *The Unintended Reformation: How a Religious Revolution Secularized Society*. Cambridge, MA: Harvard University Press, 2012.

Gregory, Jeremy. "'Establishment' and 'Dissent' in British North America: Organizing Religion in the New World." In *British North America in the Seventeenth and Eighteenth Centuries*. The Oxford History of the British Empire: Companion Series, edited by Stephen Foster, 136–69. Oxford: Oxford University Press, 2013.

Griffin, Patrick. *America's Revolution*. New York: Oxford University Press, 2012.

Gunther, Karl. *Reformation Unbound: Protestant Visions of Reform in England, 1525–1590*. New York: Cambridge University Press, 2014.

Gutjahr, Paul C. *An American Bible: A History of the Good Book in the United States, 1770–1880*. Stanford, CA: Stanford University Press, 1999.

Gutjahr, Paul. "The Letter(s) of the Law: Four Centuries of Typography in the King James Bible." In *Illuminating Letters: Typography and Literary Interpretation*, edited by Gutjahr and Megan L. Benton, 17–44. Amherst: University of Massachusetts Press, 2001.

Guyatt, Nicholas. *Providence and the Invention of the United States, 1607–1876.* New York: Cambridge University Press, 2007.

Hall, David D. "The Chesapeake in the Seventeenth Century." In Amory and Hall, *History of the Book,* 55–82.

Hall, David D. "Readers and Writers in Early New England." In Amory and Hall, *History of the Book,* 117–51.

Hall, David D. *A Reforming People: Puritanism and the Transformation of Public Life in New England.* New York: Knopf, 2011.

Hall, David D. *Worlds of Wonder, Days of Judgment: Popular Religious Belief in Early New England.* New York: Knopf, 1989.

Hall, David D., and Russell L. Martin. "Appendix Two: A Note on Popular and Durable Authors and Titles." In Amory and Hall, *History of the Book,* 519–21.

Hamlin, Hannibal, and Norman W. Jones, eds. *The King James Bible after 400 Years: Literary, Linguistic, and Cultural Influences.* New York: Cambridge University Press, 2010.

Hammond, Geordan. *John Wesley in America: Restoring Primitive Christianity.* New York: Oxford University Press, 2014.

Handbook of European History, 1400–1600, 2 vols. Leiden: Brill; Grand Rapids, MI: Eerdmans, 1995.

Haselby, Sam. *The Origins of American Religious Nationalism.* New York: Oxford University Press, 2015.

Hatch, Nathan O. *The Democratization of American Christianity.* New Haven, CT: Yale University Press, 1989.

Hatch, Nathan O. *The Sacred Cause of Liberty: Republican Thought and the Millennium in Revolutionary New England.* New Haven, CT: Yale University Press, 1977.

Hatch, Nathan O. "*Sola Scriptura* and *Novus Ordo Seclorum.*" In *The Bible in America: Essays in Cultural History,* edited by Nathan Hatch and Mark A. Noll, 59–78. New York: Oxford University Press, 1982.

Heimert, Alan. *Religion and the American Mind: From the Great Awakening to the Revolution.* Cambridge, MA: Harvard University Press, 1966.

Hempton, David. *Methodism: Empire of the Spirit.* New Haven, CT: Yale University Press, 2005.

Hempton, David. *Religion and Political Culture in Britain and Ireland: From the Glorious Revolution to the Decline of Empire.* New York: Cambridge University Press, 1996.

Herbert, A. S. *Historical Catalogue of Printed Editions of the English Bible, 1525–1961.* London: British and Foreign Bible Society; New York: American Bible Society, 1968.

Hill, Christopher. *The English Bible and the Seventeenth-Century Revolution.* London: Allen Lane/Penguin, 1993.

Hills, Margaret T. *The English Bible in America: A Bibliography of Editions of the Bible and the New Testament Published in America, 1777–1957.* New York: American Bible Society & New York Public Library, 1982.

Hoffman, Ronald, and Peter J. Albert, eds. *Religion in a Revolutionary Age.* Charlottesville: University Press of Virginia, 1994.

Holifield, E. Brooks. *Era of Persuasion: American Thought and Culture, 1521–1680.* Boston: Twayne, 1989.

Holifield, E. Brooks. *Theology in America: Christian Thought from the Age of the Puritans to the Civil War.* New Haven, CT: Yale University Press, 2003.

Holland, David F. *Sacred Borders: Continuing Revelation and Canonical Restraint in Early America.* New York: Oxford University Press, 2011.

Hoppit, Julian. *A Land of Liberty? England 1689–1727.* New York: Oxford University Press, 2000.

Hughes, Richard T., ed. *The American Quest for the Primitive Church.* Urbana: University of Illinois Press, 1988.

Hurley, Michael. *Scriptura Sola: Wyclif and his Critics.* New York: Fordham University Press, 1960.

Hutchins, Zachary McLeod. *Inventing Eden: Primitivism, Millennialism, and the Making of New England.* New York: Oxford University Press, 2014.

Hutson, James H., ed. *Religion and the New Republic: Faith in the Founding of America.* Lanham, MD: Rowman and Littlefield, 2000.

Israel, Jonathan I. *Radical Enlightenment: Philosophy and the Making of Modernity, 1650–1750.* New York: Oxford University Press, 2001.

Jacobs, Alan. *The Book of Common Prayer: A Biography.* Princeton, NJ: Princeton University Press, 2013.

Jasanoff, Maya. *Liberty's Exiles: American Loyalists in the Revolutionary World.* New York: Knopf, 2011.

Jeffrey, David Lyle, ed. *The King James Bible and the World It Made.* Waco, TX: Baylor University Press, 2011.

Johnson, Sylvester. "Colonialism, Biblical World-Making, and Temporalities in Equiano's Interesting Narrative." *Church History* 77 (2008): 1003–24.

Juhnke, James C., and Carol Hunter. *The Missing Peace: The Search for Nonviolent Alternatives in United States History.* Kitchner, ON: Pandora, 2001.

Juster, Susan. "The Evangelical Ascendency in Revolutionary America." In *The Oxford Handbook of the American Revolution*, edited by Edward G. Gray and Jane Kamensky, 407–26. New York: Oxford University Press, 2013.

Kadane, Matthew. *The Watchful Clothier: The Life of an Eighteenth-Century Protestant Capitalist.* New Haven: Yale University Press, 2013.

Keble, N. H. "C. S. Lewis, Richard Baxter, and 'Mere Christianity.'" *Christianity and Literature* 30 (1981): 27–44.

Keillor, Steven J. *This Rebellious House: American History and the Truth of Christianity.* Downers Grove, IL: InterVarsity Press, 1996.

Kennedy, Rick. *The First American Evangelical: A Short Life of Cotton Mather*. Grand Rapids, MI: Eerdmans, 2015.

Kidd, Colin. *The Forging of Races: Race and Scripture in the Protestant Atlantic World, 1600–2000*. New York: Cambridge University Press, 2006.

Kidd, Thomas S. *God of Liberty: A Religious History of the American Revolution*. New York: Basic, 2010.

Kidd, Thomas S. *The Great Awakening: The Roots of Evangelical Christianity in Colonial America*. New Haven, CT: Yale University Press, 2007.

Kidd, Thomas S. "'Let Hell and Rome Do Their Worst': World News, Anti-Catholicism, and International Protestantism in Early-Eighteenth Century Boston." *New England Quarterly* 86 (June 2003): 265–90.

Kidd, Thomas S. *Patrick Henry: First Among Patriots*. New York: Basic, 2011.

Kidd, Thomas S. *The Protestant Interest: New England after Puritanism*. New Haven, CT: Yale University Press, 2004.

"KJB: The Book that Changed the World." DVD presented by John Rhys-Davies, produced by Norman Stone. Lionsgate Home Entertainment, 2011.

Kling, David W. *The Bible in History: How the Texts Have Shaped the Times*. New York: Oxford University Press, 2004.

Knoppers, Laura Lunger, ed. *Puritanism and Its Discontents*. Newark: University of Delaware Press, 2003.

Kolb, Robert. *Martin Luther: Confessor of the Faith*. New York: Oxford University Press, 2009.

Labaree, Leonard W. "The Conservative Attitude toward the Great Awakening." *William and Mary Quarterly* 1 (July 1944): 335–52.

Lambert, Frank. *Inventing "The Great Awakening."* Princeton, NJ: Princeton University Press, 1999.

Langford, Paul. *A Polite and Commercial People: England 1727–1783*. New York: Oxford University Press, 1989.

Laplante, Eve. *The Life and Repentance of Samuel Sewall: Salem Witch Judge*. New York: HarperOne, 2007.

Legaspi, Michael C. *The Death of Scripture and the Rise of Biblical Studies*. New York: Oxford University Press, 2010.

Lemay, J. A. Leo. "Ebenezer Kinnersley." In *American National Biography*, 12:729–30.

Lemay, J. A. Leo. *Ebenezer Kinnersley: Franklin's Friend*. Philadelphia: University of Pennsylvania Press, 1964.

Lepore, Jill. *The Name of War: King Philip's War and the Origin of American Identity*. New York: Knopf, 1998.

Lewis, C. S. *English Literature in the Sixteenth Century, Excluding Drama*. New York: Oxford University Press, 1954.

Lewis, C. S. *The Literary Impact of the Authorized Version*. Fortress: Philadelphia, 1963 (orig. 1950).

Lillback, Peter. *George Washington's Sacred Fire*. Bryn Mawr, PA: Providence Forum Press, 2006.

Lindberg, Carter. *The European Reformations.* Cambridge: Blackwell, 1996.

Little, Thomas J. "The Origins of Southern Evangelicalism: Revivalism in South Carolina, 1700–1740." *Church History* 75 (Dec. 2006): 768–808.

Livingstone, David N. *Dealing with Darwin: Place, Politics, and Rhetoric in Religious Engagements with Evolution.* Baltimore, MD: Johns Hopkins University Press, 2014.

Lovelace, Richard F. *The American Pietism of Cotton Mather.* Grand Rapids, MI: Eerdmans, 1979.

Lupas, Liana. *A Light to the Nations: America's Earliest Bibles (1532–1864).* New York: MOBIA Museum of Biblical Art, 2010.

Lutz, Donald S. "The Relative Influence of European Writers on Late Eighteenth-Century American Political Thought." *American Political Science Review* 78 (Mar. 1984): 189–97.

MacCormack, Sabine. *On the Wings of Time: Rome, the Incas, Spain, and Peru.* Princeton, NJ: Princeton University Press, 2007.

MacCulloch, Diarmaid. *The Reformation: A History.* New York: Viking, 2003.

MacMaster, Richard K., Samuel L. Horst, and Robert F. Ulle. *Conscience in Crisis: Mennonite and Other Peace Charles in America, 1739–1789.* Scottsdale, PA: Herald, 1979.

Mailer, Gideon. "Anglo-Scottish Union and John Witherspoon's American Revolution." *William and Mary Quarterly* 67 (Oct. 2010): 709–46.

Malcolm, Joyce Lee. "Slavery in Massachusetts and the American Revolution." *Journal of the Historical Society* 10 (Dec. 2010): 415–36.

Malless, Stanley, and Jeffrey McQuain. *Coined by God: Words and Phrases that First Appear in the English Translations of the Bible.* New York: W. W. Norton, 2003.

Malley, Brian. *How the Bible Works: An Anthropological Study of Evangelical Biblicism.* Walnut Creek, CA: AltaMira Press, 2004.

Malley, Brian. "Understanding the Bible's Influence." In *The Social Life of Scriptures: Cross-Cultural Perspectives on Biblicism,* edited by James S. Bielo, 194–204. New Brunswick, NJ: Rutgers University Press, 2009.

Marini, Stephen. "American Protestant Hymn Project: A Ranked List of Most Frequently Printed Hymns, 1737–1960." In *Wonderful Words of Life: Hymns in American Protestant History and Theology,* edited by Richard J Mouw and Mark A. Noll, 251–64. Grand Rapids, MI: Eerdmans, 2004.

Marini, Stephen A. *Radical Sects of Revolutionary New England.* Cambridge, MA: Harvard University Press, 1982.

Marsden, George M. *Fundamentalism and American Culture: The Shaping of Twentieth-Century Evangelicalism, 1870–1925.* New York: Oxford University Press, 1980.

Marsden, George M. *Jonathan Edwards: A Life.* New Haven, CT: Yale University Press, 2003.

Marshall, P. J., ed. *The Oxford History of the British Empire* (gen. ed. Wm. Roger Louis). Vol. 2, *The Eighteenth Century.* New York: Oxford University Press, 1997.

Marshall, Peter, and David Manuel. *The Light and the Glory, 1492–1793: God's Plan for America.* Old Tappan, NJ: Revell, 1977.

Masui, Shitsuyo. "Reconsidering Calvinist Ethics in the Massachusetts Bay: Robert Keayne, 'The Last Will and Testament' (1653)." *Journal of American and Canadian Studies* (Sophia University, Tokyo) 31 (2103): 3–22 (précis in English, text in Japanese).

Mathews, Donald G. *Slavery and Methodism: A Chapter in American Morality, 1780–1845.* Princeton, NJ: Princeton University Press, 1965.

Mathisen, Keith A. *The Shape of Sola Scriptura.* Moscow, ID: Canon, 2001.

May, Henry F. *The Enlightenment in America.* New York: Oxford University Press, 1976.

May, Henry F., and David Lundberg. "The Enlightened Reader in America." *American Quarterly* 28 (1976): 262–71.

McClymond, Michael J., and Gerald R. McDermott. *The Theology of Jonathan Edwards.* New York: Oxford University Press, 2012.

McConville, Brendan. *The King's Three Faces: The Rise and Fall of Royal America, 1688–1776.* Chapel Hill: University of North Carolina Press, 2006.

McDermott, Gerald. *One Holy and Happy Society: The Public Theology of Jonathan Edwards.* University Park: Penn State University Press, 1992.

McGrath, Alister E. *Historical Theology: An Introduction to the History of Christian Thought,* 2nd ed. Malden, MA: Wiley-Blackwell, 2102.

McLeod, Hugh. *The Religious Crisis of the 1960s.* New York: Oxford University Press, 2007.

McLoughlin, William G., and Martha Whiting Davidson. "The Baptist Debate of April 14–15, 1668." *Proceedings of the Massachusetts Historical Society,* 3rd ser., 76 (1964): 91–133.

McWilliams, William Carey. "The Bible in the American Political Tradition." In *Religion and Politics: Political Anthropology.* Vol. 3, edited by Myron J. Aronoff, 11–45. New Brunswick, NJ: Transaction, 1984.

Mekeel, Arthur J. "New England Quakers and Military Service in the American Revolution." In *Children of Light,* edited by Howard H. Brinton, 241–71. New York: Macmillan, 1938.

Metzger, Bruce. Introduction to *New Testament with Psalms and Proverbs,* New Revised Standard Version. Cambridge: Cambridge University Press, 1989.

Meyer, Donald H. *The Democratic Enlightenment.* New York: G. P. Putnam Sons, 1976.

Middlekauff, Robert. *The Glorious Cause: The American Revolution, 1763–1789.* New York: Oxford University Press, 1982.

Miller, Nicholas P. *The Religious Roots of the First Amendment: Dissenting Protestants and the Separation of Church and State.* New York: Oxford University Press, 2012.

Miller, Perry. "The Garden of Eden and the Deacon's Meadow." *American Heritage,* Dec. 1955, 54–61.

Minkema, Kenneth. "Thomas Prince." In *American National Biography,* 17:881–82.

Morgan, Edmund S. *American Slavery, American Freedom: The Ordeal of Colonial Virginia.* New York: W. W. Norton, 1975.

Morgan, Edmund S. *The Puritan Dilemma: A Life of John Winthrop.* Boston: Little, Brown, 1958.

Morgan, Edmund S. *Roger Williams, the Church and the State.* New York: Harcourt, Brace & World, 1967.

Morison, Samuel Eliot. *Harvard College: The Seventeenth Century*, 2 vols. Cambridge, MA: Harvard University Press, 1936.

Morrill, John. "A Liberation Theology? Aspects of Puritanism in the English Revolution." In *Puritanism and Its Discontents*, edited by Laura Lunger Knoppers, 27–48. Newark: University of Delaware Press, 2003.

Mulder, John. "William Livingston: Propagandist against Episcopacy." *Journal of Presbyterian History* 54 (Spring 1976): 83–104.

Nelson, Eric. "Hebraism and the Republican Turn of 1776: A Contemporary Account of the Debate over *Common Sense.*" *William and Mary Quarterly* 70 (Oct. 2013): 781–812.

Nelson, Eric. *The Hebrew Republic: Jewish Sources and the Transformation of European Political Thought.* Cambridge, MA: Harvard University Press, 2010.

Nelson, Eric. "'Talmudic Commonwealthmen' and the Rise of Republican Exclusivism." *Historical Journal* 50 (Dec. 2007): 809–35.

Nicolson, Adam. *God's Secretaries: The Making of the King James Bible.* New York: HaperCollins, 2003.

Noll, Mark A. *America's God: From Jonathan Edwards to Abraham Lincoln.* New York: Oxford University Press, 2002.

Noll, Mark A. "The Bible in American Culture." In *Encyclopedia of the American Religious Experience*, Vol. 2, edited by C. H. Lippy and P. W. Williams, 1075–87. New York: Charles Scribner's Sons, 1988.

Noll, Mark A. "The Bible in North America." In *The New Cambridge History of the Bible.* Vol. 4, *From 1750 to the Present*, edited by John Riches, 391–426. New York: Cambridge University Press, 2015.

Noll, Mark A. "The Bible in Revolutionary America." In *The Bible in American Law, Politics, and Political Rhetoric*, edited by James Turner Johnson, 39–60. Philadelphia: Fortress, 1985.

Noll, Mark A. *Christians in the American Revolution.* 2nd ed. Vancouver: Regent College Publishing, 2006 (orig. 1976).

Noll, Mark A. "Jonathan Edwards' Use of the Bible: A Case Study (Genesis 32:22–32) with Comparisons." *Jonathan Edwards Studies*, vol. 2, no. 1 (2012): 30–46.

Noll, Mark A. *Princeton and the Republic: 1768–1822.* Princeton, NJ: Princeton University Press, 1989.

Noll, Mark A. *The Rise of Evangelicalism: The Age of Edwards, Whitefield, and the Wesleys.* Downers Grove, IL: InterVarsity Press, 2003.

Noll, Mark A. "Samuel Davies." In *American National Biography*, 6:159–61.

Noll, Mark A. "Science, Theology, and Society: From Cotton Mather to William Jennings Bryan." In *Evangelicals and Science in Historical Perspective*, edited by

David N. Livingstone, D. G. Hart, and M. Noll, 99–119. New York: Oxford University Press, 1999.

Noll, Mark A. "'Wee shall be as a citty upon a hill': John Winthrop's Non-American Exceptionalism." *Review of Faith and International Affairs* 10, no. 2 (2012): 5–11.

Norton, David. *A History of the Bible as Literature*, 2 vols. New York: Cambridge University Press, 1993.

Norton, David. *The King James Bible: A Short History from Tyndale to Today*. New York: Cambridge University Press, 2011.

Norton, David. *A Textual History of the King James Bible*. Cambridge: Cambridge University Press, 2005.

O'Brien, Patrick K. "Inseparable Connections: Trade, Economy, Fiscal State, and the Expansion of Empire, 1688–1815." In *Oxford History of the British Empire*. Vol. 2, edited by P. J. Marshall, 28–52. New York: Oxford University Press, 1998.

Oberman, Heiko Augustinus. *The Harvest of Medieval Theology: Gabriel Biel and Late Medieval Nominalism*. Durham, NC: Labyrinth, 1983 (orig. 1963).

Pardo, Osvaldo F. *The Origins of Mexican Catholicism: Nahua Rituals and Christian Sacraments in Sixteenth-Century Mexico*. Ann Arbor: University of Michigan Press, 2004.

Parker, Kim Ian. *The Biblical Politics of John Locke*. Waterloo, Ont.: Wilfrid Laurier University Press, 2004.

Pastena, Carla Gardina. *Protestant Empire: Religion and the Making of the British Atlantic World*. Philadelphia: University of Pennsylvania Press, 2009.

Paul, Robert S. *The Assembly of the Lord: Politics and Religion in the Westminster Assembly and the "Grand Debate."* Edinburgh: T. & T. Clark, 1985.

Paul, Robert S. *The Lord Protector: Religion and Politics in the Life of Oliver Cromwell*. Grand Rapids. MI: Eerdmans, 1964 (orig. 1954).

Pelikan, Jaroslav. *The Reformation of the Bible: The Bible of the Reformation*. New Haven. CT: Yale University Press, 1996.

Perl-Rosenthal, Nathan R. "The 'divine right of republics': Hebraic Republicanism and the Debate over Kingless Government in Revolutionary America." *William and Mary Quarterly* 66 (July 2009): 535–64.

Peterson, Mark A. "The Selling of Joseph: Bostonians, Antislavery, and the Protestant International, 1689–1733." *Massachusetts Historical Review* 4 (2002): 1–22.

Pilcher, George William. *Samuel Davies: Apostle of Dissent in Colonial Virginia*. Knoxville: University of Tennessee Press, 1970.

Pointer, Richard W. *Encounters of the Spirit: Native Americans and European Colonial Religion*. Bloomington: Indiana University Press, 2007.

Porterfield, Amanda Porterfield. *Conceived in Doubt: Religion and Politics in the New American Nation*. Chicago: University of Chicago Press, 2012.

"Preparing for the Revolution," *Mennonite Historical Bulletin*, July 1974, 6–7.

Price, Jacob M. "Holden, Samuel (1674/5–1740)," *Oxford Dictionary of National Biography* (Oxford University Press, 2004); online ed., May 2011 [http://www.oxforddnb.com/view/article/47785, accessed 10 July 2014].

Prien, Hans-Jürgen. *Christianity in Latin America*. Translated by Stephen Buckwalter. Rev. ed. Leiden: Brill, 2013.

Raboteau, Albert J. *Slave Religion: The "Invisible Institution" in the Antebellum South*, 2nd ed. New York: Oxford University Press, 2004.

Rack, Henry D. *Reasonable Enthusiast: John Wesley and the Rise of Methodism*. Philadelphia: Trinity Press, 1989.

Rahe, Paul A. *Republics Ancient and Modern: Classical Republicanism and the American Revolution*. Chapel Hill: University of North Carolina Press, 1992.

Rappleye, Charles. *Sons of Providence: The Brown Brothers, the Slave Trade, and the American Revolution*. New York: Simon & Schuster, 2006.

Reedy, Gerard, S.J. *The Bible and Reason: Anglicans and Scripture in late Seventeenth-Century England*. Philadelphia: University of Pennsylvania Press, 1985.

Reid-Maroney, Nina. *Philadelphia's Enlightenment: Kingdom of Christ, Empire of Reason*. Westport, CT: Greenwood, 2001.

Richards, Phillip M. "Phillis Wheatley and Literary Americanization." *American Quarterly* 44 (1992): 163–91.

Roeber, A. Gregg. "German and Dutch Books and Printing." In Amory and Hall, *History of the Book*, 298–313.

Rohrer, S. Scott. *Jacob Green's Revolution: Radical Religion and Reform in a Revolutionary Age*. State College: Penn State University Press, 2014.

Rupp, E. G. *Studies in the Making of the English Protestant Tradition*. New York: Cambridge University Press, 1966 (orig. 1946).

Sassi, Jonathan D. "Religion, Race, and the Founders." In Dreisbach and Hall, *Faith and the Founders*,174–99.

Savart, Claude, and Jean-Noël Aletti, eds. *Bible de tous les temps*. Vol. 8, *Le monde contemporain et la Bible*. Paris: Beauchesne, 1985.

Schama, Simon. *Rough Crossings: Britain, the Slaves and the American Revolution*. London: BBC Books, 2005.

Schlenther, Boyd Stanley. "Religious Faith and Commercial Empire." In *Oxford History of the British Empire*. Vol. 2, edited by P. J. Marshall, 128–50. New York: Oxford University Press, 1998.

Schlereth, Eric R. *An Age of Infidels: The Politics of Religious Controversy in the Early United States*. Philadelphia: University of Pennsylvania Press, 2013.

Schutz, John A. "Jonathan Belcher." In *American National Biography*, 2:490–91.

Sehat, David Sehat, *The Myth of American Freedom*. New York: Oxford University Press, 2011.

Shagan, Ethan H. *The Rule of Moderation: Violence, Religion and the Politics of Restraint in Early Modern England*. New York: Cambridge University Press, 2011.

Shalev, Eran. *American Zion: The Old Testament as a Political Text from the Revolution to the Civil War*. New Haven, CT: Yale University Press, 2013.

Shapiro, Barbara J. *Probability and Certainty in Seventeenth-Century England: A Study of the Relationships Between Natural Science, Religion, History, Law, and Literature*. Princeton, NJ: Princeton University Press, 1983.

Sheehan, Jonathan. *The Enlightenment Bible: Translation, Scholarship, Culture.* Princeton, NJ: Princeton University Press, 2005.

Sherman, William H. "'The Book Thus Put in Every Vulgar Hand': Impressions of Readers in Early English Printed Bibles." In *The Bible as Book: The First Printed Editions,* edited by Paul Saenger and Kimberly Van Kampen, 125–34. London: British Library, 1999.

Sider, Ronald J. *Andreas Bodenstein von Karlstadt: The Development of His Thought, 1517–1525.* Leiden: E. J. Brill, 1974.

Siegel, Thomas J. "Professor Stephen Sewall and the Transformation of Hebrew at Harvard." In *Hebrew and the Bible in America: The First Two Centuries,* edited by Shalom Goldman, 228–45. Hanover, NH: University Press of New England, 1993.

Silverman, David J. *Faith and Boundaries: Colonists, Christianity, and Community among the Wampanoag Indians of Martha's Vineyard, 1600–1871.* New York: Cambridge University Press, 2005.

Simms, P. Marion. *The Bible in America: Versions that Have Played their Part in the Making of the Republic.* New York: Wilson-Erickson, 1936.

Slaughter, Thomas P. *The Beautiful Soul of John Woolman, Apostle of Abolition.* New York: Hill and Wang, 2008.

Smith, Christian. *The Bible Made Impossible: Why Biblicism Is Not a Truly Evangelical Reading of Scripture.* Grand Rapids, MI: Brazos, 2011.

Smith, Kay Higuera, Jayachitra Lalitha, and L. Daniel Hawk, eds. *Evangelical Postcolonial Conversations.* Downers Grove, IL: InterVarsity Press, 2014.

Smith, Mark. "The Hanoverian Parish: Towards a New Agenda." *Past and Present* 216 (Aug. 2012): 79–105.

Smith, William (Billy). "A Heavenly Correspondence: Benjamin Colman's Epistolary World and the Dissenting Interest, 1695–1747." PhD diss., University of Notre Dame, in progress.

Smolinski, Reiner, and Jan Stievermann, eds. *America's First Bible Commentary: Essays in Reappraisal.* Tübingen: Mohr Siebeck; and Grand Rapids, MI: Baker, 2010.

Sobel, Mechal. *The World They Made Together: Black and White Values in Eighteenth-Century Virginia.* Princeton, NJ: Princeton University Press, 1987.

Stackhouse, Rochelle A. "Hymnody and Politics: Isaac Watts's 'Our God, Our Help in Ages Past' and Timothy Dwight's 'I Love Thy Kingdom, Lord'." In *Wonderful Words of Life,* edited by Richard J. Mouw and Mark A. Noll, 44–52. Grand Rapids, MI: Eerdmans, 2004.

Stein, Stephen J. "America's Bibles: Canon, Commentary, and Community." *Church History* 64 (1995): 169–84.

Stoll, Ira. *Samuel Adams: A Life.* New York: Free Press, 2008.

Stout, Harry S. *The Divine Dramatist: George Whitefield and the Rise of Modern Evangelicalism.* Grand Rapids, MI: Eerdmans, 1991.

Stout, Harry S. *The New England Soul: Preaching and Religious Culture in Colonial New England.* New York: Oxford University Press, 1986.

Stout, Harry S. "Word and Order in Colonial New England." In *The Bible in America: Essays in Cultural History*, edited by Nathan O. Hatch and Mark A. Noll, 3–18. New York: Oxford University Press, 1982.

Stout, Harry S., and Christopher Grasso. "Civil War, Religion, and Communications: The Case of Richmond." In *Religion and the Civil War*, edited by Randall M. Miller, Charles Reagan Wilson, and Harry Stout, 313–59. New York: Oxford University Press, 1998.

Stout, Harry S., and Peter Onuf. "James Davenport and the Great Awakening in New London." *Journal of American History* 70 (1983): 556–78.

Strong, Rowan. *Anglicanism and the British Empire, ca. 1700–1850*. Oxford: Oxford University Press, 2007.

Thuesen, Peter J. *In Discordance with the Scriptures: American Protestant Battles over Translating the Bible*. New York: Oxford University Press, 1999.

Tomlin, T. J. *A Divinity for All Persuasions: Almanacs and Early American Religious Life*. New York: Oxford University Press, 2014.

Tracy, Joseph. *The Great Awakening*. New York: Arno, 1969 (orig. 1841).

Turner, James. *Philology: The Forgotten Origins of the Modern Humanities*. Princeton, NJ: Princeton University Press, 2014.

Valeri, Mark. "Francis Hutcheson." In *Colonial Writers, 1735–1781*, edited by Emory Elliott, 310–17. Detroit: Gale, 1984.

Valeri, Mark. *Heavenly Merchandize: How Religion Shaped Commerce in Puritan America*. Princeton, NJ: Princeton University Press, 2010.

Valeri, Mark. "Jonathan Edwards, the Edwardians, and the Sacred Cause of Free Trade." In *Jonathan Edwards at Home and Abroad*, edited by David W. Kling and Douglas A. Sweeney, 85–100. Columbia: University of South Carolina Press, 2003.

Valeri, Mark. "The New Divinity and the Revolution." *William and Mary Quarterly* 46 (Oct. 1989): 741–69.

Van Engen, Abram. "Origins and Last Farewells: Bible Wars, Textual Form, and the Making of American History." *New England Quarterly* 86 (Dec. 2013): 543–92.

Volz, Hans, et al. "Continental Versions to ca. 1600." In *The Cambridge History of the Bible*. Vol. 3, *The West from the Reformation to the Present Day*, edited by S. L. Greenslade, 94–140. Cambridge: Cambridge University Press, 1963.

Ward, W. R. *The Protestant Evangelical Awakening*. New York: Cambridge University Press, 1992.

Wells, William V. *The Life and Public Services of Samuel Adams*, 3 vols. Boston: Little, Brown, 1865.

Wertenbaker, Thomas Jefferson. *Princeton, 1746–1896*, with a new preface by John M. Murrin. Princeton, NJ: Princeton University Press, 1996 (orig. 1946).

Wheeler, Rachel. *To Live Upon Hope: Mohicans and Missionaries in the Eighteenth-Century Northeast*. Ithaca, NY: Cornell University Press, 2008.

Whitford, David M. *The Curse of Ham in the Early Modern Era: The Bible and the Justification for Slavery*. Farnham, UK: Ashgate, 2009.

Williams, George H. *The Radical Reformation*. Philadelphia: Westminster, 1962.

Wills, Garry. "Mason Weems, Bibliopolist." *American Heritage*, Feb./Mar. 1981, 66–68.

Wimbush, Vincent. *White Men's Magic: Scripturalization as Slavery*. New York: Oxford University Press, 2012.

Winship, Michael P. *Godly Republicanism: Puritans, Pilgrims, and a City on a Hill*. Cambridge, MA: Harvard University Press, 2012.

Winship, Michael P. *Making Heretics: Militant Protestantism and Free Grace in Massachusetts, 1636–1641*. Princeton, NJ: Princeton University Press, 2002.

Winslow, Ola. *Meetinghouse Hill, 1630–1783*. New York: Norton, 1972 (orig. 1952).

Witham, Larry. *A City Upon a Hill: How Sermons Changed the Course of American History*. New York: HarperOne, 2007.

Wolosky, Shira. "Bible Republicanism: John Cotton's 'Moses His Judicials' and American Hebraism." *Hebraic Political Studies* 4 (Spring 2009): 104–27.

Wolterstorff, Nicholas. "Locke's Philosophy of Religion." In *The Cambridge Companion to Locke*, edited by Vere Chappell, 172–98. New York: Cambridge University Press, 1994.

Wood, Gordon S. *Empire of Liberty*. New York: Oxford University Press, 2009.

Worden, Blair. *God's Instruments: Political Conduct in the England of Oliver Cromwell*. New York: Oxford University Press, 2012.

Wright, John. *Early Bibles of America*. 3rd ed. New York: Thomas Whittaker, 1894.

Young, Alfred E., Gary B. Nash, and Ray Raphael, eds. *Revolutionary Founders: Rebels, Radicals, and Reformers in the Making of the Nation*. New York: Knopf, 2011.

Young, Michael P. *Bearing Witness against Sin: The Evangelical Birth of the American Social Movement*. Chicago: University of Chicago Press, 2006.

Zuckert, Michael P. "National Rights and Protestant Right." In *Protestantism and the American Founding*, edited by Michael Zuckert and Thomas S. Engerman, 21–76. Notre Dame, IN: University of Notre Dame Press, 2004.

Zuckert, Michael P. *Natural Rights and the New Republicanism*. Princeton, NJ: Princeton University Press, 1994.

General Index

Cole, Nathan, 179, 195–97

Colet, John, 22, 74

Colley, Linda, 152, 354n1, 355n18

Collinson, Patrick, 347n1

Colman, Benjamin, 159–60, 161,
 173, 242–43

Columbus, Christopher, 7, 22–25

Common Sense, 307–15, 378n75

confessional states, 12–13, 128

Congregationalists: in England, 83, 89,
 106; in America, 118, 120–22, 136

Connecticut, 14, 81, 101, 111

Connolly, Sean, 354n4

Constantine, 6

Cornelius, Janet, 361n5

Costa, Sarah (neé Jackman), 342n2

Cotton, John, 118–19, 120, 122,
 132–34, 240

covenant, 116, 137, 161, 196, 265, 282,
 283, 339; in Scotland, 92; and John
 Winthrop, 110–11

Coverdale, Miles, 55–56, 61

Cranmer, Thomas, 56, 75, 292

Crawford, Michael, 195, 358n4, 360n65

Cromwell, Oliver, 81, 90–91, 268 300

Cromwell, Thomas, 56

Crystal, David, 345n9

Cugoano, Quobana, 229–30

Cummings, Brian, 347n4

Daniell, David, 342n15, 345n5, 346n31

Davenport, James, 198–99, 232

Davenport, John, 117–18

Davidson, Martha, 352n23

Davies, Samuel, 167–69, 211

Davis, David Brion, 316, 330, 367n22,
 367n31 368n34, 368n46, 371n6,
 380n113, 380n119

Davis, Derek, 372n20

Den Hartog, Jonathan, 341n1

Devotion, John, 286, 368n42

Dickinson, Jonathan, 187

Diderot, Denis, 6

Doyle, Eric, O.F.M., 46, 345n37

Dreisbach, Daniel, 276, 371n1, 371n8,
 372n16, 372n23, 381n130

Duché, Jacob, 304

Duffy, Eamon, 346n25

Dummer's War, 158, 161

Dunbar, Samuel, 283

Edward VI, 58

Edwards, Jonathan, 155, 178, 180, 183,
 184–86, 199, 260, 287

Eliot, John, 113, 141–42

Elizabeth I, 13, 69

Endy, Melvin, 371n1, 375n23

Engel, Katherine, 244, 367n19

Enlightenment, the, 236–37, 238–39,
 255–56, 360n48, 361n90

Equiano, Olaudah, 227–29, 364n61

Erasmus, Desiderius, 22, 24, 39,
 45, 51, 52

Erben, Patrick, 368n43

Essig, James, 319, 367n22, 380n119

Estinenne, Robert (Stephanus), 59

exceptionalism: American, 20–21,
 100, 117, 201, 205, 284, 308,
 320, 329, 330, 333, 335, 339;
 English or British, 167, 207,
 265, 330, 339

Ferdinand and Isabella, 23

Ferguson, Robert, 256

Fernández-Armesto, Felipe, 342n5

Fiering, Norman, 369n53

Filmer, Robert, 96, 126

First Amendment (1791), 337

Fisher, Linford, 232, 233,
 353n28, 365n71

Fletcher, John, 323

Forty-Two Articles. See Thirty-Nine Articles

Fox, Francis, 367n21, 372n11

Foxcroft, Thomas, 162

Scripture Index

The manufacturer's authorised representative in the EU for product safety is
Oxford University Press España S.A. of el Parque Empresarial San Fernando
de Henares, Avenida de Castilla, 2 – 28830 Madrid (www.oup.es/en).

Printed in the USA/Agawam, MA
November 29, 2024

877487.105